Lecture Notes in Computer Science 13285

More information about this series at https://link.springer.com/bookseries/558

Jianying Zhou · Sridhar Adepu ·
Cristina Alcaraz · Lejla Batina ·
Emiliano Casalicchio · Sudipta Chattopadhyay ·
Chenglu Jin · Jingqiang Lin ·
Eleonora Losiouk · Suryadipta Majumdar ·
Weizhi Meng · Stjepan Picek ·
Jun Shao · Chunhua Su ·
Cong Wang · Yury Zhauniarovich ·
Saman Zonouz (Eds.)

Applied Cryptography and Network Security Workshops

ACNS 2022 Satellite Workshops
AIBlock, AIHWS, AIoTS, CIMSS, Cloud S&P, SCI, SecMT, SiMLA
Rome, Italy, June 20–23, 2022
Proceedings

 Springer

Editors
Jianying Zhou (iD)
Singapore University of Technology
and Design
Singapore, Singapore

Cristina Alcaraz (iD)
University of Malaga
Malaga, Spain

Emiliano Casalicchio (iD)
Sapienza University of Rome
Rome, Roma, Italy

Chenglu Jin (iD)
Centrum Wiskunde & Informatica
Amsterdam, The Netherlands

Eleonora Losiouk (iD)
University of Padua
Padua, Italy

Weizhi Meng (iD)
Technical University Denmark
Kongens Lyngby, Denmark

Jun Shao
Zhejiang Gongshang University
Hangzhou, China

Cong Wang (iD)
City University of Hong Kong
Hong Kong, Hong Kong

Saman Zonouz
Rutgers University
Piscataway, NJ, USA

Sridhar Adepu (iD)
University of Bristol
Bristol, UK

Lejla Batina (iD)
Radboud University Nijmegen
Nijmegen, The Netherlands

Sudipta Chattopadhyay (iD)
Singapore University of Technology
and Design
Singapore, Singapore

Jingqiang Lin (iD)
University of Science and Technology
of China
Hefei, China

Suryadipta Majumdar (iD)
Concordia University
Montreal, QC, Canada

Stjepan Picek (iD)
Delft University of Technology
Delft, The Netherlands

Chunhua Su (iD)
University of Aizu
Aizu-Wakamatsu, Japan

Yury Zhauniarovich (iD)
Delft University of Technology
Delft, The Netherlands

ISSN 0302-9743   ISSN 1611-3349 (electronic)
Lecture Notes in Computer Science
ISBN 978-3-031-16814-7   ISBN 978-3-031-16815-4 (eBook)
https://doi.org/10.1007/978-3-031-16815-4

This Springer imprint is published by the registered company Springer Nature Switzerland AG
The registered company address is: Gewerbestrasse 11, 6330 Cham, Switzerland

Preface

The proceedings contain the papers selected for presentation at the ACNS 2022 satellite workshops, which were held in parallel with the main conference (the 20th International Conference on Applied Cryptography and Network Security) during June 20–23, 2022. Due to the ongoing COVID-19 crisis, ACNS 2022 was held in Rome, Italy, in a hybrid mode while the workshops were organized as online events.

In response to this year's call for workshop proposals, there were eight satellite workshops, the same as last year. Each workshop provided a forum to address a specific topic at the forefront of cybersecurity research.

- 4th Workshop on Application Intelligence and Blockchain Security (AIBlock 2022), chaired by Weizhi Meng and Chunhua Su
- 3rd Workshop on Artificial Intelligence in Hardware Security (AIHWS 2022), chaired by Lejla Batina and Stjepan Picek
- 4th Workshop on Artificial Intelligence and Industrial IoT Security (AIoTS 2022), chaired by Sridhar Adepu and Cristina Alcaraz
- 2nd Workshop on Critical Infrastructure and Manufacturing System Security (CIMSS 2022), chaired by Chenglu Jin and Saman Zonouz
- 4th Workshop on Cloud Security and Privacy (Cloud S&P 2022), chaired by Suryadipta Majumdar and Cong Wang
- 3rd Workshop on Secure Cryptographic Implementation (SCI 2022), chaired by Jingqiang Lin and Jun Shao
- 3rd Workshop on Security in Mobile Technologies (SecMT 2022), chaired by Eleonora Losiouk and Yury Zhauniarovich
- 4th Workshop on Security in Machine Learning and its Applications (SiMLA 2022), chaired by Sudipta Chattopadhyay

This year, we received a total of 52 submissions. Each workshop had its own Program Committee (PC) in charge of the review process. These papers were evaluated on the basis of their significance, novelty, and technical quality. The review process was double-blind. In the end, 31 papers were selected for presentation at the eight workshops, with an acceptance rate of 60%.

ACNS also gave the best workshop paper award. The winning papers were selected among the nominated candidate papers from each workshop. The following two papers shared the ACNS 2022 Best Workshop Paper Award. They will also receive the monetary prize sponsored by Frontiers.

- Yuanyuan Zhou and Francois-Xavier Standaert. "S-box Pooling: Towards More Efficient Side-Channel Security Evaluations" from the AIHWS workshop
- Thijs Heijligenberg, Oualid Lkhaouni, and Katharina Kohls. "Leaky Blinders: Information Leakage in Mobile VPNs" from the SecMT workshop

This year Frontiers specifically sponsored a best AIoTS workshop paper award. The program chairs of the AIoTS workshop selected the following paper for the award.

- Alessandro Visintin, Flavio Toffalini, Eleonora Losiouk, Mauro Conti, and Jianying Zhou. "HolA: Holistic and Autonomous Attestation for IoT Networks"

Besides the regular papers presented at the workshops, there were 14 invited talks.

- "Towards Decentralized Privacy-Preserving Application Intelligence" by S. M. Chow (Chinese University of Hong Kong, Hong Kong SAR, China) at the AIBlock workshop
- "Homomorphic Computing: Achieving the Pinnacle of Data Privacy" by Rosario Cammarota (Intel, USA) and "A Fault Can Do Wonders: On Advanced Fault Attacks on Protection Mechanisms, Post-Quantum Cryptography and Deep Learning" by Shivam Bhasin (NTU, Singapore) at the AIHWS workshop
- "Fusing AI and Design to Protect Critical Infrastructure" by Aditya P. Mathur (SUTD, Singapore) and "Trustworthy AI for Securing CPS" by Tingting Li (Cardiff University, UK) at the AIoTS workshop
- "Oh What a Tangled Web We Weave - Securing ICS Networks" by Nils Ole Tippenhauer (CISPA, Germany) and "Urban Water Infrastructure: Challenges and Smart Solutions" by Zoran Kapelan (TU Delft, The Netherlands) at the CIMSS workshop
- "Notions of Security and Trust in Virtualized Infrastructures" by Vijay Varadharajan (University of Newcastle, Australia) and "Vulnerability Detection for Emerging Technologies" by Paria Shirani (Toronto Metropolitan University, Canada) at the Cloud S&P workshop
- "Hey... it's a PDF. What can go wrong?" by Christian Mainka and Vladislav Mladenov (Ruhr University Bochum, Germany) at the SCI workshop
- "Trust, But Verify: A Longitudinal Analysis of Android OEM Compliance and Customization" by Simone Aonzo (EURECOM, France) and "From the Analysis of Mobile Apps to the Analysis of the Mobile Ecosystem" by Antonio Bianchi (Purdue University, USA) at the SecMT workshop
- "Towards Trustworthy AI" by Jun Sun (SMU, Singapore) at the SiMLA workshop

There was also a poster session chaired by Emiliano Casalicchio. Five posters were included in the proceedings in the form of extended abstracts.

The ACNS 2022 workshops were made possible by the joint efforts of many individuals and organizations. We sincerely thank the authors of all submissions. We are grateful to the program chairs and PC members of each workshop for their great effort in providing professional reviews and interesting feedback to authors in a tight time schedule. We thank all the external reviewers for assisting the PC in their particular areas of expertise. We are grateful to Frontiers for sponsoring the workshops. We also thank General Chairs Mauro Conti and Angelo Spognardi and the organizing team members of the main conference as well as each workshop for their help in various aspects.

Last but not least, we thank everyone else, speakers, session chairs, and attendees for their contribution to the success of the ACNS 2022 workshops. We are glad to see the workshops have become an important part of ACNS and provide a stimulating platform to discuss open problems at the forefront of cybersecurity research. We would expect that in-person workshops will return in 2023.

June 2022   Jianying Zhou
                                                                              ACNS 2022 Workshop Chair

AIHWS 2022

Third Workshop on Artificial Intelligence in Hardware Security

21 June 2022

Program Chairs

Lejla Batina   Radboud University, The Netherlands
Stjepan Picek   Radboud University, The Netherlands

Program Committee

Aydin Aysu	North Carolina State University, USA
Ileana Buhan	Radboud University, The Netherlands
Lukasz Chmielewski	Radboud University, The Netherlands
Chitchanok Chuengsatiansup	University of Adelaide, Australia
Elena Dubrova	KTH Royal Institute of Technology, Sweden
Baris Ege	Riscure B.V., The Netherlands
Fatemeh Ganji	Worcester Polytechnic Institute, USA
Naofumi Homma	Tohoku University, Japan
Xiaolu Hou	Slovak University of Technology, Slovakia
Dirmanto Jap	Nanyang Technological University, Singapore
Luca Mariot	Radboud University, The Netherlands
Tsunato Nakai	Mitsubishi Electric Corp., Japan
Kostas Papagiannopoulos	University of Amsterdam, The Netherlands
Guilherme Perin	TU Delft, The Netherlands
Kazuo Sakiyama	University of Electro-Communications, Japan
Shahin Tajik	Worcester Polytechnic Institute, USA
Vincent Verneuil	NXP Semiconductors, Germany
Lichao Wu	TU Delft, The Netherlands
Zhengyu Zhao	CISPA Helmholtz Center for Information Security, Germany

Publicity Chair

Marina Krcek   Delft University of Technology, The Netherlands

CLOUD S&P 2022

Fourth Workshop on Cloud Security and Privacy

22 June 2022

Program Chairs

Suryadipta Majumdar   Concordia University, Canada
Cong Wang   City University of Hong Kong, HK SAR, China

Program Committee

Irfan Ahmed   Virginia Commonwealth University, USA
Prabir Bhattacharya   Thomas Edison State University, USA
Mauro Conti   University of Padua, Italy
Helei Cui   Northwestern Polytechnical University, China
Nora Cuppens   École Polytechnique de Montréal, Canada
Sabrina De Capitani   Universitá degli Studi di Milano, Italy
  di Vimercati
Carol Fung   Concordia University, Canada
Yosr Jarraya   Ericsson Security, Sweden
Kallol Krishna Karmakar   University of Newcastle, UK
Rongxing Lu   University of New Brunswick, Canada
Taous Madi   King Abdullah University of Science and Technology,
                                  Saudi Arabia
Makan Pourzandi   Ericsson Security, Sweden
Pierangela Samarati   Universitá degli Studi di Milano, Italy
Paria Shirani   Ryerson University, Canada
Lingyu Wang   Concordia University, Canada
Xingliang Yuan   Monash University, Australia
Mengyuan Zhang   Hong Kong Polytechnic University, HK SAR, China

Additional Reviewers

Mohammad Ekramul Kabir   Concordia University, Canada
Riccardo Lazzeretti   Sapienza Università di Roma, Italy

SCI 2022

Third Workshop on Secure Cryptographic Implementation

23 June 2022

Program Chairs

Jingqiang Lin   University of Science and Technology of China, China
Jun Shao   Zhejiang Gongshang University, China

Publication Chair

Bo Luo   University of Kansas, USA

Publicity Chairs

Hao Peng   Zhejiang Normal University, China
Fangyu Zheng   Chinese Academy of Sciences, China

Program Committee

Florian Caullery	HENSOLDT Cyber GmbH, Germany
Bo Chen	Michigan Technological University, USA
Jiankuo Dong	Nanjing University of Posts and Telecommunications, China
Niall Emmart	NVIDIA Corporation, USA
Johann Großschädl	University of Luxembourg, Luxembourg
Miroslaw Kutylowski	Wroclaw University of Technology, Poland
Bingyu Li	Beihang University, China
Fengjun Li	University of Kansas, USA
Ximeng Liu	Fuzhou University, China
Rongxing Lu	University of New Brunswick, Canada
Chunli Lv	China Agricultural University, China
Di Ma	ZDNS, China
Yuan Ma	Chinese Academy of Sciences, China
Ziqiang Ma	Ningxia University, China
Zhiguo Wan	Shandong University, China
Ding Wang	Nankai University, China
Juan Wang	Wuhan University, China
Fan Zhang	Zhejiang University, China
Fangyu Zheng	Chinese Academy of Sciences, China
Cong Zuo	Nanyang Technological University, Singapore

SecMT 2022

Third Workshop on Security in Mobile Technologies

20 June 2022

Program Chairs

Eleonora Losiouk   University of Padua, Italy
Yury Zhauniarovich   Delft University of Technology, The Netherlands

Program Committee

Yazan Boshmaf   Hamad Bin Khalifa University, Qatar
Marco Casagrande   EURECOM, France
Flavio Toffalini   EPFL, Switzerland
Giorgos Vasiliadis   Hellenic Mediterranean University and FORTH-ICS, Greece

SiMLA 2022

Fourth Workshop on Security in Machine Learning and its Applications

22 June 2022

Program Chair

Sudipta Chattopadhyay   Singapore University of Technology and Design, Singapore

Web Chair

Sakshi Udeshi   Singapore University of Technology and Design, Singapore

Publicity Chair

Ezekiel Soremekun   University of Luxembourg, Luxembourg

Program Committee

Amir Aminifar	Lund University, Sweden
Shuang Liu	Tianjin University, China
Chris Poskitt	Singapore Management University, Singapore
Ahmed Rezine	Linköping University, Sweden
Ezekiel Soremekun	University of Luxembourg, Luxembourg
Jingyi Wang	Zhejiang University, China

Contents

AIBlock – Application Intelligence and Blockchain Security

Universal Physical Adversarial Attack via Background Image

Yidan Xu[1], Juan Wang[1], Yuanzhang Li[1], Yajie Wang[2], Zixuan Xu[1], and Dianxin Wang[1](✉)

[1] School of Computer Science and Technology, Beijing Institute of Technology, Beijing, China
{xuyidan,wangjuan99,popular,xuzixuan,dianxinw}@bit.edu.cn
[2] School of Cyberspace Science and Technology, Beijing Institute of Technology, Beijing, China
wangyajie19@bit.edu.cn

Abstract. Recently, adversarial attacks against object detectors have become research hotspots in academia. However, digital adversarial attacks need to generate adversarial perturbation on digital images in a "pixel-wise" way, which is challenging to deploy accurately in the real world. Physical adversarial attacks usually need to paste the adversarial patches on the surface of target objects one by one, which is not suitable for objects with complex shapes and is challenging to deploy in practice. In this paper, we propose a universal background adversarial attack method for deep learning object detection, which puts the target objects on the universal background image and changes the local pixel information around the target objects so that the object detectors cannot recognize the target objects. This method takes the form of a universal background image for the physical adversarial attack and is easy to deploy in the real world. It can use a single universal background image to attack different classes of target objects simultaneously and has good robustness under different angles and distances. Extensive experiments have shown that the universal background attack can successfully attack two object detection models, YOLO v3 and Faster R-CNN, with average success rates of 74.9% and 67.8% with varying distances from 15 cm to 60 cm and angels from −90° to 90° in the physical world.

Keywords: Physical adversarial attack · Object detection · Adversarial examples

1 Introduction

In recent years, deep neural networks(DNNs) have shown excellent performance in various computer vision tasks, such as image classification, object detection, and image segmentation [7,8,11,14,15]. However, it has been demonstrated that DNNs are vulnerable to adversarial examples [19]. Adversarial examples are maliciously crafted perturbations that are imperceptible to human observers

J. Zhou et al. (Eds.): ACNS 2022 Workshops, LNCS 13285, pp. 3–14, 2022.
https://doi.org/10.1007/978-3-031-16815-4_1

but can mislead the target model and can even be generalized to the real world. Therefore, the existence of adversarial examples poses great security risks to the deployment of DNN-based systems in the real world, which makes adversarial examples become research hotspots in current academia.

Adversarial attacks can be divided into digital attacks and physical attacks according to whether the pixel values of an image can be directly modified. For digital adversarial attacks, the attackers can directly modify the pixel values of a digital image and input the modified digital adversarial examples into the target model to attack. However, physical adversarial attacks cannot directly modify the pixel values of an image. The attackers can only generate physical adversarial examples in the real world and then input them into the target model to attack after cameras capture the physical adversarial examples. In this paper, we focus on the physical attack, which is more challenging and meaningful in practical application because the physical adversarial examples in the real world need to face light, angle, distance, and other changes and easily lose effect.

Previous works focus on generating adversarial patches [2,17,20] to perform the adversarial attack. They train in the digital world to generate adversarial patches and then print them and paste them into the target object to attack target models. However, these patch-based methods generate adversarial patches in a "pixel-wise" way, which is challenging to deploy accurately in the real world. In addition, they need to modify the target object itself. When attacking multiple targets, they need to generate the adversarial patch for each category or even each target object and then paste the adversarial patch on the surface of target objects one by one. Recent research [22] has proposed a non-contact adversarial patch that can hide all objects of a specific class without touching the target object by pasting a carefully constructed translucent patch on the camera lens. However, in the actual attack, it is usually difficult for the attacker to contact and modify the imaging lens, and the attack can only be targeted at a specific category, rather than using a single adversarial patch to attack different categories of target objects.

In this paper, we study the universal physical adversarial attack, which can attack different kinds of objects in the real world. Inspired by the implicit use of context information by object detectors in reasoning, we propose a universal background physical adversarial attack method, which can generate a universal background image with the specific pattern, affect the detection of the target object placed on it, and make it hidden or misclassified by the target model. The universal background image proposed in this paper is easy to deploy in the physical world, can attack different kinds of target objects simultaneously, and has good robustness under the transformation of different angles and distances.

Our contributions are listed as follows:

- We propose a new physical adversarial attack method based on the background image, which can generate a universal background image with a specific pattern and affect the prediction of the target object detector by modifying the local contexts surrounding the target object. The attack method

is easy to deploy in the physical world and has good robustness under the transformation of different angles and distances.
- We realize a universal attack against object detectors in the real world for the first time, which can affect the detection of all objects belonging to various categories by using only a single universal background image.

2 Background and Related Work

2.1 Object Detection

Object detection is the primary task of computer vision and one of the most essential and challenging branches in the computer vision field. Existing object detection models can generally be divided into two categories: the one-stage models represented by the SSD [11] and YOLO [14] models and the two-stage models represented by Faster R-CNN [15]. The one-stage models can infer the location and classification result of target objects simultaneously, while the two-stage models are a two-step reasoning process. In the first stage, the two-stage models utilize the region proposal network(RPN) to choose the possible candidate areas of the objects. And in the second stage, the possible candidate areas are pooled and converted to a fixed size, and then features are extracted from each candidate box for classification. Although the detection speed of two-stage models is slower than that of one-stage models, the detection accuracy of two-stage models is generally higher.

2.2 Physical Adversarial Attacks

Kurakin et al. [9] verified for the first time that digital adversarial examples were still adversarial after being extended to the physical world by directly printing digital adversarial examples on paper and then collecting them with a camera and inputting them into the target model for test. However, such adversarial examples were not robust in the physical world. Since the physical adversarial examples will undergo a series of unknown transformations in the physical world, such as angle, distance, and illumination, which will affect the attack performance of the physical adversarial examples, the physical adversarial attack methods usually pay more attention to the robustness of the adversarial examples in the physical world. The adversarial patch is the most common physical adversarial attack method, first proposed in paper [2] to attack image classifiers. Eykholt et al. [5]aimed at the image classification model in the automatic driving scene, taking stop signs as the target objects and realizing the physical adversarial attack by printing some black and white stickers and pasting them on stop signs. To improve the robustness of physical adversarial attacks, Athalye et al. [1] proposed a general EoT framework for image classification, adding various physical transformations to the generation process of adversarial examples and using 3D printing technology to reproduce adversarial examples in the physical world, realizing robust physical attack at different viewpoints. Xu et al. [20] proposed Adversarial T-shirt, a robust physical adversarial example for evading person detectors even if it suffers from deformation due to a moving person's pose change. This method uses TPS interpolation to model fabric deformation to ensure that the adversarial patch does not lose effect due to fabric deformation when printed onto the T-shirt, thus hiding the specific person wearing the T-shirt with the adversarial pattern. Subsequently, Eykholt et al. [17] extended the method against image classification in [5] to object detection. This method minimizes the detection score of the object detector to make the detection score lower than the detection threshold so that the target object can not be successfully detected. Moreover, to maintain the adversarial robustness in the physical world, they added an alignment function to the loss function to process the adversarial examples and used smooth loss and non-printable loss to generate physical adversarial examples with smooth perturbation. Zhao et al. [21] further proposed a new method to attack the target object at the early hidden layer and generate adversarial examples with a reasonable semantic background to generate more effective adversarial examples. However, these works generate adversarial examples in a "pixel-wise" way that is difficult to deploy precisely in the real world.

2.3 Adversarial Attacks Using Contextual Information

Many previous works [3,6,13,18] have demonstrated that exploiting contextual information can improve object detection performance. Inspired by this, some recent works [10,12,16] have attacked the object detector by exploiting contextual information to generate adversarial patches that do not overlap with any objects of interest in the scene. These methods consider modifying global contextual information to attack object detectors and place the printed adversarial patch in the scene to hide all objects in the scene. But in the real world, when the detection distance changes, the position and the size of the adversarial patch in the scene will also change, limiting the application of the attack. DNN-based object detection models usually use the interior features of candidate regions to classify. In this paper, we consider modifying the local surrounding contextual information of the object, which can maintain effectiveness even when the position and the size of the adversarial patch change. Meanwhile, this method can also attack the object detection models that only use local context surrounding a proposal region.

3 Method

In this paper, we aim to generate a universal background image with a specific pattern to attack object detectors in the physical world, which can interfere with the detection of all categories of target objects placed on it, making them hidden or misclassified by the object detector when deployed in a specific background area in the physical world.

Existing patch-based methods are not suitable for the target objects with complex shapes and are challenging to deploy accurately in the physical world.

Therefore, we propose a universal background adversarial attack method, making it easy to deploy in the physical world. Since the circle is an axisymmetric pattern with rotation invariance, the specific pattern composed of concentric circles of different widths is adopted to design a universal background image. This symmetrical pattern helps to keep the background image robust in different angle and distance transformations in the physical world. In generating a universal background image, we constrain the pixel value in each concentric ring to be the same, and optimize the ring width as wide as possible to facilitate the deployment of the universal background image in the physical world. The universal background image and attack schematic diagram are shown in Fig. 1:

We initialize the universal background image with r concentric rings with a width of 1 pixel. Since the universal background image cannot be directly optimized like the pixel-level perturbation, we adopt a method similar to [4] to optimize the perturbation vector P with length r and then fill the vector values in the perturbation vector P into the rings of concentric rings to obtain the universal background image.

3.1 Objective Function

To ensure that the background image has good attack performance and reproducibility in the physical world, we carefully design a loss function to optimize the universal background image. The loss function consists of adversarial loss, width loss, and non-printable loss.

Adversarial Loss. Let f(x): $x \rightarrow \{p_{obj}^k, p_{cls}^k, b^k\}_{k=1}^K$ denote an object detector, which takes an image $x \in \mathbf{R}^{c,h,w}$ as input and outputs the prediction vectors of K bounding boxes, where p_{obj}^k is the probability that the k-th bounding box contains an object, p_{cls}^k is a probability vector over C classes for the object in the k-th bounding box, and a bounding box $b^k = [x^k, y^k, w^k, h^k]$ denotes the position of the k-th bounding box.

Input the adversarial example x^{adv} into the target detector f(x), and the adversarial loss attacks the mean of the product of the detection score and classification score in all the bounding boxes containing target category C, and the formula is as follows:

$$L_{adv} = \frac{1}{K} \sum_{i=1}^{K} (p_{obj}^k, p_{cls \in C}^k) \tag{1}$$

Width Loss. We use the L1 norm of the difference between adjacent vector values of the perturbation vector P to optimize the ring width. Compared with other norms, the L1 norm tends to generate sparse solutions, which helps to optimize the difference between adjacent vectors to 0, so that adjacent concentric rings have the same pixel value, thus connecting into wider rings, reducing the

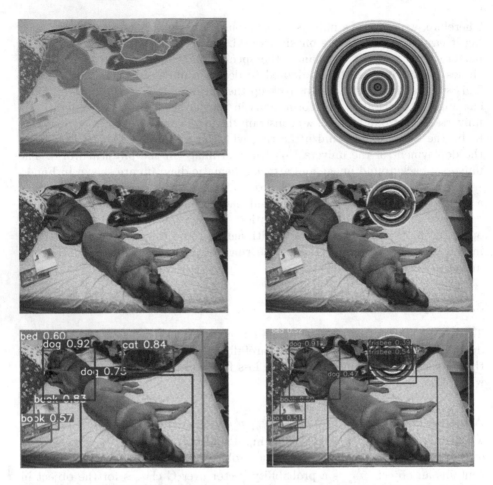

Fig. 1. The universal background image and attack schematics. Top: the left column is the result of instance segmentation, and the right column is the universal background image generated on YOLO v3 model. Middle: the left column is the clean image, and the right column is the adversarial example obtained by placing the universal background image under the target object cat. Bottom: the left column is the detection result of the clean image, where the target object cat is normally detected with high confidence of 0.84, and the right column is the detection result of the adversarial example, where the target object cat is misclassified as a frisbee.

number of rings, and thus alleviating the deployment difficulty of the physical world. The formula of ring width loss is as follows:

$$L_{width} = \sum_{i=1}^{r} |P_{i+1} - P_i| \qquad (2)$$

Non-printable Loss. We use a non-printable loss to mitigate the difference between the printer's gamut and the digital world's. We generate the universal background image in the physical world by printing. Since the colors produced by most printers do not fully cover the entire RGB color space, the colors produced by printers are somewhat different from the colors in the digital world. So we refer to related work and use NPS(non-printability score) as part of the objective function to deal with this constraint. The formula is as follows:

$$L_{nps} = \sum_{i=1}^{r} \prod_{p' \in W} |sigmoid(P_i) - p'| \tag{3}$$

where W is a set of printable colors (RGB triples).

Finally, we have a total objective function consisting of three components:

$$L_{total} = L_{adv} + \lambda_1 \cdot L_{width} + \lambda_2 \cdot L_{nps} \tag{4}$$

where λ_1 and λ_2 are hyperparameters that balance the loss terms. During the training, we set λ_1 to 0.01 and λ_2 to 5.

3.2 The Generation of the Universal Background Image

We first randomly initialize the perturbation vector $P \sim N(0,1)$ to be normally distributed. Then we use the image data set of the target category C for training to optimize the perturbation vector P. In the process of optimization, to make the value of the perturbation vector P within the effective range [0, 1], we use the sigmoid function $\Theta(x) = \frac{1}{(1+e^x)}$ to process the perturbation vector P, and obtain $\Theta(P)$. Then, the values of $\Theta(P)$ are successively filled into the ring so that all pixel values in the same ring are consistent with the corresponding values of $\Theta(P)$ to obtain the universal background image of this round. In each iteration, we place the universal background image under the target object in clean image x to get the adversarial example x^{adv}, then input it into the target detector, and calculate the loss function according to formula 4. Finally, we use the MI-FGSM method to update the perturbation vector P. MI-FGSM is a common black-box attack method, which can generate more transferable adversarial samples by introducing momentum to stabilize the update direction. Since the optimization variable in this paper is perturbation vector P, the updating formula of MI-FGSM is as follows:

$$g_{i+1} = \mu \cdot g_i + \frac{\nabla_p L_{total}}{||\nabla_p L_{total}||_1}, P_{i+1} = P_i + \alpha \cdot sign(g_{i+1}) \tag{5}$$

where μ and α are both set to 1.

During the placement of adversarial examples, we follow the following steps:

- We firstly perform instance segmentation for all objects in the clean image X;

- Then we find all target objects classified as C and scale the universal background image randomly to 1–1.5 times the size of the corresponding detection bounding box to enhance the robustness of attacking objects of different sizes. Then the universal background image is placed under the target objects to attack. The center of the universal background image is aligned with the center of the detection bounding box. If the universal background image has been added to the current background and the overlap rate exceeds 80%, the universal background image will not be added to this position.
- Finally, we place the universal background images successively under the target objects in the clean image x, and restore all the objects to their original positions according to the previous instance segmentation results to obtain the modified adversarial example X^{adv}.

4   Experiments

We evaluate our proposed universal background image in the physical world to prove its effectiveness.

4.1   Experiment Setup

We chose the first-stage model representing YOLO v3 and the second-stage model representing Faster R-CNN as target models and generate the universal background images in the digital world, respectively. We use the COCO training set for training. We randomly selected ten categories from COCO's 80 categories for training and randomly selected 100 photos from each training category, a total of 1000 photos. Then, we used Epson L4160 color printer and glossy photo paper to print the generated universal background images, fixed in 600*600 pixels. In the physical world, we select airplane, elephant, horse, and sheep as four different categories of attack objects to verify the universal attack effect, among which only airplane is the category used in training. To evaluate the attack effect of the universal background image at different distances and angles, we divided the distance between 15 cm and 60 cm into three areas, with 15 cm as an interval, and used the built-in camera of Galaxy S9 to shoot 10s videos at $0°$, $\pm30°$, $\pm60°$, and $\pm90°$ respectively. YOLO v3 model and Faster R-CNN model were used for detection. In this paper, we use random Gaussian noise background images for comparison to evaluate attack success rates at different distances and angles. In this paper, attack success is defined as the target object being hidden or misclassified by the target detector. The success rate of physical attack is $f_{succ} = N_{succ}/N_{total}$, where N_{total} stands for all frames in the video, and N_{succ} stands for the frame number of a successful attack.

We use $image_{Gauss}$ to represent random Gaussian noise background image, $image_{YOLOv3}$ to represent universal background image trained on YOLO v3 model, and $image_{FasterR-CNN}$ to represent universal background image trained on Faster R-CNN model.

Figure 2 and Fig. 3 respectively show the success rate of attacking the YOLO V3 model and the Faster R-CNN model with three universal background images at different distances and angles. The darker the background color in the region, the higher the success rate of attack.

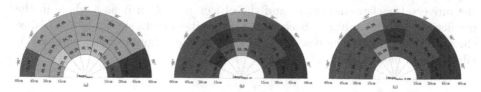

Fig. 2. The universal physical attack success rate of attacking YOLO v3 model at different angles and distances.

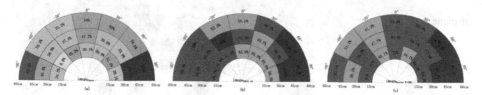

Fig. 3. The universal physical attack success rate of attacking Faster R-CNN model at different angles and distances.

4.2 Attack Success Rate

Compared with the direct application of $image_{Gauss}$, using $image_{YOLOv3}$ and $image_{FasterR-CNN}$ to attack YOLO V3 model and Faster R-CNN model have better attack effects. The average attack success rate can be increased by more than 20%. It shows that our optimization method further finds a universal background image with a better attack effect on the baseline.

4.3 The Effect of Angle and Distance

The results show that the greater the angle and distance, the more successful the attack. However, at different distances and angles, the universal background images proposed by us all be effective, which indicates that the universal background images are still robust in the physical world even without physical transformation.

4.4 The Effect of Target Model

The success rate of using background images generated by different training models to attack the same target model is very close, which indicates that the universal background image proposed by us will have excellent attack performance even if the training model and attack model are different. As can be seen from Fig. 2 and Fig. 3, the YOLO v3 model, as a first-stage model, relies more on contexts in prediction, so the attack success rate is higher than Faster R-CNN, a two-stage model.

4.5   Visualized Results

Figure 4 shows the visualized results of the physical attack. Due to the limited perturbation space, the universal background image tends to make the target object misclassified rather than hidden. We believe that the model will recognize the universal background image and the object placed on it as a whole in the prediction, and the universal background image itself looks similar to the frisbee class, so it will introduce new features so that the original object category is affected and misclassified.

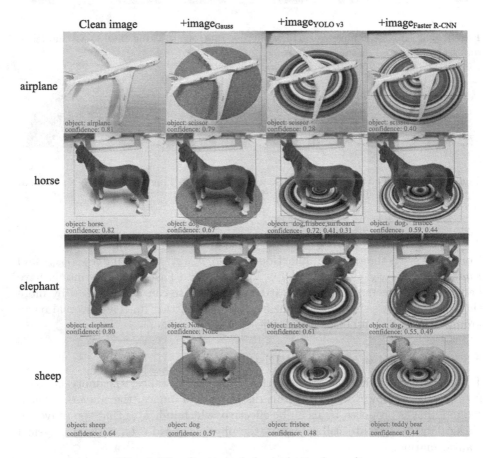

Fig. 4. Visualization of physical attack results.

5   Conclusion

In this paper, we propose a universal background adversarial attack method against object detectors, which can use a single universal background image to attack different types of target objects by modifying the local contexts around them. Unlike previous patch-based attack methods, which generate perturbations in a "pixel-wise" way, our method generates a universal background image with the specific pattern, which is much easier to deploy in the real world than "pixel-level" patches and has good robustness at different angles and distances. Extensive experiments have shown that our proposed method can achieve excellent performance against two object detection models, YOLO v3 and Faster R-CNN, with average success rates of 74.9% and 67.8% with varying distances from 15 cm to 60 cm and angels from $-90°$ to $90°$ in physical world attacks. Compared with random Gaussian noise background attack, the universal background with a specific pattern proposed in this paper has a better adversarial attack effect. Although the proposed universal background physical adversarial attack has excellent performance, as a new type of physical adversarial attack, our work still needs to be improved, and there is still a lot of room for improvement, such as further research on the automatic generation of background patterns, to find more adversarial and robust background image. In the future, we will continue to study the automatic optimization method of background images to get more effective adversarial examples.

References

1. Athalye, A., Engstrom, L., Ilyas, A., Kwok, K.: Synthesizing robust adversarial examples. In: International Conference on Machine Learning, pp. 284–293. PMLR (2018)
2. Brown, T.B., Mané, D., Roy, A., Abadi, M., Gilmer, J.: Adversarial patch. arXiv preprint arXiv:1712.09665 (2017)
3. Choi, M.J., Lim, J.J., Torralba, A., Willsky, A.S.: Exploiting hierarchical context on a large database of object categories. In: 2010 IEEE Computer Society Conference on Computer Vision and Pattern Recognition, pp. 129–136. IEEE (2010). https://doi.org/10.1109/CVPR.2010.5540221
4. Dong, X., et al.: Robust superpixel-guided attentional adversarial attack. In: Proceedings of the IEEE/CVF Conference on Computer Vision and Pattern Recognition, pp. 12895–12904 (2020). https://doi.org/10.1109/CVPR42600.2020.01291
5. Eykholt, K., et al.: Robust physical-world attacks on deep learning visual classification. In: Proceedings of the IEEE Conference on Computer Vision and Pattern Recognition, pp. 1625–1634 (2018)
6. Galleguillos, C., Belongie, S.: Context based object categorization: a critical survey. Comput. Vis. Image Underst. **114**(6), 712–722 (2010). https://doi.org/10.1016/j.cviu.2010.02.004
7. He, K., Gkioxari, G., Dollár, P., Girshick, R.: Mask R-CNN. In: Proceedings of the IEEE International Conference on Computer Vision, pp. 2961–2969 (2017). https://doi.org/10.1109/TPAMI.2018.2844175
8. Krizhevsky, A., Sutskever, I., Hinton, G.E.: ImageNet classification with deep convolutional neural networks. In: Advances in Neural Information Processing Systems, vol. 25, pp. 1097–1105 (2012). https://doi.org/10.1145/3065386
9. Kurakin, A., Goodfellow, I., Bengio, S., et al.: Adversarial examples in the physical world (2016). https://doi.org/10.1201/9781351251389-8

10. Lee, M., Kolter, Z.: On physical adversarial patches for object detection. arXiv preprint arXiv:1906.11897 (2019)
11. Liu, W., et al.: SSD: single shot multibox detector. In: Leibe, B., Matas, J., Sebe, N., Welling, M. (eds.) ECCV 2016. LNCS, vol. 9905, pp. 21–37. Springer, Cham (2016). https://doi.org/10.1007/978-3-319-46448-0_2
12. Liu, X., Yang, H., Liu, Z., Song, L., Li, H., Chen, Y.: Dpatch: an adversarial patch attack on object detectors. arXiv preprint arXiv:1806.02299 (2018)
13. Oliva, A., Torralba, A.: The role of context in object recognition. Trends Cogn. Sci. 11(12), 520–527 (2007)
14. Redmon, J., Farhadi, A.: YOLOv3: an incremental improvement. arXiv preprint arXiv:1804.02767 (2018)
15. Ren, S., He, K., Girshick, R., Sun, J.: Faster R-CNN: towards real-time object detection with region proposal networks. In: Advances in Neural Information Processing Systems, vol. 28, pp. 91–99 (2015). https://doi.org/10.1109/TPAMI.2016.2577031
16. Saha, A., Subramanya, A., Patil, K., Pirsiavash, H.: Role of spatial context in adversarial robustness for object detection. In: Proceedings of the IEEE/CVF Conference on Computer Vision and Pattern Recognition Workshops, pp. 784–785 (2020). https://doi.org/10.1109/CVPRW50498.2020.00400
17. Song, D., et al.: Physical adversarial examples for object detectors. In: 12th USENIX Workshop on Offensive Technologies (WOOT 2018) (2018)
18. Song, Z., Chen, Q., Huang, Z., Hua, Y., Yan, S.: Contextualizing object detection and classification. In: CVPR 2011, pp. 1585–1592. IEEE (2011). https://doi.org/10.1109/CVPR.2011.5995330
19. Szegedy, C., et al.: Intriguing properties of neural networks. arXiv preprint arXiv:1312.6199 (2013)
20. Xu, K., et al.: Adversarial T-Shirt! evading person detectors in a physical world. In: Vedaldi, A., Bischof, H., Brox, T., Frahm, J.-M. (eds.) ECCV 2020. LNCS, vol. 12350, pp. 665–681. Springer, Cham (2020). https://doi.org/10.1007/978-3-030-58558-7_39
21. Zhao, Y., Zhu, H., Liang, R., Shen, Q., Zhang, S., Chen, K.: Seeing isn't believing: towards more robust adversarial attack against real world object detectors. In: Proceedings of the 2019 ACM SIGSAC Conference on Computer and Communications Security, pp. 1989–2004 (2019). https://doi.org/10.1145/3319535.3354259
22. Zolfi, A., Kravchik, M., Elovici, Y., Shabtai, A.: The translucent patch: a physical and universal attack on object detectors. In: Proceedings of the IEEE/CVF Conference on Computer Vision and Pattern Recognition, pp. 15232–15241 (2021). https://doi.org/10.1109/CVPR46437.2021.01498

Efficient Verifiable Boolean Range Query for Light Clients on Blockchain Database

Jianpeng Gong, Jiaojiao Wu, Jianfeng Wang, and Shichong Tan[✉]

State Key Laboratory of Integrated Service Networks (ISN), Xidian University,
Xi'an 710071, China
{jpgong,jiaojiaowujj}@stu.xidian.edu.cn, jfwang@xidian.edu.cn,
sctan@mail.xidian.edu.cn

Abstract. Blockchain allows clients to query and verify any transactions, which requires the clients to maintain the entire blockchain database locally. This approach is inadvisable because the blockchain database is an append-only ledger and incurs significant maintenance overhead. Very recently, blockchain light client has attracted considerable concerns, which relies on a third party (i.e., a full node) to perform query processing and verification. However, the dishonest full node may return an incorrect and incomplete result of the query requests. Therefore, it remains a challenging issue to achieve secure, efficient, and rich verifiable queries for light clients. In this paper, we propose an efficient verifiable Boolean range query scheme for light clients on the blockchain database. Firstly, we design a new authenticated data structure, polynomial commitment B^+-tree (PCB-tree), which efficiently ensures the correctness and completeness of Boolean range queries for blockchain light clients. Secondly, we provide a tunable trade-off between query time and communication overhead by autonomously setting the fanout size of the PCB-tree. Moreover, our scheme can support batch processing to reduce query complexity and proof size. Finally, security analysis and performance evaluation show that our proposed scheme is secure and practical.

Keywords: Blockchain database · Light clients · Verifiable boolean range query · Data integrity

1 Introduction

Blockchain, as a revolutionary technology [10], has aroused widespread attention and research in various fields, such as smart contract platform, decentralized storage, and supply chain traceability. Meanwhile, with the popularization of blockchain technology in the finance and supply chain, the people's demand for efficient and various queries of data stored in a blockchain database has become more and more urgent. For illustration, a user, Bob, wants to query the data about his consumption in the last month that satisfy the following Boolean range conditions, such as "[2021-11-01, 2021-12-01]" and "*sender* = Bob ∨ *receiver*

J. Zhou et al. (Eds.): ACNS 2022 Workshops, LNCS 13285, pp. 15–35, 2022.
https://doi.org/10.1007/978-3-031-16815-4_2

= Bob", where $\vee$ represents Boolean logical operator OR. The result will be faithfully returned if the query is conducted in the traditional centralized systems with a trusted party. From the security perspective, if the client downloads the complete blockchain duplication as a full node, it can query and validate the integrity of transactions locally. However, The appended-only and immutable properties of blockchains result in the data increases with the generation of new blocks, which requires a large amount of storage and network overhead [7]. In the past two years, the data on the Ethereum blockchain has been growing linearly with a slope of roughly 0.424 GB/Day is significantly faster than Bitcoin, which exceeds the capability of most query clients. To address above concern, most blockchain systems introduce the light client (e.g., Simplified Payment Verification [10] and Light Ethereum Subprotocol [18]), which can download only the valid block header from the longest chain to verify whether the current block contains the interested transactions without the complete blockchain dataset.

However, the light client that stores only block header information will raise the following concerns when querying transactions:

- **The integrity of query result:** The light client relies on the query service provided by the full node. If the full node is untrusted, it probably returns fake or partial results to light clients [3], or it will obtain the privacy information of light clients by capturing some sensitive request [8,13]. Therefore, the security of current blockchain queries is still a crucial issue.
- **The query efficiency:** The increasing growth of blockchain brings heavy overhead for developers to access transactions on the blockchain. Meanwhile, the current blockchain system only supports single-type queries and has low query efficiency. Therefore, it is necessary to implement a blockchain query system with high efficiency and rich query functionalities for light clients.

There are some attempts to implement verifiable queries of blockchain for the light client. The state-of-the-art schemes either utilize the trusted execution environment or authenticated data structure to ensure the integrity of query results. Therefore, it is of great significance to design a new structure that guarantees the correctness and completeness of the query results and reduces the communication and verification costs.

1.1 Contributions

In this paper, we focus on verifiable Boolean and range queries. Motivated by the above observations, we propose an efficient and verifiable Boolean range query scheme for light clients on the blockchain database. To evaluate our design, we implement the prototype system and conducted multiple experiments based on it. Our main contributions can be summarized as follows:

- We propose a new authenticated data structure, polynomial commitment B$^+$-tree (PCB-tree), that supports the Boolean and range queries.
- We provide an adjustable trade-off between query time and communication overhead by autonomously setting the fanout size of the PCB-tree. Meanwhile, our scheme can support batch processing to reduce the proof size and verification time.

– We prove the security of the scheme in theory and implement a prototype system to evaluate the performance of our proposed scheme. The experiment results demonstrate that our scheme is efficient in terms of query, verification and communication overheads.

1.2 Related Work

In this section, we briefly review the related works on verifiable query processing over traditional outsourced databases and blockchain.

Verifiable Query Processing over Traditional Database. There are some verifiable query works that have been studied in outsourced databases. The current verifiable query is divided into two categories: circuit-based Verifiable Computation (VC) technique and Authenticated Data Structure (ADS). However, the VC-based scheme overhead is very high and sometimes impractical [11]. In comparison, the ADS-based approach is generally more efficient. The Merkle Hash Tree (MHT) is a significant component in verifiable query schemes and is extended to different types of databases, including Merkle B-tree (MB-tree) for relational data [6] and Merkle R-tree (MR-tree) for spatial data [20]. However, these works are more for the outsourced databases and insufficient for the blockchain case.

Verifiable Query Processing over Blockchain. Simplified Payment Verification (SPV) protocol[1] is the first light client protocol proposed in the Bitcoin paper [10]. It can use Merkle proof to verify whether the blockchain network accepts a transaction. However, the costs of verification and storage increase linearly with the growth of the blockchain. Some verifiable query works have been studied in blockchain systems to ensure the integrity of the query results. Xu et al. [19] present an accumulator-based ADS and implement a verifiable query framework, called vChain, that alleviates the storage and computing costs of the light client. However, the public key size of the accumulator is linear to the largest multiset size, and the large proof size leads to an expensive communication overhead for the light client. Shao et al. [16] utilize the Trusted Execution Environment (TEE) to achieve an authentication range query scheme for blockchain, but it does not discuss potential side-channel attacks against TEE. Zhu et al. [23] put forward a verifiable aggregate queries scheme based on the accumulator that supports multiple selection predicates. However, it uses the same accumulator as vChain and does not solve the linear overhead problem. Meanwhile, the construction cost of ADS is expensive since different query dimensions require different ADSs. Zhang et al. [21,22] utilize MB-tree structure and cryptographic accumulator to present a gas-efficient scheme for hybrid-storage blockchains. However, its index maintenance cost remains relatively expensive, and the query process is complicated. LineageChain [15] leverages a novel skip list index to achieve efficient provenance query processing and stores provenance information

---

[1] The concepts of payment verification and transaction verification are different in the blockchain.

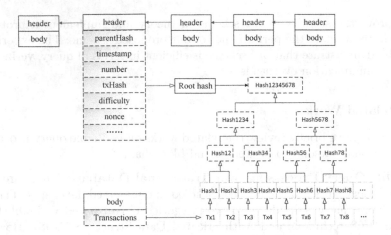

Fig. 1. Blockchain data structure

in a Merkle tree. Therefore, LineageChain only ensures the correctness of the query results, but not completeness.

2 Preliminaries

2.1 Blockchain Data Structure

From the perspective of data structure, blocks in blockchain mainly contain two parts: block header and block body. As shown in Fig. 1, all transactions are recorded in each block and organized a MHT built on top of them. The block header contains: (1) *parentHash*, which is the hash of the previous block; (2) *timestamp*, which is the time of block creation; (3) *number*, which is block height; (4) *txHash*, which is the root hash of MHT; (5) *difficulty*, which is the difficulty coefficient of mined blocks; (6) *nonce*, which is the random number constructed by the miners to solve Proof of Work (PoW) protocol problem. Other miners can append it to the blockchain after verifying the *nonce* of the new block.

2.2 B⁺-Tree

B⁺-tree [4] is a multi-branch sort tree structure that can improve the search efficiency of range queries. The numerical range query process of B⁺-tree is described as follows:

- One starts the query from the root node. If the lower bound of the range query matches the current non-leaf node, it then searches its subtree.
- When traversing to a leaf node, one adds the corresponding record into the results set if the lower bound element is found, then continue to search backwards through the pointer relationship between nodes until the upper bound is found at the end of the query.

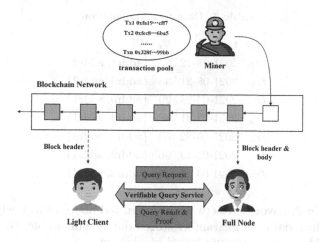

Fig. 2. Our system architecture

2.3 Constant Size Polynomial Commitment

A polynomial commitment scheme allows one to commit a polynomial with a short proof while keeping it hidden from others. The verifier can confirm the claimed statement of the committed polynomial. Kate, Zaverucha and Goldberg [5] first present polynomial commitment scheme (KZG commitments) as the following:

- **Setup**($1^\lambda, t$) generates an appropriate algebraic structure $\mathcal{G}$ and a public-private key pair $\langle \mathsf{PK}, \mathsf{SK} \rangle$ to commit to a polynomial of degree $\leq t$.
- **Commit**($\mathsf{PK}, p(x)$) generates a commitment $\mathcal{C}$ to a polynomial $p(x)$ using the public key PK.
- **CreateWitness**($\mathsf{PK}, p(x), z$) generates a witness ω for the evaluation $p(z)$ of $p(x)$ at the index z.
- **VerifyEval**($\mathsf{PK}, \mathcal{C}, z, p(z), \omega$) verifies that $p(z)$ is indeed the evaluation at the index z of the polynomial committed in $\mathcal{C}$.
- **CreateWitnessBatch**($\mathsf{PK}, p(x), S$) generates the batched witness ω_S for the value $p(i)$, where $i \in S$.
- **VerifyEvalBatch**($\mathsf{PK}, \mathcal{C}, S, r(x), \omega_S$) verifies the correctness of the witness returned by **CreateWitnessBatch** algorithm.

3 Problem Statement

In this section, we describe the system model and threat model of our scheme.

3.1 System Model

We propose a verifiable query scheme on blockchain database. Figure 2 depicts the four entities in our system framework:

Table 1. Data formal definition

tx$_{id}$	t_i	V_i	W_i
tx_1	2021-05-12	5	{addr1, addr2}
tx_2	2021-05-21	35	{addr3, addr2}
tx_3	2021-04-28	20	{addr5, addr1}
tx_4	2021-05-21	80	{addr4, addr1}
tx_5	2021-05-22	56	{addr6, addr8}
tx_6	2021-05-19	90	{addr3, addr1}
tx_7	2021-04-22	10	{addr3, addr1}

- **Blockchain Network:** A network of untrusted nodes collectively maintains the blockchain data and guarantees stored data is immutable. We assume our system is based on an account-based blockchain.
- **Full Node:** A full node downloads complete duplication of the blockchain database and can independently verify the correctness of any block/transaction [1]. Also, the full node can provide payment services for others, such as query or Application Programming Interface (API) services.
- **Light Client:** A light client only stores block headers and verifies transactions relying on full nodes. It generally runs on resource-constrained devices.
- **Miner:** A miner[2] competes to create new blocks by a consensus algorithm (*e.g.*, PoW algorithm) and appends it to the blockchain network.

In our system, when a light client wants to retrieve existing transaction data, the light client firstly synchronizes all newer block headers from the longest chain and connects to one of the full node servers to send query requests in which the client is interested. The miners are responsible for organizing all transactions within the block to construct the PCB-tree and appending root commitment to the block header to replace the traditional root hash. The full node provides rich queries for light clients and returns both query results and the corresponding proofs using our ADS structure. After that, the clients use the Verification Object (VO) to verify the correctness and completeness of returned results.

As shown in Table 1, the transaction data tx_i is defined as triple elements $\langle t_i, V_i, W_i \rangle$, where t_i is the transaction timestamp, V_i is a transaction value that represents one numerical attribute, and W_i is a set attribute that contains the address information of the sender and receiver. Each block contains multiple transaction data objects $\{tx_1, tx_2, \cdots, tx_n\}$. Light clients want to query all transactions that match the query request in a period. In this paper, we consider mainly the rich Boolean range queries based on the time window. Specifically, a Boolean range query is defined as follows: $q = \langle [t_s, t_e], [v_l, v_u], \gamma \rangle$, where t_s and t_e is the start and end time of a time window, v_l and v_u represent the lower and upper bound of the transaction query range, and γ is a Boolean query such as addr1∧(addr2∨addr3). For example, the light client may request a specific query $q = \langle [2021 - 05, 2021 - 06], [10, 40], sender = \text{addr1} \wedge receiver = \text{addr2} \rangle$ to find all the matched transactions.

---

[2] Miners can be full nodes or light nodes.

3.2   Threat Model and Assumptions

In our scheme, we assume the blockchain network is strong and does not consider some attacks against blockchain, *e.g.*, Eclipse attack, and Sybil attack. We believe that light clients are honestly reliable and randomly connect to one of the full nodes from the blockchain network to perform the query operation. Furthermore, driven by economic interests, we assume the miners are honest to faithfully execute our ADS structure, which will not lead to some underlying system security vulnerabilities. Meanwhile, we think no particular relationship between miners and full nodes. The full nodes are untrusted and regarded as potential adversaries. On the one hand, the full nodes can obtain some sensitive information (*e.g.*, account address and transaction information) by the queries of clients, which will result in the disclosure of user privacy [3,8]. On the other hand, the full nodes may return incorrect or incomplete query results to reduce the query expense [19]. Hence, the query results from the full nodes need to be validated to satisfy the following criteria:

- **Correctness.** The result data tuples indeed exist in the blockchain databases, and they have not been tampered with in any way. Meanwhile, as the results, they should satisfy the query conditions.
- **Completeness.** No satisfactory results have been omitted by the full nodes, either intentionally or unintentionally.
- **Lightweightness.** The results should have lower storage costs and communication overhead for lightweight clients than that of current schemes.

4   Polynomial Commitment B$^+$-Tree

4.1   Overview

The MHT is usually constructed for each block to authenticate transaction data in the original blockchain. However, this naive method has the following shortcomings. Firstly, the MHT supports only efficient membership queries instead of providing non-membership proofs. Secondly, the proofs of MHT can hardly be aggregated effectively, resulting in serious communication overhead and inefficient verification. To deal with the drawbacks above, we propose a novel ADS structure illuminated by [6] and [17], PCB-tree, which ensures the integrity of light client queries and avoids the problem of large public key parameters and proofs.

4.2   PCB-Tree Structure on Blockchain

For simplicity, we combine the polynomial commitment and B$^+$-tree to implement a PCB-tree supporting constant size intra-node proof and more efficient queries than MHT. Denote (k_i, tx_i) the key-value pair of PCB-tree leaf node, where k_i represents the numerical attribute (*e.g.*, transferred transaction's amount), tx_i is the corresponding transaction data. In the B$^+$-tree index, the

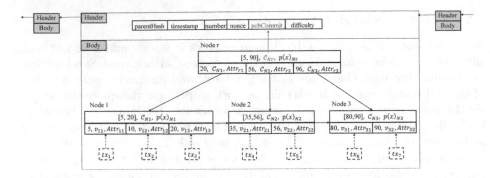

Fig. 3. The ADS structure on a block

overflow page is commonly used to deal with duplicate keys [14]. For the convenience of description, we assume there are no duplicate keys in the context.

Figure 3 shows a block structure with PCB-tree. The block header consists of the following elements: *parentHash, timestamp, number, pcbCommit, difficulty, nonce*, where *pcbCommit* is the root commitment of PCB-tree to replace the original *txHash* (Fig. 1). In the PCB-tree, each tree node has four fields: the minimum and maximum key (denoted by $[min, max]$), the node commitment value (denoted by $\mathcal{C}$), the polynomial (denoted by $p(x)$), and the transactions set of each node (denoted by S). Let $LagrangeInterpolation(\cdot)$ be a function to find a polynomial, '$\|$' be the string concatenation, $hash(\cdot)$ be Keccak-256 algorithm, respectively. The fields of a node are described as follows:

- $S = [(k_1, v_1), \ldots, (k_b, v_b)]$, where b denotes the number of key-value pairs in each node, k_i is the index. For the leaf node, v_i represents a transaction hash such that $v_i = hash(tx_i)$. For the non-leaf node, v_i represents a commitment value $\mathcal{C}_i$ of its child node.
- $k_i' = hash(k_i \| i)$, $S' = [(k_1', v_1), \ldots, (k_b', v_b)]$. To account for the sorted order of the keys and the position binding relation within the nodes, we transform the k_i to k_i'.
- $p(x)$ represents a polynomial for key-value pairs in each node such that $p(k_i') = v_i$. It can be done with the Lagrange interpolation formula or Horner's method.
- $\mathcal{C} = \mathbf{Commit}(\mathsf{PK}, p(x))$, where PK is the public key generated in $\mathbf{Setup}(\cdot)$ algorithm in advance.
- *Attr* represents attributes set for each node. For the leaf node, it is a set of transaction attributes, including the boundary keys information, the address information and so on. For the non-leaf node, $Attr_n = Attr_{l_1} \cup \ldots \cup Attr_{l_b}$, where $l_1, \ldots, l_b$ are the children of node n.

Algorithm 1 describes the ADS construction procedure, and the PCB-tree is built based on the transaction objects of the block in a bottom-up fashion. First, the miner parses each transaction tx_i in transaction set T into the formal we

---

Algorithm 1: ADS Construction (by the miner)

Input: Public key PK, Transactions set T
Output: root commitment $pcbCommit$

1	Initialize a new PCB-tree;	17	**repeat**
2	Parse T into key-value pairs $List_{tx} \leftarrow$	18	**for** $i{=}1$ to l/f **do** // non-leaf node
	$\{(k_1, tx_1, attr_1), \cdots, (k_n, tx_n, attr_n)\}$;	19	**for** $j{=}1$ to f **do**
3	Sort $List_{tx}$ according to the k_i;	20	$k_j \leftarrow k_{i+j}$;
4	Number of leaf node $l \leftarrow n/f$;	21	$v_j \leftarrow C_l$;
5	**for** $i{=}1$ to l **do** // leaf node	22	$Attr_j \leftarrow Attr_l$;
6	// entries of each node;	23	**end**
7	**for** $j{=}1$ to f **do**	24	$S_i \leftarrow [(k_1, v_1), \cdots, (k_f, v_f)]$;
8	$k_j \leftarrow k_{i+j}$;	25	$Attr_i \leftarrow [Attr_1, \cdots, Attr_f]$;
9	$v_j \leftarrow hash(tx_{i+j})$;	26	$C_i, p(x)_i \leftarrow$
10	$Attr_j \leftarrow attr_{i+j}$;		**nodeUpdate**$(S_i, node_i)$;
11	**end**	27	Insert $\langle C_i, p(x)_i, S_i, Attr_i \rangle$ to i
12	$S_i \leftarrow [(k_1, v_1), \cdots, (k_f, v_f)]$;		-th PCB-tree node;
13	$Attr_i \leftarrow [Attr_1, \cdots, Attr_f]$;	29	**end**
14	$C_i, p(x)_i \leftarrow$ **nodeUpdate**$(S_i, node_i)$;	30	$l \leftarrow l/f$;
15	Insert $\langle C_i, p(x)_i, S_i, Attr_i \rangle$ to i-th	31	**until** *all transactions is completed*;
	PCB-tree node;	32	Store root commitment $pcbCommit$ in
16	**end**		block header;

---

defined. Next, the miner inserts each transaction data to the leaf node of PCB-tree and updates the commitment value C and polynomial $p(x)$ for each node. This process is repeated until all transactions are inserted. Finally, after the tree construction is finished, the root commitment of the PCB-tree will be written in the block header as $pcbCommit$. The node update algorithm **nodeUpdate**() aims to update the value of commitment and polynomial for inserted node. We first build the binding relationship between the numerical attribute k_i and position i, then calculate the polynomial by the Lagrange interpolation formula for the node and its corresponding commitment value. The procedure is described in Algorithm 2.

Algorithm 2: PCB-tree Node Update Algorithm

1	**Function nodeUpdate**(S, *curr*)**:**
	Input: The key-value pairs of node S, The updated node *curr*
	Output: The commitment C, The polynomial $p(x)$
2	**for** $i{=}1$ to $S.size$ **do**
3	$k_i' \leftarrow hash(k_i \parallel i)$;
4	**end**
5	$S' \leftarrow [(k_1', v_1), \cdots, (k_{S.size}', v_{S.size})]$;
6	$p(x) \leftarrow LagrangeInterpolation(S')$;
7	$C \leftarrow$ **Commit**$(PK, p(x))$;
8	**return** $C, p(x)$;

Our PCB-tree leverages the feature of B^+-tree to improve the efficiency of range queries and reduce the I/O operation times of node queries. The query efficiency of our PCB-tree is higher than MHT. In this paper, the size of public key PK grows linearly with the branching factor f of the PCB-tree, rather than the largest transaction set size. It can be adjusted flexibly to make the trade-off between query efficiency and communication overhead. Meanwhile, the public-private key pair of KZG commitments can be generated by executing the Distributed Key Generation (DKG) protocol [12], and the PK can be shared to a bulletin board which can be generated once and then reused.

5   The Proposed Construction

For ease of illustration, we first focus on the range query in each block. We then extend it to the Boolean query and ensure the integrity of its results. Finally, to enhance the performance of the query service, we discuss batch processing on multiple query objects. Based on our designed PCB-tree, we explain the proof generation and verification for the range query.

5.1   Verifiable Range Query Processing

In the verifiable query phase, when the light client triggers a query request, the full node parses the query firstly and returns the correct results R and proofs VO according to Algorithm 3. Then, the light client updates the newest block headers periodically and verifies the integrity of the results through VO. Next, we will focus on the range query processing on numerical attribute V_i for the full node.

In the full node, the range query is executed in a top-down way that is similar to the range query of the B$^+$-tree. Algorithm 3 shows a range query $q = [l, u]$ on a single block. When l equals u, the range query is a point query. First, the full node can process a query from the root node. If the query condition does not intersect with the attribute of the current node, it means its subtree does not contribute to the query result. In this case, the full node will generate the proof for the root node as the VO, and the procedure is terminated. Otherwise, keep exploring its subtree. During the search process, if the keyword on the non-leaf node is equal to the given value, it only adds the corresponding proof to VO and does not terminate until the real data in leaf nodes are found. The leaf node of the PCB-tree organizes a sequence list, and we can traverse backward from the first leaf node found. The query algorithm of PCB-tree **RangeQuery()** is described in Algorithm 5 (See Appendix A), which recursively queries each level of nodes. To improve the query efficiency of internal nodes, we use an efficient localization algorithm **getPos()**. It mainly utilizes the idea of binary search to locate the query path quickly, and we use the bit vector to denote which keys are the points on the search path in each node. For example, the $\langle 0, 1, 1, 0 \rangle$ means that the second and third positions of the current node are retrieved. Algorithm 6 shows the localization procedure in detail (See Appendix A).

Algorithm 3: Range Query Processing (by full node)

Input: PCB-tree $root$, Range query condition $q = [l, u]$
Output: Query Results R, Verification Object VO

1 Initialize two empty set R, VO;
2 **if** $root.[min,max]$ *matches* q **then**
3 $\quad|\quad$ **RangeQuery**$(root, l, u, R, VO)$;
4 **else**
5 $\quad|\quad$ $R = \emptyset$;
6 $\quad|\quad$ $num \leftarrow root.$keyNum, $p(x) \leftarrow root.p(x)$;
7 $\quad|\quad$ $\omega_{min} =$ **CreateWitness**$(PK, p(x), k_0)$;
8 $\quad|\quad$ add $\langle 0, (k_0, v_0), \omega_{min} \rangle$ to VO;
9 $\quad|\quad$ $\omega_{max} =$ **CreateWitness**$(PK, p(x), k_{num})$;
10 $\quad|\quad$ add $\langle num, (k_{num}, v_{num}), \omega_{max} \rangle$ to VO;
11 **end**
12 **return** $\langle R, VO \rangle$

For example, consider a range query $q = [19, 40]$ as shown in Fig. 3. The full node traverses the keyword index from the root node to the leaf nodes, and adds the matched transaction to R. Finally, the results are $\{[(3, 20, tx_3), (1, 35, tx_4)]\}$. In this case, the full node needs to return the membership of the query results and the non-membership of the greatest and smallest elements in the range, $e.g.$, 19,40. The VO returned by the full node includes $\{[\langle 1, (20, \mathcal{C}_{N1}), \omega_{r1} \rangle, \langle 2, (56, \mathcal{C}_{N2}), \omega_{r2} \rangle], [[\langle 2, (10, v_{12}), \omega_{12} \rangle, \langle 3, (20, v_{13}), \omega_{13} \rangle], [\langle 1, (35, v_{21}), \omega_{21} \rangle, \langle 2, (56, v_{22}), \omega_{22} \rangle]]\}$, where ω_{ij} is the witness for the elements in the j-th position of the i-th node and is generated by invoking **CreateWitness**$(\cdot)$ algorithm.

Algorithm 4 describes the steps of result verification on the light client. The verification process is on the client-side from top to bottom. At first, the light client downloads all block headers from the blockchain to fetch the root commitment against the $pcbCommit$ and leverages the polynomial commitment primitive **VerifyEval**$(\cdot)$ algorithm to check the correctness of the search path elements. The binding relationship between data and position in each node ensures the completeness of query results. The validated commitment for each entry in the parent node needs to be used to verify the correctness of their child nodes. In the leaf node, the user uses the function $hash(\cdot)$ to compute $v_i = hash(tx_i)$ according to R, then invoke **VerifyEval**$(\cdot)$ algorithm to prove the correctness of returned result.

5.2   Extension to Verifiable Boolean Query

The previous section mainly discusses the range queries on the numerical attribute V_i. In real-life scenarios, the query client may consider the keyword queries on the set attributes W_i. The Boolean query on the set attributes is supported in our PCB-tree by the field $Attr$. In the non-leaf nodes, the attribute set of the parent node is the union of the attribute sets of all its child nodes. Therefore, when the full node receives a Boolean query condition $q = \{addr1 \wedge (addr3 \vee addr4)\}$, it firstly parses the query into two parts: $\{addr1\}$

Algorithm 4: Results Verification (by the light client)

Input: Query results R, Verification object VO, Query condition q
Output: The verification result: 1 or 0

1 Interpret R and VO as a list of $\langle i, k_i, tx_i \rangle$ and $\langle i, (k_i, v_i), \omega_i \rangle$, respectively;
2 $vCommit \leftarrow$ root commitment $PcbCommit$;
3 **for** *each level in VO* **do**
4 $\quad$ $vo \leftarrow \langle i, (k_i, v_i), \omega_i \rangle$;
5 $\quad$ Check the k_i is in the query range q;
6 $\quad$ Verify the i-th entry of current node is correct via the $vCommit$ and vo;
7 $\quad$ $vCommit \leftarrow v_i$;
8 $\quad$ **if** *current node is leaf and k_i matches q* **then**
9 $\quad\quad$ $value \leftarrow hash(tx_i)$ according to the R;
10 $\quad\quad$ Check the $value$ is equal the v_i of the VO;
11 $\quad$ **end**
12 **end**

---

and $\{addr3, addr4\}$. In this paper, the Boolean query is represented by a Boolean function in Conjunctive Normal Form (CNF), which is a list of AND or OR operators. The full node starts the query from the root node and compare query condition one by one with the set attribute $Attr$ in each node. However, this way is not efficient. In order to speed up the query, we introduce Bloom Filter (BF) into PCB-tree. Bloom filter is a long binary vector and a series of random mapping functions, and it can be used to test whether an element is a member of a set fastly. When constructing the index of PCB-tree, we need to create a BF bit vector for each node attribute, which means each BF represents a set attribute W_i, and the BF of non-leaf nodes denote the union of BFs in its child nodes. Therefore, when the system starts traversing from the PCB-tree root node, BF is used to determine whether the subtrees of current node have the query attributes.

In the range query, v_i is the hash of transactions tx_i, and it is seen as an authenticator of the transactions. Based on polynomial commitment, we guarantee the integrity of numerical attribute query results. In order to guarantee the integrity of the Boolean query, we need to build a binding relationship between numerical attributes, set attributes and transactions. Hence, v_i needs to be transformed into a tamper-proof digest value, such as hash value, $v_i = hash(tx_i \| W_i)$. We take v_i as the value in the key-value pair (k_i, v_i) in the leaf node for Boolean range queries.

Remark 1. In order to further reduce the communication overhead, it is necessary for supporting batch operations. The primitive **CreateWitnessBatch**($\cdot$) introduced in Sect. 2.3, which can aggregate multiple query points in the same polynomial commitment. We can aggregate the proof for multiple query points under the same node when executing range query. For example, the full node can return an aggregated proof $\omega_{r1,r2} = $ **CreateWitnessBatch**(PK, $p(x)_{Nr}$, $[(20, \mathcal{C}_{N1}), (56, \mathcal{C}_{N2})]$) for two points under the root node $\langle 1, (20, \mathcal{C}_{N1}), \omega_{r1} \rangle$ and $\langle 2, (56, \mathcal{C}_{N2}), \omega_{r2} \rangle$. The light client can apply **VerifyEvalBatch**($\cdot$) to process batch verification. Boneh et al. [2] proposes two polynomial commitment schemes which can open proof for multiple points and polynomials at the same time. We can also leverage this enhanced polynomial commitment scheme to aggregate different node in the PCB-tree which will further reduce the VO size.

5.3 Security Analysis

In this paper, we give a formal definition and analyze the security of our proposed scheme. Note that the polynomial commitment scheme is secure [5].

Definition 1 *(Security). A verifiable Boolean range query scheme is secure if the success probability of any polynomial-time adversaries in the following experiment is negligible:*

- *Run the ADS generation algorithm and send all transactions $\{tx_1, \ldots, tx_n\}$ in a block to the adversary;*
- *The adversary outputs the query q, the result R, and the VO.*

The above definition indicates that malicious full node forges an incorrect or incomplete result is negligible. Next, we will prove that our proposed scheme indeed satisfies the desired security requirements.

Theorem 1. *Our proposed verifiable Boolean range query scheme based on PCB-tree can guarantee the correctness and completeness of query result as defined in Definition 1.*

Proof. The verifiable query processing should guarantee that the returned results are correct and complete. We prove this theorem by contradiction as follows:

(1) *Correctness of query results.* The returned results R contain a transaction tx^* such that $tx^* \notin \{tx_i\}_{i=1}^n$ and pass the verification. The client will validate the integrity of the transaction with respect to the $PcbCommit$ stored in the blockchain. Therefore, the forge is impossible because the polynomial commitment scheme and the underlying consensus mechanism of the blockchain are secure.

(2) *Completeness of query results.* There exists a transaction tx_d that satisfies the query condition q, but not in the result set R. Now suppose there is a missing transaction tx_d. In our proposed PCB-tree, all transactions are stored in the leaf nodes after being sorted according to the numerical attribute k_i, and we build the binding relationship between k_i and the indexed position i for commitment. During query processing, the full node requires two additional boundary objects for non-membership proofs for query objects, falling immediately to the left and the right of tx_d. Meanwhile, the light verifier syncs the latest block headers from the blockchain network. The missing object tx_d must fall under one polynomial witness value in the VO. Thus, our proposed scheme is secure.

6 Performance Evaluation

This section describes the performance evaluation of our verifiable query scheme. We deploy all experiments on a personal laptop computer with AMD R7 4800H CPU @ 2.90 GHz, 24 GB RAM, and run a single thread to simulate the processing of the full node and the light client. In the experiments, we retrieve the Ethereum databases via a blockchain infrastructure, e.g., Infura[3]. The codes of query processing and verification programs are written in Python and Golang based on the B^+-tree structure and the KZG commitments[4].

6.1 Experiment Setting

We describe the detailed experiment configuration. The PCB-tree is built based on the real transaction dataset from Ethereum blockchain. It contains 1,000 blocks with 96,287 transactions, and each transaction is defined as ⟨timestamp, value, from, to⟩, where the timestamp is the query period, value is the amount of transaction transferred, from and to are the addresses of sender and receiver respectively.

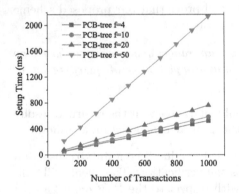 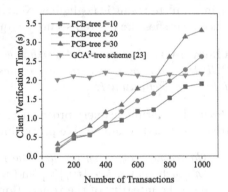

Fig. 4. Setup cost of miner   **Fig. 5.** Verification cost of light client

To evaluate the entire system's performance, we perform four sets of experiments. Firstly, we evaluate the setup cost of ADS construction for the miner. Then, we evaluate the query processing cost of the full node and compare it with the GCA^2-tree [23] which implements a verifiable query scheme using the same accumulator as vChain [19]. Finally, we measure the result verification cost on the light client and the size of the VO.

6.2 Experiment Evaluation

Setup Cost. We start with evaluating the construction time of PCB-tree on the miner-side. From Fig. 4, we can learn that the construction time increases

---

[3] https://infura.io/.
[4] https://github.com/protolambda/go-kzg.

Table 2. Time cost of proof

Fanout	Single process		Batch process (max)	
	Generation	Verification	Generation	Verification
2	0.515 ms	2.451 ms	0.514 ms	2.688 ms
10	0.609 ms	2.728 ms	0.717 ms	5.548 ms
20	1.385 ms	2.813 ms	4.97 ms	13.477 ms
30	2.281 ms	3.027 ms	17.086 ms	28.986 ms
50	7.839 ms	7.109 ms	78.115 ms	96.106 ms

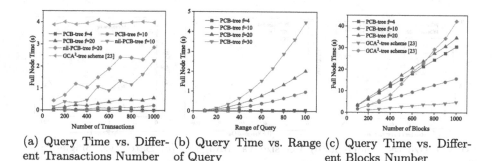

(a) Query Time vs. Different Transactions Number

(b) Query Time vs. Range of Query

(c) Query Time vs. Different Blocks Number

Fig. 6. Range query performance of full node

linearly when the number of transactions in a block grows, and as the fanout increases, the construction overhead becomes more expensive, but this ADS construction operation does not affect the performance of blockchain. On the one hand, the current block generation rate of Ethereum is 15s/block, and the average number of transactions per block does not exceed 400. Therefore, the miner can do the construction and mining processes in parallel. On the other hand, the experiment is run a personal computer with a single thread, which is impractical for the miner. Moreover, our PCB-tree ensures the integrity of query results, which is crucial for the verifiable query scheme.

Query Performance. We first test the performance of range queries from different dimensions as shown in Fig. 6 and compare the time cost of queries with the scheme in [23]. Figure 6(a) illustrates the range query performance of full nodes when the number of transactions in a block increases. The full node query performance contains two parties: results query time and proof generation time. It can be seen that the cost of queries increases only linearly with enlarging the transactions number. Meanwhile, its query time increases as the fanout increases. Compared with the single operation, proofs batch aggregation will degrade quickly the query time, where *nil-PCB-tree* represents that batch processing is not used. In theoretical analysis, the complexity of the range query is approximate $\mathcal{O}(log_f n)$. However, it is also necessary to generate proofs for the corresponding results during the query process, which is expensive and is the

Table 3. Comparison of proof size

Scheme	Commitment size	VO format	One VO size	Public parameters	Batch operation
Merkle Tree [9]	32	Hash	$10 \cdot 32 = 320$	–	N
MB-Tree [6]	32	Hash	$3 \cdot 9 \cdot 32 = 864$	–	N
vChain [19]	32	hash,π_v, Attr, Digest	$10 \cdot 288 = 2880$	$64 \cdot 1000 = 64000$	Y
PCB-Tree (this work)	64	π_{pcb}, Attr	$3 \cdot (64 + 64) = 384$	$64 \cdot 10 = 640$	Y

Note: We use a 256-bit group and BN256 elliptical curve for class groups at 128-bit security. We assume the number of transactions is $n = 1000$, the size of attribute messages is 256-bit (An 'Attr' field consists of 2 elements) and 256-bit hashes. We assume the fanout $f = 10$ for PCB-tree and MB-tree and the path height of Merkle tree is 10.

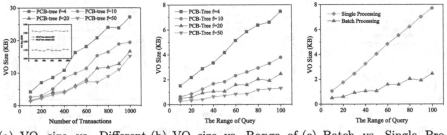

(a) VO size vs. Different Transactions Number

(b) VO size vs. Range of Query

(c) Batch vs. Single Processing

Fig. 7. Communication cost

primary cost of the full node. Furthermore, with the increase of fanout, the time of proof generation and verification increases which account for the increment of query time. The time cost of proof is shown in Table 2.

We repeat the above experiment while fixing the transactions number to 500 in a block and varying the range of queries. Figure 6(b) shows the changing trend of query time when the range of query increases. As the range of queries, the leaf proof number becomes longer, which accounts for the linear increase in our systems. Figure 6(c) shows the query performance at different block numbers. Each block contains 500 transactions and fixes the range of queries to 15. Since we mainly consider the performance of a single block in this paper, we will execute the single block query algorithm recursively for different blocks.

VO Size. Next, we measure the communication cost between the full node and the light client. Firstly, we theoretically analyze the storage cost of commitments, proof, and public parameters of various schemes, as shown in Table 3. Our public key parameters and VO size are small compared to scheme [19]. In our schemes, the proofs for non-leaf and leaf nodes are $\langle k_i, c_i, \pi_i \rangle$ and $\langle k_i, \pi_i \rangle$ respectively. The batch proofs for non-leaf and leaf nodes are $\langle m(k_i, c_i), r(k), \pi_i \rangle$ and $\langle m(k_i), r(k), \pi_i \rangle$ respectively, where m is the number of elements aggregated, $r(k)$ is the remainder of the polynomial division and the size is 32 bytes. To alleviate communication overhead, we can only send x-axis coordinates of the elliptic curve points and add additional one-bit messages to record the positive and negative. In this case, the proof size would only be 32 bytes.

Figure 7(a) illustrates the VO size with increasing numbers of transactions. It can be seen that the VO size grows linearly with the number of transactions. However, the order of magnitude of our VO size is *KB*, and the scheme [23] is *MB*. Figure 7(b) and 7(c) shows the VO size with varying query range. The transactions number is fixed to 500 at per block, and the fanout of Fig. 7(c) is 20. We observe that the VO size is small when the tree fanout is small. Meanwhile, the proof aggregation will reduce quickly the communication overhead transferred from the full node to the light client. In contrast, without batch processing, the VO size increases linearly at least $3\times$. Therefore, based on Fig. 6 and Fig. 7, we conclude that our scheme makes a trade-off between query efficiency and VO size.

Verification Cost. Finally, we evaluate the verification cost at the light client with the number of transactions queried. We mainly discuss the cost of proof verification in this experiment because it is a major overhead for the client. Figure 5 demonstrates that the verification time grows linearly with the transactions number, and the verification time of scheme [23] is a stable horizontal line. However, we discover that the clients generally query transactions they are interested in the recent period, and the experiment shows that when the numbers of transactions that are interested ≤ 800, the client verification efficiency of our scheme is better than scheme [23].

7   Conclusion

In this paper, we study the problem of verifiable query processing and propose an efficient and verifiable Boolean range query scheme for light clients on blockchain databases. Firstly, we developed a novel authenticated data structure, polynomial commitment B$^+$-tree (PCB-tree). Based on that, we achieve efficient integrity and correctness verification of Boolean and range queries for blockchain light clients. Secondly, our scheme provides a tunable trade-off between query time and communication overhead by autonomously setting the fanout size of the PCB-tree. Thirdly, our scheme can further support batch processing to reduce VO size and verification time. Finally, security analysis and experiment have substantiated that our scheme is secure and efficient.

Acknowledgements. This work is supported by the Key Research and Development Program of Shaanxi (Program No. 2022KWZ-01), the Key Research and Development Program of Shaanxi (No. 2020ZDLGY08-03), and the Fundamental Research Funds for the Central Universities (No. JB211503).

A   Pseudo Codes of the PCB-Tree Algorithms

Algorithms 5 and 6 respectively show the query processing of the PCB-tree introduced in Sect. 5.

Algorithm 5: Range Query w.r.t. PCB-tree

---

1 **Function** RangeQuery($curr,\ l,\ u,\ R,\ VO$):
    Input: Current node $curr$, Lower bound l, Upper bound u, Results
           set R, Verification object VO

2   **if** $curr$ *is not leaf* **then**

3        $left = \textbf{getPos}(curr,\ l)$;

4        $right = \textbf{getPos}(curr,\ u)$;

5        $p(x) \leftarrow curr.p(x)$;

6   **if** $left == right$ **then**

7            $\omega_{left} = \textbf{CreateWitness}(\mathsf{PK},\ p(x),\ k_{left})$;

8   add $\langle left,\ (k_{left}, v_{left}),\ \omega_{left}\rangle$ to VO;

9   **RangeQuery**($curr.children_{left},\ l,\ u,\ R,\ VO$);

10   **else**

11   **for** $i{=}left$ *to* $right;\ i\ +{=}\ 1$ **do**

12                $\omega_i = \textbf{CreateWitness}(\mathsf{PK},\ p(x),\ k_i)$;

13   add $\langle i,\ (k_i, v_i),\ \omega_i \rangle$ to VO;

14   **end**

15            $max = curr_{left}.max$;

16   **RangeQuery**($curr.children_{left},\ l,\ max,\ R,\ VO$);

17            $min = curr_{right}.min$;

18   **RangeQuery**($curr.children_{right},\ min,\ u,\ R,\ VO$);

19   **end**

20   **else**

21        $left = \textbf{getPos}(curr,\ l)$;

22   **while** $curr$ *is not None* **do**

23            $p(x) \leftarrow curr.p(x)$;

24   **for** $i \leftarrow left$ **to** $curr.size()$ **do**

25   **if** $curr.keys[i] > u$ **then**

26   break;

27   add $\langle i,\ curr.keys[i],\ tx_i \rangle$ to R;

28                $\omega_i = \textbf{CreateWitness}(\mathsf{PK},\ p(x),\ k_i)$;

29   add $\langle i,\ (k_i, v_i),\ \omega_i \rangle$ to VO;

30   **end**

31   **if** $curr.next$ *is not None* **then**

32                $curr = curr.next$;

33                $left = 0$;

34   **end**

35   **end**

36   **end**

Algorithm 6: Position Search Algorithm

```
1  Function getPos(curr, key):
      Input: The current node curr, The search key key
      Output: The position index z
2     count ← curr.keyNum;
3     z ← -1;
4     if count ≠ 0 then
          // binary search
5         lo ← 0;
6         hi ← entries;
7         while z < 0 do
8             mid ← (lo+hi) // 2;
9             diff ← key-curr.keys[mid];
10            if diff ≤ 0 then
11                if key-curr.keys[mid-1] > 0 then
12                    z ← mid;
13                else
14                    z ← -2;
15                end
16            else
17                if key-curr.keys[mid+1] ≤ 0 then
18                    z ← mid+1;
19                else
20                    z ← -3;
21                end
22            end
23            if z == -2 then
24                lo ← 0;
25                hi ← mid-1;
26            else if z == -3 then
27                lo ← mid+1;
28                hi ← hi;
29            end
30        else
31            z ← -1;
32        end
33        return z;
```

References

1. Antonopoulos, A.M.: Mastering Bitcoin: Programming the Open Blockchain. O'Reilly Media, Inc. (2017)
2. Boneh, D., Drake, J., Fisch, B., Gabizon, A.: Efficient polynomial commitment schemes for multiple points and polynomials. Cryptology ePrint Archive (2020)

3. Cai, C., Xu, L., Zhou, A., Wang, R., Wang, C., Wang, Q.: EncELC: hardening and enriching ethereum light clients with trusted enclaves. In: IEEE INFOCOM 2020-IEEE Conference on Computer Communications, pp. 1887–1896. IEEE (2020)
4. Comer, D.: Ubiquitous b-tree. ACM Comput. Surv. (CSUR) **11**(2), 121–137 (1979)
5. Kate, A., Zaverucha, G.M., Goldberg, I.: Constant-size commitments to polynomials and their applications. In: Abe, M. (ed.) ASIACRYPT 2010. LNCS, vol. 6477, pp. 177–194. Springer, Heidelberg (2010). https://doi.org/10.1007/978-3-642-17373-8_11
6. Li, F., Hadjieleftheriou, M., Kollios, G., Reyzin, L.: Dynamic authenticated index structures for outsourced databases. In: Proceedings of the 2006 ACM SIGMOD International Conference on Management of Data, pp. 121–132 (2006)
7. LongHash: Blockchain big data problem. https://www.longhash.com/en/news/2382/Blockchain's-Big-Data-Problem
8. Matetic, S., Wüst, K., Schneider, M., Kostiainen, K., Karame, G., Capkun, S.: BITE: bitcoin lightweight client privacy using trusted execution. In: 28th USENIX Security Symposium (USENIX Security 19), pp. 783–800 (2019)
9. Merkle, R.C.: A certified digital signature. In: Brassard, G. (ed.) CRYPTO 1989. LNCS, vol. 435, pp. 218–238. Springer, New York (1990). https://doi.org/10.1007/0-387-34805-0_21
10. Nakamoto, S.: Bitcoin: a peer-to-peer electronic cash system (2009). https://bitcoin.org/bitcoin.pdf
11. Parno, B., Howell, J., Gentry, C., Raykova, M.: Pinocchio: nearly practical verifiable computation. In: 2013 IEEE Symposium on Security and Privacy, pp. 238–252. IEEE (2013)
12. Pedersen, T.P.: Non-interactive and information-theoretic secure verifiable secret sharing. In: Feigenbaum, J. (ed.) CRYPTO 1991. LNCS, vol. 576, pp. 129–140. Springer, Heidelberg (1992). https://doi.org/10.1007/3-540-46766-1_9
13. Qin, K., Hadass, H., Gervais, A., Reardon, J.: Applying private information retrieval to lightweight bitcoin clients. In: 2019 Crypto Valley Conference on Blockchain Technology (CVCBT), pp. 60–72. IEEE (2019)
14. Ramakrishnan, R., Gehrke, J., Gehrke, J.: Database Management Systems, vol. 3. McGraw-Hill, New York (2003)
15. Ruan, P., Chen, G., Dinh, T.T.A., Lin, Q., Ooi, B.C., Zhang, M.: Fine-grained, secure and efficient data provenance on blockchain systems. Proc. VLDB Endow. **12**(9), 975–988 (2019)
16. Shao, Q., Pang, S., Zhang, Z., Jing, C.: Authenticated range query using SGX for blockchain light clients. In: Nah, Y., Cui, B., Lee, S.-W., Yu, J.X., Moon, Y.-S., Whang, S.E. (eds.) DASFAA 2020. LNCS, vol. 12114, pp. 306–321. Springer, Cham (2020). https://doi.org/10.1007/978-3-030-59419-0_19
17. Smith, C., Rusnak, A.: Dynamic Merkle B-tree with efficient proofs. arXiv preprint arXiv:2006.01994 (2020)
18. Wiki, E.: Ethereum light client protocol. https://eth.wiki/concepts/light-client-protocol
19. Xu, C., Zhang, C., Xu, J.: vchain: Enabling verifiable Boolean range queries over blockchain databases. In: Proceedings of the 2019 International Conference on Management of Data, pp. 141–158 (2019)
20. Yang, Y., Papadopoulos, S., Papadias, D., Kollios, G.: Authenticated indexing for outsourced spatial databases. VLDB J. **18**(3), 631–648 (2009)
21. Zhang, C., Xu, C., Wang, H., Xu, J., Choi, B.: Authenticated keyword search in scalable hybrid-storage blockchains. In: 2021 IEEE 37th International Conference on Data Engineering (ICDE), pp. 996–1007. IEEE (2021)

22. Zhang, C., Xu, C., Xu, J., Tang, Y., Choi, B.: Gem^ 2-tree: a gas-efficient structure for authenticated range queries in blockchain. In: 2019 IEEE 35th international conference on data engineering (ICDE), pp. 842–853. IEEE (2019)
23. Zhu, Y., Zhang, Z., Jin, C., Zhou, A.: Enabling generic verifiable aggregate query on blockchain systems. In: 2020 IEEE 26th International Conference on Parallel and Distributed Systems (ICPADS), pp. 456–465. IEEE (2020)

SuppliedTrust: A Trusted Blockchain Architecture for Supply Chains

Yong Zhi Lim[1,2(✉)], Jianying Zhou[1], and Martin Saerbeck[2]

[1] Singapore University of Technology and Design, Singapore, Singapore
yongzhi_lim@mymail.sutd.edu.sg, jianying_zhou@sutd.edu.sg
[2] TÜV SÜV Asia Pacific, Digital Service Centre of Excellence, Singapore, Singapore
{yong-zhi.lim,martin.saerbeck}@tuvsud.com

Abstract. The impact of COVID-19, shortage of chips and external factors has made a flurry demand, increased costs and significant delays in supply chains despite technological advancements in the supply chain management process. The blockchain technology is constantly being explored and attracts supply chains in adopting them to allow businesses to scale rapidly. In our work, we identify gaps between existing blockchain implementations and cybersecurity standards. We introduce a framework and show how we can implement secure and trusted blockchains onto the supply chains.

Keywords: Blockchain · Standards · Supply chains

1 Introduction

The advent of blockchains, arguably made popular by cryptocurrencies, brings the benefit of decentralization that attract supply chains in adopting them. In this paper, we identify directions on where and how to implement blockchains onto the supply chains. There is a current lack of literature to provide governance to bridge cybersecurity standards and the use of blockchain technology in supply chains. Even though current cybersecurity standards exist, such gaps in bridging blockchains and the supply chains pose a problem in trust for widespread adoption.

Firstly, both information (IT) and operational technology (OT) are treated as 2 separate entities in supply chains; causing friction for data in motion between these networks. Secondly, the proliferation of blockchains has enabled smarter and innovative ways to communicate; but with the lack of interoperability. With rapid advances and push for digital consumption in the cloud, our work aims to introduce an agnostic and guiding framework to bridge gaps in cybersecurity standards, provide convergence for IT and OT systems, and for various stakeholders in the supply process to move quicker towards the adoption of blockchain technology in supply chains.

Currently a blockchain is implemented on top of a supply chain and has limited consideration for cybersecurity standards and difficulty to integrate OT processes, which are usually air-gapped and separate from IT systems. As smart con-

J. Zhou et al. (Eds.): ACNS 2022 Workshops, LNCS 13285, pp. 36–52, 2022.
https://doi.org/10.1007/978-3-031-16815-4_3

tracts increase in functionality and become more sophisticated, threats against them only continue to escalate.

In this paper, we first provide a background in the current state of supply chains and existing cybersecurity standards. Secondly, we introduce an architecture which supply chains can follow in order to understand how a blockchain can be applied on top of a supply chain through a 3-layer mapping process. Thirdly, we provide a survey of existing threats. Lastly, we explore challenges and directions for future work.

2 Background

2.1 Current State of Supply Chains

It is of no doubt that the impact of COVID-19, shortage of chips and external factors has made a flurry demand, increased costs and significant delays in supply chains [16,30,32]. Despite technological advancements in the supply chain management process, supply chains still operate a centralized model to achieve competitive advantage and prevents quick transfer of information between different supply chains [56].

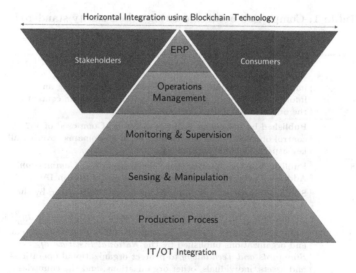

Fig. 1. Horizontal/vertical scaling in a typical supply chain

As supply chains modernize towards Industry 4.0 (i4.0), Operational Technology (OT) or Industrial Control Systems (ICS) plays a crucial link in managing machines in a supply chain. As shown in Fig. 1, rapid horizontal scaling in supply chains is needed to allow integration and better optimized flow of data and products from suppliers and vendors. This also enables fast adaptation of information across different stakeholders in the supply chain. Thus, avoiding the bullwhip effect, reducing the time needed for response and increased resilience in this process. [57] Data from actuators or sensors are typically located at the edge which are managed or connected to PLCs (Programmable Logic Controllers) and are controlled by SCADA (Supervisory Control and Data Acquisition) systems. These systems require an always uptime with high availability with minimal disruptions to business continuity.

With increasing use of Internet-of-Things (IoT) devices in the supply chain (even for use in the military [23]), the current state of such systems are no longer restrained or isolated and have achieved some level of connectivity or interfaced with other systems in the network. Even though the blockchain is secure, it is of essence that these systems not only remain connected but are also resilient against unintended behaviour or cyber attacks to ensure that data can remain trusted.

2.2   Cybersecurity Standards

As of writing, there are several published standards to guide and audit organizations to implement systems securely. Table 1 shows a quick survey of existing standards which serve to protect IT and/or OT systems.

Table 1. Comparison between existing cybersecurity standards

Standard	Description	IT	OT
ISO 27001 [17]	Security management by the *International Organization for Standardization*. Generic requirements for establishing, implementing, maintaining and continually improving an information security management system within the context of the organization	✓	
CCM v4 [4]	Published by the *Cloud Security Alliance*. Composed of 197 control objectives that are structured in 17 domains covering all key aspects of cloud technology	✓	
IEC 62443 [8]	Published by the *International Electrotechnical Commission*. Addresses cybersecurity threats and vulnerabilities in IACS		✓
ETSI [10]	Standards, articles and publications for the EU written by the *European Telecommunications Standards Institute* in conjunction with *European Union Agency for Cybersecurity* [73]	✓	✓
NIST SP 800-53 [37]	Catalog of security and privacy controls for information systems and organizations published by the *National Institute of Standards and Technology* to protect organizational operations and assets, individuals, other organizations, and the countries from a diverse set of threats and risks, including hostile attacks, human errors, natural disasters, structural failures, foreign intelligence entities, and privacy risks	✓	✓

The above shows a non-exhaustive list of standards for supply chains to follow and may not be sufficient as they do have other standards not only to increase consumers confidence, but to abide to legislatory concerns. In recent literature, evolving blockchain standards such as the ISO/TC 307 or the IEEE

SA P241x series have been published or are still undergoing research and have yet to consider OT systems as part of the ecosystem [18,61].

3 Related Work

The most current contributions in the literature are comprehensive and cover both the blockchain technology and the supply chain management in good detail [2,53,78]. Deployment of blockchains in supply chains promotes transparency, traceability and scalability. However, implementations such as [15,33] rely on a permissioned blockchain model and do not reveal an open implementation or model how to build a trusted blockchain on top of supply chains. As highlighted by [53], the most crucial challenge to be addressed is to authenticate on-chain data with its physical counterpart, which can be rapidly adopted through standardization. In [78], it describes each of the individual blockchain as frameworks to address concerns in specific supply chains, citing security concerns in consensus and popular usage of IoT devices.

They also lack an emphasis to secure the supply chain management process with the use of cybersecurity standards, given that key OT processes in the supply chain still operate in an air-gapped or isolated environment. While the state-of-the-art does indeed share current and existing blockchain implementations for different supply chains, they may adopt and implement blockchains which are closed-source and not follow standardization.

4 Framework

4.1 Overview

We introduce *SuppliedTrust*, an agnostic framework for supply chains which we identify issues, risk and problems by applying a 3-layer mapping process as shown in Fig. 2. The 3 layers are: Governance, Supply Chain and the Blockchain layers. Firstly, the Governance layer, consists of merging IT/OT operations by identifying standards relevant to their specific domains in the supply chain. Secondly, the Supply Chain layer, consists of the various stakeholders which form the individual or part of the consortium of the blockchain network. Lastly, the Blockchain layer, consists of the specific domains of the blockchain technologies that is to be applied on top of the Supply Chain layer.

4.2 Governance Layer

The Governance layer consists of 2 domains, split into information technology and operational technology.

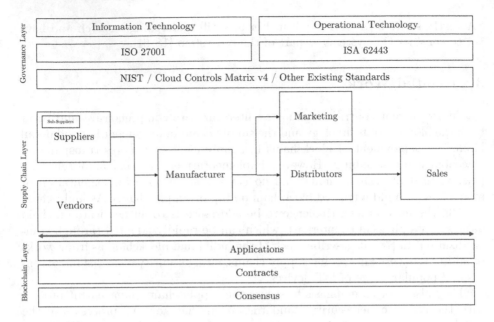

Fig. 2. *SuppliedTrust* architecture

Standards. By using established standards such as the ISO 27001 and ISA 62443, they provide guiding principles for a secure implementation of IT and OT infrastructure respectively. However, these are not sufficient as we move towards a connected world. Other existing standards such as the NIST and the Cloud Controls Matrix (CCM) currently do not consider an implementation of a blockchain on top of this secured process. Despite the release of v4, CCM currently considers the Shared Security Responsibility Model (SSRM) as a partial gap for ISO 27001 and only considers a permissioned blockchain, *Hyperledger Fabric*, for deployment [2,4]. As such, we presently identified it as a gap to enable secure and trusted exchange of information between the blockchain and the supply chain. As shown in Fig. 3, transactional data from Supply Chain X can transverse within its trusted environment (Tx_{SC_x}), but there is a concern on how data should be handled within its OT network ($\text{Tx}_{OT(SC_x)}$), when it leaves the supply chain into the cloud ($\text{Tx}_{C(SC_x)}$) for commits into the blockchain ($\text{Tx}_{BC(SC_x)}$), and eventual consumption by Supply Chain Y ($\text{Rx}_{C(SC_x)}$ and Rx_{SC_x}).

Cloud-Based Services. As cloud-based services become more popular than ever, BaaS (Blockchain-as-a-Service) are presently the easiest solutions to integrate blockchains into supply chains. Thus, supply chains can leverage on cloud services to run their blockchain nodes and feed data into the network.

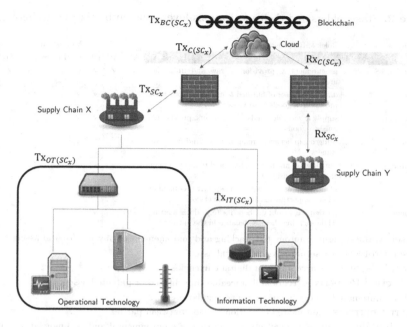

Fig. 3. Simplified OT/IT integration on a supply chain with a blockchain.

$\mathrm{Tx}_{OT(SC_x)}$: OT data from Supply Chain X
$\mathrm{Tx}_{IT(SC_x)}$: IT data from Supply Chain X
Tx_{SC_x} : Transmitted transactional data from Supply Chain X
$\mathrm{Tx}_{C(SC_x)}$: Transmitted transactional data from Supply Chain X transversing into the cloud
$\mathrm{Tx}_{BC(SC_x)}$: Transmitted transactional data from Supply Chain X committed into the blockchain
$\mathrm{Rx}_{C(SC_x)}$: Received transactional data from Supply Chain X retrieved from the cloud
Rx_{SC_x} : Received transactional data from Supply Chain X

4.3   Supply Chain Layer

The Supply Chain layer consists of the various stakeholders, their roles and responsibilities in the blockchain.

Stakeholders. In a typical supply chain, various stakeholders may include suppliers, sub-suppliers, vendors, its customers (via sales) and last but not least, the manufacturer themselves. Compared to centralized cryptocurrency exchange where the Know Your Customer (KYC) process is mandatory [39], every individual stakeholder in a supply chain are already known and well-defined. However, their interests within the supply chain management may differ since each of the individual parties may wish to gain benefits (e.g. oracle information, monetary or rewards) from joining the blockchain. An example is given in Table 2.

Table 2. Stakeholders and their motivations leveraging on blockchain technology.

Stakeholders	Roles & Responsibilities	Motivation								
		AM	AP	DP	IP	LL	SC	SU	TR	TO
Suppliers/Sub-Suppliers	procurement & provision of raw and unfinished materials	✓	✓	✓	✓	✓	✓	✓	✓	✓
Vendors	direct purchaser of finished & unfinished products, provision of goods & services	✓	✓	✓	✓	✓	✓	✓	✓	✓
Manufacturers	supply & meet demands of consumers, provision of finished goods	✓	✓	✓	✓	✓	✓	✓	✓	✓
Marketers	bridges gap between trends and demand from consumers				✓			✓	✓	
Distributors	purchaser of finished products and to meet demand & support consumers	✓	✓	✓		✓	✓		✓	✓
Sales	identifying & educating prospective consumers while supporting existing consumers						✓	✓		
Consumers	participate to obtain benefits (e.g. data sharing) while ensuring check & balance in the network			✓				✓	✓	✓

AM Asset Management - automated tracking and management of physical/digital assets
AP Asset Protection - secure physical/digital assets
DP Digital Payments - acceptance of digital currencies
IP Intellectual Property - secure and traceable copyrighted or patented assets
LL Legal - automated processing of rules and regulations
SC Smart Contracts - automated execution of code between parties
SU Sustainability - automated collection/reporting of environmental and/or financial functions
TR Tracking - traceability of physical/digital assets
TO Tokenization - non-fungible tokens, representation of physical/digital assets

4.4   Blockchain Layer

The Blockchain layer consists of 3 domains, split into applications, contracts and consensus (Fig. 2) with a dotted line indicating horizontal data flow traversing different stakeholders (regardless of direction) in the Supply Chain layer.

Applications. Decentralized applications (Dapps) or Web3, provides a front-end interface for users to interact with the blockchain.

As shown in Fig. 4, these frontend applications provide its users (or any of its stakeholders in the supply chain) an always uptime, decentralized control and benefits, thanks to JavaScript Object Notation Remote Procedure Calls (JSON-RPC) by a suitable provider, which eliminates the need for backend services. Developers can take advantage of such application programming interfaces (APIs) to interact directly with the blockchain. However, blockchains are incapable of storing large amounts of digital or physical information on-chain as this requires the use of an off-chain storage, notably decentralized storages.

Contracts. Smart contracts within the blockchain ecosystem plays a significant and important role in enabling fully automated supply chains. Not only rules are well-defined between various parties listed in the smart contract, but they also define the conditions required to provide information and/or monetary transfer [80]. This greatly speeds up the process of information transfer without the need of an intermediary.

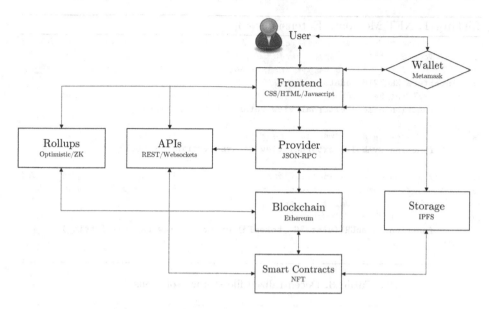

Fig. 4. A Web3 implementation in *Ethereum*

More recently so, smart contracts have been made popular via their representation of digital assets via the use of non-fungible tokens (NFTs) which could provide a possible use case for supply chains [64]. Widely perceived to be a digital representation of an artwork, NFTs have shaken the world tagged with a perceived value, then auctioned or sold onto a marketplace such as OpenSea or Rarible [6,35,79]. However, NFTs themselves should not simply be tagged with a value, as it name implies 'non-fungible', which then can be a representation of an asset stored digitally in the virtual space. According to the *ERC-721* specifications, smart contracts written in *Solidity* for *Ethereum* contains *optional* fields for its metadata extension.

As highlighted in the Applications domain (see Fig. 2, under Blockchain layer), any asset that is pointing to an off-chain resource may prove troublesome if `tokenURI` (line 15 in Listing 1) ceases to exist or a collision if another asset (e.g. non-uniqueness or identical) does indeed exist. To combat this, the use of decentralized domains or storages is a natural fit. However, current decentralized file storage solutions are partially suitable for use with supply chains.

As depicted in Table 3, supply chains may not be able to adopt some of the decentralized file storages for their usage due to lack of confidentiality, privacy or file persistence [44]. A commercial solution, *CargoX*, uses *Polygon* and the *InterPlanetary File System* (IPFS) as their part of their process [38]. However, recent research and tracking in NFTs prior to their indicated release does show that privacy in *IPFS* may not be guaranteed and may result being compromised [21,47].

Listing 1. NFT Metadata Extensions [83]

```
1   /// @title ERC-721 Non-Fungible Token Standard, optional metadata extension
2   /// @dev See https://eips.ethereum.org/EIPS/eip-721
3   ///  Note: the ERC-165 identifier for this interface is 0x5b5e139f.
4   interface ERC721Metadata /* is ERC721 */ {
5       /// @notice A descriptive name for a collection of NFTs in this contract
6       function name() external view returns (string _name);
7
8       /// @notice An abbreviated name for NFTs in this contract
9       function symbol() external view returns (string _symbol);
10
11      /// @notice A distinct Uniform Resource Identifier (URI) for a given asset.
12      /// @dev Throws if '_tokenId' is not a valid NFT. URIs are defined in RFC
13      ///  3986. The URI may point to a JSON file that conforms to the "ERC721
14      ///  Metadata JSON Schema".
15      function tokenURI(uint256 _tokenId) external view returns (string);
16  }
```

Table 3. Decentralized file storage solutions.

System	Features	File persistence	Data retention	Contracts
BitTorrent [1]	Efficient file distribution achieving pareto efficiency	Not guaranteed		
IPFS [41]	Decentralized web storage by providing content addressing and pinning	Not guaranteed		
Swarm [31]	Incentive-based decentralized storage platform	Not guaranteed		
Safe [62]	Autonomous private-guaranteed social network by providing unused computing resources	Public guaranteed, private deletable	✓	
Storj [14]	Decentralized private-guaranteed cloud storage	Determined lifetime, deletable	✓	
Arweave [52]	Archival decentralized storage	Blockweave	✓	✓ [11]
Siacoin [28]	Decentralized storage platform	Private guaranteed	✓	✓ [5]

Consensus. Consensus are mechanisms which allow a blockchain to reach a certain finality to a common decision before committing transactions onto the block. This is crucial as once they are committed onto the block, they cannot be reversed once they are written onto the chain. For different parties to inter-operate, the choice of a blockchain will determine different set of infrastructure requirements. Some examples of consensus include:

1. *Proof-of-Work* (PoW). Nakamoto introduced PoW as network timestamps transactions by hashing them into an ongoing chain of hashes, forming an immutable ledger [68]. Parties first gossip in the network whenever a new transaction is performed. Used by *Bitcoin* and *Ethereum*.

2. *Proof-of-Stake* (PoS). PoS was first introduced by Peercoin (PPCoin in August 2012) with the term 'coin age' [59]. A timestamp field is added into each transaction to determine the age of the currency held by the user. As such, each transaction is tracked by how long has the currency be held; the longer the age, the larger the influence a user has on the transaction. Used by *Algorand* and *Cardano*.

3. *Practical Byzantine Fault Tolerance* (PBFT). Termed by Castro and Liskov, PBFT works by assuming no more than $\dfrac{n-1}{3}$ users are faulty [43]. Used by *Hyperledger Fabric* and *Tendermint*.

As there are many evolving consensus algorithms (and its variants) which a supply chain may decide to commit finality of their transactions, no specific consensus is an one-size-fit-all and must be specifically tailored for different supply chains. Besides, interoperability is also a concern when communicating between different blockchains in supply chains. Despite current progress (no particular order) in *Chainlink*, *Cosmos* and *Polkadot*, these blockchains provide cross-chain bridges or a relayer to attempt to communicate with other blockchains, but require information to be off-loaded, then human or oracle-validated before it can be transferred to the destination chain [3,13,24].

4.5 Use Cases

Our proposed framework can be applied in supply chains where IT/OT integration is yet to be achieved or partially achieved, as formatted data needs to be secured and fed for other stakeholders in the blockchain. An example would be the validation of claims or features in the manufacture of products for eventual consumption by consumers. Following our proposed framework (via the use of cybersecurity standards and understanding the blockchain layer) not only ensures a secure implementation in both the IT/OT environment, but also maintains the trust needed between stakeholders across the blockchain.

5 Threats

An architecture would not be complete without considering the threats and risks should a blockchain be deployed on top of a supply chain. In this section, we perform a study of existing vulnerabilities and attacks which will need to run a trusted blockchain on a supply chain.

5.1 Web3 Vulnerabilities

Dapps or Web3 are no different from its current iteration of its Web2 counterpart. It continues to utilize the existing networking stack and protocols (e.g. DNS, TCP/IP, UDP) and suffers from the usual web vulnerabilities which were present since the 1st generation of the web [76]. According to the OWASP Top

10:2021, the most notable risks from web applications are: 1) broken access controls, 2) cryptographic failures, 3) injection, 4) insecure design, 5) security misconfiguration, 6) vulnerable and outdated components, 7) identification and authentication failures, 8) software and data integrity failures, 9) security logging and monitoring failures and 10) server-side request forgery [22].

This can be clearly seen from the given Web3 implementation given in Fig. 4, where the frontend, provider and APIs provides such avenues of attacks to occur. Although the use of *Ethereum Name Service* (ENS) or *Unstoppable Domains* can alleviate centralization issues as per compared to DNS, it does not solve the problem of fraudulent or malicious links (e.g. domain or typo-squatting) and introduces new problems introduced by smart contracts [34,84].

5.2 Smart Contract Attacks

Poorly written code in smart contracts can cause bugs or attackers to simply exploit or bypass functions. Based on the Common Weakness Enumeration (CWE) database, the Smart Contract Weakness Classification (SWC) registry has recorded a total of 136 vulnerabilities affecting *Ethereum* smart contracts, with reentrancy as the most critical [29,69].

The use of automated checking of smart contracts tools ease developers from their workload and prevent wastage of time to determine detection of false positives. Tools such as *MythX* [20] (a commercial solution spun off from *Mythril* [12]) and *Slither* [51], when used in combination, detected a total of 42/115 (37%) vulnerabilities and provides the best trade-off between accuracy and execution costs [49]. Besides, not all tools are proven to be easy to configure and may be complex to use [65]. According to [72], while such vulnerable contracts may not be exploitable in practice, it empathizes the need for best coding practices and manual auditing of source code [26,46,82].

Even though such attacks is confined mainly by *Ethereum*-based smart contracts, large-scale exploits such as The Decentralized Autonomous Organization (*TheDAO*) attack [81] and the Parity Wallet hack [71] were key examples of reentrancy and access control issues has been well-researched and documented [60].

NFT Legitimacy. NFT legitimacy can be backed by supply chains based on their branding and relationship perceived by consumers. They can present themselves as authorities and arbiters of legitimacy [40]. However, NFTs merely presents a proof of ownership on their respective blockchain and lack standards to ensure that the correctness of the JSON metadata stored off-chain (as shown in Listing 1) [19].

5.3 Consensus Attacks

Supply chains wishing to integrate a blockchain into their process must understand the risks of having insufficient parties and/or having too much influence or control over the network. Some well-explored consensus attacks are shown in Table 4.

Table 4. Common consensus attacks on PoW, PoS and PBFT protocols.

Attack	Method	PoW	PoS	PBFT
Selfish mining [50,70,75]	Withholds solved block and creates a fork	✓		
Time desynchronization [7]	Slowing down or speeding up perceived network time	✓		
33% [42,75]	Hashing power			✓
Eclipse [54,67]	Partitions network, isolates and usurp control of a node	✓	✓	
Long range [45]	Forking chain from a specific block	✓	✓	
Double spending [55]	Creation of two or more conflicting blocks with same height	✓	✓	
51% [45,75]	Hashing power	✓	✓	✓
DDoS [74]	Flooding network with extreme traffic	✓	✓	✓
Sybil [48,55]	Corrupt network by forming fake identities	✓	✓	✓

6 Challenges

Despite growing threats, several challenges also exist in overcoming barriers for the adoption of blockchains in businesses, specifically discovering use cases for supply chains.

6.1 Layer-1 Solutioning

Shared Security Responsibility Model. As explained in Sect. 4.2, BaaS poses a significant problem if supply chains select a single cloud-based provider, which defeats the very property of blockchains; decentralization. On top of that, SSRMs differ between different cloud-based providers and risk profiling must be carried out to determine if supply chains can accept failures when utilizing blockchains in the cloud [27,58,63].

Smart Contracts. As depicted in Fig. 4, smart contracts are a key-enabler in automating processes within a blockchain. However, it requires a definite solution and is difficult to code in accordance to current regulatory obligations, governance or standards that needs interpretability by humans. Besides, other blockchains such as *Hyperledger Fabric* or *Solana* utilize different programming languages, namely *Chaincode* and *Rust* respectively, which introduces different attack vectors [9,36].

6.2 Layer-2 Solutioning

Layer-2 provides scalability for blockchains via rollups and will greatly allow the horizontal scaling between stakeholders in the supply chain [25,77]. The concept of rollups is to execute resource-intensive transactions off-chain, then submit transactional data to *Layer-1* for confirmations by agreements. As minimum data is required to be computed on-chain, rollups are seen as an effective way to scale blockchains.

They are classified into three solutions; 1) optimistic rollups, 2) ZK-rollups (Zero-Knowledge), and 3) validium. The difference among these variants is the methodology and format of security proofs posted to *Layer-1* for processing. Similar to other scaling solutions, rollups suffers from inherent several short-comings. For instance, the waiting period in optimistic rollups causes delays due to the design of fraud proof challenges. The complexity of proof generation and verification may result in slow adoption of ZK-rollups. Validium seems to be promising by combining the first two solutions. However, generating a proof still requires high availability of off-chain data at any given time.

6.3   IT/OT Integration

While this paper considers both IT and OT integration of the supply chain, building a blockchain on top of these existing systems pose a huge challenge for legacy or traditional industries which may not be technologically competent or ready to migrate to a fully digitalized process [66]. Not to mention, there is a need to consider that the software lifecycle for OT is significantly delayed and differ from their IT counterparts. Different countries may adopt different standards to protect their assets and resources due to legislatory concerns.

7   Conclusion

We identified gaps in cybersecurity standards to implement trusted blockchains in supply chains. By defining clear and distinct roles and responsibilities for each of the stakeholders in the supply chain, they partake an endeavour on maintaining trust between blockchains and yet remain accountable. Supply chains can quickly implement a blockchain to ensure a secure and trusted environment by identifying potential threats and adopting *SuppliedTrust*. These will form the basis for shaping blockchains to be much more secure, should ever an implementation be integrated with a supply chain.

References

1. BitTorrent (BTT) White Paper. https://www.bittorrent.com/btt/btt-docs/BitTorrent_(BTT)_White_Paper_v0.8.7_Feb_2019.pdf
2. Blockchain/Distributed Ledger Technology (DLT) Risk and Security. https://cloudsecurityalliance.org/artifacts/blockchain-dlt-risk-and-considerations/
3. Bridges: Adding External Adapters to Nodes|Chainlink Documentation. https://docs.chain.link/docs/node-operators/
4. Cloud Controls Matrix and CAIQ v4|Cloud Security Alliance. https://cloudsecurityalliance.org/artifacts/cloud-controls-matrix-v4/
5. Contracts [Sia Wiki]. https://siawiki.tech/renter/contracts
6. Create, sell or collect digital items secured with blockchain. https://rarible.com
7. culubas: Timejacking & Bitcoin. https://culubas.blogspot.com/2011/05/timejacking-bitcoin_802.html
8. Cyber security|IEC. https://www.iec.ch/cyber-security
9. Developing with Rust|Solana Docs. https://docs.solana.com/developing/on-chain-programs/developing-rust

10. ETSI - Welcome to the World of Standards! https://www.etsi.org/
11. GitHub - ArweaveTeam/SmartWeave: Simple, scalable smart contracts on the Arweave protocol. https://github.com/ArweaveTeam/SmartWeave
12. GitHub - ConsenSys/mythril: Security analysis tool for EVM bytecode. https://github.com/ConsenSys/mythril
13. GitHub - cosmos/gravity-bridge: a CosmosSDK application for moving assets on and off of EVM based, POW chains. https://github.com/cosmos/gravity-bridge
14. GitHub - storj/whitepaper: The Storj v3 whitepaper. https://github.com/storj/whitepaper
15. IBM Food Trust - Blockchain for the world's food supply. https://www.ibm.com/blockchain/solutions/food-trust
16. Inside the GPU Shortage: Why You Still Can't Buy a Graphics Card. https://sea.pcmag.com/graphics-cards/44196/inside-the-gpu-shortage-why-you-still-cant-buy-a-graphics-card
17. ISO - ISO/IEC 27001 - Information security management. https://www.iso.org/isoiec-27001-information-security.html
18. ISO - ISO/TC 307 - Blockchain and distributed ledger technologies. https://www.iso.org/committee/6266604.html
19. Metadata Standards. https://docs.opensea.io/docs/metadata-standards
20. MythX: Smart contract security service for Ethereum. https://mythx.io/
21. NFT tracking and analytics platform. https://icy.tools
22. OWASP Top Ten Web Application Security Risks. https://owasp.org/www-project-top-ten/
23. Parvus®DuraCOR®Pi. https://www.curtisswrightds.com/products/computing/systems/sff/duracor-pi.html
24. Polkadot Bridges - Connecting the Polkadot Ecosystem with External Networks. https://polkadot.network/blog/polkadot-bridges-connecting-the-polkadot-ecosystem-with-external-networks/
25. Scaling|ethereum.org. https://ethereum.org/en/developers/docs/scaling/
26. Security Considerations|Solidity 0.8.14 documentation. https://docs.soliditylang.org/en/latest/security-considerations.html
27. Shared Responsibility Model - Amazon Web Services (AWS). https://aws.amazon.com/compliance/shared-responsibility-model/
28. Sia: Simple Decentralized Storage. https://blockchainlab.com/pdf/whitepaper3.pdf
29. Smart Contract Weakness Classification and Test Cases. https://swcregistry.io
30. Supply chain, shortages, and our first-ever price increase - raspberry pi. https://www.raspberrypi.com/news/supply-chain-shortages-and-our-first-ever-price-increase/
31. SWARM: Storage and communication infrastructure for a self-sovereign digital society. https://www.ethswarm.org/swarm-whitepaper.pdf
32. Timeline: How the Suez Canal blockage unfolded across supply chains|Supply Chain Dive. https://www.supplychaindive.com/news/timeline-ever-given-evergreen-blocked-suez-canal-supply-chain/597660/
33. Unibright IO - Unibright and Baseledger - Enterprise Blockchain Solutions from Germany. https://unibright.io/
34. Unstoppable Domains. https://unstoppabledomains.com/
35. World's first and largest NFT marketplace. https://opensea.io
36. Writing Your First Chaincode - hyperledger-fabricdocs main documentation. https://hyperledger-fabric.readthedocs.io/en/latest/chaincode4ade.html

37. Security and privacy controls for information systems and organizations. Technical report, September 2020. https://doi.org/10.6028/nist.sp.800-53r5. https://doi.org/10.6028/nist.sp.800-53r5
38. CargoX Bluepaper - Building Digital Trust with Blockchain Document Transfer, September 2021. https://cargox.io/static/files/CargoX-Bluepaper-September-2021.pdf
39. Moving Crypto Forward with Updated KYC Policies on Binance, September 2021. https://www.binance.com/en/blog/community/moving-crypto-forward-with-updated-kyc-policies-on-binance-421499824684902779
40. Baytaş, M.A., Cappellaro, A., Fernaeus, Y.: Stakeholders and value in the NFT ecosystem: towards a multi-disciplinary understanding of the NFT phenomenon. In: CHI Conference on Human Factors in Computing Systems Extended Abstracts. CHI EA 2022, New York, NY, USA. Association for Computing Machinery (2022). https://doi.org/10.1145/3491101.3519694
41. Benet, J.: IPFS - Content Addressed, Versioned, P2P File System. CoRR abs/1407.3561 (2014). https://arxiv.org/abs/1407.3561
42. Castro, M., Liskov, B.: Practical byzantine fault tolerance and proactive recovery. ACM Trans. Comput. Syst. **20**(4), 398–461 (2002). https://doi.org/10.1145/571637.571640
43. Castro, M., Liskov, B., et al.: Practical byzantine fault tolerance. In: OSDI 1999, pp. 173–186 (1999)
44. Daniel, E., Tschorsch, F.: IPFS and friends: a qualitative comparison of next generation peer-to-peer data networks. CoRR abs/2102.12737 (2021). https://arxiv.org/abs/2102.12737
45. Deirmentzoglou, E., Papakyriakopoulos, G., Patsakis, C.: A survey on long-range attacks for proof of stake protocols. IEEE Access **7**, 28712–28725 (2019). https://doi.org/10.1109/ACCESS.2019.2901858
46. Diligence, C.: Ethereum smart contract best practices. https://consensys.github.io/smart-contract-best-practices/
47. Doan, T.V., Bajpai, V., Psaras, Y., Ott, J.: Towards decentralised cloud storage with IPFS: opportunities, challenges, and future directions (2022). https://doi.org/10.48550/ARXIV.2202.06315. https://arxiv.org/abs/2202.06315
48. Douceur, J.R.: The sybil attack. In: Druschel, P., Kaashoek, F., Rowstron, A. (eds.) IPTPS 2002. LNCS, vol. 2429, pp. 251–260. Springer, Heidelberg (2002). https://doi.org/10.1007/3-540-45748-8_24
49. Durieux, T., Ferreira, J.a.F., Abreu, R., Cruz, P.: Empirical review of automated analysis tools on 47,587 ethereum smart contracts. In: Proceedings of the ACM/IEEE 42nd International Conference on Software Engineering, ICSE 2020, New York, NY, USA, pp. 530–541. Association for Computing Machinery (2020). https://doi.org/10.1145/3377811.3380364
50. Eyal, I., Sirer, E.G.: Majority is not enough: bitcoin mining is vulnerable. CoRR abs/1311.0243 (2013). https://arxiv.org/abs/1311.0243
51. Feist, J., Grieco, G., Groce, A.: Slither: a static analysis framework for smart contracts. CoRR abs/1908.09878 (2019). https://arxiv.org/abs/1908.09878
52. Galiev, A., Ishmukhametov, S., Latypov, R., Prokopyev, N., Stolov, E., Vlasov, I.: ARCHAIN: a novel blockchain based archival system. CoRR abs/1901.04225 (2019). https://arxiv.org/abs/1901.04225
53. Gonczol, P., Katsikouli, P., Herskind, L., Dragoni, N.: Blockchain implementations and use cases for supply chains-a survey. IEEE Access **8**, 11856–11871 (2020). https://doi.org/10.1109/ACCESS.2020.2964880

54. Heilman, E., Kendler, A., Zohar, A., Goldberg, S.: Eclipse attacks on bitcoin's peer-to-peer network. In: 24th USENIX Security Symposium (USENIX Security 2015), pp. 129–144. USENIX Association, Washington, D.C., August 2015. https://www.usenix.org/conference/usenixsecurity15/technical-sessions/presentation/heilman
55. Iqbal, M., Matulevičius, R.: Exploring sybil and double-spending risks in blockchain systems. IEEE Access **9**, 76153–76177 (2021). https://doi.org/10.1109/ACCESS.2021.3081998
56. Ishida, S.: Perspectives on supply chain management in a pandemic and the post-COVID-19 era. IEEE Eng. Manag. Rev. **48**(3), 146–152 (2020). https://doi.org/10.1109/EMR.2020.3016350
57. Chen, C.J.: Developing a model for supply chain agility and innovativeness to enhance firms' competitive advantage. Manage. Decis. **57**, November 2018. https://doi.org/10.1108/MD-12-2017-1236
58. Kaczorowski, M.: Exploring container security: the shared responsibility model in GKE|Google Cloud Blog. https://cloud.google.com/blog/products/containers-kubernetes/exploring-container-security-the-shared-responsibility-model-in-gke-container-security-shared-responsibility-model-gke
59. King, S., Nadal, S.: Ppcoin: peer-to-peer crypto-currency with proof-of-stake. Self-published paper, August 19, 1 (2012)
60. Kushwaha, S.S., Joshi, S., Singh, D., Kaur, M., Lee, H.N.: Systematic review of security vulnerabilities in ethereum blockchain smart contract. IEEE Access **10**, 6605–6621 (2022). https://doi.org/10.1109/ACCESS.2021.3140091
61. König, L., Korobeinikova, Y., Tjoa, S., Kieseberg, P.: Comparing blockchain standards and recommendations. Future Internet **12**(12) (2020). https://doi.org/10.3390/fi12120222. https://www.mdpi.com/1999-5903/12/12/222
62. Lambert, N., Ma, Q., Irvine, D.: Safecoin: the decentralised network token. https://docs.maidsafe.net/whitepapers/pdf/safecoin.pdf
63. Lanfear, T., Berry, D.: Shared responsibility in the cloud - Microsoft Azure|Microsoft Docs. https://docs.microsoft.com/en-us/azure/security/fundamentals/shared-responsibility
64. Lim, Y.Z., Zhou, J., Saerbeck, M.: Shaping blockchain technology for securing supply chains. In: Zhou, J., et al. (eds.) ACNS 2021. LNCS, vol. 12809, pp. 3–18. Springer, Cham (2021). https://doi.org/10.1007/978-3-030-81645-2_1
65. López Vivar, A., Sandoval Orozco, A.L., García Villalba, L.J.: A security framework for Ethereum smart contracts. Comput. Commun. **172**, 119–129 (2021). https://doi.org/10.1016/j.comcom.2021.03.008. https://www.sciencedirect.com/science/article/pii/S0140366421001043
66. Mansfield-Devine, S.: The state of operational technology security. Netw. Secur. **2019**(10), 9–13 (2019). https://doi.org/10.1016/S1353-4858(19)30121-7. https://www.sciencedirect.com/science/article/pii/S1353485819301217
67. Marcus, Y., Heilman, E., Goldberg, S.: Low-resource eclipse attacks on Ethereum's peer-to-peer network. Cryptology ePrint Archive, Report 2018/236 (2018). https://ia.cr/2018/236
68. Nakamoto, S.: Bitcoin: a peer-to-peer electronic cash system. Technical report, Manubot (2019). https://git.dhimmel.com/bitcoin-whitepaper
69. NCC Group: Decentralized Application Security Project (DASP) - Top 10 (2018). https://dasp.co/
70. Niu, J., Feng, C.: Selfish mining in Ethereum. CoRR abs/1901.04620 (2019). https://arxiv.org/abs/1901.04620
71. Palladino, S.: The parity wallet hack explained - OpenZeppelin blog (2017). https://blog.openzeppelin.com/on-the-parity-wallet-multisig-hack-405a8c12e8f7/

72. Perez, D., Livshits, B.: Smart contract vulnerabilities: vulnerable does not imply exploited. In: 30th USENIX Security Symposium (USENIX Security 2021), pp. 1325–1341. USENIX Association, August 2021. https://www.usenix.org/conference/usenixsecurity21/presentation/perez
73. Rossella, M., Cédric, L.: Methodologies for the identification of critical information infrastructure assets and services. European Union Agency for Network and Information Security (ENISA), Brussels (2015)
74. Saad, M., Njilla, L., Kamhoua, C., Kim, J., Nyang, D., Mohaisen, A.: Mempool optimization for defending against DDoS attacks in PoW-based blockchain systems. In: 2019 IEEE International Conference on Blockchain and Cryptocurrency (ICBC), pp. 285–292 (2019). https://doi.org/10.1109/BLOC.2019.8751476
75. Saad, M., et al.: Exploring the attack surface of blockchain: a systematic overview. CoRR abs/1904.03487 (2019). https://arxiv.org/abs/1904.03487
76. Secureum: Web3 Security Perspectives - Secureum #0. https://secureum.substack.com/p/web3-security-perspectives-secureum
77. Sguanci, C., Spatafora, R., Vergani, A.M.: Layer 2 blockchain scaling: a survey. CoRR abs/2107.10881 (2021). https://arxiv.org/abs/2107.10881
78. Shakhbulatov, D., Medina, J., Dong, Z., Rojas-Cessa, R.: How blockchain enhances supply chain management: a survey. IEEE Open J. Comput. Soc. 1, 230–249 (2020). https://doi.org/10.1109/OJCS.2020.3025313
79. Sharma, T., Zhou, Z., Huang, Y., Wang, Y.: "It's a blessing and a curse": unpacking creators' practices with non-fungible tokens (NFTs) and their communities (2022). https://doi.org/10.48550/ARXIV.2201.13233. https://arxiv.org/abs/2201.13233
80. Szabo, N.: Smart contracts: building blocks for digital markets. https://www.fon.hum.uva.nl/rob/Courses/InformationInSpeech/CDROM/Literature/LOTwinterschool2006/szabo.best.vwh.net/smart_contracts_2.html
81. Vessenes, P.: Deconstructing the DAO attack: a brief code tour (2016). https://vessenes.com/deconstructing-thedao-attack-a-brief-code-tour/
82. Waas, M.: Understanding the world of automated smart contract analyzers. https://soliditydeveloper.com/smart-contract-security-analyzers
83. Entriken, W., Shirley, D., Evans, J., Sachs, N.: EIP-721: ERC-721 non-fungible token standard. https://eips.ethereum.org/EIPS/eip-721
84. Xia, P., Wang, H., Yu, Z., Liu, X., Luo, X., Xu, G.: Ethereum name service: the good, the bad, and the ugly. CoRR abs/2104.05185 (2021). https://arxiv.org/abs/2104.05185

Towards Interpreting Vulnerability of Object Detection Models via Adversarial Distillation

Yaoyuan Zhang[1], Yu-an Tan[2], Mingfeng Lu[3], Lu Liu[2], Quanxing Zhang[1], Yuanzhang Li[1], and Dianxin Wang[1](✉)

[1] School of Computer Science and Technology, Beijing Institute of Technology, Beijing 100081, China
{yaoyuan,zhangqx,popular,dianxinw}@bit.edu.cn
[2] School of Cyberspace Science and Technology, Beijing Institute of Technology, Beijing 100081, China
{tan2008,liulu}@bit.edu.cn
[3] School of Information and Electronics, Beijing Institute of Technology, Beijing 100081, China
lumingfeng@bit.edu.cn

Abstract. Recent works have shown that deep learning models are highly vulnerable to adversarial examples, limiting the application of deep learning in security-critical systems. This paper aims to interpret the vulnerability of deep learning models to adversarial examples. We propose adversarial distillation to illustrate that adversarial examples are generalizable data features. Deep learning models are vulnerable to adversarial examples because models do not learn this data distribution. More specifically, we obtain adversarial features by introducing a generation and extraction mechanism. The generation mechanism generates adversarial examples, which mislead the source model trained on the original clean samples. The extraction term removes the original features and selects valid and generalizable adversarial features. Valuable adversarial features guide the model to learn the data distribution of adversarial examples and realize the model's generalization on the adversarial dataset. Extensive experimental evaluations have proved the excellent generalization performance of the adversarial distillation model. Compared with the normally trained model, the mAP has increased by 2.17% on their respective test sets, while the mAP on the opponent's test set is very low. The experimental results further prove that adversarial examples are also generalizable data features, which obeys a different data distribution from the clean data. Understanding why deep learning models are not robust to adversarial samples is helpful to attain interpretable and robust deep learning models. Robust models are essential for users to trust models and interact with the models, which can promote the application of deep learning in security-sensitive systems.

Keywords: Adversarial examples · Interpretability · Object detection · Deep learning

J. Zhou et al. (Eds.): ACNS 2022 Workshops, LNCS 13285, pp. 53–65, 2022.
https://doi.org/10.1007/978-3-031-16815-4_4

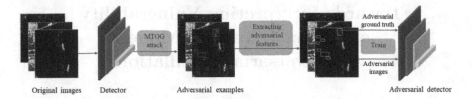

Original images   Detector   Adversarial examples   Adversarial detector

Fig. 1. A conceptual diagram of our framework. The paper adopts the MTOG attack to generate adversarial examples to make an object detector fabricate many bounding boxes. Adversarial features are extracted from these bounding boxes to construct a new dataset, called the adversarial dataset. By training an object detection model on the adversarial dataset, we obtain an adversarial distillation model.

1   Introduction

Recent works have shown that deep learning models are vulnerable to adversarial examples [1,27], which imperceptibly perturbed natural inputs to induce DNN models to make erroneous predictions. Previous work tried to explain this phenomenon from multiple perspectives, [2,24] interpret the existence of adversarial examples from the standpoint of theoretical models, and [8,18,25] focus on the demonstration based on high-dimensions quantities. However, these theories often fail to capture the behavior we observe in practice fully. More broadly, previous work in the field tends to treat adversarial examples as aberrations caused by the high dimensional nature of the input space or statistical fluctuations in the training data [8,10,27]. [13] propose a new perspective on adversarial examples. They demonstrate that adversarial examples are not bugs but features in image classification. Still, there are no explanations for adversarial examples in more complex computer vision tasks, such as object detection.

In this paper, we commit to interpreting the vulnerability of deep learning object detection models to adversarial examples, inspired by [13]. We illustrate that adversarial examples are classification features and localization features. Object detectors are vulnerable to adversarial examples because they do not learn the data distribution of adversarial examples. Object detectors tend to exploit any available features to localize the position of objects and classify them to a specific class, even those features that seem inexplicable to humans. We demonstrate that object detection models can learn valuable features on adversarial examples and be generalized to the whole data distribution, just like benign examples.

To corroborate our hypothesis, we propose adversarial distillation. Given an object detection model trained on the benign training set, we improve the TOG attack [6] to generate adversarial examples and design an extracting adversarial features module to construct an adversarial dataset. The inputs of this dataset are nearly identical to the originals, but all appear incorrectly localized and labeled. They are associated with their new ground truth (not the originals) only through small adversarial perturbations (and hence utilize only adversarial features). We train the adversarial distilled model on this adversarial dataset and evaluate the performance of this model both on the adversarial test set and the original test set. Experimental results have shown that the adversarial distilled model yields well generalization despite the lack of predictive human-visible information, which indicates that adversarial examples are features satisfying a specific data distribution but different from the distribution of benign data. We consider one class object detection dataset because this type of dataset has a simple category, and the model trained on the dataset can better focus on localization features. We further choose the SAR ship detection dataset [29] as the original dataset and implement adversarial distillation on this dataset. In summary, we make the following contributions:

- We train an object detection model on the SAR ship dataset, which obtains a great mAP. Simultaneously, We craft adversarial examples to attack this model and effectively decrease the mAP.
- We establish experiments to illustrate that adversarial examples are not vulnerabilities but well-generalizable features satisfying a specific data distribution.

The rest of this paper is organized as follows. In Sect. 2, we briefly review the related backgrounds. We present the detail of the framework in Sect. 3. Section 4 reports all experimental results. Finally, we summarize the conclusion in Sect. 5.

2   Related Works

2.1   Interpretable Adversarial Examples

[13] propose a novel explanation for the existence of adversarial examples. The standard training method can learn both useful robust and non-robust features in their work. The non-robust features are beneficial to generalization but very sensitive, which makes classifiers vulnerable to adversarial examples. The sensitivity of non-robust features should be understood as their small changes will significantly change the model's predictions. The useful, robust feature is the common feature with certain interpretability, such as cat ears and cat tail in cat classification. When performing formal training based on robust features and non-robust features, respectively, classifiers can obtain good accuracy on the standard test set. Classifiers with different structures trained on different datasets of the same distribution may learn similar non-robust features, which makes the adversarial examples transferable. [13] validates the hypothesis by extracting the image classification dataset into roust features and non-robust features and use the Gaussian distribution as an example.

2.2   Object Detection

Object detection is one of significant computer vision tasks, which detects the class and location of objects in digital images [9,15,21]. In object detection, we take YOLOv3 [22] as an example. Given an input image x, the model first generates a great number of S candidate bounding boxes $\hat{B}(x) = \{\hat{o}_1, ..., \hat{o}_S\}$ where $\hat{o}_i = (\hat{b}_i^x, \hat{b}_i^y, \hat{b}_i^w, \hat{b}_i^h, \hat{C}_i, \hat{p}_i)$ represents a candidate centered at coordinates $(\hat{b}_i^x, \hat{b}_i^y)$, and $(\hat{b}_i^w, \hat{b}_i^h)$ is width and height of the candidate. The objectness score $\hat{C}_i \in [0, 1]$ denotes whether the candidate contains an object, and a K-class probability vector $\hat{p}_i = (\hat{p}_i^1, \hat{p}_i^2, ..., \hat{p}_i^K)$ estimates the class of the corresponding candidate. The detection process usually divides the input x into grids with different scales, and each grid cell generates plenty of candidate bounding boxes based on the anchors and localizes the object centered at the cell. The candidates with low prediction confidence are excluded via applying confidence threshold, and those with high overlapping are removed by non-maximum suppression. The remaining candidates constitute the final detection result $\hat{O}(x)$.

For training an object detector, each object o_i in a training sample (x, O) is allocated to one of the S bounding boxes according to the center coordinates and the amount of overlapping with the anchors. $O = \{o_i | 1_i = 1, 1 \leq i \leq S\}$ is a set of objects in ground truth where $1_i = 1$ if the i-th bounding box is responsible for an object and 0 otherwise, $o_i = (b_i^x, b_i^y, b_i^w, b_i^h, p_i)$ with $p_i = (p_i^1, p_i^2, ..., p_i^K)$ and $p_i^c = 1$ if the class of o_i is c. Training a DNN model often begins with initializing the parameters of the model randomly and updating parameters slowly via taking the derivative of the loss function L concerning parameters θ on a mini-batch of input-output pairs $\{(x, O)\}$ with the following equation until convergence:

$$\theta_{t+1} = \theta_t - \alpha \nabla_{\theta_t} L(x, O; \theta), \tag{1}$$

where α is the learning rate. The loss function of a deep object detection network is divided into three parts, each part corresponds to describing the existence, locality, and category of a detected object. The objectness score $\hat{C}_i$ can be learned by minimizing the binary cross-entropy l_{BCE}:

$$L_{obj}(x, O; \theta) = \sum_{S}^{i=1} [1_i l_{BCE}(1, \hat{C}_i)]$$

$$L_{noobj}(x, O; \theta) = \sum_{S}^{i=1} [1 - 1_i l_{BCE}(0, \hat{C}_i)], \tag{2}$$

The spatial locality is learned by minimizing the squared error l_{SE}:

$$L_{loc}(x, O; \theta) = \sum_{S}^{i=1} 1_i [l_{SE}(x_i, \hat{x}_i) + l_{SE}(y_i, \hat{y}_i)$$
$$+ l_{SE}(\sqrt{W_i}, \sqrt{\hat{W}_i}) + l_{SE}(\sqrt{W_i}, \sqrt{\hat{W}_i})] \tag{3}$$

The K-class probabilities $\hat{p}_i$ is optimized by minimizing the binary cross-entropy:

$$L_{prob}(x, O; \theta) = \sum_{S}^{i=1} 1_i \sum_{c \in classes} l_{BCE}(p_i^c, \hat{p}_i^c) \tag{4}$$

Therefore, the deep object detection network can be optimized by the linear combination of the above loss functions:

$$L(x, O; \theta) = L_{obj}(x, O; \theta) + \lambda_{noobj} L_{noobj}(x, O; \theta)$$
$$+ \lambda_{loc} L_{loc}(x, O; \theta) + L_{prob}(x, O; \theta), \tag{5}$$

Synthetic Aperture Radar (SAR) [12,14] is a high-resolution imaging radar that can generate high-resolution two-dimensional images of range and azimuth via reflecting the emitted electromagnetic wave onto the target. For SAR can provide high-resolution images in all weather conditions, SAR images have been widely used for complex object detection and recognition tasks, such as ship object detection. With the widespread application of SAR in ship detection [28], some large-scale datasets have emerged, such as SSDD [14], OpenSARShip [12] and SAR ship dataset [29].

2.3   Adversarial Examples

Adversarial examples are first found in image classification task [23], an adversarial example x' is crafted by adding imperceptible perturbations to a clean input x, making the target model output incorrect predictions [4,10,16,17,19]. The process of generating an adversarial example can be defined as

$$min \parallel x' - x \parallel_p \quad s.t. \hat{O}(x') \neq \hat{O}(x), \tag{6}$$

where p represents the distance metric, which can be the L_0, L_2 and L_∞ norm.

Adversarial examples also exist in object detection task [3,26,30]. TOG attack is a family of adversarial attacks on object detection, including object-vanishing attack, object-fabrication attack, object-mislabeling attack and untargeted attack [6,7]. We take the untargeted attack as an example to introduce the TOG attack. TOG attack fixes the model parameters and initializes with a clean image (i.e., $x'_0 = x$), iteratively updating the adversarial example with the following equation:

$$L(x'_t, \hat{O}(x); \theta) = L_{obj}(x'_t, \hat{O}(x); \theta) + L_{noobj}(x'_t, \hat{O}(x); \theta)$$
$$+ L_{loc}(x'_t, \hat{O}(x); \theta) + L_{prob}(x'_t, \hat{O}(x); \theta), \tag{7}$$

$$x'_{t+1} = \Pi_{x,\epsilon}[x'_t + \alpha \Gamma(\nabla_{x'_t} L(x'_t, \hat{O}(x); \theta))] \tag{8}$$

where $\Pi_{x,\epsilon}[\cdot]$ is the projection onto a hypersphere with a radius ϵ centered at x in L_p norm, Γ is a sign function.

2.4   Distillation

[11] initially propose a distillation method to reduce a large model (the teacher) to a smaller distillation model (the student), thereby improving accuracy on the test set and speeding up the rate of the student predicting hard labels (ground truth). At a high level, the working principle of distillation can be summarized

into three steps: one is to train the teacher on the training set in a standard way. The second is to use the teacher to label each instance on the training set with soft labels (the output vector of the teacher). For example, the hard label on an image of a dog indicates that it is classified as a dog. At the same time, the soft label describes that it is a dog with 76% probability, a cat with 22% probability, and a cow with 0.2% probability. The third is to train the distillation model on the soft labels from the teacher instead of the hard labels from the training set. Distillation is exploited in multiple domains [5, 20].

3 Methodology

3.1 Definitions

We consider object detection with one class ($K = 1$ in Sect. 2.2), where input-output pairs $(x, O) \in X \times \{(b_i^x, b_i^y, b_i^w, b_i^h, p_i^c)\}$ are sampled from a data distribution D. Following the definition of [13], we define a function f to represents an object detector. Additionally, we define f_l as a localization function and f_c as a classification function.

- γ−valuable localization features: For an input x, we call a localization feature f_l γ−valuable ($\gamma > 0$) if it is correlated with the ground-truth bounding boxes in expectation, that is if

$$E_{(x,O)\sim D}[B(x) \cdot f_l(x)] \geq \gamma, \tag{9}$$

  where $B(x) = \{(b_i^x, b_i^y, b_i^w, b_i^h)\}$.
- ρ−valuable classification features: For an input x, we call a classification feature f_c ρ−valuable ($\rho > 0$) if it is correlated with the ground-truth label in expectation, that is if

$$E_{(x,O)\sim D}[c \cdot f_c(x)] \geq \rho. \tag{10}$$

- Valuable adversarial features: When the input is x', we define γ−valuable adversarial localization feature and ρ−valuable adversarial classification feature satisfying Eq. 9 and Eq. 10, respectively.

3.2 Framework

In this work, we elaborate on adversarial distillation for interpreting that adversarial examples are the features satisfying a specific data distribution. A conceptual description of these experiments can be found in Fig. 1. We construct an adversarial dataset where the input-output association is based on valuable adversarial features. We show that this dataset suffices to train an object detector with good performance on the adversarial test set. Still, poor performance on the original test set results from the gap between original and adversarial distribution.

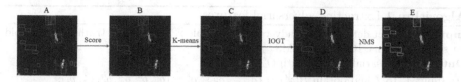

Fig. 2. An example in Sect. 3.3. A is the adversarial example generated by MTOG; B, C and D are the intermediate images selected after Score, K-means and IOGT, respectively; E is the final result selected after NMS.

3.3 Extracting Adversarial Features

We construct a dataset where the input-output association is based on valuable adversarial features, including localization and classification. To accomplish this, we modify each input-output pair (x, O) as follows. We integrate momentum into TOG attack [6] (MTOG) to generate the corresponding adversarial examples on original datasets so that the original object detector f can detect many objects which do not exist in human eyes. We then extract adversarial features via selecting these forged bounding boxes according to the following steps.

Given an adversarial example x', (1) Score: we discard bounding boxes with scores below the threshold to ensure adversarial classification features $\rho-$valuable; (2) K-means: we analyze the range of original ground-truth bounding boxes by k-means clustering algorithm and remove the bounding boxes that exceed this range to a certain threshold; (3) IOGT: we design the IOGT method to discard those bounding boxes intersecting with the original ground truth, which ensures that the selected bounding boxes do not include original localization features. IOGT can be formulated as

$$IOGT(B) = \frac{B \cap GT}{GT}, \tag{11}$$

where GT represents all original ground-truth bounding boxes $\{(b_i^x, b_i^y, b_i^w, b_i^h)\}$, B represents the candidate bounding box; (4) NMS: we exploit non-maximum suppression to ensure that the forged bounding boxes do not intersect, making the generated localization features not duplicated. The remaining bounding boxes are aligned as O' to form the new input-output pair (x', O'). Finally, the resulting input-output pairs make up the new dataset, named adversarial dataset. The whole process is described in Algorithm 1, and Fig. 2 shows an example of processing by the extracting adversarial feature module.

3.4 Adversarial Distillation

We elaborate on adversarial distillation for interpreting that adversarial examples are the features satisfying a specific data distribution. A conceptual description of these experiments can be found in Fig. 1. We first train an object detection model (the teacher) on the original dataset. Then, we use the MTOG attack to

---

Algorithm 1 Extracting adversarial features

Input: An object detector f; an adversarial example x' and ground truth O; Threshold
for score, k-means, IOGT and NMS
Output: Adversarial ground truth O'
1: Input x' to f and obtain $\hat{B}(x') = \{\hat{o}_1, ..., \hat{o}_n\}$, $\hat{o}_i = (\hat{b}_i^x, \hat{b}_i^y, \hat{b}_i^w, \hat{b}_i^h, \hat{C}_i, \hat{p}_i)$;
2: $\text{temp}_1 = \text{temp}_2 = [\,]$
3: **for** $\hat{o}_i$ in $\hat{B}(x')$ **do**
4:      **if** $\hat{p}_i >$ score **then**
5:          continue
6:      **end if**
7:      **if** $(\hat{b}_i^w, \hat{b}_i^h)$ not in k-means **then**
8:          continue
9:      **end if**
10:     **if** $\text{IOGT}(\hat{b}_i^x, \hat{b}_i^y, \hat{b}_i^w, \hat{b}_i^h) \neq 0$ **then**
11:         continue
12:         Add $\hat{o}_i$ into temp1
13:     **end if**
14: **end for**
15: temp2 = NMS(temp1)
16: $O' = $ temp2
17: **return** O'

---

generate adversarial examples against the teacher and obtain the corresponding outputs of the teacher. We next use Sect. 3.3 to craft adversarial ground
truth, thus making the adversarial dataset. Finally, we train the distilled model
(the student) on the adversarial training set from the teacher rather than on
the original training set. We find that the distilled model performs well on the
adversarial test set, which indicates that adversarial examples are features satisfying a specific data distribution. Meanwhile, the student performs poorly on
the original test set, which indicates that the gap between the adversarial and
original data distribution results in poor generalization.

4   Experiments

4.1   Setup

Datasets. We select SAR ship detection dataset consisting 43,819 ship chips [29].
We randomly allocate the training set, validation set, and test set according to
the ratio of 7: 2: 1. Meanwhile, we do the same operation on the corresponding
adversarial dataset.

MTOG Attack. The maximum perturbation ϵ is set to 8 with pixel value in
[0,255]. The number of iterations T is 20, the step size is 2 and the decay factor μ
is 1.0. We set the coefficient $\lambda = 0.2$ empirically in order to reduce the proportion
of L_{noobj} in L.

Benign   Benign GT   MTOG   Adv Result   Select

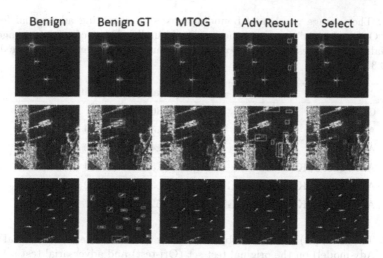

Fig. 3. Some random samples from the original SAR Ship dataset and the corresponding adversarial examples.

Extracting Adversarial Features. We set the threshold of the classification score of each candidate bounding box in the output of the model to 0.5 in order to ensure adversarial classification features ρ–valuable. We set the range of k-means clustering to [5, 104]. And the bounding box threshold of both IOU in NMS and IOGT is set to 0 to remove the intersecting bounding boxes.

Adversarial Distillation. We train three Yolov3-Mobilenet[1] models on the SAR ship detection dataset and its corresponding adversarial dataset, respectively. For each model, we divide the training process into two steps. At the first step, Adam optimization is used with a learning rate of 0.001 and a batch size of 16, and training epochs are 30. In the second step, the learning rate is 0.0001, the batch size is 16, and the training epochs are 20. After models are trained, we test these models on the original test set and adversarial test set. We evaluate the performance of models by mean Average Precision (mAP), and the threshold of IOU is set to 0.5. Our experiments are conducted on an Intel(R) Xeon(R) CPU E5-2620 v4 @ 2.10 GHz CPU, a GPU of NVIDIA GeForce RTX 2080 Ti with 11 GB, and 32 GB of memory.

4.2 Generating Adversarial Examples

Figure 3 shows test SAR images (left) with the detection results made by YOLOv3-Mobilenet on benign (the "Benign GT" column), the corresponding adversarial examples (the "MTOG" column) generated by MTOG attacks with the detection results made by YOLOv3-Mobilenet (the "Adv Result" column), and the adversarial example selected by Sect. 3.3 (the "SELECT" column).

---

[1] https://github.com/Adamdad/keras-YOLOv3-mobilenet.

Table 1. The average number of bounding boxes in extracting adversarial features module. "Ori" and "Adv" represent the average bounding boxes of original images and adversarial examples, respectively. "Score", "K-means", "IOGT", and "NMS" are defined in Sect. 3.3.

	Training	Validation	Test
Ori	1.363	1.347	1.352
Adv	13.393	13.359	13.520
Adv+Score	12.436	12.580	12.402
Adv+Score+K-means	10.840	10.954	10.789
Adv+Score+K-means+IOGT	10.343	10.452	10.289
Adv+Score+K-means+IOGT+NMS	8.528	8.557	8.490

Table 2. The mAP (%) of original object detector (Ori-model) and adversarial object detector (Adv-model) on the original test set (Ori-test) and adversarial test set (Adv-test), respectively.

	Ori-test	Adv-test	Adv-GT-test
Ori-model	86.34	83.45	0.12
Adv-model	1.19	88.51	–

From Fig. 3, we can observe that the MTOG attack fools the object detector to give many invisible objects (bounding boxes), most with high confidence and some with low confidence. After MTOG, the mAP of the detector drops to 0.12%, the results are shown in Table 2. However, some bounding boxes with natural objects still exist, some bounding boxes intersect together, and the aspect ratio of some bounding boxes does not match the k-means clustering result. After extracting adversarial features, we remove those bounding boxes with low confidence or intersect with ground truth or the aspect ratio not in k-means clustering. We keep the one with the highest confidence for the intersecting bounding boxes.

Table 1 shows the average number of bounding boxes after each step in Sect. 3.3. In Table 1, MTOG adversarial attack craft plenty of bounding boxes compared to original images. We follow the steps described in Sect. 3.3 to remove useless bounding boxes. We take the training set as an example. After an adversarial attack, the average number of bounding boxes increases from 1.363 to 13.393. After Score, it drops to 12.436. After K-means, it decreases by 1.596. Finally, the average number of bounding boxes is 8.528.

4.3 Evaluation on Adversarial Distillation

We report in Table 2 the mAP of original object detector (Ori-model) and adversarial object detector (Adv-model) on the original test set (Ori-test), adversarial test set (Adv-test) and the test set with adversarial examples and the ground truth (Adv-GT-test), respectively.

In the first column of Table 2, the data (86.34%) represents the result of training on the original dataset and evaluation on the original dataset. This data shows that YOLOv3-Mobilenet performs well on the SAR ship dataset. The data (1.19%) represents the result of training on the adversarial dataset and evaluation on the original dataset, which indicates that the gap between the adversarial and original data distribution results in poor generalization. The data (83.45%) in Table 2 is the mAP of original models evaluated on the adversarial dataset and 0.12% shows the MTOG attack successfully attack the original model. The data (88.51%) indicates that adversarial examples are features satisfying a specific data distribution, just like the original dataset. It further explains that adversarial examples are not bugs, but features, some of which are indeed valuable for localization and classification in object detection.

5   Conclusion

This paper proposes a new perspective on adversarial examples that are not aberrations but features satisfying a specific data distribution. In object detection, adversarial examples contain classification features and localization features. These features are helpful for models to generalize. We support this hypothesis by performing adversarial distillation, which constructs adversarial datasets on the teacher and trains the adversarial object detector on these datasets. We select ship detection in SAR images as an original dataset for its category is simple, and the model can better focus on localization features. We introduce the MTOG attack to generate adversarial examples to provide a basis for constructing an adversarial dataset. The experiment results show that adversarial examples are generalizable features that satisfy a specific data distribution. The model trained on the adversarial training set generalizes well on the adversarial test set. We hope that our findings can help researchers better understand the black-box deep learning models, thereby contributing to the deep development and extensive application of deep learning models.

Acknowledgements. This work was supported by the National Natural Science Foundation of China under Grant (No. 61876019, 62072037, U1936218).

References

1. Biggio, B., et al.: Evasion attacks against machine learning at test time. In: Blockeel, H., Kersting, K., Nijssen, S., Železný, F. (eds.) ECML PKDD 2013. LNCS (LNAI), vol. 8190, pp. 387–402. Springer, Heidelberg (2013). https://doi.org/10.1007/978-3-642-40994-3_25
2. Bubeck, S., Lee, Y.T., Price, E., Razenshteyn, I.: Adversarial examples from computational constraints. In: International Conference on Machine Learning, pp. 831–840. PMLR (2019)
3. Carlini, N., Wagner, D.: Adversarial examples are not easily detected: bypassing ten detection methods. In: Proceedings of the 10th ACM Workshop on Artificial Intelligence and Security, pp. 3–14 (2017)

4. Carlini, N., Wagner, D.: Towards evaluating the robustness of neural networks. In: IEEE Symposium on Security and Privacy, pp. 39–57 (2017)
5. Cheng, X., Rao, Z., Chen, Y., Zhang, Q.: Explaining knowledge distillation by quantifying the knowledge. In: Proceedings of the IEEE/CVF Conference on Computer Vision and Pattern Recognition, pp. 12925–12935 (2020)
6. Chow, K.H., Liu, L., Gursoy, M.E., Truex, S., Wei, W., Wu, Y.: TOG: targeted adversarial objectness gradient attacks on real-time object detection systems. arXiv preprint arXiv:2004.04320 (2020)
7. Chow, K.-H., Liu, L., Gursoy, M.E., Truex, S., Wei, W., Wu, Y.: Understanding object detection through an adversarial lens. In: Chen, L., Li, N., Liang, K., Schneider, S. (eds.) ESORICS 2020. LNCS, vol. 12309, pp. 460–481. Springer, Cham (2020). https://doi.org/10.1007/978-3-030-59013-0_23
8. Gilmer, J., et al.: Adversarial spheres. arXiv preprint arXiv:1801.02774 (2018)
9. Girshick, R., Donahue, J., Darrell, T., Malik, J.: Rich feature hierarchies for accurate object detection and semantic segmentation. In: Proceedings of the IEEE Conference on Computer Vision and Pattern Recognition, pp. 580–587 (2014)
10. Goodfellow, I.J., Shlens, J., Szegedy, C.: Explaining and harnessing adversarial examples. In: International Conference on Learning Representations (2015)
11. Hinton, G., Vinyals, O., Dean, J.: Distilling the knowledge in a neural network. Comput. Sci. **14**(7), 38–39 (2015)
12. Huang, L., et al.: OpenSARShip: a dataset dedicated to sentinel-1 ship interpretation. IEEE J. Sel. Top. Appl. Earth Observ. Remote Sens. **11**(1), 195–208 (2017)
13. Ilyas, A., Santurkar, S., Engstrom, L., Tran, B., Madry, A.: Adversarial examples are not bugs, they are features. In: Annual Conference on Neural Information Processing Systems (2019)
14. Li, J., Qu, C., Shao, J.: Ship detection in SAR images based on an improved faster R-CNN. In: 2017 SAR in Big Data Era: Models, Methods and Applications (BIGSARDATA), pp. 1–6. IEEE (2017)
15. Liu, W., et al.: SSD: single shot multibox detector. In: Leibe, B., Matas, J., Sebe, N., Welling, M. (eds.) ECCV 2016. LNCS, vol. 9905, pp. 21–37. Springer, Cham (2016). https://doi.org/10.1007/978-3-319-46448-0_2
16. Liu, Y., Chen, X., Liu, C., Song, D.: Delving into transferable adversarial examples and black-box attacks. In: International Conference on Learning Representations (2017)
17. Mądry, A., Makelov, A., Schmidt, L., Tsipras, D., Vladu, A.: Towards deep learning models resistant to adversarial attacks. Stat **1050**, 9 (2017)
18. Mahloujifar, S., Diochnos, D.I., Mahmoody, M.: The curse of concentration in robust learning: Evasion and poisoning attacks from concentration of measure. In: AAAI Conference on Artificial Intelligence, vol. 33, no. 01, pp. 4536–4543 (2019)
19. Papernot, N., McDaniel, P., Goodfellow, I., Jha, S., Celik, Z.B., Swami, A.: Practical black-box attacks against deep learning systems using adversarial examples. arXiv preprint arXiv:1602.02697 (2016)
20. Papernot, N., McDaniel, P., Wu, X., Jha, S., Swami, A.: Distillation as a defense to adversarial perturbations against deep neural networks. In: 2016 IEEE Symposium on Security and Privacy (SP), pp. 582–597. IEEE (2016)
21. Redmon, J., Divvala, S., Girshick, R., Farhadi, A.: You only look once: unified, real-time object detection. In: Proceedings of the IEEE Conference on Computer Vision and Pattern Recognition, pp. 779–788 (2016)
22. Redmon, J., Farhadi, A.: YOLOv3: an incremental improvement. arXiv preprint arXiv:1804.02767 (2018)

23. Russakovsky, O., et al.: ImageNet large scale visual recognition challenge. Int. J. Comput. Vis. **115**(3), 211–252 (2015)
24. Schmidt, L., Santurkar, S., Tsipras, D., Talwar, K., Madry, A.: Adversarially robust generalization requires more data. Advances Neural Inf. Process. Syst. (2018)
25. Shafahi, A., Huang, W.R., Studer, C., Feizi, S., Goldstein, T.: Are adversarial examples inevitable? In: International Conference on Learning Representations (2018)
26. Song, D., et al.: Physical adversarial examples for object detectors. In: 12th USENIX Workshop on Offensive Technologies (WOOT 2018) (2018)
27. Szegedy, C., et al.: Intriguing properties of neural networks. In: International Conference on Learning Representations (2014)
28. Wang, Y., Wang, C., Zhang, H.: Combining a single shot multibox detector with transfer learning for ship detection using sentinel-1 SAR images. Remote Sens. Lett. **9**(8), 780–788 (2018)
29. Wang, Y., Wang, C., Zhang, H., Dong, Y., Wei, S.: A SAR dataset of ship detection for deep learning under complex backgrounds. Remote Sens. **11**(7), 765 (2019)
30. Wei, X., Liang, S., Chen, N., Cao, X.: Transferable adversarial attacks for image and video object detection. arXiv preprint arXiv:1811.12641 (2018)

Vulnerability Detection for Smart Contract via Backward Bayesian Active Learning

Jiale Zhang[1] , Liangqiong Tu[1], Jie Cai[1(✉)], Xiaobing Sun[1(✉)], Bin Li[1],
Weitong Chen[1], and Yu Wang[2]

[1] College of Information Engineering, Yangzhou University, Yangzhou 225127, China
{jialezhang,xbsun,lb,wtchen}@yzu.edu.cn, jiecaiyzu@gmail.com
[2] Institute of Artificial Intelligence and Blockchain, Guangzhou University,
Guangzhou 510006, China
yuwang@gzhu.edu.cn

Abstract. Smart contract is a piece of program code running on the blockchain, which aims to realize trusted transactions without third parties. In recent years, smart contract vulnerabilities emerge one after another, resulting in huge economic losses. Machine learning technology is widely used in smart contract vulnerability detection. It is common that model training in machine learning often requires a large amount of labeled data while the unlabeled data in the current field is very rich and acquiring labels is extremely difficult. As a result, it takes a lot of manpower and time to label a vulnerability, and it is challenging to perform effective smart contract vulnerability detection. To tackle this problem, we propose *BwdBAL*, a novel framework for smart contract vulnerability detection that combines Bayesian Active Learning (BAL) and a backward noise removal method. We use BAL to remove the impact of model uncertainty on uncertainty sampling in active learning. During the backward process, we clean up the noise in the labeled dataset to reduce the negative influence on the classification model. We evaluate *BwdBAL* on 8 vulnerabilities about 4929 smart contracts with four performance indicators. The experimental results show that *BwdBAL* outperforms two baseline methods: conventional machine learning-enabled classification method and one-way active learning method.

Keywords: Smart contract · Vulnerability detection · Active learning · Uncertainty measure · Backward learning

1 Introduction

Blockchain is a new type of distributed system, which is widely applied in finance, supply chain, logistics security, and other fields [1–4]. Its one of the key components is smart contract which is a programmable code on the blockchain that

---

J. Zhang and L. Tu contributed equally to this work.

J. Zhou et al. (Eds.): ACNS 2022 Workshops, LNCS 13285, pp. 66–83, 2022.
https://doi.org/10.1007/978-3-031-16815-4_5

aims to realize trusted transactions without a third party. The number of smart contracts has been growing rapidly since Ethereum is released that the first open-source blockchain on which smart contracts can be deployed. A blockchain industry media in US Cointegraph [5] one is a company committed to analyzing blockchain ecology whose statistical results showed that the number of smart contracts deployed in the Ethereum system reached more than 1,971,000 in March 2020. Torres et al. [6], analyzed all smart contracts and transactions on Ethereum from 2015 to 2020. Their survey shows that the number of smart contracts attacked has not decreased in recent years. It is vulnerable to malicious attacks since the smart contract manages high-value virtual tokens and is immutable. Once attacked, it will cause huge economic losses. Therefore, the research on smart contract security has attracted much attention.

Smart contracts are designed and programmed by developers to realize the management activities of digital assets. Once the smart contract is deployed on the blockchain, it cannot be updated, and the vulnerability of the smart contract is inevitable. Timely detecting smart contracts vulnerabilities before deploying and calling smart contracts are critical for smart contracts quality assurance. Since vulnerability detection aims to effectively find vulnerabilities by using detection technology before they are exploited, it can help smart contract developers or testers focus on vulnerability-prone modules.

Traditional techniques based on static analysis, program verification, symbolic execution, and fuzzy testing have been studied a lot. These methods are mainly inspired by static and dynamic detection methods, such as static detection methods based on static analysis [7,8] and program verification method [9–11]. In the dynamic detection method, Loi et al. [12] based on dynamic symbols and Jiang et al. [13] based on fuzzing test. These tools can effectively detect smart contract vulnerabilities. In recent years, smart contract vulnerability detection method-based machine learning has also been widely studied. Machine learning methods significantly improve the efficiency of smart contract vulnerability detection. However the existing research still has some limitations: (1) machine learning methods often need enough training samples while most of the real data are unlabeled furthermore it requires a lot of manpower and time to label; (2) most research tools use the existing detection tools to mark, but the existing detection tools have a large false-positive rate and false-negative rate, which will reduce the accuracy of the training model; (3) some of these existing tools require specific defect patterns or specification rules defined by experts.

In order to address the above problems, Yu et al. [14] proposed using active learning to improve vulnerability inspection efficiency. Active learning selects modules from unlabeled samples to query labels from experts through a sampling strategy. The newly queried samples are merged into the labeled data set to update the training classifier, and the labeled sample size is continuously expanded through a cyclic iterative query. Active learning greatly reduces the time and cost of manually labeling data since not all data need annotation. And active learning is widely applied in image classification, text classification, defect detection and other fields [15–19]. However, the work [14] still has several limitations (to be described detailly in the next subsection), which inspired our approach.

1.1 Motivation

The most important component of active learning is sampling strategy and the key goal of active learning is how to select the most representative and informative candidate instances to achieve better efficiency with the least labeling cost [20]. The uncertainty measure based active learning method used in [14] has the limitation that only according to the prediction results of SVM, uncertainty sampling shall be carried out first, and then certainty sampling shall be carried out. This process only relies on SVM prediction results and does not consider the uncertainty of the model itself. Thus, the selected candidate sample is not a sample with higher uncertainty. In this paper, we use the Bayesian model to select more informative instances for labeling. When selecting labeled samples, this framework considers the uncertainty of the model itself, uses MC dropout [21] method to quantify the uncertainty of the model, and then comprehensively calculates the uncertainty of the samples.

The training set of machine learning needs humans to label in an unselective way, which leads to the need for a lot of marking. How to make human labor more efficient is a key point of research. In order to improve the accuracy of manual marking and reduce the impact of human errors, paper [9] proposed relabeling instances that are inconsistent results between manual marking and model prediction. The main limitation of this method is that it will increase human effort in active learning and does not consider whether the labeled dataset can have a positive impact on the model performance, namely, the labeled dataset is noisy. The noises are caused by incorrectly labeled instances or outliers of correctly labeled instances. So that they may produce a negative impact on the model. To tackle this issue, in this paper, we exploit a backward noise removal method, which explores labeled datasets to detect suspiciously unreliable instances. The performance of the model will degrade due to noisy instances. To eliminate the negative effects of noises, these noisy instances need to be processed by withdrawal from labeled datasets and re-sampling from the unlabeled datasets for labeling.

To sum up, in this paper, we propose *BwdBAL*, a novel framework for vulnerability classification for smart contracts that leverages the two mentioned-above methods: Bayesian Active Learning and backward noise removal method. Our framework consists of two major stages: forward learning and backward learning. In the first stage, *BwdBAL* exploits forward active learning to select some more informative sol files from the unlabeled dataset for querying their labels and then incorporates them with the current labeled dataset to construct a training set. This process is forward learning. In the second stage, *BwdBAL* utilizes a backward noise removal method to detect and process suspiciously unreliable instances by exploring labeled datasets for improving the generalization ability of the model. Finally, active learning is a circular process until the target effect is reached.

1.2   Contribution

In summary, we make the following contributions:

- We apply an active learning-based framework to classify smart contract vulnerability. We propose a novel framework *BwdBAL* to address an important issue in smart contract vulnerability detection: the lack of labeled data. Different from the traditional smart contracts vulnerability detection model, *BwdBAL* based on active learning learns by querying tags from Oracle and continuously selects more informative instances through query strategies for human oracle. Our framework can identify more vulnerabilities, even if there are only a small number of labeled datasets.
- The noises of the labeled dataset are caused by incorrectly labeled instances or outliers of correctly labeled instances. We utilize a backward noise removal method to detect and process suspiciously unreliable instances by exploring labeled datasets for improving the generalization ability of the model.
- We evaluate *BwdBAL* on 8 vulnerabilities about 4929 smart contracts with four performance indicators. The experimental results show that *BwdBAL* outperforms the baseline methods, and the uncertainty sampling strategy outperforms the other four sampling strategies.

The rest of the paper is organized as follows: Sect. 2 presents Research on smart contract vulnerability detection and active learning. Section 3 described our methodology. Section 4 investigates the detail of experiment designs as well as their results. Finally, we provide our conclusions and future work directions in Sect. 5.

2   Related Work

2.1   Smart Contract Vulnerability Detection

Smart contract security has received a lot of attention, and massive research on smart contract vulnerability detection has emerged in recent years. Those approaches are mainly divided into two groups: traditional technology and machine learning technology. a) Traditional technology, which mostly uses the artificial definition of rules or patterns related to smart contract vulnerabilities, then applies traditional methods such as static analysis, symbolic execution, or fuzzy testing to detect vulnerabilities. b) Machine learning technology, which extracts the corresponding features of smart contracts, and then trains the classification model based on a machine learning algorithm to detect vulnerabilities.

Traditional Technology. Early work on smart contract vulnerability detection by employing static analysis, symbolic execution, or fuzzy testing. Smart contract vulnerability detection based on static analysis method is mainly through control flow analysis. Smartcheck [7] and Slither [8] analyzes syntax of smart contract source code from control flow graph. Different from the former Vandal

[22] analyzes semantics from smart contract bytecode to detect vulnerability. Another stream of work relies on symbolic execution. Oyente [12] is the first work on security analysis of smart contracts. It uses dynamic symbolic execution technology to detect security vulnerabilities. Orisis [23] is a static analysis framework based on symbol execution and taint analysis, which mainly focuses on integer overflow vulnerability detection for Ethereum. In addition, there are some work based on Fuzzy testing. Contractfuzzer [13] generates fuzzing inputs based on the ABI specifications of smart contracts, defines test oracles to detect security vulnerabilities, which is the first work based fuzzy testing. Liu et al. [24]presented a fuzzing-based analyzer to automatically detect reentrancy bugs in Ethereum smart contracts. Traditional methods heavily rely on fixed expert rules or patterns, leading to low accuracy and poor scalability.

Machine Learning Technology. Most of the previous works in smart contract vulnerability detection are supervised, i.e., they use known vulnerabilities to train a classifier for detecting vulnerabilities. Those methods focus on smart contract source code, bytecode, or opcode. Then they extract features from AST (Abstract Syntax Tree) or CFG (Control Flow Graph). The two types of features they use for detecting smart contract vulnerabilities are smart contract security metrics and text mining features:

(1) Smart contract security metrics: Kevin et al. [25] used the Goal Question Metric (GQM) approach to find 15 security code metrics that can be applied to smart contract development. Momeni et al. [26] extracted 17 features that represented the complexity of the code from ASTs for supervised binary classifiers training and detecting. Their model predicted a number of major software vulnerabilities with an average accuracy of 95%.

(2) Text mining features: Most research has combined different language models to extract features from data related to smart contracts. Liao et al. [27] presented SoliAudit which uses machine learning and fuzz testing for smart contract vulnerability assessment. They attempted two different methods to extract features from the preprocessed opcode sequence: n-gram with term frequency-inverse document frequency and word2vec. Qian et al. [28] proposed contract snippet representations for smart contracts and used word2vec to extract features from contract snippet for Reentrancy vulnerability detection with a deep learning model. Ashizawa et al. [29] proposed Eth2Vec, a machine-learning-based static analysis tool for vulnerability detection in smart contracts. Eth2Vec could automate feature extraction for each contract by leveraging the neural networks-based PV-DM model. Mi et al. [30] proposed a framework for automating vulnerability detection in smart contracts with deep learning. They applied the CFG to get the sequence reflected the program execution semantics from bytecode and the n-gram model to form a features vector.

2.2 Active Learning

The most important component of active learning is sampling strategy, how to select the most representative and informative candidate instances to achieve better efficiency with the least labeling cost [20]. In order to alleviate the uncertainty of the machine learning model, this uncertainty will affect the uncertainty evaluation when selecting candidate label instance in active learning, [31–33] combined with the Bayesian model to comprehensively consider the uncertainty of the classification model for uncertainty sampling. To minimize the impact of human error, the previous researchers [34,35] estimate the label reliability or expertise level of labelers and then delete error-like answers, [36] requires labelers to relabel error-like labeled instances which can improve learning performance to some extent.

At present, a lot of research work has applied active learning for defect prediction. Luo et al. [37] proposed a two-stage active learning framework combining a clustering technique and support vector machine. Li et al. [38] proposed an active semi-supervised learning method to select the most helpful modules. Lu et al. [39] proposed an adaptively defect prediction framework combining supervised learning and active learning. Lu et al. [40] proposed active learning as a way to automate the development of models which improve the performance of defect prediction between successive releases. Zhou et al. [15] propose a two-phase framework that combines Hybrid Active Learning and Kernel PCA (HALKP) to select some informative and representative unlabeled modules from the current version for querying their labels and to extract representative features by embedding the original data of two versions into a high-dimension space. However, all these methods are applied to defect prediction.

Due to the limitation of their method as mentioned in this paper in Sect. 1.1, we employ a two-way active learning framework to select the more informative candidate instances and remove the noise of the labeled dataset.

3 The Proposed Method

3.1 Overview

Figure 1 depicts the overview of our smart contract vulnerability detection framework based on Bayesian Active Learning with backward noise removal method. Our framework is mainly divided into two parts: the forward learning process uses a Bayesian neural network and the backward learning process eliminates the noise in the labeled set by exploring it. Here our process to smart contract vulnerability detection goes through multiple steps. First, give an original smart contract, data cleaning is necessary such as removing blank lines, irrelevant comments, and non-ASCII characters. We then parse each cleaned smart contract into a sequence of code tokens, which are embedded into feature vector representations. Second, each cycle of active learning consists of two stages: forward learning and backward learning. In the first stage, we attempt to feed the feature vectors of labeled data to train the classifier. *BwdBAL* exploits BAL to select some more informative sol files from the unlabeled datasets for querying their labels and then incorporates them with the current labeled dataset to construct a new training set. This process is forward learning. In the second stage, *BwdBAL* utilizes a backward noise removal method to detect and process suspiciously unreliable instances by exploring labeled datasets for improving the generalization ability of the model. Finally, active learning is a circular process until the target effect is reached.

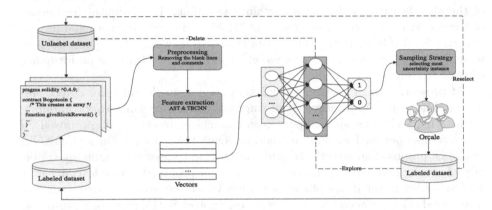

Fig. 1. Overview of the proposed smart contract vulnerability detection method.

3.2   Feature Extraction

This section explains the process of creating a feature matrix for all smart contracts. Before extracting the feature vector, it is necessary to clean the source code of the smart contract (i.e., removing the blank lines and comments). Then we use the infercode [30] tool to extract the feature vector of smart contact source code. Infercode constructs ASTs and then utilizes the TBCNN technique to generate numeric values for features in smart contracts. For each AST this tool identifies a set of subtrees, and all the subtrees are accumulated into a vocabulary of subtrees. Then an AST is fed into a Tree-Based CNN (TBCNN) encoder to produce a code vector $\vec{v_i}$. The steps of feature extraction are as follows:

(1) By traversing the AST, this tool selects a subtree whose root node is of type expr-stmt, decl-stmt, expr, condition. In addition, the tool also considers nodes that represent a single keyword, such as if, for, while. These nodes can be viewed as subtrees of size 1.
(2) After obtaining subtrees the tool uses it to learn source code encoders under the self-supervision mechanism (TBCNN). There are some differences between infercode's TBCNN and the original design itself. It builds in node initialization embedding with textual information not only just type information, and original TBCNN's dynamic node pooling is replaced with an attention mechanism to include node embedding.

Since the subtree in ASTs is regarded as the label represented by the training code without any manual marking work or expensive graphics construction overhead, we can extract the features of smart contract code more efficiently and conveniently using infercode.

3.3 Active Learning with Uncertainty Measure

The goal of active learning in the task of smart contract vulnerability detection is to create a classification model by selecting the most information sample to expand the labeled dataset. There are many strategies in active learning to select samples such as uncertainty sampling, query-by-committee, error reduction, density-weighted methods, and so on. These strategies are very different in the way of selecting the most informative samples. Uncertainty sampling is the most commonly used sampling method. From the perspective of machine learning, the uncertainty sampling strategy selects the samples that are the most uncertain sample of the model from the unlabeled set. That is, the model cannot determine its label, and the output probability of the model is close to 0.5. The classification model based on Bayesian active learning is P(.).

$$P(y^*|x^*, L) = \int P(y^*|x^*, \omega)P(\omega|L)d\omega \qquad (1)$$

where $L = \{x, y\}$ denotes training data; ω is the distribution of model parameters and $y = \{0, 1\}$ denotes labels set. In our case, where $y = 1$ represents smart contract including one or more vulnerabilities and $y = 0$ represents it without vulnerability.

Since the prior distribution $P(\omega|L)$ is difficult to calculate, function $q(\omega|\theta)$ controlled by a set of parameters $\theta = (\mu, \sigma)$ approximate the posteriori distribution $P(y^*|x^*, D)$. The parameters $\theta = (\mu, \sigma)$ are normal distribution. The μ and σ are mean value and standard deviation of distribution; KL divergence is used to optimize the distance between function q(.) and $P(\omega|L)$, and the following results are obtained:

$$\theta^* = arg \min_{\theta} \mathbb{E}_{q(\omega|\theta)}\left[log\left(\left[\frac{q(\omega|\theta)}{P(L|\omega)P(\omega)}\right]\right)\right] \qquad (2)$$

The function of minimization of KL divergence is transformed into solving the maximization function ElBO(.) and the transformed function is:

$$ELBO(q) = \mathbb{E}\left[log(P(\omega))\right] + \mathbb{E}\left[log(P(L|\omega))\right] - \mathbb{E}\left[log(q(\omega|\theta))\right] \qquad (3)$$

The uncertainty assessment method is as follows: The uncertainty measure function H(.) of sample $\vec{x_i}$ is defined as its conditional entropy given the label variable y:

$$H(y|x) = -\sum_{y \in Y} P(y|x_i, \theta_L)logP(y|x_i, \theta_L) \qquad (4)$$

where θ_D denotes the classification model θ trained on the data D; $P(y|x_i, \theta_D)$ denotes probability calculated by this model.

Alogrithm 1. Backward Bayesian Active Learning

input: The labeled source code of smart contract L; The unlabeled sourcecode of smart contract U; The probabilistic classifier θ
Output: Three Indicators of classifier θ
1: **function** FORWARDAL(L, U, θ)
2:    **repeat**
3:        **for** $x_i \in U$ **do**
4:            Select instance x_i according to Eq(1)
5:            Query the label y_{xi} of x_i
6:            Remove x_i from U($U^{'}$=U-x_i), U=$U^{'}$;
7:            Merge (x_i,y_i) into L($L^{'}$=L+(x_i,y_i)), L=$L^{'}$
8:            L, U = BackwardAL(L, θ)
9:            Train the classifier model θ based on L
10:        **end for**
11:    **until** Meeting the stop criterion
12:    **return** The result of three indicators
13: **end function**
14: **function** BACKWARDAL(L, U, θ)
15:    **for** $x_i \in L$ **do**
16:        Select x_{d1}, x_{d2} from L according to Eq(5) and Eq(6)
17:    **end for**
18:    Select x_r from U according to Eq(7)
19:    Query the label y_r of x_r
20:    Remove $\{(x_{d1}, y_{d1}), (x_{d2}, y_{d2})\}$ from L($L^{'}$=L-$\{(x_{d1}, y_{d1}), (x_{d2}, y_{d2})\}$)
21:    Merge (x_r, y_r) into L($L^{'}$=L+(x_r, y_r))
22:    $L=L^{'}$
23:    **return** L, U
24: **end function**

3.4   Active Learning with Backward Noise Removing

There is a problem that labeled dataset does not always have a positive impact on the model performance. Namely, the labeled dataset may be noisy. The noises are caused by incorrectly labeled instances or outliers of correctly labeled instances. So that they may produce a negative impact on the model. To tackle this issue, in this paper, we exploit a backward noise removal method, which explores labeled datasets to detect suspiciously unreliable instances. The performance of the model will degrade due to noisy instances. As shown in Algorithm 1, to eliminate the negative effects of noises, these noisy instances need to be processed by withdrawal from labeled datasets and re-sampling from the unlabeled datasets for labeling. The former withdrawal operation refers to selecting the samples with the least influence on the model which will be deleted from the labeled set by deleting samples or changing their labels one by one from the labeled set and then calculating the information entropy. Formula 2 $x^{'}_{d1}$ is the selected sample by deleting; Formula 3 $x^{'}_{d2}$ is the selected sample by changing its label. The latter re-sampling operation to select the sample furthest from the deleted sample in the former operation. Formula 4 $x^{'}_r$ is the selected sample that will be sent to an oracle.

$$x^{'}_{d1} = arg \min_{x \in L} \sum_{x^u \in U} (H(y^u | x^u; \theta_{L \setminus (x, y^{'}_i)})) \tag{5}$$

$$x^{'}_{d2} = arg \min_{x \in L} \frac{\sum_{i \neq i'} P(y_i | x; \theta_{L \setminus (x, y^{'}_i)}) \times \sum_{x^u \in U} H(y^u | x^u; \theta_{L | (x, y_i)})}{1 - P(y_i | x; \theta_{L \setminus (x, y^{'}_i)})} \tag{6}$$

$$x_r' = \max_{x \in U} \sqrt{(x - x_i)^2(y - y_i)^2} \tag{7}$$

where H(.) stands for definition formula of information entropy; $\theta_{L \setminus (x, y_i')}$ denotes the labeled data set with a certain labeled instance (x, y_i') excluded and $\theta_{L|(x, y_i)}$ represents the labeled data set with instance x label changed from y_i' to y_i.

4 Experiment

4.1 Experiment Set and Benchmark Detaset

The experiment uses 10-fold cross-validation to carry out experiments. Each experiment performs random division on the dataset. 30% of the dataset is used as test data, and the other data is used as training data to prevent data overlap between test and training data. A certain ratio of data is extracted from the training data for manual labeling. In this experiment, the ratio of the initial labeled data is 5%. The initial training dataset is used to train the classification model, and the remaining training data is used as an unlabeled sample pool. In the active learning stage, although there is a cost for querying labels if this process can make vulnerability prediction more effective and improve software quality, the cost is acceptable as long as we control the number of queries to a small amount, usually, less than 20% of the total number of unlabeled sample [40]. In this work, we select four thresholds, i.e., 5%, 10%, 15%, 20%. In practice, the label of candidate unlabeled instances is determined by domain experts. In this work, we endow them with the ground truth labels from the benchmark dataset to simulate the process of human inspectors checking source code files, as in work [14, 15].

We conduct extensive experiments on 4929 smart contracts containing 8 types of vulnerability. The NCC Group organization [41] proposed the Decentralized Application Security Project (DASP) TOP10 [42]. We chose to detect 8 vulnerabilities included in DASP TOP10, which are listed in Table 1. To collect enough data, we use three data sets including Smartbugs [43], SoliAudit-benchmark [44] and SolidiFi-benchmark [45]. First, we collect basic malicious smart contracts from Smartbugs. Then we collect more smart contracts as the final experimental dataset to build and evaluate our framework for smart contract vulnerability classification from two other data sets. Duplicated and blank contracts were filtered out according to their source code. Finally, Table 1 shows the information of the final experimental dataset. In this work, we label a smart contract as 1 if it contains one or more vulnerabilities. Otherwise, we label it as 0.

4.2 Performance Indicators

We measure the performance of *BwdBAL* with four indicators, namely accuracy, precision, recall, and F-measure, which are widely used in smart contract vulnerability detection [26–28, 30]. Accuracy is the most common metric employed in machine learning evaluations. Because of the imbalance of our dataset (the

Table 1. Descriptive statistics for smart contract vulnerability types grouping.

Vulnerability type	#Smart contracts	Containing types
BlockTimestamp	452	Time manipulation, bad randomness
CallDepth	403	Unchecked low level calls
Overflow	898	Arithmetic
Reentrancy	552	Reentrancy
TimeDep	1085	Time manipulation, bad randomness
TOD	937	Front running
TxOrigin	149	Access control
Underflow	453	Arithmetic
All	4929	-

proportion of vulnerable smart contracts is very small), we could not use only one metric for evaluation. Therefore, we also use other metrics. The four indicators can be derived from a confusion matrix shown in Table 2 and defined as the following formulas.

Table 2. Confusion matrix.

	Predicted as vulnerability	Predicted as non-vulnerability
Actual vulnerability	TP	FN
Actual non-vulnerability	FP	TN

(1) Accuracy: Accuracy is the proportion of correctly predicted samples in the total samples, with the value range of [0,1]. The value is larger, the prediction ability of the model is better.

$$accuracy = \frac{(TP + TN)}{(TP + FP + TN + FN)} \tag{8}$$

(2) Precision: Precision is the proportion of correct prediction in the positive samples predicted by the classifier, with the range of [0,1]. The value is larger, the prediction ability of the model is better.

$$precision = \frac{TP}{(TP + FP)} \tag{9}$$

(3) Recall: The recall is the proportion of the correct positive samples predicted by the classifier in all positive samples, with the range of [0,1]. The value is larger, the prediction ability of the model is better.

$$recall = \frac{TP}{(TP + FN)} \tag{10}$$

4.3   Experimental Results

RQ1: How effective is *BwdBAL* compared with some other algorithms?

Method: As mentioned above, our smart contract vulnerability classification framework *BwdBAL* consist of two stages: forward learning stage for selecting some more informative sol files from unlabeled dataset and backward learning stage for removing noise data from labeled dataset. This question investigates whether our framework is better than other two methods, including the method that only uses machine learning no active learning (LogisticRegression), the method that only use active learning but only forward active learning stage (AL).

Results: Table 3 shows the change in the value of the indicator when the labeled sample ratios are 5%, 10%, 15%, and 20%. The experimental results of *BwdBAL* are in bold. As to each algorithm, we repeat experiments 10 times to calculate the average. It can note that using active learning with less manual labeling has better performance than not using active learning. When the number of queries is only 5%, the active learning method is more effective, and the accuracy of all two models is basically about 50%. In addition, the accuracy of *BwdBAL* is basically higher than that of one-way active learning. Particularly in overflow, the accuracy and recall of active learning are higher than that of LogisticRegression. Our method is 68%, 50.2%; one-way active learning is 47.7%, 29.9%; LogisticRegression is 38.9%, 8.9%. As the number of queries increases, the performance of all models is gradually improving. Since the proportion of the maximum number of queries is set to 20%, we will analyze the results more detailly below. When the number of queries is 20%, the accuracy of the active learning method is higher than 80%, while the accuracy of the LogisticRegression method is slightly lower, only less than 80%. And in terms of CallDepth, Overflow, Reentrancy, TOD, and TxOrigin vulnerability, the accuracy of our two-way active learning method is slightly higher than that of the one-way active learning method. However, for BlockTimestamp, TImeDep, and Uunderflow vulnerability, the accuracy of our framework is not as high as that of the latter method. The one-way active learning is 89.1%, 75.4%, 88.7%, and ours is 89%, 74.2%, 87.6%. Especially for Txorigin vulnerability, the accuracy of *BwdBAL* can reach 96.3%. Although the precision value of the model is not very high, in general, the performance of our two-way active learning framework (*BwdBAL*) is better than the other two baseline methods with the less labeled datasets.

RQ2: How do different sampling strategies of active learning affect the performance of BwdAL4Sc?

Method: We compare BwdAL4Sc with the following five baseline approaches (1) Random: randomly select a query instance, (2) QBC [46]: select instances using query-by-committee, (3) Density [47]: select instances with taking into account the information of unmarked samples, (4) EER [48]: select instances with making the loss function reduce the most by adding one sample, and (5) Unc: select instances with the lowest uncertainty.

Results: Figure 2 shows the classification recall of different active learning approaches with a varied number of queries. In order to more intuitively see the experimental results, we use a line chart to describe the changes of the recall of different sampling strategies with different samples labeled proportions. It can be concluded from their plots that *BwdBAL* can achieve higher performance using uncertainty strategy than the other four strategies. When the percentage of labeled samples is less than 10%, the effect of uncertainty sampling strategy is not as good as Density and EER. However, with the increase in the number of queries, the uncertainty sampling strategy can achieve better performance. When the percentage of labeled samples is less than 10%, QBC has the highest recall at BlockTimestamp. For CallDepth random and QBC have a better performance when the percentage of labeled samples is less than 15%. For Overflow and Reentrancy, when the percentage of labeled samples is less than 15%, Density has a higher recall than other strategies. In terms of TimeDep, Density, QBC, Random, and EER have similar recall as a whole. For TxOrigin and Underflow, when the percentage of labeled samples is less than 15%, QBC has a higher recall than other strategies.

Table 3. The Detailed Results for *BwdBAL* and other two baseline method with different ratio of number of queries.

Data	Algorithm	Number of queries (percentage of unlabeled data)											
		5%			10%			15%			20%		
		a	p	r	a	p	r	a	p	r	a	p	r
BlockTimestamp	LogisticRegression	0.274	0.119	0.056	0.311	0.129	0.134	0.513	0.314	0.497	0.721	0.491	0.435
	ActiveLearning	0.286	0.396	0.266	0.529	0.482	0.321	0.534	0.534	0.467	0.891	0.421	0.659
	BwdBAL	0.333	0.254	0.223	0.545	0.546	0.560	0.551	0.651	0.618	0.890	0.517	0.730
CallDepth	LogisticRegression	0.305	0.202	0.104	0.481	0.317	0.344	0.688	0.360	0.509	0.748	0.443	0.501
	ActiveLearning	0.488	0.085	0.267	0.490	0.520	0.425	0.697	0.444	0.593	0.805	0.525	0.679
	BwdBAL	0.543	0.554	0.310	0.553	0.566	0.488	0.663	0.582	0.682	0.808	0.586	0.843
Overflow	LogisticRegression	0.389	0.225	0.089	0.414	0.213	0.158	0.497	0.292	0.598	0.696	0.694	0.797
	ActiveLearning	0.477	0.141	0.299	0.637	0.438	0.593	0.586	0.558	0.671	0.783	0.693	0.809
	BwdBAL	0.680	0.518	0.502	0.682	0.624	0.656	0.681	0.722	0.767	0.784	0.722	0.845
Reentrancy	LogisticRegression	0.658	0.375	0.288	0.665	0.400	0.441	0.666	0.425	0.394	0.826	0.841	0.601
	ActiveLearning	0.617	0.396	0.258	0.622	0.671	0.416	0.626	0.441	0.415	0.877	0.616	0.786
	BwdBAL	0.618	0.462	0.290	0.635	0.690	0.639	0.639	0.694	0.504	0.880	0.701	0.810
TimeDep	LogisticRegression	0.509	0.233	0.144	0.539	0.367	0.354	0.665	0.384	0.288	0.667	0.661	0.501
	ActiveLearning	0.505	0.223	0.245	0.533	0.456	0.389	0.519	0.354	0.546	0.754	0.589	0.817
	BwdBAL	0.573	0.373	0.288	0.588	0.590	0.472	0.592	0.598	0.678	0.742	0.613	0.826
TOD	LogisticRegression	0.559	0.240	0.110	0.500	0.269	0.254	0.577	0.405	0.311	0.673	0.574	0.464
	ActiveLearning	0.651	0.196	0.289	0.648	0.601	0.393	0.467	0.554	0.486	0.779	0.793	0.608
	BwdBAL	0.533	0.339	0.287	0.543	0.557	0.474	0.546	0.553	0.594	0.781	0.662	0.823
TxOrigin	LogisticRegression	0.412	0.090	0.050	0.554	0.524	0.175	0.515	0.245	0.581	0.915	0.593	0.625
	ActiveLearning	0.503	0.130	0.248	0.466	0.537	0.240	0.723	0.375	0.499	0.962	0.240	0.755
	BwdBAL	0.406	0.206	0.258	0.507	0.507	0.366	0.607	0.508	0.546	0.963	0.709	0.799
Underflow	LogisticRegression	0.603	0.106	0.030	0.605	0.114	0.062	0.610	0.388	0.181	0.751	0.610	0.643
	ActiveLearning	0.373	0.388	0.139	0.401	0.459	0.220	0.615	0.462	0.539	0.887	0.620	0.701
	BwdBAL	0.564	0.465	0.213	0.577	0.580	0.363	0.591	0.594	0.541	0.876	0.592	0.849

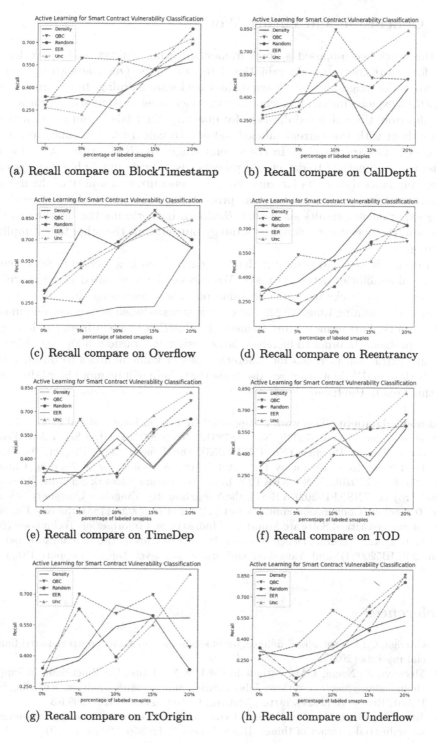

(a) Recall compare on BlockTimestamp   (b) Recall compare on CallDepth

(c) Recall compare on Overflow   (d) Recall compare on Reentrancy

(e) Recall compare on TimeDep   (f) Recall compare on TOD

(g) Recall compare on TxOrigin   (h) Recall compare on Underflow

Fig. 2. Compare on recall

5   Conclusion and Future Work

In this work, we proposed a novel framework using bidirectional active learning for smart contract vulnerabilities detection tasks. Our framework consists of two major stages: forward learning and backward learning. In the first stage, *BwdBAL* exploits uncertainty sampling strategy to select some more informative sol files from the unlabeled datasets for querying their labels and then incorporates them with the current labeled dataset to construct a training set. This process is forward learning. In the second stage, *BwdBAL* utilizes a backward noise removal method to detect and process suspiciously unreliable instances by exploring labeled datasets for improving the generalization ability of the model. Finally, active learning is a circular process until the target effect is reached. The experimental results show that *BwdBAL* outperforms the baseline methods, and the uncertainty sampling strategy outperforms the other four sampling strategies.

Besides, it needs to point out that our current work is limited to smart contract vulnerabilities detection tasks. We choose the pool-based active learning process, so the backward active learning process takes a long time. In order to shorten the running time, we plan to exploit stream-based active learning in our future work. Furthermore, this framework (*BwdBAL*) suffers from the low precision problem. In order to increase the precision, we consider adopting different feature extraction methods for different types of vulnerabilities to improve the prediction model. Moreover, we also hope that there will be more breakthroughs in this area in the future.

Acknowledgement. This work is supported by the National Natural Science Foundation of China (No. 61972335, No. 61872312, No. 62002309); the Six Talent Peaks Project in Jiangsu Province (No. RJFW-053), the Jiangsu "333" Project, the Open Funds of State Key Laboratory for Novel Software Technology of Nanjing University (No. KFKT2020B15, No. KFKT2020B16), the Future Network Scientific Research Fund Project (FNSRFP-2021-YB-47), the Yangzhou city-Yangzhou University Science and Technology Cooperation Fund Project (YZ2021157, YZ2021158), the Key Laboratory of Safety-Critical Software Ministry of Industry and Information Technology (No. NJ2020022), the Natural Science Research Project of Universities in Jiangsu Province (No. 20KJB520024), and Yangzhou University Top-level Talents Support Program (2019).

References

1. Garriga, C.: Decentralized finance: on blockchain- and smart contract-based financial markets (2021)
2. Moosavi, J., Naeni, L.M., Fathollahi-Fard, A.M., Fiore, U.: Blockchain in supply chain management: a review, bibliometric, and network analysis. Environ. Sci. Pollut. Res. 1–15 (2021). https://doi.org/10.1007/s11356-021-13094-3
3. Jiang, Y., Zhong, Y., Ge, X.: Smart contract-based data commodity transactions for industrial internet of things. IEEE Access **7**, 180856–180866 (2019)

4. Xu, B., Agbele, T., Jiang, R.: Biometric blockchain: a better solution for the security and trust of food logistics. IOP Conf. Ser. Mater. Sci. Eng. **646**, 012009 (2019)
5. [26] cointegraph1. https://cointelegraph.com/. Accessed 21 Mar 2022
6. Torres, C.F., Iannillo, A.K., Gervais, A., State, R.: The eye of horus: spotting and analyzing attacks on ethereum smart contracts. arXiv preprint arXiv:2101.06204 (2021)
7. Tikhomirov, S., Voskresenskaya, E., Ivanitskiy, I., Takhaviev, R., Marchenko, E., Alexandrov, Y.: Smartcheck: static analysis of ethereum smart contracts. In: Proceedings of the 1st International Workshop on Emerging Trends in Software Engineering for Blockchain, pp. 9–16 (2018)
8. Feist, J., Grieco, G., Groce, A.: Slither: a static analysis framework for smart contracts. In: 2019 IEEE/ACM 2nd International Workshop on Emerging Trends in Software Engineering for Blockchain (WETSEB), pp. 8–15. IEEE (2019)
9. Kalra, S., Goel, S., Dhawan, M., Sharma, S.: Zeus: analyzing safety of smart contracts. In: NDSS, pp. 1–12 (2018)
10. Park, D., Zhang, Y., Saxena, M., Daian, P., Roşu, G.: A formal verification tool for ethereum VM bytecode. In: Proceedings of the 2018 26th ACM Joint Meeting on European Software Engineering Conference and Symposium on the Foundations of Software Engineering, pp. 912–915 (2018)
11. Tsankov, P., Dan, A., Drachsler-Cohen, D., Gervais, A., Buenzli, F., Vechev, M.: Securify: practical security analysis of smart contracts. In: Proceedings of the 2018 ACM SIGSAC Conference on Computer and Communications Security, pp. 67–82 (2018)
12. Luu, L., Chu, D.-H., Olickel, H., Saxena, P., Hobor, A.: Making smart contracts smarter. In: Proceedings of the 2016 ACM SIGSAC Conference on Computer and Communications Security, pp. 254–269 (2016)
13. Jiang, B., Liu, Y., Chan, W.K.: Contractfuzzer: fuzzing smart contracts for vulnerability detection. In: 2018 33rd IEEE/ACM International Conference on Automated Software Engineering (ASE), pp. 259–269. IEEE (2018)
14. Yu, Z., Theisen, C., Williams, L., Menzies, T.: Improving vulnerability inspection efficiency using active learning. IEEE Trans. Softw. Eng. **47**(11), 2401–2420 (2019)
15. Xu, Z., Liu, J., Luo, X., Zhang, T.: Cross-version defect prediction via hybrid active learning with kernel principal component analysis. In: 2018 IEEE 25th International Conference on Software Analysis, Evolution and Reengineering (SANER), pp. 209–220. IEEE (2018)
16. Tong, S., Koller, D.: Support vector machine active learning with applications to text classification. J. Mach. Learn. Res. **2**(Nov), 45–66 (2001)
17. Hoi, S.C.H., Jin, R., Lyu, M.R.: Large-scale text categorization by batch mode active learning. In: Proceedings of the 15th International Conference on World Wide Web, pp. 633–642 (2006)
18. Tuia, D., Ratle, F., Pacifici, F., Kanevski, M.F., Emery, W.J.: Active learning methods for remote sensing image classification. IEEE Trans. Geosci. Remote Sens. **47**(7), 2218–2232 (2009)
19. Cho, J.W., Kim, D.-J., Jung, Y., Kweon, I.S.: MCDAL: maximum classifier discrepancy for active learning. IEEE Trans. Neural Netw. Learn, Syst (2022)
20. Huang, S.-J., Jin, R., Zhou, Z.-H.: Active learning by querying informative and representative examples. In: Advances in Neural Information Processing Systems 23 (2010)
21. Gal, Y., Ghahramani, Z.: Dropout as a Bayesian approximation: representing model uncertainty in deep learning. In: International Conference on Machine Learning, pp. 1050–1059. PMLR (2016)

22. Brent, L., et al.: Vandal: a scalable security analysis framework for smart contracts. arXiv preprint arXiv:1809.03981 (2018)
23. Torres, C.F., Schütte, J., State, R.: Osiris: hunting for integer bugs in ethereum smart contracts. In: Proceedings of the 34th Annual Computer Security Applications Conference, pp. 664–676 (2018)
24. Liu, C., Liu, H., Cao, Z., Chen, Z., Chen, B., Roscoe, B.: Reguard: finding reentrancy bugs in smart contracts. In: 2018 IEEE/ACM 40th International Conference on Software Engineering: Companion (ICSE-Companion), pp. 65–68. IEEE (2018)
25. Kevin N'DA, A.A., Matalonga, S., Dahal, K.: Applicability of the software security code metrics for ethereum smart contract. In: Awan, I., Benbernou, S., Younas, M., Aleksy, M. (eds.) Deep-BDB 2021. LNNS, vol. 309, pp. 106–119. Springer, Cham (2022). https://doi.org/10.1007/978-3-030-84337-3_9
26. Momeni, P., Wang, Y., Samavi, R.: Machine learning model for smart contracts security analysis. In: 2019 17th International Conference on Privacy, Security and Trust (PST), pp. 1–6. IEEE (2019)
27. Liao, J.-W., Tsai, T.-T., He, C.-K., Tien, C.-W.: SoliAudit: smart contract vulnerability assessment based on machine learning and fuzz testing. In: 2019 Sixth International Conference on Internet of Things: Systems, Management and Security (IOTSMS), pp. 458–465. IEEE (2019)
28. Qian, P., Liu, Z., He, Q., Zimmermann, R., Wang, X.: Towards automated reentrancy detection for smart contracts based on sequential models. IEEE Access **8**, 19685–19695 (2020)
29. Ashizawa, N., Yanai, N., Cruz, J.P., Okamura, S.: Eth2vec: learning contract-wide code representations for vulnerability detection on ethereum smart contracts. In: Proceedings of the 3rd ACM International Symposium on Blockchain and Secure Critical Infrastructure, pp. 47–59 (2021)
30. Mi, F., Wang, Z., Zhao, C., Guo, J., Ahmed, F., Khan, L.: VSCL: automating vulnerability detection in smart contracts with deep learning. In: 2021 IEEE International Conference on Blockchain and Cryptocurrency (ICBC), pp. 1–9. IEEE (2021)
31. Atighehchian, P., Branchaud-Charron, F., Lacoste, A.: Bayesian active learning for production, a systematic study and a reusable library. arXiv preprint arXiv:2006.09916 (2020)
32. Tsymbalov, E., Makarychev, S., Shapeev, A., Panov, M.: Deeper connections between neural networks and Gaussian processes speed-up active learning. arXiv preprint arXiv:1902.10350 (2019)
33. Kirsch, A., Van Amersfoort, J., Gal, Y.: Batchbald: efficient and diverse batch acquisition for deep Bayesian active learning. In: Advances in Neural Information Processing Systems 32 (2019)
34. Cakmak, M., Thomaz, A.L.: Eliciting good teaching from humans for machine learners. Artif. Intell. **217**, 198–215 (2014)
35. Donmez, P., Carbonell, J.G., Schneider, J.: Efficiently learning the accuracy of labeling sources for selective sampling. In: Proceedings of the 15th ACM SIGKDD International Conference on Knowledge Discovery and Data Mining, pp. 259–268 (2009)
36. Zhang, X.-Y., Wang, S., Yun, X.: Bidirectional active learning: a two-way exploration into unlabeled and labeled data set. IEEE Trans. Neural Netw. Learn. Syst. **26**(12), 3034–3044 (2015)
37. Luo, G., Ma, Y., Qin, K.: Active learning for software defect prediction. IEICE Trans. Inf. Syst. **95**(6), 1680–1683 (2012)

38. Li, M., Zhang, H., Rongxin, W., Zhou, Z.-H.: Sample-based software defect prediction with active and semi-supervised learning. Autom. Softw. Eng. **19**(2), 201–230 (2012)
39. Lu, H., Cukic, B.: An adaptive approach with active learning in software fault prediction. In: Proceedings of the 8th International Conference on Predictive Models in Software Engineering, pp. 79–88 (2012)
40. Lu, H., Kocaguneli, E., Cukic, B.: Defect prediction between software versions with active learning and dimensionality reduction. In: 2014 IEEE 25th International Symposium on Software Reliability Engineering, pp. 312–322. IEEE (2014)
41. NCC group. https://www.nccgroup.trust/us/. Accessed 21 Mar 2022
42. DASP top 10. https://dasp.co/. Accessed 21 Mar 2022
43. Durieux, T., Ferreira, J.F., Abreu, R., Cruz, P.: Empirical review of automated analysis tools on 47,587 ethereum smart contracts. In: Proceedings of the ACM/IEEE 42nd International Conference on Software Engineering, pp. 530–541 (2020)
44. SoliAudit vulnerability analyzer dataset. https://goo.gl/UAUpK5/. Accessed 21 Mar 2022
45. Ghaleb, A., Pattabiraman, K.: How effective are smart contract analysis tools? Evaluating smart contract static analysis tools using bug injection. In: Proceedings of the 29th ACM SIGSOFT International Symposium on Software Testing and Analysis, pp. 415–427 (2020)
46. Abe, N.: Query learning strategies using boosting and bagging. In: Proceedings of 15th International Conference on Machine Learning (ICML 1998) (1998)
47. Ebert, S., Fritz, M., Schiele, B.: RALF: a reinforced active learning formulation for object class recognition. In: 2012 IEEE Conference on Computer Vision and Pattern Recognition, pp. 3626–3633. IEEE (2012)
48. Roy, N., McCallum, A.: Toward optimal active learning through Monte Carlo estimation of error reduction. ICML Williamstown **2**, 441–448 (2001)

A Multi-agent Deep Reinforcement Learning-Based Collaborative Willingness Network for Automobile Maintenance Service

Shengang Hao[1], Jun Zheng[1], Jie Yang[1], Ziwei Ni[1], Quanxin Zhang[1], and Li Zhang[2](✉)

[1] School of Computer Science, Beijing Institute of Technology, Beijing 100081, China
[2] Department of Media Engineering, Communication University of Zhejiang, Hangzhou 310018, China
nythhsg@163.com

Abstract. With the growth of maintenance market scale of automobile manufacturing enterprises, simple information technology is not enough to solve the problem of uneven resource allocation and low customer satisfaction in maintenance chain services. To solve this problem, this paper abstracts the automotive maintenance collaborative service into a multi-agent collaborative model based on the decentralized partially observable Markov decision progress (Dec-POMDP). Based on this model, a multi-agent deep reinforcement learning algorithm based on collaborative willingness network (CWN-MADRL) is presented. The algorithm uses a value decomposition based MADRL framework, adds a collaborative willingness network based on the original action value network of the agent, and uses the attention mechanism to improve the impact of the collaboration between agents on the action decision-making, while saving computing resources. The evaluation results show that, our CWN-MADRL algorithm can converge quickly, learn effective task recommendation strategies, and achieve better system performance compared with other benchmark algorithms.

Keywords: Equipment manufacturing · Maintenance collaborative service · Multi-agent · Deep reinforcement learning · Value decomposition

1 Introduction

Manufacturing service industry is a manufacturing-oriented service industry. Its development helps to accelerate the transformation of manufacturing industry and upgrade the position of Chinese manufacturing enterprises in the industrial chain [1]. Product service is a new growth point of output value and profit of manufacturing enterprises. Product maintenance, as the main component of product service, is an important part of manufacturing-oriented service industry [2].

In recent years, the development of automobile industry has stimulated the rapid growth of automobile maintenance market. According to the white paper on China's auto aftermarket in 2020, the scale of China's auto maintenance market is expected to

J. Zhou et al. (Eds.): ACNS 2022 Workshops, LNCS 13285, pp. 84–103, 2022.
https://doi.org/10.1007/978-3-031-16815-4_6

reach 1.74 trillion yuan in 2025. It can be seen that the automobile maintenance industry will be the most important part of the automobile market for a long time in the future. With the further expansion of the output value in this industry, all kinds of automobile maintenance service providers enter the automobile aftermarket. Maintenance chain enterprises have become an important part of the automobile maintenance market because of their advantages such as resource integration, fast response speed and transparent price.

At present, the information technology still is the important means of supporting resource integration and efficiency improvement in maintenance chain enterprises, but it is not enough to solve the problems of unbalanced resource allocation, poor service coordination and low customer satisfaction because of the low personnel quality and the low level of information technology in this industry. With the increasing popularity of industrial Internet [3], big data, artificial intelligence and other new generation information technologies in the manufacturing field, intelligent manufacturing system has more functions of cognition and learning compared with its previous generation [4]. It makes it possible to automatically realize the distributed resource aggregation and the rational resource allocation in automobile maintenance chain services, in order to alleviate the imbalance between resource supply and resource demand in some regions.

Based on the above problems, this paper proposes a task recommendation strategy in multi-agent cooperation scenario based on deep reinforcement learning with value decomposition. In this scenario, multiple automobile maintenance stations cooperate with each other to complete the maintenance task in maintenance chain enterprises. This task recommendation strategy can automatically realize the adaptive adjustment of the maintenance tasks among multiple maintenance stations with the goal of minimizing maintenance time and maintenance cost and improving customer satisfaction, so as to achieve the effective utilization of maintenance resources among multiple stations.

The main contributions are summarized as follows:

1) Aiming at the problems of inefficient resource allocation and low customer satisfaction in the automobile maintenance market, this paper proposes a maintenance collaborative service model based on the decentralized partially observable Markov decision progress to solve the optimization problem of multi-agent joint action in the maintenance chain service scenario.

2) Based on the proposed maintenance collaborative service model, a task recommendation strategy using multi-agent deep reinforcement learning (MADRL) is proposed. This strategy uses a new network framework of MADRL, in which each agent has two network modules: action estimation network and collaborative willingness network. To improve the impact of agent cooperation on action decision-making, the attention mechanism is used in collaborative willingness network, while saving computing resources.

The rest of this article is arranged as follows: Sect. 2 briefly introduces the related works about automobile after-sales collaborative service and multi-agent deep reinforcement learning. Section 3 discusses the system model for automobile maintenance collaborative service. Next, a task recommendation strategy using MADRL is proposed in Sect. 4 and the detail algorithm implementation is presented. Section 5 gives the implementation results and the analysis. Section 6 gives the conclusion.

2 Research Background

2.1 Automobile After-Sales Collaborative Service

At present, there are few research on service collaboration in the field of auto after-sales service, mainly focusing on the research of business process and the construction of after-sales service information system. For example, workflow technology is used to study the business process in the field of automotive collaborative after-sales service [5, 6]. The automotive collaborative after-sales service system based on Service-Oriented Architecture (SOA) is designed to abstract the processes involved in various businesses of after-sales service into the reusable services and the key technologies of SOA, web service and business process choreography is analyzed in detail [7, 8]. According to the dynamic scalability requirements of the architecture of industrial chain collaborative work platform, some scholars [9, 10] use software component technology to construct the model of automobile industry chain collaborative service platform based on the concepts of business decomposition, business modeling and component abstraction. In the field of maintenance service, there are some research about the fault prediction of specific equipment. Yang et al. [11] established a Grey model based on similar information fusion, used historical samples for similarity matching, applied the Grey model to predict the future degradation trajectory, and obtained the remaining service life of engine. Yi Fei et al. [12] studied the fault pattern recognition method based on Hidden Markov model, and used the model to convert the signal characteristics of weak change into the log likelihood probability with large change to effectively identify the fault pattern. Zhou Chilean [13] proposed a prediction method of fault and remaining life based on HMM model. The experiential results show the fault prediction method are effective.

2.2 Multi-agent Deep Reinforcement Learning

Multi-agent cooperation refers to the cooperation among multiple agents to complete a task under the condition of limited time and limited resources. Deep reinforcement learning (DRL) as a deep learning method, it continuously interacts with the environment and improves its own strategies according to the feedback to maximize the expected reward by the deep neural network. Therefore, the Multi agent deep reinforcement learning (MADRL) formed by their integration has become an important research direction in the field of AI. At the present, there are two main types of MADRL algorithms.

(1) Algorithm based on value function
    This kind of algorithm can be regarded as the most basic work of multi-agent deep reinforcement learning. Its core method is to use neural network to continuously approximate the value function. After fitting the value function, you can output the estimated action value Q or state value V only by inputting the relevant information of the agent, and then select the strategy according to the value function, which is

applied to discrete action space. DQN is an algorithm based on value function, and it has many improved versions [14–16]. VDN [17, 18] is a joint q-network algorithm, which is used to learn the local model of each agent. This joint Q-network is obtained by accumulating the independent Q values of all agents. QMIX [19] is an improvement of VDN algorithm, but it uses a network called mixing network to nonlinearly combine the independent Q values of each agent. Good results have been obtained in the experiment, but how to train the network better is still a problem in research. QTRAN [20, 21] is an algorithm to further optimize QMIX and VDN algorithms. it is very difficult to approach the joint Q-value function directly with the depth network, so QTRAN first obtains the joint Q-value function with the VDN method as the estimation function of the real joint Q-value function, and then minimizes the gap between the local Q-value function and the joint Q-value function.

(2) Algorithm based on Actor-Critic

Value function is difficult to deal with a series of problems caused by non-stationary environment in complex scenes. The Actor-Critic based algorithm learns the critic network through centralized learning, but learns its own independent actor network (also called strategy network) through discrete learning. It has good scalability and can solve the problem of non-stationary environment. It is often used in continuous action space. Asynchronous advantage Actor-Critical (A3C) algorithm is an algorithm based on Actor-Critical (AC) framework, which provides asynchronous training by opening up multiple parallel environments. The Soft Actor-Critical (SAC) [22, 23] algorithm is based on the maximum entropy reinforcement learning framework. Unlike other algorithms that maximize the cumulative expected reward, SAC maximizes the entropy regularized reward. The multi-agent deep deterministic policy gradient algorithm (MADDPG) proposed by Lowe R. [24] is an extended algorithm under the actor critic framework. MADDPG is a DDPG algorithm in multi-agent environment. The algorithm sets up an independent critic network and actor network for each agent, as well as an independent reward mechanism. In this way, MADDPG algorithm can be extended to related multi-agent problems in different environments. The COMA algorithm proposed by Foerster J [25] uses the idea of counterfactual baseline to solve the credit allocation problem in multi-agent system. COMA algorithm adopts a joint critic network to calculate the difference between the comprehensive reward obtained by each agent through decision-making according to the actor network and the expectation of the agent's action value function Q. This difference is called its own advantage function, and the expectation of the action value function Q is called the counterfactual baseline.

3 System Model

This section mainly introduces the system model proposed in this paper. In the maintenance chain enterprise of a brand of automobile in a large and medium-sized city, there are N maintenance service stations $X = \{x_1, x_2, \cdots, x_N\}$ distributed in different regions of the city cooperate to complete the customer's automobile maintenance service, as shown in Fig. 1, in which each node represents one maintenance service station

$x_i (i = 1 \cdots N)$ and they are equal in the automobile cooperative maintenance service model. In order to achieve efficient handling of maintenance tasks within the city and to improve customer satisfaction, a single maintenance service station will not blindly limit customers' maintenance tasks to this site. It will decide whether to complete a maintenance task locally or to recommend it to other service stations according to its own auto parts inventory and the maintenance capacity. For example, the car connected by the red curve in Fig. 1 represents the maintenance task recommended to other stations. Assuming that the decision result of the ith maintenance service station x_i at the time step t is $d_i^j(t)$, then $d_i^j(t) \in \{0, 1\}$, and j $\in \{0, 1, 2, 3... N\}$. Specifically, $d_i^j(t) = 0$ indicates the task is done in local service station, $d_i^j(t) = 1$ indicates that the task is recommended to the jth service station, and the decision result meets the following restrictions:

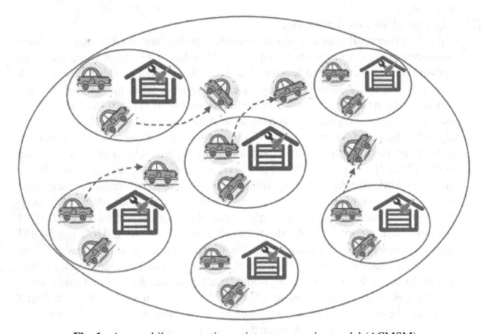

Fig. 1. Automobile cooperative maintenance service model (ACMSM)

$$\sum_{j=0}^{N} d_i^j(t) = 1 \tag{1}$$

Whether it is repaired locally or recommended to other service stations, there are two main factors affecting customer satisfaction, one is maintenance time and the other is maintenance cost. Generally, automobile maintenance mainly includes the repair and replacement of auto parts. Both of them need to spend maintenance time and bear maintenance cost. The difference between them is that the repair operation does not include the material cost of auto parts while replacement operation does. For the same maintenance task, whether it is finished locally or is recommended to other service stations, the maintenance operations of auto parts are the same. Therefore, in order to simplify the system model, we assume that the maintenance task is only to replace the damaged parts. The auto parts covered by automobile maintenance services are complex, including tires, oils, maintenance, brake pads, wipers, filters, lights, batteries, engines, screws, general security, large and small assemblies, tools, etc. In order to simplify the system model, we divide the auto parts into four categories: maintenance parts (engine oil and filter element), vulnerable parts (tire and battery), repair parts (engine and starter) and accident parts (stamping parts and condenser) according to the different replacement frequency of auto parts. In addition, it is assumed that the vector $K_i = (k_{i1}, k_{i2}, k_{i3}, k_{i4})$ represents the number of four types of auto parts to be maintained at the ith service station, where $k_{ij} \in \{0, 1, 2... m\}$ and $k_{ij} = 0$ represents that the jth type of auto parts does not need to be maintained at the ith service station, and $k_{ij} = m$ represents that the number of the jth type of auto parts to be maintained is m.

Below, we will describe the quantitative expression of maintenance time and maintenance cost required to perform maintenance tasks at different service stations.

3.1 Local Maintenance

At the time step t for the ith service station, if the maintenance task are decided to be performed in the local station, the maintenance service time T_i^L is the sum of maintenance time and diagnosis time and other time, It can be quantitatively described as

$$T_i^L = \frac{\sum_{m=1}^{4} k_i^m w_m}{f_i} + \sigma_i \tag{2}$$

where, k_i^m represents the number of the mth type of auto parts be maintained at the ith service station, w_m represents the workload required to maintain the mth type of auto parts, and f_i represents the maintenance capacity that can be allocated in the ith service station, σ_i represents the sum of maintenance preparation time, maintenance diagnosis time and equipment commissioning time of the ith service station.

When the maintenance task is performed in the local station, the maintenance cost consists of the sum of man-hour cost and material cost, which is quantitatively described as

$$C_i^L = (\frac{\sum_{m=1}^{4} k_i^m w_m}{f_i} + \sigma_i)q + \sum_{m=1}^{4} k_i^m e_m \tag{3}$$

where q is the average man-hour cost of the maintenance service station and e_m is the average price of the mth type of auto parts.

3.2 Recommending to Other Maintenance Service Stations

When the maintenance task is recommended to the jth service station by the ith service station, the maintenance service time T_i^j will include the time when the task transfers from the ith service station to the jth service station, and the sum of the maintenance time, diagnosis time and other time of the jth service station, which will be described as

$$T_i^j = \frac{D_{ij}}{s} + \frac{\sum_{m=1}^{4} k_i^m w_m}{f_j} + \sigma_j \tag{4}$$

where D_{ij} is the location distance between the ith service station and the jth service station, s is the average speed, and f_j is the maintenance capacity that can be allocated by the jth service station.

When the maintenance task is recommended to the jth service station, the maintenance cost still includes man-hour cost and material cost, which is quantitatively described as

$$C_i^j = \left(\frac{\sum_{m=1}^4 k_i^m w_m}{f_j} + \sigma_j \right) q + \sum_{m=1}^4 k_i^m e_m \tag{5}$$

No matter whether the maintenance task is finished locally or is recommended to other service stations, at the time step t, the ith service station may need to perform the multiple maintenance tasks simultaneously. Therefore, the allocatable maintenance capacity and the number of auto parts needed in the ith service station needs to meet the following conditions:

$$\sum_t d_i^j(t)f_i \le F_i$$
$$\sum_{i \in N} d_i^j(t)K_i(t) \le \mathbb{K}_i \tag{6}$$

where F_j represents the maximum maintenance capacity and $\mathbb{K}_i$ represents the maximum of auto parts in the ith service station.

3.3 Joint Optimization Problem

In order to make full use of the human resources of the automobile maintenance chain enterprise and try to reduce the system maintenance overhead to improve customer satisfaction, the optimization problem of automobile after-sales collaborative maintenance service discussed in this paper can be described as realizing the optimization solution of system maintenance overhead through the reasonable selection of maintenance decision $d_i^j(t)$. The system cost consists of maintenance time and maintenance cost. At the tth time step, the maintenance time of the system can be expressed as $T(t) = \sum_{i=1}^N (\rho_i T_i(t))$, and the maintenance cost can be expressed as $C(t) = \sum_{i=1}^N (\rho_i C_i(t))$, in which ρ_i represents the task arrival rate. When the ith service station performs maintenance tasks locally, $T_i(t) = T_i^L$ and $C_i(t) = C_i^L$. When the ith service station recommends tasks to other service stations, $T_i(t) = T_i^j$ and $C_i(t) = C_i^j$. Since the dimensions of maintenance time and maintenance cost are different, they need to be treated without dimension. As a result, the cost function of the system is expressed as:

$$\text{cost}(t) = \beta \frac{T(t)}{T^E} + (1 - \beta) \frac{C(t)}{C^E} \tag{7}$$

where β and $1 - \beta$ respectively represent the system's preference for the maintenance time and the maintenance cost. The β value can be adjusted to meet the sensitivity of system for time or cost. T^E and C^E respectively represents the sum of maintenance time of all service stations and the sum of maintenance cost of all service stations when all tasks are performed locally in one time step. Finally, the optimization problem of system maintenance overhead will be defined as the following joint optimization formula:

$$\lim_{\tau \to \infty} \frac{1}{\tau} \min \sum_{t=1}^{\tau} cost(t)$$

$$\text{s.t. C1} : d_i^j(t) \in \{0, 1\} \ (i, j) \in N, t$$

$$\text{C2} : \sum_{j=0}^{N} d_i^j(t) = 1$$

$$\text{C3} : 0 \le f_i \le F_i$$

$$\text{C4} : \sum_{i \in N} d_i^j(t) f_i \le F_i$$

$$\text{C5} : 0 \le K_i(t) \le \mathbb{K}_i$$

$$\text{C6:} \sum_{i \in N} d_i^j(t) K_i(t) \le \mathbb{K}_i \qquad (8)$$

Among these constraints, C1 indicates that there are two situations in the maintenance decision of the maintenance service station. C2 indicates that the service station i can only recommend a task to one other service station at most. C3 and C4 ensure that the sum of maintenance capacity assigned the maintenance tasks at each service station is less than the maximum of maintenance capacity in the service station.C5 and C6 ensure that the sum of auto parts required by the maintenance tasks at each service station is less than the maximum of auto parts in the service station.

In this joint optimization problem, multiple service stations make maintenance decisions in the distributed way. At the time step t, the maintenance service station observes its individual state and some global environment states, such as the number of auto parts required by the maintenance task, the assignable maintenance capacity, and the location distance from other service stations, and generates an action where to perform maintenance tasks, and then affect the available number of auto parts and the assignable maintenance capacity in the whole system, and will receive a system reward. Finally, the service station will reach a new state. This process can be described by the decentralized partially observable Markov decision progress (Dec-POMDP).

4 Dynamic Task Recommending Algorithm Based on MADRL

4.1 Dec-POMDP Formulation

As mentioned in the above section, the optimization problem of automobile collaborative maintenance service can be described by a Dec-POMDP. The process can be abstracted as an 8-tuple (A, S, U, F, R, O, Z, γ).

$A = \{1, 2, ..., N\}$ represents a finite set of agents. In the scenario of automobile collaborative maintenance service, the maintenance service station is abstracted as an agent.

S represents a collection of environmental states, $S = \{s_1(t), s_2(t), \cdots, s_N(t)\}$. For each service station m, its own state at the time step t is $s_m(t) \in S$ and $s_m(t)$ can be described as: $s_m(t) = (d_m(t), K_m(t), f_m(t), D_m(t))$, where $d_m(t)$ is the maintenance decision, $K_m(t)$ is the required number of auto parts for the maintenance task at time t and it is also a vector, $K_m(t) = (k_{m1}(t), k_{m2}(t), k_{m3}(t), k_{m4}(t))$, in which each component represents the required number of each type of auto parts. $f_m(t)$ is the assigned maintenance capacity, $D_m(t)$ is the location distance between the mth service station and other service stations. These data is provided by the information management system of the maintenance chain enterprise.

U represents the joint action space and the actions of all agents at the time step t are represented as $(\mu_1(t), \mu_2(t), ...\mu_N(t)) \in U$, in which $\mu_m(t) \in \{0, 1, 2, ...N\}$ represents the actions executed by the mth service station at time t. When $\mu_m(t) = 0$, it means the task is finished in the local service station. When $\mu_m(t) = j$, it means the task is recommended to the jth service station.

F is a state transition function that is the function of all agents transferring to the new state after performing the actions in the current state, which is represented as $F: S \times U-> S$. Assuming that the state transition function of each agent is represented as $f_m(t)$, there is $f_m(t) = P(s_m(t + 1)|s_m(t), \mu_m(t))$.

R means a set of the system rewords. Each agent can obtain the system reward $r_m(t)$ after it perform the action $\mu_m(t)$ according to the current state $s_m(t)$, in which $r_m(t) \in R$. $r_m(t)$ comprises the maintenance time reward $r_{m,T}(t)$ and the maintenance cost reward $r_{m,C}(t)$, and it is expressed as $r_m(t) = \beta * r_{m,T}(t) + (1 - \beta) * r_{m,C}(t)$, where $r_{m,T}(t) = (T_m^j - T_m^L)/T_m^L$. $r_{m,T}(t)$ is the ratio of the time difference between two maintenance strategies. Similarly, $r_{m,C}(t) = (C_m^j - C_m^L)/C_m^L$ represents the ratio of the cost difference between two maintenance strategies.

When $\mu_m(t)=0$, which represents the maintenance task is done in local service station, there is $r_{m,T}(t) = (T_m^0 - T_m^L)/T_m^L = 0$, $r_{m,C}(t) = (C_m^0 - C_m^L)/C_m^L=0$, and $r_m(t)=0$; When $\mu_m(t)=j$, which represents the maintenance task is recommended to the jth service station, $r_m(t)$ will be a non-zero real value. If the maintenance time in local service station is lower than that in other service stations, $r_{m,T}(t)$ is a positive reward; otherwise, $r_{m,T}(t)$ is a negative reward. Similarly, if the maintenance cost in local service station is lower than that in other service stations, $r_{m,C}(t)$ is a positive reward; otherwise, $r_{m,C}(t)$ is a negative reward.

Obviously, the overall reward of the system can be decomposed into the sum of the rewards obtained by each agent. By maximizing the long term cumulative reward $R_m(\tau)$, we can find out the optimal task recommendation strategy for each service station that minimizes the system maintenance overhead, i.e.,

$$\max R_m(\tau) = \max \sum_{t=1}^{\tau} \gamma^t r_m(t) \qquad (9)$$

γ Is the attenuation coefficient, which is usually set to a number less than 1.

O represents the set of joint observations and $O = \{o_1(t), o_2(t), \cdots, o_N(t)\}$, in which $o_m(t)$ is the state that each service station m can observe at the time step t and it is described as $o_m(t) = (s_m(t), s_{m1}(t), s_{m2}(t), \cdots, s_{mn}(t))$ where $s_m(t)$ represents the own state of the mth service station and $s_{mj}(t)(j = \{1, 2, \cdots n\}$ and $n < N)$ represents the state of the jth station adjacent to the mth station.

Z represents the observation probability function.

4.2 Proposed CWN-MADRL Algorithm

When one service station cooperates with other service stations to complete a maintenance task and makes the maintenance decision, it will consider not only its own state, but also the state of other service stations. In addition, the location distance between any two service stations varies, so one service station may pay different attention to other service stations. This different attention to peers will lead to different collaborative willingness between two service stations. Finally, this collaborative willingness will affect the maintenance strategy and the action made by the service station. For example, the service station will change from the action A to the action B because of influence of the collaborative willingness of adjacent station.

Based on this assumption, this paper proposes a multi-agent deep reinforcement learning algorithm based on collaborative willingness network (CWN-MADRL) to solve the optimization problem of automobile collaborative maintenance service. CWN-MADRL is an improved algorithm based on QMIX algorithm and it has three types of networks, one is called act estimation network, one is called collaborative willingness network, and the last one is mixing network of joint action value function. Each agent has an act estimation network to generate the value estimation of the action, a collaborative willingness network to generate the collaborative willingness of the agent. The mixing network combine the actions of all agents to learn a joint action value function. CWN-MADRL algorithm adopts off-policy to update the parameters of these network, so the historical experiences comprising the state, action, reward, and next state as the training data will be recorded in the replay buffer. Next, we present the detailed CWN-MADRL architecture and the learning process (as shown in Fig. 2).

Act Estimation Network

The act estimation network $\tilde{Q}_i$ of each agent i is is used to learn the act estimation function $\tilde{Q}_i$ (τ^i, μ^i_t), in which τ^i is defined as the action-observation history. Its inputs are the current individual observation o^i_t and the action μ^i_{t-1} at the previous time step t-1, as shown in Fig. 3, and its output represents the value estimation of the agent executing a certain action. $h^i_t and h^i_{t-1}$ Represents the hidden state in the current time step t and that in the previous time step t-1 respectively, and they are in the GRU network. Each MLP represents the fully connected network, and the activation function is ReLU.

Collaborative Willingness Network

The cooperation intention network C^i of each agent i is used to learn the cooperation willingness function $C^i(o^i_t)$ which indicates the willingness of the agent to cooperate with other peer agents. Its input is the observation o^i_t at the time step t and it consists of the partial environmental state observed by the agent i (including the state of other adjacent agents) and the individual state of the agent i. The structure of cooperation willingness network is shown in Fig. 4, in which the multi-head attention network is used to process the information of adjacent agents and further capture the relationship between the agent i and its adjacent agents. Here, we use a four-head attention network. Each head focuses on the connection between the agent i and its adjacent agent j, representing the willingness value of the agent j participating in cooperation with the agent i. Then the output of each head are connected to be calculated.

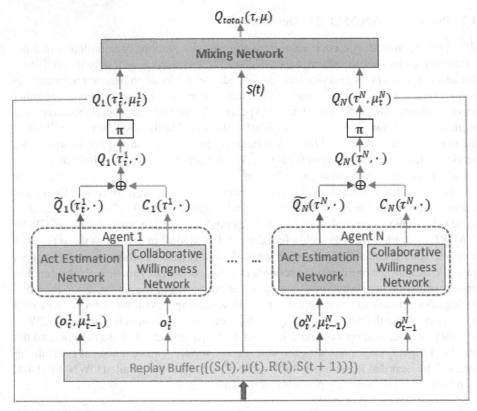

Fig. 2. The overall CWN-MADRL architecture

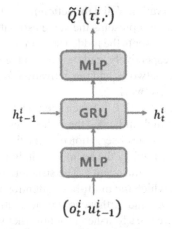

Fig. 3. Structure of act estimation network

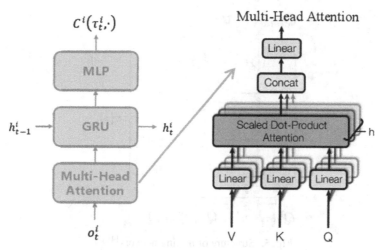

Fig. 4. Structure of collaborative willingness network

$$head_j : g_j = softmax\left(\frac{e_i \cdot e_j^T}{\sqrt{d_k}}\right)e_j'(i \neq j) \tag{10}$$

$$mutli - head : g = concat\{head_1, \cdots, head_n\}$$

In the above formulas, e_i represents the query vector and $e_i = f(o_t^i)$, e_j represents the key vector and $e_j = f(o_t^j)$, e_j' represents the value vector and $e_j' = f(o_t^j)$. There are first four adjacent agents j selected from the agents closer to agent i.

Mixing Network

The mixing network is a feed forward neural network that is used to learn a joint action value function $Q_{total}(\tau, \mu)$. Its structure is shown in Fig. 5 and it is the same as the structure of mixing network in QMIX algorithm [19]. The network input $Q^i(\tau_t^i, \mu_t^i)$ is the individual action value of each agent i at the time step t. The network output is the joint action value $Q_{total}(\tau_t, \mu_t)$ at the time step t. This network is constructed by super network [26] which is used to generate the weight parameter of the mixing network. The advantage of super network is it has less weight parameters and faster training time. W_1 and W_2 represent the generated weight parameters.

Parameter Update

In reinforcement learning, temporal-difference learning (TD learning) can directly learns from the historical experience without knowing the environment model. The value function of the current state can be updated based on the estimated values of other states. The update rules can be expressed as follows:

$$Q(s_t, a_t) \leftarrow Q(s_t, a_t) + \alpha\delta_t \tag{11}$$

where $\alpha \in (0, 1)$ is the learning step, t is the time step, and δ_t is the TD error at time t. The common methods to calculate the TD error are Q-learning [27], Sarsa [28] and Expected Sarsa [29]. These methods can be extended to n-step methods and they can also be combined with λ-return. The λ-return can average n-step return by using different

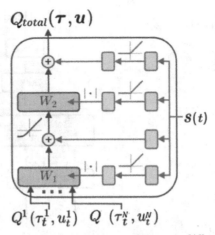

$Q_{total}(\boldsymbol{\tau}, \boldsymbol{u})$

$S(t)$

$Q^1(\tau_t^1, u_t^1) \quad Q(\tau_t^N, u_t^N)$

Fig. 5. Structure of mixing network[46]

n, and can balance between the sampling variance and the estimation deviation [30] by adjusting λ value.

Agent decision-making is continuous, so we can use a long decision sequence as a whole to estimate the impact of the current decision on the future decisions, that is, we can take the data at the current time step and that at the next N steps from replay buffer for learning policy. The action value function Q_i can be used to evaluate the current decisions and $Q_i = \tilde{Q}_i + C_i$. The joint action value function Q_{total} consists of individual action value functions Q_i, so updating Q_{total} can train the parameters in Q_i end to end.

We use the off-policy TD control algorithm Q-learning to update the mixing network parameters, because the our CWN-MADRL algorithm is trained in the centralized way and it is executed in the decentralized way. Although the Q-learning algorithm based on n-step return can reduce the deviation when updating the target, it will bring the high variance[85]. Therefore, we adopt λ- return to solve this problem. As a result, the action value function in the Q-learning algorithm combining λ- return and n-step return can be expressed as:

$$G_t^\lambda = (1 - \lambda) \sum_{n-1}^{\infty} \lambda^{n-1} G_{t:t+n}$$

$$G_{t:t+n} = \sum_{k=0}^{n-1} \gamma^k r_{t+k+1} + \gamma^n \max_\mu Q(\tau_{t+n}, \mu) \tag{12}$$

where $\lambda \in [0, 1]$ is the parameter to adjust the average degree. When $\lambda = 1$, it degenerates to Monte Carlo method. When $\lambda = 0$, it degenerates to one-step TD method. In other words, the larger λ is, the longer historical experiences need to be considered; The smaller λ is, the shorter historical experiences are. Using the above formula, the TD target can be calculated to realize the agent's processing of the whole historical experiences.

After adding λ- return into the update rules of TD learning, the update rules of joint action value function can be derived as follows:

$$Q_{total}(\tau, \mu) \leftarrow Q_{total}(\tau, \mu) + \sum_{k=t}^{min(t+n,T)-1} (\lambda\gamma)^{k-1}\delta_k$$

$$\delta_k = r_{k+1} + \gamma \max_{\mu} Q_{all}(\tau_{k+1}, \mu) - Q_{total}(\tau_k, \mu_k)$$

(13)

4.3 Algorithm Training

The proposed CWN-MADRL algorithm is trained in the centralized way. The training data comes from the historical experiences stored in the replay buffer. Multiply agents can act in parallel to obtain their action evaluation value Q_t, and they can select the appropriate actions μ_t based on ϵ-greedy policy according to the global state at the initial time and the individual observation value of each agent. By executing these actions, each agent can get the individual observation value at the next time step, the global state and the reward value at the current time step, so $\{S(t), \mu(t), R(t) and S(t + 1)\}$ can be stored into the replay buffer. In the training stage, the historical experiences are sampled from the replay buffer and the mixing network uses them to calculate the loss function of the system, and finally the parameters of all networks are updated end-to-end by minimizing the following loss function.

$$\mathcal{L}(\psi) = \sum_{i=1}^{b} \sum_{t=1}^{T-1} [(y_{i,t}^{total} - Q_{total}(\tau_{i,t}, \mu_{i,t}; \psi))^2]$$

(14)

where the TD target is $y_{i,t}^{total} = G_t^\lambda$, G_t^λ is calculated by the target mixing network with the parameter Ψ^-, b is the batch size of samples from the replay buffer. T is the max time step in each episode. In Algorithm 1, we outline the pseudocode for the implementation of CWN-MADRL.

Algorithm 1 CWN-MADRL

Input: Global state at the time step t=1 S(t)={$(s_1(1), s_2(1), \ldots, s_m(1), \ldots, s_N(1))$, Observation of each agent $\{o^i\}_{i=1}^n$, the max size d of experiences in replay buffer, the batch size b, the number M of episode.

Output: model of CWN-MADRL

Initial: the replay buffer D={}, the parameters θ of act estimation network in each agent , the parameters φ of collaborative willingness network in each agent, and the parameters ψ of mixing network, and the parameters $\theta^- = \theta, \phi^- = \phi, \Psi^- = \Psi$ of their corresponding target networks.

1: **For** episode=1 to *M* **do:**

2:     **For** t=1 to *T-1* **do:**

3:         read the u(t-1) from the experience buffer

4:         **For** each agent m **do:**

5:             Input (o_t^m, μ_{t-1}^m) to the act estimation network and obtain $\widetilde{Q}_m(\tau^m, \mu_t'^m)$

6:             Input o_t^m to the collaborative willingness Network network and obtain $C^m(o_t^m)$

7:             Calculate the evaluation value Q of the expected act $\mu_t'^m$ based on the formula

$$Q_m(\tau^m, \mu_t'^m) = \widetilde{Q}_m(\tau^m, \mu_t'^m) + C^m(o_t^m)$$

8:             Select the actual act μ_t^m according to ε-greedy policy

9:             Obtain the observation o_{t+1}^m and reward $r_m(t)$ by performing μ_t^m and transfer from $s_m(t)$ into $s_m(t+1)$

10:         **End for**

11:     Obtain the whole reward R(t) of all the agents and the global state S(t+1)

12:     Store $\{S(t), \mu(t), R(t) \ and \ S(t+1)\}$ in reply buffer D;

13:     **End for**

14:     If the number of experiences in D is greater than *d* **then**

15:         Delete the older experiences according to the principle of "first-in first-out"

16:     **Else if** the number of experiences in D is greater than *b* **then**

17:             Select b experiences from D

18:             **For** i=1 to b **do:**

19:                 Calculate the value of Q_{total} using the mixing network with hypernetwork

20:                 Calculate the target value of y_i^{total} using the target networks based on the formula (11)

21:             **End for**

22:         Update the parameters θ, φ, Ψ based on the formula (13)

23:         **End if**

24:     **End if**

25:     If update-interval steps have passed **then**

26:         Update the parameters $\theta' = \theta, \phi' = \phi, \Psi' = \Psi$ of the target networks

27:     **End if**

28:**End For**

5 Experimental Analysis

In this section, some experiments are performed to verify the performance of CWN-MADRL with simulated experimental scenarios, run with TensorFlowGPU-1.14.0 and Python-3.7 on a desktop powered by Intel Xeon W2245 and NVIDIA Titan RTX.

5.1 Experimental Setup and Comparison Algorithm

The parameters involved in the system overhead calculation in the automobile cooperative maintenance service model (ACMSM) are shown in Table 1, and the super parameters of CWN-MADRL algorithm are shown in Table 2.

Table 1. Key parameters of ACMSM

Parameter	Value
Number of Service Stations (N)	10–20
Total maintenance capacity of the ith service station (F_i)	24–40 working hours
Average allocatable maintenance capacity per task of the ith service station (f_i)	1–3 working hours
Maximum of 4 types of auto parts ($\mathbb{K}_i$)	(300, 200, 100, 40)
Average maintenance workload of four types of auto parts (W = (w1, w2, w3, w4))	(0.5, 1, 3, 5)
Average material cost of four types of auto parts (E = (e1, e2, e3, e4))	(50, 200, 2000, 5000)
Hourly maintenance cost of service station (k)	100
Distance between two service stations (D_{ij})	10–100 km
Average moving speed between two service stations (s)	30 km/h

To verify the effectiveness of CWN-MADRL, we compare it with the following benchmark algorithms.

Independent Q-learning (IQL): an algorithm in which each agent execute the exploitation action and the exploration action only according to its own reward function, and it does not consider the relationship with other agents;

Mixture Q-learning (QMIX): an algorithm in which all agents share a mixing network whose gradient can be directly transmitted backward to each agent's individual network;

Value-Decomposition Networks (VDN): an algorithm in which the global value is simply decomposed into the sum of individual action value of each agent, and the parameters in the global value network is updated by TD algorithm.

5.2 Comparison of Algorithm Performance

Reward is the metric used to measure the effectiveness of DRL-based algorithms. Figure 6 shows the normalized system reward trend of our CWN-MADRL compared

Table 2. Key parameters of CWN-MADRL

Parameter	Value
Number of episode (M)	10000
Learning rate (ρ)	0.0001
Discount factor (γ)	0.95
Max size of replay buffer (d)	5000
Batch size (b)	32
The head number of multi-head attention network (h)	4
ϵ value	$1 - \sum_{m=0}^{M} \frac{1-0.05}{M} m$
λ return (λ)	0.8

with IQL, QMIX and VDN. MADRL-RA and DQN. It can be seen that the CWN-MADRL algorithm has the best performance and the faster convergence speed. The performance of VDN algorithm is better than QMIX algorithm, because in the scenario of collaborative maintenance service, the relationship between the global action evaluation value Q_{total} and the individual action evaluation value Q_i of each agent is relatively simple, and Q_{total} can be approximated by calculating the cumulative sum of multiple Q_i. The performance of IQL algorithm is the worst, and it is difficult to converge to the stable state. It may be because the agent in IQL does not consider the cooperation with other agents. CWN-MADRL algorithm is an improved QMIX algorithm, in which the cooperation willingness network in each agent is added and the parameters of the mixing network are updated by using the TD algorithm combined with λ-return and n-step return. The experimental results show that these improvements are effective and beneficial.

Figure 7 shows the relationship between the task arrival rate (ρ_m) and the average system overhead. We find that the higher the task arrival rate results in the higher the average system overhead. Specifically, when the task arrival rate reaches more than 60%, the system cost increases significantly. The reason is that with the increase of reached workload, the processing capacity of the local maintenance service station can no longer meet the customer's service request and It is necessary to recommend the maintenance task to other service stations.

At this time, the task migration time will account for a certain proportion of the system cost, so the average system cost will increase. When the task arrival rate continues to increase, the service station that accept the recommended task may recommend the maintenance task to another service station due to the imminent depletion of resources, which further aggravates the average system cost. Importantly, compared with other benchmark algorithms, CWN-MADRL algorithm can learn the better task recommendation policy and it has the lower average system cost because it considers the global environment information and the cooperation willingness of other service stations. Compared with IRL, QMIX and VDN algorithms, the system overhead is reduced by 39.1%, 15.6% and 9.4% respectively.

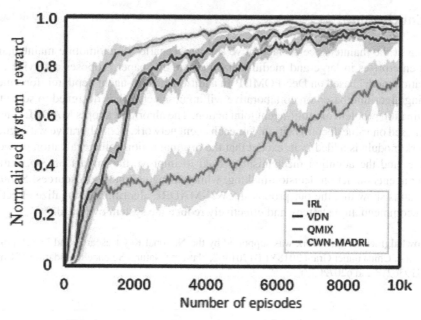

Fig. 6. Average system reward trend of different algorithms

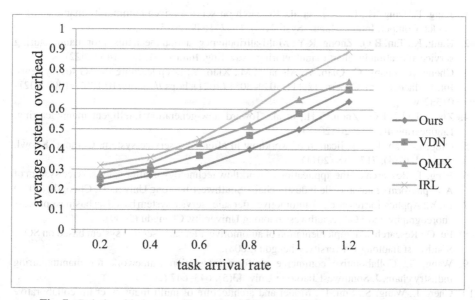

Fig. 7. Relationship between the task arrival rate and the average system overhead

6 Conclusion

Aiming at the maintenance collaborative service scenario of automobile maintenance chain enterprises in large and medium-sized cities, this paper proposes a service collaboration model based on Dec-POMDP. In addition, a multi-agent depth reinforcement learning algorithm based on collaborative willingness network is designed to solve the optimization problem of multi-agent joint action. The algorithm adopts MADRL framework based on value decomposition. For each agent network, a collaborative willingness network module is added in it, except that the original action value evaluation network module, and the attention mechanism is used to improve the impact of cooperation among agents on action decision-making, while saving computing resources. Simulation results show that the our proposed CWN-MADRL algorithm can realize effective task recommendation strategy and effectively reduce the system overhead.

Acknowledgments. This work was supported by the National Key Research and Development Program of China under Grant 2018YFB1701402, National Natural Science Foundation of China (no. U1936218 and 62072037).

References

1. Jiang, P., Ding, K., Leng, J., et al.: Research on service driven community manufacturing model. Comput. Integr. Manuf. Syst. **21**(6), 1637–1649 (2015)
2. Kang, K., Tan, B.Q., Zhong, R.Y.: Multi-attribute negotiation mechanism for manufacturing service allocation in smart manufacturing. Adv. Eng. Inform. **51**, 132–145 (2022)
3. Cheng, X., Zhang, C., Qian, Y., Aloqaily, M., Xiao, Y.: Deep learning for 5G IoT systems. Int. J. Mach. Learn. Cybern. **12**(11), 3049–3051 (2021). https://doi.org/10.1007/s13042-021-01382-w
4. Zhou, J., Li, P.G., Zhou, Y.H., et al.: Toward new-generation intelligent manufacturing. Engineering **4**(1), 11–20 (2018)
5. Qing, L., Pan, L.: Application of workflow in after-sales service system. Comput. Knowl. Technol. **07**(4), 717–718 (2011)
6. Feng, T.: Research on the application of workflow technology in after-sales service system of ASP platform of automobile industry chain. Southwest Jiaotong University, Chengdu (2011)
7. Li, X.: Application research of automotive after sales service system based on business process choreography and SOA. Southwest Jiaotong University, Chengdu (2009)
8. Fu, Q.: Research and implementation of automotive after sales service system based on SOA. Southwest Jiaotong University, Chengdu (2008).
9. Wang, S.: Collaborative commerce platform integration framework for manufacturing industry chain. J. Southwest Jiaotong Univ. **43**(5), 643–647 (2008)
10. Chen, J., Wang, S., Sun, L.: Model and architecture of multi industry chain collaborative public service platform for flexible business association. Comput. Integr. Manuf. Syst. **17**(1), 177–185 (2011)
11. Yang, X.Y., Fang, Z.G., Li, X.C., et al.: Similarity-based in- formation fusion grey model for remaining useful life prediction of aircraft engines. Grey Syst.: Theory Appl. **11**(3), 463–483 (2021)
12. Yang, Y.F., Feng, J.: Fault pattern recognition and state prediction research of ship power equipment based on HMM-SVR. Ship Eng. **40**(3), 68–72 (2018)

13. Zhou, Z.L.: Research on fault prediction of switch machine based on hidden Markov model. Southwest Jiaotong University, Chengdu (2020)
14. Rashid, T., Samvelyan, M., De Witt, C.S., Farquhar, G., Foerster, J., Whiteson, S.: Monotonic value function factorisation for deep multi-agent reinforcement learning. J. Mach. Learn. Res. 21(178), 1–51 (2020)
15. Vinyals, O., Babuschkin, I., Czarnecki, W.M., et al.: Grandmaster level in StarCraft II using multi-agent reinforcement learning. Nature 575(7782), 350–354 (2019)
16. Tang, Z., Yu, C., Chen, B., et al.: Discovering diverse multi-agent strategic behavior via reward randomization. arXiv preprint arXiv:2103.04564 (2021)
17. Son, K., Kim, D., Kang, W.J., et al.: QTRAN: learning to factorize with transformation for cooperative multi-agent reinforcement learning. In: International Conference on Machine Learning, PMLR, pp. 5887–5896 (2019)
18. Sunehag, P., Lever, G., Gruslys, A., et al.: Value-decomposition networks for cooperative multi-agent learning based on team reward. In: Proceedings of the 17th International Conference on Autonomous Agents and Multiagent Systems, IFAAMAS, Richland, USA, pp. 2085–2087 (2018)
19. Rashid, T., Samvelyan, M., Witt, C.S., et al.: QMIX: monotonic value function factorisation for deep multi-agent reinforcement learning. In: Proceedings of the 35th International Conference on Machine Learning, New York, USA, pp. 4292–4301. ACM (2018)
20. Yang, Y., Hao, J., Liao, B., et al.: Qatten: a general framework for cooperative multi-agent reinforcement learning. arXiv:2002.03939 (2020)
21. Son, K., Kim, D., Kang, W.J., et al.: QTRAN: learning to factorize with transformation for cooperative multi-agent reinforcement learning. In: Proceedings of the 36th International Conference on Machine Learning, New York, USA, pp. 5887–5896. ACM (2019)
22. Mnih, V., et al.: Playing Atari with deep reinforcement learning. arXiv preprint arXiv:1312.5602 (2013)
23. Heess, N., Silver, D., The, Y.W.: Actor-critic reinforcement learning with energy-based policies. In: European Workshop on Reinforcement Learning, PMLR, pp. 45–58 (2013)
24. Lowe, R., Wu, Y., Tamar, A., Harb, J., Abbeel, P., Mordatch, I.: Multi-agent actor-critic for mixed cooperative-competitive environments. In: Proceedings of the 31st International Conference on Neural Information Processing Systems, pp. 6382–6393 (2017)
25. Foerster, J., Farquhar, G., Afouras, T., et al.: Counterfactual multi-agent policy gradients. In: Proceedings of the 32nd AAAI Conference on Artificial Intelligence, AAAI, Palo Alto, USA, pp. 2974–2982 (2018)
26. Ha, D., Dai, A.M., Le, Q.V.: HyperNetworks. In: Proceedings of the 5th International Conference on Learning Representations. OpenReview.net, Amherst (2017)
27. Watkins, C.J.C.H.: Learning from delayed rewards. King's College, University of Cambridge (1989)
28. Rummery, G.A., Niranjan, M.: On-line q-learning using connectionist systems. University of Cambridge, Department of Engineering Cambridge, UK (1994)
29. Van Seijen, H., Van Hasselt, H., Whiteson, S., et al.: A theoretical and empirical analysis of expected sarsa. In: 2009 IEEE Symposium on Adaptive Dynamic Programming and Reinforcement Learning, pp. 177–184. IEEE, Piscataway (2009)
30. Kearns, M.J., Singh, S.P.: Bias-variance error bounds for temporal difference updates. In: Proceedings of the 13th Annual Conference on Computational Learning Theory, pp. 142–147. Morgan Kaufmann, San Francisco (2000)

Hybrid Isolation Model for Device Application Sandboxing Deployment in Zero Trust Architecture

Jingci Zhang[1]($\boxtimes$), Jun Zheng[1], Zheng Zhang[2], Tian Chen[1], Kefan Qiu[1], Quanxin Zhang[2], and Yuanzhang Li[2]

[1] School of Cyberspace Science and Technology, Beijing Institute of Technology, Beijing 100081, China
sdhrzjc@163.com
[2] School of Computer Science and Technology, Beijing Institute of Technology, Beijing 100081, China

Abstract. With recent cyber security attacks, "border defense" security protection mechanism has been repeatedly infiltrated breakthrough, and the "border defense" security protection mechanism has often penetrated and broken through, and the "borderless" security defense idea of "Never Trust, Always Verify" – Zero Trust was proposed . The device application sandbox deployment model is one of the four essential zero trust architecture device deployment models. Isolation sandboxes isolate trusted applications from potential threats. The isolation of the application sandbox directly affects the security of trusted applications. Given the security risks such as sandbox escape in the sandbox application, we propose a hybrid isolation model based on access behavior (AB-HIM) and give the formal definition and security characteristics of the model. The model dynamically determines the security identity of the subject according to the access behavior and controls the access operation of the application sandbox. Therefore, the sandbox meets the characteristics of autonomous security, domain isolation, and integrity, ensuring that the system is always in an isolated safe state and easy to use. Finally, zero trust architecture device application sandboxing deployment environment based on containers and Linux security module implements the security model. And aiming at the same container escape vulnerability, we make security comparison experiments. The experimental results show that the security model proposed in this paper effectively enhances the security of the device application sandboxing deployment model in zero trust architecture.

Keywords: Zero trust architecture · Device application sandboxing · Isolation mechanism · Access control model

1 Introduction

Significant cyber security [8] incidents have occurred frequently in recent years. Advanced Persistent Threat [6,20] continues at a high level in cyber threats.

Supported by the National Key R&D Program of China (2018YFB1004402).

The original traditional network security defense mechanism based on the idea of "border defense" has been repeatedly breached by infiltration. Once the isolation mechanism [30] between the internal and external networks is breached, attackers quickly gain control of the internal network and steal confidential data. At the same time, with the continuous development of emerging technologies such as cloud computing, big data, and the Internet of Things, corporate network architecture is changing from "boundary" to "boundless". The traditional security boundary protection concept is slowly withdrawing from the stage. The security, universality, and authority of "border defense" are significantly challenged. Accordingly, the chief analyst of Forrester formally proposed the concept of "Zero Trust" in 2010 [10]. Zero trust breaks "border defense" of the traditional defense concepts and no longer simply uses clear boundaries to determine whether to trust network entities. The core concept of Zero Trust is "Never Trust, Always Verify". When Zero trust emerged, it was so popular that the US Department of Defense (DoD) successively invested significant defense budgets in advancing the implementation of DoD Zero trust deployments [16,22]. An increasing number of outstanding international companies have also begun deploying networks that implement zero trust architecture. Research institutions have also successively released technical standards of zero trust. All of these symbolize zero trust opening a new network security defense mode. The National Institute of Standards and Technology (NIST) published 800-207 Zero Trust Architecture in August 2020 [22]. This publication expounds on the logical components of Zero Trust architecture and four typical deployment models. In particular, the fourth standard deployment model is device application sandboxing (Fig. 1). This deployment model utilizes isolated areas to run applications or processes, and the isolated areas are collectively named application sandboxes. Virtual machines, containers, or other methods are usually used as

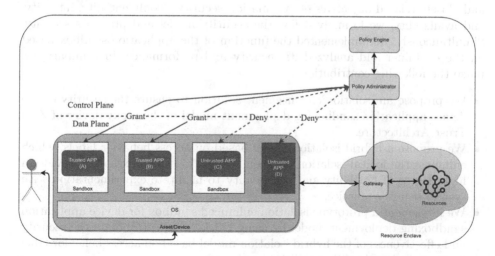

Fig. 1. Device application sandboxing deployment in zero trust architecture [22]

the implementation option of application sandboxes. Isolated regions [23] protect the security of application programs on the device. The device application sandboxing model is widely deployed in practical applications. The advantage of this deployment model is to isolate trusted applications from other applications on the device. Although the vulnerabilities existing in equipment assets fail to be scanned promptly. Host-hidden malware hardly attacks applications that are running in isolation sandboxes. However, if malware damages the isolation mechanism between sandboxes, significant security threats will infect trust applications running in the sandboxes. In addition, the trust applications running in different sandboxes have the requirement of communication with each other. The sandboxes occur cross-reading and cross-writing data for information exchange. Once one of the sandboxes is implanted with viruses, malicious attackers own the privilege to attack other trusted sandboxes as a springboard.

This paper proposes a security access control mechanism [7,25] to enhance application sandbox isolation, aiming at the security risks of weak isolation in the device application sandboxing model. The security access control mechanism controls the access behavior of the application sandbox to the resources and data of the system and manages the privilege operation of the application sandbox based on the minimum privilege principle to promote the isolation of the application sandbox. The security access control mechanism takes the hybrid isolation model based on access behavior identification as the core. It regards the running application and sandbox as a complete system entity as the minimum granularity for implementing access control. The advantages of the security access control mechanism are following: a) We enhance the isolation between the application sandboxes when they exchange the information flow. b) We control the information flow between the application sandboxes according to the security policy to ensure that the data in the application sandboxes are not leaked, added, deleted, and tampered with. Focusing on the three independent and closely related objectives of information security - confidentiality, integrity, and availability, we formally define the security model and prove its security. Simultaneously, we implemented the function of the application sandbox based on the container and analyzed its security and performance. In summary, we make the following contributions:

- We propose an isolation enhancement solution to ensure the security of the device application sandboxing deployment model of the proxy device of Zero Trust Architecture.
- We propose a hybrid isolation model based on access behavior labels, which enhances the logical isolation between application sandboxes and provides a high degree of flexibility and practicality to facilitate experimentation with system security practice.
- We implement a prototype isolation enhanced sandbox for device application sandboxing deployment model by using Docker and corroborate the security and effectiveness of the hybrid isolation model based on access behavior label by reproducing the vulnerabilities.

Table 1. Comparison of access control model

S/N	security model	Protection objects	Security attributes	Security features	Security policy contents
1	Bell-LaPadula [2, 15]	Information of system	Confidentiality	1. A computer access control model that simulates military security policies	1. Discretionary security policy: use the access control matrix representation, the elements of the matrix indicates the access authority of user to object
				2. The first strictly formalized security model	2. Mandatory security policy: security level is defined for each subject and object, security level is composed of confidentiality and scope, and there is a dominant relationship betweensecurity levels
					3. Reading up and writing down
2	Biba [3, 18]	Data	Integrity	Multi-level access control model, with full levels assigned to each subject and object	1. Writing up and reading down
					2. Information flow is always from high security level to low security level
3	Clark-Wilson [27, 28]	Commercial data	Integrity	Focused on meeting the security needs of business applications and used in banking systems to ensure data integrity, this model is slightly more complex and tailored to modern data storage technologies	1.The system accepts "UDI" and converts it to "CDI"
					2. "CDI" can only be changed by "TP"
					3. TP ensures the integrity of CDI
					4. IVP owns "CDI"
4	Chinese-wall [4, 11]	Information of customers	integrity	1. Security model applied in MSS	1. Each subject has a username and belongs to a group or has a role
				2. Application in organizations where exist conflict of interest	2. Each object has an access controllist that limits the access of subject
					3. User flags are checked each time access occurs based on access control lists to control their access rights
5	Discretionary access control [19, 26]	Specified objects	–	Allow the owner of an object to set the protection policy for that object	–

2 Related Work

2.1 Sandbox Security

M. Ali Babar et al. [1] analyzed the isolation mechanisms provided by three container engines, i.e. Docker, LXD, and Rkt. Thanh Bui et al. [5] briefly compared the security of hardware-based virtualization technology (e.g. XEN) and OS-level virtualization technology (i.e. container mechanism) from the system architecture level. Reshetova et al. [21] theoretically analyzed the security of several OS-level virtualization solutions, including FreeBSD Jails, Linux-V Server, Solaris Zones, OpenVZ, LxC and Cells etc. What's more, Some researchers [12,17] also evaluated container security using potential vulnerabilities against specific container mechanisms such as Docker. For example, A. Martin et al. [13] did a vulnerability-oriented [29] risk analysis of the container, classifying the vulnerabilities into five categories, performing a vulnerability assessment according to the security architecture, and using cases of Docker. A Mouat et al. [17] sorted the vulnerabilities of container platforms into kernel exploits, DoS, container breakouts, poisoned images, compromising secrets. Z. Jian et al. [9] summarized two models to achieve Docker container escape, proposed a defense tool by inspecting the status of namespaces, and evaluated the tool with 11 CVE vulnerabilities. Due to the small number of exploits reported in the vulnerability databases such as CVE and NVD, it was challenging to provide a persuasive security evaluation on container mechanisms. However, most of these works addressed sandbox security from the system architecture or designed principle level without forming information flow control through the security model. So those work hardly enhanced sandbox security through the quantitative method, but more through the qualitative approach. In this paper, we propose an access control model for the sandbox to improve isolation, ensuring that the trusted application in the sandbox is protected from untrusted programs or code.

2.2 Access Control Model

Es-Salhi et al. [24] proposed a new access control model for integrated ICS systems based on Domain and Type Enforcement (DTE). This new model allowed defining and applying enforced access controls for ICS timing requirements. Access controls definition was based on a high-level language that ICS administrators could use easily use. This paper also proposed an initial generic ruleset based on the ISA95 functional model. This generic ruleset simplified the deployment of DTE access controls and provided an excellent introduction to the DTE concepts for administrators. AI-Mawee et al. [14] proposed a recommendation-based trust model, called Admonita, for data integrity that applied to any structured data in a system and provided a measure of trust to applications. Admonita incorporated subjective logic to maintain the trustworthiness of data and applications in a system. Oleshchuck [19] proposed a trust-enhanced data integrity model that was based on the Biba integrity model using subjective logic. In his model, he reformulated the rules of the Biba integrity model in terms of trust and proposed how to combine Role- Based Access Control RBAC with the introduced integrity model. The Chinese Wall model was introduced by Brewer and Nash [4] in 1989. The Chinese Wall model assumed impenetrable Chinese Walls among company data sets so that no conflict of interest occurred on the same side of the wall. According to the model, subjects were only granted access to data that did not conflict with other data they possessed. However, those models cared more about access control policy or theoretical security, less caring about access behavior and security practices. In this paper, we propose a hybrid isolation model based on access behavior based on the DTE model and the security thought of Biba and the Chinese wall model, which determines the trust level of the object according to the access behavior of subjects in practice more accessible.

The comparison of common access control models is shown in Table 1.

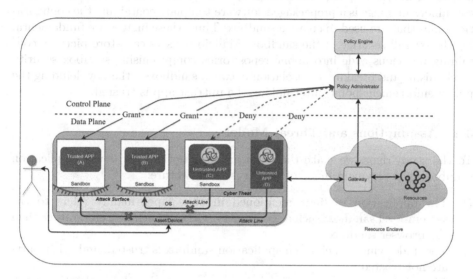

Fig. 2. Threat model for device application sandboxing deployment in zero trust architecture

3 Motivation and Threat Model

This section first identifies the attack surface of device application sandboxing deployment in zero trust architecture and then discusses the threat model of the AB-HIM model.

3.1 Attack Surface

Sandbox provides a security mechanism for separate applications, which runs in a highly controlled environment. Sandbox is often used to test unverified programs that may contain a virus or other malicious code without allowing the software to harm the host device. But sandbox is used to protect the trusted application from untrusted programs or code for device application sandboxing deployment in zero trust architecture. However, all applications running in the sandbox scenes depend on the isolation of the sandbox. Figure 2 depicts the typical architecture of device application sandboxing deployment in zero trust architecture and its attack surface. In device application sandboxing deployment, sandboxes are usually managed by the management tools via over-powerful privileged interfaces. They could be arbitrarily inspected and tampered with by not only the kernel but also the management tools in a host. That leads to compromising trusted sandbox easily by malicious applications which can access privileged interfaces (e.g., attack surface). What's more, in a virtual machine or container, an image is a prepackaged software template containing the configurations files that are used to create a sandbox. Thus, these images are fundamental for the overall security of the sandbox. Malicious users can store pictures containing malicious code into public repositories compromising sandbox security mechanisms and breaking the isolation between sandboxes, thereby deluding the policy enforcement point into thinking the untrust app is trusted.

3.2 Assumptions and Threat Models

To the study'rigor, we make the following assumptions for device application sandboxing deployment mode of zero trust architecture:

(1) The application sandbox mentioned in this paper mainly refers to the system-level sandbox, such as containers, virtual machines, etc., rather than the browser sandbox.
(2) The underlying kernel of the application sandbox is trusted, and other parts are not trusted.
(3) The minimum granularity of security access control is the application sandbox and other processes running in parallel with the application.
(4) The security purpose of security access control is mainly to ensure isolation between application sandbox without considering system confidentiality.

4 Hybrid Isolation Model Based on Access Behavior

To enhance the isolation of sandbox under the condition of limited interoperability, just as Fig. 3 shows, this paper proposes a hybrid isolation model based on access behavior (hybrid isolation model based on access behavior, AB-HIM) based on the domain isolation model DTE, combined with the security thought of integrity security model Biba and Chinese Wall. In this model, subjects are classified into corresponding security domains according to their functionality. They corresponding trust level is determined according to their credibility. The type of object (such as configuration files, executable files, etc.) is determined according to the object's attributes. The trust level of the object depends on the trust level of the subject (application sandbox) that first visited the object, if and only if the business domain where the subject is located has access to the type of the object. The access of the subject to the object doesn't produce low trust. Only when the level of information flows to a high level of trust, the subject's access to the object is allowed. The AB-HIM model ensures the integrity of the application sandbox and data files, thereby enhancing sandbox isolation while dynamically determining the trust level of the object based on the initial access behavior of the subject, ensuring flexibility and practicality of the model.

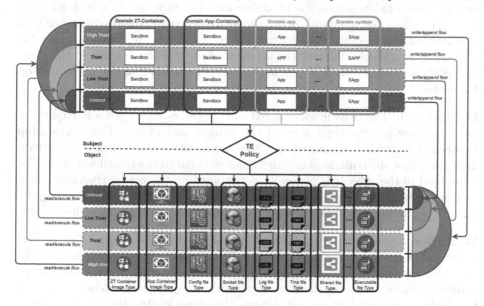

Fig. 3. Schematic diagram of AB-HIM

4.1 Security Objectives

According to system security requirements and security design principles, the model has three security goals:

(1) Application sandbox only accesses objects consistent with their functional requirements.
(2) Application sandbox only has the minimum privilege to complete its function.
(3) Information flow cannot be generated between application sandboxes from high-security level to low-security level.

4.2 Definitions

Definition 1. The subject is denoted as $S = \{s_1, s_2, s_3, \cdots\}$, which includes application sandbox, system process and sandbox management process, etc. The object is denoted as $O = \{o_1, o_2, o_3, \cdots\}$, and include entities such as files, directories, sandbox images, and applications. Access operations are denoted as $P = \{r, w, a, e\}$, which refer to operations such as reading, writing, adding, and executing respectively. Furthermore, two special access operations are denoted as $P' = \{create, del\}$, which are object creation operations and deletion operations.

Definition 2. The security domains are denoted as $D = \{d_1, d_2, d_3, \cdots\}$, indicating the security domain identification of the subject. The system divides the subject into multiple security domains (such as authentication domain, business domain, etc.) based on the identification. The type notation is denoted as $T = \{t_1, t_2, t_3, \cdots\}$, which is used to identify the type of the object (such as executable files, directory files, configuration files, etc.). The domain type table is denoted as , which indicates the access authority of the domain to the type. The users are denoted as $U = \{u_1, u_2, u_3, \cdots\}$, indicating that the users exist on the system.

Definition 3. The trust level, denoted as $C = \{c_1, c_2, c_3, \cdots\}$, is a partial-order set that identifies the trust level of the subject and object. The relationship between trust levels is expressed as a dominance relationship, denoted as $c_i \triangleright c_j$, indicating that the trust level of c_i is higher or equal to the trust level of c_j. The trust level of the subject is generally determined by the actual trustworthiness metric of the subject, while the trust level of an object is determined by its initial trust level or the trust level of the subject who first accesses the object.

Definition 4. Security label, donated as L, is used to characterize the security context of security attributes of the subject and object. The security label of the subject is denoted as $Ls = (d, c, u)$, d denotes the security domain to which the subject belongs, c denotes the trust level of the subject, and u denotes the user to which the subject belongs, acl denotes the access control list of the object.

Definition 5. The system state space, denoted as $V = (A, U, DT, L)$, is used to describe the access control state of the system $A = S \times O \times P$, which represents the current set of allowed access to the system. The access decision set is denoted as $W = \{allow, deny, ?\}$, $allow$ represents access control request, $deny$ represents rejecting the current access control request, and ? represents an unjudged exception.

Definition 6. The AB-HIM model system is denoted as $\sum = v_0, V, R \times W, F$, v_0 is the initial state, V is the spatial state, $R \times W$ represents the request input set and decision output set in the current state. F represents the state transition function, it is the transition rule between states.

4.3   Security Characteristics

To describe whether a system state is in an isolated and safe condition, the following security characteristics are defined.

(1) Autonomous security. For the system state v, $\forall a \in v.A$, $s \in a.S$, $o \in a.O$, $\forall p \in a.P$ and $uk = U(s)$, $uh = U(o)$, $lo = Lo(o)$, all make $(uk, uh, p) \in lo \cdot acl$ to be true, then the state v satisfies the autonomous security.
(2) Domain isolation feature. For the system state v, $\forall a \in v.A$, $s \in a.S$, $o \in a.O$, $\forall p \in a.P$, $d_i = D(s)$ and $t_j = T(o)$, all make $p \in v.DT_{ij}$ to be true, then the state v satisfies the isolation characteristic.

(3) Integrity characteristics. For the system state $v, \forall a \in v.A, s \in a.S, o \in a.O, p \in a.P$ and $ls = Ls(s)$, when $p \in \{w\}$, $lo = Ls(o)$, ff $l_s.c \triangleright l_o.c \wedge l_o.c \triangleright l_s.c$ is established; when $p \in \{a\}$, ff $l_s.c \triangleright l_o.c$ is established; when $p \in \{r, e\}$, $ff l_o.c \triangleright l_s.c$ is established. When the above conditions are met, the system state v is said to meet the confidentiality characteristics.

A system state is isolated and secure if and only if it satisfies both the autonomous security, domain isolation, and integrity properties.

4.4 Security Level Management

AB-HIM model implements access control for system entities based on the security label of system entities. Security attributes such as security domains, types, users, and access control lists in the security label are determined when the subject and object are created. Except for the interference of the security administrator, the security attributes, as mentioned above, will not change during the access process of the subject and object. Still, the trust level will vary according to the access behavior of the subject and object. Currently, the security level of most multi-level security models determines the security level of the subject and object when they are created, remaining unchanged during the entire operation. It is difficult to adapt to the inherent requirements of system dynamic operation safety and makes the model less flexible and practicable. It is not easy to popularize and use the model (such as the multi-level security module of SELinux). It isn't easy to achieve the security goal of protecting the system. Because of the above problems, in the AB-HIM model, the trust level of the subject is determined according to its business function, permission requirement, and risk assessment. And the highest trust level (initial trust level) of the object is determined by automatic methods such as virus detection and vulnerability assessment. At the same time, the trust level of the object is associated with the trust level of the subject. The final trust level of the object depends on its initial trust level and the trust level of the subject who first accesses the object. This makes the model meet the dynamic security requirements, realize more strict integrity protection and ensure the practicability of the model. The change of the trust level of the subject and the object in the whole life cycle is shown in Fig. 4. It mainly includes three stages, the initialization stage, the access stage, and the transfer stage.

(1) Initialization stage: When the subject is created, according to the security domain to which the subject belongs, combined with the authority of the subject requirements and risk assessment results, the subject is given the level of trust C_{s-init} that the subject should have. In creating the object, through automatic methods such as file source screening, virus detection, and vulnerability assessment, the trust of the object is comprehensively evaluated, and the highest trust level C_{o-max} can be obtained to ensure flexibility and practicability. Objects transfer trust level only when they are accessed.

(2) Access stage: From the creation of the object to the scene before the subject accesses it for the first time, the trust level of the object C_{o-max} remains unchanged, and the trust level of the subject C_{s-init} remains unchanged. When the subject accesses the object for the first time, if it is authorized to access it, the trust level of the object is assigned to the trust level of the subject, that is $C_o = C_s$. If it is not authorized, the trust level of the object remains unchanged. When the subject does not access the object for the first time, the trust level of the object remains unchanged. Objects transfer trust levels only when they are accessed.

(3) Transition stage: System administrators change the trust level of the corresponding subject and object in the system according to the system operation requirements. The security management process must have the appropriate privileges. At the same time, the following trust level transfer rules must be satisfied for the subject-object trust level transfer under the model security objectives.

① Transition Rule of Subject Trust Level: For the subject s, the current trust level is C_s, and the trust level after the Transition C'_s must satisfy $C_s \triangleleft C'_s$.

② Transition Rule of Object Trust Level: For the object o, the current trust level is C_o. If the access operation of the subject to the object is writing or adding, the transferred trust level C'_o must satisfy $C'_o \triangleleft C_o$. If the access operation of the subject to the object is reading, the trust level after the transition C'_o must satisfy $C'_o = C_o$.

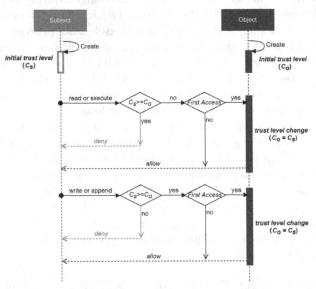

Fig. 4. Trust level transition of object during access

In the security label management of the AB-HIM model and the trust level management, the access control list, privilege management, and ownership are all maintained by the system administrators. Without violating the security objectives of the model, the administrator decides the decision-making matters and some privileged operation authorization within the scope of autonomous access control to ensure the practicability of the model.

4.5 Security State Transition Rules

When the subject in the system accesses the object, the system's state may change. This paper establishes the corresponding state transition rules to ensure that the system is safe before and after state transition.

(1) Read access state transition rules
When system state $V = (S \times O \times P, U, DT, L)$ is accessed by request (S, O, r), the following rules are required: $s \in S$, $o \in O$, and $u_k = U(s)$, $u_h = U(o)$, $l_s = L_s(s)$, $l_o = L_o(o)$, $d_i = D(s)$, $t_j = T(o)$.

$$(s, o, r) \Rightarrow \begin{cases} (u_k, u_h, r) \in l_o.acl \wedge r \in V.DT_{ij} \wedge l_s.c \vartriangleleft l_o.c, allow; \\ ((u_k, u_h, r) \notin l_o.acl \vee r \notin V.DT_{ij} \vee l_s.c \ \not\!\!\vartriangleleft l_o.c), deny; \\ other \quad conditions, ?. \end{cases}$$

(2) Write access state transition rules
When system state $V = (S \times O \times P, U, DT, L)$ is accessed by request (S, O, w), the following rules are required: $s \in S$, $o \in O$,and $u_k = U(s)$, $u_h = U(o)$, $l_s = L_s(s)$, $l_o = L_o(o)$, $d_i = D(s)$, $t_j = T(o)$.

$$(s, o, w) \Rightarrow \begin{cases} (u_k, u_h, w) \in l_o.acl \wedge w \in V.DT_{ij} \wedge l_s.c \vartriangleright l_o.c, allow; \\ (u_k, u_h, w) \notin l_o.acl \vee w \notin V.DT_{ij} \vee l_s.c \ \not\!\!\vartriangleright l_o.c, deny; \\ other \quad conditions, ?. \end{cases}$$

(3) Append access state transition rules
When system state $V = (S \times O \times P, U, DT, L)$ is accessed by request (S, O, a), the following rules are required: $s \in S$, $o \in O$, and $u_k = U(s)$, $u_h = U(o)$, $l_s = L_s(s)$, $l_o = L_o(o)$, $d_i = D(s)$, $t_j = T(o)$.

$$(s, o, a) \Rightarrow \begin{cases} (u_k, u_h, a) \in l_o.acl \wedge a \in V.DT_{ij} \wedge l_o.c \vartriangleleft l_s.c, allow; \\ (u_k, u_h, a) \notin l_o.acl \vee a \notin V.DT_{ij} \vee l_o.c \ \not\!\!\vartriangleleft l_s.c, deny; \\ other \quad conditions, ?. \end{cases}$$

(4) Execute access state transition rules
When system state $V = (S \times O \times P, U, DT, L)$ is accessed by request (S, O, e), the following rules are required: $s \in S$, $o \in O$, and $u_k = U(s)$, $u_h = U(o)$, $l_s = L_s(s)$, $l_o = L_o(o)$, $d_i = D(s)$, $t_j = T(o)$.

$$(s, o, e) \Rightarrow \begin{cases} (u_k, u_h, e) \in l_o.acl \wedge e \in V.DT_{ij} \wedge l_s.c \vartriangleleft l_o.c, allow; \\ (u_k, u_h, e) \notin l_o.acl \vee e \notin V.DT_{ij} \vee l_s.c \ \not\!\!\vartriangleleft l_o.c, deny; \\ other \quad conditions, ?. \end{cases}$$

5 Security Analysis

Theorem 1: Security Preservability of system state transition rule. If the system state $V = (S \times O \times P, U, DT, L)$ is safe, then the system state is also safe after a state transition according to any AB-HIM model state fitting rule.

Contradiction: If the system state is safe, it must satisfy autonomous security, domain isolation characteristics, and integrity characteristics simultaneously.

Firstly, it is proved that the system state transformation rule is secure under the read access state transformation rule. Assuming that the system cannot enter a secure state under read access rule, the system state V' is not insecure. Then there must be a read access operation (S, O, r) that converts the security state V into an unsafe state V'. It can be seen from the read access state transition rules $(u_k, u_h, r) \notin l_o.acl$, $(u_k, u_h, r) \in l_o'.acl$, or $r \notin v.DT_{ij}$, $r \in v'.DT_{ij}$, or $l_s.c$ $\lhd l_o.c$, $l_s'.c \lhd l_o'.c$, that all of them are established. The state satisfies autonomous controllability, isolation and confidentiality at the same time, that is, it is a safe state.

When the state transition rule is the write access state transition rule, the additional access state transition rule, and the execution access state transition rule, the proof method such as the read access state transition rule will not be repeated. In summary, we can know that the security retention theorem of the system state transition rule holds.

Theorem 2: Secure Preservability of Trust Level Transferring Rule. For any trust level transferring rules in the AB-HIM model, the information flow from low trust level to high trust level is not generated when the rules are processed.

Proof: Using the contradiction method proves that after the trust level transferring is carried out according to the model's two trust level transferring rules, the system will not generate an information flow from low trust level to high trust level.

(1) Assuming that the system generates the flow of information from low trust level to high trust level when the system performs trust level transferring according to the subject trust level transferring rules. The Flow of information from low trust level object O_1 to high trust level object O_2 is generated. The subject first accesses the low trust level object O_1 with a read operation. The subject writes or appends the read information to O_2. According to the model state transition rules, the trust level of the subject before transferring is not higher than the trust level of O_1, the trust level after the trust level transferring is not lower than the trust level of O_2. Therefore, the trust level of the subject increases after the trust level transfers. Still, according to the subject trust level transferring rule, the trust level of the transferred subject should decrease. It contradicts the conclusion derived from the hypothesis. Therefore, we conclude that the subject trust level transferring rule has security retention.

(2) Assuming that the system generates the flow of information from low trust level to high trust level when the system performs trust level transferring according to the object trust level transferring rule. The information flow from low trust subject S_1 to high trust subject S_2 is generated. Then, subjects S_1 with low trust level access object O by writing or adding operations. According to the model state transition rules, the trust level of the object

before the trust level transferring is not higher than the trust level of S_1. After the trust level transferring is not lower than the trust level of S_2. Therefore, after the object is transferred to the security level, the trust level increases. However, according to the transferring rule of the object trust level, when the access operation before the transferring of the object trust level is written or added, the object trust level must be reduced, which contradicts the conclusion deduced according to the hypothesis. At the same time, if the access operation before transferring of the trust level of the object is read, the trust level of the object becomes higher after the transferring of trust level. However, the object's essential attributes of have not changed, which does not conform to the actual situation of the system. And the subject that has unable to read their contents now own privileges to read their data, violating the security goals of the system. In consequence, when the access operation before the object trust level transferring is read operation, the security level of the object only remains unchanged after the trust level transferring. Therefore the trust level transferring rule of the object has security retention.

In summary, it can be concluded that the trust level transfer rule of the model satisfies the security retention of the trust level transfer rule, which means that the theorem holds.

6 Experiment

We implement a deployment environment based on CentOS and the container solution Docker for the device application sandboxing deployment model in zero-trust architecture and implement the AB-HIM model based on the Linux Security Module (LSM). At the same time, aiming at the Docker container escape vulnerability, we confirm that AB-HIM is safe and effective by comparing the success of vulnerability exploitation before and after enabling the AB-HIM security model.

6.1 Prototype

In the AB-HIM model prototype, the main subjects are containers, system processes, and service processes, divided into system domains, agent container domains, application container domains, application domains, and so on. Subjects are denoted as $\{system\_d, zt\_container\_d, app\_container\_d, app\_d, ...\}$. The subject is expressed in an 8-bit integer. The objects are mainly application images, documents, directories, sockets, configuration files, and executables, divided into proxy images, application images, configuration files, executables, log files, shared files, and so on. Objects are denoted as $\{zt\_image\_t, app\_image\_t, config\_t, exec\_t, socket\_t, ...\}$. The object is expressed in an 8-bit integer. The trust level is classified as untrustworthy, low-trustworthy, trusted, and high-trustworthy, denoted as $\{Untrust, Low\_Trust, Trust, High\_Trust\}$. The trust level is expressed in 8-bit characters. The security policy format of the AB-HIM model prototype is

$\{domin, type, op\}$, and the prototype is implemented in the form of a domain-type table with a cross-linked data structure, which is used to determine domain-to-type access operations. The prototype of the AB-HIM model is a Linux kernel security module that enhances container isolation based on the open-source code of SELinux and the autonomous access control mechanism of Linux, according to the security characteristics, security label management, and state transition rules of the AB-HIM model. All above expressions are summarized in Table 2, Table 3, and Table 4.

Table 2. The domain of subjects

Subject	Denotes	Expression
System management	system_d	8-bit
Agent container	zt_container_d	8-bit
Application container	app_container_d	8-bit
Application	app_d	8-bit

Table 3. The type of objects

Object	Denotes	Expression
Proxy images	zt_image_t	8-bit
Application images	app_image_t	8-bit
Configuration files	config_t	8-bit
Executables	exec_t	8-bit
Log filesshared files	socket_t	8-bit

Table 4. The trust level

Trust level	Mark as	Expression
Untrustworthy	Untrust	8-bit
Low-trustworthy	Low_Trust	8-bit
Trusted	Trust	8-bit
High-trustworthy	High_Trust	8-bit

6.2   Security Evaluation

In this paper, we focus on the Docker container escape vulnerability CVE-2020-15257 to test whether the exploit is successful with or without AB-HIM to confirm the practicality and feasibility of the AB-HIM model. The software environment of the experiment is shown in Table 5, and the CVE-2020–15257 vulnerability exploitation schematic is just shown in Fig. 7. The result of the container escape attack at docker is shown in Fig. 5, which protects without the AB-HIM security Model. While the result of the container escape attack at docker is shown in Fig. 6, which is protected by AB-HIM security Model. The experiment result shows that AB-HIM effectively defends against the container escape vulnerability CVE-2020-15257 and confirms the effectiveness of the AB-HIM model. We compare AB-HIM and Container-SELinux in terms of security policy size, access control granularity, flexibility, security attributes, and simplicity. The result is shown in Table 7.

Table 5. The version of software in experiment

OS	CentOS 7
docker-ce version	19.03.10
Docker-ce-cli version	19.03.10
Container.io version	1.3.7
Security Module	AB-HIM
Docker Images	Ubuntu:18.04

Fig. 5. The result of exploiting CVE-2020-15257 without AB-HIM

Fig. 6. The result of exploiting CVE-2020-15257 with AB-HIM

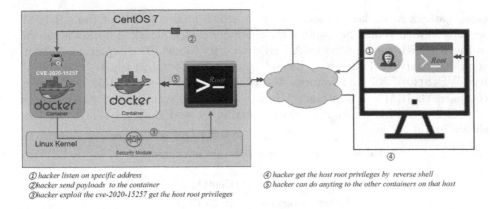

① hacker listen on specific address   ④ hacker get the host root privileges by reverse shell
② hacker send payloads to the container   ⑤ hacker can do anyting to the other containers on that host
③ hacker exploit the cve-2020-15257 get the host root privileges

Fig. 7. CVE-2020-15257 Vulnerability exploitation schematic

Table 6. Hardware configuration in performance experiment

Memory	4GB
CPU	4x Intel® Core™ i7-7700 CPU @3.60 GHz
NIC	Intel® Ethernet Connection (5) 1219-LM

Table 7. The result of AB-HIM and sVirt through contrastive analysis

Security module	Policy magnitude	Control granularity	Flexibility	Security attributes	Simplicity
AB-HIM	Hundreds	Container	High	Integrity	Good
Container-SElinux	Thousands	Container	Low	Confidentiality	So-so

6.3   Performance Evaluation

In order to analyze the performance overhead of the AB-HIM model in terms of
access control, data-intensive and network-intensive test procedures are mainly
selected for performing experiments. In order to analyze the performance overhead brought by the access control of the AB-HIM model, data-intensive and
network-intensive test programs are mainly selected for performing experiments.
Based on fio and netperf benchmark tools, this paper tests the performance of the
container with AB-HIM model, SELinux, and without mandatory access control
model. The hardware configuration is shown in Table 6, and the software environment is shown in Table 5. The results of the network-intensive performance
experiments are shown in Fig. 8. The results of the data-intensive performance
experiments are shown in Fig. 9. The experimental results show that the AB-
HIM security module has less impact on network and disk access performance
than Container-SELinux.

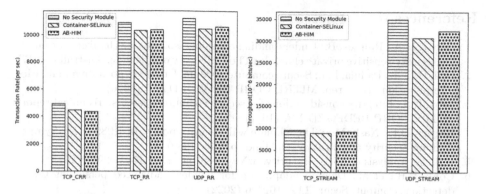

Fig. 8. The result of benchmarking of network with different security module

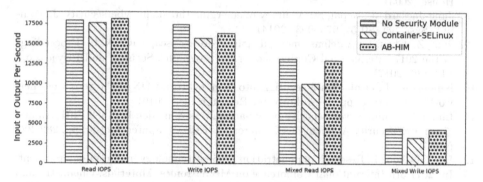

Fig. 9. The result of benchmarking of disk access with different security module

7   Conclusion

Aiming at the isolation problems such as the escape of the sandbox of the zero trust architecture device application sandboxing deployment mode, we design hybrid isolation model based on access behavior label (AB-HIM) model based on the DTE model and the security thought of Biba and Chinese wall model. The model determines the object's trust level according to the subject's access behavior, prevents the flow of information flow from the low trust level to the high trust level, and ensures the flexibility and availability of the model while ensuring the isolation and credibility of the system. We introduce the definition of the model in detail and prove its security characteristics. Finally, we implement a prototype of the model based on SELinux and do the comparative experiment. The experiment results show that the model is safe and effective to ensure the isolation of the sandboxes.

References

1. Babar, M.A., Ramsey, B.: Understanding container isolation mechanisms for building security-sensitive private cloud. In: The University of Adelaide, Australia (2017)
2. Bell, D.E., La Padula, L.J.: Secure computer system: Unified exposition and multics interpretation. Tech. rep. MITRE CORP BEDFORD MA (1976)
3. Biba, K.J.: Integrity considerations for secure computer systems. Technical report MITRE CORP BEDFORD MA (1977)
4. Brewer, D.F., Nash, M.J: The Chinese wall security policy. In: 1989 IEEE Symposium on Security and Privacy, Oakland, p. 206 (1989)
5. Bui, T.: Analysis of docker security. arXiv preprint arXiv:1501.02967 (2015)
6. Coulter, R., et al.: Domain adaptation for windows advanced persistent threat detection. Comput. Secur. **112**, 102496 (2022)
7. Ferraiolo, D., Kuhn, D.R., Chandramouli, R.: Role Based Access Control. Artech House (2003)
8. Jang-Jaccard, J., Nepal, S.: A survey of emerging threats in cybersecurity. J. Comput. Syst. Sci. **80**(5), 973–993 (2014)
9. Jian, Z., Chen, L.: A defense method against docker escape attack. In: Proceedings of the 2017 International Conference on Cryptography, Security and Privacy, pp. 142–146 (2017)
10. Kindervag, J., et al.: Build security into your network's DNA: the zero trust network architecture, pp. 1–26. Forrester Research Inc. (2010)
11. Lin, T.Y.: Chinese wall security policy-an aggressive model. In: 1989 Fifth Annual Computer Security Applications Conference. IEEE Computer Society, pp. 282–283 (1989)
12. Lu, T., Chen, J.: Research of penetration testing technology in docker environment. In: 2017 5th International Conference on Mechatronics, Materials, Chemistry and Computer Engineering (ICMMCCE 2017), pp. 1354–1359. Atlantis Press (2017)
13. Martin, A., et al.: Docker ecosystem-vulnerability analysis. Comput. Commun. **122**, 30–43 (2018)
14. Al-Mawee, W., Carr, S., Mayo, J.: Admonita: a recommendationbased trust model for dynamic data integrity. In: ICISSP, pp. 273–282 (2021)
15. McLean, J.: A comment on the 'basic security theorem' of Bell and LaPadula. Inf. Processing Lett. **20**(2), 67–70 (1985)
16. Mehraj S., Banday, M.T.: Establishing a zero trust strategy in cloud computing environment. In: 2020 International Conference on Computer Communication and Informatics (ICCCI), pp. 1–6. IEEE (2020)
17. Mouat, A.: Docker Security: Using Containers Safely in Production. O'Reilly Media (2015)
18. Oleshchuk, V.: Trust-enhanced data integrity model. In: 2012 IEEE 1st International Symposium on Wireless Systems (IDAACS-SWS), pp. 109–112. IEEE (2012)
19. Osborn, S., Sandhu, R., Munawer, Q.: Configuring role based access control to enforce mandatory and discretionary access control policies. ACM Trans. Inf. Syst. Secur. (TISSEC) **3**(2), 85–106 (2000)
20. Panahnejad, M., Mirabi, M.: APT-Dt-KC: advanced persistent threat detection based on kill-chain model. J. Supercomput. **78**(6), 8644–8677 (2021). https://doi.org/10.1007/s11227-021-04201-9
21. Reshetova, E., Karhunen, J., Nyman, T., Asokan, N.: Security of OS-level virtualization technologies. In: Bernsmed, K., Fischer-Hübner, S. (eds.) NordSec 2014. LNCS, vol. 8788, pp. 77–93. Springer, Cham (2014). https://doi.org/10.1007/978-3-319-11599-3_5

22. Rose, S.W., et al.: Zero trust architecture (2020)
23. Rutkowska, J., Wojtczuk, R.: Qubes OS architecture. In: Invisible Things Lab Technical report, vol. 54 , p. 65 (2010)
24. Es-Salhi, K., Espes, D., Cuppens, N.: DTE access control model for integrated ICS systems. In: Proceedings of the 14th International Conference on Availability, Reliability and Security, pp. 1–9 (2019)
25. Samarati, P., de Vimercati, S.C.: Access control: policies, models, and mechanisms. In: Focardi, R., Gorrieri, R. (eds.) FOSAD 2000. LNCS, vol. 2171, pp. 137–196. Springer, Heidelberg (2001). https://doi.org/10.1007/3-540-45608-2_3
26. Sandhu R., Munawer, Q.: How to do discretionary access control using roles. In: Proceedings of the Third ACM Workshop on Role-Based Access Control, pp. 47–54 (1998)
27. Shockley, W.R.: A9 implementing the Clark/Wilson integrity policy using current technology. Comput. Sci. Technol. **1**(11), 1 (1989)
28. Xu, Q., Liu, G.: Configuring Clark-Wilson integrity model to enforce flexible protection. In: 2009 International Conference on Computational Intelligence and Security, vol. 2, pp. 15–20. IEEE (2009)
29. Zhao, B., et al.: Research on container-oriented isolation control technology. J. Phys.: Conf. Ser. **1871**(1), 012016 (2021)
30. Zhao L., et al.: A lightweight isolation mechanism for secure branch predictors. arXiv preprint arXiv:2005.08183 (2020)

AIHWS – Artificial Intelligence in Hardware Security

On the Effect of Clock Frequency on Voltage and Electromagnetic Fault Injection

Stefanos Koffas[1(✉)] and Praveen Kumar Vadnala[2]

[1] Delft University of Technology, Delft, The Netherlands
s.koffas@tudelft.nl
[2] Riscure BV, Delft, The Netherlands
vadnala@riscure.com

Abstract. We investigate the influence of clock frequency on the success rate of a fault injection attack. In particular, we examine the success rate of voltage and electromagnetic fault attacks for varying clock frequencies. Using three different tests that cover different components of a System-on-Chip, we perform fault injection while its CPU operates at different clock frequencies. Our results show that the attack's success rate increases with an increase in clock frequency for both voltage and EM fault injection attacks. As the technology advances push the clock frequency further, these results can help assess the impact of fault injection attacks more accurately and develop appropriate countermeasures to address them.

Keywords: RISC-V · System-on-chip · Voltage and electromagnetic fault injection

1 Introduction

Fault Injection (FI) attacks have been used to attack cryptographic implementations for over two decades. It is now well known that both symmetric and asymmetric cryptosystems are vulnerable to Differential Fault Analysis (DFA) attacks [7–9,15]. However, breaking cryptographic implementations is just one of the many possibilities for FI attacks. They have been frequently used to break the security of smart cards and embedded devices [10,25–27]. FI attacks have been successfully used to break secure boot, e.g., bypassing the authentication of the code stored in flash memory, allowing attackers to run their code on the device. Further, FI has been used for privilege escalation or to extract firmware from the device.

Previous Work. Boneh, DeMillo, and Lipton demonstrated how faults induced in hardware could be exploited to recover the secret key used in RSA [9]. In this attack, a fault is injected while the device performs an RSA operation, leading to incorrect output. Given several incorrect outputs and the correct output, recovering the secret key used with a DFA attack is possible. Similar attacks have

J. Zhou et al. (Eds.): ACNS 2022 Workshops, LNCS 13285, pp. 127–145, 2022.
https://doi.org/10.1007/978-3-031-16815-4_8

been later proposed for other public, and symmetric-key algorithms [1,2,7,8,15]. A survey of these successful fault attacks can be found in [5].

Moreover, existing published results use FI to break the non-cryptographic security mechanisms. In [26], Timmers, Spruyt, and Witteman showed that FI could be used to load attacker-controlled data into the Program Counter (PC) register in an ARM 32-bit platform, allowing an attacker to gain runtime control of the device by setting the PC to an address where the attacker's payload is stored. In [20], the authors performed FI on the instruction cache of ARMv7-M architectures and modified the control flow of a program. Cui and Housley used FI to corrupt the data stored in DRAM, thereby breaking the secure boot of an embedded device [11]. A laser FI attack has been successfully used to break the secure boot of a smartphone in [27]. In [25], FI has been successfully used to escalate the privileges in Linux from user mode to kernel mode. Recently, FI has also been used to extract the firmware from several commercial devices [10].

Contributions. Unlike smart cards, many embedded systems in use today are implemented using multi-core System-on-Chips (SoCs) that are complex and host CPUs that run at hundreds of MHz to few GHz. Most of these SoCs can operate at different frequencies, and they often provide an option to configure their frequency externally or internally. Moreover, some SoCs start booting directly from an external clock that is relatively slow and switch to PLL (Phase Locked Loop) sometime during the boot flow. This switch leads to a natural question: *does the FI's attack success rate depend on the operating frequency?*

The success rate of an FI test is defined as the number of successful faults divided by the number of total attempts. So, naturally, as the success rate increases, the effort required to perform a successful attack decreases. Although dependency between the EM pulse voltage and the clock frequency along with success rate was briefly discussed in [18] within the context of FPGA, to the best of our knowledge, no extensive study examined the relationship between the clock frequency and the success rate of an FI attack. In this work, we address this gap for Voltage FI (VFI) and ElectroMagnetic FI (EMFI) within the context of an SoC. We use SiFive's HiFive1 development board for our experiments, which houses the FE310-G000 chip, the first commercially available RISC-V SoC.

Organization. The rest of the paper is organized as follows. We provide a brief introduction to different FI attacks and fault models in Sect. 2. Next, we describe the three different test applications used in our testing in Sect. 3. The hardware and the software tools used for the experiments are listed in Sect. 4. The results from our experiments for both VFI and EMFI on HiFive1 are presented in Sect. 5. We provide possible reasons for the observed behaviour in Sect. 6. Finally, we conclude the paper in Sect. 7.

2   Preliminaries

Fault injection attacks are a class of physical attacks that try to actively modify the intended behavior of the device in order to bypass its security. Faults can be injected into the targeted device through different means, e.g., varying the supply voltage or the clock speed, or using electromagnetic emissions or laser beams [4]. In this section, we describe the common techniques used to inject faults. We also recall various fault models from the literature.

Clock Fault Injection. A fault is injected by tampering with the target's clock signal [3]. For example, the target is supplied with a clock signal higher than its operating frequency for a short period reducing the length of a single clock cycle. Thus, it may cause setup time constraint violations [28] changing the program's control flow, which could result in breaking a security mechanism.

Voltage Fault Injection. A fault is injected by changing the target's supply voltage [28]. This change is applied when the targeted operation is executed, making it possible to induce the desired effect in the device. As shown in [28], voltage fault injection causes setup time violations like the clock fault injection.

Electromagnetic Fault Injection. A fault is injected by applying a transient or a harmonic EM pulse [6,12,17]. A fault injection probe consisting of a coil generates such pulses after a high voltage pulse is applied to the coil, inducing eddy currents into the chip. These eddy currents cause faulty behavior that could be used to break a security mechanism.

Optical Fault Injection. A fault is injected into the target device with the help of a light pulse [24]. The applied light pulse induces a photo-electric current in the device, causing faults in the computations. The light pulse can be generated using a low-cost camera flashlight, but often this is not precise. For higher precision, a laser beam is used to induce the desired light pulse.

Fault Models. The behavior of a device can be affected in various ways due to fault injection attacks. These attacks can influence both the CPU's execution unit and the static components that store data and instructions like the registers and the caches [25]. In general, it is difficult to determine the exact reason behind a successful fault injection attack. Therefore, we use high-level fault models that describe the effect of faults on the device's behavior on the instruction set architecture level [26]. Commonly used fault models include:

- **Instruction Manipulation:** The fault modifies the instruction, leading to unexpected behavior. For example, a bit flip in the opcode field of an instruction converts a subtraction operation into an addition.
- **Instruction Skipping:** This is a special case of instruction manipulation that results in a modified instruction that has no impact on the device's behavior. This can happen, for example, when the operands of the modified instruction have been changed to something that is not used later by the program or when a branch instruction has been changed to a *nop*, i.e., no operation.
- **Memory Corruption:** The fault affects the values loaded from a register or memory, which can cause unexpected effects on the program execution. This can happen when the data loaded to a register from the data cache

is corrupted. Alternatively, when the data read from the main memory is corrupted, the data or instruction cache stores the corrupted value.

3   Test Applications

In this section, we propose three test applications that aim to capture the effects of faults on different SoC components. These tests are based on the characterization test presented in [26] and intend to cover the effect of faults on an SoC more extensively. At a high level, a fault can modify the instructions being executed or the data being processed through a single or multiple bit flips. Such modifications can occur in any SoC component, like the CPU or the memory, or during data exchange. We aim to cover different scenarios where a fault could modify the data or instructions.

Our tests are designed to cover the effects on various SoC components. We implemented them in assembly to fully control what is being executed on the CPU and avoid any undesired effects caused by compiler optimizations. We show these tests in Listing 1.1, Listing 1.2, and Listing 1.3 in an assembly-like pseudo-code that can be easily translated into any Instruction Set Architecture (ISA). In all these tests, we use two general-purpose registers named $t0$ and $t1$. Their names come from the temporary registers defined in RISC-V but all ISAs have such registers.

3.1   Register-Based Loop

In the register-based loop, we only use the CPU registers to implement a loop. We use two counters: one that goes up and the other goes down. These counters are initialized to 0 ($t0$ register) and n ($t1$ register), respectively. The test consists of a loop that increments and decrements $t0$ and $t1$, respectively, in steps of 1, until $t1$ becomes 0. The rest of the registers are initialized with a known fixed value (e.g., 0xdeadbeef) to monitor if the fault modified the source or destination registers in an instruction. The test uses only two registers to store the counters, and hence the data cache will not be used. Additionally, as the code size is small, it should most likely fit in the instruction cache.

A successful fault is identified by checking the value of the registers at the end of the loop. In some cases, the registers $t0$ and $t1$ do not hold the values n and zero due to the injected fault. Alternatively, the fault could also affect the value in the unused registers.

```
1    # Push a known value to all the registers
2    # N: the number of registers in the ISA
3    (t2, ..., tN) ← 0xdeadbeef
4    t0 ← 0
5    t1 ← n
6    reg_loop:
7        t0 ← t0 + 1
8        t1 ← t1 - 1
9        if t1 > 0 then goto reg_loop
```

Listing 1.1. Register based test

3.2 Memory-Based Loop

The memory-based loop is similar to the register-based loop but the counters are loaded/saved from/to the memory (using load and store instructions) in every iteration. Again, the loop ends when $t1$ is 0 (Listing 1.2). After the first load, a copy of the data is kept in the data cache, and hence faults would only affect the data cache and its transfers inside the loop. The loop code should fit in the instruction cache due to its size. We also initialize all the unused registers to a fixed value to track any corruptions in their contents or verify whether a different register was used in a loop iteration due to the fault. A successful fault is determined by examining the registers and comparing their values with the expected ones.

```
1    # Push a known value to all the registers
2    # N: the number of registers in the ISA
3    (t2, ..., tN) ← 0xdeadbeef
4    t0 ← 0
5    stack[sp - 4] ← t0
6    t1 ← n
7    stack[sp - 8] ← t1
8    mem_loop:
9        t0 ← stack[sp - 4]
10       t1 ← stack[sp - 8]
11       t0 ← t0 + 1
12       t1 ← t1 - 1
13       stack[sp - 4] ← t0
14       stack[sp - 8] ← t1
15       if t1 > 0 then goto mem_loop
```

Listing 1.2. Memory based test

3.3 Unrolled Loop

In this test, we implement a fully unrolled loop. We use one up-counter ($t0$) initialized to 0, that is incremented n times through an unrolled loop. Similar to the other two tests, we also initialize all the unused registers to a fixed value.

In general, this test can be used in two different ways according to the loop's number of increment instructions. First, if a small n is used, the program can fully fit in the instruction cache, which results in no cache misses during the execution of the test. As a result, only transfers between the instruction cache and the CPU are affected. This way, it is possible to pinpoint the sensitivity of the instruction cache and the corresponding bus to FI attacks. On the other hand, if a large n is used and the program cannot fit in the instruction cache, there will be instruction cache misses during the execution of the test, which results in loading the instructions from the main memory. The CPU to main memory bus's sensitivity to FI attacks could also be determined in such cases.

```
1    # Push a known value to all the registers
2    # N: the number of registers in the ISA
3    (t1, ..., tN) ← 0xdeadbeef
4    t0 ← 0
5    t0 ← t0 + 1
6    t0 ← t0 + 1
7    t0 ← t0 + 1
8    ...
9    t0 ← t0 + 1
```

Listing 1.3. Unrolled loop

A successful fault is detected when the value in $t0$ is not equal to n or when the value in any of the unused registers is corrupted.

4 Setup

Performing automatic execution of FI attacks requires both hardware and software tools. In this section, we describe the tools used for our experiments. We also briefly discuss the characteristics of the target used for the experiments.

4.1 Target of Evaluation

Our target is the FE310-G000 (fabricated in TSMC CL018G 180 nm [22]) which is included in the development board HiFive1. FE310-G000's maximum supported frequency is 320 MHz and the CPU requires 1.8 V or 3.3 V supply voltage to operate [21]. We did not decap the chip due to its thin package as was also described in [14]. The tests presented in Sect. 3 are implemented as part of a user-defined program that runs on bare-metal (without an operating system), as described in Subsect. 4.3.

4.2 Hardware Tools

During our experiments, various faults (also referred to as attempts in this paper) are injected into the device in order to identify suitable parameters for success. For that reason, a fully automated setup has been created using commercially available tools from Riscure [19]. We used the following hardware tools for testing:

- **Glitch Generator:** An FPGA based workbench that can be programmed to interact with embedded devices. The "brain" of this device consists of two finite state machines (up to 255 states each), which are responsible for the correct generation of every signal that is needed for our experiments. To handle inputs/outputs, the device consists of 32 GPIO pins that can interact with the target. We use this device to generate the glitch used for the fault injection. The Glitch Generator consists of six analog voltage outputs, and it can also provide the input voltage for small embedded devices.
- **Glitch Amplifier:** This analog device is used in conjunction with the Glitch Generator. It is used to generate sharper and more accurate voltage glitches that are essential in voltage fault injection attacks.
- **EMFI Transient Probe:** The Glitch Generator controls this device. It generates an electromagnetic pulse lasting for 50 ns after the Glitch Generator triggers it. The probe is made of a copper winding around a ferrite core, and its tip is a flat circle with a diameter of 1.5 mm.

4.3 Software Tools

We implemented a simple bare-metal application in C and RISC-V assembly that runs on the FE310-G000 chip. This application accepts messages from the PC through the UART interface and runs one of the three characterization tests described in Sect. 3. The message from the UART determines which test should run every time. Right before the test starts, a GPIO pin is set to high, and the same pin is set to low when the test

Table 1. The list of commands used to communicate with the board

Command	Functionality
"#1"	Run the register based loop (test 1)
"#2"	Run the memory based loop (test 2)
"#3"	Run the unrolled loop (test 3)
"#4"	Enable the PLL at 320 MHz (fast EMFI configuration)
"#5"	Disable the PLL and use 16 MHz (slow configuration)
"#6"	Enable the PLL at 90 MHz (medium configuration)
"#7"	Enable the PLL at 240 MHz (fast VFI configuration)

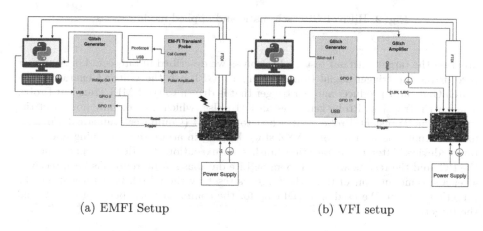

(a) EMFI Setup   (b) VFI setup

Fig. 1. Setups used for the experiments.

ends. This pin is used in the synchronization between the Glitch Generator and the target device. The application can alter the chip's operating frequency dynamically by enabling or disabling the PLL. We used three clock configurations to investigate the effect of different operating frequencies on both VFI's and EMFI's attack success rate. The first configuration operates at 16 MHz (*slow* configuration) and does not use the PLL clock generator. However, the *medium* and the *fast* configurations use the PLL. The *medium* configuration operates at 90 MHz. The *fast* configuration operates at 320 MHz and 240 MHz for the EMFI and the VFI, respectively. We had to operate the device slightly slower than the maximum allowed frequency for VFI due to the instabilities introduced after the board was modified (see Subsect. 4.5). In Table 1, we show a summary of the protocol used between the PC and the board.

4.4 EMFI Setup

Our experimental setup used for the EMFI is shown in Fig. 1a. The target board is powered using an external power supply. A Python script that runs in the PC controls the target through the UART interface and configures the state machine inside the Glitch Generator through a user-friendly API. This state machine consists of one state that produces the glitch when the trigger is generated from the target device. We

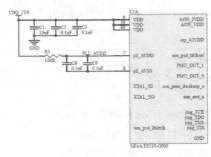

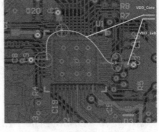

(a) HiFive1 CPU schematic [23]

(b) Power cuts in HiFive1 for effective voltage fault injection

Fig. 2. HiFive1 CPU schematic and applied modifications.

program the target with our test application as we described in Subsect. 4.3. A jumper wire drives the trigger signal from the target's GPIO to the Glitch Generator. The Glitch Generator produces another trigger that is driven to the EMFI Transient Probe. The EMFI Transient Probe generates an EM pulse, which may or may not affect the target. The Transient Probe is attached to a CNC (Computer Numerical Control) machine that acts as a movable XYZ stage helping in accurate positioning above the target device. After the application finishes its execution, the device replies back to the PC, and the results are saved to an SQLite database. If no reply has been received after a specific amount of time, the target is reset by the Glitch Generator using the target's reset pin. We used an FTDI chip for the communication between the PC and the target.

4.5 VFI Setup

In Fig. 2a, the schematic that describes the circuit around the FE310-G000 chip in the HiFive1 development board is shown [23]. We see that pins 6, 30, and 46 are used for the CPU's power supply. To create a stable power supply line that is not affected by small variations in the input voltage, some filter capacitors are connected directly to these pins. To increase the effectiveness of the VFI, the glitch should be applied directly to the CPU without having to pass through the filter circuit. Therefore, we modified the HiFive1 board used for our experiments. The applied power cuts are shown in Fig. 2b. In particular, pins 6, 30, and 46 are cut from the rest of the circuit and soldered to an external pin so that it is possible to connect them to a 1.8 V power supply directly (VDD_Core in the Fig. 2b).

The experimental setup we used for VFI is shown in Fig. 1b. For this experiment, the development board was powered from an external power supply at 5 V. The power cuts isolated the SoC from the rest of the board, and hence we powered it separately. In particular, we connected the Glitch Amplifier directly to the external pin that powers it. When there is no glitch, the output of the Glitch Amplifier is set at 1.8 V, as suggested in [21]. We verified that the chip correctly operated in this setup even though the filter capacitors have been removed. Like the EMFI, the target generates a trigger when the application starts. The trigger is then driven to the Glitch Generator. Next, the Glitch Generator produces the glitch, which is fed to the Glitch Amplifier. The glitch drops the V_{in} to a random value smaller than 1.8 V (from 1.0 V to 1.6 V) for a short time.

We chose a broad range of values for the glitch to investigate the chip's behavior under various circumstances. When we need to perform an attack, we can narrow this range and use values that yield a high probability of a successful attack. A Python script controlled this process, and an FTDI chip was used for the communication between the PC and the target.

4.6 Results Classification

The output from a fault injection attempt is categorized as follows:

- **Expected:** The test has completed its execution and the expected results (e.g., $t0 = n$ and $t1 = 0$) were sent back to the PC.
- **Crash/Mute:** The impact of the glitch was strong, and the target crashed, or there was no reply from the target before the timeout expired. In this case, the glitch either affects the execution path and the application cannot continue or causes the target to reset.
- **Successful:** The counter values ($t0$ and $t1$) returned to the PC were different from the expected ($t0 \neq n$ or $t1 \neq 0$). Therefore, the injected fault produced an undesirable effect on the program execution without causing a crash.

Note that the success rate of an experiment is defined as the number of successful attempts divided by the total number of attempts.

5 Experimental Results

To investigate how clock frequency affects FI success rate, we performed VFI and EMFI experiments while the CPU was clocked at different frequencies. In this section, we present the results from these experiments.

Parameter Space. The glitch applied in every fault injection attempt is fully defined through a set of configurable parameters. These parameters form the parameter space for the experiment, and they are different for every type of FI attack.

5.1 EMFI

The effectiveness of the EMFI depends on the location of the probe. Thus, we need to identify the location that gives the maximum success rate. For that reason, we performed a scan over the 6×6 mm chip's package [21] in a two-dimensional grid of points. On every point in the grid, we performed multiple FI attempts for statistical analysis. In general, the grid's density (distance between different points) depends on the size of the chip and its package and the transient probe tip's area. When the probe tip is small, a dense grid can be used. On the other hand, when the probe tip is large, a sparse grid should be used. If the grid remains dense even with a large tip, every EMFI experiment can affect multiple points in the grid, introducing redundancy in the results. We used an 8×8 grid of 64 points for our scan, which resulted in a step of 0.75 mm. The diameter of our probe tip is 1.5 mm, and such a step is reasonable to avoid interference between different grid points. The grid's origin ($X = 0$, $Y = 0$) corresponds to the lowest left corner of the chip's resin package (see FE310-G000 pinout in [21]).

The parameter space for the EMFI consists of the following:

- **Glitch power:** The EM pulse's amplitude as a percentage of the Transient Probe's maximum supported power. The maximum supported power corresponds to a 470V pulse. We saw that values above 80% resulted in many resets and below 40% seemed ineffective. For that reason, we used values between 40% and 80% of the maximum power.
- **Glitch delay:** The time between the trigger and the glitch. This should not be larger than the whole duration of the test that runs on the CPU. There was no need for exact timing in our experiments as they were loops and our aim was to draw a sensitivity map. Thus, the delay used was a random value between the 35% and 65% of each test's execution time. As expected, the exact ranges are different for every test and every clock frequency.
- **X:** The X coordinate (in micrometers) of the grid point.
- **Y:** The Y coordinate (in micrometers) of the grid point.

We scanned the whole chip package in this experiment. At each point, we performed a number of attempts with varying glitch delay and glitch power, both of which were selected randomly from the above predefined ranges. We set n equal to 10000 (0x2710). The results of this experiment are summarized in Fig. 3, Fig. 4, and Fig. 5. In these graphs, the x and y axes show the X and Y co-ordinates of the grid point, respectively. The *green* color represents *expected* results, the *yellow* color *crashes/mutes*, and the *red successful* results (see Subsect. 4.6). We add a small random value (0–400 μm) to each experiment's X and Y coordinates so that they are not plotted on top of each other.

We see from Fig. 3 and Fig. 4 that for the slow (16 MHz) and the medium (90 MHz) clock configurations, successful glitches occurred only in the unrolled loop (Listing 1.3). These glitches occurred around the pins that communicate with the SPI flash memory (see F310-G000 pinout in [21]). The unrolled loop (Listing 1.3) consists of 10000 additions, and it requires an instruction cache of 10000 instructions ∗ 4 bytes per instruction = 40000 ≈ 39 KiB. However, FE310-G000 has only a 16 KiB instruction cache. Thus, our faults were most likely affecting the instruction transfers from the flash. On the other hand, the code perfectly fits in the instruction cache when the number of loop iterations is small, i.e., 300. In this case, no successful glitch appeared around the region where we observed successful glitches previously. After the first iteration of the loop, the code is copied into the instruction cache, and there is no more interaction with the SPI flash memory. We saw no successful glitches in that case (slow and medium clock configurations), and we concluded that transfers from the instruction cache to the CPU were robust in these experiments.

In Table 2, we summarize some of the observed successful attempts. For all the successful attempts in the unrolled loop test, the returned value is less than the expected 10000 (0x2710). If the returned counter value is close to 0x2710, it is safe to conclude that some **add** instructions were skipped due to the fault. This happened when $t0$ is 0x2700, 0x2708, and 0x270f for 16 MHz, 90 MHz, and 320 MHz, respectively. In the remaining cases (i.e., 0x256e, 0x26c2, 0x2660), there is a significant difference between the returned and the expected values, so we cannot assume that only a few instructions were skipped. Even though the glitch lasts for 0.8, 4.5, and 16 cycles for the slow, medium, and fast clock configurations, the returned values differ by 418, 88, and 176 from the expected value. In [14], it was verified that an EMFI attack could affect multiple instructions at once. However, the probability of this effect dropped significantly for more than six instructions. Thus, in all these cases, some instructions were altered completely. Such alterations require multiple bit-flips for each altered instruction that

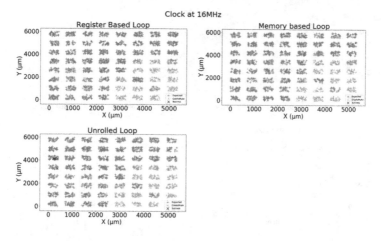

Fig. 3. EMFI results of all three tests at 16 MHz (PLL bypassed).

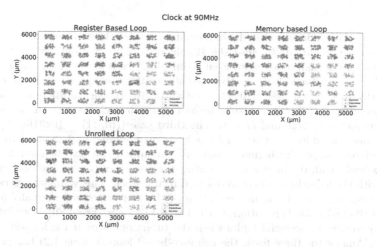

Fig. 4. EMFI results of all three tests at 90 MHz (PLL enabled).

is not aligned with the state-of-the-art fault models like the sampling [18] or the charge-based [16]. Additionally, the successful attempts in this area were not increased as the operating frequency increased, which contradicts the charge-based fault model [16]. We concluded that this behavior was possible due to the retrieval of instructions from the external SPI flash. Therefore, these errors were not of particular interest for this work because the external SPI flash is unprotected in this board, and an attacker could directly attack it.

The other two tests have successful faults only when the chip operates at 320 MHz, verifying the charge-based fault model [16]. In particular, we conclude that the branch instruction can be skipped in the register-based test, as one of the results was $(t0, t1)$ = (7190, 2810) = (0x1c16, 0xafa). In that case, everything was run as expected until the branch instruction because $t0 + t1 = 10000$. Additionally, in two cases a result larger than 10000 was saved in $t0$ (0x2e20 and 0x29ef), but the loop exited normally

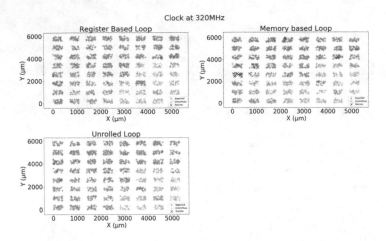

Fig. 5. EMFI results of all three tests at 320 MHz (PLL enabled).

(i.e., $t1 = 0$). This indicates that the immediate values of the additions can be altered (instruction manipulation) because the significant difference from 10000 cannot be explained by a few instruction skips even if our glitch lasts for 16 clock cycles.

For the memory-based loop, we observed all possible faults when the chip operated at 320 MHz. In the first case $((t0, t1) = (0x270f, 0x0))$, one addition was skipped. In the second case $((t0, t1) = (0x62f, 0x20e1))$, the branch instruction was skipped because $t0 + t1 = 0x2710$ and $t1 \neq 0$. The third case $((t0, t1) = (0x31fe, 0))$ shows that the constant added or subtracted has been manipulated and changed to a completely different value. Furthermore, memory corruption can also be seen when $(t0, t1) = (0xdeadde040, 0)$. In this case, during the loop's execution, the contents of a register with the value 0xdeadbeef were saved in the stack. This value was retrieved in the next loop iteration. Then, the execution of the loop continued normally for 8529 (0xdeade040 - 0xdeadbeef) iterations until $t1$ was set to zero. From Fig. 5, we infer that it is easier to induce successful faults when the target operates at the highest possible frequency. Among the three tests, the memory-based loop (Listing 1.2) has produced a higher percentage of successful faults because memory operations (i.e., loads and stores) are highly vulnerable to faults. Additionally, we practically verified that each program behaves differently under the same EMFI attacks highlighting the need for a profiling phase before targeting an application. Such a profiling phase could define the susceptibility of different assembly instructions to EMFI.

5.2   VFI

For an effective Voltage fault injection, we have removed the chip's filter capacitors (see Subsect. 4.5). The CPU was powered directly from the Glitch Generator. Its supply voltage should be 1.8 V ($\pm 10\%$) to function normally. For the glitch, the input voltage was dropped for a small amount of time, different for every clock configuration.

The parameter space for the VFI consists of the following:

- **glitch voltage:** The voltage provided to the target during the glitch. This voltage takes values from 1 V to 1.6 V.

Table 2. Output from some of the successful faults in EMFI

Frequency	Test	t0	t1	Comment
16 MHz	Register based loop	–	–	–
	Memory based loop	–	–	–
	Unrolled loop	0x256e	–	Instruction manipulation (add)
		0x2700	–	Instruction skipping (add)
90 MHz	Register based loop	–	–	–
	Memory based loop	–	–	–
	Unrolled loop	0x26c2	–	Instruction manipulation
		0x2708	–	Instruction skipping (add)
320 MHz	Register based loop	0x1c16	0xafa	Instruction skipping (branch)
		0x2e20	0x0	Instruction manipulation (add)
		0x29ef	0x0	Instruction manipulation (add)
	Memory based loop	0x270f	0x0	Instruction skipping (add)
		0x62f	0x20e1	Instruction skipping (branch)
		0x31fe	0x0	Instruction manipulation (add)
		0xdeade040	0x0	Memory corruption
	Unrolled loop	0x2660	–	Instruction manipulation
		0x270f	–	Instruction skipping (add)

- **glitch length:** The amount of time that the glitch (voltage drop) is applied to the target. In our experiments, this takes up to a small number of clock cycles.
- **glitch delay:** The amount of time between the trigger and the glitch. It should be smaller than the total execution time of the test that runs on the CPU. Similar to the EMFI experiments, the delay used was a random value from 35% to 65% of the test's execution time.

In our experiments, we varied all three parameters for each attempt. The values for these parameters were chosen randomly from the allowed ranges. Similar to the EMFI, we chose n equal to 10000 (0x2710). We show the results from the VFI experiment in Figs. 6, 7 and 8 for the slow, medium, and fast clock, respectively. The X-axis shows the glitch voltage in volts and the Y-axis shows the glitch length in nanoseconds. Here, the *expected* results, *crashes/mutes*, and *successful* results are marked in *green*, *yellow*, and *red*, respectively (Subsect. 4.6). The highest frequency that the application could run normally, when no glitch is applied, is 240 MHz due to the instabilities that we mentioned in Subsect. 4.5.

Our experiments show that the largest number of successful glitches appear in the fast clock configuration (240 MHz), and the smallest number of successful glitches appear when the circuit operates at 16 MHz. In [28], it was shown that VFI increases signal propagation delays creating timing constraint violations. Such violations become easier when the circuit operates in a higher clock frequency due to the decreased clock period.

In Table 3, we show some of the observed successful attempts. Their classification is based on the analysis we presented in Subsect. 4.6. When the clock operated at 16 MHz, we see that the branch instruction can be skipped in both the register-based loop and the memory-based loop. Here, we got $(t0, t1) = (0x1a5, 0x256b)$ for the

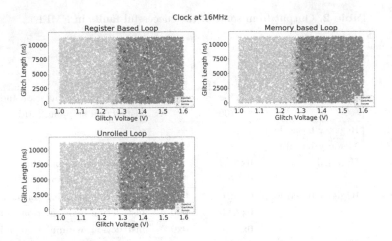

Fig. 6. VFI results of all three tests at 16 MHz (PLL bypassed).

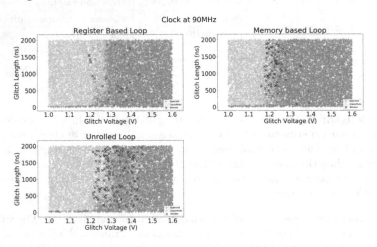

Fig. 7. VFI results of all three tests at 90 MHz (PLL enabled).

register based loop and $(t0, t1) = (0x1182, 0x158e)$ and $(t0, t1) = (0x1adb, 0x1adc)$ for the memory-based loop. In the second case for the memory-based loop, $t0 + t1 \neq 0x2710$, meaning that apart from the branch skipping, one more operation (**add/sub**) was also manipulated. Instruction manipulation was possible in both the register-based loop $((t0, t1) = (0x25b6, 0))$ and the unrolled loop $(t0 = 0x26e0)$. Furthermore, the **add** instruction was also successfully skipped both in the memory-based loop $((t0, t1) = (0x270f, 0))$ and in the unrolled loop $(t0 = 0x270f)$.

Similarly, when the clock operated at 90 MHz various faults have been observed. The branch instruction was successfully skipped for both the register-based loop $((t0, t1) = (0xeb2, 0x185e))$, and the memory-based loop $((t0, t1) = (0xc37, 0x19d9))$, $(t0, t1) = (0x608, 0x2109)$, $(t0, t1) = (0xa3d, 0xdeadbeee))$. Apart from branch skipping, we also observed memory corruption for the memory-based loop $((t0, t1) = (0xa3d, 0xdeadbee))$. Here, after the wrong value was loaded in $t1$, the subtraction was per-

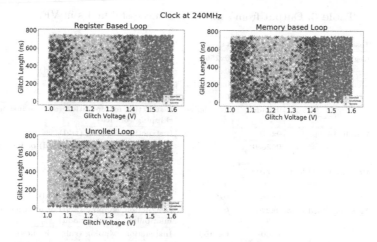

Fig. 8. VFI results of all three tests at 240 MHz (PLL enabled).

formed and then the branch was skipped. In one case, both the **sub** and the branch instructions have been skipped $((t0, t1) = (0x608, 0x2109))$ because the sum is 0x2711 and $t0 \neq 0$. The rest of the experiments (register-based: $(t0, t1) = (0x2700, 0)$, memory-based: $(t0, t1) = (0x270e, 0)$, unrolled: $t0 = 0x2f0f$, $t0 = 0x2711$) indicate some kind of instruction manipulation in the constants that were added or subtracted.

When the clock operated at 240 MHz, similar results have been observed. In this frequency, there were multiple cases of branch skipping (register-based: $(t0, t1) = (0xb85, 0xdeadbeed)$, $(t0, t1) = (0x5f0, 0x2120)$, memory-based: $(0xada, 0x1c36)$, $(t0, t1) = (0xcaa, 0xdeadbeee)$). There were also multiple examples of memory corruption for both the register-based loop $((t0, t1) = (0xb85, 0xdeadbeed))$ and the memory-based loop $((t0, t1) = (0xdeadce5f, 0)$, $(t0, t1) = (0xcaa, 0xdeadbeee))$. For one of these cases (memory-based: $(t0, t1) = (0xdeadce5f, 0)$), the wrong value was loaded to $t0$ and the loop continued normally for 0xdeadce5f - 0xdeadbeef = 0xf70 iterations before it stopped. In the other two cases, the predefined value, i.e., 0xdeadbeef was loaded to $t1$, and the **sub** instruction decreased $t1$ by 1 (normal execution) or 2 (instruction manipulation), and the branch instruction was skipped in the same loop iteration. In one case for the register-based loop, we got $(t0, t1) = (0x2711, 0)$. This happened either because one addition was manipulated and a 2 was added instead of 1, or one subtraction was skipped and thus, the loop was executed for 1 more iteration. The rest of the experiments are either instruction manipulations (memory-based: $(t0, t1) = (0x1c0f, 0)$, unrolled: $t0 = 0x2720$, $t0 = 0x181c$) or addition skipping (unrolled: $t0 = 0x270f$).

6   Discussion

In this section, we present possible explanations for the observed results. The observed results are compatible with earlier analyses of the effects of FI on digital integrated circuits. VFI causes timing constraint violations [28], which in turn cause computation faults. The timing constraints essentially dictate that the time taken by a circuit to process data must be lower than the clock period of the target for it to function

Table 3. Output from some of the successful faults in VFI

Frequency	Test	t0	t1	Comment
16 MHz	Register based loop	0x1a5	0x256b	Instruction skipping (branch)
		0x25b6	0x0	Instruction manipulation (add)
	Memory based loop	0x1182	0x158e	Instruction skipping (branch)
		0x270f	0x0	Instruction skipping (add)
		0x1adb	0x1adc	Instruction manipulation (add) + instruction skipping (branch)
	Unrolled loop	0x270f	–	Instruction skipping (add)
		0x26e0	–	Instruction manipulation (add) or instruction skipping (add)
90 MHz	Register based loop	0x2700	0x0	Instruction manipulation (add)
		0xeb2	0x185e	Instruction skipping (branch)
		0x4b38	0x0	Instruction manipulation (add)
	Memory based loop	0x270e	0x0	Instruction skipping (add) or instruction manipulation (sub or add)
		0x608	0x2109	Instruction skipping (sub + branch)
		0xa3d	0xdeadbeee	Memory corruption + instruction skipping (branch)
		0xc37	0x19d9	Instruction skipping (branch)
	Unrolled loop	0x2f0f	–	Instruction manipulation (add)
		0x2711	–	Instruction manipulation (add)
240 MHz	Register based loop	0x2711	0x0	Instruction manipulation (add) or instruction skipping (sub)
		0xb85	0xdeadbeed	Memory corruption + instruction skipping (branch)
		0x5f0	0x2120	Instruction skipping (branch)
	Memory based loop	0x1c0f	0x0	Instruction manipulation (add or sub)
		0xada	0x1c36	Instruction skipping (branch)
		0xdeadce5f	0x0	Memory corruption
		0xcaa	0xdeadbeee	Memory corruption + instruction skipping (branch)
	Unrolled loop	0x2720	–	Instruction manipulation (add)
		0x181c	–	Instruction manipulation (add) or instruction skipping (add)
		0x270f	–	Instruction skipping (add)

correctly. So, by increasing the data processing time using FI, it is possible to violate the above constraint and induce faults in the computation. As the operating frequency of the target increases, the clock period decreases. Hence, it is relatively easier to violate the setup time constraint, thereby increasing the success rate of VFI.

In EMFI, we did not see only timing faults, but we also observed bit sets, resets, and flips, meaning that our experiments are aligned with the charge-based fault model [14] instead of the sampling fault model [18]. The sampling fault model [18] states that the susceptibility windows of the DFFs are independent of the operating frequency, but the distance of these windows decreases as the clock period gets smaller [13]. As a result, one could claim that a glitch injected randomly during the execution of a program has a higher probability of causing a successful fault when the chip operates at a high frequency. However, the fact that we were able to successfully inject faults (not related to the SPI flash) only when the chip operated at 320 MHz suggests that the charge-based fault model is more accurate in this case.

In theory, the same success rate can be achieved when the target operates at a lower frequency, e.g., by inducing more powerful voltage glitches or EM pulses. However, the power of glitches cannot arbitrarily be increased in practice without causing the target to reset. This behavior was also observed in our experiments: when the target was running at 240 MHz (VFI), we could get many successful faults, where glitch duration was less than 800 ns (see Fig. 8). However, we needed to increase the glitch duration for the slower clock speeds, i.e., 2000 ns and 12000 ns for 90 MHz and 16 MHz respectively (see Fig. 7 and Fig. 6). Such longer glitches inevitably make the target dysfunctional, leading to more resets, as seen from these results. To conclude, when the target operating frequency is low, the success rate decreases due to more resets caused by the increased glitch power. This might also explain the higher success rate when the operating frequency is higher.

7 Conclusion

Many embedded systems in use today are implemented using multi-core SoCs that are complex and host CPUs that run at hundreds of MHz to few GHz. The security of these devices faces different challenges compared to other simple devices like smart cards. In this paper, we investigated the effect of clock frequency on the success rate of VFI and EMFI on such SoCs. To determine the effect of faults more holistically, we developed three test applications that target different components of the SoC. We performed both VFI and EMFI on a RISC-V-based SoC while it was executing our tests. The experimental results showed that the probability of success for fault injection attacks increases as the clock frequency increases. We saw this behavior in both VFI and EMFI. Finally, we provided theoretical justification for the observed results.

References

1. Anderson, R., Kuhn, M.: Low cost attacks on tamper resistant devices. In: Christianson, B., Crispo, B., Lomas, M., Roe, M. (eds.) Security Protocols 1997. LNCS, vol. 1361, pp. 125–136. Springer, Heidelberg (1998). https://doi.org/10.1007/BFb0028165
2. Aumüller, C., Bier, P., Fischer, W., Hofreiter, P., Seifert, J.-P.: Fault attacks on RSA with CRT: concrete results and practical countermeasures. In: Kaliski, B.S., Koç, K., Paar, C. (eds.) CHES 2002. LNCS, vol. 2523, pp. 260–275. Springer, Heidelberg (2003). https://doi.org/10.1007/3-540-36400-5_20
3. Balasch, J., Gierlichs, B., Verbauwhede, I.: An in-depth and black-box characterization of the effects of clock glitches on 8-bit MCUs. In: 2011 Workshop on Fault Diagnosis and Tolerance in Cryptography, pp. 105–114. IEEE (2011)
4. Bar-El, H., Choukri, H., Naccache, D., Tunstall, M., Whelan, C.: The sorcerer's apprentice guide to fault attacks. Proc. IEEE 94(2), 370–382 (2006)
5. Barenghi, A., Breveglieri, L., Koren, I., Naccache, D.: Fault injection attacks on cryptographic devices: theory, practice, and countermeasures. Proc. IEEE 100(11), 3056–3076 (2012)
6. Bayon, P., et al.: Contactless electromagnetic active attack on ring oscillator based true random number generator. In: Schindler, W., Huss, S.A. (eds.) COSADE 2012. LNCS, vol. 7275, pp. 151–166. Springer, Heidelberg (2012). https://doi.org/10.1007/978-3-642-29912-4_12

7. Bayon, P., et al.: Contactless electromagnetic active attack on ring oscillator based true random number generator. In: Schindler, W., Huss, S.A. (eds.) COSADE 2012. LNCS, vol. 7275, pp. 151–166. Springer, Heidelberg (2012). https://doi.org/10.1007/978-3-642-29912-4_12

8. Biham, E., Shamir, A.: Differential fault analysis of secret key cryptosystems. In: Kaliski, B.S. (ed.) CRYPTO 1997. LNCS, vol. 1294, pp. 513–525. Springer, Heidelberg (1997). https://doi.org/10.1007/BFb0052259

9. Boneh, D., DeMillo, R.A., Lipton, R.J.: On the importance of checking cryptographic protocols for faults. In: Fumy, W. (ed.) EUROCRYPT 1997. LNCS, vol. 1233, pp. 37–51. Springer, Heidelberg (1997). https://doi.org/10.1007/3-540-69053-0_4

10. Bozzato, C., Focardi, R., Palmarini, F.: Shaping the glitch: Optimizing voltage fault injection attacks. IACR Trans. Cryptogr. Hardw. Embed. Syst. **2019**, 199–224 (2019)

11. Cui, A., Housley, R.: BADFET: defeating modern secure boot using second-order pulsed electromagnetic fault injection. In: 11th USENIX Workshop on Offensive Technologies (WOOT 17) (2017)

12. Dehbaoui, A., Dutertre, J.-M., Robisson, B., Tria, A.: Electromagnetic transient faults injection on a hardware and a software implementations of AES. In: 2012 Workshop on Fault Diagnosis and Tolerance in Cryptography, pp. 7–15. IEEE (2012)

13. Dumont, M., Lisart, M., Maurine, P.: Electromagnetic fault injection : How faults occur. In: 2019 Workshop on Fault Diagnosis and Tolerance in Cryptography (FDTC), pp. 9–16 (2019). https://doi.org/10.1109/FDTC.2019.00010

14. Elmohr, M.A., Liao, H., Gebotys, C.H.: EM fault injection on ARM and RISC-V. In: 2020 21st International Symposium on Quality Electronic Design (ISQED), pp. 206–212 (2020). https://doi.org/10.1109/ISQED48828.2020.9137051

15. Giraud, C.: DFA on AES. In: Dobbertin, H., Rijmen, V., Sowa, A. (eds.) AES 2004. LNCS, vol. 3373, pp. 27–41. Springer, Heidelberg (2005). https://doi.org/10.1007/11506447_4

16. Liao, H., Gebotys, C.: Methodology for EM fault injection: charge-based fault model. In: 2019 Design, Automation Test in Europe Conference Exhibition (DATE), pp. 256–259 (2019). https://doi.org/10.23919/DATE.2019.8715150

17. Moro, N., Dehbaoui, A., Heydemann, K., Robisson, B., Encrenaz, E.: Electromagnetic fault injection: towards a fault model on a 32-bit microcontroller. In: 2013 Workshop on Fault Diagnosis and Tolerance in Cryptography, pp. 77–88. IEEE (2013)

18. Ordas, S., Guillaume-Sage, L., Tobich, K., Dutertre, J.-M., Maurine, P.: Evidence of a larger EM-induced fault model. In: Joye, M., Moradi, A. (eds.) CARDIS 2014. LNCS, vol. 8968, pp. 245–259. Springer, Cham (2015). https://doi.org/10.1007/978-3-319-16763-3_15

19. Riscure. Inspector fault injection (2020). https://getquote.riscure.com/en/inspector-fault-injection.html. Accessed 19 Aug 2022

20. Riviere, L., Najm, Z., Rauzy, P., Danger, J.L., Bringer, J., Sauvage, L.: High precision fault injections on the instruction cache of ARMv7-M architectures. In: 2015 IEEE International Symposium on Hardware Oriented Security and Trust (HOST), pp. 62–67. IEEE (2015)

21. SiFive. FE310-G000 Datasheet (2017). https://sifive.cdn.prismic.io/sifive%2Ffeb6f967-ff96-418f-9af4-a7f3b7fd1dfc_fe310-g000-ds.pdf. Accessed 19 Aug 2022

22. SiFive. FE310-G000 Manual (2019). https://static.dev.sifive.com/FE310-G000.pdf. Accessed 19 Aug 2022
23. SiFive. HiFive1 Schematics (2016). https://sifive.cdn.prismic.io/sifive%2F080cdef9-4631-4c9b-b8f5-7937fbdec8a4_hifive1-a01-schematics.pdf. Accessed 19 Aug 2022
24. Skorobogatov, S.P., Anderson, R.J.: Optical fault induction attacks. In: Kaliski, B.S., Koç, K., Paar, C. (eds.) CHES 2002. LNCS, vol. 2523, pp. 2–12. Springer, Heidelberg (2003). https://doi.org/10.1007/3-540-36400-5_2
25. Timmers, N., Mune, C.: Escalating privileges in linux using voltage fault injection. In: 2017 Workshop on Fault Diagnosis and Tolerance in Cryptography (FDTC), pp. 1–8 (2017)
26. Timmers, N., Spruyt, A., Witteman, M.: Controlling pc on ARM using fault injection. In: 2016 Workshop on Fault Diagnosis and Tolerance in Cryptography (FDTC), pp. 25–35 (2016)
27. Vasselle, A., Thiebeauld, H., Maouhoub, Q., Morisset, A., Ermeneux, S.: Laser-induced fault injection on smartphone bypassing the secure boot. IEEE Trans. Comput. **69**, 1449–1459 (2018)
28. Zussa, L., Dutertre, J.-M., Clediere, J., Tria, A.: Power supply glitch induced faults on FPGA: an in-depth analysis of the injection mechanism. In: 2013 IEEE 19th International On-Line Testing Symposium (IOLTS), pp. 110–115. IEEE (2013)

S-box Pooling: Towards More Efficient Side-Channel Security Evaluations

Yuanyuan Zhou[1,2](✉) and François-Xavier Standaert[1](✉)

[1] Crypto Group, ICTEAM Institute, UCLouvain, Louvain-la-Neuve, Belgium
{yuanyuan.zhou,fstandae}@uclouvain.be
[2] SGS Brightsight, Delft, The Netherlands

Abstract. Nowadays, profiled attacks are the standard penetration tests for security evaluations. Often the security evaluators have to perform profiled attacks on each S-box to quantify the security strength of the target symmetric cryptographic algorithm implementations more accurately. The required time to conduct such profiled attacks is very long due to the number of profiling traces (for many certification bodies, at least 1,000,000 are mandated). It is getting even more time-consuming after introducing deep learning profiled attacks. Furthermore, some certification bodies instruct up to 5,000,000 or 10,000,000 profiling traces because modern embedded secure IC products have more and more countermeasures against side-channel attacks. It is a challenge to simultaneously decrease the number of required profiling traces and the required profiling time while retaining the attack performance for profiled attacks. In this work, we propose a simple yet remarkably effective pooling approach to address this problem for security evaluations. That is, pooling over the S-boxes to build a large profiling set and perform the profiling on this large set once. Intensive experiments are conducted with this pooling approach using different profiling tools (template attack and its pooled variant, stochastic model and deep learning) on three different AES implementations (a sequential S-box software AES implementation without masking, a sequential S-box software AES implementation with first-order masking and a parallel S-box hardware AES implementation with first-order masking). The experimental results have shown that the proposed pooling approach can lead to similar attack performance while decreasing both the required number of profiling traces and the required profiling time by a factor of 8 or even 16.

1 Introduction

1.1 The Context of This Work

In Kocher's seminal work [8], Side-Channel Attacks (SCA) were proposed to extract secret keys of cryptographic algorithms implementations via the timing side channel. Since then, SCA have drawn plenties of attention in the community. On the one hand, it is extended to different side channels, *e.g.*, power consumption [9], electromagnetic radiation [13]. On the other hand, different

J. Zhou et al. (Eds.): ACNS 2022 Workshops, LNCS 13285, pp. 146–164, 2022.
https://doi.org/10.1007/978-3-031-16815-4_9

distinguishers and new approaches are also adapted to SCA. Amongst them, profiled attacks are considered the most powerful SCA after Chari *et al.* published the novel template attacks [2]. Various research works have focused on improving profiled attacks from different perspectives, *e.g.*, for efficiency purposes [3,14], or portability and robustness. It is worth noting that there are two types of profiled attacks depending on what we are profiling, either profiling the key itself or profiling some intermediate data that depends on it (*e.g.*, S-box output). Generally speaking, profiling the key directly is more studied in the asymmetric cases, profiling key-dependent values (*e.g.*, S-box output) is more studied in the symmetric cases, and key transportation is rarely studied (though applies in all cases).

Concretely, SCA are a pillar for security evaluations of information security products[1], and profiled attacks are a de facto standard penetration test for cryptographic algorithms. For security evaluations, based on the rating policy to gain so-called AVA_VAN.5 security assurance[2], such a standard profiled attacks-based penetration test typically costs 3 to 4 weeks in total for an experienced security evaluator. It is grey-box testing although the security evaluators often can get access to the detailed design information (hardware and/or software) of the implemented symmetric algorithms being evaluated. The outline of time division (in total 3 to 4 weeks) for such a standard profiled attacks-based penetration test starting from scratch is below:

– Stage 1 (1–2 weeks): Understand the target implementation and narrow down the target interval as much as possible through SPA (**S**imple **P**ower **A**nalysis)/SEMA (**S**imple **E**lectro**M**agnetic **A**nalysis) and CPA (**C**orrelation **P**ower **A**nalysis)/CEMA (**C**orrelation **E**lectro**M**agnetic **A**nalysis) (or similar techniques). It also includes the scripting time of the measurement and measurement/analysis time. It is vital to narrow down the target interval as much as possible because the sampling rate for measuring EM (Electro-Magnetic Radiation) traces can be very high (5 GHz to 10 GHz). Hence, the number of sample points within the interesting interval can be the bottleneck of the subsequent profiled attacks. Another critical step in this stage is to choose the appropriate EM signal after surface scans of the chip. It is easier when the location of the symmetric algorithm co-processor is known to the evaluators, but if it is not known, this task can become very time-consuming.
– Stage 2 (0.5–1 week): Measure at least 1,000,000 (recently some certification bodies demand 5,000,000 or up to 10,000,000 because of more and more security countermeasures in the modern secure microcontrollers) profiling traces and at least 150,000 attack traces (50,000 for each of 3 different attack keys).
– Stage 3 (1–1.5 weeks): Preprocess the measured traces (*e.g.*, align them [17]) and conduct template and deep learning profiled attacks on all S-boxes (*e.g.*, 16 in the AES case) in an attempt to recover those three different attack keys (3 sets of attack traces as mentioned in Stage 2). It also includes the reporting

---

[1] https://www.sogis.eu/uk/supporting_doc_en.html.
[2] https://www.sogis.eu/documents/cc/domains/sc/JIL-Application-of-Attack-Potential-to-Smartcards-v3-1.pdf.

time. More precisely, due to the implemented countermeasures such as jitters and random delays, often the evaluators have to re-synchronize (align) the traces step by step to get closer and closer to where the S-box operations are supposed to take place [17]. It commonly costs 1 or 2 days considering the number of traces and the number of sample points of every trace. Afterwards, the evaluators need to perform both template and deep learning attacks on each S-box one by one. Currently, the best practice is to execute profiling and attacking on each S-box one by one [4]. It naturally requires lots of time taking into account the number of sample points (normally a few thousand sample points for one S-box considering the EM traces) and the amount of the traces. With deep learning evaluations now being mandated by certification bodies, this issue further amplifies. Because usually, compared to the classical template attacks, the training of the neural networks requires much more time owing to the many hyperparameters to be tuned.

1.2 Problem to Be Addressed

To simplify the task of the evaluators, there is not much we can do considering Stage 1 and Stage 2. Also, we cannot skip or shorten the necessary re-synchronization preprocessing for Stage 3 [17]. One may argue that deep learning profiled attacks can be effective to tackle this, however, re-synchronization pre-processing makes deep learning attacks more efficient from security evaluation perspective according to [17] and the same target implementations are considered in this work. Hence, the only option left is to *find a more efficient way to decrease both the number of required profiling traces and the required profiling time while preserving the attack performance*. Somewhat surprisingly, there have been limited attempts to characterize and improve such practical challenges. In this work, therefore, we aim to study it for popular profiled distinguishers and various target implementations.

1.3 Our Contribution

The general idea of our work is S-box pooling. It is to first reconstruct a larger set of profiling traces by pooling the profiling traces corresponding to each S-box. The second step is to execute profiling only once on this new profiling traces set. Finally, it is to attack all the S-boxes to disclose all the subkeys (*e.g.*, 16 in the AES case) using the attack traces.

Our contributions in this context are twofold: First, from a data complexity point of view, the proposed S-box pooling approach can decrease the required amount of profiling traces by a factor of 8 or 16 while preserving the attack performance as shown in Table 2. In other words, the evaluators can measure eight or even sixteen times fewer profiling traces during Stage 2. The extra benefit will be reducing the preprocessing time of Stage 3 because 8 or 16 times fewer traces need to be re-synchronized. Second, from the time complexity perspective, the proposed S-box pooling approach can decrease the required profiling time by a factor of 8 or 16 (considering the AES case) while preserving the attack performance.

1.4   Related Work

We note that a recent and independent work investigated a similar technique (S-box pooling, which they denote as cross-subkey training) from a different perspective [6]. Namely, their focus is to improve the attack performances when the number of profiling traces is overly limited. They use the accuracy metric while we use the guessing entropy metric for attack performance comparison. In their work, only deep learning profiled attacks are considered so accuracy could be a suitable metric. They have observed significant accuracy improvement with cross-subkey training compared to the case where the amount of profiling traces is overly limited. It can be explained by the fact that sufficient profiling traces are available by using cross-subkey training and all 16 S-boxes are expected to leak in a very similar way because of the unmasked sequential software AES S-box implementation. Both factors lead to the better generalization of the deep learning model they are using. We relatively aim to optimize the profiling complexity when this number is sufficient. We also cover more target devices (they only target an unprotected AES software implementation: we additionally cover a masked AES software implementation and a masked hardware one) and distinguishers (they only consider one deep learning distinguisher: we additionally cover other state-of-the-art profiling tools). Overall, their conclusions are complementary to ours and show that S-box pooling can also improve attack performances when the number of profiling traces is limited.

1.5   Organization of the Paper

The rest of this paper is organized as follows. Section 2 introduces the necessary background on profiled attacks used in this work. Then, we describe our proposed S-box pooling approach and methodology in Sect. 3. Finally, Sect. 4 demonstrates the effectiveness of this pooling approach based on the intensive experimental results on three different AES implementations, for different profiling tools.

2   Background

Since Chari et al. have introduced template attacks in their pioneering work [2], profiled attacks have gradually become the commonly recognized most powerful side-channel attacks. Profiled attacks consist of two phases, i.e., the profiling phase and the attack phase. During the profiling phase, an attacker/evaluator uses a profiling device (and has control of the key or at least knows the key) to model the leakage characteristic of the target key-dependent sensitive data (typically the S-box output of symmetric algorithms) with the side-channel traces of the target implementation. The outcome of the profiling phase is the built leakage characteristic models for every possible target sensitive data value, e.g., 256 values of the AES S-box output[3]. During the attack phase, the attacker/evaluator

---

[3] That is, the identity model is used for labeling as what we do in this work. The Hamming Weight model can also be used for labeling.

uses the victim device to measure the side-channel traces of the target implementation. And then, he/she matches the traces with the previously built leakage characteristic models of the target sensitive data. For each attack trace, the adversary calculates the target sensitive data based on the known input and the guessed key unit (*e.g.*, one key byte). A score is computed for each possible guessed key unit value (256 possible values for one byte of AES key) per each trace. In the end, for each hypothesised key unit value, the scores for all the attack traces are combined using *e.g.*, the maximum likelihood method to get a combined score of that specific guessed key unit value. The combined score of each possible hypothesised key unit value is compared to find the highest one. The hypothesised key unit value with the highest score is considered the recovered key unit. This attack process is repeated for all key units to reveal the complete key.

In this work, we use four different state-of-the-art profiled attacks, namely, template attack (TA) and its pooled variant (TA$_p$), stochastic attack (SA) and deep learning attack (DL), to experimentally investigate the efficiency of our proposed pooling profiling traces approach.

2.1 Template Attack

From an information-theoretic viewpoint, TA is believed to be the most powerful type of SCA [2] when (1) the noise of side-channel traces follows the Gaussian distribution and (2) an unlimited number of traces are available. It makes use of a multivariate normal distribution to model the probability density function of each possible target sensitive data given a leakage observation, so it is parameterized as

$$p(L = l | S = s) = \frac{1}{\sqrt{(2\pi)^d |\sigma_s|}} e^{-\frac{1}{2}(l-\mu_s)^{\top} \sigma_s^{-1}(l-\mu_s)}. \tag{1}$$

In this equation, d is the number of sample points. $|\sigma_s|$ denotes the determinant of the covariance matrix and $\top$ indicates the transpose. In practice, usually, some points of interest (POIs) are detected first for dimension reduction purpose.

In the attack phase, the probability $p(L = l | K = g)$ for each key candidate is set by $p(L = l | S = s)$ given a known input of each attack trace. The classification of each key guess is then computed based on Bayes' Theorem as follows:

$$p(K = g | L = l) = \frac{p(L = l | K = g) \cdot p(K = g)}{p(L = l)}. \tag{2}$$

Based on an assumption that all attack traces are independent, to make use of all available attack traces for each key guess, a final score of each key guess is calculated as below:

$$p_g = p(g|L) = \frac{\displaystyle\prod_{m=1}^{M} p(L = l_m | K = g) \cdot p(K = g)}{\displaystyle\prod_{m=1}^{M} p(L = l_m)}. \tag{3}$$

In practice, the p_g is usually calculated using the sum of the log-posterior to avoid the potential arithmetic underflow problem. The highest p_g indicates the correct key candidate g^*. The pooled variant of the TA, next denoted TA$_p$, is proposed in [3]. It uses only a single pooled covariance matrix σ to reduce the profiling complexity, which is dominated by the estimation of the covariance. The rest is the same as normal TA.

2.2 Stochastic Model Attack

SA [14] relies on linear regression to build the leakage characteristic models of sensitive data. It assumes that the side-channel leakage observation of the target sensitive data s at time t consists of two parts $l_t(s) = h_t(s) + R_t$, where $h_t(s)$ is the key-dependent part and the latter one is a non-key dependent noise term with zero mean. Similar to TA, the profiling also contains two parts, the linear approximation $\hat{h}_t$ of h_t and the estimation of noise-related covariance matrix σ. The estimation of $\hat{h}_t$ for each time instantiation is done in a chosen suitable u-dimensional vector subspace $\mathcal{F}_{u;t}$. In this work, we choose the subspace $\mathcal{F}_9$ by utilizing the bitwise coefficients of the AES S-box output. Afterwards, d_1 POIs are chosen based on the estimated $\hat{h}_t$ to compute the covariance matrix σ. The profiling results in a Gaussian multivariate density $\hat{f} : \mathbb{R}^{d_1} \to \mathbb{R}$.

During the attack phase, we only consider the maximum likelihood principle to recover the key following [4,14]. More specifically, the correct key guess g^* is the one that maximizes:

$$p_g = p(g|L) = \prod_{m=1}^{M} \hat{f}(\mathbf{l_t}(s_{m,k}) - \hat{\mathbf{h}}_t(s_{m,g})). \tag{4}$$

In this equation, k indicates the unknown correct subkey to be revealed.

2.3 Deep Learning DPA Attack

Different from the above-mentioned classical profiled attacks, DL makes no assumption of the leakage characteristic. It exploits the features (sample points with regard to side-channel traces) to classify the labels (sensitive data in the SCA context) using neural networks (details arrive in Subsect. 4.1). The training process of neural networks (corresponds to the profiling) aims to construct a classifier function $F(.) : \mathbb{R}^d \to \mathbb{R}^{|S|}$. This function maps the input trace $\mathbf{l} \in R^d$ to the output vector $\mathbf{p} \in R^{|S|}$ of scores. During the training, for each training batch, the backpropagation method [7] is used to update the trainable parameters of the neural network model aiming at minimizing the loss, which is calculated to quantize the classification error over each training batch. In the attack phase, the built trained model (*i.e.* $F(.)$ with all the final updated trainable parameters) is used to classify each attack trace to obtain its score vector $\mathbf{p}[s_{m,g}]$. Afterwards, the final score vector of each key candidate $\mathbf{p}[g]$ is calculated using all the attack traces (similar to Eq. 3). The key candidate $g^* = \text{argmax } \mathbf{p}[g]$ is considered the right subkey.

3 Methodology

As discussed in Subsect. 1.2, the problem to be solved in this work is: to simultaneously decrease both the required number of profiling traces and the required profiling time while the performance of the online attack is essentially unchanged.

In the following, we first introduce the proposed S-box pooling approach and how it resolves this challenge for security evaluators. We then describe the methodology, which we will use to systematically investigate the soundness of the proposed pooling approach in a profiled attacks context. It includes the metric for comparing profiling performance, the metrics used for training neural networks, the knowledge of POIs assumption, the POI selection approach, and the choice of parameters for different profiled attacks in our experiments. For simplicity, we will only discuss the AES case. But the principle can be easily extended to other symmetric cryptographic algorithms.

3.1 S-box Pooling Profiled Attack

The core idea of this pooling approach is: to extract the profiling traces of each S-box and to stack the extracted profiling traces for all S-boxes in order to build a new large set of profiling traces. In theory, this approach is based on improving the signal-to-noise ratio of the profiling traces by increasing the amount of the profiling traces. Instead of directly measuring a lot of profiling traces, it is to gather enough profiling traces by extracting and stacking all available S-box calculation segments of each side-channel trace. For instance, we measure 1,600 profiling traces of the first round of AES encryption. So we have 1,600 traces for each S-box. By extracting and stacking then we build a new set of 25,600 ($=$ $16 \times 1,600$) profiling traces since there are 16 S-boxes. In the ideal situation where the S-boxes are leaking according to the same model, this strategy will lead to a reduction of the number of profiling traces by a factor of 16 (for the AES). Furthermore, the profiling time will be reduced by the same factor (In this work we only considered that the same deep learning model is used for performance comparison with and without S-box pooling.) since only a single model will have to be built. Of course, in practice, the situation may not be ideal and it is the goal of our following investigations to clarify the extent to which S-box pooling is a good trade-off for concretely relevant case studies. For this purpose, we used the following 4-step method:

1. Step 1: Measure enough profiling traces (the number of profiling traces marked as N_{ori}) being able to retrieve the AES key, perform TA, TA_p, SA and DL profiled attacks on each S-box separately to recover all 16 subkeys. Make them the baseline attack performance for later use and comparison.
2. Step 2: Determine the minimum required number of profiling traces (denoted as N_{min}) to achieve similar profiling performance as the baseline using a binary search algorithm. That is, starting from $N_{ori}/2$ profiling traces to conduct profiled attacks to compare the profiling performance with the baseline until profiling performance similar to the baseline obtained using N_{min} profiling traces.

3. Step 3: Build four new sets of profiling traces by pooling the profiling traces of each S-box based on the predefined S-box pooling ratio (labelled as PR) of 16, 8, 4 and 2 with the determined N_{min}, in which the pooling ratio of 16 means pooling $N_{min}/16$ profiling traces of each S-box to build the new set of profiling traces. Meanwhile, construct another four new sets of profiling traces without pooling the profiling traces of each S-box, *i.e.*, directly taking N_{min}/PR profiling traces from the original measurement for each S-box.

4. Step 4: For each S-box pooling ratio PR, perform TA, TA_p, SA and DL profiled attacks on each S-box using the new built set of profiling traces with pooling and using the newly constructed set of profiling traces without pooling. Note that, with pooling, we only need profiling once. While without pooling, we need profiling 16 times because we have to execute profiling for each S-box one by one following the current best practice.

Eventually, compare the profiling performance with and without pooling to the baseline.

3.2   Knowledge of POIs Assumption

There is an implicit assumption about the knowledge of the POIs to apply this pooling approach. That is, evaluators can figure out the rough timing interval of each S-box of one AES round calculation in the side-channel traces. Through SPA/CPA and SEMA/CEMA as mentioned in Stage 1 in Subsect. 1.1, this is feasible for most of the evaluated security products in the security evaluation grey-box testing context. For instance, the evaluators can vary the input length and/or the key length, perform correlation analyses on the input and output data, make use of the design information such as the location of the AES co-processor in the glue logic area or temporarily switch off some countermeasures like jitters.

Concerning the POI selection for classical profiled attacks TA, TA_p and SA, we use the popular SOST (Sum Of Squared pairwise T-differences) [4] for POI selection, since typically the masking countermeasure is implemented in the evaluated products. It does not require any secret information about the implementation, and it can be easily, efficiently computed. It is also commonly used by security evaluators for profiled attacks.

3.3   Metrics and Selection of Parameters

In order to compare the profiling complexity of different tools, information-theoretic metrics like mutual information (MI) are natural candidates [15]. Yet, it requires that all the investigated profiling methods give rise to probabilistic outcomes. In some cases, the tools we consider fairly output scores that do not directly embed such a probabilistic meaning. Therefore, we will preferably evaluate our strategy based on the guessing entropy (GE) metric [16]. Note that both metrics have the same comparative value and are thus equally good for our purposes (but computing guessing entropy curves is generally more expensive than estimating information-theoretic metrics).

Regarding the metrics used to train the neural networks, we use the Negative Log-Likelihood (NLL) loss function [1] for DL profiled attacks, because it is proved that minimizing the NLL loss is equivalent to maximizing the Perceived Information and thus to minimize the online attack complexity, thanks to the recent work [11].

For SA profiled attack, since we do not precisely know which model is followed by the target sensitive intermediate data, we choose a linear 9-element basis (the eight S-box output bits together with a constant), which is the standard choice for this distinguisher [14].

4 Experimental Results

To confirm the soundness of the proposed pooling approach in security evaluations, in this section, we apply the pooling approach to three different representatives of AES implementations, from easy to hard. That is, we consider a sequential S-box software AES without masking, a sequential S-box software AES with first-order masking [12] and a parallel S-box hardware AES with first-order masking. The first DUT (Device Under Test) in Subsect. 4.2 represents a sort of ideal case: all the S-boxes are supposed to leak in almost the same way, because all the S-boxes are executed sequentially, and no countermeasures are involved. The aim is to verify how the proposed S-box pooling approach behaves in an almost ideal leakage context. In Subsect. 4.3, the second DUT is going further: to investigate how efficient the proposed S-box pooling approach will be in a more realistic scenario. In this case, because all the S-boxes are still executed sequentially, there should be no interference regarding leakage characteristics between them. Finally, the third DUT in Subsect. 4.4 is the scenario closest to the security evaluations, because it is a hardware AES co-processor implementation with random masking, which is just the case for most modern evaluated products. In this case, multiple S-boxes are executed in parallel, so the leakage characteristic of each S-box will be affected by the others being executed at the same time. The involved random masking of each S-box will also introduce more discrepancy in the leakage characteristic given a limited amount of profiling traces. It is therefore essential to know how much profiling efficiency the evaluators can gain in this realistic scenario. We label those three DUTs as DUT1, DUT2 and DUT3 in the rest of this paper.

4.1 Common Settings

For all the three DUTs, we compare the profiling performance with and without S-box pooling using four different state-of-the-art profiled attacks, namely, TA, TA_p, SA and DL profiled DPA attacks. For each DUT, the same device is used for the profiling and attacking phase. All these four profiled attacks are implemented in Python and PyTorch version 1.7.1 with an NVIDIA GTX 1080Ti GPU. The following common settings are used for all the experiments in this work,

Table 1. MLP model details

MLP
nb_epoch = 50
batch_size_training = 32
Dense(50, activation="relu", input_shape=(nb_samples,))
BatchNormalization()
Dense(100, activation="relu")
BatchNormalization()
Dense(256, activation="softmax")
compile(loss='categorical-crossentropy', optimizer='adadelta', metrics=['accuracy'])
learning_rate_policy = ReduceLROnPlateau(optimizer, 'min', factor=0.05, verbose=True)

1. No matter whether the masking countermeasure is present or not, the target of all profiled attacks in this work is the first round S-box output of AES encryption. That is, $Sbox(p[i] \oplus k[i])$, in which p denotes a 16-byte AES input and k corresponds to a 16-byte AES key, with i the index of the S-box. Note that we focus on the common scenario where the masked randomness is not given to evaluators. Our conclusions would apply identically in the more worst-case scenario where this randomness is known for profiling. But the concrete gains would be less significant (because we expect the profiling task to be significantly simplified in that case).

2. The used DL neural network model for DL attacks is a published MLP (Multi-Layer Perceptron) [10]. The structure of this model is simple and shallow, while it showed pretty good performance for similar DUTs (similar to our DUT1 and DUT2) in that paper. It also showed great performance for all the three DUTs in our work. In addition, we use the *Adadelta* optimizer and adopt the adaptive learning rate policy *ReduceLROnPlateau* to gradually decrease the learning rate (we used the default Adadelta optimizer initial learning rate of 1.0) with a factor of 0.05 if the training stagnates. We use a batch size of 32 and 50 as the number of epochs for all the DL experiments. All the profiling traces and attack traces used for DL experiments are normalized using the *StandardScalar* function from the Scikit-learn library by removing the mean and scaling to unit variance. For all the DL experiments, we isolate 15% profiling traces as a validation set. This is due to the fact that a validation data set is critical to DL performance as it provides a way to timely detect overfitting [5]. We used the trained model with the highest validation accuracy for the DL attacks. As aforementioned, all the DL experiments utilize the NLL loss to train the model. The details of the used DL model and the hyperparameters are described in Table 1.

3. As mentioned in Step 2 of Subsect. 3.1, we need to determine the minimum number of required profiling traces N_{min} for each DUT before the performance comparison for different profiled attacks. To this end, we use DL attacks to determine the N_{min} for each DUT because only DL attacks can fully recover all the subkeys for all three DUTs as shown in the eprint version of the paper.

4.2 Setting #1: An Unmasked Sequential AES S-boxes Implementation

DUT1 is the ChipWhisperer unmasked software AES with 16 sequential S-boxes. It is expected that all the 16 S-boxes of this AES implementation leak in the same way (or with negligible discrepancy) because of the sequential implementation of the S-box layer without masking. The goal of using this DUT is to verify whether the proposed pooling approach can achieve similar profiling performance using 16 times fewer profiling traces in such an almost ideal context, which is the optimum result we are seeking in terms of decreasing the required number of profiling traces and the required profiling time.

Implementation Settings. This software AES implementation is based on an 8-bit ATXmega128D4-AU microcontroller. The 16 S-boxes are executed one by one. A set of 11,000 power consumption traces of 3,000 sample points each has been measured via the on-board ADC of the ChipWhisperer Lite board for the experiments. The CPU is running at 7.37 MHz and the sampling rate is 29.48 MHz. More specifically, 10,000 profiling traces have been measured with random key data and random input data, 1,000 attack traces have been measured with a fixed random key and random input data.

Based on the knowledge of POIs assumption discussed in Subsect. 3.2, we first identify the time intervals of each S-box in the power traces utilizing SPA and CPA. In the end, we cut 50 sample points (*e.g.* sample points 110–160 for S-box 1, 206–256 for S-box 2, ..., 1550–1600 for S-box 16) for each S-box from the originally measured power traces to build 16 new subsets of traces, where each new subset corresponds to one S-box. These 16 subsets of traces as a whole are denoted as nPR_1.

Following our designed methodology in Subsect. 3.1, we first perform TA, TA_p, SA and DL attacks on these 16 new sets of traces as the baseline of attack performance. This baseline is marked with nPR_1 in the subsequent GE results. Second, the minimum required number of profiling traces N_{min} is determined using a binary search algorithm. In this case, N_{min} is 6,700 based on the DL attack results as explained in Subsect. 4.1.

Next, we make use of the proposed pooling approach to build four new sets of profiling traces according to the PR of 16, 8, 4 and 2. They are denoted as PR_16, PR_8, PR_4 and PR_2 respectively. Also, another four sets of profiling traces without pooling are constructed by directly taking N_{min}/PR profiling traces for each S-box from the previously built trace sets nPR_1. They are denoted as nPR_16, nPR_8, nPR_4 and nPR_2 respectively. Similar to nPR_1, each of nPR_16, nPR_8, nPR_4 and nPR_2 consists of 16 subsets, and each subset corresponds to one S-box. We then conduct TA, TA_p, SA and DL attacks on PR_16, PR_8, PR_4, PR_2, nPR_16, nPR_8, nPR_4 and nPR_2.

For the sets with pooling the profiling traces PR_16, PR_8, PR_4 and PR_2, we only perform profiling once followed by attacking all 16 S-boxes to retrieve the subkeys. On the contrary, for the sets without pooling the profiling traces nPR_16, nPR_8, nPR_4 and nPR_2, we need to perform profiling 16 times, each profiling is for one S-box followed by attacking that single S-box.

Finally, we compare all the conducted profiled attacks results (with and without pooling profiling traces) with the baseline results.

Attack Results. By comparing the aforementioned profiled attacks results with the baseline GE results as shown in Fig. 1, it is demonstrated that using S-box pooling can decrease both the number of profiling traces and profiling time by a factor of 16 considering the DL attack results. For readability, here we only present the results for 3 different sets, *i.e.*, the baseline GE results (nPR_1, 6,700 profiling traces), the GE results with pooling with PR of 16 (PR_16, 6,700 = 16 × 418 profiling traces) and the GE results without pooling with PR of 16 (nPR_16, 418 profiling traces). The full comparison is given in the eprint version of the paper.

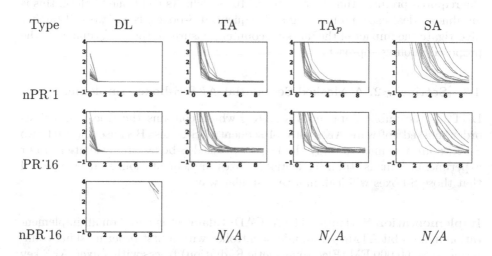

Fig. 1. DUT1 guessing entropy results, X-axis: number of attack traces, Y-axis: guessing entropy.

Considering the GE results of different profiled attacks on this DUT in the same setting (the same PR, with pooling or not), it is worth noting that DL shows the best attack performance. It suggests that the DL attack has a better generalization for this DUT. TA and its variant TA_p show similar but slightly worse attack performance while SA shows the worst attack performance for this DUT, which is in line with the observations in [4][4]. For the nPR_16 setting, the GE results of TA, TA_p and SA attacks are not available due to very few profiling

---

[4] It is out of scope because the goal of this work is to verify the efficacy of the proposed pooling approach in terms of decreasing both the required number of profiling traces and the required profiling time.

traces for each class of S-box output, which leads to singular results during the profiling.

More interestingly, this trend is the same when we consider the impact of pooling profiling traces. It can be observed that the DL attack performance of the PR_16 case using pooling is already comparable to the baseline DL attack performance, while the DL attack performance of the nPR_16 case without using pooling is way worse than the baseline DL attack performance. The DL attack performance of the PR_8 case using pooling already outperforms the baseline DL attack performance. Hence, these GE results show that pooling can decrease the required number of profiling traces by a factor of 16 without reducing the attack performance. This is the optimal result one can achieve and it most likely holds because all 16 S-boxes are leaking in almost the same way. From a time complexity point of view, using a pooling ratio of 16 means using the same total amount of profiling traces as the baseline case, while only profiling once in the pooling case and profiling 16 times in the baseline case. It results in decreasing the required profiling time by a factor of 16 as well. As mentioned before, this is an almost ideal case: no masking and sequential S-boxes. Next, we will further investigate the impact of the masking countermeasure on the performance of the proposed pooling approach.

4.3   Setting #2: A Masked Sequential AES S-boxes Implementation

DUT2 is the public data set ASCADv1, which contains the traces of a first-order masked software AES with 14 sequential S-boxes. Because the first two S-boxes are not masked, only the last 14 masked S-boxes are evaluated in our experiments. This is still a sequential S-boxes implementation, so it is expected that those S-boxes will leak in a very similar way.

Implementation Settings. The ASCADv1 data set is based on an implementation in an 8-bit ATMega8515 microcontroller with a first-order masking countermeasure. 60,000 EM (Electromagnetic Radiation) traces with a fixed AES key were acquired using an EM coil at a sampling rate of 2 GHz, in which 50,000 are the profiling traces and the remaining 10,000 traces are the attack traces. Each trace consists of 100,000 sample points.

Based on the knowledge of POIs assumption, we narrowed down the time intervals of each S-box in the EM traces. In the end, 700 sample points (*e.g.*, sample points 45400–46100 for S-box 3, 32910–33610 for S-box 4, ..., 18330–19030 for S-box 16) for each S-box were cut out from the originally acquired EM traces to build 14 new subsets of traces. These 14 subsets of traces as a whole are denoted as nPR_1. TA, TA_p, SA and DL attacks are then conducted on nPR_1 as the baseline of attack performance. The minimum required number of profiling traces N_{min} of 37,000 was found based on the DL attack results.

We further constructed four new sets of profiling traces according to the PR of 14, 7, 4 and 2. They are denoted as PR_14, PR_7, PR_4 and PR_2 respectively. In addition, their counterparts without S-box pooling, *i.e.*, nPR_14,

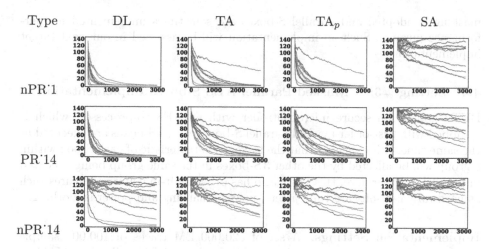

Fig. 2. DUT2 guessing entropy results, X-axis: number of attack traces, Y-axis: guessing entropy.

nPR_7, nPR_4 and nPR_2 were constructed as well. TA, TA$_p$, SA and DL attacks were then performed on these 8 sets of traces and the results are compared with the baseline.

Attack Results. Figure 2 displays our results. For the same reason as in the previous case, only the results of nPR_1 (37,000 profiling traces), PR_14 (37,000 = 14×2,642 profiling traces) and nPR_14 (2,642 profiling traces) are shown here, our eprint version of the paper provides the full results. Again, the DL attack results suggest that using pooling can decrease both the number of profiling traces and profiling time by a factor of 14.

Our observations regarding the different performances of different profiles distinguishers are similar to the ones made for DUT1. Namely, the DL attack shows slightly better results than TA and its variant TA$_p$, while SA shows the worst performance.

The same trend is also observed with regard to the impact of pooling profiling traces: PR_14 already gives slightly better results than the baseline nPR_1 considering the DL attacks. The results without using pooling are significantly worse than the baseline ones. In short, from both the data complexity and time complexity viewpoints, using pooling can decrease the required number of profiling traces and required profiling time by a factor of 14, which is the optimal result. Most likely all those 14 masked S-boxes leak in a very similar way.

In this sequential masked S-boxes case, using pooling also leads to optimal attack performance. It further confirms that S-box pooling can be used for protected implementations in security evaluations. To further assess the impact of other implementation factors on the performance of the pooling approach, a very realistic scenario is finally brought into our scope. Namely, many modern secure microcontrollers have a dedicated AES co-processor, in which random masking is adopted and parallel S-boxes are sometimes implemented for performance purpose. Such an implementation will be assessed in our next target implementation.

4.4   Setting #3: A Masked Parallel AES S-boxes Implementation

DUT3 is a 90 nm secure microcontroller with an AES co-processor, which is equipped with first-order masked parallel S-boxes, *i.e.*, 4 S-boxes are executed at the same time. It is expected that the leakage characteristic of each S-box within a group will be affected by the other 3 S-boxes in the same group being executed in parallel. Furthermore, this DUT also has other built-in countermeasures such as hardware and software time jitters, power balancing and power smoothing.

Implementation Settings. A set of 520,000 EM traces of 100,000 sample points each has been measured via an SGS Brightsight EM coil using a LeCroy Waverunner 620Zi oscilloscope at a sampling rate of 10 GHz. The coil is located on top of the AES co-processor from the back side of the chip. The operating frequency of the AES co-processor is 32 MHz with variable internal clock enables. 480,000 profiling traces have been measured with random key data and random input data. 40,000 attack traces have been measured with a fixed random key and random input data.

In accordance with the knowledge of POIs assumption, using SPA/CPA and SEMA techniques with the knowledge of the AES co-processor location, the time intervals of each group of 4 parallel S-boxes were figured out in the EM traces. For instance, different key lengths and different input lengths were used to execute the AES encryption to observe the difference they caused in the power and EM traces. Different numbers of AES rounds could be distinguished in the EM traces and each round contains 4 groups of EM peaks, with each group corresponding to the execution of 4 parallel S-boxes. It has to be mentioned that multiple alignments steps had to be done because the measured EM traces were heavily misaligned. We used the same re-synchronization method as in [17], which exploits correlation to align each group of EM peaks in the traces. It is a 3-step procedure.

1. Manually select a searching interval S that contains the operation to be aligned among all the traces.
2. Manually choose a smaller reference interval R_{T_i} specific to each trace T_i.
3. Within the whole interval S of each trace, search for the segment to be aligned by computing the Pearson's correlation between each segment (the same length as R_{T_i}) and the reference feature R_{T_i}. The right segment is the one showing the highest correlation within the whole interval S. The trace is abandoned if the highest correlation is lower than a pre-defined threshold chosen by the evaluator.

During the measurement campaign, it was not possible to trigger the oscilloscope close to the first AES round. Therefore, the EM traces were aligned several times to get close to the first AES round step by step, followed by more local alignments within the first AES round because there are 4 groups of EM peaks to be aligned one by one. Targeting different time intervals (for both the searching interval and reference interval), we applied this alignment method multiple times to the EM traces. In general, we chose new intervals when the misalignment was getting larger, and we repeated this process until the target interval was well aligned. In this way, we can gradually align each group of EM peaks corresponding to 4 parallel S-boxes being executed.

After all the alignments, 500 sample points for each group of 4 parallel S-boxes were kept from the original EM traces to build 16 new subsets of traces and as a whole, they are marked as nPR_1. We used each segment 4 times, targeting each S-box once. TA, TA_p, SA and DL attacks were then conducted on nPR_1 as the baseline of attack performance. The minimum required number of profiling traces N_{min} of 410,000 was further determined based on the DL attack results.

Similar to previous DUTs, we prepared eight new sets of profiling traces with or without pooling the profiling traces, *i.e.*, PR_16, PR_8, PR_4 and PR_2 and nPR_16, nPR_8, nPR_4 and nPR_2. We performed TA, TA_p, SA and DL attacks on these 8 sets of traces and compared the results with the baseline.

Attack Results. The comparison of results is shown in Fig. 3. Once again, we only present the results of nPR_1 (410,000 profiling traces), PR_16 (410,000 = 16 × 25,625 profiling traces), PR_8 (820,000 = 16 × 51,250 profiling traces) and nPR_8 (51,250 profiling traces). The full results are provided in the eprint

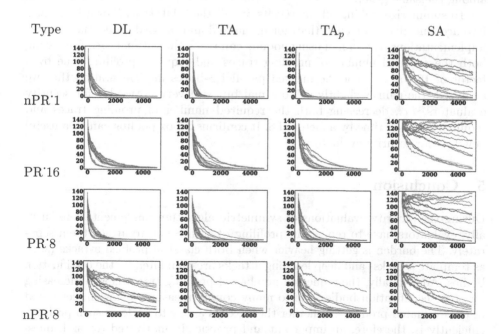

Fig. 3. DUT3 guessing entropy results, X-axis: number of attack traces, Y-axis: guessing entropy.

Table 2. Summary of the experiments of 3 DUTs

	PR	N_{ori}	N_{min}	Samples	Implementation	Data complexity gain	Time complexity gain
DUT1	16/8/4/2	10,000	6,700	50	SW sequential	16 (*optimal*)	16 (*optimal*)
DUT2	14/7/4/2	50,000	37,000	700	Masked SW sequential	14 (*optimal*)	14 (*optimal*)
DUT3	16/8/4/2	480,000	410,000	500	Masked HW parallel	$\geqslant 8$ (*sub-optimal*)	$\geqslant 8$ (*sub-optimal*)

version of the paper. This time the DL attack results demonstrate that using pooling can decrease both the number of profiling traces and profiling time by a factor of at least 8.

Different from the previous two DUTs, the TA and its variant TA_p show better results than DL for all the 5 sets of profiling traces without pooling, *i.e.* nPR_16, nPR_8, nPR_4, nPR_2 and the baseline nPR_1. The other way around is observed if the proposed S-box pooling approach is adopted: DL then slightly outperforms TA and TA_p. Focusing on the pooling cases and the DL results, using PR of 16 achieves slightly worse results compared to the baseline, while using PR of 8 leads to better results than the baseline. These observations put forward that even when evaluating a more challenging (and therefore more practically relevant) hardware implementation with masking, the S-box pooling approach remains effective. It does not lead to an optimal factor gain of 16 for the data and time complexity but still reduces these complexities to a significant factor 8. This sub-optimal gain is most likely caused by the parallel execution of 4 S-boxes. The leakage model of a single S-box is interfered by other 3 S-boxes among the same group.

To summarize, taking all the results for all the 3 DUTs as shown in Table 2 into account, it is concluded that, for unmasked and masked sequential S-boxes implementations, the gain of using pooling can reach the optimal, *i.e.*, decreasing both the required number of profiling traces and required profiling time by a factor of 16 (or 14). For the masked parallel S-boxes implementation that we analyzed, the gain is slightly sub-optimal but still very noticeable for security evaluators, *i.e.*, decreasing both the required number of profiling traces and required profiling time by a factor of 8. It confirms S-box pooling can be a useful new tool for security evaluators.

5   Conclusion

During the security evaluations of symmetric algorithm implementations, usually, evaluators have to repeat the profiling of each S-box to attack them separately. The burden is getting heavier when both classical profiled attacks (such as template attacks) and deep learning attacks are mandated by the certification bodies. Additionally, the requested number of profiling traces is also increasing for some certification bodies due to many countermeasures being implemented in the evaluated products. Whether there exists a way to perform such profiling efficiently is, therefore, an important and practically motivated research question. To this end, the community so far mostly focused its efforts on improving the attack performance targeting one S-box. In this work, we analyze the complementary approach of trying to decrease the profiling (data and time) complexity thanks to S-box pooling.

Intensive experiments on three different AES implementations were performed with 108 different configurations. The results demonstrate that, for representative unmasked software sequential S-boxes implementation and the masked software sequential S-boxes implementation, using this S-box pooling approach can decrease both the required number of profiling traces and required profiling time by a factor of 16 (or 14), which corresponds to the optimal gain. For the masked hardware parallel S-boxes implementation that we analyzed, the gain is still sub-optimal in terms of data complexity and time complexity. Nevertheless, we can decrease both the required number of profiling traces and required profiling time at least by a factor of 8 in this practically relevant setting. We used only the first round S-box computations for simplicity, indeed this S-box pooling can be extended to all S-box computations of all AES rounds. The goal of the paper is to show that in some practically-relevant contexts, S-box pooling can lead to significant gains but there are admittedly implementations for which it may not be applicable, *e.g.*, if the S-boxes leak differently.

We believe these results show that the efficient exploitation of profiling measurements, for example, thanks to S-box pooling, can be a useful addition to the evaluators' toolbox. On the one hand, it is easy to adopt and integrate into existing toolchains. On the other hand, there are contexts in which this simple optimization can lead to significant gains (remembering that concretely, a factor 16 is highly relevant for evaluation tasks that can take days).

Acknowledgements. We would like to express our gratitude to anonymous reviewers for their insightful comments. François-Xavier Standaert is a senior research associate of the Belgian Fund for Scientific Research (F.R.S.-FNRS). This work has been funded in parts by the ERC project SWORD (Grant Number 724725).

References

1. Cagli, E., Dumas, C., Prouff, E.: Convolutional neural networks with data augmentation against jitter-based countermeasures. In: Fischer, W., Homma, N. (eds.) CHES 2017. LNCS, vol. 10529, pp. 45–68. Springer, Cham (2017). https://doi.org/10.1007/978-3-319-66787-4_3
2. Chari, S., Rao, J.R., Rohatgi, P.: Template attacks. In: Kaliski, B.S., Koç, K., Paar, C. (eds.) CHES 2002. LNCS, vol. 2523, pp. 13–28. Springer, Heidelberg (2003). https://doi.org/10.1007/3-540-36400-5_3
3. Choudary, O., Kuhn, M.G.: Efficient template attacks. In: Francillon, A., Rohatgi, P. (eds.) CARDIS 2013. LNCS, vol. 8419, pp. 253–270. Springer, Cham (2014). https://doi.org/10.1007/978-3-319-08302-5_17
4. Gierlichs, B., Lemke-Rust, K., Paar, C.: Templates vs. stochastic methods. In: Goubin, L., Matsui, M. (eds.) CHES 2006. LNCS, vol. 4249, pp. 15–29. Springer, Heidelberg (2006). https://doi.org/10.1007/11894063_2
5. Guyon, I.: A scaling law for the validation-set training-set size ratio. AT & T Bell Laboratories (1997)

6. Hu, F., Wang, H., Wang, J.: Cross-subkey deep-learning side-channel analysis. Cryptology ePrint Archive, Report 2021/1328 (2021). https://ia.cr/2021/1328

7. Kelley, H.J.: Gradient theory of optimal flight paths. ARS J. **30**(10), 947–954 (1960)

8. Kocher, P.C.: Timing attacks on implementations of Diffie-Hellman, RSA, DSS, and other systems. In: Koblitz, N. (ed.) CRYPTO 1996. LNCS, vol. 1109, pp. 104–113. Springer, Heidelberg (1996). https://doi.org/10.1007/3-540-68697-5_9

9. Kocher, P., Jaffe, J., Jun, B.: Differential power analysis. In: Wiener, M. (ed.) CRYPTO 1999. LNCS, vol. 1666, pp. 388–397. Springer, Heidelberg (1999). https://doi.org/10.1007/3-540-48405-1_25

10. Maghrebi, H.: Deep learning based side-channel attack: a new profiling methodology based on multi-label classification. IACR Cryptol. ePrint Arch. **2020**, 436 (2020). https://eprint.iacr.org/2020/436

11. Masure, L., Dumas, C., Prouff, E.: A comprehensive study of deep learning for side-channel analysis. IACR Trans. Cryptogr. Hardw. Embed. Syst. **2020**(1), 348–375 (2020). https://doi.org/10.13154/tches.v2020.i1.348-375

12. Prouff, E., Strullu, R., Benadjila, R., Cagli, E., Dumas, C.: Study of deep learning techniques for side-channel analysis and introduction to ASCAD database. IACR Cryptol. ePrint Arch. 53 (2018). http://eprint.iacr.org/2018/053

13. Quisquater, J.-J., Samyde, D.: ElectroMagnetic Analysis (EMA): measures and counter-measures for smart cards. In: Attali, I., Jensen, T. (eds.) E-smart 2001. LNCS, vol. 2140, pp. 200–210. Springer, Heidelberg (2001). https://doi.org/10.1007/3-540-45418-7_17

14. Schindler, W., Lemke, K., Paar, C.: A stochastic model for differential side channel cryptanalysis. In: Rao, J.R., Sunar, B. (eds.) CHES 2005. LNCS, vol. 3659, pp. 30–46. Springer, Heidelberg (2005). https://doi.org/10.1007/11545262_3

15. Standaert, F.-X., Koeune, F., Schindler, W.: How to compare profiled side-channel attacks? In: Abdalla, M., Pointcheval, D., Fouque, P.-A., Vergnaud, D. (eds.) ACNS 2009. LNCS, vol. 5536, pp. 485–498. Springer, Heidelberg (2009). https://doi.org/10.1007/978-3-642-01957-9_30

16. Standaert, F.-X., Malkin, T.G., Yung, M.: A unified framework for the analysis of side-channel key recovery attacks. In: Joux, A. (ed.) EUROCRYPT 2009. LNCS, vol. 5479, pp. 443–461. Springer, Heidelberg (2009). https://doi.org/10.1007/978-3-642-01001-9_26

17. Zhou, Y., Standaert, F.-X.: Deep learning mitigates but does not annihilate the need of aligned traces and a generalized ResNet model for side-channel attacks. J. Cryptogr. Eng. **10**(1), 85–95 (2019). https://doi.org/10.1007/s13389-019-00209-3

Deep Learning-Based Side-Channel Analysis Against AES Inner Rounds

Sudharshan Swaminathan[1], Łukasz Chmielewski[2,3]([✉]), Guilherme Perin[1], and Stjepan Picek[1]

[1] Delft University of Technology, Delft, The Netherlands
[2] Radboud University Nijmegen, Nijmegen, The Netherlands
[3] Riscure, Delft, The Netherlands
lukchmiel@gmail.com

Abstract. Side-channel attacks (SCA) focus on vulnerabilities caused by insecure implementations and exploit them to deduce useful information about the data being processed or the data itself through leakages obtained from the device. There have been many studies exploiting these leakages, and most of the state-of-the-art attacks have been shown to work on AES implementations. The methodology is usually based on exploiting leakages for the outer rounds, i.e., the first and the last round. In some cases, due to partial countermeasures or the nature of the device itself, it might not be possible to attack the outer rounds. In this case, the attacker needs to resort to attacking the inner rounds.

This work provides a generalization for inner round side-channel attacks on AES and experimentally validates it with non-profiled and profiled attacks. We *formulate the computation of the hypothesis values of any byte in the intermediate rounds*. The more inner the AES round is, the higher is the attack complexity in terms of the number of bits to be guessed for the hypothesis. We discuss the main limitations for obtaining predictions in inner rounds and, in particular, we compare the performance of Correlation Power Analysis (CPA) against deep learning-based profiled side-channel attacks (DL-SCA). We show that because trained deep learning models require fewer traces in the attack phase, they also have fewer complexity limitations to attack inner AES rounds than non-profiled attacks such as CPA. This paper is the first to propose deep learning-based profiled attacks on inner rounds of AES to the best of our knowledge.

1 Introduction

In the past twenty years, much academic and industrial research provided methods to attack and protect the Advanced Encryption Standard (AES) implementations. Among these attacks, side-channel analysis (SCA) targets unintentional leakages from software and hardware implementations. The aim can be twofold: from the designer's perspective (the defensive side), a side-channel analysis indicates a potential source of leakages in the implemented algorithm. Additionally,

J. Zhou et al. (Eds.): ACNS 2022 Workshops, LNCS 13285, pp. 165–182, 2022.
https://doi.org/10.1007/978-3-031-16815-4_10

the analysis provides important directions to design countermeasures to mitigate such attacks. On the other hand, an evaluator (offensive side) is interested in verifying the worst-case security to advise the manufacturer or certify the implementation against specific types of SCAs and applications. Besides different perspectives, one must consider different types of side-channel attacks. One common division is into non-profiled and profiled attacks. New forms of non-profiled and profiled SCA encounter in AES a suitable target to validate proposed methods. In this sense, most works concentrate on attacking the first and last AES (encryption or decryption) rounds, leaving the attacks on inner rounds out of scope.

The reason stems from the attack complexities and assumptions: attacking the outer rounds requires a minimal effort in terms of key guessing and the number of measurements. On the other hand, several design reasons could limit a side-channel attack application on the outer (i.e., first and last) rounds. Countermeasures (as they add costs overheads to the design) could be applied only to these outer rounds, leaving inner rounds unprotected. In this case, the only side-channel attack mitigations are the inherent sources of noise and misalignments. Additionally, it is common to implement several AES rounds within a single clock cycle for faster encryption or decryption processes, which is a highly adopted mechanism for hardware-based implementations. This limits the leakages of the AES intermediate bytes that do not coincide with the clock cycles edges.

The past (and not very recent) literature already proposed various differential power analysis (DPA) attacks on inner AES rounds. In [11], the authors described a DPA attack on round 2, requiring the same attack complexity (8 bits) as attacking round 1 and with an overhead in the required number of measurements due to the chosen-input nature of the attack. Lu et al. investigated how many rounds of an AES implementation should be protected to be secure against power analysis attacks [13]. They provided two main conclusions: attacking the inner rounds of AES is possible at the cost of increasing the data complexity, and any attack requiring a DPA on more than 32 bits is considered infeasible.

In this work, we extend the formulation of [13] and provide a theoretical generalization of such an attack on the inner rounds of AES-128. This generalization provides the designers with a comprehensive understanding of the complexity of the attack at each round and the threat profile that the attacker needs to have to make a successful attack. We assume that inner rounds are not protected by specific countermeasures (e.g., first-order masking or multiple rounds within a single clock cycle) but only by inherent noise and misalignment. Under this assumption, we run both non-profiled attacks (CPA) and profiled attacks (deep learning-based SCA) and show that deep learning-based SCA reaches significantly better attack performance and succeeds in scenarios where CPA does not indicate a successful key recovery.

Our Contributions.

1. Based on related works, we first analyze the computation of the hypothesis for any byte in the intermediate rounds for AES-128 in the encryption mode

with some predefined conditions in mind and use the same to determine the relative difficulty of such attacks. Due to the non-linear substitutions in each AES round, targeting any intermediate byte after n S-boxes requires an attack complexity of $8 \times n$ bits. The attack complexity in terms of the number of bits represents the bit-length of guessed hypothesis. This introduces significant time and memory overheads to mount such a complex attack.

2. To make our analysis more realistic, we consider potential countermeasures (such as Gaussian noise and misalignment) to power traces collected from an unprotected AES.

3. The training phase of a deep learning-based profiled attack on inner rounds is not affected by the increased attack complexity. Consequently, we show that the attack phase from the deep learning-based approach is a considerable improvement over limitations faced by non-profiled CPA due to the added countermeasures, especially when the attack complexity is higher than 16 bits. In this case, the attacker faces strong time and memory limitations in processing attack traces.

4. In scenarios when CPA cannot succeed due to implicit countermeasures (which is a practical case shown in this paper on encryption round 3), a convolutional neural network-based profiled attack can easily recover the key even with a very limited number of attack traces.

2 Preliminaries

2.1 Correlation Power Analysis (CPA)

CPA is a statistical method used to correlate the side-channel traces with the observed leakage [3]. There, an attacker has to perform numerous encryptions/decryptions and collect the traces. A hypothesis for each key guess can then be obtained by using a leakage model. CPA uses Pearson Correlation for differentiating between the modeled and the actual power traces.

2.2 Deep Learning Methodologies

Deep learning-based SCA (DL-SCA) provides an improvement over other profiled attacks such as template attacks [5] in terms of efforts during pre-processing of traces and effectiveness of the attack. Deep learning methodologies take the traces along with their labels in the profiling phase across the selected data points in time, run them through the defined model, and determine the weights according to the defined criteria such as high accuracy and minimal loss. The labels here depend on the leakage function and the key hypotheses. The input layer of the DL model contains the measurements of the traces across the data points in time, and the output layer contains output nodes for each of the classes defined by the leakage model. These trained weights are then used in the attack phase to determine the probabilities of each of the classes given by the intermediate value corresponding to each key guess. The key guess having the highest probability values would indicate the most likely secret key.

In this work, we use convolutional neural networks (CNNs) to conduct deep learning-based SCA. We employ CNN with VGG-like architecture as it is a prominent model used for SCA, see, e.g., [1,10]. The original model was developed for image classification, where the input signal has multiple input dimensions starting from 2. As SCA has only one spatial dimension considering its data points in time, the main difference that VGG-like architectures introduce is how it handles 1-dimension signal on each of its convolution and pooling operations.

2.3 Attack Evaluation Methodology

The most commonly used metric for evaluating the performance of a side-channel attack is key rank. We use the same for evaluating the performance of the attacks carried out in this work. An average key rank (denoted guessing entropy) represents the average number of keys the attacker needs to go through during the attack to reveal the actual key successfully [20]. As seen in the above sections, we obtain a posterior distribution of probabilities for each of our defined classes as the output of the attacks. The key guess contributing the most to the highest probable predicted class across the attack traces is predicted to be the key byte being used. Consequently, the output vector that is obtained during the attack is of the form $\mathbf{k} = [k_0, k_1, k_2, ..., k_{|K|-1}]$, where $|K|$ is the size of the keyspace. These key guesses contained in the vector $\mathbf{k}$ are then ordered in the decreasing order of probability, that is, k_0 is the most probable key guess, also known as the best guess, and $k_{|K|-1}$ is the least probable key guess. We then check the position at which the actual key byte resides in this ordered list, and this position of the actual key byte is termed the key rank.

3 Related Work

The first and the last rounds, being dependent on a relatively small fraction of the key, are more vulnerable and are therefore primary targets of side-channel attacks. As we go into the inner rounds, every intermediate byte would depend on an increasing number of key bytes due to the diffusion properties of AES, thereby increasing the data complexity of the attack. The trade-off, therefore, focuses on protecting the first and the last rounds and leaving other intermediate rounds unprotected or with very simple countermeasures [7,21]. In some cases of hardware implementation, it is also possible that multiple rounds are executed within one clock cycle. This would result in the inner rounds being exposed, i.e., it would then be possible to capture traces corresponding to the inner rounds. In such cases, the hypothesis built for the first round would not correlate to the captured traces, and the attack would not work. *Such cases, along with the hindrance caused by the partial countermeasures, raise the need to look into attacks on unprotected or even partially protected inner rounds and understand the resources that the attacker would need to launch such attacks.*

While Jaffe et al. already described a DPA attack after the SubBytes of round 2 [11], Lu et al. answered an important question about how many rounds of an AES implementation should be protected for it to be secure against power analysis attacks [13]. To this end, they show that it is possible to attack the inner rounds of AES at the cost of increasing the data complexity of the attack. They define the feasibility of an attack by the number of bits required to launch the DPA/CPA and set this threshold to 32 bits. Consequently, any DPA attack requiring more than 32 bits is considered infeasible and, as such, not investigated.

We extend on the same and formulate a generalization of such an attack on the inner rounds. We also analyze the feasibility of such generalization.

Many approaches have been developed in SCA, from statistical methods such as CPA/DPA to template attacks and machine learning-based approaches. While the former has been studied extensively, attacks based on profiling involving machine learning and deep learning are still developing. Already studies appearing one decade ago showed that machine learning could be used to mount successful side-channel attacks that are also more effective than template attacks [8,9]. Machine learning methods such as SVM have also been used to defeat masked implementations, as shown by Lerman et al. [12]. Extending on the same, Gilmore et al. showed that neural networks could also be used to tackle the masking countermeasure and are more effective than the other machine learning-based approaches [6]. However, these implementations depend on a crucial assumption that the random masks are available to the attacker during the profiling phase, which as mentioned by [6] is an impractical assumption. As discussed before, most of the practical and efficient countermeasure implementations involve only the outer rounds [7,21]. Therefore, we can bypass these countermeasures if we attack the inner rounds directly, which would also not necessitate having the random masks used by the target implementation.

Deep learning (more precisely, convolutional neural networks and multilayer perceptrons) has been successfully used to attack AES implementations, as first shown by Maghrebi et al. [15]. Next, Cagli et al. showed that convolutional neural networks could break implementations protected with the jitter countermeasure, especially if the attack is augmented with synthetic data obtained from data augmentation techniques [4]. Kim et al. discussed the VGG-like architecture that showed good attack performance for several datasets, where some were using masking or hiding countermeasures [10]. Benadjila et al. introduced the ASCAD dataset, which is a dataset used in most of the SCA studies today, and also investigated the hyperparameter tuning to find architectures leading to successful attacks [1]. Picek et al. showed that metrics commonly indicating the performance of machine learning algorithms are not appropriate to assess the SCA performance [17]. Zaid et al. proposed a methodology to design convolutional neural network architectures that have a small number of trainable parameters and that result in efficient attacks [24]. Wouters et al. further discussed the methodology perspective, providing even smaller neural network architectures that perform well [23]. Perin et al. explored how deep learning-based SCA generalized to previously unseen examples and showed that ensembles of random neural networks could outperform even state-of-the-art neural network architectures [16]. Rijsdijk et al. introduced the reinforcement learning approach for designing neural networks that perform well and are as small as possible [18].

These studies represent only a fraction of works exploring machine learning-based side-channel attacks, but to the best of our knowledge, none of those works consider attacking inner rounds of AES.

4   First-Order Non-profiled Attacks on AES Inner Rounds

Lu et al. [13] give five general principles for attacking bytes in the inner rounds of AES using first and second-order DPA. These principles consider the attack to be feasible as long as the attack is on less than 32 bits. We focus on the following two principles listed by [13] that are based on the first-order DPA:

1. Attacking from input: any intermediate byte before the MixColumns operation of round 3 can be exploited by conducting a first-order DPA attack and will depend on the part of the plaintext bytes being fixed.
2. Attacking from the output: any intermediate byte resulting from the AddRoundKey operation of round 7 can be exploited to conduct a first-order DPA attack and will depend on some of the ciphertext bytes being fixed. **Note:** Although Lu et al. [13] consider any byte after the AddRoundKey operation of round 7, we noticed that it was also possible to attack from output before the AddRoundKey of round 7 while considering single bit DPA attacks.

In this section, we briefly analyze these attacks and comment on possible extensions or lack of them.

4.1   Notations

Before describing the attacks, we present the notations that we use in this section.

- Plaintext bytes are denoted by p_i, where i is the index of the byte. Similarly, ciphertext bytes are denoted by c_i.
- The output byte of an S-box in any round is denoted by v_i^n, where i is the index of the byte and n indicates the round. For example, v_0^1 is the first byte obtained after the S-box in round 1. Similarly, bytes after the MixColumns operation are denoted using u_i^n, while the output bytes of a round, i.e., bytes after the AddRoundKey are denoted by w_i^n.
- The key bytes are denoted by k_i^n and the round key they belong to is denoted by K_n. The initial key would then be $\{k_0^0, k_1^0, ..., k_{15}^0\} \in K_0$, while the last round key would be $\{k_0^{10}, k_1^{10}, ..., k_{15}^{10}\} \in K_{10}$
- S-box in round n is denoted as S_n and we denote its application on an input byte u as $S_n(u)$. The inverse of the S-box is denoted as S_n^{-1}.
- Terms such as γ, δ, θ are used to denote 8-bit constants.

4.2   On the Attack Feasibility After the S-box at Rounds 2, 3, and 4

The attack on rounds 2 and 3 are presented in Lu et al. [13], and due to space constraints, we omit them here. Here, we consider attacking a byte immediately after the S-box in round 4 (S_4). Let this be the first byte v_0^4. Let w_0^3 denote a byte obtained after round 3 and u_0^3 a byte after the MixColumns of round 3. Then with $k_0^3 \in K_3$, we have:

$$v_0^4 = S_4(w_0^3) \text{ and } w_0^3 = u_0^3 \oplus k_0^3. \tag{1}$$

The byte u_0^3 results from MixColumns in round 3 and can be written as:

$$u_0^3 = 02 * v_0^3 \oplus 03 * v_5^3 \oplus 01 * v_{10}^3 \oplus 01 * v_{15}^3, \tag{2}$$

where $(v_0^3, v_5^3, v_{10}^3, v_{15}^3)$ are bytes resulting from the S-box operation of this same round 3. Consider $\theta = 03 * v_5^3 \oplus 01 * v_{10}^3 \oplus 01 * v_{15}^3 \oplus k_0^3$. Now, using Eq. (2) and deriving the value of v_0^3 from[1]

$$v_0^3 = S_3(02 * S_2(02 * S_1(p_0 \oplus k_0^0) \oplus \delta) \oplus \gamma), \tag{3}$$

we can rewrite the byte v_0^4 as:

$$v_0^4 = S_4(02 * S_3(02 * S_2(02 * S_1(p_0 \oplus k_0^0) \oplus \delta) \oplus \gamma) \oplus \theta). \tag{4}$$

Here, θ depends on $(v_5^3, v_{10}^3, v_{15}^3)$. From Eq. (3), it can be observed that each of these bytes depend on the set (δ, γ, p_i), where p_i is some plaintext byte not included in either δ or γ. Combining the plaintext bytes that this set depends on, it can be concluded that $(v_5^3, v_{10}^3, v_{15}^3)$ depend on 16 bytes of plaintext each. Thus, θ effectively depends on all 16 plaintext bytes. This way, implementing an attack to recover k_0^0 by predicting v_0^4 requires fixing the 16 plaintexts for each side-channel measurement. Also, we would have to guess the variables of the set $(k_0^0, \delta, \gamma, \theta)$ in this case, that is, the attack would have to guess 32 bits in order to find one key byte. Therefore, this turns this statistical DPA attack infeasible in practice. On the other hand, a profiled attack can still vary k_0^0 (and keeping all remaining key bytes from K_0 fixed), which allows collecting profiling traces with at most 256 different intermediate values for v_0^4. Although the profiling phase allows larger variability, the attack phase is still restricted to a single plaintext-key combination.

4.3   Attacking a Byte Before AddRoundKey at Round 7

Since this attack is not presented by Lu et al. [13], we list it here. We formulate an attack on round 7 from the output in encryption mode, which would require an adaptive chosen-ciphertext attack. The process is similar to that noticed in the case of encryption. Attacking the byte u_0^7 we have:

$$u_0^7 = k_0^7 \oplus S_8^{-1}(v_0^8), \tag{5}$$

---

[1] Equation (3) is derived from: $v_0^3 = S_3(02 * S_2(u_0 \oplus k_0^1) \oplus \gamma) \implies v = S_3(02 * S_2(02 * v_0^1 \oplus \delta) \oplus \gamma)$.

where v_0^8 is a byte from after S_8 and $k_0^7 \in K_7$. The byte v_0^8 affects 4 bytes of the resultant state after the MixColumns of round 8.

The value v_0^8 can be expressed as follows:

$$v_0^8 = 0e * u_0^8 \oplus 0b * u_1^8 \oplus 0d * u_2^8 \oplus 09 * u_3^8, \tag{6}$$

where $(u_0^8, u_1^8, u_2^8, u_3^8)$ are bytes from the state after the MixColumns operation of round 8. These 4 bytes can then be written in terms of another 4 bytes from after S_9. That is, for $(v_0^9, v_1^9, v_2^9, v_3^9)$ being bytes after S_9 and $k_0^8, k_1^8, k_2^8, k_3^8$ being bytes of K_8, we have:

$$u_0^8 = S_9^{-1}(v_0^9) \oplus k_0^8, u_1^8 = S_9^{-1}(v_1^9) \oplus k_1^8, u_2^8 = S_9^{-1}(v_2^9) \oplus k_2^8, \text{ and } u_3^8 = S_9^{-1}(v_3^9) \oplus k_3^8. \tag{7}$$

Consider $0b * u_1^8 \oplus 0d * u_2^8 \oplus 09 * u_3^8 \oplus k_0^8 = \gamma$. Plugging the value of u_0^8 into Eq. (6), and subsequently, the value of v_0^8 into Eq. (5), we obtain:

$$u_0^7 = k_0^7 \oplus S_8^{-1}(0e * S_9^{-1}(v_0^9) \oplus \gamma). \tag{8}$$

Expanding v_0^9, which affects 4 bytes after MixColumns of round 9, we get:

$$v_0^9 = 0e * u_0^9 \oplus 0b * u_1^9 \oplus 0d * u_2^9 \oplus 09 * u_3^9, \tag{9}$$

where $u_0^9, u_1^9, u_2^9, u_3^9$ are the first 4 bytes from after the MixColumns operation of round 9. Each of these bytes go through the S-box and ShiftRows of round 10 and the last AddRoundKey before giving out ciphertext bytes. Therefore, u_i^9 can be represented as:

$$\begin{aligned} u_0^9 &= S_{10}^{-1}(c_0 \oplus k_0^{10}) \oplus k_0^9, & u_1^9 &= S_{10}^{-1}(c_{13} \oplus k_{13}^{10}) \oplus k_1^9, \\ u_2^9 &= S_{10}^{-1}(c_{10} \oplus k_{10}^{10}) \oplus k_2^9, & u_3^9 &= S_{10}^{-1}(c_7 \oplus k_7^{10}) \oplus k_3^9, \end{aligned} \tag{10}$$

where $(c_0, c_7, c_{10}, c_{13})$ are ciphertext bytes. Considering $0b * u_1^9 \oplus 0d * u_2^9 \oplus 09 * u_3^9 \oplus k_0^9 = \delta$, we can rewrite Eq. (8) as:

$$u_0^7 = k_0^7 \oplus S_8^{-1}(0e * S_9^{-1}(0e * S_{10}^{-1}(c_0 \oplus k_0^{10}) \oplus \delta) \oplus \gamma). \tag{11}$$

The term δ depends on the bytes u_1^9, u_2^9, u_3^9, which in turn depend on one ciphertext byte each, as seen above. γ depends on (u_1^8, u_2^8, u_3^8) which in turn depend on (v_1^9, v_2^9, v_3^9) that are similar to v_0^9. We can observe from Eq. (9) that v_0^9 would be affected by four ciphertext bytes, which would actually be the case with $v_1^9, v_2^9,$ and v_3^9 as well. We can conclude that γ would depend on 12 ciphertext bytes.

A statistical attack on the S-box in this case, such as DPA, would therefore include an attack on 32 bits of the set $(k_0^7, k_0^{10}, \delta, \gamma)$ and require 15 ciphertext bytes to be constant. An improvement can be achieved here by performing a bitwise attack such as a single-bit DPA as indicated in [13]. Here, k_0^7, being XORed, would not affect the magnitude of the difference but would only affect the sign. Performing a single-bit DPA attack and taking the absolute of the difference would therefore cancel out the influence of k_0^7. A similar observation can be made for CPA attacks as well. This would bring the attack complexity down to 24 bits as then we would have to attack only $(k_0^{10}, \delta, \gamma)$.

As we see, based on the analysis of the attacks on round 4, the approach considered by us is not feasible for further rounds (e.g., round 5).

5   Experimental Results

5.1   Setup

We use a general setup for capturing the power traces for all of our experiments. The traces contain power measurements collected from a Piñata development board[2] based on a 32-bit STM32F4 microcontroller with an ARM-based architecture, running at the clock frequency of 168 MHz. We acquired power traces from a standard unprotected AES-128 look-up table implementation running on the target device. The setup consisted of a Riscure current probe[3], a Lecroy Waverunner 610Zi oscilloscope, and a computer to communicate with the equipment and store the acquired traces. The power traces were measured at a sampling frequency of 1GS/sec and consisted of 220 000 samples. We perform power acquisitions specifically for rounds 2 and 3 and use the chosen plaintext strategy for the attacks as was discussed in Sect. 4.

For round 2, we need four acquisitions to attack all the key bytes since it is possible to attack 4 bytes at once. We collect 10 000 traces per acquisition, with 20% of the traces having a fixed key which is also the target key. We use Gaussian noise as a test against countermeasure while attacking both rounds 2 and 3. The mean and the standard deviation of the original traces dataset have been used to generate the Gaussian noise that is added to each trace. That is, the new traces with the noise were computed as follows,

$$X^* = X + \mathcal{N}(\mu_x, \sigma_x^2), \tag{12}$$

where $\mathcal{N}(\mu_x, \sigma_x^2)$ is the Gaussian distribution formed using the mean μ_x and the variance σ_x^2 of the original traces X itself. For round 3, we have to perform 16 acquisitions for attacking all key bytes since only one key byte can be attacked at a time. We collect 3 000 traces per acquisition for round 3, with all the traces having the fixed target key. The traces collected were misaligned during the time of acquisition, and we use this misalignment for an additional countermeasure in this case. That is, we first align the traces and perform the attacks, followed by attacking the original dataset to compare the results in the presence of misalignment. We employ a standard pattern-based approach to do the alignment.

5.2   The Deep Learning Model Architecture

We use the benchmarked model architecture CNN$_{best}$, which has been proven to outperform other models such as VGG-16 and MLP$_{best}$ as shown by Benadjila et al. [1]. The architecture CNN$_{best}$ contains five convolutional blocks to begin with, where each block is made up of 1 convolutional layer and one average pooling layer. Each convolutional layer has filters for each block as (64, 128, 256, 512, 512), the kernel size as 11 (effectively indicating *same* padding), and uses ReLU as the activation function. The convolutional blocks are followed by two

---

[2] Piñata Board: https://www.riscure.com/product/pinata-training-target/.
[3] Current probe: https://www.riscure.com/product/current-probe.

fully connected layers, each containing 4 096 units. Finally, the output layer uses Softmax and gives the probabilities for all the classes, which in our case would be the probabilities for each of the 9 Hamming Weight classes. The model uses categorical cross-entropy as the loss function, which is the most prominent of the loss function used in such case scenarios, as has been mentioned in Sect. 2.2.

For hyperparameter tuning, CNN_{best} works with the RMSprop backpropagation optimizer, a learning rate of 10^{-5}, and trains for 75 or 100 epochs for a batch size of 200. While we do not change the optimizer and the learning rate, Benadjila et al. [1] also showed CNN_{best} has an equally good performance with 50 epochs as well. We observed that while 50 epochs give better results for round 3, 100 epochs worked better while attacking a byte at round 2. Further, we also noticed better performance in the attack phase (w.r.t. the number of traces taken to guess the correct key byte) when using a smaller batch size, which is then fixed to be 64 in our experiments. Accordingly, the input layer then has the shape of $(2\,960 \times 64)$ where $2\,960$ is the number of PoIs (or features) selected. The number of PoIs selected in this case correspond to the traces of the S-box computation of the third round. Table 1 shows the benchmarked values used for CNN_{best} and the values that we consider for this work.

We also test randomized CNN architectures with up to 4 convolutional layers each having the kernel size ranging from 10 to 20 and a stride of either 5 or 10, followed by 3 dense layers each having up to 1 000 neurons and a layer weight initializer randomly picked from (random_uniform, glorot_uniform, he_uniform). The activation function for all layers was randomly selected from (relu, selu, elu, and tanh). We observed that most of these random architectures also showed good results in breaking the inner rounds.

Table 1. Summary of the benchmarked values of the hyperparameters.

Hyperparameters	Benchmarked choice	Our setup
Training hyperparameters		
Epochs	Up to 100	50 (R3)/100(R2)
Batch size	200	64
Architecture hyperparameters		
Blocks	5	5
CONV layers	1	1
Filters	64	64
Kernel size	11	11
FC layers	2	2
ACT function	ReLU	ReLU
Pooling layer	Average	Average
Padding	With zeros	With zeros

5.3   Attacking a Byte After Round 2 S-box

To attack a byte after the S-box of round 2, each target byte needs three plaintext bytes to be fixed in the target dataset, allowing us to target four key bytes with each acquisition of power traces. For example, to target key bytes (0, 4, 8, 12), we need to have the other 12 plaintext bytes fixed. Therefore, trace set acquisition is made accordingly, where these 4 bytes of the plaintext are randomly defined, and the others remain fixed. An attack to find all the 16 key bytes would therefore require four such acquisitions in total. We chose to attack the 0th key byte for showcasing our results. We compute the hypothesis for attacking key byte 0 as:

$$hyp = HW[S(02 * S(p_0 \oplus k_0) \oplus \delta)], \tag{13}$$

where $\delta = 03 * S(p_5 \oplus k_5) \oplus 01 * S(p_{10} \oplus k_{10}) \oplus 01 * S(p_{15} \oplus k_{15}) \oplus k_0^1$. As can be seen here, we need to keep the plaintext bytes (5, 10, 15) fixed in order to make the attack possible, and the hypothesis hyp itself depends on only p_0 and k_0 of the input trace. For DL-SCA, we label the traces during the profiling phase using the hypothesis and then guess the bytes (k_0, δ) during the attack phase. We set the hyperparameters as discussed in Sect. 5.2. Training and validation are done for 7 500 and 500 traces, respectively, and on variable keys that do not consist of the target key bytes while having the constant plaintext bytes as 0x00 for simplicity. The attack is performed on a set of 2 000 traces with a fixed key. In the case of DL-SCA, we observe that the attack yields the key after 238 traces, as shown in Fig. 1 when the rank becomes 0. We generalize the term to *rank* here since we are guessing another byte apart from the key byte itself, and therefore, it is of the order 10^4 denoting roughly the 65 536 possibilities while guessing 16 bits (2^{16} possibilities). We can then deduce that the attack takes 238 traces to start recognizing the correct trend from profiling, thereby leading to correct guesses thereafter, which we can see from the drop of the rank to 0.

We then launch CPA on a set of 2 000 traces with a fixed key derived from the same dataset used above. We first compute the hypothesis for all the 2^{16} guesses and as given in Eq. (13). The correlation is then computed for all the guesses per trace, and the guess with the highest value is chosen to be the most likely guess as in any CPA attack. This experiment is then repeated 100 times for each batch of shuffled traces, and the highest correlation value is then averaged out, resulting in an average rank for each batch. The results of this attack are shown in Fig. 1. The average rank achieved by CPA is six after 2 000 traces. As we notice a decreasing trend in the average ranks, we believe that CPA would eventually find the key if given more traces during the attack.

Now we add Gaussian noise as described in Sect. 5.1 and observe the performance of the attacks. With the added noise, DL-SCA finds the key after 139 traces as seen in Fig. 2, while CPA does not find the key even with 2 000 traces despite a downward trend, as visible in Fig. 2. The average rank for CPA is 352 after 2 000 traces while it attempts to recover 16 bits of information.

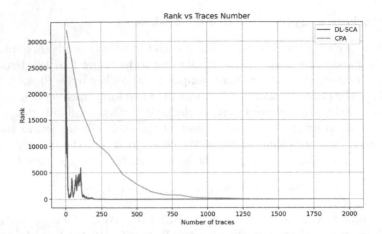

Fig. 1. DL-SCA and CPA for key byte 0 after S-box on encryption round 2.

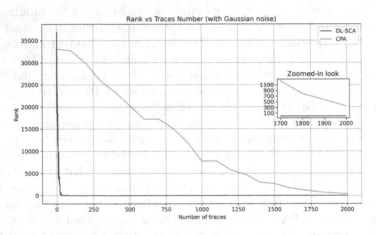

Fig. 2. DL-SCA and CPA for key byte 0 with adding Gaussian Noise.

5.4 Attacking a Byte After Round 3 S-box

Round 3 requires the attacker to acquire a separate trace set per each key byte. Here we specifically target k_0 and we then compute the hypothesis as follows,

$$hyp = HW[S(02 * S(02 * S(p_0 \oplus k_0) \oplus \delta) \oplus \gamma)], \qquad (14)$$

where hyp is the 8-bit hypothesis computed for one input trace while p_0 and k_0 are the first bytes of plaintext and key for that input trace, respectively. Since this depends on p_0, we gather the acquisition set with the first byte as variable and the rest of the bytes as constant, which we set as 0x00 for simplicity. As discussed in Sect. 5.1, we first perform the attacks on aligned traces, followed by attacks on the misaligned ones. For DL-SCA on the aligned set of traces, since we have only 3 000 traces collected per acquisition in our dataset, we use the first 2 000 traces for the profiling phase, the following 500 for validation and attack the next 500 traces. The model used is as described in Sect. 5.2. As done for round 2, the label for each trace is computed using Eq. (14) for profiling, where (δ, γ) can be set to any constant including 0x00. During the attack we attempt to guess 3 bytes (k_0, δ, γ). On performing the attack in this case, we successfully attain the key byte k_0 along with the correct values of δ and γ after 11 traces. The result is shown in Fig. 3 (here too, we generalize the term to *rank* since we are guessing 3 bytes in total). Similar to the result seen for round 2, the rank is of the order 10^6, indicating the 2^{24} possible guesses (approximately 16 million possibilities) for 24 bits of data. The attack takes just 11 traces to start recognizing the trend and guessing the correct key.

For CPA, we compute the hypothesis and subsequently the correlation for all the 2^{24} guesses, similar to what was done for round 2. The result of this attack is then shown in Fig. 3. The correct key converges towards the highest correlation value as expected from a successful CPA attack, and the correct key is obtained after 50 traces and again at 110 traces. Here, we restrict the computation of key ranks to only 1 experiment instead of 100 as done in the case of round 2. Therefore, the results for CPA on round 3 are given as a proof of concept for the attack. This is because of the CPU-intensive operations done while brute-forcing 24 bits on a standard personal computer. The experiments were done using Intel Core i9 8-core processor and 16GB RAM. Computation of hypothesis for 500 traces takes approximately 27 min, followed by an average of 9 min for computing the key rank for each batch of traces. With an increment of 10 traces per batch, completing 1 experiment for all the batches ranging from 10 to 500 traces (50 batches) takes approximately 7.35 h. Multi-processing can be used to speed up the experiments, but storing 2^{24} possibilities for each trace is memory intensive, thereby making the use of multiple processes more expensive (in terms of speed-memory trade-off) for a standard personal computer.

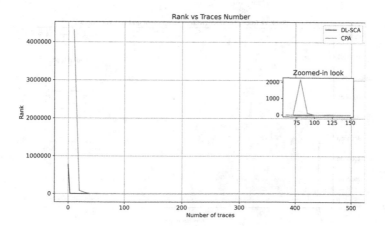

Fig. 3. DL-SCA and CPA on aligned traces for byte 0 after S-box in round 3.

We now use the misaligned traces to compare the performance of DL-SCA and CPA in the presence of such an implicit countermeasure. We use the same DL model (along with the hyperparameters) and the samples interval to perform DL-SCA on the misaligned traces. The attack reveals the key after ten traces. The comparison of DL-SCA and CPA on the misaligned traces is shown in Fig. 4. As expected, a CPA attack fails in this case due to misalignment.

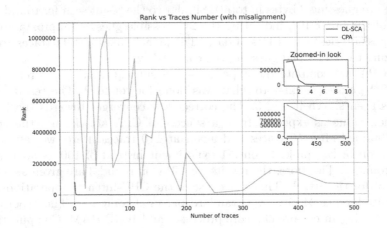

Fig. 4. DL-SCA and CPA on misaligned traces for byte 0 after S-box in round 3.

We further compare the performance of DL-SCA with CPA by adding Gaussian noise to the misaligned traces. The results can be seen in Fig. 5. While DL-SCA finds the key after 34 traces, CPA is unable to do so even after going through our entire attack set of 500 traces.

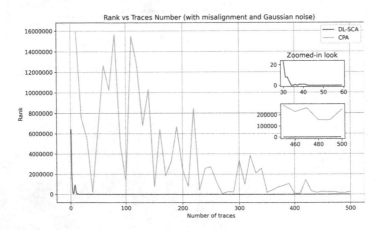

Fig. 5. DL-SCA and CPA on misaligned traces with Gaussian noise added for key byte 0 after S-box in round 3.

While DL-SCA successfully finds the key in all the above cases, CPA is successful only when the traces are aligned. The effectiveness of DL-SCA is further proven when attacking misaligned traces since it succeeds with as few as ten traces, while CPA is unsuccessful. *We can therefore conclude that DL-SCA outperforms CPA by a significant margin when attacking the inner rounds.*

5.5 Attacking a Byte After Round 4 S-box

To attack the byte after the round 4 S-box, we need to guess 32 bits comprising the set of $(k_0, \delta, \gamma, \theta)$, as can also be seen from Eq. (4). Although attacking 32 bits is still feasible, the usage of the aforementioned three constants implies that all the 16 bytes of plaintext and the key need to be fixed for this particular attack to work. However, profiling using the same plaintexts and the same key would result in the same labels and consequently would result in the overfitting of the model.

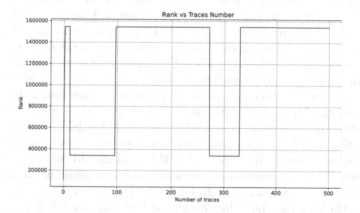

Fig. 6. DL-SCA on round 4 S-box with different plaintexts used for training and constant one for attacking. A fixed key was used both for profiling and for attack.

Another case scenario would involve profiling using different plaintext but a constant key. This would mean calculating the exact values of δ, γ, and θ, which in turn leads to a properly trained model. However, the assumption in the attack phase while computing the four target bytes is that these 4 bytes are constant during the profiling as well and, by extension, should ideally have different Hamming Weights as labels than what was computed. As an example, two plaintexts having the same first byte should have the same label and, therefore, similar traces. However, since we are using different plaintexts for each trace during profiling, the training factor that the constants bring in is totally eliminated. This effectively means that the training phase and the attacking phase are carried out on data that are completely different from each other, thereby rendering the attack unsuccessful. The results for the same are shown in Fig. 6, and it can be observed that the rank never converges to a correct guess and does not show a decreasing trend either. A similar result was also seen while using the same plaintext but different keys. This is because the values of δ, γ, and θ not only depend on the plaintext but also on the keys and the subsequent round keys. *As of now, we conclude that an attack on any byte after the round 4 S-box is infeasible within the boundaries considered by our work.*

6   Conclusions and Future Work

In this work, we proposed general formulations to attack any intermediate byte in AES encryption mode. Results indicated that attacks on rounds 2 and 3 are practical besides the increased complexity in the hypothesis guessing (16 and 24 bits, respectively). We demonstrated in practice that because profiled attacks are less restricted from fixed plaintext limitations in the profiling phase, DL-SCA can easily succeed in recovering the key in scenarios without or with (noise and misalignment) countermeasures. On the other hand, non-profiled attacks, such as CPA, becomes highly constrained by time and memory limitations as a consequence of the increased complexity to guess intermediates from inner rounds. As mentioned by several related works, for several targets, DL-SCA shows easier key recovery in comparison to non-profiled attacks if the profiling phase is done appropriately. Therefore, as shown in this paper, DL-SCA becomes a strong candidate to attack (not properly protected) inner rounds from AES.

Moreover, we observed that the results from Sect. 5 have certain limitations. Most notably, the presented approach fails at attacking further than round 3. Therefore, the most interesting open question is whether it is possible to attack rounds between 4 and 6. We believe that this goal should be achievable using deep learning. The first, more straightforward approach would be to attack both S-box input and output using multi-label DL [14]. We envision that in this approach, attacking the Hamming Weight of both intermediates would be the most efficient. By targeting these two intermediate states at once, the attack would be able to recover the key in a similar way to [2,19,22]. Note that such method can be applied even without requiring access to input and output for AES[4].

The second approach would be to attack a combination of S-box input and output. For example, we envision that it might be sufficient to use an XOR of S-box input and output as a label. The traces might not be directly leaking that XOR value, but the neural network might be able to combine S-box input and output leakages and classify the XORed value correctly, in a similar way to which neural networks were shown to combine leakages in masked AES traces [12].

Acknowledgements. Łukasz Chmielewski is partially supported by the Technology Innovation Institute (TII), https://www.tii.ae/, and by European Commission through the ERC Starting Grant 805031 (EPOQUE) of Peter Schwabe.

---

[4] Similar results might be achievable using template attacks, but our choice is deep learning as it has been shown to outperform template attacks multiple times.

References

1. Benadjila, R., Prouff, E., Strullu, R., Cagli, E., Dumas, C.: Study of deep learning techniques for side-channel analysis and introduction to ASCAD database. ANSSI, France and CEA, LETI, MINATEC Campus, France. Online verfügbar unter https://eprint.iacr.org/2018/053.pdf, zuletzt geprüft am 22 (2018)
2. Le Bouder, H., Lashermes, R., Linge, Y., Thomas, G., Zie, J.-Y.: A multi-round side channel attack on AES using belief propagation. In: Cuppens, F., Wang, L., Cuppens-Boulahia, N., Tawbi, N., Garcia-Alfaro, J. (eds.) FPS 2016. LNCS, vol. 10128, pp. 199–213. Springer, Cham (2017). https://doi.org/10.1007/978-3-319-51966-1_13
3. Brier, E., Clavier, C., Olivier, F.: Correlation power analysis with a leakage model. In: Joye, M., Quisquater, J.-J. (eds.) CHES 2004. LNCS, vol. 3156, pp. 16–29. Springer, Heidelberg (2004). https://doi.org/10.1007/978-3-540-28632-5_2
4. Cagli, E., Dumas, C., Prouff, E.: Convolutional neural networks with data augmentation against Jitter-based countermeasures. In: Fischer, W., Homma, N. (eds.) CHES 2017. LNCS, vol. 10529, pp. 45–68. Springer, Cham (2017). https://doi.org/10.1007/978-3-319-66787-4_3
5. Chari, S., Rao, J.R., Rohatgi, P.: Template attacks. In: Kaliski, B.S., Koç, K., Paar, C. (eds.) CHES 2002. LNCS, vol. 2523, pp. 13–28. Springer, Heidelberg (2003). https://doi.org/10.1007/3-540-36400-5_3
6. Gilmore, R., Hanley, N., O'Neill, M.: Neural network based attack on a masked implementation of AES. In: 2015 IEEE International Symposium on Hardware Oriented Security and Trust (HOST), pp. 106–111. IEEE (2015)
7. Herbst, C., Oswald, E., Mangard, S.: An AES smart card implementation resistant to power analysis attacks. In: Zhou, J., Yung, M., Bao, F. (eds.) ACNS 2006. LNCS, vol. 3989, pp. 239–252. Springer, Heidelberg (2006). https://doi.org/10.1007/11767480_16
8. Heuser, A., Zohner, M.: Intelligent machine homicide. In: Schindler, W., Huss, S.A. (eds.) COSADE 2012. LNCS, vol. 7275, pp. 249–264. Springer, Heidelberg (2012). https://doi.org/10.1007/978-3-642-29912-4_18
9. Hospodar, G., Gierlichs, B., De Mulder, E., Verbauwhede, I., Vandewalle, J.: Machine learning in side-channel analysis: a first study. J. Cryptogr. Eng. $1(4)$, 293 (2011). https://doi.org/10.1007/s13389-011-0023-x
10. Kim, J., Picek, S., Heuser, A., Bhasin, S., Hanjalic, A.: Make some noise. Unleashing the power of convolutional neural networks for profiled side-channel analysis. IACR Trans. Cryptographic Hardware Embed. Syst. 148–179 (2019)
11. Kocher, P.C., Jaffe, J., Jun, B., Rohatgi, P.: Introduction to differential power analysis. J. Cryptogr. Eng. $1(1)$, 5–27 (2011). https://doi.org/10.1007/s13389-011-0006-y
12. Lerman, L., Bontempi, G., Markowitch, O.: A machine learning approach against a masked AES. J. Cryptogr. Eng. $5(2)$, 123–139 (2015). https://doi.org/10.1007/s13389-014-0089-3
13. Lu, J., Pan, J., den Hartog, J.: Principles on the security of AES against first and second-order differential power analysis. In: Zhou, J., Yung, M. (eds.) Applied Cryptography and Network Security, 8th International Conference, ACNS 2010, Beijing, China, 22–25 June 2010. Proceedings. Lecture Notes in Computer Science, vol. 6123, pp. 168–185 (2010). https://doi.org/10.1007/978-3-642-13708-2_11
14. Maghrebi, H.: Deep learning based side-channel attack: a new profiling methodology based on multi-label classification. IACR Cryptol. ePrint Arch. **436** (2020). https://eprint.iacr.org/2020/436

15. Maghrebi, H., Portigliatti, T., Prouff, E.: Breaking cryptographic implementations using deep learning techniques. In: Carlet, C., Hasan, M.A., Saraswat, V. (eds.) SPACE 2016. LNCS, vol. 10076, pp. 3–26. Springer, Cham (2016). https://doi.org/10.1007/978-3-319-49445-6_1

16. Perin, G., Chmielewski, L., Picek, S.: Strength in numbers: Improving generalization with ensembles in machine learning-based profiled side-channel analysis. IACR Trans. Cryptographic Hardware Embed. Syst. (4), 337–364 (2020). https://doi.org/10.13154/tches.v2020.i4.337-364, https://tches.iacr.org/index.php/TCHES/article/view/8686

17. Picek, S., Heuser, A., Jovic, A., Bhasin, S., Regazzoni, F.: The curse of class imbalance and conflicting metrics with machine learning for side-channel evaluations. IACR Trans. Cryptographic Hardware Embed. Syst. **2019**(1), 209–237 (2018). https://doi.org/10.13154/tches.v2019.i1.209-237, https://tches.iacr.org/index.php/TCHES/article/view/7339

18. Rijsdijk, J., Wu, L., Perin, G., Picek, S.: Reinforcement learning for hyperparameter tuning in deep learning-based side-channel analysis. IACR Trans. Cryptographic Hardware Embed. Syst. (3), 677–707 (2021). https://doi.org/10.46586/tches.v2021.i3.677-707, https://tches.iacr.org/index.php/TCHES/article/view/8989

19. Saha, S., Bag, A., Basu Roy, D., Patranabis, S., Mukhopadhyay, D.: Fault template attacks on block ciphers exploiting fault propagation. In: Canteaut, A., Ishai, Y. (eds.) EUROCRYPT 2020. LNCS, vol. 12105, pp. 612–643. Springer, Cham (2020). https://doi.org/10.1007/978-3-030-45721-1_22

20. Standaert, F.-X., Malkin, T.G., Yung, M.: A unified framework for the analysis of side-channel key recovery attacks. In: Joux, A. (ed.) EUROCRYPT 2009. LNCS, vol. 5479, pp. 443–461. Springer, Heidelberg (2009). https://doi.org/10.1007/978-3-642-01001-9_26

21. Tillich, S., Herbst, C., Mangard, S.: Protecting AES software implementations on 32-Bit processors against power analysis. In: Katz, J., Yung, M. (eds.) ACNS 2007. LNCS, vol. 4521, pp. 141–157. Springer, Heidelberg (2007). https://doi.org/10.1007/978-3-540-72738-5_10

22. Veyrat-Charvillon, N., Gérard, B., Standaert, F.-X.: Soft analytical side-channel attacks. In: Sarkar, P., Iwata, T. (eds.) ASIACRYPT 2014. LNCS, vol. 8873, pp. 282–296. Springer, Heidelberg (2014). https://doi.org/10.1007/978-3-662-45611-8_15

23. Wouters, L., Arribas, V., Gierlichs, B., Preneel, B.: Revisiting a methodology for efficient CNN architectures in profiling attacks. IACR Trans. Cryptographic Hardware Embed. Syst. (3), 147–168 (2020). https://doi.org/10.13154/tches.v2020.i3.147-168, https://tches.iacr.org/index.php/TCHES/article/view/8586

24. Zaid, G., Bossuet, L., Habrard, A., Venelli, A.: Methodology for efficient CNN architectures in profiling attacks. IACR Trans. Cryptographic Hardware Embedded Systems **2020**(1), 1–36 (2019). https://doi.org/10.13154/tches.v2020.i1.1-36, https://tches.iacr.org/index.php/TCHES/article/view/8391

A Side-Channel Based Disassembler for the ARM-Cortex M0

Jurian van Geest$^{(\boxtimes)}$ and Ileana Buhan

Digital Security Group, Radboud University, Nijmegen, The Netherlands
jurianvgeest@gmail.com, ileana.buhan@ru.nl

Abstract. The most common application for side-channel attacks is the extraction of secret information, such as key material, from the implementation of a cryptographic algorithm. However, using side-channel information, we can extract other types of information related to the internal state of a computing device, such as the instructions executed and the content of registers. We used machine learning to build a side channel disassembler for the ARM-Cortex M0 architecture, which can extract the executed instructions from the power traces of the device. Our disassembler achieves a success rate of 99% under ideal conditions and 88.2% under realistic conditions when distinguishing between groups of instructions. We also provide an overview of the lessons learned in relation to data preparation and noise minimization techniques.

Keywords: Side-channels · Disassembler · Machine-learning

1 Introduction

The extraction of information using side channels is extensively studied in an adversarial setting, where the target of the attack is the implementation of a cryptographic algorithm. There are two classes of side-channel attacks. The first are *non-profiled* attacks, where the adversary can choose the input data, observe the encryption output, and monitor the side-channel information. The second is *profiled* attacks, where the adversary has access to a clone device to learn the behavior of the algorithm. Side channel attacks have a long history of success [1] in extracting key information from power or electromagnetic traces collected during the execution of a cryptographic algorithm.

However, monitoring the side-channel information of an embedded system has also been proven to be useful for defense purposes [2]. A *side-channel disassembler* monitors the control flow of an application at run-time by translating side-channel information, such as power traces, into assembly code consisting of instructions and operands. The applications of a side-channel disassembler are multiple. An example is the detection of security breaches, such as malware attacks. To detect malware using a side-channel disassembler, the signature information of the healthy device at run-time is collected. This information is used to

J. Zhou et al. (Eds.): ACNS 2022 Workshops, LNCS 13285, pp. 183–199, 2022.
https://doi.org/10.1007/978-3-031-16815-4_11

verify the integrity of the code running on the device. A flag is raised if a deviation from normal operation mode is detected. Another application is reverse engineering of the firmware of a target device. Side-channel disassemblers have been shown to successfully recognize both the opcode and the operands for a given device and instruction set architecture.

Problem Statement. Translating a power trace into a sequence of instructions is a challenge. The first challenge is that an instruction is typically executed once for an execution path, so there is relatively little information to use for identification. The second challenge is that the power signature of an instruction is influenced by other instructions in the pipeline [3], changing the side-channel signature of an instruction. The third challenge is that the implementation of the microarchitecture of an embedded device is a trade secret, and hidden storage elements influence the interaction of instructions [4].

Contribution. Building on previous work, we investigate the use of machine learning models for side-channel disassembly of instructions running on an ARM-Cortex M0 processor, which is a popular choice for IoT due to its ultralow gate count. Its side-channel leakage has been extensively studied in the context of *leakage simulators*. Unlike *side-channel disassemblers* which extract the assembly instruction from a power trace, *leakage simulators* aim to construct the power trace for a set of assembly instructions. This is the first attempt at modeling a 32-bit architecture with a 3-stage pipeline; previous work has focused on 8-bit processors with 2-stage pipelines. 32-bit architectures are more complex and typically add more components, increasing the difficulty of recognizing instructions in power traces. Using the information collected from the power traces, we performed experiments to identify the groups of instructions as suggested in [5] and individual instructions. Under ideal conditions, our side-channel disassembler reaches a success rate of 99%, while under realistic conditions, we observe a success rate of 88.2%.

Paper Organization. Section 2 describes the related work. The experimental setup that we used to validate our results is presented in Sect. 3 and the datasets we collected are described in Sect. 4. The challenges of selecting mixed-instruction sequences are described in Sect. 5. Our results are presented in Sect. 6 and conclusions are presented in Sect. 7. The KL-based feature selection proposed in [6] is discussed in more detail in Sect. A (appendix).

2   Related Work

Side-Channel Disassemblers. Park *et al.* [6] have created a side-channel disassembler targeting the Atmega 328P microcontroller and report a success rate of 99.03% in instruction identification. The first step of the disassembler is to collect power traces. Next, all instructions are divided into groups on the basis of their operands. Since the microcontroller used has a two-stage pipeline, the target instruction is preceded and succeeded by a random instruction to fill the pipeline. After the traces are collected, the difference between each trace and a reference trace containing only nop's is computed to remove electrical noise. This work is the starting point for the results presented in this paper. We extensively experimented with the proposed special feature selection and combined it with several machine learning algorithms. Eisenbarth et al. [7] targets a PIC16F687 microcontroller, running at 1 MHz that features a set of 35 instructions (most are 1 cycle instructions). Their goal is to reconstruct the instructions executed and their order from a single measurement. They use templates to model the power consumption of a single instruction. They also use instruction frequency analysis to determine the probability that instructions appear in a piece of code and feed this information to the distinguisher function. They report a recognition rate of 70%. Msgna et al. [8] targets an 8-bit ATMega163 microcontroller, running at 4 MHz, which features a set of 130 instructions. For the experiments, they only used 39 instructions and report a 100% recognition rate.

Side-Channel Leakage for the ARM-Cortex M0. McCann et al. [5] created ELMO, a leakage simulator for the ARM-Cortex M0/M4 family. ELMO is instruction-accurate, which easily allows the identification of a leaky instruction in the context of side channels. An exciting feature of ELMO is the support for *sequence dependency*. The critical observation is that the power consumption of different instructions depends on the instructions executed before. Following a cluster analysis to identify similar instructions (i.e., those that leak information in the same way), the authors identified five groups that correspond to the same processor component. In this work, we use the grouping of instructions proposed by [5]. In addition, the authors find remarkable consistency in the data-dependent leakage of different physical boards. Shelton et al. [4] improves the side channel model of ELMO by capturing interactions that span multiple cycles. ELMO [5] is augmented to account for storage elements, which play a critical role in the security of masked implementations. A novel feature of ELMO* [4] is a systematic battery of small code sequences that can be used to highlight the interaction of instructions through storage elements. The idea of finding hidden storage elements is generic and could be used for any other architecture. Bazangani et al. [9] propose a new leakage simulator ABBY, for the ARM-Cortex M0 architecture based on machine learning. The advantage of ABBY compared to ELMO is twofold. The first advantage is that no reverse engineering of the target device is required, and the second is that ABBY can learn nonlinear leakage models. Arora et al. [3] compare the manufacturing variability between different physical devices from the same manufacturer. The study targets an ARM-Cortex M0 architecture and shows that the power trace signature of a sequence of instructions depends on microarchitecture implementation. The implication of this work is that the existence of a generic side-channel disassembler, which is identified with high-accuracy instructions on ARM-Cortex M0 cores produced by different manufacturers, is improbable.

3   Experimental Setup

For training or profiling, power traces are collected from an ARM-Cortex M0 microcontroller, STM32F0 Discovery (STM32F051R8). The CPU is clocked at 8 MHz. To improve the signal-to-noise ratio in the measured power traces, the capacitors between VDD and GND are removed, since they reduce the signal-to-noise ratio in the power traces (Fig. 1a). The oscilloscope is set to 1.25GS, resulting in 156.25 samples per cycle. The power consumption of the board is measured using an AC current probe since it ignores the DC component, which can vary between different measurements. An overview of the setup can be found in Fig. 1b.

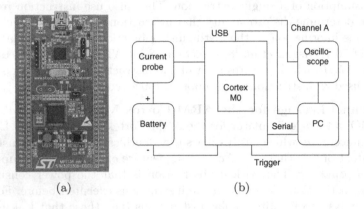

(a)   (b)

Fig. 1. Overview of the setup used to collect the traces. (a) Frontal view of the STM32F030R8 board, where the removed capacitors: C18, C19, C20, C21 are highlighted. (b) Schematic overview of the setup used to collect traces.

4   The Datasets

The ARM-Cortex M0 implements the ARMv6-M instruction set, which consists of most of the 16 bit Thumb instructions and some of the 32 bit Thumb-2 instructions. For this project, we select the core instructions relevant for cryptographic operations, similar to [5], who observed that the power consumption of the selected instructions can be divided into five different groups by performing a cluster analysis. The resulting groups and instructions are shown in Table 1.

Table 1. Overview of the division of instructions into groups.

Group 1 (ALU)	adds, ands, cmp, eors, movs, orrs, subs
Group 2 (SHIFTS)	lsls, lsrs, rors
Group 3 (LOADS)	ldr, ldrb, ldrh
Group 4 (STORES)	str, strb, strh
Group 5 (Multiplications)	muls

Since the microcontroller board has a limited amount of memory, the data sets collected consist of multiple *acquisitions*. The *acquisitions* are created from multiples *programs*. A *program* is a sequence of assembly instructions. For our

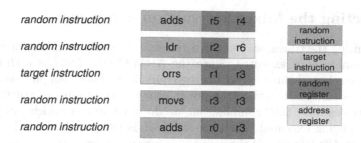

Fig. 2. Snippet of a *program*. Note that 10 **nops** are executed before and after this fragment to ensure an accurate acquisition.

data sets, a *program* is constructed as follows: ten **nops**, two *random instructions*, one *target instruction* followed by two *random instructions* and ten **nop** instructions. An example can be seen in Fig. 2.

The **nop** instructions do not use operands. The operands used for the other instructions in *program* are random values in random registers. Since loads and stores instructions need an actual memory address to load from and store to, one register (**r6**) is reserved for this and filled with an existing memory address. The other free registers (**r0-r5**) are filled with new random 32-bit values before each program is executed.

Three datasets are created for different purposes. To be able to apply the proposed feature selection in [6], dataset A is created that matches the settings required for this special feature selection. Dataset B is created for the recognition of the five instruction groups, and dataset C is created for the recognition of instructions within the largest instruction group: group 1.

Dataset A contains sixty *programs* targeting three instructions. Two additional programs consisting of **nop** instructions are used as a baseline to remove electrical noise. The three *target instructions* are: **adds**, **ands** (from group 1) and **muls** (group 5). For each *target instruction*, we generate 20 programs by randomizing the *random instructions*. The *random instructions* are taken from groups 1, 2, and 5. For each *program* 300 power traces are acquired, with 6000 samples per trace. The collection of traces is done in one acquisition campaign.

Dataset B contains a total of 12,500 *programs*, with *target instructions* in the five groups. Each group contains 2,500 *programs*. The *target instruction* is randomly selected from all instructions in the group. For each *program*, 20 traces are collected, with 6000 samples each. An average is taken over these 20 power traces to reduce electrical noise. Only 500 *programs* fit into the memory of the board, so the data set consists of 25 different acquisitions.

Dataset C contains 17,500 *programs* targeting instructions from group 1. For each of the seven *target instructions* in the group, 2500 *programs* are created. For each *program*, 20 traces are collected with 6000 samples each. To reduce electrical noise, an average is taken over these 20 power traces. The data set is collected in 35 acquisition campaigns.

5 Selecting the Mixed-Instruction Sequence

After acquiring the traces, we want to determine the samples in the trace related to the assembly code executed. Since the ARM-Cortex M0 has a three-stage pipeline, we selected three cycles (or the equivalent of 469 samples) since each of the stages can contribute to the power usage of the target instruction. The collected traces have 6000 samples, but we do not know at which samples our assembly is being executed. With our setup, it is not possible to calculate the time between the trigger and the moment our assembly code starts executing. In the power traces, we can see the influence of the executed assembly, but since we have a three-stage pipeline (Fig. 3) we do not know which stage of the pipeline causes the change in power consumption or which instructions are in the pipeline at that exact moment.

Fig. 3. Executed instructions in the pipeline. The target instruction is expected to influence the power trace in cycle 3–5.

To select the samples in the power trace corresponding to *target instruction*, we explore two techniques. The first is *sample-eviction*, which works by removing a window of three cycles from the traces by replacing them with zero values and then calculating the classification score. By evicting samples at different intervals in the trace, we expect the lowest score[1] to indicate the location of the most important samples. The second technique is *moving-window*, where we calculate the classification score in a moving window of three cycles. The highest score indicates the three cycles that contain the most useful information for the machine learning model. For both techniques, we chose to use a Multilayer Perceptron model as discussed in Subsect. 6.1.

The top graph in Fig. 4 shows a processed power trace where noise and nop were subtracted to give a better visualization of where random and target instructions influence the power trace. The middle and bottom graphs in Fig. 4 show the result of the *sample-eviction* and *moving-window* technique, respectively. Note that, for both techniques, the score for a given sample is calculated over the 469-sample window, which starts at that specific sample. The gray lines are plotted with intervals of one cycle, or 156.25 samples. The starting point of the cycle is not known, so the lines could be out of phase.

There are different options to interpret the available information. Looking at the top graph of Fig. 4 there are six cycles clearly influenced by the executed

---

[1] A poor classification score indicates the relevant samples are missing.

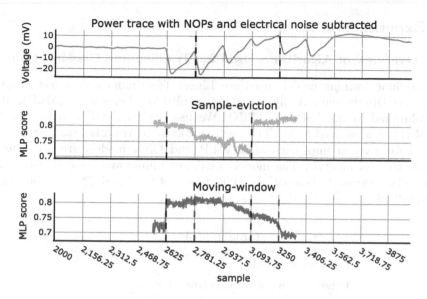

Fig. 4. Power-trace (top) and the applied techniques for selecting the samples to be used in further analysis (middle and bottom). (color figure online)

assembly. An estimation could be that the pipeline fetch stage uses the least power, so the six cycles would be cycle 2–7 in Fig. 3. The corresponding cycles where the target instruction is in the pipeline are marked with black dashed lines on the top graph of Fig. 4.

In the middle graph Fig. 4, *sample-eviction* the score is lowest just before sample 3100 and begins to increase rapidly after that. This could indicate that the most important cycles are happening before that moment (between the black dashed lines). Using the *moving-window* technique, we could use the three cycles just after the significant increase in the score (between black dashed lines) or the three-cycle window used to calculate the maximum score (between purple dashed lines).

These techniques and information do not give a clear location for the most important samples in the power trace. Since the machine learning algorithm used will receive a 469 sample input similar to *moving-window*, we take the maximum score for *moving-window* in sample 2780 as a starting point for our experiments. To check whether other samples would contain additional information, we explore using more than 469 samples as input in Subsect. 6.2.

For the selection of KL divergence-based features, the location of relevant samples in the trace is followed by the continuous wavelet transform and KL divergence. In Sect. A (Appendix), this is discussed in more detail.

6   Experimental Results

6.1   Overview of Algorithms Used for Training and Classification

The machine learning models used are Linear Discriminant Analysis (LDA), Quadratic Discriminant Analysis (QDA), Multilayer Perceptron (MLP), and Convolutional Neural Network (CNN). We use LDA and QDA to implement two of the models used in [6]. The package `sklearn.discriminant_analysis` is used for Python implementation. MLP and CNN models are often used for side-channel analysis. The models used are simple and created using the `tensorflow.keras` Python package. The details of MLP and CNN can be found in Table 2 and Table 3.

Table 2. MLP

Layer type	Details
Dense	units = 200, activation = selu
Dense	units = 200, activation = selu
Dense	units = 200, activation = selu
Dense	units = 200, activation = selu
Dense	units = classes, activation = softmax

Table 3. CNN

Layer type	Details
Conv	filters = 8. kernel size = 20, activation = relu
Flatten	
Dense	units = 128, activation = relu
Dropout	
Dense	units = 128, activation = relu
Dense	units = classes, activation = softmax

Before computing the MLP and CNN scores, the data have to be normalized first. This is done using `sklearn.preprocessing.StandardScaler`. For both the MLP and CNN models, they are set on 100 epochs, since the accuracy did not increase for more epochs. For all machine learning models, the scores are calculated using 5-fold cross-validation.

6.2   Choosing the Configuration for the Dataset

Most instructions take one cycle to execute; however, all loads and stores take two cycles. This means that the starting sample of *target instruction* can change depending on whether one or both of the two random instructions that precede the target instruction are load or store. To overcome this problem, while loading the traces, we check whether load/stores occurs before *target instruction* and increase the offset by the right amount of samples if there are. In Table 4 can be seen that for each of the machine learning models the score increases, for LDA and QDA there is even a significant improvement when adjusting the offset.

Table 4. Dataset B. Offset vs. none

	LDA	QDA	MLP	CNN
Normal offset	65.9%	50.6%	80.4%	79.6%
Adjusted offset	84.4%	70.7%	85.6%	87.8%

When different acquisitions are run, the power traces can be slightly different due to variables such as temperature. To check whether this influences the scores for our dataset, we ran scores for three different configurations. The first configuration uses only one acquisition file per group, resulting in 500 programs per group. The second configuration uses the complete datasets with five acquisition files per group, and the training and testing parts are taken randomly. For the last configuration, the training part consists of 4 acquisition files per group, and the last file is used for testing. The results for each configuration can be found in Table 5. Note that for the highlighted cell the QDA calculation warned that the variables are collinear, so this result should not be considered accurate. The partial data set performs worse than the complete dataset, so increasing the number of programs increases the accuracy despite adding multiple acquisition files. When using configuration 3 the scores are similar to configuration 2, so the influence of changing environmental variables on different acquisitions seems to be limited.

Table 5. Dataset B. Machine learning scores for different input configurations.

	LDA	QDA	MLP	CNN
Configuration 1: partial dataset	81.0%	31.3%	78.9%	76.9%
Configuration 2: complete shuffled	84.4%	70.7%	85.6%	88.3%
Configuration 3: complete	84.3%	71.0%	85.8%	88.1%

Since we do not have a perfect method for selecting the right samples in the power traces, we compare different amounts of samples in Table 6. Note that again the highlighted cell should not be considered accurate, since its calculation gave a collinearity warning. 469 samples selected using the sample-eviction and moving window, 781 samples using the previous selection and the cycle before and after that, and 3000 samples to ensure that all our assembly is in the selection. The differences between 469 and 781 samples are relatively small, which could indicate that our feature selection is close to the actual most important samples. The two additional instructions covered by the extra samples barely increase the scores. When taking a large 3000 sample selection, the scores are close to the other selections or even significantly lower in the case of MLP.

Table 6. Dataset B. Using different amounts of samples.

Samples	LDA	QDA	MLP	CNN
3000	84.9%	31.4%	79.6%	88.5%
781	85.4%	67.3%	88.8%	88.8%
469	84.4%	70.7%	87.9%	87.9%

For the next sections, we will use the all the acquisition files in the datasets with shuffled traces, an adjusted offset and a selection of 469 samples.

6.3 Amount of Traces per Program

In Sect. 4 is indicated that for each program in dataset B and C an average trace is taken over 20 traces. In Table 7 can be seen what the scores are with different approaches than averaging. When taking only a single trace, the score drops significantly. If we use all 20 traces for machine learning, the score increases to 93.7%. However, in this scenario (*identical-program*) the traces for training and testing are taken randomly, which means that testing can be done on traces generated with the same program as some of the traces used for training. When making the train-test division based on program rather than traces, this problem is avoided, but the score drops to 77.8% (*different-program*). This means that averaging the 20 traces results in the best score (84.7%) for a realistic scenario.

Table 7. Dataset B. Using different methods to divide all traces into training and testing sets.

Traces per program	Method	MLP score
1	-	79.5%
20	*Identical-program*	93.7%
20	*Different-program*	77.8%
20	Averaged	84.7%

6.4   Training and Classification for Groups of Instructions

The scores for the classification of different groups are given in Table 8. Note that the CNN score for the first row is not given since the number of input variables after the selection of features is too low. The KL-based feature selection can only be applied to dataset A, for which the scores are very close to random guessing (50%). However, when we use the same samples for our analysis, the score increases to 99.9%. This means that there is enough information in the samples to get an almost perfect classification score, but the KL-based feature selection cannot extract this information. Possible reasons for this can be found in Sect. A (appendix). However, this is a best-case scenario (*identical-program*), where two instructions from different groups are compared with a data set that contains power traces in its training and testing set that are based on the same program. To create a similar but more realistic scenario (*different-program*) for dataset B we took only two groups instead of all five in row three (*Dataset B (group 1 vs group 5)*), and this still gives a accuracy of 94.5%. When using the complete dataset, the accuracy drops to a maximum score of 88.2%.

Table 8. Dataset A vs. B groups.

Dataset	Feature selection	LDA	QDA	MLP	CNN
Dataset A (adds vs muls)	Yes [6]	50.3%	50.2%	50.1%	-
Dataset A (adds vs muls)	No	69.2%	66.8%	99.9%	99.8%
Dataset B (group 1 vs group 5)	No	95.4%	77.2%	93.4%	95.4%
Dataset B (all groups)	No	84.4%	70.7%	86.4%	88.2%

The confusion matrix in Fig. 5 shows the MLP result for all groups in dataset B. Since the training and testing data are randomly divided, the expected amount of traces per group, and therefore the maximum score in the matrix, is 500. It can be seen that the score is the worst for group 2 (shifts). The loads and stores can be distinguished best. Although they can be distinguished on the basis of their two-cycle duration compared to the one-cycle duration of the other instructions, loads are also not classified as stores or the other way around.

6.5   Training and Classification Results for Individual Instructions

The scores for the classification of different instructions are given in Table 9. Again, KL-based feature selection can only be applied to dataset A. The scores for KL-based feature selection are just above random guessing of instructions, but when machine learning is used on the same traces, the score increases to 99.9% (*identical-program*). This shows that although KL-based feature selection performs better for instructions than for groups, there is still a lot of information in the dataset. Moving to a more realistic scenario (*different-program*), however, in dataset C, the machine learning models perform significantly worse than for

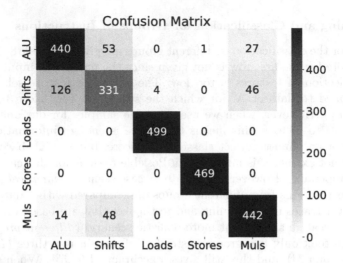

Fig. 5. Confusion matrix groups. Row indicates true label, column indicates predicted label.

groups with maximum scores of 58.1% for two classes and 25.5% for seven classes. Note that the expected score for random guessing is 50% and 14.3% for two and seven classes, respectively.

Table 9. Dataset A vs. C instructions.

Dataset	Feature selection	LDA	QDA	MLP	CNN
Dataset A (adds vs ands)	Yes [6]	56%	55.4%	51.6%	51.8%
Dataset A (adds vs ands)	No	88.1%	78.5%	99.9%	99.9%
Dataset C (adds vs ands)	No	54.7%	49.8%	58.1%	51.8%
Dataset C (all instructions)	No	20.1%	15.5%	25.5%	25.2%

The confusion matrix in Fig. 6 shows an MLP result for all instructions in dataset C. Since the training and testing data are randomly divided, the expected amount of traces per instruction and therefore the maximum score in the matrix is 500. Since the score is significantly lower than the score for groups, the matrix shows a lot of false positives and false negatives. The only instruction classified correctly in more than 50% of the cases is orrs.

6.6 Discussion

We use the term *identical-program* to describe the classification results obtained when traces of the same *program* are used to train the model and report the classification results. We use the term *different-program* to describe the classification results obtained when traces of different *programs* using the same *target instruction* are used to train the model and report the classification results. The

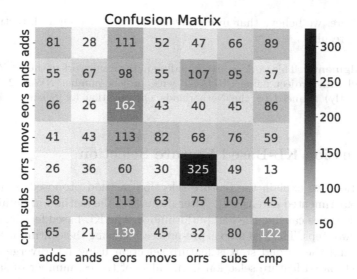

Fig. 6. Confusion matrix instructions. Row indicates true label, column indicates predicted label.

different-program setting is more challenging compared to *identical-program* for classification, but is also more realistic.

Our side-channel disassembler reached a success rate of 99% in the *identical-program* setting, which is in line with most state-of-the-art results reported in the literature. However, we observe a decrease in the success rate (95.4%) when using the *different program* strategy. When we include all five groups, our model success rate reaches 88.2%.

We observe the same behavior when analyzing results related to instruction classification. Our side-channel disassembler reached a success rate of 99.9% in the *identical-program* setting when used to distinguish between two instructions (in the same group). The same classification task in the *different program* strategy results in a success rate of 58.1%. However, when we include all the instructions, our model success rate reaches only 25.5%.

7   Conclusions and Future Work

In this work, we present the first side-channel disassembler that targets the ARM-Cortex M0, a 32-bit microcontroller. Previous side-channel disassemblers target simple 8-bit architectures. We show that the training and classification strategies used have a substantial impact on the performance reported in the model. Under ideal conditions, our side-channel disassembler reaches a success rate of 99%, while under realistic conditions, we observe a success rate of 88.2%. To our surprise, the use of sophisticated methods for feature selection did not prove helpful, and the best results we obtained with unprocessed features. As a result, creating data sets is a simpler task. The present study only examined relatively simple deep learning models, which we did not optimize for the task. Therefore, we believe that more advanced deep learning architectures can improve the results.

Acknowledgments. This work received funding in the framework of the NWA Cyber-security Call with project name PROACT with project number NWA.1215.18.014, which is (partly) financed by the Netherlands Organisation for Scientific Research (NWO).

A   Discussion KL-Based Feature Selection

In this section, we explain the feature selection method proposed by [6], with which we experimented extensively. After discussing the method in detail, we go over possible issues causing the bad performance. The KL-based feature analysis consists of two steps. The first step is pre-processing using the continuous wavelet transform, and the second step is feature selection using KL divergence. The input for KL-based feature selection is (number of traces, number of samples), resulting in output shape (number of traces, number of features).

A.1   Background

Continuous Wavelet Transform(CWT). is used to transform traces from the time domain to the time-frequency region. The wavelet used is a standard Ricker wavelet included in the `scipy.signal` package. The width used for the `scipy.signal.cwt` function is 50. The result is a two-dimensional array of shapes (50,469). This means that for each power trace, we end up with $50 * 469 = 23450$ data points. These data points are used as input for the next step: feature selection.

KL-Based Feature Selection. Kullback-Leibler (KL) divergence is the statistical distance between two probability distributions. This means that before we can use the KL divergence, the acquired data has to be transformed to probability distributions. This has to be done for each of the 23450 data points in the processed power traces. When comparing two programs or target instructions, for each data point the probability distribution is taken over the 300 (program) or 6000 (target instruction) traces. Computing the probability distributions is done with `numpy.histogram` using the Freedman-Diaconis rule for determining the bin width. For the actual KL divergence calculation we use the `scipy.special.kl_div` function.

The resulting two-dimensional array has the same shape (50,469) as all input power traces after the CWT. On the basis of the KL-divergence values at each of the sample points in this array, the features to be used in machine learning can be selected.

Not-Varying Feature Points. For each target instruction the KL divergence is computed for each unique combination of its programs. This results in 190 KL divergence arrays. To select points with a low KL divergence value, for each of the arrays a list of coordinates (*list*) is created that includes only the sample points that have a value below a certain threshold. The *not-varying feature points* are selected using Eq. 1.

$$NVP_{target} = list_1 \cap list_2 \cap \cdots \cap list_{190} \tag{1}$$

Distinct Points. Between the different target instructions, the KL is also computed, using all the programs together instead of comparing the programs. For each of the 23450 sample points in the power traces, the probability distribution is taken over the $20 * 300 = 6000$ power traces. Since there is only one combination for which the KL divergence has to be computed, the result is just one array compared to the 190 for *not-varying feature points*. To avoid collinearity, only local maximum values are used instead of taking points above a certain threshold [6]. A list of the sample points that have a local maximum value is computed; this list is called $DP_{targetA\,vs.\,targetB}$.

The final result of the selection of features is a combination of *not-varying feature points* and *distinct points*:

$$feature\,points = NVP_{targetA} \cap NVP_{targetB} \cap DP_{targetA\,vs.\,targetB} \tag{2}$$

The selected points should not vary much when the same target instruction is executed, but should vary much when different target instructions are executed and therefore contain much information for classification.

A.2   Results of Feature Selection

The final amount of *feature points* is determined using Eq. 2. The amount of *not-varying feature points* depends on the threshold used, while the amount of *distinct points* is fixed. The latter therefore is the limiting factor for the amount of resulting *feature points*. The different number of points to compute feature points for adds vs. muls and adds vs. ands is given in Table 10.

Table 10. Results for KL-based feature selection

Threshold	adds vs. muls	adds vs. ands
Not-varying feature points	795	1540
Distinct feature points	155	435
Feature points	7	112
LDA score	50.3%	56%

The first point of interest is the low amount of *feature points* for adds versus muls, but doubling the KL threshold to 0.8 only increases the amount of *feature points* to 8. The low amount of *feature points* could be an influence for the low results, however adds vs. ands does not perform much better with 112 *feature points*.

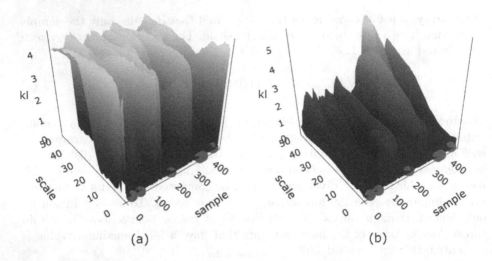

Fig. 7. KL divergence graphs with selected *feature points* for **adds** vs. **muls**. (a) **muls** program 1 vs. program 2. (b) **adds** vs. **muls**.

When plotting *feature points* in the KL divergence graphs, one of the possible causes for the low classification rates can be seen. The *not-varying feature points* are selected to be below a certain threshold and therefore should have a low KL value. This is true for both comparisons, as can be seen in Fig. 7a and Fig. 8a. However, when looking at *distinct points* (Fig. 7b and Fig. 8b) the selected *feature points* also have a very low KL value, whereas they should have a high KL value.

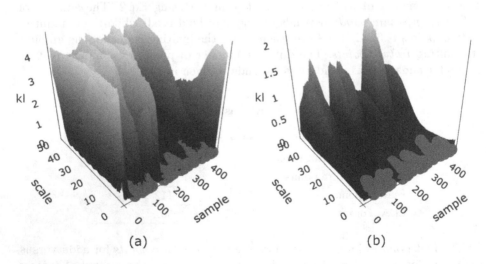

Fig. 8. KL divergence graphs with selected *feature points* for **adds** vs. **ands**. (a) **ands** program 1 vs. program 2. (b) **adds** vs. **ands**.

The low KL values for *distinct points* are possible because there is no threshold for *distinct points* to be above. The only requirement is that the selected points be a local maximum. This does not exclude points with a high KL value, but they are not present. When comparing these graphs with the results of [6], we notice that the shape of our figures is different. Whereas the high KL values for both comparing target instructions and comparing programs with the same target instruction are located mainly on the higher scales, this is different for the results in [6]. For their results, the low KL values for comparing different programs with the same target instruction are located at the same scales as the high values for comparing different target instructions. The cause of this could be related to the exact implementation, which the authors of [6] do not specify, or due to architectural differences between the different microcontrollers.

References

1. Kocher, P.C., Jaffe, J., Jun, B.: Differential power analysis. In: Wiener, M. (ed.) CRYPTO 1999. LNCS, vol. 1666, pp. 388–397. Springer, Heidelberg (1999). https://doi.org/10.1007/3-540-48405-1_25
2. Park, J., Rahman, F., Vassilev, A., Forte, D., Tehranipoor, M.: Leveraging side-channel information for disassembly and security. J. Emerg. Technol. Comput. Syst. **16**(1) (2019). https://doi.org/10.1145/3359621. ISSN 1550-4832
3. Arora, V., Buhan, I., Perin, G., Picek, S.: A tale of two boards: on the influence of microarchitecture on side-channel leakage. In: Grosso, V., Pöppelmann, T. (eds.) CARDIS 2021. LNCS, vol. 13173, pp. 80–96. Springer, Cham (2022). https://doi.org/10.1007/978-3-030-97348-3_5
4. Shelton, M.A., Samwel, N., Batina, L., Regazzoni, F., Wagner, M., Yarom, Y.: Rosita: towards automatic elimination of power-analysis leakage in ciphers. In: 28th Annual Network and Distributed System Security Symposium, NDSS 2021, Virtually, 21–25 February 2021. The Internet Society (2021). https://www.ndss-symposium.org/ndsspaper/rosita-towards-automatic-elimination-of-power-analysis-leakage-inciphers/
5. McCann, D., Oswald, E., Whitnall, C.: Towards practical tools for side channel aware software engineering: grey box' modelling for instruction leakages. In: Proceedings of the 26th USENIX Conference on Security Symposium, SEC 2017, Vancouver, BC, Canada, pp. 199–216. USENIX Association (2017). ISBN 9781931971409
6. Park, J., Xu, X., Jin, Y., Forte, D., Tehranipoor, M.: Power-based sidechannel instruction-level disassembler. In: 2018 55th ACM/ESDA/IEEE Design Automation Conference (DAC), pp. 1–6 (2018). https://doi.org/10.1109/DAC.2018.8465848
7. Eisenbarth, T., Paar, C., Weghenkel, B.: Building a side channel based disassembler. In: Gavrilova, M.L., Tan, C.J.K., Moreno, E.D. (eds.) Transactions on Computational Science X. LNCS, vol. 6340, pp. 78–99. Springer, Heidelberg (2010). https://doi.org/10.1007/978-3-642-17499-5_4
8. Msgna, M., Markantonakis, K., Mayes, K.: Precise instruction-level side channel profiling of embedded processors. In: Huang, X., Zhou, J. (eds.) ISPEC 2014. LNCS, vol. 8434, pp. 129–143. Springer, Cham (2014). https://doi.org/10.1007/978-3-319-06320-1_11 ISBN 978-3-319-06320-1
9. Bazangani, O., Iooss, A., Buhan, I., Batina, L.: Abby: automating the creation of fine-grained leakage models, Cryptology ePrint Archive, Report 2021/1569 (2021). https://ia.cr/2021/1569

Towards Isolated AI Accelerators with OP-TEE on SoC-FPGAs

Tsunato Nakai[1,2]([✉]), Daisuke Suzuki[1], and Takeshi Fujino[2]

[1] Mitsubishi Electric Corporation, Tokyo, Japan
nakai.tsunato@dy.mitsubishielectric.co.jp
[2] Ritsumeikan University, Kyoto, Japan

Abstract. An artificial intelligence (AI) accelerator is a specialized hardware accelerator designed to accelerate machine learning applications. The machine learning applications may require an isolated execution for the confidentiality of model information and processing data and the integrity of the application tasks. For example, when critical applications such as biometrics use machine learning, the applications are required to execute in a trusted environment isolated not to be compromised by the other applications. The isolated execution of a machine learning application using an AI accelerator is often achieved with a proprietary hardware architecture consisting of dedicated security circuits for the accelerator. On the other hand, several previous works have proposed using open-source or general-purpose security functions for the isolation execution to reduce design costs and commonly apply to various accelerators. This paper proposes an isolated execution method of AI accelerators using OP-TEE, an open-source Trusted Execution Environment (TEE) implementing the Arm TrustZone technology. The contribution is to analyze the security threats of AI accelerators, propose the countermeasure based on OP-TEE, and evaluate the implementation of the isolated execution.

Keywords: Trusted execution environment · Arm TrustZone · NVDLA · ZynqMPSoC

1 Introduction

An artificial intelligence (AI) accelerator is a high-performance computation machine for the efficient processing of machine learning applications in terms of processing speed and memory. Especially machine learning applications implemented on embedded devices use AI accelerators for real-time processing or power consumption. Many companies are developing a diversity of AI accelerators.

The machine learning applications may require an isolated execution for security and privacy. For example, machine learning applications that require reliability, such as biometric authentication, should be executed in a trusted environment isolated from the other applications. The processing data of such applications is related to data privacy. In addition, model information, such

J. Zhou et al. (Eds.): ACNS 2022 Workshops, LNCS 13285, pp. 200–217, 2022.
https://doi.org/10.1007/978-3-031-16815-4_12

as the network configuration and parameters, can be regarded as the intellectual property of model creators. Moreover, if the model information is revealed, it is easy to carry out several attacks such as adversarial example attacks [1] and model inversion attacks [2]. Therefore, several machine learning applications require the confidentiality of model information and processing data and the integrity of the application tasks. Recent works have proposed several methods using trusted execution environments (TEEs) to protect the trained models, the processing data, and the execution tasks [3–5]. TEEs provide an isolated environment that malicious software cannot manipulate.

Several machine learning applications using AI accelerators often achieve isolated execution with a proprietary hardware architecture consisting of dedicated security circuits for the accelerators. For example, according to the Apple Platform Security report [6], the machine learning applications related to security and privacy, such as Face ID, achieve isolated execution by using a dedicated secure subsystem (Secure Enclave), which is separated from the main processor. Only Secure Enclave can access the AI accelerator (Neural Engine) for security and privacy. In one of the previous works, Hua et al. applied the isolated execution to an open-source AI accelerator of Xilinx (CHaiDNN [7]) by implementing a dedicated controller with a specific instruction set around the accelerator [8].

Several previous works have proposed that open-source or general-purpose security functions are used for the isolation execution of AI accelerators to reduce design costs and commonly apply to various accelerators. Xie et al. apply the isolated execution to an open-source AI accelerator (VTA [9]) by using Intel SGX, a TEE, and plugging in a dedicated security interface circuit to VTA [10]. However, only the VTA and the security interface circuit have been implemented and evaluated. The paper does not show the implementation and evaluation of the connection to Intel SGX.

This paper proposes an isolated execution method of AI accelerators using OP-TEE [11], an open-source TEE implementing the Arm TrustZone technology, and reports the implementation of the isolated execution. The proposed method applied the isolated execution to an open-source AI accelerator of NVIDIA (NVDLA [12]) by mainly using OP-TEE, XMPUs, and XPPUs. The XMPUs and XPPUs [13] are general-purpose security functions provided by Xilinx on SoC-FPGAs (Zynq UltraScale+ MPSoC). The paper analyzes the security threats of AI accelerators and clarifies the scope of the proposed countermeasures using open-source or general-purpose security functions.

The contributions of this work can be summarized as follows:

- The proposed method provides the isolated execution of AI accelerators based on open-source and general-purpose security functions (Sect. 3). This paper focuses on the following topics that previous works have not discussed: the isolated execution of AI accelerators using OP-TEE and the security functions in recent SoC-FPGAs.
- The security threats of AI accelerators are analyzed (Sect. 2), and the scope of the proposed countermeasures is clarified (Sect. 3).
- The experiments show the implementation and evaluation of the proposed method.

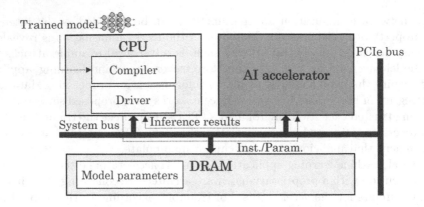

Fig. 1. System architecture of a typical AI accelerator

2 Security Analysis

This section describes the security threats of AI accelerators. In addition, the section describes previous works of isolated execution countermeasures against the threats.

2.1 AI Accelerators

Several machine learning applications use an AI accelerator which has more computing power than the main processor. In particular, there is a diversity of AI accelerators for deep learning, such as TPU [14], VTA [9], and NVDLA [12]. Most AI accelerators typically have dedicated instruction sets and compilers. For example, NVDLA includes register instructions for each functional module and the corresponding compiler.

Figure 1 shows the system architecture of a typical AI accelerator. The AI accelerator system consists of a software stack and a hardware stack. The software stack consists mainly of a compiler and a driver. The compiler analyzes the network of a trained model and generates the instruction flow from a dedicated instruction set to execute the trained model on the AI accelerator. Furthermore, the compiler converts the parameters of the trained model into a dedicated data format. The driver sends and receives data with the AI accelerator based on the model information converted by the compiler. The hardware stack consists primarily of the CPU, DRAM, and AI accelerator. Due to the large size of trained model parameters, the parameters are often deployed in the off-chip DRAM. The AI accelerator executes the inference process using instructions from the main processor and data stored in the DRAM.

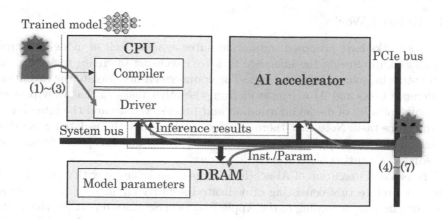

Fig. 2. Attack path to a typical AI accelerator

2.2 Threat Model

The attacker's goal is to steal model information or compromise the inference task. For example, model information can be regarded as intellectual property because it may contain the know-how of the model creator. In addition, when a biometric authentication uses machine learning, the attacker may bypass the authentication by compromising the inference task.

An attacker could launch both software and hardware attacks on an AI accelerator. Figure 2 shows the paths of each attack on the system architecture of a typical AI accelerator. Each attack is categorized by reference to the paper [10]. In software, the following attacks are possible.

(1) Direct access to the main memory excluding CPU reserved areas.
(2) Access the AI accelerator via memory-mapped I/O and send commands.
(3) Unauthorized driver API calls or tampering.

This paper assumes that an attacker can compromise the OS or hypervisor to execute malicious software at the privilege level.

In hardware, the following attacks are possible.

(4) Direct access to the main memory by connecting a malicious device to the external I/O interface (DMA attacks).
(5) Direct access to the off-chip memory (DRAM) when the off-chip memory is available.
(6) Access the AI accelerator via a malicious device and send commands.
(7) Eavesdropping on the system and Peripheral Component Interconnect Express (PCIe) bus.

The CPU and AI accelerator packages themselves are assumed to be trusted here. The hardware such as memory, storage, and peripherals may be compromised. Note that side-channel attacks using execution time and memory access patterns and DoS attacks are outside the scope of this paper.

2.3   Related Works

Previous works have proposed countermeasures against theft of model information and compromising the inference task by executing inference tasks and AI accelerators in isolated environments. The countermeasures isolate the execution of inference tasks and AI accelerators from the other tasks so that they protect the confidentiality of model information and processed data and the integrity of the inference task. Note that there are also works about the isolated execution of machine learning applications using GPUs [15–17], but this paper focuses on the isolated execution of AI-specific hardware.

The isolated execution of AI accelerators is often achieved with a proprietary hardware architecture consisting of dedicated security circuits for the accelerators. For example, according to the Apple Platform Security report [6], the applications related to security and privacy with the AI accelerator (Neural Engine), such as Face ID, achieve isolated execution by using a dedicated secure subsystem (Secure Enclave), which is separated from the main processor. The latest devices (A14 and M1 or later) further divide the operation of Secure Enclave into normal and secure modes. The applications related to security and privacy, such as Face ID, access the Neural Engine in the secure mode. In addition, there is a mechanism to reset the state of the Neural Engine when the mode is switched so that both the normal and secure modes can use the Neural Engine. The Secure Enclave uses memory encryption as well as memory isolation.

In contrast to the isolated execution with proprietary hardware, several previous works have proposed using open-source or general-purpose security functions to reduce design costs and commonly apply to various accelerators. Hua et al. implement a dedicated controller with a specific instruction set around an open-source AI accelerator of Xilinx (CHaiDNN [7]) for the isolated execution [8]. On the other hand, Xie et al. use Intel SGX, a TEE, and plug in a dedicated security interface circuit to access the open-source AI accelerator (VTA [9]) for the isolated execution [10]. TEEs can achieve the isolated execution of AI accelerators without a dedicated controller with a specific instruction set, as in the method of Hua et al.

Xie et al. proposed the isolated execution method of AI accelerator with low design cost by using TEEs. However, its implementation and evaluation are not well shown. Specifically, only the VTA and the security interface circuit have been implemented and evaluated. The paper does not show the implementation and evaluation of the connection to Intel SGX.

Although recent SoC-FPGAs support memory protection units (MPUs) and TEEs against DMA attacks related to the threat of (4), previous works have not discussed the application of AI accelerators to isolated execution. For example, Zynq UltraScale+ MPSoC, an SoC-FPGA of Xilinx, can use the Arm TrustZone technology. Furthermore, it has the Xilinx Memory Protection Units (XMPUs) and Xilinx Peripheral Protection Units (XPPUs) to complement the security functions of the Arm TrustZone technology [13,18].

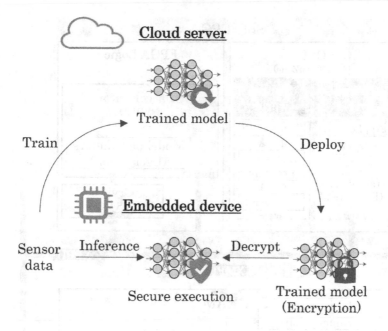

Fig. 3. Use case of the isolated execution

3   Proposed Method

This section proposes the isolated execution method of AI accelerators based on open-source or general-purpose security functions. The proposed method mainly uses OP-TEE on the Arm TrustZone technology, XMPUs, and XPPUs. First, the section describes the overview of the proposed method. Next, the components: NVDLA, Arm TrustZone, OP-TEE, XMPUs, and XPPUs, are explained. Finally, the correspondence between threats of (1) to (7) and the security function of the proposed method is summarized.

3.1   Overview

Figure 3 shows a use case of the isolated execution of AI accelerators. The use case shows that an embedded device executes a real-time inference with an AI accelerator using sensor data as input on-site. A cloud server gathers the sensor data from the embedded device and generates a trained model for the embedded device. The generated model in the cloud server is fed back to the embedded device for making it suitable. In such a service, the trained model can be a key component. The service can be required to protect the trained model from theft. The use case shows that the encrypted model is securely decrypted and executed for inference.

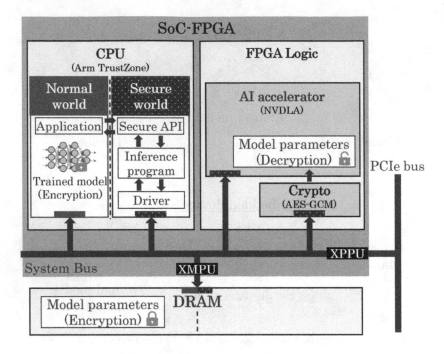

Fig. 4. Overview of the proposed method

Figure 4 shows the overview of the proposed method. In Fig. 4, the proposed method is applied to NVDLA, an AI accelerator. The security functions mainly include Arm TrustZone, XMPUs, and XPPUs. The cryptographic circuit, AES-GCM, is optional. Section 3.3 explains its necessity. The Arm TrustZone isolates applications executed on the CPU. In particular, isolating the driver of the NVDLA restricts access to the NVDLA. The XMPUs isolate the access to the DRAM. The XPPUs isolate the access from peripherals. The next section describes the details of each function.

The execution flow of the proposed method is as follows. First, a deep learning application is launched from the normal execution environment (the normal world). The application sends input data and model information (the network configuration and parameters) to the isolated execution environment (the secure world) via specific APIs. The model information is encrypted in advance. The inference program in Secure world decrypts the network configuration and sends instructions regarding the network configuration to NVDLA via the driver. The encrypted model parameters are sent to the NVDLA via DRAM. The cryptographic circuit decrypts the model parameters and passes them to the NVDLA. The NVDLA reads the decrypted model parameters via the cryptographic circuit according to the commands from the inference program in the secure world. The inference results are obtained by repeating the above operations between the inference program in the secure world and NVDLA.

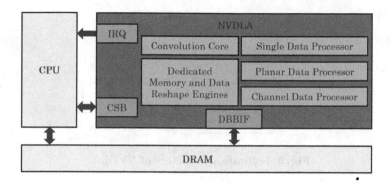

Fig. 5. Hardware architecture of NVDLA (Small)

3.2 NVDLA

NVDLA is a deep learning accelerator framework that NVIDIA open-sourced in 2017. The maintenance of the NVDLA project ended in the middle of development in 2019. However, the NVDLA has recently attracted attention, with several companies utilizing it and the release of a product combined with RISC-V, an open-source CPU.

The hardware of the NVDLA includes Small-NVDLA for IoT devices and Large-NVDLA for performance-oriented devices. Figure 5 shows the hardware architecture of the Small-NVDLA. The Small-NVDLA consists of a convolution core, a single data processor, a planner data processor, a channel data processor, and Dedicated memory and data reshape engines. The convolution core is an optimized high-performance convolution engine. The single data processor is a look-up engine for the activation function. The planar data processor is a matrix averaging engine for pooling. The channel data processor is a matrix averaging engine for normalization functions. The dedicated memory and data reshape engines are acceleration engines for tensor reshape and copy operations. The data backbone interface (DBBIF) is an AMBA AXI4-compliant interface for the dedicated memory engines of the NVDLA to access the DRAM. The configuration space bus (CSB) is an address and data interface to access and configure the NVDLA register set. The states of the NVDLA, such as operation completion and error conditions, are asynchronously reported to the CPU that commands the NVDLA via the external interrupt (IRQ) interface.

The software of NVDLA consists of a compiler and a driver. Figure 6 shows the software architecture of NVDLA. The compiler converts trained models with Caffe [19], an open-source deep learning framework, into a Loadable file which is a proprietary file format of NVDLA. The driver reads the loadable file and sends the instructions to NVDLA for each layer of the trained model, their scheduling, and the parameters. The NVDLA project designs the driver to separate the parts that depend on the implementation platform, making it easy to port to various execution platforms, including Linux and FreeRTOS.

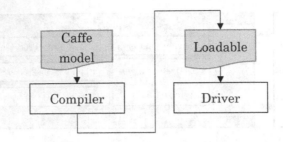

Fig. 6. Software architecture of NVDLA

3.3   Arm TrustZone and OP-TEE

The Arm TrustZone technology is a security function that enables a TEE in Arm Cortex-A/M processors. The Arm TrustZone isolates the computer resources such as registers, cache, and memory between a normal world and a secure world. The secure world is an isolated execution environment that is not directly accessible from the normal world and allows the execution of security-critical software.

The firmware of the Arm TrustZone (Arm Trusted Firmware) has a secure monitor. The secure monitor is a system that provides that a context switch is managed between the normal world and the secure world when a secure monitor call (SMC) is received to switch each world. The communication between the normal world and the secure world is only via a specific API.

The Arm TrustZone can also be deployed on SoC-FPGAs with Cortex-A processors. The Arm TrustZone enables to isolate the access of circuits (PL: Programmable Logic). In FPGA-SoC of Xilinx, the ARPROT[0]/AWPROT[0] bits and AXI Interconnect are used to set the isolation function. The master of the AXI bus sets the ARPROT[0]/AWPROT[0] bits to configure read/write security settings. The slaves of the AXI bus can be protected by setting to secure or non-secure. The slaves with the secure setting can only be accessed from the secure world.

OP-TEE is an open-source TEE that has a secure OS running on the Arm TrustZone technology. The OP-TEE supports the evaluation board of Zynq Ultrascale+ MPSoC, which is the SoC-FPGA of Xilinx.

3.4   XMPUs and XPPUs

The memory and peripheral isolation function of the Xilinx Zynq Ultrascale+ MPSoC are described. The isolation function consists of the Xilinx Memory Protection Units (XMPUs) and the Xilinx Peripheral Protection Units (XPPUs). Compared to the Arm TrustZone, the XMPUs and XPPUs can precisely configure the isolation in units of AXI bus masters.

Table 1. Correspondence between threats and the security functions

Security functions	Threats						
	(1)	(2)	(3)	(4)	(5)	(6)	(7)
Arm TrustZone	✓	✓	✓	✓	-	✓	-
XMPUs	-	✓	-	-	✓	-	-
XPPUs	-	✓	-	✓	✓	✓	-
Parameter encryption	✓	-	-	✓	✓	-	✓

The Xilinx Memory Protection Units (XMPUs) provide memory protection by isolating memory areas. The XMPUs check whether access to an address is allowed from a definition of memory areas for memory accesses from AXI bus masters. The definition of memory areas lists the address range and the AXI bus masters that are allowed to access the address range. In addition, the configured memory areas can be isolated into a normal world and a secure world by the Arm TrustZone support. The memory areas tagged as secure can only be accessed by authorized secure masters.

Xilinx Peripherals Protection Units (XPPUs) provide peripheral protection and control registers. The XPPUs define the address areas of peripherals and control registers and check whether access to the addresses is allowed from AXI bus masters. In addition, the configured access of peripherals and control registers can be isolated into the normal world and a secure world by the Arm TrustZone support.

3.5   Threats and Countermeasures

Table 1 shows the correspondence between the security functions of the proposed method and the security threats of (1) to (7) in Sect. 2.2.

The threats of (1) to (3) on software can be mainly addressed by the Arm TrustZone technology. The attacker is assumed to attack from the normal world.

(1) Against the direct access to the main memory excluding CPU reserved areas, the memory isolation of the Arm TrustZone functionality restricts access from the normal world to the main memory where the model information is stored. In addition, model information accessed from the normal world is encrypted and stored.

(2) Against the access to the AI accelerator via memory-mapped I/O, the memory isolation of the Arm TrustZone prevents access from the normal world via memory-mapped I/O is restricted. The XMPUs also restrict access to the DRAM.

(3) Against the unauthorized driver API calls or tampering with the driver, the memory isolation of the Arm TrustZone prevents the unauthorized driver API calls from the normal world. The driver implemented in the secure world is not tampered with from the normal world.

The threats of (4) to (7) on hardware can be mainly addressed by XMPUs, XPPUs, and the cryptographic circuit.

(4) Against the direct access to the main memory by connecting a malicious device to the external I/O interface, the memory isolation of the Arm Trust-Zone allows the main memory used by the secure world cannot be accessed.
(5) Against the direct access to the off-chip memory (DRAM) when the off-chip memory is available, the access to DRAM is restricted by the XMPUs.
(6) Against the access to the AI accelerator via a malicious device, the PL isolation of the Arm TrustZone allows the unauthorized access is restricted.
(7) Against eavesdropping on the system and PCIe bus, the cryptographic circuit achieves that model information flowing on the bus is encrypted.

The threats of (4) to (6) are addressed by the peripheral isolation of XPPUs to prevent DMA attacks. The cryptographic circuit also serves as countermeasures for (4) to (5) in addition to (7).

The open-source or general-purpose security functions such as the Arm Trust-Zone, XMPUs, and XPPUs can address the threats of (1) to (6). For the threat of (7), it is necessary to build the cryptographic circuit to the AI accelerator for parameter encryption. Compared with previous works, the method proposed by Hua et al. [8] addresses the threats of (1) to (7) with access control and parameter encryption by a dedicated controller. The method proposed by Xie et al. [10] addresses the threats of (1) to (7) with Intel SGX and parameter encryption. The proposed method does not require the design of a dedicated controller as in the method proposed by Hua et al. On the other hand, the proposed method requires the implementation of a cryptographic circuit for parameter encryption against the threat of (7). The proposed method is similar to the method proposed by Xie et al., however, this paper reveals that the open-source and general-purpose security functions of the proposed method can address the threats of (1) to (6). Note that this section does not cover attacks that exploit vulnerabilities in security functions, side-channel attacks, and denial-of-service attacks.

4   Experiments

This section describes experiments to evaluate the implementation of the proposed method. In the experiments, the overhead of the execution time is evaluated due to the security functions.

4.1   Experimental Setup

The experiments are performed on the ZCU102 [20], a Zynq Ultrascale+ MPSoC evaluation board. Since the OP-TEE supports the ZCU102, the OP-TEE is implemented on the Arm TrustZone of the Zynq Ultrascale+ MPSoC. However, the publicly available code has bugs and parts that are not compatible with the latest ZCU102. The code of the OP-TEE is modified for the experiments.

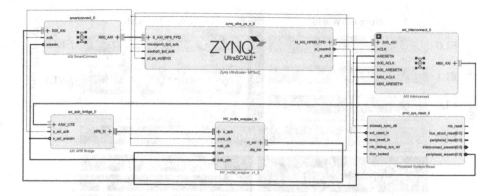

Fig. 7. Hardware block diagram of the implemented NVDLA

Table 2. Trained models in the experiments

Trained models	Number of layers	Parameter size [MB]	Training dataset
LeNet-5	7	0.19	MNIST
Resnet18	18	44	Cifar10

Figure 7 shows the hardware block diagram of the implemented NVDLA. The NVDLA is implemented to PL on the ZCU102 and connected to the Zynq Ultrascale+ MPSoC via AXI Interconnect. The clock frequency is 100 MHz. The DRAM areas used by the NVDLA are restricted to access from the normal world by the XMPUs configuration of AXI Interconnect. The restricted areas are used to store instruction data and intermediate values of operations for the NVLDA. The unrestricted areas are mainly used in the normal world, where the encrypted model information is stored for the NVDLA. The peripheral used in the normal world is restricted to access to the secure world by the XPPUs configuration of AXI Interconnect.

Note that no cryptographic circuit is implemented in this experiment because it is optional in the proposed method. For the protection of the trained models, the model information is encrypted by the AES-GCM-128 for confidentiality and integrity [4]. It is stored in the normal world. In the experiments, the model information is decrypted by the software in the secure world, not by the cryptographic circuit. In addition, note that the encryption of parameters is decrypted by the software in the secure world, so it does not protect against eavesdropping on the system bus and PCIe bus (the threat of (7)).

Figure 8 shows the software stack of the implemented NVDLA. It is necessary to port the driver to operate the NVDLA. The driver provided by the NVDLA project can be directly ported to the OS (Petalinux) in the normal world of OP-TEE. On the other hand, the driver can not be directly ported to the OS in the secure world, because the OS has minimal functionality and lacks a kernel that depends on the driver. The driver is configured with separate platform-dependent

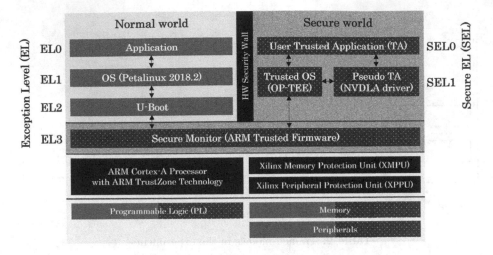

Fig. 8. Software stack of the implemented NVDLA

portions. However, these dependent portions must be developed for the OS of the secure world. The part of the driver for the secure world is developed by using a Pseudo Trusted Application (PTA), the implementation method for the kernel module of the secure world for OP-TEE. The inference application is implemented as a user Trusted Application (TA). The application in the normal world launches the TA via the OP-TEE API. Only the application in the secure world can access the NVDLA.

Table 2 shows trained models in the experiments. The experiments are performed by implementing LeNet-5 [21] and Resnet18 [22] to be accelerated by NVDLA. The trained model of LeNet-5 is trained to identify the handwriting sample MNIST [23]. The trained model of Resnet18 is trained to identify CIFAR10 object images [24]. Each model is generated by Caffe and converted to a loadable file by the compiler for NVDLA.

4.2 Experimental Results

The overhead of the execution time for inference is evaluated. First, the overhead of hardware acceleration is evaluated due to the differences between the normal and secure world. Next, the whole overhead of the inference application is evaluated, including the overhead of context switching.

A comparison of the execution time of NVDLA is shown in Table 3 and Fig. 9. The purpose of the comparison is to analyze the overhead which is caused by each security function, Arm TrustZone, XMPUs, and XPPUs. The execution time is measured from the launch of the NVDLA driver to the end of the inference to analyze the impact on hardware acceleration. The overhead of switching the worlds and parameter encryption is not included in the execution time. According to the results, there actually is not much of a difference between

Table 3. Execution time of hardware acceleration in the normal and secure world

	Call from Normal world	Call from Secure world	
		without XMPUs & XPPUs	with XMPUs & XPPUs
Execution time [ms]			
LeNet-5	2.29	2.46	2.63
Resnet18	10.20	10.36	11.53

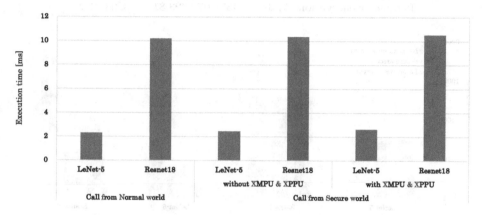

Fig. 9. Comparison of execution time of hardware acceleration in the normal and secure world

the accelerations in the normal and secure world on each trained model. More-over, the overhead of the call from the secure world is negligible. Because the XMPUs and XPPUs are implemented in hardware. The results show that Arm TrustZone, XMPUs, and XPPUs have a small impact on the execution time of hardware acceleration.

Table 4 and Fig. 10 show a comparison of the whole execution time for the inference application. The results show the whole overhead of the inference on NVDLA compared to the software implementation on ARM Cortex-A53 of ZCU102. The execution time is measured from the launch of the application to the end of the inference. The secure execution uses OP-TEE, XMPUs, and XPPUs. The parameter encryption includes the decryption of the model param-eters by the software on the secure execution. The comparison of the implemen-tation on ARM Cortex-A53 and NVDLA shows that the NVDLA acceleration improves the processing speed by a factor of 14 for LeNet-5 and by a factor of 35 for Resnet18. There is an overhead of about 4 ms in the secure execution on each trained model, comparing no countermeasures (the execution in the normal world) to secure execution. The time of the secure execution includes the over-head of context switching because the application in the secure world is called from the normal world. The parameter encryption increases the execution time for each trained model. The execution time includes the time of decryption for encrypted model information in the secure world. The overheads are about 20

Table 4. Execution time of the whole execution time for the inference application

	ARM Cortex-A53		NVDLA	
	LeNet-5	Resnet18	LeNet-5	Resnet18
Execution time [ms]				
No countermeasures	32.68	365.69	2.29	10.2
Secure execution	36.85	370.66	6.43	14.32
Parameter encryption	54.31	4351.07	23.81	3993.91

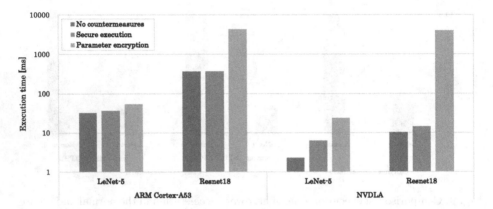

Fig. 10. Comparison of execution time of the whole execution time for the inference application

ms on LeNet-5 and 4 s on Resnet18. The results show an increase by a factor of 3 to 285 from the execution time of the secure execution. It depends on the size of the model parameters for the decryption. Therefore, parameter encryption by the software accounts for the large overhead of the proposed method.

5 Discussion

This section discusses future works for the proposed method, including parameter encryption, combined use of AI accelerators, and hardware security.

5.1 Parameter Encryption

The parameter encryption against the threat of (7) requires that the cryptographic circuitry be integrated into an AI accelerator. In the experiments, the decryption for encrypted parameters is performed by software in the secure world, the overhead of the execution time is dominant. Therefore, the hardware implementation of the cryptographic circuit is expected to reduce the overhead.

5.2   Combined Use of AI Accelerators

AI accelerators could be used in both the normal and secure world. For example, devices of Apple divide the operations of an AI accelerator into normal and secure modes. Each mode can use the AI accelerator [6]. The isolated execution of AI accelerators is not only on Apple devices. NVIDIA's latest GPU architecture (H100), announced in 2022, has confidential computing (CC) mode, which switches to the isolated execution with TEEs by turning the CC mode on and off.

The proposed method restricts access to the AI accelerator to the secure world only. Therefore, it is necessary to consider a mechanism to use AI accelerators in both the normal and secure world.

5.3   Hardware Security

Side-channel attacks are not covered by the proposed method. On the other hand, Xu et al. [25] organize the threats and countermeasures against hardware trojans, side-channel attacks, and fault injection attacks against AI accelerators. Wang et al. [26] also incorporate side-channel attack countermeasures into AI accelerators. Therefore, it is necessary to consider such hardware attacks, including the extent to which countermeasures should be taken.

The proposed method leverages the security functions of hardware support such as Arm TrustZone, XMPUs, and XPPUs. On the other hand, attacks against Arm TrustZone, XMPUs, and XPPUs have also been studied [27,28]. The security of Arm TrustZone, XMPUs, and XPPUs should also be evaluated.

6   Conclusion

This paper proposes an isolated execution method based on open-source and general-purpose security functions for AI accelerators to reduce design costs and commonly apply to various accelerators. The proposed method mainly uses Arm TrustZone (OP-TEE), XMPUs, and XPPUs as the open-source and general-purpose security functions. In the security analysis, the paper showed that open-source and general-purpose security functions can provide several countermeasures, but not to the extent of countermeasures against eavesdropping on the system and PCIe bus. In the experiments, the proposed method is implemented by using OP-TEE and NVDLA, an AI accelerator, on Zynq UltraScale+ MPSoC, an SoC-FPGA. The experiments show that the execution time of parameter encryption by the software accounts for the large overhead (up to 285 times increase) compared to the overhead of Arm TrustZone, XMPUs, and XPPUs in the proposed method. The overhead of Arm TrustZone, XMPUs, and XPPUs have a small impact on the execution time of hardware acceleration. Therefore, AI accelerators require a cryptographic circuit in the case of the countermeasure against eavesdropping model parameters on the bus and the acceleration of the parameter encryption.

Acknowledgments. This work was supported by JST-Mirai Program Grant Number JPMJMI19B6, Japan.

References

1. Szegedy, C., et al.: Intriguing properties of neural networks. arXiv preprint arXiv:1312.6199 (2013)
2. Fredrikson, M., Jha, S., Ristenpart, T.: Model inversion attacks that exploit confidence information and basic countermeasures. In: Proceedings of the 22nd ACM SIGSAC Conference on Computer and Communications Security, pp. 1322–1333 (2015)
3. Isakov, M., Gadepally, V., Gettings, K.M., Kinsy, M.A.: Survey of attacks and defenses on edge-deployed neural networks. In: 2019 IEEE High Performance Extreme Computing Conference (HPEC), pp. 1–8. IEEE (2019)
4. Nakai, T., Suzuki, D., Fujino, T.: Towards trained model confidentiality and integrity using trusted execution environments. In: Zhou, J., et al. (eds.) ACNS 2021. LNCS, vol. 12809, pp. 151–168. Springer, Cham (2021). https://doi.org/10. 1007/978-3-030-81645-2_10
5. ETSI GR SAI 004.: GROUP REPORT V1.1.1 Securing Artificial Intelligence (SAI); Problem Statement (2020). https://www.etsi.org/deliver/etsi_gr/SAI/001_ 099/004/01.01.01_60/gr_SAI004v010101p.pdf
6. Apple Secure Enclave. https://support.apple.com/ja-jp/guide/security/ sec59b0b31ff/1/web/1
7. Xilinx CHaiDNN-v2. https://github.com/Xilinx/CHaiDNN
8. Hua, W., Umar, M., Zhang, Z., Edward Suh, G.: GuardNN: secure DNN accelerator for privacy-preserving deep learning. arXiv preprint arXiv:2008.11632 (2020)
9. Moreau, T., et al.: A hardware-software blueprint for flexible deep learning specialization. IEEE Micro **39**(5), 8–16 (2019)
10. Xie, P., Ren, X., Sun, G.: Customizing trusted AI accelerators for efficient privacy-preserving machine learning. arXiv preprint arXiv:2011.06376 (2020)
11. Linaro OP-TEE. https://www.op-tee.org
12. NVIDIA Deep Learning Accelerator. https://nvdla.org
13. Isolation Design Example for the Zynq UltraScale+ MPSoC. https://japan.xilinx. com/support/documentation/application_notes/xapp1336-isolation-design-flow-example-mpsoc.pdf
14. Jouppi, N.P., et al.: In-datacenter performance analysis of a tensor processing unit. In: Proceedings of the 44th Annual International Symposium on Computer Architecture, pp. 1–12 (2017)
15. Park, H., Lin, F.X.: Safe and practical GPU acceleration in trustzone. arXiv preprint arXiv:2111.03065 (2021)
16. Hashemi, H., Wang, Y., Annavaram, M.: Privacy and integrity preserving training using trusted hardware. CoRR, abs/2105.00334 (2021)
17. NVIDIA H100 Tensor Core GPU Architecture, Exceptional Performance, Scalability, and Security for the Data Center. https://www.nvidia.com/en-us/data-center/ solutions/confidential-computing/
18. Benhani, E.M., Bossuet, L., Aubert, A.: The security of ARM TrustZone in a FPGA-based SoC. IEEE Trans. Comput. **68**(8), 1238–1248 (2019)
19. Jia, Y., et al.: Caffe: convolutional architecture for fast feature embedding. arXiv preprint arXiv:1408.5093 (2014)

20. Zynq UltraScale+ MPSoC ZCU102. https://japan.xilinx.com/products/boards-and-kits/ek-u1-zcu102-g.html
21. LeCun, Y., Haffner, P., Bottou, L., Bengio, Y.: Object recognition with gradient-based learning. In: Shape, Contour and Grouping in Computer Vision. LNCS, vol. 1681, pp. 319–345. Springer, Heidelberg (1999). https://doi.org/10.1007/3-540-46805-6_19
22. He, K., Zhang, X., Ren, S., Sun, J.: Deep residual learning for image recognition. In: Proceedings of the IEEE Conference on Computer Vision and Pattern Recognition, pp. 770–778 (2016)
23. Lecun, Y., Bottou, L., Bengio, Y., Haffner, P.: Gradient-based learning applied to document recognition. Proc. IEEE **86**(11), 2278–2324 (1998)
24. Krizhevsky, A., Hinton, G., et al.: Learning multiple layers of features from tiny images (2009)
25. Xu, Q., Arafin, Md.T., Qu, G.: Security of neural networks from hardware perspective: a survey and beyond. In: 2021 26th Asia and South Pacific Design Automation Conference (ASP-DAC), pp. 449–454 (2021)
26. Wang, X., Hou, R., Zhu, Y., Zhang, J., Meng, D.: NPUFort: a secure architecture of DNN accelerator against model inversion attack. In: Proceedings of the 16th ACM International Conference on Computing Frontiers, pp. 190–196 (2019)
27. Gross, M., Jacob, N., Zankl, A., Sigl, G.: Breaking TrustZone memory isolation through malicious hardware on a modern FPGA-SoC. In: Proceedings of the 3rd ACM Workshop on Attacks and Solutions in Hardware Security Workshop, pp. 3–12 (2019)
28. Stajnrod, R., Yehuda, R.B., Zaidenberg, N.J.: Attacking TrustZone on devices lacking memory protection. J. Comput. Virol. Hacking Tech. 1–11 (2021)

Order vs. Chaos: Multi-trunk Classifier for Side-Channel Attack

Praveen Kulkarni[1,2(✉)] and Vincent Verneuil[1]

[1] NXP Semiconductors Germany GmbH, Hamburg, Germany
{praveen.kulkarni,vincent.verneuil}@nxp.com
[2] Radboud University, Nijmegen, The Netherlands
praveen.kulkarni@ru.nl

Abstract. There is a revived interest in applying machine learning techniques for side-channel attacks, focusing on utilizing advancements in deep learning techniques. Most of the recent research work focuses on using a discriminative-learning-based classifier approach for profiled attacks, which we henceforth denote as a standard classifier approach. The standard classifier learns the intermediate target value in the training phase using a training loss function designed with classification accuracy. At the same time, the performance metric used for reporting results on a real attack dataset is generally key guessing entropy.

Although the standard classifiers are popular, they severely suffer from low classification accuracy (almost close to random guessing accuracy) on the attack and validation dataset. This also poses a problem in model selection with early stopping, and most of the literature does model selection at some arbitrary number of training epochs. This raises the concern that the standard classifier approach is ill-posed for the side-channel attack task, and it motivated us to investigate alternative ways of performing a side-channel attack.

This paper will introduce a novel multi-trunk binary classifier (MTOvC) approach as an alternative to a standard classifier. It exhibits good validation and attack dataset accuracies, suggesting that the resulting loss function is more suitable for the side-channel attack task. Moreover, good validation accuracies allow us to perform sensible model selection with early stopping in the case of multi-trunk classifiers.

Keywords: Multi-trunk · Low accuracy · Data-augmentation · Improve accuracy · Order vs. chaos

1 Introduction

The term *side-channel analysis* (SCA) in computer security indicates an attack based on the physical implementation of the algorithm, rather than the weakness in the actual algorithm. In cryptanalysis, side-channel attack aims to recover the encryption key based on information gained from side channels of the device performing the cryptographic operations like timing information [12], power consumption [11], thermal radiation, electromagnetic emanations [7,24], and even

J. Zhou et al. (Eds.): ACNS 2022 Workshops, LNCS 13285, pp. 218–232, 2022.
https://doi.org/10.1007/978-3-031-16815-4_13

acoustic emanations [8]. When it comes to SCA attack, *profiled attacks* are the most popular and powerful within the machine learning community. In the case of *profiled attacks*, the evaluators have access to the test device, and they know about the possible target intermediate values. Using a test device, evaluators first estimate the conditional distribution associated with each sensitive variable (i.e., intermediate value). Then, for SCA attack, the evaluator uses a target device containing a secret to predict the sensitive variable. Using these predictions over multiple traces on the target device can bring down the entropy of the secret and hence attack the device. The first such profiled attack called *template-attack* (TA) was introduced in 2002 [5].

The major drawback of TA is its data complexity [6] when dealing with high dimensional data, and it also needs preprocessing steps like trace alignment. Recently, machine learning, and more specifically, deep learning techniques, are gaining quite some traction in the SCA community and are shown to outperform TA [4,15,23,25]. This can be attributed to auto-feature selection and hierarchical feature learning capabilities offered by these techniques [3,9,14]. For SCA attacks, auto-feature selection avoids the need for the point-of-interest selection step needed for TA. At the same time, multi-layered hierarchical feature learning allows learning non-linear relationships between features, which is not possible with TA as it can be thought of as a single-layered network. Furthermore, to avoid the use of preprocessing steps like trace alignment, and to overcome common jitter-based countermeasure, *convolution neural networks* are proving to be an excellent choice [4,18,25,28]. This is possible as *convolution neural networks* are architecturally invariant to shift and distortion, which is made possible by three core ideas, namely local receptive fields, replicated weights, and spatial or temporal subsampling [13]. The first core idea, i.e., local receptive field capture low-level features, which is fed to higher layers to learn more complex features. The second core idea, replicated weights, allow keeping the parameter count low while constraining each feature map within a convolution layer to perform the same operations across the image/signal. And last third core idea, i.e., spatial or temporal subsampling, which can be used optionally, enables dimensionality reduction and thus helps in bringing down computational complexity. Finally, even more recently, there were several works showcasing that point-of-interest selection before feeding the features into neural networks is not even needed, as with "raw" features, the attack performance can be even better [16,22].

The common setup among most of the recent publications [4,10,18,19,25, 28] on machine learning-based approaches for the SCA attack is to use some variant of discriminative classifiers [20,21]. We call this approach as standard classifier approach. In Sect. 2, we will introduce and highlight some problems with the standard classifier approach when used for SCA attacks. In Sect. 3, we introduce our approach, which we call *multi-trunk order vs. chaos* (MTOvC) binary classifier, and discuss its possible advantages. Finally, we will close this paper with results and conclusion in Sects. 4 and 5, respectively.

2 Standard Classifiers

This section will discuss a typical standard classifier used for side-channel attacks. In Sect. 2.1, we will formulate and describe the standard classifier architecture, while in Sect. 2.2, we will describe evaluation of attack phase. This will be followed by a thought experiment in Sect. 2.3, which will help us to understand the disadvantages associated with the standard classifier. Finally, in Sect. 2.4, we will discuss the disadvantages of the standard classifier, which will help us understand the motivation behind this paper.

2.1 Architecture

A typical standard classifier has stacked neural network layers like convolution, dense, pooling followed by a final softmax layer [9]. Figure 1 shows such a typical standard classifier based on discriminative learning [20,21], used for SCA attacks [4,10,18,19,25,28]. The M training tuples for such a classifier is as follows:

$$\left(t_i^{(label)}, (label) \right) \quad \forall i \in \{1, ..., M\}, \tag{1}$$

with:

(label) — A target intermediate value defined as $label \in Z = f(P, K)$, where P is some public variable e.g., a plaintext, and K is the part of a secret key the attacker wants to retrieve. If the target intermediate value is 8 bit, then *label* can take one of 256 (i.e., 2^8) values. Notation *(label)* is always surrounded by round brackets and can have actual value instead of variable *label* e.g. $(000), (001), ..., (255)$.

C — The number of discrete values a *(label)* can take. This depends on the leakage model and number of bits in the target intermediate value.

M — The number of side-channel measurements (i.e., traces) used for profiling.

$t_i^{(label)}$ — The ith out of M side-channel measurement t (i.e., trace) with corresponding target intermediate-value *(label)*.

The goal of such a classifier is to learn an objective function f that maps an input measurement, i.e., trace, to a discrete output label as given in Equation (2) below.

$$f : t_i^{(label)} \rightarrow (label). \tag{2}$$

2.2 Evaluation

A standard classifier that is trained on M profiling traces as given by the training tuple in Equation (1) is then fed with A attack traces to obtain a prediction

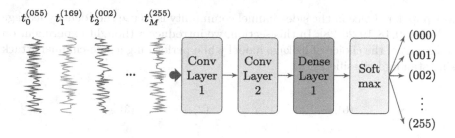

Fig. 1. Standard multi-class classifier

vector **P** of dimension $A \times C$. Then, we compute a sum of log probabilities S for a given guess key k as follows:

$$S(k) = \sum_{i=1}^{A} log(\mathbf{P}_{i,y}), \tag{3}$$

with:

A — The number of side-channel measurements (i.e., traces) used for attack.

$\mathbf{P}_{i,y}$ — Is the probability for the given guess key k and the corresponding guess label y. Note that the guess label y depends on the choice of a cryptographic algorithm, the intermediate target value, and the corresponding datum (i.e., plaintext or ciphertext).

The computations in Eq. (3) are then repeated for each possible guess key. These sums of log probabilities (S) are then sorted based on their value. The position of the secret key k^* in this sorted array is then the key-rank. Furthermore, it is usual to estimate effort to obtain the secret key k^* with the guessing entropy (GE) metric [26]. GE represents the average position of the secret key k^* (i.e., average key-rank) over multiple experiments. Multiple experiments can be obtained by taking multiple random subsets of the vector **P**. In this paper, GE is estimated over 100 experiments. Finally, we define T_{GE0} as the number of side-channel measurements required to reach guessing entropy (GE) equal to zero. This is the metric that is widely used to report the strength of a side-channel attack.

2.3 Thought Experiment

Without loss of generality, let us consider an 8-bit target intermediate value. In this case, the leakage can take one of 256 (2^8) values if we assume the Identity leakage model (ID). Similarly, if we assume the Hamming-weight (HW) leakage model, we have nine possible values and if we assume, let us say, least-significant-bit (LSB), then we have two possible values. In reality, we do not know the actual leakage model, and we heuristically assume some leakage model. The most popular choice in the side-channel community is to use the Identity leakage model [4,10,18,19,25,28]. In this section, we introduce a thought experiment on the impact of the choice of leakage model while performing a side-channel attack using standard classifiers.

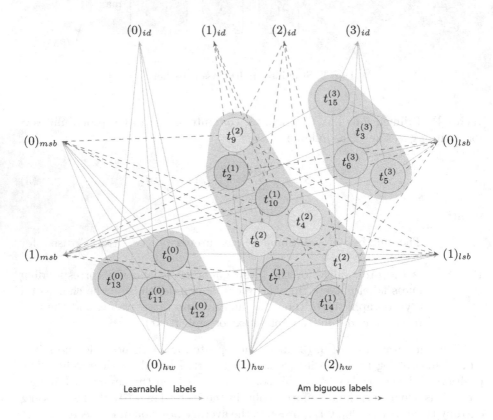

Fig. 2. Learnable labels vs. ambiguous labels

Assume a toy dataset with sixteen traces, and also assume a 2-bit target intermediate value. This toy dataset is specifically designed to leak the Hamming-weight of the intermediate value. Figure 2 shows the 2D embedding for such a dataset. The 2D-embedding is a visual representation of a higher dimensional trace in a 2D plane for visual inspection. Visualizing such embeddings is a powerful tool to analyze any dataset [17], and one of the most popular choices is t-SNE [17]. Every point in the figure is a trace, and there are three clusters (in gray) because we have simulated a Hamming-weight leakage model (hw), which can take one of three values. If we had used the Identity leakage model (id), there would have been four clusters; two in case we would have simulated either the least-significant-bit leakage model (lsb) or the most-significant-bit leakage model (msb).

In our toy dataset case, we know what exactly is leaking, but that is not true with real datasets. Under such circumstances, one can heuristically or, based on experimentation, use different labeling strategies. For the thought experiment, we label the traces of the dataset with the following four labeling strategies corresponding to the leakage models msb, lsb, id, and hw. The labeling is shown on the left, right, top, and bottom respectively of Fig. 2. One can think of more labeling strategies, but for our discussion, this will suffice. We use continuous green lines to indicate that the labels can be learned, while red dashed lines indicate ambiguous and hence difficult to learn labels. The labels that have a one-to-one mapping from the leakage cluster (in gray) to the corresponding label are easy to learn. On the other hand, the labels that are hard to learn, have a one-to-many relationship between the leakage cluster and the labels.

Table 1. Accuracies for different leakage model assumptions

Dataset	Accuracy type	id (%)	lsb (%)	msb (%)	hw (%)
2-bit toy dataset	Acc_{base}	25	50	50	37.5
	Acc	75	75	75	100
8-bit toy dataset	Acc_{base}	0.39	50	50	19.63
	Acc	3.52	56.25	56.26	100

We can expect a 100% accuracy if the labeling strategy used is the Hamming-weight (HW) as there is a one-to-one mapping between the leakage clusters and the labels. However, using the id, lsb, and msb labeling strategies, we can get 50% traces labeled wrongly, and hence we can achieve maximum accuracy of 75%. To test this empirically, we made two toy datasets, one for 2-bit and the other for 8-bit values, and simulated hw leakage so that there are three and nine clusters, respectively. Then, we trained a simple MLP (multi-layer perceptron) neural network with these datasets and recorded the highest validation accuracy (Acc) observed within a training session in Table 1. One can see that the higher the number of bits – and hence the number of classes–, the lower the maximum possible accuracy is. We also provide the baseline-classifier accuracy (Acc_{base}). Acc_{base} is the accuracy of the `tensorflow.estimator.BaselineClassifier` provided in tensorflow software [1]. Note that such classifier ignores input data and will learn to predict the average value of each label. In short it will predict the probability distribution of the classes as seen in the labels. These numbers are more desirable especially in case of class-imbalance.

We can see that we might not be able to learn meaningful information from some traces because of a wrong choice of labeling strategy. Furthermore, this phenomenon of low validation and attack dataset accuracies can be observed with all the networks that use standard classifier-based approach [4,10,18,19,25,28] indicating that the approach might be ill-posed. Although we might not be able to get rid of the problem completely, we still present a novel approach called *multi-trunk order vs. chaos* (MTOvC), which has better validation and attack dataset accuracies and also has improved T_{GE0} metric under certain conditions, as will be discussed in Sect. 4.

2.4 Ambiguous Labels and Low Accuracies (*Acc*)

Based on Sect. 2.3 above, we make some comments on low accuracies and problems in training with ambiguous labels.

- Given that the validation and attack dataset accuracies of the trained standard classifiers are low and close to random guessing accuracies, the loss function based on classification accuracy might be ill-posed for the task at hand.
- Generally, one can correctly assume that noise is the cause for low accuracies, but the toy dataset we used to report numbers in Table 1 has no noise, and with a known leakage model, we can easily achieve 100% accuracy. So, we can infer that ambiguous labels are also a major cause of low accuracies.
- Irrespective of the low accuracy, neural networks are still capable of succeeding at T_{GE0} metric [4,10,18,19,25,28]. We argue that this is possible due to the fraction of traces that have easy to learn labels, as shown in Fig. 2 with green continuous lines.
- Continuing with the point above, we can also infer that the network is not learning anything valuable from the remaining fraction of traces that have hard-to-learn labels, thus reducing the number of useful traces for the attack.

3 Introducing MTOvC classifiers

This section introduces our approach, which we call *multi-trunk order vs. chaos* (MTOvC). In Sect. 3.1, we formulate and describe the MTOvC binary classifier architecture, while in Sect. 3.2, we describe evaluation of attack phase. Finally, in Sect. 3.3, we discuss the advantages and disadvantages of the MTOvC classifier in comparison to a standard classifier.

3.1 Architecture

In Fig. 3, we present a simplified diagram of the MTOvC binary classifier architecture. The network comprises multiple trunks, consisting of stacked neural network layers like convolution, dense, and optional pooling layers. Then, a concatenation layer concatenates the output of all trunks and feeds it to a stack of dense layers. Unlike standard classifier, the output of our network is a sigmoid layer with one output: two labels representing order (◉) and chaos (✪) . A sigmoid layer or a soft-max layer with two outputs is mathematically equivalent, but we prefer a sigmoid layer as it reduces the number of trainable parameters by two in the final dense layer and also reduces overfitting considerably, as observed during our experimentation.

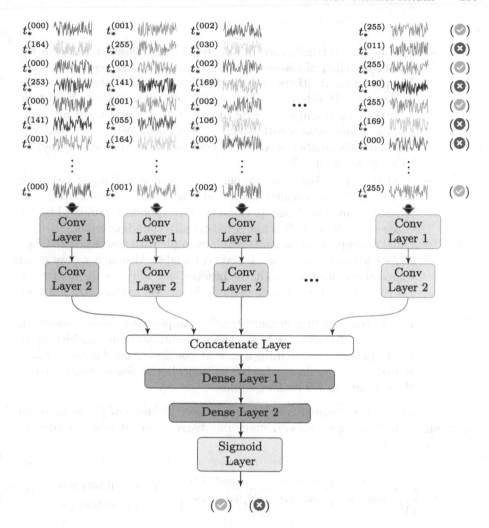

Fig. 3. Multi-trunk order vs. chaos (MTOvC) binary classifier

We present hereafter the training tuple that is used to train this network, i.e., how we feed this network. Note that there are two parts: the first part corresponds to ordered examples, and the second part to chaos examples. We extract M_* examples from the profiling dataset with M traces. Half of the multi-trunk examples are ordered, and the remaining half is not (chaos examples). In practice, we shuffle the examples and feed them to the MTOvC network, as can be seen in the top part of Fig. 3.

$$\left((t_*^{(label=000)}, t_*^{(label=001)}, ..., t_*^{(label=Tr)}), (\checkmark) \right)$$
$$\left((t_*^{(label\neq000)}, t_*^{(label\neq001)}, ..., t_*^{(label\neq Tr)}), (\times) \right) \tag{4}$$

with:

Tr — The number of trunks used in MTOvC binary classifier. It is exactly equal to number of classes C used in standard classifier.

M_* — The number of multi-trunk examples extracted from profiling dataset made up of M side channel measurements (i.e., traces). Note that each training example is made up of Tr traces and there are huge possible combinations with which we can make such tuples. But you can limit this number to M_* to be comparatively very larger than M let's say $M_* \approx M \times 10$.

$t_*^{(label)}$ — A randomly picked side-channel measurement t (i.e., trace) from subset of M traces which has target intermediate-value $(label)$. For ordered examples $(label)$ is same as corresponding trunk while for chaos examples $(label)$ is not equal to corresponding trunk.

(✓) — Label corresponding to multi-trunk example with traces ordered, i.e., a trace fed to correct trunk based on its label Although we are using a special icon for the label in the bracket, in reality, we use float value 1.0 to indicate the ordered-example label. We extract M_* / 2 such examples.

(✗) — Label corresponding to multi-trunk example with traces unordered, i.e., a trace fed to a randomly chosen trunk without considering its label. Although we are using a special icon for the label in the bracket, in reality, we use float value 0.0 to indicate the chaos-example label. We extract M_* / 2 such examples.

The goal of such a classifier is to learn an objective function f that maps an input multi-trunk example to a corresponding discrete output label, as given in Equation (5) below.

$$f : \begin{cases} \left(t_*^{(label=000)}, t_*^{(label=001)}, ..., t_*^{(label=Tr)} \right) \rightarrow (✓), & \text{if ordered} \\ \left(t_*^{(label\neq000)}, t_*^{(label\neq001)}, ..., t_*^{(label\neq Tr)} \right) \rightarrow (✗), & \text{otherwise} \end{cases} \quad (5)$$

3.2   Evaluation

The evaluation of an attack using a MTOvC binary classifier is similar to a standard classifier with slight differences, as will be explained below. The MTOvC classifier is trained on M_* multi-trunk example tuples that are extracted from the profiling dataset with M traces, as shown in Equation (4). This trained classifier is then fed with A_* multi-trunk example tuples extracted from the attack dataset with A traces. This network then provides a prediction vector $\mathbf{P}$ of dimension $A_* \times 1$. Note that the second dimension is one instead of two, as we are using a sigmoid layer with one output. Using this prediction vector, we then compute a sum of log probabilities S for a given guess key k as follows:

$$S(k) = \sum_{i=1}^{A_*} log(\mathbf{P}_i), \quad (6)$$

with:

$\mathbf{P}_i$ — The probability for the given guess key k for i_{th} multi-trunk attack example.

A_* — The number of multi-trunk examples extracted from attack dataset made up of A side channel measurements (i.e., traces). Note that each attack example is made up of Tr traces and there are huge possible combinations with which we can make such tuples. But you can limit this number to A_* to be comparatively very larger than A let's say $A_* \approx A \times 10$.

The computations in Equation (6) are then repeated for each possible guess key. These sums of log probabilities (S) are then sorted based on their value. The position of the secret key k^* in this sorted array is then the key-rank. Furthermore, it is usual to estimate effort to obtain the secret key k^* with the guessing entropy (GE) metric [26]. GE represents the average position of the secret key k^* (i.e., average key-rank) over multiple experiments. In case of MTOvC classifier, multiple experiments can be obtained by re-computing the vector $\mathbf{P}$ for different subsets of A attack measurements. Similar to standard classifier for MTOvC classifier, we estimate GE over 100 experiments. Finally, we define T_{GE0} as the number of side-channel measurements required to reach guessing entropy (GE) equal to zero.

3.3 Advantages and Disadvantages over Standard Classifier

We will now summarize some advantages and disadvantages of the MTOvC classifier.

Advantages

– MTOvC classifier exhibits high accuracy on validation and attack dataset. This suggests that the resulting loss function of our classifier is more suitable for the side-channel attack task.
– During training M_* can be significantly larger than M, as the multi-trunk dataset is produced with randomly sampling traces for each trunk. The combinations of traces that we can sample from all trunks to make a multi-trunk example are exponentially related to the number of trunks. Similarly, during attack A_* can be significantly larger than A. For this paper, we have heuristically set $M_* \approx M \times 10$ and $A_* \approx A \times 10$. Thus, the multi-trunk dataset generator offers implicit data augmentation as a by-product.
– MTOvC approach allows training with more than one trace simultaneously due to its multi-trunk architecture.

Disadvantages

– The computational complexity of the MTOvC binary classifier is linearly proportional to the number of trunks.

- The data pipeline for generating multi-trunk datasets is complex and occupies 256 times more memory. We still managed to keep the memory footprint low by yielding one batch at a time.
- The number of parameters is nearly 256 times more than that of the standard classifier. This is because we use the same architecture as the standard classifier and repeat it 256 times per trunk.
- Minimum 256 unique traces are required to see any benefit from the multi-trunk architecture. With some fake traces per trunk, we can still manage to attack with traces less than 256, but then the performance is similar to that of the standard classifier.

4 Results

In Sect. 4.1, we will first introduce public datasets that we have used and the datasets we have created. Then, in Sect. 4.2, we will discuss results that are summarized in Table 2.

4.1 Datasets

We consider four datasets for our experiments that will be explained in this section.

simulated. This dataset is similar to **8-bit toy dataset** discussed in Sect. 2.3 with the difference that the number of samples is 33 instead of two. The target we use is first round S-Box processing on the third byte. We have simulated the Hamming-weight of the target in actual traces. There is no masking countermeasure implemented for this dataset. The sole purpose of this dataset is to experiment with our MTOvC architecture quickly. In this dataset, we have added very small noise, such that the T_{GE0} metric is less than 256 for the standard classifier. We use 100000 traces for profiling and 10000 traces for the attack. Additionally, we use a 90%–10% split for training and validation during the profiling phase.

simulated-noisy. This dataset is similar to **simulated**, but the added noise is larger. The noise added is such that the T_{GE0} metric should be greater than 256 for the standard classifier. The remaining settings for profiling and attack datasets are the same as **simulated**.

ascad-v1-fk. The ASCAD dataset [2] is a widely used dataset, especially with deep learning techniques. It has measurements protected with masking countermeasure. We use a $desync = 0$ version that is the traces with no simulated desynchronization. The original dataset has 100000 samples per trace obtained for a masked AES implementation running on an 8-bit ATmega8515 smart card. We use the same settings as provided by [2] with 700 samples that contain information on the first round S-Box processing for the third byte. This simplifies the neural network architecture, limiting the input dimension to 700. Also, note that we use 50000 traces for profiling, with 90%–10% split for training and validation.

While for the attack, we use 10000 traces. Furthermore, note that this dataset uses the same fixed key for profiling and attack datasets.

ascad-v1-vk. This dataset is also from the same authors [2], but it uses random keys for the profiling dataset. It has measurements protected with masking countermeasure. While the target for attack is the same as ascad-v1-fk, the number of samples is different, i.e., the authors recommend using 1400 samples per trace. Note that this dataset has 200000 traces for profiling and 100000 for the attack, but we use 50000 for profiling and 10000 for the attack. Furthermore, for profiling, we train networks with a 90%–10% split for training and validation.

4.2 Discussion

Table 2 summarizes all our results. For each dataset, we have provided results for our implementations of standard classifier and MTOvC classifier. All the numbers reported use the Identity leakage model, i.e., there are 256 classes in the case of the standard classifier and 256 trunks in the case of the MTOvC classifier. While for datasets ascad-v1-fk and ascad-v1-vk, apart from our implementations, we also provide results for standard classifiers from publications in the public domain [27,28]. These results are marked with corresponding citations in column "Model". Note that our standard classifier implementation for the dataset ascad-v1-fk is very similar to that of [28], and hence the T_{GE0} number is almost the same. But in addition, we also report the Acc metric. Similarly, for dataset ascad-v1-vk for the standard classifier, we borrow the implementation from [27] and additionally report the Acc metric.

Table 2. Results for standard and MTOvC classifier

Dataset	Model	Acc_{base} (%)	Acc (%)	T_{GE0}
simulated	Standard	0.39	3.44	21
	MTOvC	50.0	100.0	107
simulated-noisy	Standard	0.39	3.21	412
	MTOvC	50.0	96.78	272
ascad-v1-fk	Standard [28]	0.39	—	191
	Standard [27]	0.39	—	160
	Standard	0.39	0.71	190
	MTOvC	50.0	95.46	174
ascad-v1-vk	Standard [28]	0.39	—	—
	Standard [27]	0.39	—	3144
	Standard	0.39	0.64	3121
	MTOvC	50.0	91.36	2583

The T_{GE0} metric we report is a median of over 100 attacks. The Acc reported is accuracy on the entire attack dataset for corresponding datasets. We also

230 P. Kulkarni and V. Verneuil

provide the baseline-classifier accuracy (Acc_{base}). Acc_{base} is the accuracy of the `tensorflow.estimator.BaselineClassifier` provided in tensorflow software [1]. Note that such classifier ignores input data and will learn to predict the average value of each label. In short it will predict the probability distribution of the classes as seen in the labels. These numbers are more desirable especially in case of class-imbalance.

For the `simulated` dataset, the standard classifier performs superior to the MTOvC classifier. As discussed in Sect. 3.3, this is because the MTOvC classifier has 256 trunks and needs a minimum of 256 attack-dataset traces to take any advantage of the MTOvC architecture. Nevertheless, due to the artificial noise added in the `simulated-noisy` dataset, the standard classifier has deteriorated from 21 to 412. This gives the MTOvC classifier an advantage and can be seen in the results. Note that the classification accuracy Acc of MTOvC is superior to that of the standard classifier.

Finally, we see similar results on real datasets `ascad-v1-fk` and `ascad-v1-vk`. Since the T_{GE0} metric for `ascad-v1-fk` dataset is less than 256, our implementation of MTOvC is similar to the standard classifier. While on `ascad-v1-vk`, since the standard classifier takes more than 256 traces, we have some advantages when using the MTOvC classifier.

5 Conclusion

Our preliminary results on `ascad-v1-fk` and `ascad-v1-vk` [2] show that the performance of the multi-trunk classifier is similar to that of state-of-art standard classifiers when the considered datasets are relatively easy to attack and can be attacked with less than 256 traces. With more complex datasets that cannot be attacked with 256 traces, then we see some advantages when using the MTOvC classifier. Furthermore, compared to standard classifiers, the results demonstrate a superior classification accuracy, and we also benefit from implicit data augmentation offered by the multi-trunk dataset generator. Nevertheless, when it comes to the MTOvC classifier, as highlighted in Sect. 3.3, there are some disadvantages like computational complexity, a high number of trainable parameters needed, and a minimum cap of 256 traces during the attack to see any benefits. In the future, we plan to investigate further approaches to simplify the architecture or perform training of trunks in a distributed fashion. Additionally, we plan to investigate the independent performance of trunks, i.e., how much each trunk contributes to the attack performance.

References

1. Abadi, M., et al.: TensorFlow: large-scale machine learning on heterogeneous distributed systems. arXiv:1603.04467 [cs] (2016). http://arxiv.org/abs/1603.04467
2. Benadjila, R., Prouff, E., Strullu, R., Cagli, E., Dumas, C.: Deep learning for side-channel analysis and introduction to ASCAD database. J. Cryptogr. Eng. **10**(2), 163–188 (2019). https://doi.org/10.1007/s13389-019-00220-8

3. Bishop, C.M.: Pattern Recognition and Machine Learning. Information Science and Statistics, Springer, New York (2006)
4. Cagli, E., Dumas, C., Prouff, E.: Convolutional neural networks with data augmentation against jitter-based countermeasures. In: Fischer, W., Homma, N. (eds.) CHES 2017. LNCS, vol. 10529, pp. 45–68. Springer, Cham (2017). https://doi.org/10.1007/978-3-319-66787-4_3
5. Chari, S., Rao, J.R., Rohatgi, P.: Template attacks. In: Kaliski, B.S., Koç, K., Paar, C. (eds.) CHES 2002. LNCS, vol. 2523, pp. 13–28. Springer, Heidelberg (2003). https://doi.org/10.1007/3-540-36400-5_3
6. Choudary, O., Kuhn, M.G.: Efficient template attacks. IACR Cryptol. ePrint Arch, 770 (2013). http://eprint.iacr.org/2013/770
7. Gandolfi, K., Mourtel, C., Olivier, F.: Electromagnetic analysis: concrete results. In: Koç, Ç.K., Naccache, D., Paar, C. (eds.) CHES 2001. LNCS, vol. 2162, pp. 251–261. Springer, Heidelberg (2001). https://doi.org/10.1007/3-540-44709-1_21
8. Genkin, D., Shamir, A., Tromer, E.: Acoustic cryptanalysis. J. Cryptol. $30(2)$, 392–443 (2016). https://doi.org/10.1007/s00145-015-9224-2
9. Goodfello, I., Bengio, Y., Courville, A.: Deep Learning. MIT Press (2016). http://www.deeplearningbook.org
10. Hospodar, G., Gierlichs, B., De Mulder, E., Verbauwhede, I., Vandewalle, J.: Machine learning in side-channel analysis: a first study. J. Cryptogr. Eng. $1(4)$, 293 (2011). https://doi.org/10.1007/s13389-011-0023-x
11. Kocher, Paul, Jaffe, Joshua, Jun, Benjamin: Differential power analysis. In: Wiener, Michael (ed.) CRYPTO 1999. LNCS, vol. 1666, pp. 388–397. Springer, Heidelberg (1999). https://doi.org/10.1007/3-540-48405-1_25
12. Kocher, P.C.: Timing attacks on implementations of Diffie-Hellman, RSA, DSS, and other systems. In: Koblitz, N. (ed.) CRYPTO 1996. LNCS, vol. 1109, pp. 104–113. Springer, Heidelberg (1996). https://doi.org/10.1007/3-540-68697-5_9
13. LeCun, Y., Bengio, Y.: Convolutional networks for images, speech, and time series. Handb. Brain Theory Neural Netw. $3361(10)$, 1995 (1995)
14. LeCun, Y., Bengio, Y., Hinton, G.: Deep learning. Nature $521(7553)$, 436–444 (2015). http://www.nature.com/articles/nature14539
15. Lerman, L., Bontempi, G., Markowitch, O.: Power analysis attack: an approach based on machine learning. Int. J. Appl. Cryptograp. 3, ied Cryptography (2014)
16. Lu, X., Zhang, C., Cao, P., Gu, D., Lu, H.: Pay attention to raw traces: a deep learning architecture for end-to-end profiling attacks. IACR Trans. Cryptograph. Hardware Embed. Syst. 235–274 (2021). https://tches.iacr.org/index.php/TCHES/article/view/8974
17. van der Maaten, L., Hinton, G.: Visualizing data using t-SNE. J. Mach. Learn. Res. $9(86)$, 2579–2605 (2008). http://jmlr.org/papers/v9/vandermaaten08a.html
18. Maghrebi, H., Portigliatti, T., Prouff, E.: Breaking cryptographic implementations using deep learning techniques. In: Carlet, C., Hasan, M.A., Saraswat, V. (eds.) SPACE 2016. LNCS, vol. 10076, pp. 3–26. Springer, Cham (2016). https://doi.org/10.1007/978-3-319-49445-6_1
19. Martinasek, Z., Zeman, V.: Innovative method of the power analysis. Radioengineering $22(2)$, 9 (2013)
20. Memisevic, R.: An introduction to structured discriminative learning. Technical report, University of Toronto, Toronto, Canada, Technical report (2006)
21. Ng, A.Y., Jordan, M.I.: On discriminative vs. generative classifiers: a comparison of logistic regression and naive bayes. In: Dietterich, T.G., Becker, S., Ghahramani, Z. (eds.) Advances in Neural Information Processing Systems 14 [Neural Information Processing Systems: Natural and Synthetic, NIPS

2001(December), pp. 3–8, 2001. Vancouver, British Columbia, Canada], pp. 841–848. MIT Press (2001). https://proceedings.neurips.cc/paper/2001/hash/7b7a53e239400a13bd6be6c91c4f6c4e-Abstract.html

22. Perin, G., Wu, L., Picek, S.: Exploring feature selection scenarios for deep learning-based side-channel analysis. Technical report 1414, na (2021). https://eprint.iacr.org/2021/1414

23. Picek, S., Heuser, A., Guilley, S.: Template attack vs bayes classifier. IACR Cryptol. ePrint Arch (2017)

24. Quisquater, Jean-Jacques., Samyde, David: Electromagnetic analysis (ema): measures and counter-measures for smart cards. In: Attali, Isabelle, Jensen, Thomas (eds.) E-smart 2001. LNCS, vol. 2140, pp. 200–210. Springer, Heidelberg (2001). https://doi.org/10.1007/3-540-45418-7_17

25. Rijsdijk, J., Wu, L., Perin, G., Picek, S.: Reinforcement learning for hyperparameter tuning in deep learning-based side-channel analysis. IACR Trans. Cryptographic Hardware Embed. Syst. 677–707 (2021). https://tches.iacr.org/index.php/TCHES/article/view/8989

26. Standaert, F.-X., Malkin, T.G., Yung, M.: A unified framework for the analysis of side-channel key recovery attacks. In: Joux, A. (ed.) EUROCRYPT 2009. LNCS, vol. 5479, pp. 443–461. Springer, Heidelberg (2009). https://doi.org/10.1007/978-3-642-01001-9_26

27. Wu, L., Perin, G., Picek, S.: I Choose you: automated hyperparameter tuning for deep learning-based side-channel analysis. IACR Cryptol. ePrint Arch, 1293 (2020). https://eprint.iacr.org/2020/1293

28. Zaid, G., Bossuet, L., Habrard, A., Venelli, A.: Methodology for efficient CNN architectures in profiling attacks. IACR Trans. Cryptographic Hardware Embed. Syst. 1–36 (2020). https://tches.iacr.org/index.php/TCHES/article/view/8391

AIoTS – Artificial Intelligence and Industrial IoT Security

Framework for Calculating Residual Cybersecurity Risk of Threats to Road Vehicles in Alignment with ISO/SAE 21434

Ahmed Khan[✉], Jeremy Bryans, and Giedre Sabaliauskaite

Center for Future Transport and Cities, Coventry University, Coventry, UK
khana270@uni.coventry.ac.uk, {ac1126,ad5315}@coventry.ac.uk

Abstract. Safety-critical Cyber-Physical Systems, such as high-tech cars, require new risk management approaches to investigate and address their cybersecurity risks. The current standard for automotive security ISO/SAE 21434 presents such a framework, which discusses the threats, the associated risk, and the chosen treatment, which can be risk reduction through the implementation of a countermeasure or defense. This paper presents a residual cybersecurity risk management framework aligned with the ISO/SAE 21434 framework. The proposed approach audits the applied defenses over the generated attack paths for the identified threats and associated system components. Flow networks are used to calculate the reduced or mitigated risk and the remaining risk of the threat in the presence of the selected countermeasure. The feasibility of the method is explained using a simple automotive system example.

Keywords: Cybersecurity · ISO/SAE 21434 · Risk management framework · Residual risk · Attack tree · Flow graph

1 Introduction

A few decades ago, vehicles had few basic Electronic Control Units (ECUs) connected to actuators and sensors for small-scale communication. Over time, cars used artificial intelligence-enhanced components, became connected to the Internet and the adjacent vehicles and the roadside infrastructure. These improvements were only possible because of the complex integration of control units, sensors, actuators, and different communication systems [1]. There are up to 150 ECUs in any modern vehicle with complex integration of these ECUs using multiple in-vehicle networks including the Controller Area Network (CAN) [26]. ECUs receive inputs from numerous sensors, for instance, acceleration sensors, Tyre Pressure Monitoring Sensor (TPMS), and wheel speed sensors among others. Systematic connections and communications between sensors and control units gave rise to Cyber-Physical Systems (CPS). On the other hand, Vehicle to Vehicle (V2V) and Vehicle to infrastructure (V2I) communication needs a

J. Zhou et al. (Eds.): ACNS 2022 Workshops, LNCS 13285, pp. 235–247, 2022.
https://doi.org/10.1007/978-3-031-16815-4_14

fusion of Bluetooth, Wi-Fi, and 4G/5G technologies [1]. This integration leads us towards a more complex and vulnerable system as more attack surfaces will be available in a system[2]. Several published attacks show that it is possible to exploit these attack surfaces and these attacks can also affect the operational safety of a vehicle [3,4].

According to available reports [26], it is possible to attack core functions of vehicles, such as disconnecting the brakes from the engine. In 2015 there were about 1.4 million cars recalled by Chrysler because of a discovered vulnerability using which hackers can remotely take control of the digital system of a Jeep over the Internet [5]. The Tesla Model S was hijacked remotely from 12 miles away as reported in [6]. Recently, researchers have found 14 vulnerabilities in the infotainment system of multiple BMWs series [8]. The above mentioned studies show that it is crucial to address automotive cybersecurity throughout the development process. The standard ISO/SAE 21434 was compiled to address the issues of integration of automotive cybersecurity in the whole product life cycle of a modern vehicle [7].

The complex infrastructure of modern vehicles increases the risk of cyber-attacks as the cyber risk of the whole system is composed of the risk of an individual interconnected component. ISO/SAE 21434 [15] suggests including cybersecurity aspects at multiple stages of vehicle development. It also includes risk determination and treatment of the assets. Clause 15, Threat analysis and risk assessment (TARA) method is designed for the risk assessment and the treatment decision. Currently, the standard considers the risk treatment decision as the very last step of TARA. Still, it does not advise identifying the residual risk after applying appropriate risk treatment decisions. Thus if a countermeasure is chosen there is no calculation of the residual risk.

In ISO 26262, there is consideration of residual risk (defined there as risk remaining after the deployment of safety measures) but ISO/SAE 21434 [15] has not included the corresponding security concept as of yet. We define residual risk as to the remaining risk after applying the chosen threat defenses [9]. It is vital to consider the effectiveness of the used control measures over the identified threat. According to [10] after evaluation, the mitigated risk after applying the defenses is less than expected. Multiple risk management frameworks are designed according to the standards such as ISO 31000 [11], NIST SP800-30 [12], but there is a need to have one that is aligned with the ISO/SAE 21434.

This work aims to fill the above gap by proposing a novel residual risk management framework. The framework considers the qualitative and recurrent process to reduce the residual risk to an acceptable level while considering the standard risk management practices. Possible threats of a component will be identified from the exploitable vulnerabilities, whereas the attack trees will be generated from the given architecture. Appropriate defenses will be applied against the generated attack paths to observe the residual risk. The contribution of this paper includes the proposed residual risk management framework considering continual risk assessment. We will also present a method to calculate the residual risk of a system. Lastly, we will apply the proposed method to a headlamp system example from ISO/SAE 21434 and evaluate its benefits.

Table 1. Threat Modeling Methods applicable to Automotive

Name	Definition	Reference Method	Required detail level
ATA Model [21]	Visualizing threats against a system in the form of a tree.	Attack Tree	Detailed system design
SW Vulnerability Analysis	Examining software to avoid vulnerabilities		Code examination
FMVEA [22]	Failure Mode and Failure Effect model for both safety and security	STRIDE	Detailed system design
SAHARA [23]	Combination of HARA and STRIDE, traces impact of security breaches on system safety.	STRIDE	High level design
SHIELD	Security, Privacy and Dependability assessing method.		Detailed system design
CHASSIS	Analysis Trade-off between safety and security.	Use Case Diagram	High level Design
BDMP	Combine Fault tree and Attack tree.	Attack Tree	Detailed system design
Threat Matrix [24]	Threat data is presented in the form of threats	FMEA	Detailed system design
BRA	10 binary decisions in the form of questions		High level design

The rest of the paper is structured as follows. Section 2 gives a brief introduction to ISO/SAE 21434 standard, requirements of the risk management framework, and related work. Section 3 walks through the proposed risk management framework and headlamp example, borrowed from ISO/SAE 21434. In Sect. 4 we discusses the scope of our work with respect to available methods. Finally, Sect. 5 gives a conclusion about the paper and discusses ways we might extend this work.

2   Background

This section will discuss the requirements of the risk management framework. Furthermore, it includes a brief introduction to ISO/SAE 21434 and summarizes the related work.

2.1   Requirements Of Risk Management Framework

The induction of new technologies in the modern vehicle has revolutionized the automotive industry. Risk management frameworks play a vital role in building a more robust and resilient system. We have identified the following requirements of the risk management framework for the automotive based on work from [13,14].

- The framework must follow well-established standards and practices for risk management such as ISO 31000 [11], NIST SP800-3 [12].
- It should be a comprehensive framework that ensures that the risk of the automotive system is managed effectively and efficiently.

- The risk management framework should be generic so that it can support the relations and entities involved in the process not bound to specific domain.
- It must be scalable as new interfaces and technology are integrated in the automotive domain.
- The framework should support automation and parameterization.
- It should also integrate the assurance to verify the effectiveness of the applied countermeasures.
- It should be a continual process so it can adopt any change in the respective environment.
- The risk management framework should handle the propagation of risk between different entities.
- There should be a mechanism that can give intuitive ranking indicators to measure the results obtained from the risk management framework considering the acceptable criteria.

2.2 ISO/SAE 21434

As discussed earlier, Connected and Autonomous Vehicles (CAV) have introduced new targets for hackers and therefore risks for users concerning the security and safety of a vehicle. To deal with these emerging problems, SAE and ISO have invested in the development of an industry Standard ISO/SAE 21434 [15] that is a successor of SAE J3061 [16]. The purpose for creating ISO/SAE 21434 [15] was to define a structured process for cyber-secure design, reducing risks of a successful attack and providing information regarding how to react while facing cybersecurity threats. To assess the risk of threats on a system there are various risk assessment methods which are discussed in detail in clause 15 of ISO/SAE 21434. Considering the vehicle life cycle for safety that is adopted from ISO 26262 [17], there are three major phases: the concept phase, product development phase, and production, operation, and maintenance phase. In the concept phase, an item is defined. An item represents a system or number of systems that are implemented in a vehicle considering ISO 26262 [17]. There are nested models in the product development phase, such as a) product development at the system level. b) product development at the hardware level. c) product development at a software level. The production, operation, and maintenance phase has to ensure that cybersecurity specifications are implemented in the development phase. It ensures that implemented processes prevent new vulnerabilities from being part of the system. Continual monitoring and incident response handling is also done in this phase.

2.3 Related Work

Cybersecurity engineering standards were developed in several projects, including EVITA and HEAVENS. The EVITA project [19] proposed a method for risk assessment for automotive that utilized the generic approaches from ISO/IEC 18045 [18]. Later on, it and HEAVENS were incorporated in SAE J3061 [16] - The Cybersecurity Guidebook for Cyber-Physical Vehicle Systems. It was stated by the HEAVENS researchers in 2016 that EVITA was the project that made the first move towards risk assessment in the automotive industry. The National Highway Traffic Safety Administration (NHTSA) [20] proposed a composite threat model designed for the automotive industry in 2014. SAE J3061 [16] was released in 2016, and EVITA and HEAVENS are recommended threat models in it. A few other mentioned models apply to automotive systems, such as Attack Tree Analysis and Software Vulnerability Analysis. A few other methods are not mentioned in SAE J3061 but those apply to automotive systems. A brief overview of the other methods can be found in Table 1.

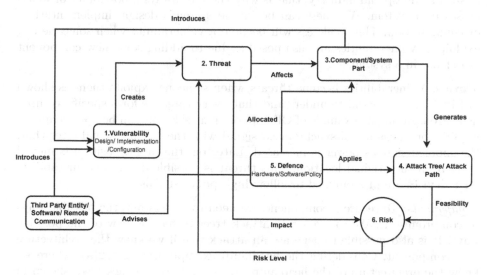

Fig. 1. Residual Risk Management Framework

The risk management process relies upon the set of guidelines and principles that can be followed across the organization to support design, implementation, integration, and evaluation. ISO 31000 [11] is an example of a general risk management framework. Cyber-physical systems are a complex integration of components required to perform respective functionality. This complex integration also increases the cyber risk of the system because there is a significant chance of an attack on the closely connected components. In [25] the authors proposed a risk assessment method for cyber-physical systems that can help to analyze the risk propagation as well as aggregation. In addition to risk assessment, they have proposed a technique utilizing evolutionary programming to select the appropriate control measures from the available list of measures. In paper [25], the authors have presented an integrated risk management framework that assesses and proactively manages the risk in a cyber-physical system. They followed the existing risk management practices and principles, such as identifying assets and then evaluating the effect of vulnerabilities over that asset. They have used the power grid system as an example and followed the standard to determine the risk level and the impact of threats and vulnerabilities to the assets.

3   Residual Risk Management Framework

This section describes the proposed residual risk assessment framework for automotive systems, while considering ISO/SAE 21434. The framework is based on the taxonomy shown in Fig. 1.

Vulnerabilities: The automotive system is the composition of multiple integrated components produced by different members of the Original Equipment Manufacturers (OEMs) supply chain. It is difficult to maintain the same level of assurance in such a widespread industry; that is why there is always a possibility of weaknesses in a system. Weakness can be in the system's design, implementation, or configuration. This weakness will become a vulnerability when someone can exploit it. Vulnerabilities are also possible due to adding some new component or defense in a system.

Threats: Vulnerabilities become threats when someone exploits them as shown in Fig. 1. It is essential to understand that every threat is for a specific component. Considering an example of GPS spoofing attack that can be done remotely requires broadcasting of synchronized signal with the original signal after that, the spoofed signal's power is increased. Later on, the target position is moved away from the original location. This threat is possible due to a vulnerability: GPS devices are programmed to follow high power signals.

Components: To secure a component, we need to understand the possible ways to compromise it. We can generate attack trees to have a view of the possible ways. It is also possible to generate an attack tree if we know the architecture of a component. Considering the headlamp example from Fig. 2(a), where we know the architecture of the headlamp, we can generate attack trees shown in Fig. 2(b).

Attack Path: Every attack path has the feasibility of exploitation. Feasibility would be high or low considering the complexity of an attack path. There is a possibility that an attack path is relatively short, but its complexity is high. Therefore, we consider the feasibility of the attack path as a factor to calculate risk as suggested in ISO/SAE 21434.

Defense: To avoid those threats becoming an attack, defenses can be applied that could be an integration of new hardware or fixing some software bug. It is also possible that the cause of the threat is some third-party entity or software. In that case, we advises some policy for interaction. In Fig. 1., we can observe that defenses are connected to components and attack paths because one defense is for some specific component. It is connected to attack paths because it will help to visualize the placement of defense in the attack path. As discussed earlier, due to the widespread nature of the automotive industry, there is always a possibility of introducing new weaknesses that will become vulnerabilities into a system. There is also a possibility that applied defenses might introduce new vulnerabilities in a system, as shown by the link from component to the vulnerabilities in Fig. 1.

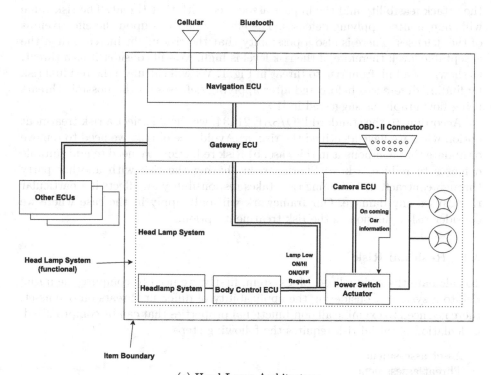

(a) Head Lamp Architecture

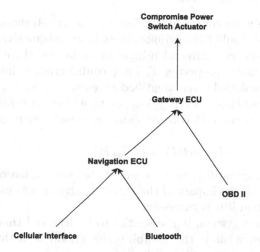

(b) Attack tree for headlamp system

Fig. 2. Example from ISO/SAE 21434 Annex-H[15]

We can calculate associated risk to a component of specific by considering the attack feasibility and the impact associated with that threat. The risk value will change after applying defenses. The efficacy depends upon the effectiveness of the defenses. There is also a possibility that the risk might increase than the acceptable level; therefore, if the risk level is high, we will consider it as a threat, as shown by a link from risk to threat in Fig. 1. We will calculate the residual risk by finding differences before and after applying defenses on the possible threats using flow graphs as suggested in [10].

According to the standard ISO/SAE 21434, we should select a risk treatment option when we have identified the risk. a) Avoidance of risk: we need to remove or update that component in this case. b) Risk reduction: we need to add suitable defenses to reduce risk. c) Sharing risk: sharing the risk with another party through contract. d) Retaining risk: takes responsibility for effects if a particular risk causes any damage. Our framework will only apply in the case where we consider risk reduction as the risk treatment option.

3.1   Residual Risk

To calculate the residual risk of a system, firstly, we need to compute the initial risk to a system. Considering the applicability of different threats on one asset, there is a need to examine all non-functional properties that can be compromised. Calculation of initial risk requires the following steps.

- Asset assessment
- Threat assessment
- Impact and Likelihood calculation

One system part/ component might have multiple assets A_i those are required to be identified first. We could have various assets in an automotive system such as CAN frame, firmware, etc. After identification of assets, there is a need to associate the non-functional properties P_i i.e. (confidentiality, integrity, availability) those can be exploited given identified threats.

Every threat has associated severity/impact to it. Let us consider we have an asset A_i, and if its property P_i is being violated, then severity or impact I of that would be

$$Impact(I) = f(A_i, P_i) \tag{1}$$

The impact will be quantified as a score(1–4) for severe, major, moderate, negligible, respectively. If the impact of the threat is high, it means it can cause more damage to a system if it is successful.

To calculate risk to a system, it is essential to understand that considering the impact of a threat, what is the feasibility/likelihood of a threat T_i. The likelihood L_i of a threat on an asset will be

$$Likelihood(L) = f(A_i, P_i, T_i) \tag{2}$$

The risk is calculated as a lookup matrix in ISO/SAE 21434, and can also be defined by company (OEM). The total risk associated with an asset can be considered as

$$R(_{A,P}) = \sum_{A_i,P_i,T_i} R(_{A_i,P_i})$$ (3)

The residual risk is risk remaining after applying appropriate control measures against threats, and that would be updated risk as R_u. The residual risk would be

$$Residual Risk = R_i - R_u$$ (4)

3.2 Head Lamp Example

We are considering a headlamp example from ISO 21434 annex H. The item boundary of this system is shown in Fig. 2(a) redrawn from ISO 21434. Navigation ECU is connected with Bluetooth and a cellular interface; those are two attack surfaces that can be used for compromising the headlamp system remotely. The other attack surface is the OBD-II connector which needs physical access to the system.

To specify the assets, we will follow the asset identification process as suggested in ISO 21434. In this example, two assets are specified, i.e. CAN frame and firmware. Multiple damage scenarios are mentioned in the standard, whereas the impact of each scenario is identified. The impact rating process includes impact category as well as impact level. In the scope of this paper, we are only considering the damage scenario with a severe impact rating. The headlamp ON/OFF message malfunction is a severe safety hazard while night driving. The integrity and availability of the CAN frame are compromised in such a case. The next step will be an attack path generation and attack feasibility rating. Majorly three possible attack surfaces i.e., cellular, Bluetooth, and OBD-II can be exploited. The attack paths can be seen in Fig. 2(b). The attack path with the highest feasibility is the one with the cellular interface as an attack surface. Its feasibility value is high because an attacker has to be in a car or very close to a moving car for the other two attack paths, which does not have a high feasibility. As discussed in equation (3), the risk value will be determined as we have an impact and the likelihood of the attack paths. The next step in standard is suggesting to reduce the risk. We will reduce the risk by applying appropriate defense while considering their effectiveness.

3.3 Calculating Residual Risk Using Flow Graphs

We can model the residual risk problem as a maximum flow problem using flow graphs. In the maximum flow problem, we have to route the flow as much as possible from source to sink. Flow graphs are used in this problem, and we will be using them for calculating the residual risk of a system. A flow graph is a directed graph in which the arch has capacities indicating the link's upper bound. Flow originates from sources and ends at the sink without any dispersion in flow graph.

We define a graph G=(V, E, c) where V is composed of assets A_i, properties P_i, source s, sink t. E is associated with edges, and c is the capacity of each link.

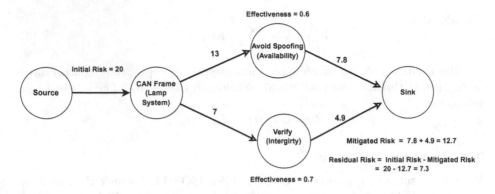

Fig. 3. Residual Risk Calculation using Flow Graph

We model a flow graph from standard practices; s and t are added to select the start and end of the flow graph. The remaining nodes follow the property of the bipartite graph.

We consider total risk as an inward flow of the flow graph, as shown in Fig. 3. Defense vertices should reduce the flow of risk after passing through them as every defense has respective effectiveness. So we can obtain the mitigated risk by multiplying the effectiveness of control measures against attacks. We have drawn Fig. 3. from the assets taken from the headlamp example in Sect. 3.2. The asset is a CAN frame of the headlamp system, whereas the control measures are verification and anti-spoofing to improve the integrity and availability of the whole system. The incoming flow is 20, and the effectiveness of defenses is 60% and 70%. These mechanisms mitigate risk, and the remaining risk that reaches the sink is 7.3 as calculated using Eq. 4.

3.4 Evaluation

To evaluate the proposed framework, we can compare it with the requirements of the risk management framework to understand that it satisfies all of the requirements as discussed in Sect. 2.1.

- Our framework is well-aligned and following NIST-SP 800 as it considers the whole life cycle. Our proposed approach is also aligned with ISO 21434.
- Our framework is comprehensive enough to deal with risk reduction considering it as a risk treatment decision. In the scope of this work, our framework does not deal with other risk treatment decisions, e.g., risk avoidance, risk sharing, and risk retaining.
- Our proposed approach is quite generic as we can apply it to other domains, e.g., Cyber-Physical Systems.
- The proposed framework is scalable. We can consider multiple defenses and attacks against any type of threat. Our work focusses on risk reduction as the risk treatment option considered.

- In further work we will be designing automated and algorithmic solutions for combining attacks trees and finding appropriate defenses, and our intention is that this framework will support automation.
- Considering the effectiveness of the countermeasures to select it against specific attacks, we will be integrating assurance techniques with our approach.
- Our framework follows a continuous process, as shown in Fig. 1.
- We will be combining attack trees to improve visualization; this fusion will allow us to understand and handle the risk propagation from one asset to another.
- To calculate the severity level of any threat, we are using the look-up matrix discussed in ISO 21434 that gives the ranking indicators about the threat. In the future, we will be looking at graph-oriented techniques for ranking.

4   Discussion

Our proposed approach strictly follows the guidelines provided by ISO 31000 as discussed in Sect. 2.1, a general framework that guides us to follow a set of standard practices to do a system's risk assessment. CAVs are one of the complex CPS, and our approach is generic enough that we can use it to do the risk assessment of other CPS. Currently, we are only using the application of automotive in the scope of this paper. There are a few other studies, such as [25], in which authors have proposed the risk assessment framework aligned with standards. [25] follows a manual approach to identify the vulnerabilities and appropriate countermeasures using the approach of the American National Highway Traffic Safety Administration; however, we are considering an automated process to generate attack trees and determine appropriate controls assessing their effectiveness. We integrated a continual process to reduce the risk to an acceptable level. Another work, [27], did a risk assessment for automotive but they did not consider residual risk. The major challenge in our work is to quantify threats and the effectiveness of controls as numerous defense mechanisms are proposed in the literature. Still, evaluating the countermeasures for effectiveness in some environments is very rarely available. This knowledge gap introduces a big challenge in our approach. To a great extent this approach requires considerable domain knowledge, and it will also complement TARA for better assessment.

5   Conclusion And Future Works

Identifying and mitigating risk is essential in developing the automotive system. Considering the remaining risk after applying defenses is vital as defenses are not usually 100% effective. In this paper, we have presented a modern risk management framework aligned with standards and requirements. It incorporates the impact of the threats, the feasibility of the attacks, and vulnerabilities introduced by new defenses and third parties. Our approach is centered around the non-functional properties of the automotive system. We have presented the work by discussing it using the example available in ISO/SAE 21434. We have evaluated our proposed framework with the requirements of the risk management framework discussed in Sect. 2.1 and found out that it is closely aligned with requirements. In the future, we will be increasing that alignment by introducing algorithms for attack tree combinations for some other examples that will lead us towards risk propagation, scalability, and a broader view of the whole system. We will also be considering the method to identify the most suitable defenses against attacks.

References

1. Dibaei, M., et al: An overview of attacks and defences on intelligent connected vehicles (2019). arXiv preprint arXiv:1907.07455
2. Sommer, F., Dürrwang, J., Kriesten, R.: Survey and classification of automotive security attacks. Information **10**(4), 148 (2019)
3. Blank, R.M.: Guide for conducting risk assessments (2011)
4. Shostack, A.: Threat Modeling: Designing for Security. John Wiley & Sons, Hoboken (2014)
5. https://www.wired.com/2016/08/jeep-hackers-return-high-speed-steering-acceleration-hacks/
6. https://www.theguardian.com/technology/2016/sep/20/tesla-model-s-chinese-hack-remote-control-brakes
7. Liedtke, T.: Risk assessment according to the ISO/SAE 21434: 2021 (2021)
8. https://www.helpnetsecurity.com/2018/05/23/hack-bmw-cars/
9. Birch, J., et al.: Safety cases and their role in ISO 26262 functional safety assessment. In: Bitsch, F., Guiochet, J., Kaâniche, M. (eds.) SAFECOMP 2013. LNCS, vol. 8153, pp. 154–165. Springer, Heidelberg (2013). https://doi.org/10.1007/978-3-642-40793-2_15
10. Anisetti, M., Ardagna, C.A., Bena, N., Foppiani, A.: An assurance-based risk management framework for distributed systems. In: 2021 IEEE International Conference on Web Services (ICWS), pp. 482–492. IEEE (2021)
11. Risk management - Guidelines, International Organization for Stan-dardization, Geneva, CH, Standard (2018)
12. Joint Task Force Transformation Initiative, Guide for Conducting Risk Assessments, National Institute of Standards and Technology, Gaithersburg, MD, Technical Report NIST Special Publication (SP) 800–30, Rev. 1 (2012)
13. Nurse, J.R., Creese, S.,De Roure, D.: Security risk assessment in Internet of Things systems. IT Prof. **19**(5), 20–26 (2017)
14. Methods for Testing & Specification; Risk-based Security Assessment and Testing Methodologies, European Telecommunications Standards Institute, Sophia Antipolis Cedex, France, Standard (2016)
15. ISO/IEC, ISO/SAE DIS 21434 - Road Vehicles - Cybersecurity Engineering, International Organization for Standardization, Geneva, CH (2020)
16. SAE International, Cybersecurity Guidebook for Cyber-Physical Vehicle Systems, Technical Report J3061, SAE International (2016)
17. ISO - International Organization for Standardization. ISO 26262 Road vehicles. Functional Safety Part 1-10 (2011)

18. ISO/IEC, ISO/IEC 18045:2008(E): Information technology - Security techniques-Methodology for IT security evaluation, International Organization for Standardization, Geneva, CH (2008)
19. The EVITA consortium, EVITA Threat and risk analysis (2009). https://www.evita-project.org
20. McCarthy, C., Harnett, K., Carter, A.: Characterization of Potential Security Threatsin Modern Automobiles: A Composite Modeling Approach, National HighwayTraffic Safety Administration (2014)
21. Schneier, B.: Attack trees. Dr. Dobb's J. **24**(12), 21–29 (1999)
22. Schmittner, C., Ma, Z., Smith, P.: FMVEA for safety and security analysis of intelligent and cooperative vehicles. In: Bondavalli, A., Ceccarelli, A., Ortmeier, F. (eds.) SAFECOMP 2014. LNCS, vol. 8696, pp. 282–288. Springer, Cham (2014). https://doi.org/10.1007/978-3-319-10557-4_31
23. Macher, G., Sporer, H., Berlach, R., Armengaud, E., Kreiner, C.: SAHARA a security-aware hazard and risk analysis method. In: 2015 Design, Automation & Test in Europe Conference & Exhibition (DATE), pp. 621–624. IEEE (2015)
24. McCarthy, C., Harnett, K., Carter, A.: Characterization of potential security threats in modern automobiles: A composite modeling approach. No. DOT HS 812 074. United States. National Highway Traffic Safety Administration (2014)
25. Kure, H.I., Islam, S., Razzaque, M.A.: An integrated cyber security risk management approach for a cyber-physical system. Appl. Sci. **8**(6), 898 (2018)
26. Koscher, K., et al.: Experimental security analysis of a modern automobile. In: 2010 IEEE Symposium on Security and Privacy, pp. 447–462. IEEE (2010)
27. Wang, Y., Wang, Y., Qin, H., Ji, H., Zhang, Y., Wang, J.: A systematic risk assessment framework of automotive cybersecurity. Automot. Innov. **4**(3), 253–261 (2021). https://doi.org/10.1007/s42154-021-00140-6

Output Prediction Attacks on Block Ciphers Using Deep Learning

Hayato Kimura[1,2]($\boxtimes$), Keita Emura[2], Takanori Isobe[2,3], Ryoma Ito[2], Kazuto Ogawa[2], and Toshihiro Ohigashi[1,2]

[1] Tokai University, Minato-ku, Japan
h_kimura@star.tokai-u.jp
[2] National Institute of Information and Communications Technology (NICT),
Koganei, Japan
[3] University of Hyogo, Kobe, Japan

Abstract. In this paper, we propose deep learning-based output prediction attacks in a blackbox setting. As preliminary experiments, we first focus on two toy SPN block ciphers (small PRESENT-[4] and small AES-[4]) and one toy Feistel block cipher (small TWINE-[4]). Due to its small internal structures with a block size of 16 bits, we can construct deep learning models by employing the maximum number of plaintext/ciphertext pairs, and we can precisely calculate the rounds in which full diffusion occurs. Next, based on the preliminary experiments, we explore whether the evaluation results obtained by our attacks against three toy block ciphers can be applied to block ciphers with large block sizes, e.g., 32 and 64 bits. As a result, we demonstrate the following results, specifically for the SPN block ciphers: (1) our attacks work against a similar number of rounds that the linear/differential attacks can be successful, (2) our attacks realize output predictions (precisely ciphertext prediction and plaintext recovery) that are much stronger than distinguishing attacks, and (3) swapping or replacing the internal components of the target block ciphers affects the average success probabilities of the proposed attacks. It is particularly worth noting that this is a deep learning specific characteristic because swapping/replacing does not affect the average success probabilities of the linear/differential attacks. We also confirm whether the proposed attacks work on the Feistel block cipher. We expect that our results will be an important stepping stone in the design of deep learning-resistant symmetric-key ciphers.

Keywords: Deep learning · Block cipher · SPN · Feistel

1 Introduction

Unlike public-key cryptography, where security is reduced to mathematically difficult problems, the security of symmetric-key cryptography is evaluated by

This work was done when the first author, Hayato Kimura, was a master student at the Tokai University, Japan, and was a research assistant at the National Institute of Information and Communications Technology (NICT), Japan.

J. Zhou et al. (Eds.): ACNS 2022 Workshops, LNCS 13285, pp. 248–276, 2022.
https://doi.org/10.1007/978-3-031-16815-4_15

resistance against classical attacks, e.g., differential, linear, and integral attacks. Specifically, the corresponding statistical characteristics, e.g., differential, linear, and integral characteristics, are searched by automatic evaluation programs and tools, e.g., SAT and MILP solvers. If there is a considerable security margin against these characteristics, the cipher can be considered to be secure against these attacks. Generally, these evaluations require the deep knowledge of target algorithms and state-of-the-art cryptanalysis techniques because automatic evaluation programs and tools must be customized for different target algorithms and attacks.

Recently, deep learning-based cryptanalysis has received considerable attention in the symmetric-key cryptography field [1,5–8,10–14,17,21,22,25,33,37–39]. Remarkably, this type of attack does not require the knowledge of target ciphers, except algorithm interfaces, i.e., the attack is feasible even if the adversary does not know the algorithm of target ciphers. Such cryptanalysis in a blackbox setting is extremely strong, i.e., the adversary can mount an attack with the minimum knowledge of target ciphers and cryptanalysis techniques. In this context, we must consider deep learning-based cryptanalysis when designing symmetric-key ciphers. However, previous studies have not clarified the features or internal structures that affect the success probabilities. Recently, Benamira et al. [8] and Chen et al. [12] confirmed whether characteristics explored by Gohr [17] can be employed in the classical distinguishing attacks. These results may be used to design deep learning-resistant symmetric-key ciphers; however, it does not seem to be sufficient because they did not identify any deep learning specific characteristic in such a manner that it affects the success probabilities of deep learning-based attacks but does not affect those of classical attacks such as linear/differential attacks. Such a deep learning specific characteristic is important because it may cause vulnerabilities against deep learning-based cryptanalysis. Thus, the usage of previous results of these attacks to design such deep learning-resistant symmetric-key ciphers is difficult.

1.1   Our Contribution

In this study, we present new deep learning-based attacks on block ciphers in a *blackbox setting* where the adversary does not know the algorithm of target ciphers, except algorithm interfaces such as key and block sizes. In a blackbox setting, deep learning-based cryptanalysis allows us to use pre-obtained input/output pairs to construct deep learning models for our attacks, such as ciphertext prediction and plaintext recovery, and then we can use these models to evaluate these attacks. The next step is to examine correlations between evaluation results obtained by deep learning-based cryptanalysis as well as the characteristics of target block ciphers. For this purpose, we apply a *whitebox analysis* technique to our evaluation phase using deep learning models. The whitebox analysis explores the relationship between the ability of deep learning-based attacks and classical attacks such as linear/differential attacks; therefore, it may be possible to clarify correlations between evaluation results obtained by deep learning-based cryptanalysis and the characteristics of target block ciphers.

To obtain highly accurate results from the whitebox analysis in a blackbox setting, we should perform comprehensive analyses using all input/output pairs, i.e., it is not appropriate to target the reduced-round block ciphers because they have the same block size as the original block ciphers, e.g., 64 or 128 bits, and we cannot use all input/output pairs. For this reason, we first focus on toy block ciphers with a small block size such as 16 bits and perform the whitebox analysis against these toy block ciphers as preliminary experiments. Based on the preliminary experiments, we apply the proposed attacks to block ciphers with large block sizes, e.g., 32 and 64 bits, and consider the whitebox analysis against the target block ciphers. The details of our contributions in this study are given as follows.

New Deep Learning-Based Output Prediction Attacks. To perform the whitebox analysis against block ciphers with large block sizes, we first focus on two toy SPN block ciphers (16-bit block variants of PRESENT [9] called small PRESENT-[4] and an AES-like cipher called small AES-[4]) and one toy Feistel block cipher (a type-II generalized Feistel structure with 4 branches called small TWINE-[4]). This allows us to accurately compare the effectiveness of the proposed deep learning-based attacks, which guess the ciphertext/plaintext from the corresponding plaintext/ciphertext without any knowledge of keys with that of classical attacks. Due to the page limitation, our target ciphers, two SPN block ciphers and one Feistel block cipher (and their toy ciphers), are introduced in Appendix A.

Because of its small internal structures with a block size of 16 bits, we can develop deep learning models by exploiting the maximum number of plaintext/ciphertext pairs, and we can precisely calculate linear/differential probability for each round. We demonstrate that the proposed attacks are effective against the similar number of rounds as linear/differential attacks. For small PRESENT-[4], we successfully mount output prediction attacks on 4 rounds, while the number of rounds that the differential distinguisher can work is also 4. For small AES-[4] and small TWINE-[4], we can mount prediction attacks on 1 and 3 rounds, while differential distinguishing attacks can reach 2 and 7 rounds, respectively. Note that our attacks realize output predictions (i.e., ciphertext prediction and plaintext recovery) that are considerably stronger than distinguishing attacks even without knowing the algorithm of target ciphers. Nevertheless, for small TWINE-[4], the number of rounds that the proposed attacks can be successful is significantly less than that of linear/differential attacks. To clarify this cause, additional studies will be required in future.

Next, based on evaluation results for toy block ciphers, we apply the proposed attacks to the target block ciphers with a block size of 64 bits, i.e., PRESENT [9], AES-like, and TWINE-like ciphers. Consequently, we consider that by increasing the amount of training data, the whitebox analysis against block ciphers with large block sizes can be regarded as equal to or greater than the whitebox analysis against toy block ciphers with a block size of 16 bits; thus, the whitebox analysis against the target block ciphers with large block sizes can be summarized as follows:

- For PRESENT, the maximum number of rounds that the proposed attacks can be successful is at least equal to that of classical linear/differential attacks.
- For AES-like and TWINE-like ciphers, we conjecture that the maximum number of rounds that the proposed attacks can be successful also becomes equal to that of classical linear/differential attacks when the amount of training data increases more.

In addition, we conduct additional experiments with 10,000 trials (rather than 100 trials) to confirm the accuracy of the success probability calculated from the proposed attacks. Consequently, we demonstrate that the additional experiments with a small number of secret keys are sufficient to obtain the best success probability, and therefore the proposed attacks lead to reliable results.

Whitebox Analysis for Deep Learning-Based Attacks. We swap or replace internal components on the toy SPN block cipher, particularly on the 4-round small PRESENT-[4], to investigate the relationship between the internal components and success probability of our deep learning-based attacks, and evaluate the impact of these modifications on the success probability of the prediction attacks. The toy Feistel block cipher, i.e., small TWINE-[4], is excluded from this investigation because Feistel block ciphers generally use the same components for both encryption and decryption algorithms. Consequently, we find that swapping or replacing the internal components significantly affects the average success probabilities of the proposed attacks. It is particularly worth noting that this is a deep learning specific characteristic because component swapping and replacing that we did in this study did not affect success probabilities of linear/differential attacks. We expect that our results will be an important foundation in the design of deep learning-resistant symmetric-key ciphers.

1.2 Comparison with Existing Studies

Due to the page limitation, we give a comparison among the proposed attacks and existing deep learning-based attacks [1,5–8,10–14,17,21–23,25,33,37–39] in Table 8 in Appendix B. For comparison, we particularly focused on whether these attacks correspond to a deep learning-based attack in a *blackbox setting* and a deep learning-based attack with the *whitebox analysis*. When an adversary performs a deep learning-based attack in a non-blackbox setting, the adversary must be familiar with the target ciphers as well as state-of-the-art cryptanalysis techniques. This degrades the original function of a deep learning-based attack in such a way that it does not require any knowledge of target ciphers and state-of-the-art cryptanalysis techniques, except algorithm interfaces. In addition, even if an adversary uses the whitebox analysis in a non-blackbox setting to perform a deep learning-based attack, this should not result in accurate evaluations of the attack. In summary, it is important to perform a deep learning-based attack with the whitebox analysis in a blackbox setting. As shown in Table 8, the proposed attacks are the first deep learning-based output prediction attacks with *whitebox analysis* on both SPN and Feistel structures in a *blackbox setting*.

Organization. This paper is organized as follows. The proposed deep learning-based output prediction attacks in a blackbox setting are introduced in Sect. 2. Our whitebox analysis is performed in Sect. 3 that explores the evaluation results obtained by our attacks against three toy block ciphers can be applied to block ciphers with large block sizes. An extended whitebox analysis on small PRESENT-[4] is introduced in Sect. 4. Finally, Sect. 5 concludes this study.

2   Methodology

In this section, we present the proposed deep learning-based output prediction attacks in a blackbox setting. To realize the proposed attacks, we construct deep learning models for ciphertext prediction and plaintext recovery, respectively. In the following, we first discuss the goals of these attacks and then explain the construction of deep learning models and their evaluation.

2.1   Goals of Attack

To date, the relationship between the abilities classical attacks and deep learning-based ones has not been clarified. Here, we focus on clarifying this relationship. We then revisit the common sense in previous works using deep learning-based attacks. The targets of this work are summarized as follows:

1. We clarify the difference in capabilities between the classical and deep learning-based attacks. Specifically, we compare the success probabilities of deep learning-based attacks with those of classical attacks.
2. Swapping or replacing the internal components in the target block ciphers does not affect the success probability of linear/differential cryptanalysis. We clarify how such modifications to cipher's algorithms affect the success probability of deep learning-based attacks.

We evaluate the success probabilities of attacks using the following settings.

Known-plaintext attack setting: In this setting, the adversary is given multiple plaintext/ciphertext pairs relating to a single secret key, and the pairs are used as training data to construct a deep learning model.

Blackbox setting: In this setting, the adversary does not have knowledge about the target block ciphers, except algorithm interfaces such as key and block sizes.

In both of these settings, the adversary is a very weak cryptographic attacker.

The blackbox setting assumes that the adversary does not know the internal structures of the cipher. In addition, the adversary does not know the cipher is a permutation. The blackbox setting also assumes that the adversary only knows the input-output format and possesses deep learning knowledge.

Regarding attack settings, a ciphertext-only attack setting, which allows the adversary to obtain only the ciphertext, is the weakest setting. However, information-theoretically no information is provided to the adversary in the setting except for several special cases, e.g., the broadcast setting of RC4 [31]. In fact, the attack in this setting is practically impossible. The known-plaintext attack is the next weakest setting. In this setting, the adversary can obtain some information from the given plaintext/ciphertext pairs and use these pairs for the attacks. The other attack settings, e.g., chosen-plaintext attack setting, require the adversary to possess some knowledge about the ciphertext, and the adversary in this setting is stronger than the adversary in the known-plaintext attack setting. Thus, we employ the known-plaintext attack setting.

In these settings, we decide the adversary's goal to output predictions (i.e., ciphertext prediction and/or plaintext recovery), and we evaluate the success probabilities of these attacks. The ciphertext prediction and plaintext recovery attacks are summarized as follows:

Ciphertext prediction attack: In this attack, the adversary obtains multiple plaintext/ciphertext pairs regarding a secret key, where n is the block size. Then, the adversary predicts a ciphertext of a plaintext not included in the previously given pairs.

Plaintext recovery attack: In this attack, the adversary obtains multiple plaintext/ciphertext pairs regarding a secret key, and then the adversary recovers a plaintext of a ciphertext that is not included in the pairs given previously.

If the ciphertext prediction attack is possible, forgery of the Cipher-based Message Authentication Code (CMAC) is possible. If the plaintext recovery attack is possible, the adversary can obtain the plaintext of any ciphertext without possessing the secret key used for encryption.

2.2   Neural Network and Hyperparameters

Deep learning allows us to automatically extract features unlike statistical machine learning techniques, e.g., Bayesian inference. Deep learning treats non-linear separable problems; thus, it appears to work well for simulating cryptographic functions with nonlinearity. Hyperparameters such as the initial learning rate, number of hidden nodes (neurons), and optimizers, are defined prior to the learning phase and are used to construct models. These parameters affect model performance; thus, they are optimized using assessment metrics.

In this paper, we consider ciphertext prediction and plaintext recovery as regression problems with supervised learning where plaintext/ciphertext pairs are used as training data. To this end, we must extract numerous features from the plaintext/ciphertext pairs obtained under the known-plaintext attack; therefore, we employ long short-term memory (LSTM) which is a type of recurrent

Table 1. Hyperparameters

Hyperparameters	Search ranges
Number of hidden nodes	100, 200, 300, 400, 500
Initial value of learning rates	0.0001, 0.001, 0.01
Number of hidden layers	1, 2, 3, 4, 5, 6, 7
Optimizers	SGD, Adam [26], RMSprop [36]

neural networks (RNN) [20]. The LSTM, which is a general technique for mapping sequences to sequences with neural networks, is used in the field of machine translation [34]. As the LSTM can realize the mapping between sequences in machine translation, we consider that it can also realize the mapping between sequences (i.e., between plaintexts and ciphertexts) in encryption/decryption of permutation-based block ciphers. In addition, we consider that numerous features can be extracted from plaintext/ciphertext pairs, i.e., the inputs to our deep learning models, by using the LSTM, which enables long-term memory of input sequences. In fact, we have confirmed that the use of the LSTM induces better experimental results than that of the convolutional neural network (CNN), as described in Appendix C for more details. We then optimize hyperparameters, e.g., number of hidden nodes, initial learning rates, number of hidden layers, and optimizers. Table 1 shows the search range for each hyperparameter. During the hyperparameter optimization, we use different secret keys from those used in the construction of deep learning models because we strictly evaluate the success probabilities of ciphertext prediction and plaintext recovery without depending on secret keys. In the following, the procedure to optimize hyperparameters is similar to constructing deep learning models, with the exception of the number of secret keys.

2.3 Deep Learning Models and Their Evaluation

We construct and evaluate deep learning models for ciphertext prediction according to the following procedure. Note that we show the plaintext recovery case in parentheses.

Step 1. The adversary obtains multiple plaintext/ciphertext pairs under the known-plaintext attack. In our experiments, we randomly select multiple plaintexts and generate ciphertexts corresponding to the selected plaintexts.

Step 2. The adversary uses the obtained plaintext/ciphertext pairs as training data to construct deep learning models. Then, the adversary constructs a deep learning model for ciphertext prediction (plaintext recovery) using the plaintexts (ciphertexts) as inputs and the ciphertexts (plaintexts) as the correct outputs.

Step 3. The adversary uses all or part of the remaining plaintexts (ciphertexts), which were not used as training data, to evaluate the constructed deep learning models. The adversary uses these plaintexts (ciphertexts) as the input to the constructed deep learning models. Then, the adversary predicts the unknown ciphertext (plaintext) corresponding to each plaintext (ciphertext).

Step 4. The adversary calculates the percentage of exact match between the predicted ciphertext (plaintext) and the correct ciphertext (plaintext) as the predicted probability.

To evaluate the predicted probabilities, we use 2^x plaintext/ciphertext pairs as training data and 2^y plaintext/ciphertext of the remaining plaintext/ciphertext pairs as test data when applying the proposed attacks against the target block ciphers with a block size of $4n$ bits. It should be noted here that $2^x + 2^y \leq 2^{4n}$. In this case, if the predicted probability is greater than $(2^{4n} - 2^x)^{-1}$, we consider the proposed attacks to be successful. This means that an attacker without knowledge of the target algorithms can predict the output value with a higher probability than a random probability.

3 Whitebox Analysis

In this section, we perform the whitebox analysis to explore the relationship between the ability of deep learning-based attacks and the classical attacks such as linear/differential attacks against three block ciphers based on our methodology presented in Sect. 2. We first use three toy block ciphers with a block size of 16 bits as a testbed for the proposed attacks. Based on these preliminary experiments, we then apply the proposed attacks to block ciphers with large block sizes, such as 32 and 64 bits. Finally, we conduct additional experiments to ensure that our whitebox analysis is accurate.

3.1 Application to Toy Block Ciphers

In this subsection, we apply the proposed attacks to three toy block ciphers, i.e., small PRESENT-[4], small AES-[4], and small TWINE-[4], as preliminary experiments. We first explain the experimental procedure for our whitebox analysis and then demonstrate experimental results to compare the number of rounds that the proposed attacks can be successful to that of existing classical attacks.

Experimental Procedure. In our experiments, we implement the proposed attacks using Keras[1], which is a deep learning library, and we employ Tensor-Flow as the backend. The following is our experimental environment: 8 Linux machines with 14 NVIDIA GPUs (RTX 2080 SUPER, GeForce GTX 1080 Ti, TITAN Xp, Tesla K40m, and Quadro P600 Mobile). For developing LSTM models by Keras, e.g., `model.add(LSTM(...))`, we specify only `units`, `input_shape`, and `return_sequences` as its arguments[2]. As an initial setting, we use common experimental hyperparameter values (see Table 2). Our experiments involve the following two sub-experiments, i.e., Experiment 1 and Experiment 2.

---

[1] https://github.com/keras-team/keras.
[2] https://keras.io/ja/layers/recurrent/.

Table 2. Experimental hyperparameters

Hyperparameters	Values
Number of input layer nodes	1
Number of output layer nodes (i.e., block sizes)	16, 32, 64
Batch size	250
Number of epochs	100

Experiment 1: In each round, we optimize hyperparameters for the target block ciphers using the proposed attacks, as described in Sect. 2.2. For our hyperparameter optimization, we use Optuna[3], which is an automatic optimization tool, and use its default search algorithm. The indication for our hyperparameter optimization is the success probability of ciphertext prediction or plaintext recovery. In our hyperparameter optimization, we obtain 100 hyperparameter candidates from the plaintext/ciphertext pairs generated by 20 secret keys. From these candidates, we select the optimized hyperparameter with the highest average success probabilities of ciphertext prediction or plaintext recovery. To this end, we use 2^{15} plaintext/ciphertext pairs as training data and remaining 2^{15} plaintext or ciphertext as testing data; thus, each average success probability is calculated from 2^{15} randomly generated plaintext/ciphertext pairs. If the average success probabilities of ciphertext prediction or plaintext recovery with the optimized hyperparameter is greater than 2^{-15}, then the number of rounds for finding the optimized hyperparameter is incremented by one; otherwise, the second sub-experiment is executed using the optimized hyperparameter.

Experiment 2: We use randomly generated 100 secret keys and the optimized hyperparameters obtained in Experiment 1 to execute the proposed attacks for ciphertext prediction or plaintext recovery; then, we compute the average success probabilities of ciphertext prediction or plaintext recovery. The secret keys used in Experiment 2 are not the same as those used in Experiment 1. After clarifying the number of attacked rounds for target block ciphers by Experiment 2, we use experimental results and linear/differential probability of the target block ciphers to compare the proposed attacks to the classical linear/differential attacks.

Experimental Results. Table 3 shows the experimental results of Experiment 2 using the optimized hyperparameter obtained in Experiment 1. Based on these experimental results, we discuss the whitebox analysis against three toy block ciphers, i.e., small PRESENT-[4], small AES-[4], and small TWINE-[4].

First, we compare the proposed and classical linear/differential attacks for small PRESENT-[4]. From the experimental results, the proposed attacks succeed up to 5 rounds for ciphertext prediction and up to 4 rounds for plaintext recovery against small PRESENT-[4]. Although the average success probability of ciphertext prediction for the 5-round small PRESENT-[4] is nearly 2^{-15}, the average success probability of plaintext recovery for the 4-round small

---
[3] https://github.com/optuna/optuna.

Table 3. Average success probabilities of ciphertext prediction/plaintext recovery using the proposed attacks against three toy block ciphers with a block size of 16 bits. We use 2^{15} training data and the remaining 2^{15} testing data. CP:=Ciphertext Prediction and PR:=Plaintext Recovery.

Cipher	Round	Category of attack	# nodes of hidden layer	# layers of hidden layer	Initial learning rate	Optimizer	Succ. prob.
small PRESENT-[4]	1	CP	400	5	0.001	Adam	1
		PR	100	2	0.001	RMSprop	1
	2	CP	400	4	0.001	RMSprop	1
		PR	400	1	0.001	Adam	1
	3	CP	300	6	0.001	RMSprop	1
		PR	300	5	0.001	RMSprop	1
	4	CP	300	4	0.01	Adam	$2^{-5.63}$
		PR	300	1	0.01	Adam	$2^{-14.50}$
	5	CP	200	7	0.001	Adam	$2^{-14.08}$
		PR	300	6	0.001	Adam	$2^{-15.73}$
small AES-[4]	1	CP	300	4	0.001	RMSprop	1
		PR	200	4	0.001	RMSprop	1
	2	CP	300	1	0.01	Adam	$2^{-16.02}$
		PR	200	2	0.01	Adam	$2^{-15.00}$
small TWINE-[4]	1	CP	300	3	0.001	RMSprop	1
		PR	300	2	0.001	Adam	$2^{-0.01}$
	2	CP	400	4	0.001	RMSprop	$2^{-0.01}$
		PR	500	3	0.001	RMSprop	$2^{-0.01}$
	3	CP	300	2	0.001	RMSprop	$2^{-10.46}$
		PR	400	2	0.001	RMSprop	$2^{-9.72}$
	4	CP	200	4	0.001	RMSprop	$2^{-14.61}$
		PR	100	1	0.01	RMSprop	$2^{-15.49}$
	5	CP	300	5	0.01	RMSprop	$2^{-15.64}$
		PR	500	4	0.001	RMSprop	$2^{-15.16}$

PRESENT-[4] is sufficiently greater than 2^{-15}. In other words, we consider that the proposed attacks can be successful for a maximum of 4 rounds. On the other hand, from the precisely calculated differential probability of small PRESENT-[4] (see Table 10 in Appendix D), the maximum number of rounds that the differential attack can be successful is 4. Similarly, based on the precisely calculated linear probability, the maximum number of rounds that a linear attack can be successful is also 4. Therefore, for small PRESENT-[4], the maximum number of rounds that the proposed attack can be successful is equal to that of classical linear/differential attacks.

Next, we compare the proposed and classical linear/differential attacks for small AES-[4]. From Table 3, we evaluate the maximum number of rounds that the proposed attacks can be successful is 1. From the precisely calculated linear/differential probabilities, the maximum number of rounds that the differential attack can be successful is 2, whereas that of the linear attack is 3. Similarly, we compare the proposed attacks and classical linear/differential attacks for small TWINE-[4]. We discovered that the proposed attack can be successful for a maximum of 3 rounds with the differential attack lasting 7 rounds and the linear attack lasting 9 rounds. In summary, for small AES-[4] and small TWINE-[4], the maximum number of rounds that the proposed attacks can be successful is less than that of the classical linear/differential attacks. It should be noted here that the proposed attacks realize much stronger ciphertext prediction and plaintext recovery than the distinguishing attacks of the classical linear/differential cryptanalysis. Nevertheless, for small TWINE-[4], the maximum number of rounds that the proposed attacks can be successful is significantly smaller than that of the classical linear/differential attacks. This cause will be clarified in a future study.

Whitebox Analysis with the Smaller Amount of Training Data. To perform the whitebox analysis with the smaller amount of training data against three toy block ciphers (i.e., 1-, 2-, 3-, 4-round small PRESENT-[4], 1-round small AES-[4], and 1-, 2-, 3-round small TWINE-[4]), we conduct additional experiments in the same procedure described above, but we vary the amount of training data in the range of from 2^2 to 2^{14} and use all the remaining plaintexts or ciphertexts as testing data. In these additional experiments, we use the optimized hyperparameters obtained in Experiment 1 (see Table 3).

We show the details of the additional experimental results in Appendix E. Table 11 shows the minimum amount of training data required for successful ciphertext prediction/plaintext recovery against three toy block ciphers. In addition, Table 12 shows more detailed results regarding the average success probabilities of ciphertext prediction/plaintext recovery by the proposed attacks against three toy block ciphers with a block size of 16 bits. If the predicted probability is greater than 2^{-15}, we consider the proposed attacks to be successful[4]. Consequently, we demonstrate successful ciphertext prediction/plaintext recovery with a smaller amount of training data than 2^{15} against three toy block ciphers, with the exception of the 4-round small PRESENT-[4].

3.2   Application to Block Ciphers with Large Block Sizes

In this subsection, we apply the proposed attacks to three block ciphers with large block sizes based on the preliminary experiments as described in Sect. 3.1. To examine the evaluation results obtained by our whitebox analysis against three toy block ciphers can be applied to the target block ciphers with large block sizes, we conduct Experiment 2 in the same procedure as described in Sect. 3.1, but we change the block sizes of the target block ciphers, e.g., 32 and 64 bits. In our experiments, we use the optimized hyperparameters obtained in Experiment 1 (see Table 3 in Sect. 3.1).

We show the details of the experimental results in Appendix F. Tables 13 and 14 show the minimum amount of training data required for successful ciphertext prediction/plaintext recovery against three block ciphers with block sizes of 32 and 64 bits, respectively. We vary the amount of training data in the range of from 2^8 to 2^{17} or from 2^{10} to 2^{19} and use 2^{16} of the remaining plaintexts or

---

[4] This assumption is strictly incorrect, but we use it for simple discussion.

ciphertexts as testing data against three toy block ciphers with block sizes of 32 or 64 bits, respectively; thus, if the predicted probability is greater than the threshold derived by equation $(2^{4n} - 2^x)^{-1}$ shown in Sect. 2.3, we consider the proposed attacks to be successful for both cases. In this case those thresholds are $(2^{32} - 2^8)^{-1}$ to $(2^{32} - 2^{17})^{-1}$ or from $(2^{64} - 2^{10})^{-1}$ to $(2^{64} - 2^{19})^{-1}$. In addition, Tables 15 and 16 in Appendix F show more detailed results regarding the average success probabilities of ciphertext prediction/plaintext recovery by the proposed attacks against three block ciphers with block sizes of 32 and 64 bits.

From Tables 13 and 15, we report that the average success probabilities of ciphertext prediction/plaintext recovery by the proposed attacks against the target block ciphers with a block size of 32 bits are not zero, excluding the 4-round small PRESENT-[8]. Expressed differently, this fact should indicate that the proposed attacks against the target block ciphers with large block sizes can be successful by simply increasing the amount of training data; thus, we consider that the proposed attack against the target block ciphers with additional rounds could be successful by using more training data than 2^{17}.

From Tables 14 and 16, we can confirm that except for the 4-round small PRESENT-[16] and the 3-round small TWINE-[16], the average success probabilities of ciphertext prediction/plaintext recovery by the proposed attacks against the target block ciphers with a block size of 64 bits are not zero. In these cases, we consider that the proposed attacks against the target block ciphers with additional rounds could be successful with more training data than 2^{19}.

As demonstrated by these results, the proposed attacks can be performed regardless of the block size of the target block ciphers by simply increasing the amount of training data. In addition, as the amount of training data increases, the larger the block size, the greater the rate of increase in the success probability (see Tables 12, 15, and 16 for more details). Therefore, we consider that by increasing the amount of training data, the whitebox analysis against block ciphers with large block sizes can be regarded as equal to or greater than the whitebox analysis against toy block ciphers with a block size of 16 bits. As discussed in Sect. 3.1, the maximum number of rounds that the proposed attacks can be successful against small PRESENT-[4] is equal to that of the classical linear/differential attacks, while the maximum number of rounds that the proposed attacks can be successful against small AES-[4] and small TWINE-[4] is less than that of the classical linear/differential attacks. Nevertheless, we consider that the whitebox analysis against the target block ciphers with large block sizes can be summarized as follows, based on the above consideration:

– For small PRESENT-[16] (i.e., PRESENT), the maximum number of rounds that the proposed attacks can be successful is at least equal to that of the classical linear/differential attacks.
– For small AES-[16] (i.e., AES-like) and small TWINE-[16] (i.e., TWINE-like), we conjecture that the maximum number of rounds that the proposed attacks can be successful also becomes equal to that of classical linear/differential attacks. To clarify the correctness of this conjecture, we should conduct addi-

tional experiments with a larger amount of training data than 2^{19}. This will be our future work.

3.3 Accuracy of Experimental Results

In Sect. 3.1, we have presented the experimental results of Experiment 1 with 20 secret keys and Experiment 2 with 100 secret keys. These experimental results may appear to be correct. However, because of the small number of secret keys used in these experiments, we should have an additional discussion to ensure that the experimental results are accurate. To this end, this subsection shows two additional experimental results on the 3-round small TWINE-[4] with 100 secret keys for Experiment 1 and 10000 secret keys for Experiment 2, respectively. The following explains why we chose the 3-round small TWINE-[4] for confirming the accuracy: If we choose a target with a probability of 1 or 2^{-15}, it appears difficult to see how the number of secret keys affects the accuracy. As shown in Table 3, the average success probabilities of ciphertext prediction and plaintext recovery by the proposed attacks in the 3-round small TWINE-[4] are approximately $2^{-10.46}$ and $2^{-9.72}$, respectively. We choose the 3-round small TWINE-[4] as the best target for additional experiments because these probabilities possibly vary significantly if the number of keys affects the accuracy.

Experimental Procedure. We explain the following two additional experiments, i.e., Experiment 1' and Experiment 2'.

Experiment 1': We use the same procedures as in Experiment 1 to optimize the hyperparameters for the 3-round small TWINE-[4]. Unlike Experiment 1, we use plaintext/ciphertext pairs generated by 100 secret keys rather than 20 secret keys in this experiment. In the hyperparameter optimization, we examine the impact of the number of secret keys used in Experiment 1' on the experimental results.

Experiment 2': We obtain the average success probabilities of ciphertext prediction/plaintext recovery for the 3-round small TWINE-[4] in the same procedures of Experiment 2 using the hyperparameters optimized by Experiment 1 (see Table 3). Unlike Experiment 2, we use the plaintext/ciphertext pairs generated by 10000 secret keys rather than 100 secret keys. In the ciphertext prediction/plaintext recovery, we explore the influence of the number of secret keys used in Experiment 2' on the experimental results.

Experimental Results. Table 4 shows a comparison of the experimental results in Experiment 1 and Experiment 1' for the 3-round small TWINE-[4]. From the table, in the hyperparameter optimization for ciphertext prediction, the highest average success probabilities obtained from Experiment 1 and Experiment 1' are nearly equal, such as $2^{-11.42}$ and $2^{-11.26}$. Conversely, in the hyperparameter optimization for the plaintext recovery, the highest average success probability obtained from Experiment 1 is much higher than that obtained from

Table 4. Comparison of the experimental results in Experiment 1 and Experiment 1' for the 3-round small TWINE-[4].

Category of attack	# keys	# trials	# nodes of hidden layer	# layers of hidden layer	Initial learning rate	Optimizer	Succ. prob.	Ref.
Ciphertext	20	100	300	2	0.001	RMSprop	$2^{-11.42}$	Experiment 1
Prediction	100	40	300	7	0.001	RMSprop	$2^{-11.26}$	Experiment 1'
Plaintext	20	100	400	2	0.001	RMSprop	$2^{-7.80}$	Experiment 1
Recovery	100	40	100	4	0.001	RMSprop	$2^{-12.82}$	Experiment 1'

Table 5. Comparison of experimental results in Experiment 2 and Experiment 2' for the 3-round small TWINE-[4]. We use the optimized hyperparameters obtained in Experiment 1 (see Table 3).

Attack	# keys	Succ. prob.	Ref.
Ciphertext	100	$2^{-10.46}$	Experiment 2
Prediction	10000	$2^{-10.64}$	Experiment 2'
Plaintext	100	$2^{-9.72}$	Experiment 2
Recovery	10000	$2^{-9.22}$	Experiment 2'

Experiment 1', such as $2^{-7.80}$ and $2^{-12.82}$. As per these experimental results, optimizing the hyperparameters with a small number of secret keys is sufficient to obtain hyperparameters with the best average success probability; therefore, we consider that the hyperparameter optimization presented in Sect. 3.1 has led to reliable results.

Table 5 shows a comparison of experimental results in Experiment 2 and Experiment 2' for the 3-round small TWINE-[4]. We can see from the table that in both ciphertext prediction and plaintext recoveries, the average success probabilities obtained from Experiment 2 and Experiment 2' are nearly equal, such as $2^{-10.46}$ and $2^{-10.64}$ in the ciphertext prediction and $2^{-9.72}$ and $2^{-9.22}$ in the plaintext recovery. According to these experimental results, the additional experiments with a small number of secret keys are sufficient to obtain the best average success probability; therefore, we consider that the ciphertext prediction/plaintext recovery presented in Sects. 3.1 and 3.2 has led to reliable results.

4   Extended Whitebox Analysis on Small PRESENT-[4]

As shown in Table 3, the average success probability of ciphertext prediction by the proposed attack on the 4-round small PRESENT-[4] is approximately 2^9 times greater than that of plaintext recovery. However, the security of the encryption and decryption is thought to be equivalent in terms of the linear/differential probabilities on small PRESENT-[4]; thus, the experimental result of the proposed attacks on the 4-round small PRESENT-[4] seems contrary to intuition. We speculate that this can be a deep learning specific characteristic.

In this section, we redesign the 4-round small PRESENT-[4] by swapping or replacing the internal components, e.g., S-box and bit permutation, and execute

Table 6. Average success probabilities when swapping or replacing components on the 4-round small PRESENT-[4]. We use 2^{15} training data and 2^{15} testing data. CP:=Ciphertext Prediction and PR:=Plaintext Recovery.

	Category of attack	# nodes of hidden layer	# layers of hidden layer	Initial learning rate	Optimizer	Succ. prob.
Original small PRESENT-[4]	CP	300	4	0.01	Adam	$2^{-5.63}$
	PR	300	1	0.01	Adam	$2^{-14.50}$
Replacing the components (Enc: sLayer-inv → pLayer) (Dec: pLayer → sLayer)	CP	200	4	0.01	Adam	$2^{-3.75}$
	PR	500	1	0.001	Adam	$2^{-12.13}$
Swapping the components (Enc: pLayer → sLayer) (Dec: sLayer-inv → pLayer)	CP	500	1	0.001	Adam	$2^{-12.21}$
	PR	400	7	0.001	Adam	$2^{-13.74}$

Experiment 1 and Experiment 2 against the new designs of the 4-round small PRESENT-[4] to reveal the relationship between the designs of block ciphers and average success probability of the proposed attacks.

4.1 Experimental Procedure

We discuss two types of experiments to investigate the average success probabilities of ciphertext prediction and plaintext recovery by the proposed attacks under the conditions that (1) the substitution layer (sLayer) and its inverse function (sLayer-inv) are replaced, and (2) the order of the sLayer and permutation layer (pLayer) is swapped in the encryption and decryption algorithms. The target toy block ciphers are the 4-round small PRESENT-[4] and the 2-round small AES-[4], and small TWINE-[4] is excluded from the target of these experiments. This is because the Feistel block ciphers generally use the same components for both encryption and decryption algorithms. The order of the sLayer and pLayer is the same in both the encryption and decryption algorithms, and sLayer-inv is not used in neither the encryption nor decryption algorithms. Rather than the experiments described in this section, we should compare the maximum number of rounds that the proposed attacks can be successful against small TWINE-[4] (a type-II generalized Feistel cipher) to that on the other types of the Feistel block ciphers, such as classical, unbalanced, alternating, type-I and type-III generalized Feistel ciphers. This will be our future study.

4.2 Experimental Results

Table 6 shows experimental results for new designs of the 4-round small PRESENT-[4]. The average success probability of ciphertext prediction is greater than that of the original small PRESENT-[4] when the sLayer is replaced with the sLayer-inv, as shown in the table. However, when the order of the sLayer and pLayer is swapped, the average success probability of ciphertext prediction is less than that of the original small PRESENT-[4]. We believe that swapping the component order affects the average success probabilities of the proposed attacks because the difference in these average success probabilities is relatively large. Given that swapping or replacing components does not affect linear/differential probabilities, we expect that our results can be an important stepping stone for designing deep learning-resistant symmetric-key ciphers.

Nevertheless, the average success probability of plaintext recovery for both cases is greater than that of the original small PRESENT-[4]; this result tends to differ from ciphertext prediction. Because the probabilities are nearly 2^{-15}, the results require more detailed analyses to increase reliability, which we leave as a future work.

In the experimental results of the 2-round small AES-[4], all average success probabilities for ciphertext prediction/plaintext recovery by the proposed attacks are less than 2^{-15}. Therefore, these results do not show whether swapping or replacing the components has any effect on the average success probabilities of the proposed attacks in the 2-round small AES-[4].

5   Conclusion

In this study, we presented deep learning-based output prediction attacks on three block ciphers with a block size of 64 bits in a blackbox setting. We clarified the following results by examining the relationship between the ability of deep learning-based attacks and classical attacks such as linear/differential attacks:

- For PRESENT, the maximum number of rounds that the proposed attack can be successful is at least equal to that of classical linear/differential attacks.
- For AES-like and TWINE-like ciphers, we conjecture that the maximum number of rounds that the proposed attacks can be successful also becomes equal to that of classical linear/differential attacks when the amount of training data is increased more.

In addition, we redesigned the 4-round small PRESENT-[4] by swapping or replacing the internal components, and we used the whitebox analysis technique to examine the relationship between the new target cipher designs and the success probability of the proposed attacks. Consequently, we clarified that swapping or replacing the internal components did not affect success probabilities of the classical linear/differential attacks, whereas it affects the average success probabilities of the proposed deep learning-based attacks; thus, we have obtained a deep learning specific characteristic. The obtained results are expected to be a foundation for designing deep learning-resistant symmetric-key ciphers.

Acknowledgments. This work was supported in part by the JSPS KAKENHI Grant Number 19K11971.

A   Our Target Ciphers

In this section, we introduce two SPN block ciphers (PRESENT [9] and AES-like cipher), one Feistel block cipher (TWINE-like cipher), and their toy ciphers (small PRESENT-[n] [27], small AES-[n], and small TWINE-[n]).

PRESENT and Small PRESENT-[n]: PRESENT [9] is a lightweight SPN block cipher with a 64-bit block size, 31 rounds, and a key size of either 80 or 128 bits. To analyze PRESENT, a toy model of PRESENT called small PRESENT-[n] [27] has been proposed. We show the round function of small PRESENT-[n] in Fig. 1. Since the block size is $4n$, small PRESENT-[16] is equivalent to the original PRESENT. The variant n, which specifies the block size and round key length, allows us to control the round of full diffusion. The S-box has 4-bit input and output. We provide the correspondence table in Table 7 that maps $\mathbb{F}_2^4 \to \mathbb{F}_2^4$. The pLayer is described as bit permutation $P(i)$, which is defined as follows. Note that this is a generalization of that of PRESENT and is equivalent to that of PRESENT when $n = 16$. $P(i)$ is used for encryption and $P^{-1}(i)$ is used for decryption.

$$P(i) = \begin{cases} n \times i \bmod (4n - 1) & (0 \le i < 4n - 1) \\ 4n - 1 & (i = 4n - 1) \end{cases}$$

$$P^{-1}(i) = \begin{cases} 4 \times i \bmod (4n - 1) & (0 \le i < 4n - 1) \\ 4n - 1 & (i = 4n - 1) \end{cases}$$

For key scheduling, the key scheduling algorithm of PRESENT-80, which is a variant of PRESENT with a key length of 80, is executed; furthermore, the $4n$ rightmost bits are used as round keys rk_i.

AES-Like and Small AES-[n]: We design AES-like cipher with a 64-bit block size, called AES-like for short. To analyze AES-like, we design its toy model called small AES-[n]. The round function of small AES is shown in Fig. 1. As with the case of PRESENT, small AES-[16] is equivalent to AES-like since the block size is $4n$. The S-box and key scheduling are the same as those of PRESENT. The maximum distance separable (MDS) matrix (over $GF(2^4)$ defined by the irreducible polynomial $x^4 + x + 1$) is the same as that of Piccolo [32], which is expressed as follows.

$$M = \begin{pmatrix} 2 & 3 & 1 & 1 \\ 1 & 2 & 3 & 1 \\ 1 & 1 & 2 & 3 \\ 3 & 1 & 1 & 2 \end{pmatrix}$$

When a 16-bit input $X_{(16)}$ is given, the output is computed as ${}^t(y_{0(4)}, y_{1(4)}, y_{2(4)}, y_{3(4)}) \leftarrow M \cdot {}^t(x_{0(4)}, x_{1(4)}, x_{2(4)}, x_{3(4)})$.

TWINE-Like and Small TWINE-[n]: We design TWINE-like cipher with a 64-bit block size, called TWINE-like for short. To analyze TWINE-like, we design its toy model called small TWINE-[n]. For our design, we adopt the

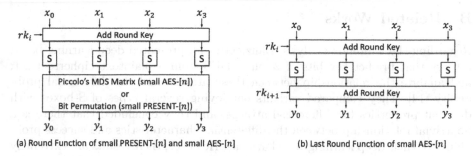

Fig. 1. (a) Round Functions of small PRESENT-$[n]$ and small AES-$[n]$, (b) Last Round Function of small AES-$[n]$.

Table 7. S-box (PRESENT and small PRESENT-$[n]$)

x	0	1	2	3	4	5	6	7	8	9	A	B	C	D	E	F
$S[x]$	C	5	6	B	9	0	A	D	3	E	F	8	4	7	1	2

Fig. 2. Round Function of small TWINE-$[n]$

type-II generalized Feistel structure with n branches and similar F function as TWINE, which comprises round key operation and 4-bit S-box, as shown in Fig. 2.

As with the case of PRESENT, small TWINE-[16] is equivalent to TWINE-like since the block size is $4n$. The S-box and key scheduling are the same as those of PRESENT. The pLayer is described as round permutation RP, which is defined as follows:

$$RP : (y_0, y_1, \ldots, y_{n-2}, y_{n-1}) \leftarrow (x_1, x_2, \ldots, x_{n-1}, x_0).$$

Two sub-round keys, rk_i^s for $s \in \{0, 1, \ldots, \frac{n}{2} - 1\}$, are used in each round, which are generated from the round key rk_i as follows:

$$rk_i^s = (rk_i \gg (4n - (4s + 4))) \ \& \ \text{0xF},$$

where $\gg$ and $\&$ are bitwise right shift operation and bitwise AND operation, respectively.

B   Related Works

Regarding the whitebox analysis, Danziger et al. presented deep learning-based attacks that predict key bits of 2-round DES from a plaintext/ciphertext set, and analyze the relationship between these attacks and the differential probability [14]. They compared variants employing several types of S-boxes with different properties for differential attacks, and they concluded that there is a nontrivial relationship between the differential characteristics and success probability of their deep learning-based attacks. However, their results are extremely limited because they targeted a two-round Feistel construction, which is quite insecure even if the component is ideal function. It is unclear how much the property of internal components affects the security of the whole construction. In addition to improve Gohr's deep learning-based attack [17], Benamira et al. [8] and Chen et al. [12] improved the success probability of traditional distinguishers using characteristics that are expected to be reacted by Gohr's attack. Their work confirms whether characteristics explored by Gohr can be employed in the traditional distinguishing attacks and they did not identify any deep learning specific characteristic. However, we calculated the ability of traditional distinguisher and our deep learning-based attack and compared them to investigate a relationship between them. Then, we identified a deep learning specific characteristic of small-PRESENT. To summarize, to the best of our knowledge, our results are the first ones that perform the whitebox analysis.

Alani and Hu reported plaintext recovery attacks on DES, 3-DES, and AES [2,24] that guess plaintexts from given ciphertexts. They claimed that attacks on DES, 3-DES, and AES are feasible with 2^{11}, 2^{11} and 1741 ($\simeq 2^{10.76}$) plaintext/ciphertext pairs, respectively. However, Xiao et al. doubted the correctness of their results [2,24] because they could not be reproduced. Baek et al. also pointed this out in the literature [4]. Therefore, we exclude these results in Table 8. Mishra et al. reported that they mounted output prediction attacks on full-round PRESENT; however, it did not work well [16]. In addition, certain results have yielded classical ciphers such as Caesar cipher, Vigenere, and Enigma ciphers [15,18,19,30].

Other machine learning-based analyses have also been reported, e.g., [28,29]. Tan et al. demonstrated that deep learning can be used to distinguish ciphertexts encrypted by AES, Blowfish, DES, 3-DES, and RC5, respectively [35], for detecting the encryption algorithm that the malware utilizes. Alshammari et al. attempted to classify encrypted Skype and SSH traffic [3].

C   Experimental Results Using the CNN

To confirm that the use of the LSTM induces better experimental results than that of the CNN, we conducted experiments using the CNN in the same procedure described in Sect. 3.1. In our experiments, we optimize activation functions in addition to the hyperparameters shown in Table 1. The following is the search range for activation functions: Tanh, Sigmoid, and ReLU. For developing

Table 8. Comparison of deep learning-based cryptanalysis. OP:=Output Prediction, PR:=Plaintext Recovery, KR:=Key Recovery, DD:=Differential Distinguisher, LD:=Linear Distinguisher, and DLD:=Differential-Linear Distinguisher.

Reference	Cipher (Block size)	Structures	Blackbox setting	Target	#Round (#Full)	Whitebox analysis
BSS08 [5]	Serpent (128 bits)	SPN	No	DD	7 (32)	No
AAAA12 [1]	Simplified DES (12 bits)	Feistel	Yes	OP	2 (N/A[b])	No
DH14 [14]	Simplified DES (12 bits)	Feistel	Yes	KR/DD	2 (N/A[b])	No
Gohr19 [17]	Speck32/64 (32 bits)	Feistel	No[a]	KR/DD	12 (22)	Yes
XHY19 [38]	DES (64 bits)	Feistel	Yes	PR	2 (16)	No
CY20 [10]	Speck32/64 (32 bits)	Feistel	No	KR/DD	13 (22)	Yes
CY20 [10]	DES (64 bits)	Feistel	No	KR/DD	8 (16)	Yes
HLZW20 [21]	DES (64 bits)	Feistel	No	KR/LD	5 (16)	No
So20 [33]	Simplified DES (8 bits)	Feistel	No	KR/LD	8 (8)	No
So20 [33]	Speck32/64 (32 bits)	Feistel	No	KR/LD	22 (22)	No
So20 [33]	Simon32/64 (32 bits)	Feistel	No	KR/LD	32 (32)	No
BBDC21 [6]	Gimli-Perm. (384 bits)	SPN	No	DD	8 (48)	No
BBDC21 [6]	ASCON-Perm. (320 bits)	SPN	No	DD	3 (16)	No
BBDC21 [6]	KNOT-256 (256 bits)	Feistel	No	DD	10 (28)	No
BBDC21 [6]	KNOT-512 (512 bits)	Feistel	No	DD	12 (52)	No
BBDC21 [6]	CHASKEY-Perm. (128 bits)	ARX	No	DD	4 (12)	No
BGMLT21 [7]	Speck32/64 (32 bits)	Feistel	No	KR/DD	13 (22)	Yes
BGMLT21 [7]	Simon32/64 (32 bits)	Feistel	No	KR/DD	16 (32)	Yes
BGPT21 [8]	Speck32/64 (32 bits)	Feistel	No	DD	7 (22)	No
BGPT21 [8]	Simon32/64 (32 bits)	Feistel	No	DD	8 (32)	No
CY21 [12]	CHASKEY-Perm. (128 bits)	ARX	No	DLD	4 (12)	Yes
CY21 [12]	DES (64 bits)	Feistel	No	DLD	6 (16)	Yes
CY21 [12]	Speck32/64 (32 bits)	Feistel	No	DLD	7 (22)	Yes
CY21 [13]	Speck32/64 (32 bits)	Feistel	No	KR/DD	13 (22)	Yes
CY21 [13]	Speck48/72 (48 bits)	Feistel	No	KR/DD	12 (22)	Yes
CY21 [13]	Speck48/96 (48 bits)	Feistel	No	KR/DD	12 (23)	Yes
CY21 [11]	DES (64 bits)	Feistel	No	DD	6 (16)	No
CY21 [11]	Speck32/64 (32 bits)	Feistel	No	KR/DD	11 (22)	No
CY21 [11]	PRESENT (64 bits)	SPN	No	DD	7 (31)	No
HRC21 [22]	Simon32/64 (32 bits)	Feistel	No	KR/DD	13 (32)	No
HRC21 [23]	Simon32/64 (32 bits)	Feistel	No	KR/DD	13 (32)	Yes
HRC21 [23]	Simon48/96 (48 bits)	Feistel	No	KR/DD	14 (36)	Yes
HRC21 [23]	Simon64/128 (64 bits)	Feistel	No	KR/DD	13 (44)	Yes
HRC21 [23]	Speck32/64 (32 bits)	Feistel	No	DD	8 (22)	Yes
HRC21 [23]	Speck48/96 (48 bits)	Feistel	No	DD	7 (23)	Yes
HRC21 [23]	Speck64/128 (64 bits)	Feistel	No	DD	8 (27)	Yes
ITYY21 [25]	TWINE (64 bits)	Feistel	No	DD	8 (36)	No
YK21 [39]	Speck32/64 (32 bits)	Feistel	No	DD	9 (22)	Yes
YK21 [39]	Simon32/64 (32 bits)	Feistel	No	DD	12 (32)	Yes
YK21 [39]	GIFT 64 (64 bits)	SPN	No	DD	8 (28)	Yes
WW21 [37]	Speck32/64 (32 bits)	Feistel	No	DD	12 (22)	Yes
WW21 [37]	Speck48/72 (48 bits)	Feistel	No	DD	15 (22)	Yes
WW21 [37]	Speck64/96 (64 bits)	Feistel	No	DD	18 (26)	Yes
This paper	**PRESENT (64 bits)**	SPN	Yes	OP	4 (31)	Yes
This paper	**AES-like (64 bits)**	SPN	Yes	OP	1 (N/A[b])	Yes
This paper	**TWINE-like (64 bits)**	Feistel	Yes	OP	3 (N/A[b])	Yes

[a]Gohr described in his paper [17] that *we consider it interesting that this much knowledge about the differential distribution of round-reduced Speck can be extracted from a few million examples by black-box methods*. However, his *black-box methods* are different from our defined blackbox setting. For this reason, we consider his proposed model as a non-blackbox setting.

[b]Because the simplified DES, AES-like, and TWINE-like ciphers, which are the modified versions of original ciphers, do not specify the number of full rounds, we described the number of full rounds of these modified versions as 'N/A'.

Table 9. Average success probabilities of ciphertext prediction/plaintext recovery using the proposed attacks against three toy block ciphers with a block size of 16 bits. We employ the CNN and use 2^{15} training data as well as remaining 2^{15} testing data. CP:=Ciphertext Prediction and PR:=Plaintext Recovery.

Cipher	Round	Category of attack	# nodes of hidden layer	# layers of hidden layer	Initial learning rate	Optimizer	Activation	Succ. prob.
small PRESENT-[4]	1	CP	100	5	0.001	Adam	Tanh	1
		PR	300	3	0.0001	RMSprop	Tanh	1
	2	CP	200	1	0.01	SGD	ReLU	$2^{-11.72}$
		PR	400	3	0.001	Adam	Sigmoid	$2^{-11.69}$
	3	CP	200	2	0.01	RMSprop	ReLU	$2^{-14.58}$
		PR	300	2	0.0001	RMSprop	Sigmoid	$2^{-14.57}$
	4	CP	300	7	0.0001	Adam	Tanh	$2^{-15.02}$
		PR	200	1	0.01	SGD	ReLU	$2^{-15.20}$
small AES-[4]	1	CP	100	4	0.0001	Adam	ReLU	$2^{-11.88}$
		PR	400	5	0.0001	Adam	Tanh	$2^{-11.83}$
	2	CP	100	4	0.01	SGD	ReLU	$2^{-15.76}$
		PR	100	7	0.001	RMSprop	Sigmoid	$2^{-15.00}$
small TWINE-[4]	1	CP	300	2	0.001	RMSprop	Sigmoid	$2^{-8.01}$
		PR	500	5	0.01	RMSprop	ReLU	$2^{-8.03}$
	2	CP	100	4	0.0001	SGD	Tanh	$2^{-15.86}$
		PR	300	2	0.0001	RMSprop	Tanh	$2^{-15.62}$

CNN models by Keras, e.g., `model.add(Conv1D(...))`, we specify only `filters`, `kernel_size`, `activation`, and `input_shape` as its arguments[5].

Table 9 shows experimental results using the CNN. Consequently, we clarify the following facts by comparing the experimental results using the LSTM and CNN based on Tables 3 and 9:

- For small PRESENT-[4], the maximum number of rounds that the proposed attacks using the LSTM and CNN can be successful is 4 and 3, respectively.
- For small AES-[4], the maximum number of rounds that the proposed attacks using the LSTM and CNN can be successful is 1 for each case. In addition, the average success probabilities of ciphertext prediction (plaintext recovery) by the proposed attacks against the 1-round small AES-[4] using the LSTM and CNN are 1 (1) and $2^{-11.88}$ ($2^{-11.83}$), respectively.
- For small TWINE-[4], the maximum number of rounds that the proposed attacks using the LSTM and CNN can be successful is 3 and 1, respectively.

To summarize the foregoing facts, we conclude that the use of the LSTM induces better experimental results of all the target block ciphers compared to the use of the CNN.

---

[5] https://keras.io/ja/layers/convolutional/.

Table 10. Maximum differential probabilities of small PRESENT-[4], small AES-[4], and small TWINE-[4]

Round	Maximum differential probability		
	small PRESENT-[4]	small AES-[4]	small TWINE-[4]
1	2^{-2}	2^{-2}	2^0
2	2^{-4}	2^{-9}	2^{-2}
3	2^{-7}	2^{-11}	2^{-4}
4	2^{-8}	2^{-11}	2^{-6}
5	2^{-14}	2^{-11}	2^{-7}
6	2^{-15}	2^{-11}	2^{-9}
7	2^{-15}	2^{-11}	2^{-9}
8	2^{-15}	2^{-12}	2^{-11}
9	–	–	2^{-11}
10	–	–	2^{-11}

D   Maximum Differential Probabilities of small PRESENT-[4], small AES-[4], and small TWINE-[4]

Table 10 shows the maximum differential probabilities of small PRESENT-[4], small AES-[4], and small TWINE-[4].

E   More Detailed Results in Sect. 3.1

Table 11 shows the minimum amount of training data required for successful ciphertext prediction/plaintext recovery against three toy block ciphers. In addition, Table 12 details the experimental results shown in Table 11. If the predicted probability is greater than 2^{-15}, we consider the proposed attacks to be successful[6].

---

[6] This assumption is strictly incorrect, but we use it for simple discussion.

Table 11. Minimum amount of training data required for successful ciphertext prediction/plaintext recovery using the proposed attacks against three toy block ciphers with a block size of 16 bits. We use the optimized hyperparameters obtained in Experiment 1 (see Table 3). CP:=Ciphertext Prediction and PR:=Plaintext Recovery.

Cipher	Round	Attack	# training data	Succ. prob.
small PRESENT-[4]	1	CP	2^3	$2^{-14.76}$
		PR	2^3	$2^{-13.40}$
	2	CP	2^4	$2^{-14.57}$
		PR	2^4	$2^{-14.56}$
	3	CP	2^{11}	$2^{-12.11}$
		PR	2^{11}	$2^{-14.55}$
	4	CP	2^{15}	$2^{-5.63}$
		PR	2^{15}	$2^{-14.50}$
small AES-[4]	1	CP	2^9	$2^{-13.32}$
		PR	2^8	$2^{-14.82}$
small TWINE-[4]	1	CP	2^4	$2^{-13.58}$
		PR	2^3	$2^{-14.93}$
	2	CP	2^{11}	$2^{-11.73}$
		PR	2^{11}	$2^{-13.18}$
	3	CP	2^{14}	$2^{-13.54}$
		PR	2^{14}	$2^{-13.02}$

Table 12. Average success probabilities of ciphertext prediction/plaintext recovery using the proposed attacks against three toy block ciphers with a block size of 16 bits. We vary the amount of training data in the range of from 2^2 to 2^{14} and use all remaining plaintexts or ciphertexts as testing data. Moreover, we use the optimized hyperparameters obtained in Experiment 1 (see Table 3). CP:=Ciphertext Prediction and PR:=Plaintext Recovery.

Cipher	Round	Attack	Success probability for each amount of training data												
			2^2	2^3	2^4	2^5	2^6	2^7	2^8	2^9	2^{10}	2^{11}	2^{12}	2^{13}	2^{14}
small PRESENT-[4]	1	CP	$2^{-16.57}$	$2^{-14.76}$	$2^{-14.46}$	$2^{-13.83}$	$2^{-13.78}$	$2^{-13.99}$	$2^{-12.90}$	$2^{-9.76}$	$2^{-6.08}$	$2^{-0.76}$	1	1	1
	1	PR	$2^{-15.44}$	$2^{-13.40}$	$2^{-12.28}$	$2^{-11.79}$	$2^{-11.65}$	$2^{-11.62}$	$2^{-10.56}$	$2^{-8.70}$	$2^{-5.65}$	$2^{-1.53}$	$2^{-0.01}$	1	1
	2	CP	–	$2^{-15.63}$	$2^{-14.57}$	$2^{-14.81}$	$2^{-14.60}$	$2^{-14.94}$	$2^{-14.83}$	$2^{-12.80}$	$2^{-7.96}$	$2^{-2.49}$	$2^{-0.01}$	1	1
	2	PR	–	$2^{-15.08}$	$2^{-14.56}$	$2^{-14.46}$	$2^{-14.46}$	$2^{-14.51}$	$2^{-14.32}$	$2^{-14.38}$	$2^{-13.81}$	$2^{-10.44}$	$2^{-2.46}$	1	1
	3	CP	–	–	–	–	–	–	–	–	$2^{-15.02}$	$2^{-12.11}$	$2^{-10.34}$	$2^{-7.80}$	$2^{-0.01}$
	3	PR	–	–	–	–	–	–	–	–	$2^{-15.54}$	$2^{-14.55}$	$2^{-14.43}$	$2^{-13.89}$	$2^{-12.86}$
	4	CP	–	–	–	–	–	–	–	–	–	–	–	$2^{-15.16}$	$2^{-15.01}$
	4	PR	–	–	–	–	–	–	–	–	–	–	–	$2^{-16.09}$	$2^{-15.42}$
small AES-[4]	1	CP	–	–	–	–	–	$2^{-15.04}$	$2^{-15.24}$	$2^{-13.32}$	$2^{-9.22}$	$2^{-4.42}$	$2^{-0.29}$	$2^{-0.01}$	1
	1	PR	–	–	–	–	–	$2^{-15.17}$	$2^{-14.82}$	$2^{-13.67}$	$2^{-10.47}$	$2^{-7.58}$	$2^{-4.35}$	$2^{-0.05}$	$2^{-0.01}$
small TWINE-[4]	1	CP	$2^{-15.54}$	$2^{-15.09}$	$2^{-13.58}$	$2^{-13.48}$	$2^{-13.19}$	$2^{-13.24}$	$2^{-12.99}$	$2^{-11.05}$	$2^{-8.12}$	$2^{-4.97}$	$2^{-1.64}$	$2^{-0.01}$	1
	1	PR	$2^{-16.99}$	$2^{-14.93}$	$2^{-13.28}$	$2^{-12.51}$	$2^{-11.87}$	$2^{-11.77}$	$2^{-12.06}$	$2^{-10.19}$	$2^{-7.28}$	$2^{-3.75}$	$2^{-1.93}$	1	$2^{-0.02}$
	2	CP	–	–	–	–	–	–	–	–	$2^{-15.86}$	$2^{-11.73}$	$2^{-7.62}$	$2^{-4.55}$	$2^{-0.58}$
	2	PR	–	–	–	–	–	–	–	–	$2^{-15.63}$	$2^{-13.18}$	$2^{-9.72}$	$2^{-5.03}$	$2^{-1.06}$
	3	CP	–	–	–	–	–	–	–	–	–	–	–	$2^{-15.47}$	$2^{-13.54}$
	3	PR	–	–	–	–	–	–	–	–	–	–	–	$2^{-15.40}$	$2^{-13.02}$

F   More Detailed Results in Sect. 3.2

Tables 13 and 14 show the minimum amount of training data required for successful ciphertext prediction/plaintext recovery against three block ciphers with block sizes of 32 and 64 bits, respectively. In addition, Tables 15 and 16 detail the experimental results shown in Tables 13 and 14, respectively.

We vary the amount of training data in the range of from 2^8 to 2^{17} or from 2^{10} to 2^{19} and use 2^{16} of the remaining plaintexts or ciphertexts as testing data against three toy block ciphers with block sizes of 32 or 64 bits, respectively; thus, if the predicted probability is greater than the threshold derived by equation $(2^{4n} - 2^x)^{-1}$ shown in Sect. 2.3, we consider the proposed attacks to be successful for both cases. In this case, those thresholds are $(2^{32} - 2^8)^{-1}$ to $(2^{32} - 2^{17})^{-1}$ or from $(2^{64} - 2^{10})^{-1}$ to $(2^{64} - 2^{19})^{-1}$.

Table 13. Minimum amount of training data required for successful ciphertext prediction/plaintext recovery using the proposed attacks against three block ciphers with a block size of 32 bits. We use the optimized hyperparameters obtained in Experiment 1 (see Table 3). CP:=Ciphertext Prediction and PR:=Plaintext Recovery.

Cipher	Round	Attack	# training data	Succ. prob.
small PRESENT-[8]	1	CP	2^{10}	$2^{-19.47}$
		PR	2^9	$2^{-22.64}$
	2	CP	2^{11}	$2^{-21.64}$
		PR	2^{14}	$2^{-1.20}$
	3	CP	2^{15}	$2^{-6.34}$
		PR	2^{17}	$2^{-2.24}$
	4	CP	N/A	N/A
		PR	N/A	N/A
small AES-[8]	1	CP	2^{12}	$2^{-17.78}$
		PR	2^{11}	$2^{-22.64}$
small TWINE-[8]	1	CP	2^{11}	$2^{-20.32}$
		PR	2^{10}	$2^{-21.64}$
	2	CP	2^{14}	$2^{-20.32}$
		PR	2^{14}	$2^{-14.49}$
	3	CP	2^{16}	$2^{-22.64}$
		PR	2^{17}	$2^{-19.18}$

Table 14. Minimum amount of training data required for successful ciphertext prediction/plaintext recovery using the proposed attacks against three block ciphers with a block size of 64 bits. We use the optimized hyperparameters obtained in Experiment 1 (see Table 3). CP:=Ciphertext Prediction and PR:=Plaintext Recovery.

Cipher	Round	Attack	# training data	Succ. prob.
small PRESENT-[16] (PRESENT)	1	CP	2^{13}	$2^{-18.00}$
		PR	2^{14}	$2^{-17.68}$
	2	CP	2^{14}	$2^{-6.64}$
		PR	2^{16}	$2^{-2.27}$
	3	CP	2^{17}	$2^{-1.30}$
		PR	2^{19}	$2^{-3.14}$
	4	CP	N/A	N/A
		PR	N/A	N/A
small AES-[16] (AES-like)	1	CP	2^{15}	$2^{-0.24}$
		PR	2^{15}	$2^{-0.06}$
small TWINE-[16] (TWINE-like)	1	CP	2^{15}	$2^{-0.30}$
		PR	2^{14}	$2^{-15.91}$
	2	CP	2^{19}	$2^{-12.50}$
		PR	2^{19}	$2^{-7.05}$
	3	CP	N/A	N/A
		PR	N/A	N/A

Table 15. Average success probabilities of ciphertext prediction/plaintext recovery using the proposed attacks against three block ciphers with a block size of 32 bits. We vary the amount of training data in the range of from 2^8 to 2^{17} and use 2^{16} of the remaining plaintexts or ciphertexts as testing data. Moreover, we use the optimized hyperparameters obtained in Experiment 1 (see Table 3). CP:=Ciphertext Prediction and PR:=Plaintext Recovery.

Cipher	Round	Attack	Success probability for each amount of training data									
			2^8	2^9	2^{10}	2^{11}	2^{12}	2^{13}	2^{14}	2^{15}	2^{16}	2^{17}
small PRESENT-[8]	1	CP	0	0	$2^{-19.47}$	$2^{-13.47}$	$2^{-0.51}$	1	1	1	1	1
		PR	0	$2^{-22.64}$	$2^{-20.64}$	$2^{-13.76}$	$2^{-7.61}$	$2^{-1.80}$	$2^{-0.01}$	$2^{-0.01}$	$2^{-0.01}$	$2^{-0.01}$
	2	CP	0	0	0	$2^{-21.64}$	$2^{-17.35}$	$2^{-6.22}$	$2^{-0.57}$	$2^{-0.54}$	$2^{-0.05}$	$2^{-0.02}$
		PR	0	0	0	0	0	0	$2^{-1.20}$	$2^{-0.06}$	$2^{-0.13}$	$2^{-0.05}$
	3	CP	0	0	0	0	0	0	0	$2^{-6.34}$	$2^{-3.32}$	$2^{-2.35}$
		PR	0	0	0	0	0	0	0	0	0	$2^{-2.24}$
	4	CP	0	0	0	0	0	0	0	0	0	0
		PR	0	0	0	0	0	0	0	0	0	0
small AES-[8]	1	CP	0	0	0	0	$2^{-17.78}$	$2^{-8.25}$	$2^{-0.12}$	$2^{-0.01}$	$2^{-0.01}$	1
		PR	0	0	0	$2^{-22.64}$	$2^{-20.64}$	$2^{-13.43}$	$2^{-0.01}$	$2^{-0.01}$	$2^{-0.01}$	$2^{-0.01}$
small TWINE-[8]	1	CP	0	0	0	$2^{-20.32}$	$2^{-17.47}$	$2^{-4.41}$	$2^{-0.01}$	$2^{-0.01}$	$2^{-0.01}$	$2^{-0.01}$
		PR	0	0	$2^{-21.64}$	$2^{-16.45}$	$2^{-12.62}$	$2^{-3.86}$	$2^{-1.69}$	$2^{-0.76}$	$2^{-0.76}$	$2^{-0.27}$
	2	CP	0	0	0	0	0	0	$2^{-20.32}$	$2^{-4.97}$	$2^{-4.84}$	$2^{-2.84}$
		PR	0	0	0	0	0	0	$2^{-14.49}$	$2^{-16.62}$	$2^{-8.78}$	$2^{-12.68}$
	3	CP	0	0	0	0	0	0	0	0	$2^{-22.64}$	$2^{-15.71}$
		PR	0	0	0	0	0	0	0	0	0	$2^{-19.18}$

Table 16. Average success probabilities of ciphertext prediction/plaintext recovery using the proposed attacks against three block ciphers with a block size of 64 bits. We vary the amount of training data in the range of from 2^{10} to 2^{19} and use 2^{16} of the remaining plaintexts or ciphertexts as testing data. Moreover, we use the optimized hyperparameters obtained in Experiment 1 (see Table 3). CP:=Ciphertext Prediction and PR:=Plaintext Recovery.

Cipher	Round	Attack	Success probability for each amount of training data									
			2^{10}	2^{11}	2^{12}	2^{13}	2^{14}	2^{15}	2^{16}	2^{17}	2^{18}	2^{19}
small PRESENT-[16] (PRESENT)	1	CP	0	0	0	$2^{-18.00}$	$2^{-0.01}$	1	1	–	–	–
		PR	0	0	0	0	$2^{-17.68}$	$2^{-8.04}$	$2^{-0.37}$	$2^{-0.01}$	$2^{-0.01}$	–
	2	CP	0	0	0	0	$2^{-6.64}$	$2^{-2.64}$	$2^{-2.31}$	$2^{-1.68}$	$2^{-0.60}$	–
		PR	0	0	0	0	0	0	$2^{-2.27}$	$2^{-0.39}$	$2^{-0.08}$	–
	3	CP	0	0	0	0	0	0	0	$2^{-1.30}$	$2^{-1.68}$	$2^{-0.74}$
		PR	0	0	0	0	0	0	0	0	0	$2^{-3.14}$
	4	CP	0	0	0	0	0	0	0	0	0	0
		PR	0	0	0	0	0	0	0	0	0	0
small AES-[16] (AES-like)	1	CP	0	0	0	0	0	$2^{-0.24}$	$2^{-0.06}$	$2^{-0.01}$	$2^{-0.01}$	–
		PR	0	0	0	0	0	$2^{-0.06}$	$2^{-0.01}$	$2^{-0.01}$	$2^{-0.01}$	–
small TWINE-[16] (TWINE-like)	1	CP	0	0	0	0	0	$2^{-0.30}$	$2^{-0.04}$	$2^{-0.01}$	$2^{-0.01}$	–
		PR	0	0	0	0	$2^{-15.91}$	$2^{-5.72}$	$2^{-5.16}$	$2^{-3.99}$	$2^{-2.45}$	$2^{-1.16}$
	2	CP	0	0	0	0	0	0	0	0	0	$2^{-12.50}$
		PR	0	0	0	0	0	0	0	0	0	$2^{-7.05}$
	3	CP	0	0	0	0	0	0	0	0	0	0
		PR	0	0	0	0	0	0	0	0	0	0

References

1. Alallayah, K.M., Alhamami, A.H., AbdElwahed, W., Amin, M.: Applying neural networks for simplified data encryption standard (SDES) cipher system cryptanalysis. Int. Arab J. Inf. Technol. 9(2), 163–169 (2012)
2. Alani, M.M.: Neuro-cryptanalysis of DES and Triple-DES. In: Huang, T., Zeng, Z., Li, C., Leung, C.S. (eds.) ICONIP 2012. LNCS, vol. 7667, pp. 637–646. Springer, Heidelberg (2012). https://doi.org/10.1007/978-3-642-34500-5_75
3. Alshammari, R., Nur Zincir-Heywood, A.: Machine learning based encrypted traffic classification: identifying SSH and Skype. In: IEEE CISDA, pp. 1–8 (2009)
4. Baek, S., Kim, K.: Recent Advances of Neural Attacks against Block Ciphers. SCIS (2020). https://caislab.kaist.ac.kr/publication/paper_files/2020/scis2020_SG.pdf
5. Bafghi, A.G., Safabakhsh, R., Sadeghiyan, B.: Finding the differential characteristics of block ciphers with neural networks. Inf. Sci. **178**(15), 3118–3132 (2008). Nature Inspired Problem-Solving
6. Baksi, A., Breier, J., Chen, Y., Dong, X.: Machine learning assisted differential distinguishers for lightweight ciphers. In: DATE, pp. 176–181 (2021)
7. Bao, Z., Guo, J., Liu, M., Ma, L., Yi, T.: Conditional differential-neural cryptanalysis. IACR Cryptology ePrint Archive 2021:719 (2021)

8. Benamira, A., Gerault, D., Peyrin, T., Tan, Q.Q.: A deeper look at machine learning-based cryptanalysis. In: Canteaut, A., Standaert, F.-X. (eds.) EURO-CRYPT 2021. LNCS, vol. 12696, pp. 805–835. Springer, Cham (2021). https://doi.org/10.1007/978-3-030-77870-5_28

9. Bogdanov, A., et al.: PRESENT: an ultra-lightweight block cipher. In: Paillier, P., Verbauwhede, I. (eds.) CHES 2007. LNCS, vol. 4727, pp. 450–466. Springer, Heidelberg (2007). https://doi.org/10.1007/978-3-540-74735-2_31

10. Chen, Y., Yu, H.: Neural aided statistical attack for cryptanalysis. IACR Cryptology ePrint Archive 2020:1620 (2020)

11. Chen, Y., Yu, H.: A new neural distinguisher model considering derived features from multiple ciphertext pairs. IACR Cryptology ePrint Archive 2021:310 (2021)

12. Chen, Y., Yu, H.: Bridging machine learning and cryptanalysis via EDLCT. IACR Cryptology ePrint Archive 2021:705 (2021)

13. Chen, Y., Yu, H.: Improved neural aided statistical attack for cryptanalysis. IACR Cryptology ePrint Archive 2021:311 (2021)

14. Danziger, M., Amaral Henriques, M.A.: Improved cryptanalysis combining differential and artificial neural network schemes. In: ITS, pp. 1–5 (2014)

15. Focardi, R., Luccio, F.L.: Neural cryptanalysis of classical ciphers. In: ICTCS, pp. 104–115 (2018)

16. Mishra, G., Krishna Murthy, S.V.S.S.N.V.G., Pal, S.K.: Neural network based analysis of lightweight block cipher PRESENT. In: Yadav, N., Yadav, A., Bansal, J.C., Deep, K., Kim, J.H. (eds.) Harmony Search and Nature Inspired Optimization Algorithms. AISC, vol. 741, pp. 969–978. Springer, Singapore (2019). https://doi.org/10.1007/978-981-13-0761-4_91

17. Gohr, A.: Improving attacks on round-reduced speck32/64 using deep learning. In: Boldyreva, A., Micciancio, D. (eds.) CRYPTO 2019. LNCS, vol. 11693, pp. 150–179. Springer, Cham (2019). https://doi.org/10.1007/978-3-030-26951-7_6

18. Gomez, A.N., Huang, S., Zhang, I., Li, B.M., Osama, M., Kaiser, L.: Unsupervised cipher cracking using discrete GANs. CoRR, abs/1801.04883 (2018)

19. Greydanus, S.: Learning the enigma with recurrent neural networks. CoRR, abs/1708.07576 (2017)

20. Hochreiter, S., Schmidhuber, J.: Long short-term memory. In: Neural Computation, vol. 9, no. 8, pp. 1735–1780 (1997)

21. Hou, B., Li, Y., Zhao, H., Wu, B.: Linear attack on round-reduced DES using deep learning. In: Chen, L., Li, N., Liang, K., Schneider, S. (eds.) ESORICS 2020. LNCS, vol. 12309, pp. 131–145. Springer, Cham (2020). https://doi.org/10.1007/978-3-030-59013-0_7

22. Hou, Z., Ren, J., Chen, S.: Cryptanalysis of round-reduced SIMON32 based on deep learning. IACR Cryptology ePrint Archive 2021:362 (2021)

23. Hou, Z., Ren, J., Chen, S.: Improve neural distinguisher for cryptanalysis. IACR Cryptology ePrint Archive 2021:1017 (2021)

24. Hu, X., Zhao, Y.: Research on plaintext restoration of AES based on neural network. Secur. Commun. Netw. **2018**, 6868506:1–6868506:9 (2018)

25. Idris, M.F., Teh, J.S., Yan, J.L.S., Yeoh, W.-Z.: A deep learning approach for active S-box prediction of lightweight generalized Feistel block ciphers. IEEE Access **9**, 104205–104216 (2021)

26. Kingma, D.P., Ba, J.: Adam: a method for stochastic optimization. In: ICLR (2015)

27. Leander, G.: Small scale variants of the block cipher PRESENT. IACR Cryptology ePrint Archive 2010:143 (2010)

28. Lee, T., Teh, J.S., Liew, J., Yan, S., Jamil, N., Yeoh, W.-Z.: A machine learning approach to predicting block cipher security. In: CRYPTOLOGY (2020)

29. Lee, T.R., Teh, J.S., Jamil, N., Yan, J.L.S., Chen, J.: Lightweight block cipher security evaluation based on machine learning classifiers and active S-boxes. IEEE Access **9**, 134052–134064 (2021)
30. Liu, Y., Chen, J., Deng, L.: Unsupervised sequence classification using sequential output statistics. In: NIPS, pp. 3550–3559 (2017)
31. Mantin, I., Shamir, A.: A practical attack on broadcast RC4. In: Matsui, M. (ed.) FSE 2001. LNCS, vol. 2355, pp. 152–164. Springer, Heidelberg (2002). https://doi.org/10.1007/3-540-45473-X_13
32. Shibutani, K., Isobe, T., Hiwatari, H., Mitsuda, A., Akishita, T., Shirai, T.: *Piccolo*: an ultra-lightweight blockcipher. In: Preneel, B., Takagi, T. (eds.) CHES 2011. LNCS, vol. 6917, pp. 342–357. Springer, Heidelberg (2011). https://doi.org/10.1007/978-3-642-23951-9_23
33. So, J.: Deep learning-based cryptanalysis of lightweight block ciphers. Secur. Commun. Netw. **2020**, 3701067 (2020)
34. Sutskever, I., Vinyals, O., Le, Q.V.: Sequence to sequence learning with neural networks. In: NIPS, pp. 3104–3112 (2014)
35. Tan, C., Ji, Q.: An approach to identifying cryptographic algorithm from ciphertext. In: ICCSN, pp. 19–23 (2016)
36. Tieleman, T., Hinton, G.: Lecture 6.5-RMSprop: divide the gradient by a running average of its recent magnitude. COURSERA: Neural Netw. Mach. Learn. **4**(2), 26–31 (2012)
37. Wang, G., Wang, G.: Improved differential-ML distinguisher: machine learning based generic extension for differential analysis. In: Gao, D., Li, Q., Guan, X., Liao, X. (eds.) ICICS 2021. LNCS, vol. 12919, pp. 21–38. Springer, Cham (2021). https://doi.org/10.1007/978-3-030-88052-1_2
38. Xiao, Y., Hao, Q., Yao, D.D.: Neural cryptanalysis: metrics, methodology, and applications in CPS ciphers. In: IEEE DSC, pp. 1–8 (2019)
39. Yadav, T., Kumar, M.: Differential-ML distinguisher: machine learning based generic extension for differential cryptanalysis. In: Longa, P., Ràfols, C. (eds.) LATINCRYPT 2021. LNCS, vol. 12912, pp. 191–212. Springer, Cham (2021). https://doi.org/10.1007/978-3-030-88238-9_10

HolA: Holistic and Autonomous Attestation for IoT Networks

Alessandro Visintin[1]([✉]), Flavio Toffalini[2,3], Eleonora Losiouk[1], Mauro Conti[1], and Jianying Zhou[3]

[1] University of Padua, Padua, Italy
alessandro.visintin@studenti.unipd.it , elosiouk@math.unipd.it,
mauro.conti@unipd.it
[2] EPFL, Lausanne, Switzerland
flavio.toffalini@epfl.ch
[3] SUTD, Singapore, Singapore
jianying_zhou@sutd.edu.sg

Abstract. Collective Remote Attestation (CRA) is a well-established approach where a single *Verifier* attests the integrity of multiple devices in a single execution of the challenge-response protocol. Current CRA solutions are well-suited for Internet of Things (IoT) networks, where the devices are distributed in a mesh topology and communicate only with their physical neighbours. Recent advancements on low-energy protocols, though, enabled the IoT devices to connected to the Internet, thus disrupting the concept of physical neighbour. In this paper, we propose HolA (Holistic and Autonomous Attestation), the first CRA scheme designed for Internet-like IoT networks. HolA provides defence against attacks targeting both the nodes and the network infrastructure. We deployed HolA on both a network of real devices (*i.e.,* 5 Raspberry Pis) and a simulated environment (*i.e.,* 1M devices in an Omnet++ network). Our results demonstrate that HolA can resist against a disruptive attacker that compromises up to half of the network devices and that tampers with network traffic. HolA can verify the integrity of 1M devices in around 12 s while the state-of-the-art requires 71 s. Finally, HolA requires 7 times less memory per device compared with the state-of-the-art.

Keywords: IoT network · Remote attestation · Distributed IoT services

1 Introduction

Internet of Things (IoT) refers to a category of small independent devices that, when connected to a network, can autonomously collaborate to accomplish complex tasks [4]. The widespread use of IoT technologies attracted the attention of adversaries, leading to the development of a broad class of attacks. These attacks are often partitioned into two groups: (i) *software attacks* that install malicious

J. Zhou et al. (Eds.): ACNS 2022 Workshops, LNCS 13285, pp. 277–296, 2022.
https://doi.org/10.1007/978-3-031-16815-4_16

software inside the device [26,27,45]; (ii) *physical attacks* that tamper directly with the hardware [13,14,24,25]. While *software attacks* are remotely executed by leveraging classic hacking techniques, *physical* ones require an adversary to remove a device from a network for a non negligible amount of time (*e.g.,* 10 min [23,30]).

In this scenario, Remote Attestation (RA) is a major solution for validating the integrity (*software* or *physical*) of remote devices [21]. The classic RA scheme [20] involves a trusted entity (*i.e., Verifier*) that challenges a remote device (*i.e., Prover*) to provide a measurement of its current status. Over the past few years, researchers proposed Collective Remote Attestation (CRA) schemes that better fit the *mesh-like* environment of IoT (*i.e.,* networks with devices communicating only with physically-close neighbours). However, the IoT world is increasingly moving from *mesh-like* to *Internet-like* networks [12,34]. Here, the concept of physical neighbour vanishes and current CRA schemes show limitations in terms of scalability and security. We consider the adoption of *Internet-like* networks prominent in light of the research on new energy-save Wireless protocols (*e.g.,* 6LoWPAN [40], Thread [22]) that promise to connect many more IoT devices to the Internet itself.

In light of these considerations we propose HolA, the first Holistic and Autonomous Attestation protocol for *Internet-like* IoT networks that: (i) guarantees an effective, efficient, and scalable periodic attestation of the whole IoT network; (ii) makes the IoT network resilient to the well-known attacks targeting *mesh-like* networks and the new ones addressing the *Internet-like* networks. We implemented HolA on real devices equipped with a trusted anchor [31] for storing keys and performing cryptographic operations (*i.e.,* 5 Raspberry Pi 3 and a Raspberry Pi 0 for performance reference). We also evaluated HolA performance in a large scale simulated network (*i.e.,* 1M devices) through Omnet++ [43]. To validate our approach, we conducted several attacks in both real and virtual scenarios, encompassing software tampering, lost packets, and corrupted devices.

2   Background

2.1   Remote Attestation

RA schemes consist in protocols that permits the verification of a remote entity. Usually, RA schemes involve two distinct roles: *Verifier* and *Prover*. The *Verifier* is considered trusted and is usually physically protected from attacks (*e.g.,* a remote server). The *Verifier* duty is to verify the integrity of a *Prover* that may be corrupted (*e.g.,* due to a malware). RA schemes require a *Verifier* to start the protocol by sending a challenge to the *Prover*, which measures some properties of its state (*e.g.,* compute a hash of a piece of software) and returns a report. Then, the *Verifier* can validate the *Prover* status by matching the returned report with a database of correct measurements.

In IoT scenarios, it is a common practice to perform *single-device* RA and *collective* RA. In the former, any network device can play the role of the *Verifier* and issue a challenge to another network device, *i.e.,* a *Prover*, to attest its status.

In the latter, only a device from a set of predefined ones can verify the current status of all the other network nodes, *i.e.*, *Provers*, and generate a cumulative report.

2.2 Trusted Anchor

Modern RA schemes require nodes mounting specific hardware, called *trusted anchor*, that correctly implement minimal hardware features for attestation [20]. The nodes use Read-Only Memory (ROM) and Memory Protection-Unity (MPU) to partition the device memory into two zones: (i) *untrusted*, containing general purpose software; (ii) *trusted*, a protected memory region shielding sensitive information, such as cryptographic algorithms, keys, and secure random number generators. In short, the *trusted anchor* guarantees that only the protocol code accesses the cryptographic keys, and the node is booted correctly. Recent works show that Off-The-Shelf IoT devices already provide *trusted anchors* with a minimal hardware features set [39].

2.3 Chord

Chord [41,46] is a Distribushed Hash Table (DHT) protocol for managing distributed hash tables. In Chord, each node is identified by an *m-bit* number computed by a hash function. Using these identifiers, nodes are linked to their predecessors and successors, thus creating a ring. To improve resilience, nodes maintain a list of successors called *successors list*. The routing of messages around the ring is made efficient by the introduction of the *fingers table*, which results in an average routing complexity of $O(\log_2(n))$ and renders the operation scalable *w.r.t.* the number of nodes in the network. Chord permits dynamicity in the network by introducing three maintenance tasks [46]: (i) the *join* task, where an outside node contacts a member of the ring to join the topology; (ii) the *stabilize* task, where a node contacts its direct successor to check its presence and possibly adjust disruptions using the *successors list*; (iii) the *rectify* task, where a node receives notification of presence from its predecessor. The *join* task is performed only when a node is entering the network, while the *stabilize* and the *rectify* tasks are periodically executed by all the nodes to maintain the ring topology.

3   Assumptions

3.1 System Model

HolA focuses on *Internet-like* networks where devices are equipped with a trusted anchor. Devices communicate with each other over a secure and reliable channel. The security of the communication is guaranteed by the adoption of known protocols (*e.g.*, Diffie-Hellman [17]) on top of the Internet ones (*e.g.*, WiFi [8], 6loWPAN [40] and TCP/IP [37]), while the reliability comes from the TCP properties Each device is uniquely identified by a certificate signed by a Certification Authority (CA) controlled by the network owner. The device private key is stored within the trusted anchor, while the public key is shared with other nodes to issue a secure channel. Finally, we assume nodes are already equipped with countermeasures against side channel attacks and having clocks loosely synchronized, as already assumed by previous works [23,28,30].

3.2 Threat Model

The goal of an attacker is to gain control of a network device and compromise it, meanwhile preventing its detection from the rest of the network. To achieve this goal, the attacker can use two different strategies:

- *Software attack (i.e., A_{sw}):* working from a remote location, the attacker can gain control of the untrusted zone of one or more network nodes through classic exploitation techniques, but not of the trusted one. Moreover, she can gain control of one or more network infrastructure nodes (*i.e.,* Dolev-Yao model [18]).
- *Hardware attack (i.e., A_{hw}):* the attacker can gain control of both the trusted and untrusted zone of one or more network nodes by manually tampering with the hardware node. Thus, the attacker needs to be in a physical range with the device, to remove it from the network for a time T_a (*e.g.,* 10 min [13,14,23–25,30]) and compromise it.

Adopting the above-mentioned strategies, the attacker can complete two attacks:

- *Injection attack:* through a A_{hw}, the attacker can inject a compromised device into the network.
- *Compromising attack:* through either a A_{hw} or a A_{sw}, the attacker can compromise a node already belonging to the network.

To inject a compromised device into the network, an adversary needs a valid certificate. Thus, she can either obtain a valid certificate from the CA or steal the certificate from another network node. While the first option is unfeasible, the second one is doable provided that the original owner is excluded from the network. In addition, the adversary can rely on A_{hw} to manipulate the network infrastructure and tamper with the protocol.

To compromise a network node, the attacker can rely on A_{hw} or on A_{sw}. Through A_{hw}, the attacker physically removes a node from the network for a time T_a, installs malicious code inside it, compromising the trusted zone, and makes the node rejoining the network. Moreover, the compromised node might manipulate the network traffic to prevent its detection. Through A_{sw}, the attacker reaches a network node from a remote location, installs malicious code inside it, compromising the untrusted zone, and manipulates the network traffic, either from the compromised node or from a network infrastructure node, to prevent the node detection.

In this work, we do not consider destructive Denial of Service (DoS) attacks that utterly interrupt any communication.

4 Motivation

4.1 CRA Limitations in Internet-Like Networks

To motivate our claim, we discuss here the impact of deploying the following three different CRA schemes in an *Internet-like* network: SANA [6], one of the most scalable protocols and currently used as a baseline; SCAPI [28], one of the CRA schemes that are the most resistant to physical attacks; PASTA [30], a scalable and physical attack resistant CRA scheme, that does not require an external *Verifier*.

Unlike *mesh-like* networks, the *Internet-like* ones do not assume physical connections among nodes and each device is logically connected to any other one. To represent the connections among devices in an *Internet-like* network, SANA and SCAPI schemes can either save the status of the whole network in each single node (S1) or define only a subset of nodes as logical neighbors (S2). S1 requires a high amount of memory allocated for each node, while S2 implies an adaptation of the current protocols. A similar approach may be applied by PASTA, which should require a node to store a key for each other network device or to include a novel mechanism to trace logical neighbor status. *Thus, current CRA schemes lack a mechanism to define logical connections in a Internet-like network.*

From a security perspective, *Internet-like* networks introduce more attack surfaces. The attacker can gain control of the devices from a remote location. Moreover, she can even target network infrastructure components (*e.g.*, switches) to tamper with the packets. In general, the remote access enables the attacker to launch wider attacks that may simultaneously affect a large number of devices. PASTA is the only work that considers such scenario, but its evaluation is limited (up to 10 devices).

4.2 Security Properties

To effectively defend against *injection* and *compromising* attacks, a CRA scheme designed for *Internet-like* networks should have three properties: (i) *neighbourhood attestation*; (ii) *absence detection*; (iii) *network obfuscation*.

Neighbourhood Attestation – It refers to the capability of each network node to verify the integrity of its neighbours. Neighbourhood attestation permits to detect any compromised node that managed to join the network through a *compromising* attack. Neighbourhood attestation is the consequence of removing a central *Verifier* in CRA schemes and distributing its attestation responsibility to all the nodes.

Absence Detection – It is the capability of a CRA scheme to detect whenever a device goes offline for a certain amount of time or even forever. In particular, the absence detection recognizes if a node becomes offline for a time T_a due to an *injection attack* performed through A_{hw}.

Network Obfuscation – This property refers to any strategy adopted by a CRA scheme to harden the network packet inspection and the consequent selective drop. This property prevents any attempt to manipulate the network traffic, which can be either performed during an *injection* or a *compromising* attack through A_{hw} or A_{sw}. Current CRA schemes do not provide any defence against attacks to the network infrastructure, since they assume the network is self-contained.

5   HolA Overview

HolA is a CRA scheme specifically designed for *Internet-like* networks, which guarantees the security properties illustrated in Sect. 4.2. HolA organizes the network devices in a ring by relying on the Chord protocol. To achieve this aim, each device needs to be equipped with specific data structures (Sect. 5.1) and to manage a specific life cycle (Sect. 5.2).

5.1   HolA Device Architecture

As specified in the system model, network devices are equipped with a trusted anchor (Sect. 5.2). Chord algorithms, together with HolA data structures and logic, are saved in the trusted anchor of each device. Table 1 shows the main components of each device and details are provided below.

`cert` – Every node is equipped with a certificate signed with `privCAKey` and defined as a tuple containing `pubKey`, `role` and `nodeId`. The `nodeId` is an incremental integer used as the index of the node inside the Status List (SL). The certificate represents the device identity, is signed offline by a CA, and used to authenticate messages exchanged among devices. We accept only trusted CAs that are controlled by the network administrators (Sect. 3.1).

`SL` – The SL keeps track of the network devices status. Each entry is a triplet defined as follows:

- `deviceStatus` (`trusted/offline/compromised`): a device is considered `trusted` as long as it succeeds the attestation from its neighbors. It eventually moves to `offline` status when it becomes inactive. Finally, a device is set as `compromised` when it stays `offline` for more than T_a or it fails the attestations.
- `exitTimestamp`: it is the exact time when a device is found to be `offline`.
- `sessionId`: it is a monotonic counter increasing every time a device enters the network. We use the `sessionId` to handle devices that temporarily go `offline` for less than T_a and that are willing to re-join the network.

We maintain a full copy of the SL in each device for two reasons: (R1) it makes the HolA scheme more robust in case of a simultaneous failure of multiple devices; (R2) it permits any device to be aware of the whole network status, thus efficiently implementing both *single-device* and *collective* attestations (Sect. 6.2).

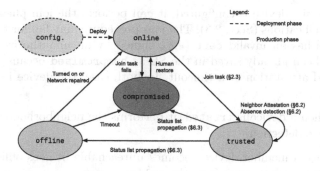

Fig. 1. Lifecycle of a network node deployed in the HolA CRA scheme.

Table 1. Main components of the HolA devices.

Data Structure	Short Description
successors list	List of the direct successors of a device [a]
finger table	List of intermediate devices in the network [a]
nodeId	a progressive unique number that identifies a device in the network
pubKey/privKey	keys used for issuing secure communication channels.
cert	A certificate representing the device identity [b]
pubCAKey	the CA pubKey used for certificate validation
Status List (SL)	a structure containing the status of each device in the network [b]
verifySF()	Function to ascertain the healthy status of a device [2, 3, 11, 16, 30, 42, 47]
role	the privilege of a device [2]

[a] See Chord protocol in (Sect. 2.3) for more info.
[b] See Device architecture in (Sect. 5.1)

A memory-efficient way to implement the SL is to create a list indexed by the nodeIds.

role – it represents the device privilege, which could be:

- *User*: generic IoT device, that can add devices to the SL, but not remove them.
- *Admin*: dedicated devices, that can perform network maintenance and remove a device from the SL.

5.2 HolA Device Lifecycle

The HolA device lifecycle is depicted in Fig. 1 and it involves the following states: configuration, online, trusted, offline and compromised.

configuration – Before a device is turned on, the network administrator installs the cryptographic material in the trusted anchor. In particular, the administrator provides the cert, the pubKey/privKey, and sets the role and the nodeId.

`online` – once the device is configured, it can perform the join phase following the Chord specifications (Sect. 2.3). The join procedure may fail for two reasons: (1) the device has an invalid `cert` (*e.g.,* signed by an unauthorized CA), (2) the node has been already saved in the SL as `compromised` because of a failed neighbourhood attestation or a timeout. In both case, the device is considered `compromised`.

`trusted` – When a device is `trusted`, it performs the neighborhood attestation and the absence detection.

`offline` – Once a member device becomes unreachable, it goes offline and has to re-join the network starting from the `online` status.

`compromised` – A member device can be set as `compromised` by other member devices, thus becoming isolated. A `compromised` device can be restored only due to manual intervention from the network administrator. In this case, the device passes to `online` and starts the join again.

6 HolA: Design

6.1 Status List Propagation

The SL is a data structure containing information about the status of all network devices (*i.e.,* `trusted`, `offline`, `compromised`) and each network device has a local and up-to-date copy of it. Whenever a device intercepts an event that requires an update to its local SL, the device will then propagate the information to the network devices to make them update their local copies of the SL. The events that can cause an SL update are:

- *New device joining the network*: when a new device enters the network, it performs the Chord *join* operation. The *successor* of the new device receives information about the new entrance, updates its own SL and propagates the information to the network.
- *Neighbourhood attestation*: thanks to the properties of Chord, each device periodically attests its *successor*. If the device finds the *successor* either `compromised` or `offline`, it updates its own SL and propagates the information to the network.
- *Absence detection*: if a device has some items in its SL marked as `offline`, it periodically verifies if any of those devices go `online`. If a device is found `offline` for more than T_a, it is marked as `compromised` in the local SL and the information is propagated to the network.

The update of the local SL occurs through a set of priority policies. Given two SL entries (*i.e.,* E_1 and E_2), we assume E_1 has priority over E_2 if (i) the `deviceStatus` of E_1 is `compromised` and the `deviceStatus` of E_2 is not `compromised`; **OR** (ii) the `sessionId` of E_1 is greater than `sessionId` of E_2. Condition (i) makes the network more conservative towards `compromised` devices, which might become again `trusted` only through the intervention of an *Admin* device. While a tampered node may be able to change its state from `compromised` to `trusted`, it would not be able to propagate it to other nodes as this particular state transition is locked by construction. Condition (ii) handles the scenario where a device turns `online` again, after being `offline`, without the network detecting its exit. The propagation of the SL update to the whole network refers only to the entries that need to be updated, thus reducing the amount of transferred information. A device receives the whole SL only when it joins the network.

6.2   Neighborhood Attestation and Absence Detection

Neighborhood attestation enables the detection of any compromised node that managed to join the network through a *compromising* attack. Absence detection permits to monitor any device going `offline` and the amount of time it stays unreachable. In HolA, each network device periodically performs a neighborhood attestation against its *successor*. During neighborhood attestation the *successor* receives a challenge asking to check its status through the `verifySF()` function (*i.e.,* healthy or compromised), save it into a `report`, and return it to the sender. The attestation report can depict three outcomes: *correct*, in which case nothing is done; *fail*, in which case the *successor* is marked as `compromised` in the local SL; *timeout*, in which case the *successor* is marked `offline`.

Any update update to the SL is eventually propagated to the neighbors. This local and up-to-date copy of the SL allows each network devices to perform:

- *Single-device attestation* - A device A can verify the integrity of a device B, even if B is not one of A's neighbours by inquiring its SL. Previous works [3, 29] focused only on A_{sw}, while the *single-device* attestation in HolA detects both A_{sw} and A_{hw}.
- *Collective attestation* - an operator connects to a node with *Admin* `role` and looks for `compromised` devices in the SL. The operator can also manually remove the `compromised` nodes from the SL. We remark that the node `role` is part of the `cert`. Thus, an adversary cannot impersonate an *Admin* node, unless she breaks the CA signature or steals a node with *Admin* `role`.

6.3   Network Obfuscation

In our threat model, we assume that the attacker may perform statistical analysis over the exchanged packets (Sect. 3.2). For instance, she may detect and stop those packets belonging to the SL propagation, thus stopping the updates on `compromised` nodes. Since we assume the devices employ secure cryptography primitives, we exclude man-in-the-middle attacks. However, the adversary can still observe the sender IP, the receiver IP, and the packet size. Previous works showed that this information is enough to denanonymize the packets [15, 32]. To mitigate this issue, we harden the packet analysis by employing network obfuscation strategies. In particular, we took inspiration from two techniques used in the mix-networks [1]: (i) all the exchanged messages have the same size by design, and (ii) any device sends extra random packets to a fixed set of devices. These techniques avoid any intermediate device to distinguish between SL propagation, neighborhood attestation, or Chord routines. In addiction, this disrupts a frequency analysis to discover the *successors* of a device [19]. We analyze the packet size and quantify the network overhead in (Sect. 7.7) and (Sect. 7.5), respectively.

7   HolA: Evaluation

7.1   Experimental Setup

We used three setups: Raspberry Pi 0 [35], Raspberry Pi 3 [36], and a simulated network on Omnet++ [43].

We used a Raspberry Pi 0 [35] as a constrained environment to estimate the cost of cryptographic operations used by HolA. A Raspberry Pi 0 mounts a 1 GHz single-core CPU with 512 MB RAM. Each received message requires three cryptographic operations to be performed: (i) authentication, (ii) key negotiation, and (iii) decryption. The authentication mechanism uses an RSA schema with a 2048 bits long key. The certificate verification required on average 0.589 ms (0.02 ms std). The key generation phase produces an AES 256B long key using a Diffie-Hellman exponentiation. This operation required on average 5.92 ms (0.0522 ms std). The decryption mechanism uses an AES-GCM [38] with a 256B long key. It required on average 0.0833 ms (0.126 ms std).

We used a network of 5 Raspberry Pi 3 [36] to prove the feasibility of HolA on real devices mounting ARM TrustZone [44]. We developed the prototype on top of OP-TEE [33] by using the C language. We implemented network communication using two TCP sockets opened in the *untrusted zone*.

We used Omnet++ to simulate an IoT TCP/IP network with up to 1M devices. We set a delay of 10 ms to simulate message processing based on the measurements on the Raspberry Pi 0. We set the communication rate to 250 Kbps based on the defined data-rate of the 6loWPAN specifications [40].

We compared the results of our experiments with state-of-the-art solutions [6,28,30]. Each work has proposed its own experiments and units of measure. We therefore tried to proposed a thorough comparison with the information available.

7.2   HolA Resiliency

HolA requires that the underlying ring is preserved to automatically repair itself in case of disrupted nodes. Therefore, the overall security of our protocol is strictly related to this property. We can adjust the resilience of our network by tuning the *successors list* length ($SLEN$). In particular, $SLEN$ must be longer than the longest sequence of consecutive disrupted nodes.[1] Fig. 2a shows

---

[1] With consecutive nodes, we mean nodes with a consecutive position in the Chord ring.

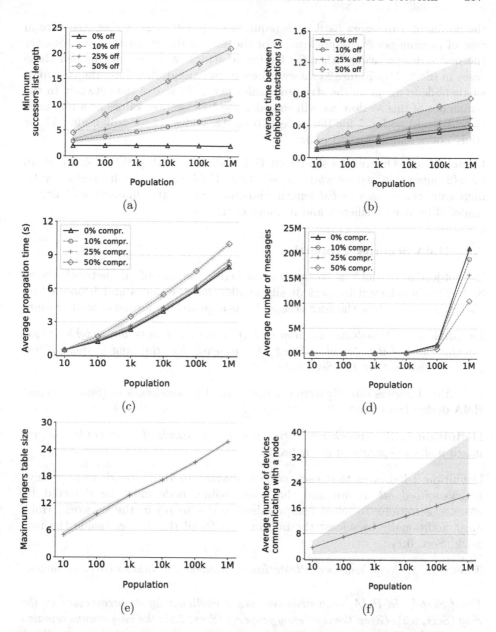

Fig. 2. Minimum successors list length required for preserving the ring structure (a), average time between two consecutive challenges received by a node (b), average time required for an information to be broadcasted (c), average number of messages required to broadcast an information (d), maximum fingers list size (e), average number of devices communicating with a specific node (f). The graphs are the results of 100 experiments run with 6 different populations. The lines represent different percentages of offline nodes (a, b) and compromised nodes (c, d). The points represent the average value and the shaded area the standard deviation. The x-axis has logarithmic base.

the minimum *successors list* length required for preserving the ring structure in case of random nodes disappearing. For the sake of this evaluation, we consider the nodes disappearing either for failure or attack, while we distinguish these cases in (Sect. 7.3). Figure 2a shows a logarithmic trend, therefore, the cost for a single node to maintain the structure scales *w.r.t.* the size of the network. In the remainder of this section, we will consider the 50% average values as a reference (*i.e.,* 4 for 10 nodes, 7 for 100 nodes, 10 for 1K nodes, 14 for 10K nodes, 17 for 100K nodes and 20 for 1M nodes).

Conclusion – Our results show that HolA is in line with [28] by tolerating up to $n/2$ outages in the network. In addition, HolA can adjust its resiliency by increasing the *successors list* length, thus introducing the unique possibility to trade-off between resiliency and memory overhead.

7.3   HolA Security Properties

The objective of HolA is to maintain a healthy status of the network (Sect. 3.2). This is achieved by periodically challenging the nodes and broadcasting the updates. We show the correctness of this approach by formal demonstration.

Definition 1. *A node is compromised if it does not pass the neighbourhood attestation or if it is found offline by the absence detection and it stays offline for more than a time T_a (Sect. 6.2).*

Definition 1 derives directly from the threat model considerations (Sect. 3.2) and HolA design (Sect. 6).

Definition 2. *A network attestation protocol is secure if it prevents compromised nodes to operate in the network.*

Definition 2 indicates that each node belonging to the network must receive *neighbourhood attestation* and that each offline node must be detected by *absence detection*. To avoid compromised nodes to rejoin the network, HolA must additionally broadcast the information to all the devices inside the network (Sect. 6.1).

Theorem 1. *Neighbourhood attestation guarantees continuous check of nodes.*

Proof Sketch. In HolA, each node receives a challenge by its predecessor in the ring (Sect. 6.2). *Given the resiliency property* (Sect. 7.2), *the ring always remains intact during HolA operations. Therefore, a node participating to the protocol will always have a predecessor.*

In HolA, a node continuously receives challenges to check its status and eventually detect a *compromising attack* carried out through A_{sw} or A_{hw} (Sect. 4.2). Therefore, it is crucial that any node is constantly verified by the other nodes; this time may vary due to the presence of offline nodes. For instance, a node immediately after a disruption needs to wait for the protocol to repair the ring before receiving its next challenge. We deepen this aspect in (Sect. 7.4).

Theorem 2. *Absence detection guarantees the detection of offline nodes.*

Proof Sketch. Each node periodically sends a challenge to its successor and expects a response. In case the communication times out, the node flags the successor as offline in the status list, removes it from the successors list and propagates this information. The sequence of operations is repeated until the node finds the first online device in the successors list. The resiliency property (Sect. 7.2) assures that at last one node will eventually find an online device. Each node participating to the protocol performs this task. Hence, using again the resiliency property, there will always be a node detecting and propagating the information about its offline successors.

Since each node of the network is continuously proved, HolA avoids *injection attacks* (Sect. 4.2).

Theorem 3. *Status list propagation reaches all online devices.*

Proof sketch. Each node propagates the information to its successors list. Given the resiliency property (Sect. 7.2), the ring always remains intact during HolA operations. Hence, the information will be routed around the circle and will eventually reach all the nodes.

Without losing in generality, we considered a limit case in which a node has an empty *finger list*, thus only relying on its *successor list*. In reality, the *finger table* usually has some entries that can be used to improve the broadcast speed. We measure the impact of the *finger table* in (Sect. 7.5). Moreover, we distinguish between a random attacker and a selective attacker. Section 7.5 treats the first case demonstrating the robustness of the process with different percentages of compromised nodes. For the second case, a selective attacker needs to physically compromise $SLEN$ consecutive nodes in the ring to block the propagation around the ring. Since we include network obfuscation techniques (Sect. 6.3), an adversary cannot exactly locate the *successors*. To successfully remove all the successors, an adversary must control all the devices contacted by a target node and those contacted by its *successor list*. In practice, in a network of 1M of device, considering a $SLEN$ of 20, and a finger list of 24 devices (more detail in Fig. 2e), an attacker must control 24^{20} devices (around 4×10^{27}) at the same time to block the SL propagation. To summarize, the network obfuscation enables a secure SL propagation to resist against a *compromising attack*.

7.4   Time Delay for Neighbourhood Attestation

We evaluated the time delay that neighbourhood attestations could suffer due to network disruptions. We experimented with 6 different populations presenting 4 different percentages of random offline nodes (from 0 to 50%). Figure 2b shows a logarithmic trend, therefore, the time period scales *w.r.t.* network size. The largest period is reached with a population of 1M device, where the maximum expected period is 1.3 s.

Conclusion – Despite major disruptions, the neighbourhood attestation procedure demonstrates optimal performance in terms of scalability and availability.

7.5   SL Propagation Performance

Theorem 3 demonstrates the correctness of HolA propagation. However, the over-all performance of the naive implementation (*i.e.,* propagating only to *successors list* nodes) are linear *w.r.t.* the network size. To improve it, we experimented with a more efficient propagation where the information is additionally sent to one entry in the *finger table*. From the propagation perspective, this is equivalent to spread the information using a binary tree topology. We measured the time and number of messages required for the propagation to reach every node in the network. We experimented with 6 different populations and 4 different percent-ages of random offline nodes. For the *successors list* lengths, we considered the suggested values in (Sect. 7.2).

Figure 2c shows the average propagation time required for HolA to propagate an information to the whole network. The propagation time is almost logarith-mic, demonstrating the scalability of the process *w.r.t.* the network size and that the process is slightly affected by the rate of offline nodes. The propagation time ranges from 8 s to 10 s with a population of 1M devices. In terms of messages, Fig. 2d shows the average number of messages required increases linearly with the online population and the number of messages sent by each node. In fact, each online node sends out an exact number of messages (all the successors plus a finger). As an example, for a population of 1M devices where 50% of them are offline we measured exactly $10,500,000$ messages $(50\% \times 1M) \times (20 + 1)$, where 20 is the *successors list* length and 1 the additional finger. This simplifies the estimate of the burden introduced by extra random packets (Sect. 6.3). In fact, the number of random packets sent proportionally affects the global number of packets exchanged. In other words, r extra random packets per each node would bring an increase of r-times in the messages.

Conclusion – HolA guarantees an efficient network propagation that scales quasi-logarithmically *w.r.t.* the network size. A complete execution of the proto-col comprising both the attestation and the propagation takes an average time period of around 12 s (Sect. 7.4). This is a major improvement *w.r.t.* to previous works, where the elapsed time could be as long as 71.7 s [30] and 1421 s [6]. The time required by PASTA [30] highly depends on the network's state, ranging from 3 s to 71.7 s while our results are more stable.

7.6   Memory Consumption

Successor List – The *successor list* size $(SLEN)$ is a constant value to be set before deploying the network. Each entry in the *successor list* stores an IP address (4B) together with the pubKey of the related node (128B), for a total of 132B. Hence, a complete *successor list* requires $(132 \times SLEN)$B.

Finger Table – Every entry of the *finger table* requires 132B as for the *successor list* (4B for the IP plus 128B for the pubKey). The total number of entries in the *finger table* depends on the network size. Figure 2e shows the maximum number of fingers of the *finger table* with different network populations (up to

1M devices). The plot shows a logarithmic trend, suggesting that the *fingers table* scales *w.r.t.* the network size. In particular, a *finger table* contains $132 \times log_2(n)$B.

Status List – Each SL entry stores a `deviceStatus` (1B), an `exitTimestamp` (8B) and a `sessionId` (1B), totalling 10B. The SL must contain all the devices in the network, hence the overall memory overhead is $(10 \times n)$B.

Cache – We introduced a cache for storing the `pubKey` and `nodeId` of other devices and speed up the communications. In particular, we tune the cache to contain as many entries as the expected number of nodes to contact (Fig. 2f). The graph indicates a logarithmic growth *w.r.t.* the global population of the network. This suggests that a cache could reduce the burden of certificate verification without imposing too much overhead on the memory. Each entry in cache occupies 130B (128B for the `pubKey` and 2B for the `nodeId`), setting the cache memory to $(130 \times log_2(n))$B.

Conclusion – The overall memory used for data structures is $10 \times n + 262 \times log_2(n) + 132 \times SLEN$. The other decentralized autonomous network (PASTA [30]) claims an overall memory cost of at most $(78, 140 + |token| \times 1,280)$B (around 700 Kb). In the same scenario (*i.e.*, 10K), HolA has an overhead of at most $(103, 668 + 132 \times SLEN)$B. Considering 14 as $SLEN$ (Sect. 7.2), the size becomes $105, 516$B (around 100 Kb), that is seven times less overhead *w.r.t.* PASTA.

7.7   Communication Overhead

We measure the communication overhead in terms of message size. In our implementation, the messages contains a header of 274B, where the majority part is dedicated to a *certificate* (256B) and the rest is for the HolA internal working. The payload of a message depends in which phase HolA is operating: (i) *join phase*, and (ii) *operational phase*. During the *join phase*, the largest message sent has size $(10 \times n + 132 \times SLEN + 274)$B and it is sent once. The *operational phase*, instead, comprises all the tasks executed by a node during its permanence inside the ring. Since we adopt network obfuscation techniques, all the *operational* messages has the same length, which is of $(264 \times (SLEN + 1))$B. In case of a network of 10K devices and a resiliency rate of 50% (Sect. 7.2), the HolA *operational* messages have a weight of 3,960B.

Conclusion – SANA [6] has a communication costs in the same order of magnitude of HolA. The same can be said for SCAPI [28] that claims an average cost of 1,314B for a network of 10K devices.

8   Related Works

CRA on Spanning Tree Topology – SEDA [7], SANA [6], and LISA [10] are the first CRA schemes. They initiate a spanning tree topology over the network and use it for distributing the burden of computation among all the devices. A limitation regarding these approaches is the static topology assumption that forces the devices to not disrupt the tree during the protocol execution. Moreover, they do not consider hardware attackers [6,7,10], they provide coarse-grained results [7] or expensive aggregation methods [6] and they propose inefficient secret keys management [7,10].

Physical Attacks Detection – Due to the increasing size of the networks, researchers investigated mechanisms to detect *physical* adversaries that may capture the devices. These works assume a *physical* adversary removes a device from the network for a non-negligible amount of time. DARPA [24] and SCAPI [28] are the main works in this direction. They both rely on an heartbeat token exchanged between neighbors that permits an external *Verifier* to detect devices' absence. These works act as overlays placed above existing solutions (SEDA [7], SANA [6]). Thus, they inherit both the complexity and the limitations of the underlying attestation scheme.

CRA for Highly Dynamic Swarms – To tackle the static topology issue of first CRA schemes, more recent ones proposed a scheme that incrementally creates a complete snapshot of the network status. SALAD [29] and PADS [5] achieve this goal through a shared structure that contains the status of all the devices, and an external *Verifier* that needs to retrieve the structure from a random device.

Autonomous Networks – A new branch of CRA works proposes autonomous networks that do not rely on an external *Verifier* to maintain their healthy status. DIAT [3] assumes a *mesh-like* connection and focuses on *software* adversaries and run-time RA (*i.e.,* they validate runtime device status). US-AID [23] can detect both *software* tampering and device disconnections. PASTA [30] handles both *software* and *physical* adversaries by relying on a periodical generation of tokens that attests the integrity of all the devices that participated in its generation. These autonomous CRA schemes focus on *mesh-like* networks where a device can only connect with its physical neighbours. Hence, they do not provide support for those environments in which a device can potentially connect with all the others.

9   Discussion

Certificate Revocation/Expiration – In our design, we ruled out the certification revocation and expiration. This may let adversaries forge fake certificates and allow malicious devices to join the network. We can overcome this issue with the introduction of probabilistic filters, as described in previous works [9].

False Positive – A device is considered `compromised` through A_{hw}, if it is `offline` for more than T_a. However, this does not mean a device has been actually under attack. This is also considered as an open problem in previous works [23,28,30]. In HolA, we mitigate this issue by relying on *Admin* devices that can manually control the network status and restore outage devices.

Devices Loosely Synchronized – As assumed also in previous works [23,28, 30], the network devices require some clock synchronization strategy to detect a A_{hw}. We aim at overcoming this limitation by storing the relative time at which a device becomes offline, instead of the absolute timestamp. However, this introduces other synchronization challenges, such as considering random network propagation delays. We plan to investigate new solutions for this issue in future versions of HolA.

10   Conclusion

In this paper, we proposed HolA, the first Holistic and Autonomous Attestation protocol for *Internet-like* networks. HolA guarantees a strong defence against both *compromising* and *injection* attacks.

We demonstrated the feasibility of the HolA protocol over real devices (*i.e.*, Raspberry Pi 0 and 3) and on a network of 1M of simulated devices (*i.e.*, Omnet++). In our evaluation, we stressed the resilience of HolA against a network with 50% of nodes disrupted. HolA showed an attestation time in between 8 s and 12 s, that is similar and more stable than previous works (*i.e.*, from 3 s to 72 s [30]). In addition, HolA can resist to adversaries that perform network analysis and selectively drop packets. In terms of scalability, HolA requires only 100 Kb per device in a network of 10K nodes, which is in contrast with the 700 Kb required by previous works [30].

Acknowledgements. The work is supported by A*STAR under its RIE2020 Advanced Manufacturing and Engineering (AME) Industry Alignment Fund - Pre Positioning (IAF-PP) Award A19D6a0053. Any opinions, findings and conclusions or recommendations expressed in this material are those of the author(s) and do not reflect the views of A*STAR.

References

1. Abe, M.: Mix-networks on permutation networks. In: Lam, K.-Y., Okamoto, E., Xing, C. (eds.) ASIACRYPT 1999. LNCS, vol. 1716, pp. 258–273. Springer, Heidelberg (1999). https://doi.org/10.1007/978-3-540-48000-6_21
2. Abera, T., et al.: C-FLAT: control-flow attestation for embedded systems software. In: Proceedings of the 2016 ACM SIGSAC Conference on Computer and Communications Security, CCS 2016, pp. 743–754. ACM, New York (2016). https://doi.org/10.1145/2976749.2978358, https://doi.acm.org/10.1145/2976749.2978358
3. Abera, T., Bahmani, R., Brasser, F., Ibrahim, A., Sadeghi, A., Schunter, M.: DIAT: data integrity attestation for resilient collaboration of autonomous systems. In: 26th Annual Network & Distributed System Security Symposium (NDSS). The Internet Society (2019). http://tubiblio.ulb.tu-darmstadt.de/110632/
4. Alaba, F.A., Othman, M., Hashem, I.A.T., Alotaibi, F.: Internet of things security: a survey. J. Netw. Comput. Appl. **88**, 10–28 (2017)

5. Ambrosin, M., Conti, M., Lazzeretti, R., Rabbani, M.M., Ranise, S.: PADS: practical attestation for highly dynamic swarm topologies. In: 2018 International Workshop on Secure Internet of Things (SIoT), pp. 18–27 (2018). https://doi.org/10.1109/SIoT.2018.00009

6. Ambrosin, M., Conti, M., Ibrahim, A., Neven, G., Sadeghi, A.R., Schunter, M.: SANA: secure and scalable aggregate network attestation. In: Proceedings of the 2016 ACM SIGSAC Conference on Computer and Communications Security, CCS 2016, pp. 731–742. ACM, New York (2016). https://doi.org/10.1145/2976749.2978335, https://doi.acm.org/10.1145/2976749.2978335

7. Asokan, N., et al.: SEDA: scalable embedded device attestation. In: Proceedings of the 22Nd ACM SIGSAC Conference on Computer and Communications Security, CCS 2015, pp. 964–975. ACM, New York (2015). https://doi.org/10.1145/2810103.2813670, http://doi.acm.org/10.1145/2810103.2813670

8. Bhatt, A., Patoliya, J.: Cost effective digitization of home appliances for home automation with low-power WiFi devices. In: 2016 2nd International Conference on Advances in Electrical, Electronics, Information, Communication and Bio-Informatics (AEEICB), pp. 643–648 (2016). https://doi.org/10.1109/AEEICB.2016.7538368

9. Broder, A., Mitzenmacher, M.: Network applications of bloom filters: a survey. Internet Math. $\mathbf{1}$(4), 485–509 (2004). https://doi.org/10.1080/15427951.2004.10129096

10. Carpent, X., ElDefrawy, K., Rattanavipanon, N., Tsudik, G.: Lightweight swarm attestation: a tale of two LISA-s. In: Proceedings of the 2017 ACM on Asia Conference on Computer and Communications Security, ASIA CCS 2017, pp. 86–100. ACM, New York (2017). https://doi.org/10.1145/3052973.3053010, http://doi.acm.org/10.1145/3052973.3053010

11. Challener, D.: Trusted platform module. In: Encyclopedia of Cryptography and Security, pp. 1308–1310 (2011)

12. Cisco Systems, I.: Why IP is the right foundation for the smart grid. https://www.cisco.com/c/dam/assets/docs/c11-581079-wp.pdf. Accessed November 2020

13. Conti, M., Di Pietro, R., Gabrielli, A., Mancini, L.V., Mei, A.: The smallville effect: social ties make mobile networks more secure against node capture attack. In: Proceedings of the 8th ACM International Workshop on Mobility Management and Wireless Access, pp. 99–106 (2010)

14. Conti, M., Di Pietro, R., Mancini, L.V., Mei, A.: Emergent properties: detection of the node-capture attack in mobile wireless sensor networks. In: Proceedings of the First ACM Conference on Wireless Network Security, pp. 214–219 (2008)

15. Conti, M., Rigoni, G., Toffalini, F.: ASAINT: a spy app identification system based on network traffic. In: Proceedings of the 15th International Conference on Availability, Reliability and Security, pp. 1–8 (2020)

16. Dessouky, G., et al.: Lo-fat: Low-overhead control flow attestation in hardware. In: Proceedings of the 54th Annual Design Automation Conference 2017, pp. 1–6 (2017)

17. Diffie, W., Hellman, M.: New directions in cryptography. IEEE Trans. Inf. Theory $\mathbf{22}$(6), 644–654 (1976)

18. Dolev, D., Yao, A.C.: On the security of public key protocols. In: Proceedings of the 22Nd Annual Symposium on Foundations of Computer Science. In: SFCS 1981, pp. 350–357. IEEE Computer Society, Washington, DC (1981). https://doi.org/10.1109/SFCS.1981.32

19. Feistel, H.: Cryptography and computer privacy. Sci. Am. $\mathbf{228}$(5), 15–23 (1973)

20. Francillon, A., Nguyen, Q., Rasmussen, K.B., Tsudik, G.: A minimalist approach to remote attestation. In: 2014 Design, Automation & Test in Europe Conference & Exhibition (DATE), pp. 1–6. IEEE (2014)
21. Gong, B., Zhang, Y., Wang, Y.: A remote attestation mechanism for the sensing layer nodes of the internet of things. Futur. Gener. Comput. Syst. **78**, 867–886 (2018)
22. Thread Group: Thread. https://www.threadgroup.org/. Accessed November 2020
23. Ibrahim, A., Sadeghi, A.R., Tsudik, G.: US-AID: unattended scalable attestation of IoT devices. In: 37th IEEE International Symposium on Reliable Distributed Systems (2018). https://doi.org/10.1109/SRDS.2018.00013, https://ieeexplore.ieee.org/document/8613950
24. Ibrahim, A., Sadeghi, A.R., Tsudik, G., Zeitouni, S.: DARPA: device attestation resilient to physical attacks. In: Proceedings of the 9th ACM Conference on Security & Privacy in Wireless and Mobile Networks, WiSec 2016, pp. 171–182. ACM, New York (2016). https://doi.org/10.1145/2939918.2939938, http://doi.acm.org/10.1145/2939918.2939938
25. Ibrahim, A., Sadeghi, A.R., Zeitouni, S.: SeED: secure non-interactive attestation for embedded devices. In: Proceedings of the 10th ACM Conference on Security and Privacy in Wireless and Mobile Networks, pp. 64–74 (2017)
26. Islam, S.A., Katkoori, S.: SafeController: efficient and transparent control-flow integrity for RTL design. In: 2020 IEEE Computer Society Annual Symposium on VLSI (ISVLSI), pp. 270–275. IEEE (2020)
27. Jeong, S., Hwang, J., Kwon, H., Shin, D.: A CFI countermeasure against got overwrite attacks. IEEE Access **8**, 36267–36280 (2020)
28. Kohnhäuser, F., Büscher, N., Gabmeyer, S., Katzenbeisser, S.: SCAPI: a scalable attestation protocol to detect software and physical attacks. In: Proceedings of the 10th ACM Conference on Security and Privacy in Wireless and Mobile Networks, WiSec 2017, pp. 75–86. ACM, New York (2017). https://doi.org/10.1145/3098243.3098255, http://doi.acm.org/10.1145/3098243.3098255
29. Kohnhäuser, F., Büscher, N., Katzenbeisser, S.: SALAD: secure and lightweight attestation of highly dynamic and disruptive networks. In: Proceedings of the 2018 on Asia Conference on Computer and Communications Security, ASIACCS 2018. Association for Computing Machinery, New York (2018). https://doi.org/10.1145/3196494.3196544
30. Kohnhäuser, F., Büscher, N., Katzenbeisser, S.: A practical attestation protocol for autonomous embedded systems. In: 4th IEEE European Symposium on Security and Privacy (EuroS&P 2019) (2019). https://doi.org/10.1109/EuroSP.2019.00028, http://tubiblio.ulb.tu-darmstadt.de/114633/
31. Kylänpää, M., Rantala, A.: Remote attestation for embedded systems. In: Bécue, A., Cuppens-Boulahia, N., Cuppens, F., Katsikas, S., Lambrinoudakis, C. (eds.) CyberICS/WOS-CPS -2015. LNCS, vol. 9588, pp. 79–92. Springer, Cham (2016). https://doi.org/10.1007/978-3-319-40385-4_6
32. Liberatore, M., Levine, B.N.: Inferring the source of encrypted http connections. In: Proceedings of the 13th ACM Conference on Computer and Communications Security, CCS 2006, pp. 255–263. Association for Computing Machinery, New York (2006). https://doi.org/10.1145/1180405.1180437, https://doi.org/10.1145/1180405.1180437
33. Linaro: Op-tee (2015). https://github.com/OP-TEE/optee_os. Accessed June 2019
34. Mandula, K., Parupalli, R., Murty, C.A., Magesh, E., Lunagariya, R.: Mobile based home automation using internet of things (IoT). In: 2015 International Confer-

ence on Control, Instrumentation, Communication and Computational Technologies (ICCICCT), pp. 340–343. IEEE (2015)

35. Pi, R.: Raspberry pi zero. https://www.raspberrypi.org/products/raspberry-pi-zero/

36. Pi, R.: Raspberry pi 3 model b (2015). https://www.raspberrypi.org

37. Rayes, A., Salam, S.: The internet in IoT. In: Internet of Things From Hype to Reality, pp. 37–65. Springer, Heidelberg (2019)

38. Salowey, J., Choudhury, A., McGrew, D.: AES galois counter mode (GCM) cipher suites for TLS. Request for Comments 5288 (2008)

39. Schulz, S., Schaller, A., Kohnhäuser, F., Katzenbeisser, S.: Boot attestation: secure remote reporting with off-the-shelf IoT sensors. In: Foley, S.N., Gollmann, D., Snekkenes, E. (eds.) ESORICS 2017. LNCS, vol. 10493, pp. 437–455. Springer, Cham (2017). https://doi.org/10.1007/978-3-319-66399-9_24

40. Shelby, Z., Bormann, C.: 6LoWPAN: The Wireless Embedded Internet, vol. 43. Wiley, Hoboen (2011)

41. Stoica, I., et al.: Chord: a scalable peer-to-peer lookup protocol for internet applications. IEEE/ACM Trans. Netw. **11**(1), 17–32 (2003). https://doi.org/10.1109/TNET.2002.808407, http://dx.doi.org/10.1109/TNET.2002.808407

42. Toffalini, F., Losiouk, E., Biondo, A., Zhou, J., Conti, M.: SCARR: scalable runtime remote attestation for complex systems. In: 22nd International Symposium on Research in Attacks, Intrusions and Defenses (RAID 2019), pp. 121–134. USENIX Association, Chaoyang District, Beijing (2019). https://www.usenix.org/conference/raid2019/presentation/toffalini

43. Varga, A.: OMNet++. In: Wehrle, K., Güneş, M., Gross, J. (eds.) Modeling and Tools for Network Simulation, pp. 35–59. Springer, Heidelberg (2010). https://doi.org/10.1007/978-3-642-12331-3_3

44. Winter, J.: Trusted computing building blocks for embedded linux-based arm trust-zone platforms. In: Proceedings of the 3rd ACM Workshop on Scalable Trusted Computing, STC 2008, pp. 21–30. ACM, New York (2008). https://doi.org/10.1145/1456455.1456460, http://doi.acm.org/10.1145/1456455.1456460

45. Xia, H.: Capability memory protection for embedded systems. Ph.D. thesis, University of Cambridge (2020)

46. Zave, P.: How to make chord correct (using a stable base). CoRR abs/1502.06461 (2015). http://arxiv.org/abs/1502.06461

47. Zeitouni, S., et al.: ATRIUM: runtime attestation resilient under memory attacks. In: 2017 IEEE/ACM International Conference on Computer-Aided Design (ICCAD), pp. 384–391. IEEE (2017)

CIMSS – Critical Infrastructure and Manufacturing System Security

The Etiology of Cybersecurity

Michele Ambrosi, Francesco Beltramini, Federico De Meo, Oliviero Nardi,
Mattia Pacchin, and Marco Rocchetto(✉)

V-Research, Verona, Italy
{michele.ambrosi,francesco.beltramini,mattia.pacchin,
marco.rocchetto}@v-research.it, research@demeo.eu,
olivieronardi@gmail.com

Abstract. The objective of this research is to lay the foundations for
the development of a scientific theory that determines (all and only) the
possible insecure and secure configurations of any abstract system to
be used for the risk assessment of systems. We claim that cybersecurity
weaknesses (i.e. errors) are at the beginning of the causality chain that
leads to cybersecurity attacks. We formulate a hypothesis that we use
to predict the weaknesses in the architectural design of a system. Our
hypothesis allows for the definition of a mathematical formula which
describes the cybersecurity of a system. We implemented a prototype
cybersecurity risk assessment tool that, based on our hypothesis, predicts
the weaknesses in a UML model of a (cyber-physical) system.

Keywords: Risk management · Cyber-physical systems · Risk
assessment · Security framework

1 Introduction

A *scientific theory* is an explanation of a phenomenon such that the explanation
follows the scientific method. The *scientific method* is an *empirical* method that
aims at mitigating potential fallacies in theories. Karl Popper famously argued
(e.g. in [15]) that a scientific theory can never be verified but only falsified, that
a theory should not be conceived by using the principle of induction,[1] and that
empirical experiments should be considered as the only evidence to support the
non-falseness of a scientific theory. In [7], Cormac Herley explores what he calls
"an asymmetry in computer security", which he defines as follows: "Things can
be declared insecure by observation, but not the reverse. There is no observation
that allows us to declare an arbitrary system or technique secure". With security, Herley only focuses on cybersecurity (we also use security and insecurity, in
this paper, only to refer to cyber-insecurity and cybersecurity) and his intuition
is that there is no scientific theory that can predict the cybersecurity of a system, nor a theory that can predict all possible insecurities of a system (which,
by negation, may be used as a theory of cybersecurity). Herley then uses this
argument to show that "claims that any measure is necessary for security are

---

[1] Einstein to Popper: "[...] and I think (like you, by the way) that theory cannot be
fabricated out of the results of observation, but that it can only be invented." [15].

J. Zhou et al. (Eds.): ACNS 2022 Workshops, LNCS 13285, pp. 299–319, 2022.
https://doi.org/10.1007/978-3-031-16815-4_17

empirically unfalsifiable". The goal of this paper is to address this issue and to lay the foundations of a scientific cybersecurity theory. We consider the problem raised by Herley not confined to "computer security" but rather we reason on any abstract system (so that our scientific hypothesis[2] may be tested in any sound implementation such as a network, a mechanical, cyber, or cyber-physical system, or even a single computer or a single device such as a hard-drive). Instead of starting from reasoning about what makes a system secure or insecure, we reason about what causes insecurities. We focus on insecurities only caused by the exploitation of cybersecurity attacks, and we assume that achieving cybersecurity means preventing all those attacks from being exploitable or exploited. Our hypothesis is that *cybersecurity attacks are only caused by the presence of errors in the design or implementation of a system* (i.e. cybersecurity weaknesses). With our approach, a list of weaknesses emerges from the mathematical formulation of a system in a framework called $\mathcal{ABF}$ (as in Assertions, Beliefs, Facts in [18])[3] predicts 4 main classes of weaknesses. Those classes are used to calculate all the insecurity configurations of all the components of a system, obtaining a precise estimation of all potential cybersecurity-related risks in any given system. Our hypothesis can be falsified by means of experiments, testing if all the predicted weaknesses are present in the system under consideration, or testing if other (not predicted by our hypothesis) weaknesses are present. In fact, if any cybersecurity weaknesses were to be found in a system and not predicted by our hypothesis, the hypothesis could be declared incomplete. If a cybersecurity weakness would be predicted by our hypothesis but found to be impossible to realize, our hypothesis could be declared as wrong.

2   Literature Review

Cybersecurity attacks seem to be related to the creativity of the attacker and thus unpredictable. Currently, the most complete understanding of insecurity issues is stored into a network of databases of weaknesses (e.g. CWE [3]), vulnerabilities (e.g. CVE [13], NVD [21]), and attacks (e.g. CAPEC [2], ATT&CK [12]). Those insecurity issues can be related to the violation of one or more requirements (explicit or implicit) in the specification, design or implementation of a system. The correlation between insecurity flaws and cybersecurity requirements has been used to define standards such as the IEC 62443-1-3 (the Industrial communication networks - Network and system security – Part 3-3: System security requirements and security levels) which defines requirements as "confidentiality of information in transit/at-rest". More generally, the idea of defining cybersecurity requirements as properties of a system was initially defined in 1970s with the CIA triad (Confidentiality, Integrity, Availability) and

---

[2] In the remainder of this paper, we will use the word hypothesis to refer to "scientific hypothesis" as a proposed scientific theory that has not gone through an extensive series of tests. We use "logical theory" to refer to a set of formal logical axioms.

[3] Intuitively, as we will see later, assertions correspond to an exchange of information between agents, beliefs to internal information considered true by the agent, and facts to requirements.

refined over the decades introducing related concepts such as authenticity or non-repudiation, or introducing new ones such as "responsibility" in the RITE approach (see [17] for an overview of the evolution of the CIA triad). The link between cybersecurity requirements and vulnerabilities is reported in the NVD databases by the CVSS [11] scoring system. The CVSS evaluates of the severity of a vulnerability by means of different metrics (such as attack complexity and user interaction) and quantitatively evaluates the impact on the CIA triad. While cybersecurity requirements, weaknesses, vulnerabilities, and attacks have been extensively studied and implemented both in academia and industry to provide tools for the testing or verification of systems, no scientific falsifiable theory correlates cybersecurity requirements to necessary and sufficient conditions (e.g. mitigations) to declare a system secure [7]. Nonetheless, the extensive body of literature has scientific foundations, for example, providing formal frameworks for the verification of properties for cybersecurity. As a driver for our argumentation, we start by reviewing the key concepts in the cybersecurity domain.

2.1   Terminology

We provide a baseline for a definition of the terms that structure our current understanding of cybersecurity.

Vulnerability. As defined in [14] (and adopted in [1]), is a "weakness in an information system, system security procedures, internal controls, or implementation that could be exploited by a threat source".

Weakness. The definition given by the MITRE in [4] of weakness is: " a type of mistake that, in proper conditions, could contribute to the introduction of vulnerabilities within that product. This term applies to mistakes regardless of whether they occur in implementation, design, or other phases of a product lifecycle." A vulnerability, such as those enumerated on the Common vulnerabilities and Exposures (CVE) List, is a mistake that can be directly used by an attacker to gain access to a system or network. The definition is circular if we interpret the word "error" and "mistake" with the same semantics: a weakness is an error that leads to a vulnerability and a vulnerability is a mistake which, in turn, is a weakness. The only difference between a weakness and vulnerability seems to be that one can consider weakness as a ground term and state that a vulnerability is caused by a weakness.

Exploit "[. . .] (from the English verb to exploit, meaning to use something to one's own advantage) is a piece of software, a chunk of data, or a sequence of commands that takes advantage of a bug or vulnerability to cause unintended or unanticipated behavior to occur on computer software, hardware, or something electronic (usually computerized)." [8].

Attack. As defined by the International Standard ISO/IEC 27000, is an "attempt to destroy, expose, alter, disable, steal or gain unauthorized access to or make unauthorized use of an asset"; where an *Asset* is "anything that has value to the organization". We do not consider ethical hackers as attacking a system. In fact, we consider the term *hack* as non-malicious (as, e.g. in [20]).

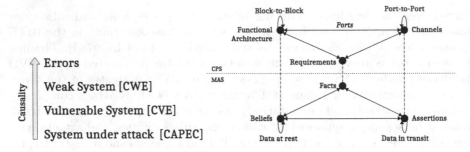

Fig. 1. Etiology of cybersecurity (left). Mapping epistemological concepts to (cyber-physical) systems engineering (right).

Threat. As defined in [14], is "Any circumstance or event with the potential to adversely impact organizational operations (including mission, functions, image, or reputation), organizational assets, individuals, other organizations, or the Nation through an information system via unauthorized access, destruction, disclosure, modification of information, and/or denial of service".

As in Fig. 1, in order to define a theory on cybersecurity we may say that the presence of vulnerabilities is a necessary condition to cause an attack in the system. Those vulnerabilities are, in turn, caused by the presence of weaknesses in the system. Weaknesses are errors in the design or implementation of a system and a theory on cybersecurity should first predict the errors in a system design.

3   A Cybersecurity Hypothesis in the $\mathcal{ABF}$-Framework

To address the problem raised by Herley, we define how to distinguish between a secure and an insecure system in the following steps of the engineering process:

1. *System Specification*: the *functional* and *physical requirements* are defined.
2. *Architecture Design*: the specification is structured into *functional* and *physical architectures*.
3. *Cybersecurity Risk Assessment*: potential *weaknesses* (errors) and *cybersecurity requirements* are identified.

We changed the focus from the attacker as the source of insecurity to the potential design errors of a system. We now define a framework for the definition of a system that we use to identify weaknesses as potential design errors.

3.1   Mereo-Topological Reasoning

Following [18], we define a system as a hierarchy of agents. Furthermore, we model an agent as a meronomy (a hierarchy of part-whole relations) over the aforementioned constituents (assertions, beliefs, and facts), based on a standard definition of mereology (i.e. based on the definition of parthood relation between

Table 1. RCC3 and RCC5 relations between regions X, Y and Z

RCC3	RCC5	Terminology	Notation	Definition
		Connects with	$C(X, Y)$	Reflexive and symmetric
		Disconnected from	$\neg C(X, Y)$	Irreflexive or antisymmetric
		Part of	$P(X, Y)$	$\forall Z\ C(Z, X) \rightarrow C(Z, Y)$
		Overlaps	$O(X, Y)$	$\exists Z\ P(Z, X) \wedge P(Z, Y)$
●	●	**Equal to**	$EQ(X, Y)$	$P(X, Y) \wedge P(Y, X)$
●		**Overlaps not equal**	$ONE(X, Y)$	$O(X, Y) \wedge \neg EQ(X, Y)$
●	●	**DiscRete from**	$DR(X, Y)$	$\neg O(X, Y)$
	●	**Partial-Overlap**	$PO(X, Y)$	$O(X, Y) \wedge \neg P(X, Y) \wedge \neg P(Y, X)$
	●	**Proper-Part-of**	$PP(X, Y)$	$P(X, Y) \wedge \neg P(Y, X)$
	●	**Proper-Part-of-***inverse*	$PPi(X, Y)$	$P(Y, X) \wedge \neg P(X, Y)$

parts). Due to the necessity of considering different relations between parts (as we will show afterwards) we extend the mereology to a mereo-topology [16,19,24], considering the relations in Table 1. For the sake of readability, we use the term *region* both to refer to a mereological part and to a topological region. Our aim is to create a meronomy (hierarchy of part-whole relations) instead of the taxonomies (categorization based on discrete sets) such as the one provided in [13,21] so that we don't need to rely on a scoring system (such as the CVSS) to assign a quantitative evaluation of the cybersecurity of each entry. Instead, we want a precise calculation of the number of insecure configurations of a system to emerge from the mathematical formulation of our cybersecurity hypothesis. A mereotopology, as defined in [16], is a mathematical structure where the basic relation between regions is the reflexive and symmetric relation *Connects With*, that we use to order a universe of agents Ag (see in Tab. 1). We use the Region Connection Calculus (RCC), as defined in [6,9], to provide an axiomatization of the mereo-topological concepts. In its broader definition, the RCC theory is composed by eight axioms, and is known as RCC8 [6]. Using RCC5 instead of RCC8 prevents us from considering tangential connections between spatial regions. However, tangential connections in RCC8 can be considered as special cases of the more general spatial relations considered in RCC5. In Table 1, we summarize the axioms of the RCC (see, e.g., [6]). We can now define a system over the mereotopology using the RCC calculus, as follows, where $rcc(X, Y)$ on two generic regions X, Y represents one of the possible RCC relations between X and Y. We note that all the RCC relations are symmetric with the exception of those that have an explicit (related) inverse.

Definition 1. System State – *A Cyber-Physical System (CPS), or a sub-system, state is defined as a tuple* $s = \langle rcc(\mathcal{F}, \mathcal{B}),\ rcc(\mathcal{F}, \mathcal{A}),\ rcc(\mathcal{B}, \mathcal{A}) \rangle$, *where* $\mathcal{A}, \mathcal{B}$, *and* $\mathcal{F}$ *are regions of assertions, beliefs (i.e. the beliefs generated by the behavior), and facts respectively, expressed as requirements.*

As in [18], it follows that, by defining a system as a fixed number of regions, there exists an upper-bound to the number of possible configuration of a system, defined by the possible relations between the different regions. The general

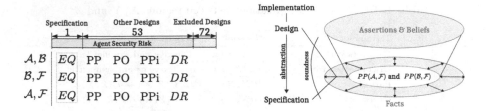

Fig. 2. Cybersecurity risk for a single agent (left). Example relation between facts, and assertions and beliefs (right).

Table 2. RCC5 composition table over 3 regions generates the ideal risk matrix (green the low-risk state, red the high-risk state, and a gradient of intermediate risk states). $T(\mathcal{A},\mathcal{F}) = \{DR(\mathcal{A},\mathcal{F}), PO(\mathcal{A},\mathcal{F}), PP(\mathcal{A},\mathcal{F}), PPi(\mathcal{A},\mathcal{F}), EQ(\mathcal{A},\mathcal{F})\}$

	$DR(\mathcal{A},\mathcal{B})$	$PO(\mathcal{A},\mathcal{B})$	$PP(\mathcal{A},\mathcal{B})$	$PPi(\mathcal{A},\mathcal{B})$	$EQ(\mathcal{A},\mathcal{B})$
$DR(\mathcal{B},\mathcal{F})$	$T(\mathcal{A},\mathcal{F})$	$DR(\mathcal{A},\mathcal{F})$ $PO(\mathcal{A},\mathcal{F})$	$DR(\mathcal{A},\mathcal{F})$	$DR(\mathcal{A},\mathcal{F})$ $PO(\mathcal{A},\mathcal{F})$	$DR(\mathcal{A},\mathcal{F})$
$PO(\mathcal{B},\mathcal{F})$	$DR(\mathcal{A},\mathcal{F})$ $PO(\mathcal{A},\mathcal{F})$ $PP(\mathcal{A},\mathcal{F})$	$T(\mathcal{A},\mathcal{F})$	$DR(\mathcal{A},\mathcal{F})$ $PO(\mathcal{A},\mathcal{F})$ $PP(\mathcal{A},\mathcal{F})$	$PO(\mathcal{A},\mathcal{F})$ $PPi(\mathcal{A},\mathcal{F})$	$PO(\mathcal{A},\mathcal{F})$
$PP(\mathcal{B},\mathcal{F})$	$DR(\mathcal{A},\mathcal{F})$ $PO(\mathcal{A},\mathcal{F})$ $PP(\mathcal{A},\mathcal{F})$	$PO(\mathcal{A},\mathcal{F})$ $PP(\mathcal{A},\mathcal{F})$	$PP(\mathcal{A},\mathcal{F})$	$PO(\mathcal{A},\mathcal{F})$ $EQ(\mathcal{A},\mathcal{F})$ $PP(\mathcal{A},\mathcal{F})$ $PPi(\mathcal{A},\mathcal{F})$	$PP(\mathcal{A},\mathcal{F})$
$PPi(\mathcal{B},\mathcal{F})$	$DR(\mathcal{A},\mathcal{F})$	$DR(\mathcal{A},\mathcal{F})$ $PO(\mathcal{A},\mathcal{F})$ $PPi(\mathcal{A},\mathcal{F})$	$T(\mathcal{A},\mathcal{F})$	$PPi(\mathcal{A},\mathcal{F})$	$PPi(\mathcal{A},\mathcal{F})$
$EQ(\mathcal{B},\mathcal{F})$	$DR(\mathcal{A},\mathcal{F})$	$PO(\mathcal{A},\mathcal{F})$	$PP(\mathcal{A},\mathcal{F})$	$PPi(\mathcal{A},\mathcal{F})$	$EQ(\mathcal{A},\mathcal{F})$

formula to calculate the number of different types of agents is $r^{\binom{n}{k}}$, where r is the number of relations with arity k, between n different regions. In our case, $\binom{n}{k} = 3$ since we consider 3 regions ($\mathcal{A}$, $\mathcal{B}$, and $\mathcal{F}$), and all the relations considered in the RCC are binary. Hence, we have up to 125 different types of agents but only 54 of the 125 (as showed in [6]) combinations are topologically correct. For RCC5 there are $5^3 = 125$ theoretical combinations but only 54 are correct with respect to the axioms.

In the quantitative evaluation of a single agent, as in Fig. 2, we argue that only 1 configuration represents the nominal (expected) behavior of the agent while the other configurations are either impossible to implement or diverge from the intended nominal behavior. We note that the numbers reported here do not consider the details of the engineering process and should be considered a limit of an abstract representation of the system.

3.2 Qualitative Evaluation of Agent Space in $\mathcal{A}, \mathcal{B}, \mathcal{F}$

While a quantitative analysis reveals how many possible configurations of an agent (i.e. a system) exist w.r.t. the $\mathcal{ABF}$-framework (e.g., 54/125 in RCC5), a qualitative analysis of the different configurations describe the configurations allowed by the $\mathcal{ABF}$-framework, and how those configurations can be categorized. In Table 2, we provide the generic composition table of RCC5 over 3 regions instantiated over $\mathcal{A}, \mathcal{B}, \mathcal{F}$, which shows the whole state space for a single agent. The color coding of the table represents the cybersecurity risk related to a generic agent, the risk is highest on the top left corner of the matrix, lowest on the bottom right corner. In Fig. 2, the relation between facts, and assertions and beliefs (as inputs and outputs of the behavior of an agent) is illustrated. Assertions and beliefs generated by the design of a system may not be exactly aligned with what the facts mandate (i.e. what the specification mandates). The relation between facts, and assertions and beliefs can be used as a metric to determine the soundness of the design with respect to the specification. We now analyze the relations between each pair of regions (i.e., $\mathcal{A}, \mathcal{B}, \mathcal{F}$). For the sake of simplicity, soundness is opposed to non-soundness in the following, however, with the RCC, one could consider different "degrees" of non-soundness. For example, in RCC5, if we consider EQ between two regions as representing soundness, DR over the same regions represents "total" non-soundness; while PP, PO, and PPi each represent different degrees of non-soundness. A similar argument can be done for completeness.

$rcc(\mathcal{A}, \mathcal{B})$ – *Collaboration.* By definition, assertions are defined as transfer of information between two agents. An agent has two main categories of assertions, input and output assertions. Given an agent a and a collection of asserted predicates Φ, the input assertions are those received by a from an agent s acting as a sender, $\mathcal{A}_{s \to a}\Phi$; similarly, output assertions are sent from a to a receiver r, $\mathcal{A}_{a \to r}\Phi$. With a slight abuse of notation, in the text we drop the Φ when the content of the assertions is not relevant. We shall consider two pairs of regions:

– $rcc(\mathcal{A}_{s \to a}, \mathcal{B})$, where the relation between input-assertions and beliefs describes the soundness of the execution of the functional architecture w.r.t. input elicitation. If all the inputs (assertions) are correctly handled in the functional specification (beliefs) the specification is complete.
– $rcc(\mathcal{A}_{a \to r}, \mathcal{B})$, where the relation between behavior and outputs describes the completeness of the behavior defined in the specification w.r.t. the input elicitation. If all the outputs (assertions) of the functional architecture can be produced, the functional architecture is complete.

$rcc(\mathcal{A}, \mathcal{F})$ *and* $rcc(\mathcal{B}, \mathcal{F})$ – *Honesty and Competence.* The relation of assertions and beliefs with facts determines the quality with respect to the nominal (specified) system. Given that facts define what needs to be true in the system, the relation of assertions and facts determines the degree of quality between the real information circulating in a system (or within an agent) and the one specified.

Since the transfer of information through assertions generates beliefs, a dishonest agent may circulate false information, generating false beliefs. The relation between beliefs and facts determines the competence (on the subjects defined by the facts) of an agent (i.e. the more competent an agent is, the more likely a belief of that agent is true).

$\mathcal{A}, \mathcal{B}, \mathcal{F}$ **CyberSecurity Enumeration (CSE).** The following cybersecurity requirement for a CPS specification can be summarized:

CSE-1 Proper interaction between correctly-behaving agents is defined as $EQ(\mathcal{A}_a, \mathcal{B}_a)$ for an agent a, and can be detailed as follows when multiple agents are considered.

  CSE-1.1 The equality relation $EQ(\mathcal{A}_{s \to a}, \mathcal{B}_a)$ describes the intended secure behavior as: the beliefs generated by the behavior of the functional architecture shall be complete w.r.t. the specified inputs of the agent. Therefore, *the assertions received by an agent or a system shall be compliant with the expected inputs of the functional architecture.*

  CSE-1.2 Similarly, the equality relation $EQ(\mathcal{A}_{a \to r}, \mathcal{B}_a)$ defines that the outputs of an agent a shall be the outputs of the functional architecture.

CSE-2 The proper adherence of the data transmitted between agents with respect to requirements, is defined as $EQ(\mathcal{A}, \mathcal{F})$.

CSE-3 The proper adherence of the behavior (in terms of input and output beliefs) with respect to requirements is defined as $EQ(\mathcal{B}, \mathcal{F})$.

We note that our CSE define the properties of a secure system, and correlated weaknesses can be found in the CWE dataset. For example, CSE-1 can be seen as correlated to the weakness class of "Improper Interaction Between Multiple Correctly-Behaving Entities" defined by the CWE–435, CSE-2 with the "Insufficient Control Flow Management" defined by MITRE in the CWE–691, and CSE-3 with the "Improper Calculation" defined by MITRE in the CWE–682. All those CWE are in the top "view" of the "research concepts" in [3], while the other classes of weaknesses do not have a direct counterpart in our hypothesis; we believe they can be seen as sub-classes, but a full comparison with the CWE is out of the scope of this article. We can now define what a secure system is (with respect to the $\mathcal{ABF}$-framework) and, based on that definition, what the cybersecurity risk is and how to quantify it in a risk matrix. The following definition holds for abstract systems defined in the $\mathcal{ABF}$-framework but will be refined for CPS afterwards in the paper.

Definition 2. Cybersecurity of a System or an Agent − *A secure system is a system where CSE-1, CSE-2, and CSE-3 holds for each agent of the system.*

The ISO 31000 consider risk as the "effect of uncertainty on objectives" and refers both to positive and negative consequences of uncertainty. Accordingly, we consider risk as follows.

Definition 3. Risk − *The risk is the uncertainty related to the whole space of potential designs resulting from a specification in the $\mathcal{ABF}$-framework.*

The definition of Risk leads to the risk matrix in Table 2, defined as follows.

Definition 4. Risk Matrix − *The risk matrix, as summarized in Table 2, is a function of the three relations $s = \langle rcc(\mathcal{F}, \mathcal{B}), rcc(\mathcal{F}, \mathcal{A}), rcc(\mathcal{B}, \mathcal{A}) \rangle$, where the maximum risk is defined by the DR relation between the three groups of regions, and the minimum risk by the EQ relation over the same regions. In between the two extremes, the granularity of possible intermediate configuration is defined by the calculus used (RCC5 in our case).*

While a risk matrix is often defined as a function of the likelihood and impact of attacks (based on quantitative ad-hoc estimation of how likely it is that an attacker will exploit one or more vulnerabilities and what is the magnitude of the incidents produced by this exploitation), we suggest that cybersecurity weaknesses are all equally likely to be exploited if there's a connection between the weakness and the asset that an attacker wants to impact. When the whole system is considered an asset, all weaknesses are equally likely to be exploited. Therefore, a risk matrix should capture the number of insecure configurations of a system, rather than predicating over likelihoods of weaknesses exploitation.

4   Prediction of Cybersecurity Weaknesses

Several standards mandate a secure-by-design approach in which cybersecurity shall be considered at the very early stages of the design process. Standards do not describe in detail how to perform a cybersecurity risk assessment and only vaguely define the overall objective, which can be summarized as to provide an understanding of the potential cybersecurity risks. All the methodologies and tools we reviewed (e.g. Threatmodeler [22], CORAS [10], SECRAM [5]) rely on the expertise of the person who performs the risk assessment for the identification of threats and for the quantitative estimation of risks. In contrast, in this section, we define how to specify a CPS in the $\mathcal{ABF}$-framework and we identify a cybersecurity metric.

4.1   From Multi-agent to Cyber-Physical Systems

As in Fig. 1, we relate MAS (Multi-Agent System) and CPS as follows.

- We consider a System as a hierarchy of agents. So, we map agents to *systems, sub-systems, or devices*, depending on the granularity of the design. For example, a modeler can model a specific device as a system not decomposed into sub-systems or devices (and the device is considered as an agent).
- Agents reason over beliefs (i.e. transform beliefs into other beliefs) and each *component of a CPS* (system, sub-system, or device) is composed by a *functional architecture* that transforms input-beliefs into output-beliefs.
- Components of a CPS have *ports* to exchange information with the outer environment (which may be a sub-system), similarly to agents. The transfer of information in a CPS is defined by *channels*.
- The concept of facts is related to the *requirements* that describe how the CPS shall behave and its *physical architecture*.

Input and Output Ports. Since the $\mathcal{ABF}$-framework is a theory of agents, we could consider ports as agents that allow the exchange of information between a channel and another agent. However, we considered a port as a special type of agent to avoid an *infinite regress*, as described in the following. While a channel transfers information between agents, and a functional architecture processes information, a port is simply a connector between a channel and a functional architecture. One, however, may argue that a similar connection is needed between a channel and the port itself. While this is not excluded by the $\mathcal{ABF}$-framework, it would obviously lead to an infinite nested structure of ports. To avoid this infinite structure, we assume that a port doesn't require any other means to transfer information from/to a channel or from/to a functional architecture.

Definition 5. Input or Output Port – *A port forwards information from the outside of an agent's boundary to the inside (input-port) or vice versa (output-port). There exist two types of ports with the following behavior: an input-port transforms assertions from a sender s ($\mathcal{A}_{s \to a}$) to beliefs of an agent a ($\mathcal{B}_a$), while an output-port transforms beliefs into assertions.*

The *quality of a port* is determined by the rcc relation between the assertions received or sent and the belief, i.e. $rcc(\mathcal{A}_{s \to a}, \mathcal{B}_a)$ for input-port or $rcc(\mathcal{A}_{a \to r}, \mathcal{B}_a)$, for output-port. A port is, in fact, syntactic sugar to express the relation between assertions and beliefs. We note that the definition of an input/output port can be considered "secure", meaning that we implicitly formulated the requirement that a port always forwards the information without modifying it in any way. This is assumed since we defined a port as if the RCC equality relation holds between the input/output assertions and the input/output beliefs. In contrast, assuming any *other* RCC relation between inputs and outputs of a port can be considered as generating a weakness.

Port Weaknesses. We now apply the $\mathcal{ABF}$-framework to list all possible cybersecurity weaknesses of a port. From our definition of ports, the following holds.

Theorem 1 (Port Weaknesses). *There exist only the following six types of weaknesses, generating six types of insecure port in RCC5:*

W1) Replace port, *where assertions reach the port but are replaced with different and un-related information before passing the boundary.*
W2) Drop port, *where assertions reach the port but do not pass the boundary of the agent (i.e. do not become belief of the agent).*
W3) Insertion port, *where new information is transferred along with the information incoming from a channel, and then sent to the recipient (agent).*
W4) Injection port, *where part of the incoming information is substituted with new information and transferred to the intended recipient.*
W5) Selective port, *where some information passes the port and part is either: (W5.1) Dropped or (WP5.2) Replaced.*

Proof. An input port is, in the $\mathcal{ABF}$-framework, defined secure as long as the relation between the two regions of input assertions $\mathcal{A}$ and output beliefs $\mathcal{B}$ are equal, i.e. $EQ(\mathcal{A}, \mathcal{B})$. Therefore, any other relation should result in a weakness (related to an insecurity flaw) of that input port. Using RCC5, there exist exactly other 4 different types of relations, one of which is the discrete-from (DR) relation, i.e. $DR(\mathcal{A}, \mathcal{B})$. When two regions are related by the DR relations, they have no subregion in common. Let us define a function weight $|X|$ such that, for any region X, it represents the smallest possible cardinality of a (mereo)topological base for X; where a base is a collection of regions in a (mereo)topology such that every region can be written as union of elements of that base. We distinguish between regions that are related to information and regions that are not (i.e., regions A such that $|A| = 0$) by writing the latter as $\emptyset$.

1. If $EQ(\mathcal{A}, \mathcal{B})$ then either $\mathcal{A} = \mathcal{B} = \emptyset$ (no communication) or $\mathcal{A} = \mathcal{B} \neq \emptyset$ (forward communication).
2. If $DR(\mathcal{A}, \mathcal{B})$ then $\mathcal{A} = \emptyset \oplus \mathcal{B} = \emptyset$ (we call *insert* the former, *full drop* the latter case), or $\mathcal{A} \neq \emptyset \wedge \mathcal{B} \neq \emptyset \wedge \mathcal{A} \neq \mathcal{B}$ called *replace* (i.e. drop and insert).
3. If $PP(\mathcal{A}, \mathcal{B})$ then $\mathcal{B}$ contains and extend $\mathcal{A}$ which we call *insertion*.
4. If $PPi(\mathcal{A}, \mathcal{B})$ then $\mathcal{A}$ contains and extend $\mathcal{B}$ which we call *drop* (or selective drop to stress the difference with the full drop).
5. If $PO(\mathcal{A}, \mathcal{B})$ then a part of the $\mathcal{A}$ is contained in the $\mathcal{B}$ which is a combination of *selective drop and generation* which we call *injection*.

Communication Channels. In this work, we only consider mono-directional channels and communication but the extension to bi-directional channel can be considered as the union of two unidirectional channels. A mono-directional channel is defined by the assertions sent or received (over the channel). We consider first the difference between a (communication) mono-directional channel (channel from now on) and an agent, as we did for the ports, since the $\mathcal{ABF}$-framework is a logical theory of agents. In fact, if a channel were considered an agent (channel-agent) then the question would be how an agent would transfer its assertions to the channel-agent. If the channel between the agent and the channel-agent is again an agent, we would generate an *infinite regress*. Therefore, we do allow channel-agents but we assume a finite depth (of detail) for a channel, where there exists a bottom-channel which is not an agent. For now, we do not constrain a channel-agent in any way so there is no difference between a channel agent and agent. Therefore, we consider channels to be bottom-channels, defined as agents with the pre-defined behavior (i.e. defined in an axiomatic way) of forwarding any input-assertion as output-assertion, without modifying it.[4]

Definition 6. Mono-directional Channel (bottom-channel) – *A mono-directional channel between two agents (s → r) is an agent whose behavior is defined as: to forward any assertion received from s over an input-port, to the output-port where r is listening to.*

---

[4] Nothing prevents us from introducing additional constraints to the channel as storing assertions that are transferred over the channel, or filter out some input-assertions.

The *quality of a mono-directional* channel is defined as the *rcc* relation between the assertions of the sender and the ones received by the receiver, i.e. $rcc(\mathcal{A}_s, \mathcal{A}_r)$.

Channel Weaknesses. Given that a mono-directional bottom-channel is assumed to be perfectly forwarding any assertion (as we assumed for ports) from its input-port to its output-port, there is no insecure behavior but only the combination of the weaknesses of the input and output port; therefore there exist $(7^2) - 1 = 48$ theoretical configurations (7^2 because there are 6 insecure types of port – see Theorem 1 – plus 1 secure type, on both input and output side; and we exclude the configuration with 2 secure types as input and output, hence the -1); where only 44 are possible.

W6) *Secure output port* and *input drop port.*
W7) *Secure output port* and *input insertion port.*
W8) *Output drop port* and *input drop port.*
W9) *Output drop port* and *input insertion port.*
W10) *Output drop port* and *input secure port.*
W11) *Output injection port* and *input secure port.*

For the sake of readability, we reported 6 examples but the proof by exhaustion (up to W49) over all the possible cases is straightforward.

Cybersecurity Weaknesses – The RIDI-Hypothesis. All the results of the application of the $\mathcal{ABF}$-framework to channels (the analysis of the RCC relations between output and input assertions of an agent) lead to the same results of the analysis of a pair of an input and output port. So far we have considered information generated by a port P_I and then sent through a channel C to another (recipient) port P_O. In this scenario, where ports and channels are atomic (otherwise raising infinite regress), we can only consider the relations between ports and channel; considering both input-port to channel and channel to output-port. In fact, the weaknesses of a channel are defined in terms of the weaknesses of ports. The same result can be obtained by analyzing the relation between the outputs of a functional block and the inputs of another functional block, where functional blocks are constituents of the functional architecture as described afterwards. To define a functional block without encountering an infinitely recursive definition, we must reach the same conclusions as for the channel. So, describing the information as flowing over a channel or in a functional block is purely syntactic sugar. We can summarize these results by saying that the relations between assertions and beliefs, output assertions of an agent and input assertions of another agent, or output beliefs of a functional block and input beliefs of another block can *only* be affected by the following weaknesses: replace, drop, injection, insertion, selective drop, and selective drop + insertion. We call this the RIDI-Hypothesis, being the four main categories of weaknesses: Replace, Insertion, Drop, Injection. We can, then, deduce the following cybersecurity properties to mitigate cybersecurity weaknesses of a port or a channel (between ports, functional blocks, or both).

- *Order-preserving* – it shall be known if information is *replaced*.
- *Availability* – it shall be known if information is *dropped* or *selectively dropped*.
- *Integrity* – it shall be known if information is *injected*.
- *Authentication* – it shall be known if information is *inserted*.

Functional Architecture. A functional architecture takes information as input-beliefs and transforms the information into output-beliefs. Those transformations occur within the functional architecture, where functional blocks transform beliefs into other beliefs. Similarly to channels, we could consider a functional block as a functional architecture occurring in an infinite regress. Therefore, we consider functional blocks as executing an abstract undefined behavior, of which we only observe the inputs and the resulting outputs (beliefs).

Definition 7. Functional Block and Architecture – *A functional block of an agent takes beliefs as inputs (input-beliefs) and returns output-beliefs. A functional architecture is an interconnected system of functional blocks.*

The quality of a functional block cannot be determined by the difference between its inputs and outputs (as we did for ports and channels), because the behavior of a functional block cannot be determined in general; since any functional block will have its own purpose based on functional requirements. Therefore, while the semantics of a port is determined by the relation between assertions and beliefs, the semantics of a functional block is determined by the relation between facts/requirements and I/O beliefs. In other words, a functional block is a generic agent with no pre-defined general behavior (while ports and channels have a pre-defined behavior). In the following, for the sake of simplicity, we use the generic region $\mathcal{B}$ to refer to the behavior (i.e. the beliefs generated by the behavior).

W50) $PO(\mathcal{B}, \mathcal{F})$ the component has a Byzantine behavior. Not all the inputs are handled properly, nor all the expected outputs are always generated when correct inputs are given.
W51) $PP(\mathcal{B}, \mathcal{F})$ some expected outputs are not generated with the correct inputs.
W52) $PPi(\mathcal{B}, \mathcal{F})$ the components correctly perform the expected behavior when the correct inputs are provided but is subject to input injections.
W53) $DR(\mathcal{B}, \mathcal{F})$ the component never performs the expected behavior (e.g. physical damage).

Requirements as Facts. During the specification phase, for any agent, channel, port, functional block and architecture, there may exist a requirement (fact) predicating over them. In other words, any requirement is defined as a fact since they must be true in any design or implementation. As in Sect. 4 and depicted in Fig. 2, facts are definitory rules that define how the system shall behave (by specification), while reality may be shown to be insecure (i.e. diverging from the expected behavior). As an example, considering a functional block that performs the summation of two inputs defined by the requirement $r := b_3 = b_1 + b_2$ for any b_1 and b_2. The possible relations between the beliefs generated by the behavior of the functional block and the requirements (i.e. $rcc(\mathcal{B}, \mathcal{F})$ is determined by the relations between the I/O beliefs $sum(b_1, b_2) = b_3$ and the requirement $sum(b_1, b_2) = b_1 + b_2$, as follows.

- $EQ(\mathcal{B}, \mathcal{F}) = EQ(\mathcal{B}_3, \mathcal{B}_{1+2})$, where $\mathcal{B}_3$ represents the region of the outputs of sum while $\mathcal{B}_{1+2}$ the expected outputs of an ideal implementation of the requirement r. The functional block correctly implements the requirements.
- $DR(\mathcal{B}, \mathcal{F}) = DR(\mathcal{B}_3, \mathcal{B}_{1+2})$, the functional block does not implement the requirements.
- $PP(\mathcal{B}, \mathcal{F}) = PP(\mathcal{B}_3, \mathcal{B}_{1+2})$, the block produces incorrect outputs for some inputs.
- $PPi(\mathcal{B}, \mathcal{F}) = PPi(\mathcal{B}_3, \mathcal{B}_{1+2})$, not all outputs result from a summation of two inputs (but with the expected inputs the function outputs correctly).
- $PO(\mathcal{B}, \mathcal{F}) = PO(\mathcal{B}_3, \mathcal{B}_{1+2})$, Byzantine behavior where occasionally outputs are produced with the correct inputs. Not all the inputs are handled properly, nor all the expected outputs are generated when correct inputs are given.

Assertions and Facts. The whole reasoning on the relation between beliefs and facts can be duplicated for the relation between assertions and facts; we cannot appreciate the difference at this level of abstraction. If the functional architecture would be extended to capture the semantics (i.e. the logic) of the communication and cybersecurity protocols, with the relation between assertions and facts we would compare protocol logics with the requirements. We won't consider the verification of the functional architecture and protocol logic in this paper since we focus on the architecture specification step of the engineering process without going into the design of the behavior of agents. We summarize our results by categorizing the weaknesses predicted by our hypothesis into: data-flow-related and functionality-related weaknesses; as in Table 3. Functional weaknesses can be seen as a general formulation of our hypothesis, while data-flow weaknesses as an application of our hypothesis to components with defined behavior/requirements.

4.2   Security and Insecurity of a System

We are ready to state our main hypotheses.

Hypothesis 1 System Security Design – *A system security design (in the $\mathcal{ABF}$-framework) is given by a precise system specification over the physical and functional architectures that uniquely defines the design to be built on top of those requirements.*

Hypothesis 2 System Insecurity Design – *If, given a system specification as a collection of requirements, there exist a non-unique design with respect to those requirements, the number of possible designs that fulfill the requirements quantitatively defines the magnitude of insecurity of a system design with respect to the specification.*

Table 3. Weaknesses categorization

RCC5	Quantity: data flow	Quality: requirements adherence
EQ	Expected/Nominal	Expected/Nominal
DR	Drops all inputs and inserts new data	The component never performs/carries the expected behavior/information
PP	Selectively drops inputs	Part of the expected outputs are not generated in response to the correct inputs
PPi	Forwards all the inputs but crafts and inserts new malicious data	The components correctly performs/carries the expected behavior/information when the correct inputs are provided but is subject to input injections
PO	Selectively drops inputs and inserts new data	Byzantine behavior. Occasionally outputs the expected output given the correct inputs. Not all inputs are handled properly, nor all expected outputs always generated on correct inputs

Based on these hypothesis, we can formulate the concepts of security and insecurity (in the $\mathcal{ABF}$-framework) as mathematical equations. Let us consider a CPS S, represented as a graph $G = \langle V, E \rangle$ where V represents the set of functional blocks and ports of S, and $E \subseteq V \times V$ is the set of pairs representing the channels and connections (data flows) between functional blocks. We define $R \subseteq V \times F$, where F is the set of all the requirements of S, and extend G as $G' = \langle V', E' \rangle$ with $V' = V \cup F$ and $E' = E \cup R$. Let $\pi : E' \rightarrow RCC$ (where RCC is the set of relations in the RCC) be the total function associating an RCC relation to each edge in G', and Π be the set of all different permutations of RCC relations over E' (i.e. $\Pi = \{\langle \pi(e_0) = EQ, \ldots, \pi(e_n) = EQ \rangle, \ldots, \langle \pi(e_0) = DR, \ldots, \pi(e_n) = DR \rangle\}$ where $e_i \in E'$ for $0 \leq i \leq n$ and $|E'| = n$). If $\sigma : \Pi \rightarrow \{0, 1\}$ is an evaluation function such that $\sigma(p) = 1$ (where $p \in \Pi$) iff the input configuration is satisfiable with respect to the logical theory defining the algebraic structure (mereotopology) and constraints of the calculus RCC (otherwise σ returns 0),[5] we define:

$$I = \sum_{p \in (\Pi \setminus \pi_{eq})} \sigma(p)$$

Here, $\pi_{eq} \in \Pi$ is the output of the function π that associates only EQ relations to any $e \in E'$, and $I \in \mathbb{N}$ represents all the insecurity configurations of the CPS S where, at least, one of the RCC relations isn't EQ. In other words, we consider π_{eq} as the only secure configuration.

---

[5] In other words, σ returns 1 if and only if a configuration is satisfiable with the respect to the axioms of the RCC.

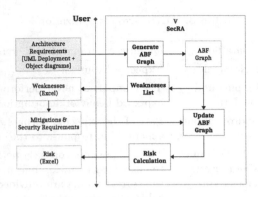

Fig. 3. Cybersecurity risk assessment tool

4.3   Cybersecurity Risk Assessment

To test our hypothesis we implemented a tool-chain (open-source with AGPLv3 license, available at [23]) for the identification of weaknesses and the calculation of potential insecure configurations. The engineering of the $\mathcal{ABF}$-framework for CPS is summarized in the UML Class diagram in Fig. 6 (in appendix). As in Fig. 3, the cybersecurity risk assessment process starts with the definition of the use cases and architectural requirements. In our process, the specification is manually translated into a UML design where:

– A *deployment diagram* describes the *physical architecture*. Each agent is defined as an UML node with (physical) ports, and agent's ports are connected via UML information flow connectors, representing the physical channel.
– A *functional architecture* is linked to each agent in the deployment diagram and is defined by an *object diagram*. The object diagram is composed by instances of functional blocks, connected via information flow connectors.
– The connection between the two diagrams is implemented by "sockets", functional blocks connected to a physical port.

The tool generates a graph-like structure which represents the specification ($\mathcal{ABF}$-graph). The $\mathcal{ABF}$-graph defines the system as a number of regions of assertions, beliefs, and facts. Those regions are connected by a generic relation which is evaluated as follows (according to the formula in Sect. 4.2). The graph is translated into a logical formula that represents the specification in the $\mathcal{ABF}$-framework and, along with the axiomatization of the RCC5 calculus, is given as input to the Z3 SMT solver. The solver identifies all possible configurations of the system and, in turn, identifies all potential weaknesses. The $\mathcal{ABF}$-graph can be viewed as PDF and the results are reported into an spreadsheet file. The

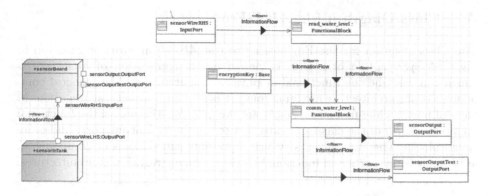

Fig. 4. Sensor board object (left) and water level reader deployment (right) diagrams.

spreadsheet file also reports the total number of configurations as indicating the cybersecurity risk associated to the specification. A user can change the status of each weakness in the spreadsheet file from the default status (open) to "mitigated" and the risk is re-calculated on-the-fly, i.e. without the need of running the tool again, based on annotations and formulas in the spreadsheet file. In our approach, cybersecurity requirements are not imposed by the specification but are automatically extracted by our tool as mitigations to potential weaknesses, which are related to the insecure configurations of the specified system.

Case Study. We report here the results of the evaluation of a water level reader (sensor ad-hoc example). As in Fig. 4 (left), we defined 2 agents: sensorInTank and sensorBoard, as the physical reader that needs to be placed in a tank, and the board that interprets the readings and outputs them as signals. The two components are connected by a wire. In Fig. 4 (right), we report the functional architecture that receives the incoming communications from the sensor in the tank and communicates them encrypted. The tool (Appendix B) reports 16777216 scenarios in which at least one component diverge from the specification.

5   Conclusion and Future Work

We proposed a hypothesis for a foundational theory on security, arguing that cybersecurity-related issues are not linked to the maliciousness of an agent but to the vagueness in the design processes. We provided a prototype tool for the quantitative estimation of the cybersecurity risk based on a UML model of a system. The verification and test-case generation will be our next steps.

316 M. Ambrosi et al.

A   Class Diagram for $\mathcal{ABF}$-Framework

The Class Diagram for the Engineering of the $\mathcal{ABF}$-framework is reported in Fig. 6. A *specification* of a CPS is viewed as an aggregation of *architectures* which can describe the functional or physical requirements. The physical components of the architecture are input/output *ports* and *channels* (aggregations of pairs of ports) while *functional blocks* are the only constituents of the functional architecture. All of the classes are abstract except input/output ports and functional blocks. Therefore, agents (which represents sub-systems or components) are composed by ports and functional blocks, as an aggregation of architectures.

B   Overview of the Results of the Tool

In Fig. 5 we show a screenshot of the results reported by our tool.

RISK				16777216	
The total risk is the total number of insecure configurations of the system					
B	C	D	E		F
Agent	Component	Comp. Type	Weakness		Status
sensorBoard	sensorWireRHS	inputport	selectively drops inputs and inserts new malicious data		open
root	sensorWireLHS2sensorWireRHS	channel	selectively drops inputs and inserts new malicious data		open
sensorInTank	sensorWireLHS	outputport	selectively drops inputs and inserts new malicious data		open
sensorInTank	sensorWireLHS	outputsocket	the component has a Byzantine behavior where occasionally outputs the expected output given the correct inputs. Not all the inputs are handled properly, nor all the expected outputs are always generated when correct inputs are given.		open

Fig. 5. Partial View of the results in the spreadsheet file

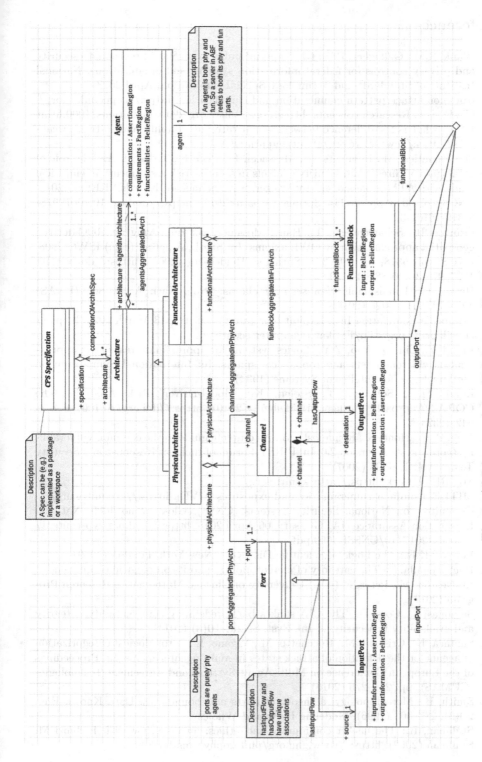

Fig. 6. $\mathcal{ABF}$-framework for CPS design – Class Diagram

References

1. Blank, R.M., Gallagher, P.D.: NIST special publication 800-53 revision 4 - security and privacy controls for federal information systems and organizations. National Institute of Standards and Technology Special Publication, April 2013
2. Common attack pattern enumeration and classification. https://capec.mitre.org/
3. CWE view: Research concepts. https://cwe.mitre.org/data/definitions/1000.html
4. FAQ - what is the difference between a software vulnerability and software weakness? https://cwe.mitre.org/about/faq.html#A.2
5. de Gramatica, M., Labunets, K., Massacci, F., Paci, F., Tedeschi, A.: The role of catalogues of threats and security controls in security risk assessment: an empirical study with ATM professionals. In: Fricker, S.A., Schneider, K. (eds.) REFSQ 2015. LNCS, vol. 9013, pp. 98–114. Springer, Cham (2015). https://doi.org/10.1007/978-3-319-16101-3_7
6. Grütter, R., Scharrenbach, T., Bauer-Messmer, B.: Improving an RCC-derived geospatial approximation by OWL axioms. In: Sheth, A., et al. (eds.) ISWC 2008. LNCS, vol. 5318, pp. 293–306. Springer, Heidelberg (2008). https://doi.org/10.1007/978-3-540-88564-1_19
7. Herley, C.: Unfalsifiability of security claims. Proc. Natl. Acad. Sci. (PNAS) **113**(23), 6415–6420 (2016)
8. Wikipedia Foundation Inc., Exploit (computer security), 18 March 2022. https://en.wikipedia.org/wiki/Exploit_(computer_security)
9. Lin, T.Y., Liu, Q., Yao, Y.Y.: Logics systems for approximate reasoning: approximation via rough sets and topological spaces. In: International Symposium on Methodologies for Intelligent Systems (1994)
10. Lund, M.S., Solhaug, B., Stølen, K.: Model-Driven Risk Analysis: The CORAS Approach. Springer, Heidelberg (2010). https://doi.org/10.1007/978-3-642-12323-8
11. Mell, P., Scarfone, K., Romanosky, S.: A complete guide to the common vulnerability scoring system version 2.0. In: FIRST-Forum of Incident Response and Security Teams, vol. 1, p. 23 (2007)
12. MITRE. Att&ck. https://attack.mitre.org/
13. MITRE. Common vulnerabilities and exposures (CVE). https://cve.mitre.org/
14. Committee on National Security Systems (CNSS). Glossary no 4009. National Information Assurance (IA) Glossary, 06 April 2015. https://rmf.org/wp-content/uploads/2017/10/CNSSI-4009.pdf
15. Popper, K.R.: The Logic of Scientific Discovery. New York, London (1959)
16. Rachavelpula, S.: The category of mereotopology and its ontological consequences. In: Neaton, M., Peter, P. (eds.) University of Chicago Mathematics Research Program (2017)
17. Samonas, S., Coss, D.: The CIA strikes back: redefining confidentiality, integrity and availability in security. J. Inf. Syst. Secur. **10**(3) (2014)
18. Santacà, K., Cristani, M., Rocchetto, M., Viganò, L.: A topological categorization of agents for the definition of attack states in multi-agent systems. In: Proceedings of the European Conference on Multi-Agent Systems and Agreement Technologies (EUMAS), pp. 261–276 (2016)
19. Smith, B.: Mereotopology: a theory of parts and boundaries. Data Knowl. Eng. **20**(3), 287–303 (1996). Modeling Parts and Wholes
20. Stallman, R.: The hacker community and ethics: an interview with Richard M. Stallman (2002). https://www.gnu.org/philosophy/rms-hack.html

21. National Institute of Standards and Technologies (NIST). National vulnerability database. https://nvd.nist.gov/
22. Threatmodeler. Threatmodeler. https://threatmodeler.com/
23. V-Research. V-research cybersecurity repository. https://github.com/v-research/cybersecurity
24. Varzi, A.C.: On the boundary between mereology and topology. In: Proceedings of the International Wittgenstein Symposium, pp. 261–276 (1994)

Outsider Key Compromise Impersonation Attack on a Multi-factor Authenticated Key Exchange Protocol

Zhiqiang Ma and Jun He[✉]

Chongqing University of Technology, Chongqiang 400054, China
hejun@cqut.edu.cn

Abstract. Authenticated key exchange (AKE) protocol is a security mechanism that ensures two parties communicate securely on a public channel and keeps the legal client interacting with the honest server. Recently, Zhang et al. proposed a multi-factor authenticated key exchange (MFAKE) scheme for mobile communications. In this paper, we present the cryptoanalysis of their MFAKE scheme. We find out their MFAKE scheme has a security flaw that renders it insecure against man-in-the-middle (MITM) attacks and outsider key compromise impersonation (KCI) attacks. We present a simple case of MITM attacks and illustrate how an adversary impersonates the client to the server if just compromising the key of the server. And an improved MFAKE scheme is proposed to overcome the weakness of Zhang's MFAKE scheme with minimum changes. We give the formal security proof of the improved MFAKE scheme in the random oracle model.

Keywords: Multi-factor · Authenticated key exchange · Key compromise impersonation attack

1 Introduction

With the rapid development of communication technologies, mobile devices have been popular in daily life. Advances in mobile telecommunication technology lay the foundation for accessing critical infrastructure (e.g., industrial manufacturing, energy, healthcare, transportation, and public safety infrastructures). People interact with these systems to obtain personal services. However, adversaries could intercept, modify or replay messages, as well as impersonate a legal user to access the protected resource. Communication security has become one of the most crucial issues when accessing critical infrastructure for service.

Authenticated key exchange (AKE) protocol allows two parties to share a common session key for secure communication over insecure public channels and verify the legitimacy of each other. Legitimate access to any information system requires authentication of the user accessing the protected information. Thus, password-based authenticated key exchange (PAKE) protocols [5,6,11,14] have received significant attention in client/server systems. PAKE protocols assume a realistic scenario that secret keys are not uniformly distributed over a large keyspace, but chosen from a small and low-entropy keyspace. It is a realistic scenario in which the users tend to choose short easily-rememberable passwords since they may require to remember many passwords and change the password frequently. Thus, passwords are vulnerable to many brute-force and dictionary-based attack tools. The simple password-based authentication has proven to be more and more inadequate [2,15] since the existing solutions cannot sufficiently prevent password-cracking, data-stealing, and data-phishing practices. Various schemes [20] are proposed in succession to reduce the affection of the password-cracking and the compromised password database.

With the growing number of innovative ways to authenticate users, there are three main approaches [18] for authentication: something you *know* (e.g., passwords), something you *have* (e.g., smartphones and smart cards), and something you *are* (e.g., biometric characteristics). In certain circumstances, however, the above factors may be insecure. When the honest user types in the correct password, the malicious user could peep the input. The smart card might be lost, stolen, or cloned. Once an adversary obtains the smart card, all the information stored could be lost. The biometric characteristics are irrevocable. Once copied by the adversary, this will cause permanent damage. Various multi-factor authenticated key exchange (MFAKE) schemes [9,16,19,23] were proposed successively by combining three factors in an authentication process to reduce the damage caused by compromising an authentication factor.

1.1 Motivations

User authentication is becoming more widely used to protect sensitive information from the illegitimate user. However, research over the past decade has shown that designing a secure authenticated key exchange scheme is very difficult. MFAKE schemes aim to achieve higher security by combining the three factors within the same authentication process. Intuitively, an adversary would have to break the three factors to break the MFAKE scheme. However, an adversary could compromise less than three factors to break the scheme if the scheme is not well designed.

An AKE protocol is provable security if and only if the security proof is correct. Several results [12,21,22] show that even several of the proposed AKE protocols that have provided security proof cannot achieve their security aims since the security proof might be flawed. Constructing a multi-factor authentication protocol remains hard work. Analysis of defects of existing protocols can make us avoid these shortcomings when designing a new scheme.

1.2 Contributions

In this paper, we revisit Zhang's MFAKE protocol [23] and analyze its security. We hope our analysis would help avoid such mistakes when designing a new MFAKE protocol in the future. The contributions of this paper are listed as follows:

1. We show this protocol has a vital security flaw, which may lead the protocol insecure against man-in-the-middle (MITM) attacks and outsider key compromise impersonation (KCI) attacks. The main problem of Zhang's MFAKE is the protocol message transcript is not bound to the session key. We give the details of a simple MITM attack and an outsider KCI attack in Sect. 5.
2. We propose an improved MFAKE protocol to fix the problem of Zhang's MFAKE protocol with minimum changes. All protocol messages include in the session key generation algorithm.
3. Finally, we provide the formal security proof of improved MFAKE protocol in the random oracle model.

1.3   Organization of the Rest Article

The rest of the paper is organized as follows. In Sect. 2, we review the related works. In Sect. 3, we introduce the basic definitions for Zhang's MFAKE protocol. In Sect. 4, we give the security model. In Sect. 5, we review Zhang's MFAKE protocol, analyze the drawback of Zhang's MFAKE protocol, propose an improved MFAKE protocol and provide the formal security proof in the random oracle model. We conclude the paper in Sect. 6.

2   Related Work

Bellovin and Merritt [5] proposed the first password-based authenticated key exchange protocol, Encrypted Key Exchange (EKE), which allows the client and server to share the plaintext password and exchange key material to derive a common session key. Then the augmented EKE protocol proposed by Bellovin and Merritt [6], replaced the requirement that the server stores the plaintext password with a one-way transformed value of the password. Augment EKE protocol prevents the adversary from impersonating the honest user. They presented two ways to accomplish this goal, digital signatures and a family of commutative one-way functions. However, the EKE and augment EKE are not given formal security analysis since the lack of a proper security model. The first formal security model of AKE protocols between two parties was introduced by Bellare and Rogaway [4]. Bellare et al. [3] proposed the security model of PAKE protocols by extending the definition of Bellare and Rogaway [4]. And this PAKE security model has been followed extensively in papers [7,10,17].

The protocols referred to above build on the single authentication factor. Recently, MFAKE which is a valuable and challenging goal has wildly caught researchers' attention [9,16,19]. Many papers claim security by combining all three factors in a protocol. Pointcheval and Zimmer [19] defined a new security model for MFAKE protocols and proposed a multi-factor AKE protocol that is proved to be secure in their security model. They claim their MFAKE protocol remains semantically secure if there are at most two corrupt queries. Namely, an adversary must break all three factors to win the game. Liu et al. [16] proposed a three-party MFAKE protocol by extending Pointcheval's protocol [19]. They provided the formal security proof of their three-party MFAKE protocol in the random oracle model. However, Hao and Clarke [12] found out Pointcheval's protocol and Liu's protocol are insecure. If an adversary has compromised the client's password, it could impersonate the server to compromise the other two factors, thus breaking the entire system. Fleischhacker et al. [9] introduced and modeled a general framework for (α, β, γ)-MFAKE by extending the three-factor AKE model from [19]. And they defined a generalized notion of *tag-based* multi-factor authentication, extending the preliminary concepts from [13] that considered the use of tags (auxiliary strings) in public key-based challenge-response scenarios. In this way, they avoided the problems identified in [12] for the protocol in [19]. Hossein et al. [8] proposed a hash-chain-based provably secure MFAKE scheme and analyse the security of their scheme in the real-or-random (ROR) model [1].

Most recently, Zhang et al. [23] proposed a multi-factor authenticated key exchange (MFAKE) scheme based on the security model from [19]. It claims to reduce the security of protocol to the Decisional Diffie-Hellman (DDH) hard problem. In this work, however, we found two weaknesses that lead to Zhang's MFAKE insecurity. One problem is that an adversary could easily modify the exchanged message to lead two non-partnered sessions to compute the same session key. Another is that once an adversary compromises the server, it could impersonate the client to the server.

3   Preliminaries

Let $\lambda \in \mathbb{N}$ be the security parameter and 1^{λ} be a string that consists of λ bits. $\emptyset$ denotes an empty string. $\|$ is the string concatenation operation. $\oplus$ is the XOR operation. For $n \in \mathbb{N}$, $[n] := \{1, 2, \ldots, n\}$ denotes the set of integers between 1 and n. If X is a set, $x \xleftarrow{\$} X$ denotes the operation of sampling a uniform random element x from X. If A is a probabilistic algorithm, $a \xleftarrow{\$} A$ means that a is the output of running A with fresh random coins. The hash function $h(\cdot) : \{0,1\}^* \rightarrow \{0,1\}^{\lambda}$ is modeled as a random oracle.

3.1   Metric Space

A *metric space* is a set $\mathcal{M}$ with a distance function $\mathsf{Dist} : \mathcal{M} \times \mathcal{M} \rightarrow [0, \infty)$. Commonly, *Hamming distance* is used to measure the distance from one value to another value. $\mathsf{Dist}(w, w')$ is the number of positions in which the strings $w \in \mathcal{M}$ and $w' \in \mathcal{M}$ differ. For an element $w \in \mathcal{M}$, let $\mathsf{Dist}(w) := \mathsf{Dist}(w, 0)$.

3.2   Min-Entropy and Statistical Distance

Definition 1 (Min-Entropy). *The min-entropy of X is $H_{\infty}(X) = -\log_2(\max_x \Pr[X = x])$.*

Definition 2 (Statistical Distance). *The statistical distance between two random variables A and B with the same domain $\mathcal{M}$ is $\mathbf{SD}(A, B) = \frac{1}{2} \sum_{w \in \mathcal{M}} |\Pr[A = w] - \Pr[B = w]|$. If $\mathbf{SD}(A, B) \leq \epsilon$, A and B are called ϵ-statistically indistinguishable.*

3.3   Public Key Encryption Scheme

Generally, we consider a public key encryption scheme PKE that consists of three probabilistic polynomial time (PPT) algorithms PKE = (PKE.KeyGen, PKE.Enc, PKE.Dec). The PKE scheme is associated with public keyspace $\mathcal{PK}_{\mathsf{PKE}}$, private keyspace $\mathcal{SK}_{\mathsf{PKE}}$, message space $\mathcal{M}_{\mathsf{PKE}}$ and ciphertext space $\mathcal{C}_{\mathsf{PKE}}$. The algorithms of PKE are defined as follows:

- $(\mathsf{pk}, \mathsf{sk}) \xleftarrow{\$} \mathsf{PKE.KeyGen}(1^\lambda)$: This algorithm takes as input the security parameter 1^λ and outputs a pair of public/private keys $(\mathsf{pk}, \mathsf{sk})$, where the public key $\mathsf{pk} \in \mathcal{PK}_{\mathsf{PKE}}$ and the private key $\mathsf{sk} \in \mathcal{SK}_{\mathsf{PKE}}$.
- $c \xleftarrow{\$} \mathsf{PKE.Enc}(\mathsf{pk}, m)$: This is the encryption algorithm that generates a ciphertext $c \in \mathcal{C}_{\mathsf{PKE}}$ for a message $m \in \mathcal{M}_{\mathsf{PKE}}$ with the public key pk.
- $m \xleftarrow{\$} \mathsf{PKE.Dec}(\mathsf{sk}, c)$: This is the decryption algorithm which takes as input a private key sk, a ciphertext c, and outputs a message m. The correctness requirement is for all pairs $(\mathsf{pk}, \mathsf{sk}) \xleftarrow{\$} \mathsf{PKE.KeyGen}(1^\lambda)$, we have $m \equiv \mathsf{PKE.Dec}(\mathsf{sk}, \mathsf{PKE.Enc}(\mathsf{pk}, m))$.

Definition 3 (Public Key Encryption Scheme). *We say that a public key encryption scheme* PKE = (PKE.KeyGen, PKE.Enc, PKE.Dec) *is* $(q, t, \epsilon_{\mathsf{PKE}})$*-secure (indistinguishable) against adaptive chosen-ciphertext attacks, if* $|\Pr[\mathsf{EXP}_{\mathsf{PKE},\mathcal{A}}^{ind\text{-}cca}(\lambda) = 1] - 1/2| \leq \epsilon_{\mathsf{PKE}}$ *holds for all adversaries* $\mathcal{A}$ *running in time at most* t *in the following experiment:*

$$
\begin{array}{l|l}
\mathsf{EXP}_{\mathsf{PKE},\mathcal{A}}^{ind\text{-}cca}(\lambda): & \mathcal{O}_{\mathsf{PKE.Dec}}(\mathsf{sk}, c): \\
\quad (\mathsf{pk}, \mathsf{sk}) \xleftarrow{\$} \mathsf{PKE.KeyGen}(1^\lambda); & \quad \textit{if } c = c^*, \textit{ return a failure } \bot, \\
\quad (m_0, m_1) \xleftarrow{\$} \mathcal{A}(pk); & \quad \textit{otherwise } m \xleftarrow{\$} \mathsf{PKE.Dec}(\mathsf{sk}, c) \\
\quad b \xleftarrow{\$} \{0, 1\}; & \quad \textit{return } m; \\
\quad c^* \xleftarrow{\$} \mathsf{PKE.Enc}(\mathsf{pk}, m_b); & \\
\quad b' \xleftarrow{\$} \mathcal{A}^{\mathcal{O}_{\mathsf{PKE.Dec}}(\mathsf{sk}, \cdot)}(pk, c^*); & \\
\quad \textit{if } b = b' \textit{ then return } 1, & \\
\quad \textit{otherwise return } 0\,. &
\end{array}
$$

where $\epsilon_{\mathsf{PKE}} = \epsilon_{\mathsf{PKE}}(\lambda)$ *is a negligible function in the security parameter* λ *and the number of queries* q *is bound by time* t.

3.4   Message Authentication Code Scheme

We consider a message authentication code scheme MAC that consists of three probabilistic polynomial time (PPT) algorithms MAC = (MAC.KeyGen, MAC.Tag, MAC.Vfy). The MAC scheme is associated with tag space $\mathcal{T}_{\mathsf{MAC}}$, message space $\mathcal{M}_{\mathsf{MAC}}$ and private keyspace $\mathcal{SK}_{\mathsf{MAC}}$. The algorithms of MAC are defined as follows:

- $\mathsf{sk}_{\mathsf{MAC}} \xleftarrow{\$} \mathsf{MAC.KeyGen}(1^\lambda)$: This is the key generation algorithm which takes as input 1^λ and outputs a secret key $\mathsf{sk}_{\mathsf{MAC}} \in \mathcal{SK}_{\mathsf{MAC}}$.
- $\tau \xleftarrow{\$} \mathsf{MAC.Tag}(\mathsf{sk}_{\mathsf{MAC}}, m)$: The generation algorithm is run by a party. It generates a tag $\tau \in \mathcal{T}_{\mathsf{MAC}}$ for a message $m \in \mathcal{M}_{\mathsf{MAC}}$ with the generation key $\mathsf{sk}_{\mathsf{MAC}}$.

– $\{0,1\} \xleftarrow{\$}$ MAC.Vfy($\mathsf{sk_{MAC}}, \tau, m$): The verification algorithm is run by the verifier. It takes as input a private key $\mathsf{sk_{MAC}}$, a tag τ, and a message m. Then it outputs 1 if τ is a valid tag for m under $\mathsf{sk_{MAC}}$, and 0 otherwise.

Definition 4 (Message Authentication Code Scheme). *We say that a message authentication code scheme* MAC = (MAC.KeyGen, MAC.Tag, MAC.Vfy) *is* (q, t, ϵ_{MAC})-*secure against strongly existential forgeries under chosen message attacks, if* $|\Pr[\mathrm{EXP}_{MAC,\mathcal{A}}^{seuf-cma}(\lambda) = 1] - 1/2| \leq \epsilon_{MAC}$ *holds for all adversaries* $\mathcal{A}$ *running in time at most* t *in the following experiment:*

$\mathrm{EXP}_{MAC,\mathcal{A}}^{seuf-cma}(\lambda)$:

  $\mathsf{sk_{MAC}} \xleftarrow{\$}$ MAC.KeyGen(1^λ);

  $(m^*, \tau^*) \xleftarrow{\$} \mathcal{A}^{\mathcal{O}_{MAC.Tag}(\mathsf{sk_{MAC}},\cdot)}$;

  return 1 if the following conditions are held:

  1. MAC.Vfy($\mathsf{sk_{MAC}}, \tau^*, m^*$) = 1 *and*

  2. $\mathcal{A}$ *didn't submit* m^* *to* MAC.Tag($\mathsf{sk_{MAC}}, \cdot$),

  and 0 otherwise;

where $\epsilon_{MAC} = \epsilon_{MAC}(\lambda)$ *is a negligible function in the security parameter* λ, *on input message* m *the oracle* $\mathcal{O}_{MAC.Tag}(\mathsf{sk_{MAC}}, \cdot)$ *returns* $\tau \xleftarrow{\$}$ MAC.Tag($\mathsf{sk_{MAC}}, m$) *and the number of queries* q *is bound by time* t.

If $\mathsf{sk_{MAC}}$ *is a one-time authentication key of* MAC *scheme, then* MAC *scheme is known as a one-time message authentication code (OTMAC) scheme which is* $(1, t, \epsilon_{MAC})$-*secure.*

3.5 Fuzzy Extractor

We consider a fuzzy extractor FE that consists of a pair of probabilistic polynomial time (PPT) algorithms FE = (FE.Gen, FE.Rep). The FE is associated with metric space $\mathcal{M}_{FE}$, randomness space $\mathcal{RS}_{FE}$, extracted string space $\mathcal{ES}_{FE}$ and helper string space $\mathcal{HS}_{FE}$. The algorithms of FE are defined as follows:

– $(R, P) \xleftarrow{\$}$ FE.Gen(crs, w): This is the generation algorithm that takes as input $crs \in \mathcal{RS}_{FE}$ and $w \in \mathcal{M}_{FE}$ and outputs an extracted string $R \in \mathcal{ES}_{FE}$ and a helper string $P \in \mathcal{HS}_{FE}$. Note that $\mathbf{SD}((R, P), (U_\lambda, P)) \leq \epsilon_{FE}$, where U_λ is uniform distribution on $\{0,1\}^\lambda$.
– $R \xleftarrow{\$}$ FE.Rep(w', P): This is the reproduce algorithm that takes as input a string $w' \in \mathcal{M}_{FE}$ and a helper string $P \in \mathcal{HS}_{FE}$. If Dist(w, w') is no more than a predetermined threshold ts and $(R, P) \xleftarrow{\$}$ FE.Gen(crs, w), this algorithm outputs FE.Rep(w', P) = R. Otherwise, no guarantee is provided about the output of FE.Rep.

Definition 5 (Fuzzy Extractor). *Let* $\mathcal{W}$ *be a family of distributions over metric space* $\mathcal{M}_{FE}$ *with* $H_\infty(\mathcal{W}) \geq min$, *where* min *is min-entropy of* $\mathcal{M}_{FE}$. *We say that a fuzzy extractor* FE = (FE.Gen, FE.Rep) *is* $(min, ts, q, t, \epsilon_{FE})$-*secure* *(indistinguishable), if* $| \Pr[\mathsf{EXP}^{ind}_{\mathsf{FE},\mathcal{A}}(\lambda) = 1] - 1/2| \leq \epsilon_{\mathsf{FE}}$ *holds for all adversaries* $\mathcal{A}$ *running in time at most* t *in the following experiment:*

$$\mathsf{EXP}^{ind}_{\mathsf{FE},\mathcal{A}}(\lambda):$$
$$crs \xleftarrow{\$} \mathcal{RS}_{\mathsf{FE}};$$
$$w \xleftarrow{\$} \mathcal{W}, U_\lambda \xleftarrow{\$} \{0,1\}^\lambda;$$
$$b \xleftarrow{\$} \{0,1\};$$
$$(R^*, P^*) \xleftarrow{\$} \mathsf{FE.Gen}(crs, w);$$
$$R_0 = U_\lambda, R_1 = R^*;$$
$$b' \xleftarrow{\$} \mathcal{A}^{\mathcal{O}_{\mathsf{FE.Gen}}(\cdot,\cdot)}(crs, R_b, P^*);$$
$$\text{if } b = b' \text{ then return } 1,$$
$$\text{and } 0 \text{ otherwise.}$$

$$\mathcal{O}_{\mathsf{FE.Gen}}(crs, w + \delta_i):$$
$$\text{if } \mathcal{A} \text{ submits a shift } \delta_i \in \mathcal{M}_{\mathsf{FE}}$$
$$\text{and } 0 < \mathsf{Dist}(\delta_i) \leq s,$$
$$(R_i, P_i) \xleftarrow{\$} \mathsf{FE.Gen}(crs, w + \delta_i),$$
$$\text{return } (R_i, P_i);$$
$$\text{else, return a failure } \perp.$$

where $\epsilon_{\mathsf{FE}} = \epsilon_{\mathsf{FE}}(\lambda)$ *is a negligible function in the security parameter* λ *and the number of queries* q *is bound by time* t.

Definition 6 (DDH Assumption). *We say the DDH assumption holds, given parameters* $(\mathbb{G}, p, g)$ *where* $\mathbb{G}$ *is a cyclic group of prime order* p *and* g *as a generator of* $\mathbb{G}$, *if it is hard to distinguish triples of the form* (g^x, g^y, g^{xy}) *from triples of the form* (g^x, g^y, g^z), *where* x, y, *and* z *are random chosen from* $\mathbb{Z}_p^*$. *Namely, the DDH problem is* $(t, \epsilon_{\mathsf{DDH}})$-*hard, if* $| \Pr[\mathsf{EXP}^{\mathsf{DDH}}_{\mathbb{G}, p, g, \mathcal{A}}(\lambda) = 1] - 1/2| \leq \epsilon_{\mathsf{DDH}}$ *holds for all adversaries* $\mathcal{A}$ *running in time at most* t *in the following experiment:*

$$\mathsf{EXP}^{\mathsf{DDH}}_{\mathbb{G}, p, g, \mathcal{A}}(\lambda):$$
$$g \xleftarrow{\$} \mathbb{G}, (x, y, z) \xleftarrow{\$} \mathbb{Z}_p^*;$$
$$b \xleftarrow{\$} \{0,1\};$$
$$\text{if } b = 0 \text{ then } X \xleftarrow{\$} g^{xy}, \text{ otherwise } X \xleftarrow{\$} g^z;$$
$$b' \xleftarrow{\$} \mathcal{A}(\mathbb{G}, p, g, g^x, g^y, X);$$
$$\text{return } 1, \text{ if } b = b', \text{ and } 0 \text{ otherwise;}$$

where $\epsilon_{\mathsf{DDH}} = \epsilon_{\mathsf{DDH}}(\lambda)$ *is a negligible probability in the security parameter* λ.

4 Security Model

4.1 Execution Environment

In the execution environment, we fix a set of honest parties $\mathcal{IDS} = \{\mathsf{id}_1, \ldots, \mathsf{id}_l\}$ for $l \in \mathbb{N}$, where id_i $(i \in [l])$ is the identity of client or server. Each identity id_i is associated with a pair of long-term keys $(\mathsf{pk}_i, \mathsf{sk}_i) \in (\mathcal{PK}_{\mathsf{PKE}}, \mathcal{SK}_{\mathsf{PKE}})$. Each honest party id_i can sequentially and concurrently execute the protocol multiple times with different intended partners. We may realize a collection of oracles $\{\Pi^s_{\mathsf{id}_i} : i \in [l], s \in [d]\}$ for $(l, d) \in \mathbb{N}$ that represent the protocol executions of a set of honest parties. Each oracle $\Pi^s_{\mathsf{id}_i}$ works as the s-th protocol instance performed by party id_i. Moreover, we assume each oracle $\Pi^s_{\mathsf{id}_i}$ maintains a list of independent internal state variables with semantics listed in Table 1.

All those variables of each oracle are initialized with the empty string $\emptyset$. At some point, each oracle $\Pi^s_{\mathsf{id}_i}$ may complete the execution and decide the internal state $\Phi^s_i \in \{\mathsf{accept}, \mathsf{reject}\}$. Additionally, we assume that the real session

Table 1. Internal states of oracles

Variable	Description
pid_i^s	Identity of id_i's intended communication partner
sid_i^s	Session identity of an oracle $\Pi_{\text{id}_i}^s$, $\text{sid}_i^s \xleftarrow{\$} 1^\lambda$
Φ_i^s	Internal state of an oracle $\Pi_{\text{id}_i}^s$, $\Phi_i^s \in \{\text{accept}, \text{reject}\}$
K_i^s	Session Key of an oracle $\Pi_{\text{id}_i}^s$, $K_i^s \in \mathcal{K}$
sT_i^s	Transcript of messages sent by an oracle $\Pi_{\text{id}_i}^s$
rT_i^s	Transcript of messages received by an oracle $\Pi_{\text{id}_i}^s$

key is assigned to the variable K_i^s iff oracle $\Pi_{\text{id}_i}^s$ has reached an internal state $\Phi_i^s = \text{accept}$.

4.2 Adversarial Model

The adversary $\mathcal{A}$ considers being a probabilistic polynomial time (PPT) Turing Machine, having complete control of the communication network. The adversary $\mathcal{A}$ could interact with the challenger $\mathcal{C}$ by issuing the following queries:

- Execute($\text{id}_i, s, \text{id}_j, t$): If the client oracle $\Pi_{\text{id}_i}^s$ and server oracle $\Pi_{\text{id}_j}^t$ have not been used, this query will carry out an honest execution of the protocol between two oracles, and return the transcripts sT_i^s and sT_j^t to $\mathcal{A}$. This query models the capability of $\mathcal{A}$ passively eavesdrops on plenty of honest executions.
- Send(id_i, s, m): This query allows $\mathcal{A}$ to send a message m of his own choice to the oracle $\Pi_{\text{id}_i}^s$. The oracle $\Pi_{\text{id}_i}^s$ will send back the response message m' (if any) according to the protocol specification and its internal states. After answering a Send query, the variables of $\Pi_{\text{id}_i}^s$ will be updated depending on the specific protocol. This query models the active attacks in the real world.
- Reveal(id_i, s): If the oracle $\Pi_{\text{id}_i}^s$ has reached an internal state $\Phi_i^s = \text{accept}$ (holding a session key) and a Test query has not been made to $\Pi_{\text{id}_i}^s$ or its partner oracle (if it exists), it responds with the contents of the variable K_i^s. Otherwise, a failure symbol $\perp$ is returned. This query models the leakage of the session key agreed by the two parties.
- Corrupt(client, a): This query will respond with the password pwd for $a = 0$, biometric data W for $a = 1$, and private key sk for $a = 2$. By issuing this query, $\mathcal{A}$ could obtain a-th authenticated factor $\{\text{pwd}, \text{W}, \text{sk}\}$ of client. This query models corruption capabilities of $\mathcal{A}$.
- Corrupt(server): This query will return server's private key sk to $\mathcal{A}$.
- Test(id_i, s): $\mathcal{C}$ first flips a coin $b \in \{0, 1\}$ uesd for all Test queries. If the oracle $\Pi_{\text{id}_i}^s$ has state $\Phi_i^s = \text{reject}$ or $K_i^s = \emptyset$, then this query returns a failure symbol $\perp$. Otherwise, $\mathcal{C}$ samples a random element K_r from session key space $\mathcal{K}$, and sets $K_0 = K_r$ and $K_1 = K_i^s$. Finally, this query responses with K_b. The oracle $\Pi_{\text{id}_i}^s$ selected by the adversary in this query is called as *test oracle*. This query does not model any actual capabilities of $\mathcal{A}$. It is used to measure the semantic security of session keys.

4.3   Secure AKE Protocols

We first review the notion regarding the partnership of two oracles, i.e. *matching sessions* [3].

Definition 7 (Matching Sessions). *In an MFAKE protocol, we say that the oracle $\Pi_{\mathsf{id}_i}^s$ and oracle $\Pi_{\mathsf{id}_j}^t$ are matching sessions, if both of them have been accept, hold $(K_i^s, \mathsf{sid}_i^s, \mathsf{pid}_i^s)$ and $(K_j^t, \mathsf{sid}_j^t, \mathsf{pid}_j^t)$, respectively, and all of the following hold:*

1. $\mathsf{sid}_i^s = \mathsf{sid}_j^t$ *and* $K_i^s = K_j^t$.
2. $\mathsf{id}_i \in$ client, $\mathsf{id}_j \in$ server, *and vice versa*.
3. $\Pi_{\mathsf{id}_i}^s$ *has* $\mathsf{pid}_i^s = \mathsf{id}_j$ *and* $\Pi_{\mathsf{id}_j}^t$ *has* $\mathsf{pid}_j^t = \mathsf{id}_i$.
4. $sT_i^s = rT_j^t$ *and* $rT_i^s = sT_j^t$.

Correctness. We say an AKE protocol Π is correct, if an oracle $\Pi_{\mathsf{id}_i}^s$ has a *matching session* to an oracle $\Pi_{\mathsf{id}_j}^t$ and they both accept with the same session key, i.e. $K_i^s = K_j^t$.

To define the security of the session key, we need the notion of *freshness* of an oracle.

Definition 8 (Freshness). *We assume that a client instance $\Pi_{\mathsf{id}_i}^s$ has been accept with its intended server id_j. And a server instance $\Pi_{\mathsf{id}_j}^t$ (if it exists) is an oracle with intended client id_i, such that $\Pi_{\mathsf{id}_i}^s$ has a matching session to $\Pi_{\mathsf{id}_j}^t$. Then the oralce $\Pi_{\mathsf{id}_i}^s$ is said to be fresh if none of the following conditions holds:*

1. $\mathcal{A}$ *queried* Reveal(id_i, s).
2. *If* $\Pi_{\mathsf{id}_j}^t$ *exists,* $\mathcal{A}$ *queried* Reveal(id_j, t).
3. $\mathcal{A}$ *queried* Corrupt(client, a) *for all three factors.*
4. *If* $\Pi_{\mathsf{id}_j}^t$ *exists,* $\mathcal{A}$ *queried* Corrupt(server).

4.4   Security Experiment $\mathsf{EXP}_{\Pi,\mathcal{A}}^{\mathsf{MFAKE}}(\lambda)$

The security experiment is processed as a game between the challenger $\mathcal{C}$ and adversary $\mathcal{A}$ based on MFAKE protocol Π, where the following steps are performed:

1. With the security parameter λ, the challenger $\mathcal{C}$ first implements the collection of oracles $\{\Pi_{\mathsf{id}_i}^s : i \in [l], s \in [d]\}$, and generates l long-term key pairs $(\mathsf{pk}_i, \mathsf{sk}_i)$ for all honest parties id_i where identity $\mathsf{id}_i \in \mathcal{IDS}$ of each party is chosen uniquely. $\mathcal{C}$ flips a coin $b \in \{0, 1\}$ uesd for all Test queries. $\mathcal{C}$ will give all public parameters to $\mathcal{A}$ and keep track of all variables of the execution environment.
2. $\mathcal{A}$ may interact by issuing the polynomial number of queries as aforementioned, namely, $\mathcal{A}$ makes queries: Execute, Send, Reveal and Corrupt.
3. At some point of time during the game, $\mathcal{A}$ may issue a Test(id_i, s) query.

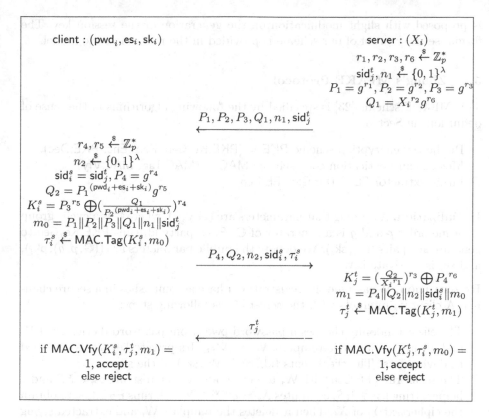

client : $(\text{pwd}_i, \text{es}_i, \text{sk}_i)$ server : (X_i)

$$r_1, r_2, r_3, r_6 \xleftarrow{\$} \mathbb{Z}_p^*$$
$$\text{sid}_j^t, n_1 \xleftarrow{\$} \{0,1\}^\lambda$$
$$P_1 = g^{r_1}, P_2 = g^{r_2}, P_3 = g^{r_3}$$
$$Q_1 = X_i^{r_2} g^{r_6}$$

$\xleftarrow{\quad P_1, P_2, P_3, Q_1, n_1, \text{sid}_j^t \quad}$

$$r_4, r_5 \xleftarrow{\$} \mathbb{Z}_p^*$$
$$n_2 \xleftarrow{\$} \{0,1\}^\lambda$$
$$\text{sid}_i^s = \text{sid}_j^t, P_4 = g^{r_4}$$
$$Q_2 = P_1^{(\text{pwd}_i + \text{es}_i + \text{sk}_i)} g^{r_5}$$
$$K_i^s = P_3^{r_5} \bigoplus \left(\frac{Q_1}{P_2^{(\text{pwd}_i + \text{es}_i + \text{sk}_i)}} \right)^{r_4}$$
$$m_0 = P_1 \| P_2 \| P_3 \| Q_1 \| n_1 \| \text{sid}_j^t$$
$$\tau_i^s \xleftarrow{\$} \text{MAC.Tag}(K_i^s, m_0)$$

$\xrightarrow{\quad P_4, Q_2, n_2, \text{sid}_i^s, \tau_i^s \quad}$

$$K_j^t = \left(\frac{Q_2}{X_i^{r_1}} \right)^{r_3} \bigoplus P_4^{r_6}$$
$$m_1 = P_4 \| Q_2 \| n_2 \| \text{sid}_i^s \| m_0$$
$$\tau_j^t \xleftarrow{\$} \text{MAC.Tag}(K_j^t, m_1)$$

$\xleftarrow{\quad \tau_j^t \quad}$

if $\text{MAC.Vfy}(K_i^s, \tau_j^t, m_1) =$ if $\text{MAC.Vfy}(K_j^t, \tau_i^s, m_0) =$
1, accept   1, accept
else reject   else reject

Fig. 1. MFAKE protocol

4. $\mathcal{A}$ may continue to make the above queries. The binding constraints on this experiment are that: $\mathcal{A}$ cannot make a Reveal query on either the test session or its partnered session; $\mathcal{A}$ can make Corrupt query no more than twice if id_i is a client.

5. Finally, $\mathcal{A}$ terminates and outputs its guess b'. The experiment returns 1 if $b = b'$, and 0 otherwise.

Definition 9 (Session Key Security). *A correct MFAKE protocol Π is called (t', ϵ)-session-key-secure, if for all adversaries $\mathcal{A}$ running within time t' in the above MFAKE security experiment $\text{EXP}_{\Pi,\mathcal{A}}^{\text{MFAKE}}(\lambda)$, it holds that:*

$$| \Pr[\text{EXP}_{\Pi,\mathcal{A}}^{\text{MFAKE}}(\lambda) = 1] - 1/2 | \leq \epsilon,$$

where $\epsilon = \epsilon(\lambda)$ is a negligible probability in the security parameter λ.

5 Security Analysis and Improvement of Zhang's MFAKE Protocol

In this section, we first review Zhang's MFAKE protocol in Fig. 1. Then we analyze the drawbacks of Zhang's MFAKE protocol. Finally, an improved scheme is proposed with slight modification on the generation of the session key. The formal security proof of our scheme is provided in the random oracle model.

5.1 Zhang's MFAKE Protocol

This MFAKE scheme [23] is specified by the following algorithms in the sense of definitions in Sect. 3:

- Public key encryption scheme PKE = (PKE.KeyGen, PKE.Enc, PKE.Dec).
- Message authentication code scheme MAC = (MAC.Tag, MAC.Vfy).
- Fuzzy extractor FE = (FE.Gen, FE.Rep).

Initialization. Assuming that parameters are $(\mathbb{G}, p, g)$, where $\mathbb{G}$ is a cyclic group of prime order p and g is a generator of $\mathbb{G}$. Each party id_i runs PKE.KeyGen to generate key pairs (pk_i, sk_i). We denote the public parameters are $((\mathbb{G}, p, g), pk_i)$, and sk_i is a private key.

Registration. We assume the registration phase accomplishes in a secure channel. A client id_i interacts with the server id_j as following steps:

- The client randomly chooses a password pwd_i from password dictionary $\mathcal{PW}$ and creates a biometric template $W_i \in \mathcal{M}_{FE}$. Its private key sk_i is regarded as device data. The client sents (id_i, pwd_i, W_i, sk_i) to the server.
- The server runs FE.Gen with W_i to obtain an extracted string $es_i \in \mathcal{ES}$ and a helper string $hs_i \in \mathcal{HS}$, computes $X_i = g^{(pwd_i + es_i + sk_i)}$, runs PKE.Enc to obtain the ciphertext Y_i of X_i. Then it deletes the template W_i and extracted string es_i and returns hs_i to the client.
- Finally, the client stores hs_i, and the server stores identity id_i of client and Y_i.

Login-Authentication. An honest client id_i first inputs pwd_i, W_i', runs FE.Rep and sends its identity as an *authentication request* to a server id_j. If there exists a Y_i corresponding to id_i, the server computes $X_i \xleftarrow{\$} $ PKE.Dec(sk_j, Y_i). After that, the client id_i and server id_j hold (pwd_i, es_i, sk_i) and X_i, respectively, where $X_i = g^{(pwd_i + es_i + sk_i)}$. The MFAKE protocol performs as the following steps (as shown in Fig. 1):

- The server samples four ephemeral keys r_1, r_2, r_3, r_6 from $\mathbb{Z}_p^*$, a current session identity sid_j^t and a random nonce n_1. Then it computes $P_1 = g^{r_1}$, $P_2 = g^{r_2}$, $P_3 = g^{r_3}$ and $Q_1 = X_i^{r_2} g^{r_6}$. The *authentication challenge* $(P_1, P_2, P_3, Q_1, n_1, sid_j^t)$ sends to the client.
- After receiving the *authentication challenge*, the client samples two ephemeral keys r_4, r_5 from $\mathbb{Z}_p^*$ and a random element n_2. It sets $sid_i^s = sid_j^t$, computes $P_4 = g^{r_4}$, $Q_2 = P_1^{(pwd_i + es_i + sk_i)} g^{r_5}$ and $K_i^s = P_3^{r_5} \bigoplus (\frac{Q_1}{P_2^{(pwd_i + es_i + sk_i)}})^{r_4}$. The client runs MAC.Tag to generate a tag τ_i^s of $m_0 = P_1 \| P_2 \| P_3 \| Q_1 \| n_1 \| sid_j^t$, and sends $(P_4, Q_2, n_2, sid_i^s, \tau_i^s)$ as *authentication response* to server.

- After receiving the *authentication response*, the server can compute $K_j^t = (\frac{Q_2}{X_i^{r_1}})^{r_3} \bigoplus P_4^{r_6}$. It runs MAC.Tag to generate a tag τ_i^s of $m_1 = P_4\|Q_2\|n_2\|\mathsf{sid}_i^s\|m_0$, and sends τ_j^t to the client.
- Finally, the client and server run MAC.Vfy(K_i^s, τ_j^t, m_1) and MAC.Vfy(K_j^t, τ_i^s, m_0), respectively. The internal state of the party sets to be accept if the output is 1, and reject otherwise.

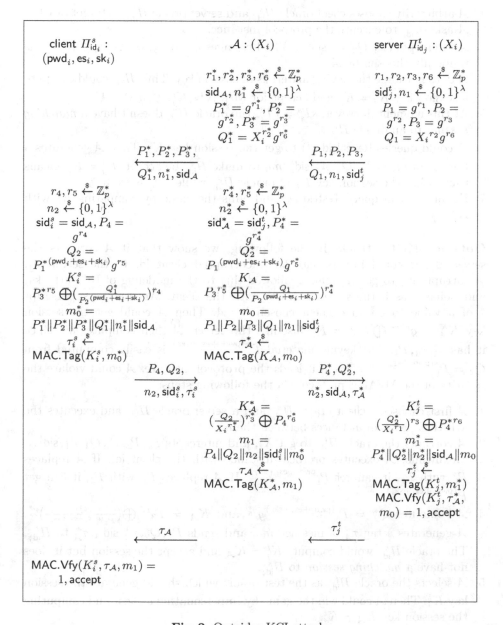

Fig. 2. Outsider KCI attack

5.2 The Insecurity of Zhang's MFAKE Scheme

Man-in-the-Middle Attack. In the following, we present a man-in-the-middle (MITM) attack on Zhang's MFAKE scheme. We assume that an adversary $\mathcal{A}$ intervenes in communication between the client and server. $\mathcal{A}$ could receive, forward, and modify the message exchanged between them.

The concrete MITM attack steps are performed as below:

1. $\mathcal{A}$ arbitrarily chooses client oracle $\Pi_{\mathsf{id}_i}^s$ and server oracle $\Pi_{\mathsf{id}_j}^t$ as target oracles.
2. $\mathcal{A}$ asks $\Pi_{\mathsf{id}_i}^s$ to execute the protocol instance.
3. $\mathcal{A}$ intercepts $(P_4, Q_2, n_2, \mathsf{sid}_i^s, \tau_i^s)$ and changes n_2 to n_3, where $n_3 \in \{0,1\}^\lambda$ is randomly choosen by $\mathcal{A}$.
4. $\mathcal{A}$ does not forge the keying materials of session key. Thus $\Pi_{\mathsf{id}_j}^t$ could compute a session key $K_j^t = K_i^s$ and accept for $\mathsf{MAC.Vfy}(K_j^t, \tau_i^s, m_0) = 1$.
5. At this moment, however, $sT_i^s \neq rT_j^t$, the oracle $\Pi_{\mathsf{id}_i}^s$ doesn't have a *matching session* to an oracle $\Pi_{\mathsf{id}_j}^t$.
6. $\mathcal{A}$ could queries $\mathsf{Reveal}(\mathsf{id}_j, t)$ to get the session key K_j^t. Then $\mathcal{A}$ generates a tag $\tau_j^{t^*}$ of $m_1 = P_4\|Q_2\|n_2\|\mathsf{sid}_i^s\|m_0$ to make $\Pi_{\mathsf{id}_i}^s$ be accept. $K_j^t = K_i^s$ means that $\mathcal{A}$ has the session key K_i^s of oracle $\Pi_{\mathsf{id}_i}^s$ while $\Pi_{\mathsf{id}_i}^s$ is fresh.
7. Finally, $\mathcal{A}$ can query $\mathsf{Test}(\mathsf{id}_i, s)$ and wins the game by comparing K_b with K_i^s.

Outsider KCI Attack. In the following, we show that if $\mathcal{A}$ corrupts the server id_j, it could impersonate an uncorrupted client id_i to the server id_j. $\mathcal{A}$ corrupts id_j to get X_i (this is allowed due to the modeling of KCI attacks) and behaves as if the server interacts with the client. We use the superscript * of a value to be an element chosen by $\mathcal{A}$. Then $\mathcal{A}$ could get the session key $K_{\mathcal{A}}^* = g^{r_3^* r_5} \bigoplus P_4^{r_6^*} = K_i^s$ just like the server. $\mathcal{A}$ then computes g^{r_5} since it has r_3^*, r_6^*, P_4. The keying material $P_1^{*(\mathsf{pwd}_i + \mathsf{es}_i + \mathsf{sk}_i)}$ is easily computed from $Q_2 = P_1^{*(\mathsf{pwd}_i + \mathsf{es}_i + \mathsf{sk}_i)} g^{r_5}$ and it leads the protocol insecure. $\mathcal{A}$ could violate the security of the MFAKE protocol via the following steps:

1. $\mathcal{A}$ first chooses a client oracle $\Pi_{\mathsf{id}_i}^s$ and a server oracle $\Pi_{\mathsf{id}_j}^t$ and executes the MFAKE protocol instances between them.
2. $\mathcal{A}$ corrupts the oracle $\Pi_{\mathsf{id}_j}^t$ to get X_i, and intercepts $P_1, P_2, P_3, Q_1, n_1, \mathsf{sid}_j^t$.
3. Meanwhile, $\mathcal{A}$ executes protocol instance with the client id_i. If $\mathcal{A}$ replaces P_1^* with P_1, it can get $P_1^{(\mathsf{pwd}_i + \mathsf{es}_i + \mathsf{sk}_i)}$. If $\mathcal{A}$ replaces P_1^* with P_2, it can get $P_2^{(\mathsf{pwd}_i + \mathsf{es}_i + \mathsf{sk}_i)}$.
4. $\mathcal{A}$ computes $Q_2^* = P_1^{(\mathsf{pwd}_i + \mathsf{es}_i + \mathsf{sk}_i)} g^{r_5^*}$ and $K_{\mathcal{A}} = P_3^{r_5^*} \bigoplus (\frac{Q_1}{P_2^{(\mathsf{pwd}_i + \mathsf{es}_i + \mathsf{sk}_i)}})^{r_4^*}$. $\mathcal{A}$ generates a tag $\tau_{\mathcal{A}}^*$ of message m_0, and sends $P_4^*, Q_2^*, n_2^*, \mathsf{sid}_{\mathcal{A}}, \tau_{\mathcal{A}}^*$ to $\Pi_{\mathsf{id}_j}^t$. The oracle $\Pi_{\mathsf{id}_j}^t$ would compute $K_j^t = K_{\mathcal{A}}$ and accept the session but it does not have a *matching session* to $\Pi_{\mathsf{id}_i}^s$.
5. $\mathcal{A}$ selects the oracle $\Pi_{\mathsf{id}_j}^t$ as the test oracle which should generate the session key K_j^t. Then $\mathcal{A}$ could win the game by impersonating a client and computing the session key $K_{\mathcal{A}} = K_j^t$.

The details of this attack are shown in Fig. 2. $\mathcal{A}$ succeeds in impersonating the honest client id_i to server id_j's oracle $\Pi^t_{\mathsf{id}_j}$ and id_i has no *matching session* to $\Pi^t_{\mathsf{id}_j}$.

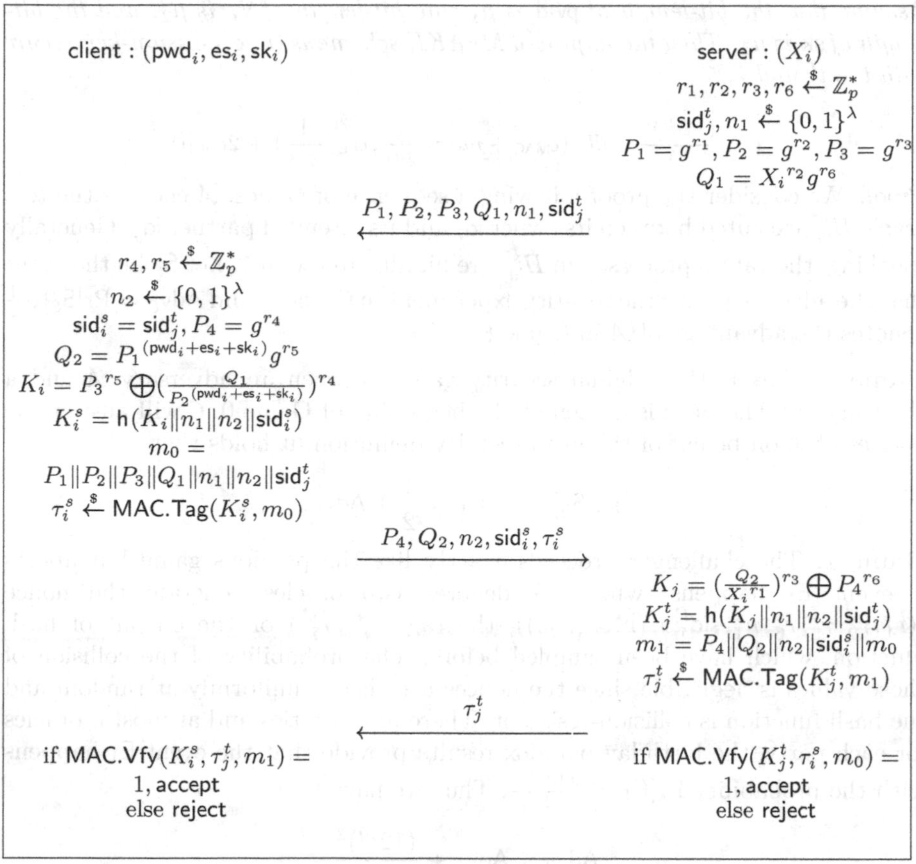

client : $(\mathsf{pwd}_i, \mathsf{es}_i, \mathsf{sk}_i)$

server : (X_i)
$$r_1, r_2, r_3, r_6 \overset{\$}{\leftarrow} \mathbb{Z}_p^*$$
$$\mathsf{sid}_j^t, n_1 \overset{\$}{\leftarrow} \{0,1\}^\lambda$$
$$P_1 = g^{r_1}, P_2 = g^{r_2}, P_3 = g^{r_3}$$
$$Q_1 = X_i^{r_2} g^{r_6}$$

$$\xleftarrow{\quad P_1, P_2, P_3, Q_1, n_1, \mathsf{sid}_j^t \quad}$$

$$r_4, r_5 \overset{\$}{\leftarrow} \mathbb{Z}_p^*$$
$$n_2 \overset{\$}{\leftarrow} \{0,1\}^\lambda$$
$$\mathsf{sid}_i^s = \mathsf{sid}_j^t, P_4 = g^{r_4}$$
$$Q_2 = P_1^{(\mathsf{pwd}_i + \mathsf{es}_i + \mathsf{sk}_i)} g^{r_5}$$
$$K_i = P_3^{r_5} \bigoplus \left(\frac{Q_1}{P_2^{(\mathsf{pwd}_i + \mathsf{es}_i + \mathsf{sk}_i)}} \right)^{r_4}$$
$$K_i^s = \mathsf{h}(K_i \| n_1 \| n_2 \| \mathsf{sid}_i^s)$$
$$m_0 =$$
$$P_1 \| P_2 \| P_3 \| Q_1 \| n_1 \| n_2 \| \mathsf{sid}_j^t$$
$$\tau_i^s \overset{\$}{\leftarrow} \mathsf{MAC.Tag}(K_i^s, m_0)$$

$$\xrightarrow{\quad P_4, Q_2, n_2, \mathsf{sid}_i^s, \tau_i^s \quad}$$

$$K_j = \left(\frac{Q_2}{X_i^{r_1}} \right)^{r_3} \bigoplus P_4^{r_6}$$
$$K_j^t = \mathsf{h}(K_j \| n_1 \| n_2 \| \mathsf{sid}_j^t)$$
$$m_1 = P_4 \| Q_2 \| n_2 \| \mathsf{sid}_i^s \| m_0$$
$$\tau_j^t \overset{\$}{\leftarrow} \mathsf{MAC.Tag}(K_j^t, m_1)$$

$$\xleftarrow{\quad \tau_j^t \quad}$$

if $\mathsf{MAC.Vfy}(K_i^s, \tau_j^t, m_1) =$
1, accept
else reject

if $\mathsf{MAC.Vfy}(K_j^t, \tau_i^s, m_0) =$
1, accept
else reject

Fig. 3. Improved MFAKE protocol

5.3 An Improvement Solution of Zhang's MFAKE Scheme

We have shown that Zhang's MFAKE scheme is vulnerable to MITM and outsider KCI attacks since the protocol message transcript is not fully bound to the keying material. We are trying to circumvent the above attacks by modifying the key derivation function. A hash function takes as input $K_i(K_j), n_1, n_2, \mathsf{sid}_i^s(\mathsf{sid}_j^t)$ and outputs the session key $K_i^s(K_j^t)$. More specifically, our improved scheme is shown in Fig. 3.

Theorem 1. *Suppose that the public key scheme* PKE *is* $(d, t, \epsilon_{\mathsf{PKE}})$*-secure against adaptive chosen-ciphertext attacks, the message authentication code scheme* MAC *is* $(1, t, \epsilon_{\mathsf{MAC}})$*-secure against strongly existential forgeries under chosen message attacks, the fuzzy extractor* FE *is* $(min, ts, d, t, \epsilon_{\mathsf{FE}})$*-secure, the hash function* h *is collision-resistant and the DDH problem is* $(t, \epsilon_{\mathsf{DDH}})$*-hard. Assume that the bit-length of* pwd *is* μ_1*, the bit-length of* W *is* μ_2*, and the bit-length of* sk *is* μ_3*. Then the improved MFAKE scheme is* (t', ϵ)*-session-key-secure with* $t \approx t'$ *and*

$$\epsilon \leq \frac{(12dl)^2}{2^\lambda} + dl \cdot (\epsilon_{\mathsf{MAC}} + max\{\frac{1}{2^{\mu_1}}, \epsilon_{\mathsf{FE}}, \frac{1}{2^{\mu_3}}\} + 2\epsilon_{\mathsf{DDH}}),$$

Proof. We consider the proof following a sequence of games. $\mathcal{A}$ chooses the test oracle $\Pi^{s^*}_{\mathsf{id}_i}$ executed between its owner id_i and its intended partner id_j. Generally speaking, the values processed in $\Pi^{s^*}_{\mathsf{id}_i}$ are highlighted with *. Let S_ξ be the event that the adversary wins the security experiment in Game ξ, and $\mathsf{Adv}_\xi = \Pr[\mathsf{S}_\xi] - \frac{1}{2}$ denotes the advantage of $\mathcal{A}$ in Game ξ.

Game 0. This is the original security game between an adversary $\mathcal{A}$ and a challenger $\mathcal{C}$. The bit b is chosen at the beginning of Game 0. $\mathcal{C}$ will answer the queries of $\mathcal{A}$ on behalf of the instances. By definition, it holds that

$$\Pr[\mathsf{S}_0] = \frac{1}{2} + \epsilon = \frac{1}{2} + \mathsf{Adv}_0.$$

Game 1. The challenger proceeds exactly like the previous game but aborts if event E_1 happens, where E_1 denotes two oracles generate the nonce $((r_1^*, r_2^*, r_3^*, r_6^*, n_1^*, \mathsf{sid}_j^{t^*}), (r_4^*, r_5^*, n_2^*))$, the tag $(\tau_i^{s^*}, \tau_j^{t^*})$ or the output of hash function, which have been sampled before. The probability of the collision of those values is negligible since the nonces are chosen uniformly at random and the hash function is collision-resistant. There are l parties and at most d oracles for each party, the birthday paradox results provide that the event E_1 happens with the probability $\Pr[\mathsf{E}_1] \leq \frac{(12dl)^2}{2^\lambda}$. Thus we have that

$$\mathsf{Adv}_0 \leq \mathsf{Adv}_1 + \frac{(12dl)^2}{2^\lambda}.$$

Game 2. In this game, $\mathcal{C}$ aborts when event E_2 happens. We define the event E_2 which happens if $\Pi^s_{\mathsf{id}_i}$ receives messages with a valid tag τ_j^t which is not send by its intended partner oracle $\Pi^t_{\mathsf{id}_j}$. We have $\mathsf{Adv}_1 \leq \mathsf{Adv}_2 + \Pr[\mathsf{E}_2]$.

If the event E_2 happens with overwhelming probability, then we could construct a tag forger $\mathcal{F}_2$ against the security of the message authentication code scheme as follows. The forger $\mathcal{F}_2$ simulates the challenger for $\mathcal{A}$. It first guesses an oracle that the adversary can forge, i.e. $\Pi^{t^*}_{\mathsf{id}_j}$. Next $\mathcal{F}_2$ generates all other secret keys honestly as the challenger in the previous game. If $\mathcal{A}$ outputs a message with a valid tag not generated by $\mathcal{F}_2$, then $\mathcal{F}_2$ could use the tag to break security. Since there are at most dl oracles for all parties, the event E_2 happens with the probability $\Pr[\mathsf{E}_2] \leq dl \cdot \epsilon_{\mathsf{MAC}}$. Thus it holds that

$$\mathsf{Adv}_1 \leq \mathsf{Adv}_2 + dl \cdot \epsilon_{\mathsf{MAC}}.$$

Game 3. In this game, C aborts if A asks the Send query with client's keys $(\mathsf{pwd}_i^*, \mathsf{es}_i^*, \mathsf{sk}_i^*)$ or server's key X_i^*. We let $pes^* = \mathsf{pwd}_i^* + \mathsf{es}_i^* + \mathsf{sk}_i^*$. Due to definition of three-factors security, A can only compromise two factors. Since there are l parties and at most d oracles for each party, A can ask dl Send queries. The three possible cases might occur as follows:

1. If W_i^* and sk_i^* are leaked, A could try to guess low-entropy passwords using the password dictionary attacks. A could guess correctly in this case with probability $\frac{dl}{2^{\mu_1}}$.
2. If pwd_i^* and sk_i^* are leaked, A could guess the extracted string es_i^* from helper string hs_i^* with the FE.Rep$(\cdot)$ function. Due to the use of the fuzzy extractor, A has an additional advantage ϵ_{FE}. Namely, A could guess correctly in this case with probability $dl \cdot \epsilon_{\mathsf{FE}}$.
3. If pwd_i^* and W_i^* are leaked, A still has no information about sk_i^* which means pes^* is still random for A. A could guess correctly in this case with probability $\frac{dl}{2^{\mu_3}}$.

Then, we have that

$$\mathsf{Adv}_2 \leq \mathsf{Adv}_3 + dl \cdot max\{\frac{1}{2^{\mu_1}}, \epsilon_{\mathsf{FE}}, \frac{1}{2^{\mu_3}}\}.$$

Game 4. In this game, C change the computations of Q_1^* and Q_2^* by $Q_1^* = g^{r_6^*}$ and $Q_2^* = g^{r_5^*}$. Similarly, the computations of K_i^* and K_j^* change to $K_i^* = P_3^{*r_5^*} \oplus Q_1^{*r_4^*}$ and $K_j^* = Q_2^{*r_3^*} \oplus P_4^{*r_6^*}$. We change this game that C will answer the Test oracle with a random key and abort if event E_4 happens. We define the event E_4 which happens if A asks hash oracle with valid K_i^*. If E_4 happens with non-negligible probability, we can build an algorithm A_4 against the DDH challenge. The A_4 receives values (g^x, g^y, g^z) such that either $z = xy$ or $z \xleftarrow{\$} \mathbb{Z}_p^*$ and runs the adversary A as a subroutine. If A_4 receives a Diffie-Hellman triple, this game proceeds exactly as Game 3, otherwise it is identical to Game 4. If A can distinguish with non-negligible probability whether $g^z = g^{xy}$ or not, then A_4 can use A to break the DDH assumption. There are at most dl oracles for all parties. Due to the security of DDH assumption, it holds that

$$\mathsf{Adv}_3 \leq \mathsf{Adv}_4 + 2dl \cdot \epsilon_{\mathsf{DDH}}$$

In this game, the answer of each Test query is a random key that is independent of the bit b. Thus, the advantage that A wins is $\mathsf{Adv}_4 = 0$.

Summing up all the probabilities from Game 0 to Game 4, we hold the result of this theorem.

6   Conclusion

In this paper, we have studied the MFAKE protocol proposed by Zhang et al. [23]. As described above, we prove that the security of the MFAKE protocol has some flaws. A simple man-in-the-middle attack and an outsider key compromise

336 Z. Ma and J. He

impersonation attack have been shown in detail. To remedy these weaknesses, an improvement MFAKE scheme has been proposed, which is secure against the attacks mentioned above. The security of the improved protocol was verified in the random oracle model.

Acknowledgments. We would like to thank Zengpeng Li for insightful comments and discussions. This work was supported by the Natural Science Foundation of China (Grant No. 61872051) and the Action Plan for high-quality Development of Graduate Education of Chongqing University of Technology (No. gzlcx20223226).

References

1. Abdalla, M., Fouque, P.-A., Pointcheval, D.: Password-based authenticated key exchange in the three-party setting. In: Vaudenay, S. (ed.) PKC 2005. LNCS, vol. 3386, pp. 65–84. Springer, Heidelberg (2005). https://doi.org/10.1007/978-3-540-30580-4_6
2. Agrawal, S., Miao, P., Mohassel, P., Mukherjee, P.: PASTA: password-based threshold authentication. In: Proceedings of the 2018 ACM SIGSAC Conference on Computer and Communications Security, pp. 2042–2059. ACM, New York (2018)
3. Bellare, M., Pointcheval, D., Rogaway, P.: Authenticated key exchange secure against dictionary attacks. In: Preneel, B. (ed.) EUROCRYPT 2000. LNCS, vol. 1807, pp. 139–155. Springer, Heidelberg (2000). https://doi.org/10.1007/3-540-45539-6_11
4. Bellare, M., Rogaway, P.: Entity authentication and key distribution. In: Stinson, D.R. (ed.) CRYPTO 1993. LNCS, vol. 773, pp. 232–249. Springer, Heidelberg (1994). https://doi.org/10.1007/3-540-48329-2_21
5. Bellovin, S., Merritt, M.: Encrypted key exchange: password-based protocols secure against dictionary attacks. In: Proceedings 1992 IEEE Computer Society Symposium on Research in Security and Privacy, pp. 72–84. IEEE Computer Society, Los Alamitos (1992)
6. Bellovin, S.M., Merritt, M.: Augmented encrypted key exchange: a password-based protocol secure against dictionary attacks and password file compromise. In: Proceedings of the 1st ACM Conference on Computer and Communications Security, pp. 244–250. ACM, New York (1993)
7. Boyko, V., MacKenzie, P., Patel, S.: Provably secure password-authenticated key exchange using Diffie-Hellman. In: Preneel, B. (ed.) EUROCRYPT 2000. LNCS, vol. 1807, pp. 156–171. Springer, Heidelberg (2000). https://doi.org/10.1007/3-540-45539-6_12
8. Far, H.A.N., Bayat, M., Das, A.K., Fotouhi, M., Pournaghi, S.M., Doostari, M.: LAPTAS: lightweight anonymous privacy-preserving three-factor authentication scheme for WSN-based IIoT. Wirel. Netw. **27**(2), 1389–1412 (2021)
9. Fleischhacker, N., Manulis, M., Azodi, A.: A modular framework for multi-factor authentication and key exchange. In: Chen, L., Mitchell, C. (eds.) SSR 2014. LNCS, vol. 8893, pp. 190–214. Springer, Cham (2014). https://doi.org/10.1007/978-3-319-14054-4_12
10. Groce, A., Katz, J.: A new framework for efficient password-based authenticated key exchange. In: Proceedings of the 17th ACM Conference on Computer and Communications Security, pp. 516–525. ACM, New York (2010)

11. Gu, Y., Jarecki, S., Krawczyk, H.: KHAPE: asymmetric PAKE from key-hiding key exchange. In: Malkin, T., Peikert, C. (eds.) CRYPTO 2021. LNCS, vol. 12828, pp. 701–730. Springer, Cham (2021). https://doi.org/10.1007/978-3-030-84259-8_24

12. Hao, F., Clarke, D.: Security analysis of a multi-factor authenticated key exchange protocol. In: Bao, F., Samarati, P., Zhou, J. (eds.) ACNS 2012. LNCS, vol. 7341, pp. 1–11. Springer, Heidelberg (2012). https://doi.org/10.1007/978-3-642-31284-7_1

13. Jager, T., Kohlar, F., Schäge, S., Schwenk, J.: Generic compilers for authenticated key exchange. In: Abe, M. (ed.) ASIACRYPT 2010. LNCS, vol. 6477, pp. 232–249. Springer, Heidelberg (2010). https://doi.org/10.1007/978-3-642-17373-8_14

14. Jarecki, S., Krawczyk, H., Xu, J.: OPAQUE: an asymmetric PAKE protocol secure against pre-computation attacks. In: Nielsen, J.B., Rijmen, V. (eds.) EURO-CRYPT 2018. LNCS, vol. 10822, pp. 456–486. Springer, Cham (2018). https://doi.org/10.1007/978-3-319-78372-7_15

15. Li, Z., Yang, Z., Szalachowski, P., Zhou, J.: Building low-interactivity multifactor authenticated key exchange for industrial internet of things. IEEE Internet Things J. 8(2), 844–859 (2021)

16. Liu, Y., Wei, F., Ma, C.: Multi-factor authenticated key exchange protocol in the three-party setting. In: Lai, X., Yung, M., Lin, D. (eds.) Inscrypt 2010. LNCS, vol. 6584, pp. 255–267. Springer, Heidelberg (2011). https://doi.org/10.1007/978-3-642-21518-6_18

17. Nam, J., et al.: Password-only authenticated three-party key exchange with provable security in the standard model. Sci. World J. 2014 (2014)

18. Ometov, A., Bezzateev, S., Mäkitalo, N., Andreev, S., Mikkonen, T., Koucheryavy, Y.: Multi-factor authentication: a survey. Cryptography 2(1) (2018)

19. Pointcheval, D., Zimmer, S.: Multi-factor authenticated key exchange. In: Bellovin, S.M., Gennaro, R., Keromytis, A., Yung, M. (eds.) ACNS 2008. LNCS, vol. 5037, pp. 277–295. Springer, Heidelberg (2008). https://doi.org/10.1007/978-3-540-68914-0_17

20. Wu, L., Wang, J., Choo, K.R., He, D.: Secure key agreement and key protection for mobile device user authentication. IEEE Trans. Inf. Forensics Secur. 14(2), 319–330 (2019)

21. Xie, Q., Tang, Z., Chen, K.: Cryptanalysis and improvement on anonymous three-factor authentication scheme for mobile networks. Comput. Electr. Eng. 59, 218–230 (2017)

22. Yang, Z., Li, S.: On security analysis of an after-the-fact leakage resilient key exchange protocol. Inf. Process. Lett. 116(1), 33–40 (2016)

23. Zhang, R., Xiao, Y., Sun, S., Ma, H.: Efficient multi-factor authenticated key exchange scheme for mobile communications. IEEE Trans. Dependable Secur. Comput. 16(4), 625–634 (2019)

Toward Safe Integration of Legacy SCADA Systems in the Smart Grid

Aldar C.-F. Chan[1](✉) and Jianying Zhou[2]

[1] University of Hong Kong, Pok Fu Lam, Hong Kong
aldar@graduate.hku.hk
[2] Singapore University of Technology and Design, Singapore, Singapore
jianying_zhou@sutd.edu.sg

Abstract. A SCADA system is a distributed network of cyber-physical devices used for instrumentation and control of critical infrastructures such as an electric power grid. With the emergence of the smart grid, SCADA systems are increasingly required to be connected to more open systems and security becomes crucial. However, many of these SCADA systems have been deployed for decades and were initially not designed with security in mind. In particular, the field devices in these systems are vulnerable to false command injection from an intruding or compromised device. But implementing cryptographic defence on these old-generation devices is challenging due to their computation constraints. As a key requirement, solutions to protect legacy SCADA systems have to be an add-on. This paper discusses two add-on defence strategies for legacy SCADA systems—the data diode and the detect-and-respond approach—and compares their security guarantees and applicable scenarios. A generic architectural framework is also proposed to implement the detect-and-respond strategy, with an instantiation to demonstrate its practicality.

1 Introduction

A SCADA (Supervisory, Control And Data Acquisition) system is a cyber network of communicating devices used for instrumentation and control of a distributed infrastructure, such as an electric power grid, in order to manage the respective physical processes. The SCADA system of a power grid can monitor and control various electric equipment along the power delivery path—including various transformers, circuit breakers, protective relays and automatic re-closers—while acquiring different measurements, which provide information about the loading conditions at different parts of the power grid and health conditions of transmission lines, etc. Hence, correct operation of a SCADA system is critical to the reliability of any power distribution system [2,3].

A successful malicious attack targeting at the SCADA system could potentially cause extensive power outage. Such service disruption could even have cascading effects onto other critical infrastructures [3]. However, most of the SCADA systems currently in active use have been deployed for decades and very few of them were originally designed with security in mind [19,22,29]. These legacy SCADA systems were assumed to operate in isolation at first, with obscurity and physical isolation being the

J. Zhou et al. (Eds.): ACNS 2022 Workshops, LNCS 13285, pp. 338–357, 2022.
https://doi.org/10.1007/978-3-031-16815-4_19

main security strategy. But nowadays, this design assumption is challenged not only by new security threats—including demonstrated break-in's of power substations [28], discovered worms on PLCs (Programmable Logic Controllers) and other industrial control system platforms [17,23], and the exposure of supposedly obstructed documents (such as SCADA system configuration and operation manuals) on the Internet [19]—but also by the changing operational model which desires a higher level of integration with relatively open systems [14], such as the AMI (Advanced Metering Infrastructure), in the envisioned smart grid for data sharing and orchestration of process control.

The increasing connectivity of these legacy SCADA systems with external smart grid systems, with comparatively more open access, could increase the attack surface for attackers to compromise devices inside the SCADA systems or send forged data or commands directly from outside. Nonetheless, these legacy SCADA systems will take decades to be phased out from operation since they are so highly integrated with the power equipment they monitor [7,22]. It is thus essential to devise protection mechanisms to safeguard legacy SCADA systems as they are increasingly integrated with newer smart grid systems.

In particular, legacy SCADA systems are typically vulnerable to forged data or commands sent from intruding or compromised devices (i.e. insider attacks) [2,7,13,19,22, 26]. For instance, a compromised SCADA RTU (Remote Terminal Unit) could launch a false command attack whereby an attacker impersonates the master station to send false control commands to other RTUs, say, to maliciously trip a particular circuit breaker. On the other hand, false readings from compromised instrumentation devices could present a distorted picture of the system status to the master station, thus possibly triggering a false alarm and disruptive actions [13]. Currently, most legacy SCADA systems could have little defense to this kind of attacks as no source authentication or command verification mechanism is in place [2,4,7,19,22,26].

Implementing cryptographic defence on the old-generation devices in these SCADA systems is impossible due to their resource constraints, and protection has to resort to the bump-in-the-wire approach [29], which is generally regarded as very inefficient. While authentication and authorization frameworks (such as IEC62351-8)—which are increasingly applied for authentication and access policy enforcement in distributed smart grid and newer SCADA systems [2,26]—can avoid or minimize false command injection, it remains challenging to deploy them in some legacy SCADA systems and protocols due to the computational and communication overheads involved, as well as, the need of modifications at both the protocol and device level. To avoid protocol modification, legacy-compliant message authentication [7] is proposed to embed authentication data as an additional payload of some specific SCADA protocols. However, it requires modifications of the device software and is applicable only to a few, usually newer SCADA protocols and devices that are powerful enough to run common cryptographic primitives. Generic strategies through enhanced incident management [1] or better process monitoring [3] could improve SCADA system security but require a higher degree of human involvement and intervention. It is fair to say truly add-on, non-intrusive protection for legacy SCADA systems and protocols remains challenging.

This paper studies and compares two different strategies to secure legacy SCADA systems for safe integration with smart grid systems. Both approaches do not require any modification on the devices, protocols or communication channels, and are scalable for different numbers of devices. The need of human intervention is also minimized. The first approach, called the "data diode" approach [10, 24, 30], is commonly adopted in the industry and aims to preserve the isolation of a legacy SCADA system while facilitating outward information flow to newer smart grid systems. The second approach aims to open up a legacy SCADA system for bidirectional information flow, with mechanisms in place to detect and identify false commands sent by intruding devices or compromised nodes. This paper proposes a high-level, architectural framework for the second approach to implement a detect-and-respond strategy to neutralize the effects of false command attacks on a SCADA field network. While this paper focuses on false command detection based on verification against an authenticated copy of each command received through a secure channel, the framework provides a general basis for incorporating other attack detection methods [12, 13, 18] to implement a defence strategy. This paper will also compare the applicability and usability of the two approaches.

The contributions of this paper is two-fold. First, a generic architectural framework is proposed to implement the detect-and-respond strategy for the protection of legacy SCADA systems against false command attacks, with a view to opening up these SCADA systems for integration with relatively more open smart grid systems. The proposed technique is non-intrusive and truly add-on without requiring modifications on existing devices and systems. It is also scalable in the sense that only one defending device is needed per field network. To demonstrate the practicality of the proposed framework, an instantiation of the detect-and-respond strategy on the Siemens Sinaut 8FW protocol [27]—a common industrial protocol for legacy SCADA systems—is presented with performance results. Second, this paper presents a comprehensive review of the current landscape of research in legacy SCADA system protection. It compares the data diode and detect-and-respond approaches, discussing their benefits and limitations, and provides practical guidelines for their application.

The rest of this paper is organized as follows. In the next section, legacy SCADA systems and false command attacks against them are discussed. The data diode strategy and the detect-and-respond strategy are presented in Sect. 3 and Sect. 4 respectively. Finally, Sect. 5 concludes with a comparison of the two strategies.

2 False Command Attacks Against Legacy SCADA Systems

A typical SCADA system, as depicted in Fig. 1, consists of PLCs and RTUs in the older versions and IEDs (Intelligent Electronic Devices) in the newer versions as the basic units for deployment in power substations or remote sites (for monitoring transmission lines) at different geographic locations. Each of these field devices has interfaces to sensors and actuators used to monitor and control equipment in a power delivery system. The field devices in a substation or remote site form a local area network, known as the field network, and are usually connected together over a broadcast medium to a sub-master or data concentrator, which in turn is connected to the MTU (Master Terminal Unit) or master station at the main control center through leased lines over a telecom operator's network. While various topologies are in use for connecting field devices with the sub-master, a broadcast channel—such as EIA-485 serial ports in the party-line mode over a pilot cable (as shown in Fig. 2) or DNP3 in the multi-drop or data concentrator mode[1]—is typically used in SCADA systems.

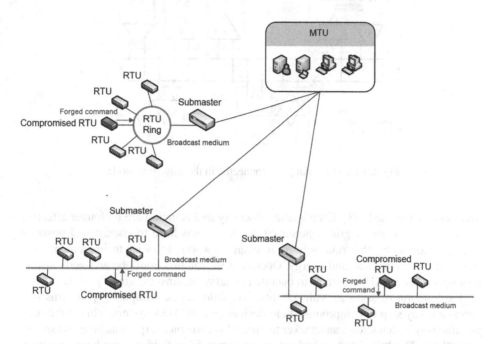

Fig. 1. A typical legacy SCADA system and the possibility of false command attacks

Despite cost efficiency achieved in cable layout and maintenance, the use of broadcast channels also eases insider attacks from compromised devices. For example, a compromised RTU can pose the MTU to issue a forged command to another RTU or PLC, causing the latter to behave abnormally. Experiments have been repeatedly reported to demonstrate the possibility of using off-the-shelf protocol analyzer software to intercept control messages and inject false commands in some legacy SCADA systems [13], with some showing the possibility to trip a circuit breaker maliciously. In a few cases, even though the circuit breaker signaled the master station that it had opened, the master station did not respond as it had not instructed the circuit breaker to open.

This type of attacks was inconceivable in the original design of SCADA systems, and SCADA devices have little resource to defend against them. Obscurity in system design, command formats and operation, combined with physical isolation, have long been the main and possibly the only strategy for securing legacy SCADA systems. However, the effectiveness of obscurity may have become unreasonable. For instance, it has been demonstrated that fuzzing can effectively discover or recover unknown SCADA commands of a SCADA device [6]. Physical break-in's to power substations have been

---

[1] Earlier SCADA systems were designed based on proprietary protocols. DNP3 is a standard adopted in newer SCADA systems for connecting RTUs and IEDs with an MTU.

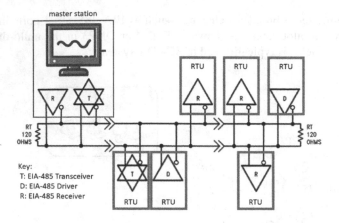

Fig. 2. EIA-485 serial ports connected in the party-line mode

occasionally reported [28]. Even worse, obscurity and isolation are no longer effective in the envisioned smart grid, wherein SCADA systems have to coexist and possibly communicate with other relatively more open networks, in order to implement two-way flow of information and energy. Operation in isolation could be an overly strong assumption for SCADA systems to operate nowadays against the smart grid backdrop.

Exploitation of software vulnerabilities on field device computing platforms is a necessary, key step to compromise field devices in a SCADA system. This is the only possible way which allows an attacker to install his code on a target machine and spread it to others. The belief that embedded processors used in field devices have relatively less exploitable software vulnerabilities or it is difficult to compromise an embedded system has become untenable, as demonstrated by the case of the Stuxnet worm discovered in 2010, which has a rootkit to infect PLCs over a proprietary SCADA system and damaged a number of centrifuge equipment in an Iranian nuclear facility [17,23]. Subsequent generations of Stuxnet were also discovered. In fact, it has been demonstrated that with crafted instructions and data, compromising an embedded processor is within reach to attackers in general. These compromises could normally go undetected by the MTU since, as demonstrated by the Stuxnet worm, a compromised device could play man-in-the-middle to conceal all malicious activities from the MTU.

In addition, should a physical break-in to a substation or remote site be possible, an attacker could simply tap in his own attacking devices directly onto the SCADA network to manipulate other innocent devices. With the increasing connectivity with other systems in the smart grid, this threat is particularly real since these newer smart grid systems typically allow more open access to general users. For instance, a smart meter may be accessible to a household user's computer for reading meter data and setting consumption patterns and alerts. Similarly, an electric vehicle (EV) charging station in a public car park could have a digital interface open for the general public for functionalities like making reservation or checking charging status of an EV.

3   Data Diode Approach

A data diode is a unidirectional gateway, similar to a firewall, which sets a digital barrier to enforce network perimeter control for a restricted network (such as a SCADA system) and fend off unwanted accesses from the less secure networks it is connected to (such as smart grid systems). Yet a data diode provides a stronger security guarantee than a firewall since strict one-way communication—from the restricted network to the less secure network only—is enforced by a certain physical law rather than digital logic, with little chance of reverse communication. Data diodes are often built using fibre optics coupler or transceivers, through the removal of the transmitter component from one side of the communication and the respective receiver component from the opposite side.[2] This makes it physically impossible to compromise such devices to achieve reverse connectivity. Moreover, they usually do not contain firmware, thus requiring minimal or no configuration at all, or have minimal software supported by micro-kernels that can be formally verified. Whereas, firewalls are often prone to configuration mistakes and relatively accessible for exploit by skilful attackers. While firmware upgrade is regularly needed in firewall maintenance, patching is seldom needed for data diode deployment. Finally, data diodes are the only devices receiving the EAL7 (Evaluation Assurance Level 7), the highest grade in the Common Criteria [9] (an international standard evaluating the level of security of equipment).

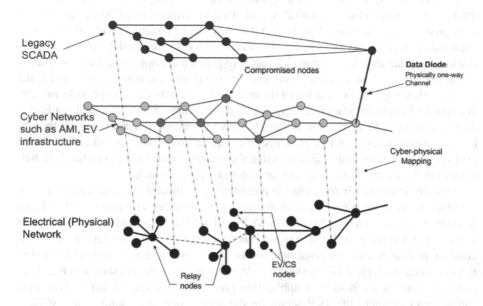

Fig. 3. Deployment scenario of the data diode approach

---

[2] Although different hardware implementations of a data diode exist, supporting different physical channels (e.g. RS-232, EIA-485, USB, Ethernet), most implementations make use of optical couplers to guarantee physical isolation.

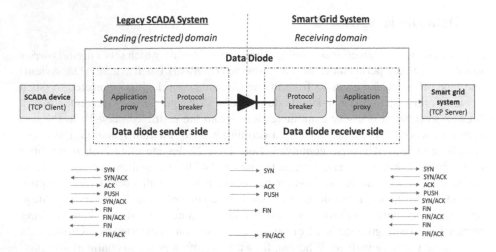

Fig. 4. TCP message flow in a unidirectional gateway [10]

Data diodes allow organisations to retrieve valuable data generated at the process level from a critical infrastructure for consumption by a wider group of users in a relatively more open system while assuring the isolation and integrity of the critical infrastructure. As shown in Fig. 3, a data diode allows data acquired by SCADA field devices to be pushed from the SCADA system so that they can be combined with other datasets captured by smart grid systems like AMI and EV systems which poll the physical conditions of the same electric power grid, in order to give a more holistic and precise picture of the conditions of the electric power grid for more accurate data analysis and hence resource planning. The correlation of these different datasets can also provide valuable insights for fault identification and predictive maintenance. Should the analysis lead to desired actions to be carried out in the SCADA system, the feedback will be through human communications. While existence of compromised nodes is possible in the smart grid systems, the data diode guarantees that they cannot send in false commands to field devices in the legacy SCADA system or infect/compromise them.

Despite similarities in the isolation mechanism, commercially available data diode solutions differ in supported services and protocols. In order to support TCP/IP-based SCADA protocols, such as MODBUS/TCP and DNP3, data diodes usually have to make use of additional software components for each side of the unidirectional link to emulate the bidirectional message flow for the three-way handshake and acknowledgements needed in a typical TCP session. As demonstrated by [10] and shown in Fig. 4, the software components include an application proxy and a protocol breaker. The application proxy emulates the TCP server on the sender side to respond to the SCADA device (TCP client) with TCP connection-oriented messages and acknowledgements while forwarding messages from the TCP client to the unidirectional link. Similarly, the application proxy emulates the TCP client on the receiver side. But it does not forward any message from the TCP server on the receiver side to the unidirectional link. Note that only TCP connection messages sent from the SCADA system to the smart grid system are allowed by the data diode. The protocol breaker acts as a middleware for packet encapsulation and possibly applying encryption and forward error correction (FEC) to data transferred over the unidirectional link. FEC is especially important to ensure correct data delivery for the noisy environment of typical SCADA systems.

4 Detect-and-Respond Approach

While data diodes provide strong security and isolation/decoupling assurance for legacy SCADA systems, sometimes they are too restrictive for certain application scenarios of the smart grid. Neither is it optimal to rely on human communications for feedback to a SCADA system. There is a realistic need for two-way flow of data between a SCADA system and a smart grid system. Proposals such as [30] therefore emerged to add a reverse channel to data diodes. But whether the advantages of a data diode over a typical firewall can be preserved in such a modification is highly uncertain. More importantly, to what degree that the security assurance of a data diode is undermined with the addition of a reverse channel needs to be assessed carefully. In scenarios requiring bidirectional data exchange between a SCADA system and a smart grid system, it is therefore more reasonable to assume the existence of compromised devices in the SCADA system [12, 13, 16, 18, 19, 22, 23] and devise mechanisms to detect false commands [13, 16, 18, 19] and/or identify compromised nodes [19, 22]. In general, a detect-and-respond strategy is preferred despite that many of the proposed schemes in the literature merely cover attack detection. Once a false command is detected, its impacts should be voided or neutralised promptly, and ideally, in an automatic manner with minimum human intervention required.

This paper presents a generic, high-level architectural framework to implement the detect-and-respond strategy for legacy SCADA systems. An embodiment in the form of a trusted protection agent is also given to illustrate typical steps needed to neutralise the effects of false commands injected by compromised field devices. The notion of the protection agent is similar to that of a trust node in [12]. The difference is that the protection agent actively neutralises the effects of false commands, whereas, the trust node only serves as a trusted routing agent to selectively relay messages between field devices and the master station. Since the framework is defined in a general setting, it should be applicable to different types of SCADA protocols and provide a basis for systematically crafting defence mechanisms fit for different SCADA systems and field devices. Besides, there is flexibility for incorporating different detection algorithms or mechanisms such as [13, 18] into the framework. The framework is also complementary to and could be combined with other approaches [1, 3, 7] for securing SCADA systems.

The underlying assumption for implementing the detect-and-respond strategy with a protection agent is that the protection agent is well protected with different protection mechanisms in place to implement the defence-in-depth strategy so as to minimize the probability of its compromise. In practice, there are various conventional techniques to achieve the security hardening of the protection agent effectively, which will be discussed in Sect. 4.1 and 4.4. In the worst case, if a physical break-in to a power substation happens, the protection agent could be compromised. But the question is, if an attacker successfully breaks in to a power station, he could actually tap in his own device to launch any type of attacks. The only reason for him to compromise the protection agent is to stop the protection agent from alerting the master station in order to conceal his attacks. That is, even for physical break-in's, the protection agent would only increase the difficulty for an attacker to launch attacks sneakily.

4.1 Protection Agent

As depicted in Fig. 5, a protection agent is installed as an add-on device in each field network of a SCADA system, which can be made up of PLCs, RTUs or IEDs. Leveraging on the broadcast medium typically found in most field networks, the protection agent— as a network sniffer—monitors commands issued to all the field devices on the network to detect malicious activities. As a safe assumption, the protection agent is generally a much more powerful machine than typical field devices, given that the underlying processor used in the protection agent could be generations away from those used in the field device of a legacy SCADA system. In addition, compared to the low-bandwidth physical channel used by these field devices (typically, in the range of 1.2–19.2 kbps [20,27,29]), the protection agent can easily be equipped with a wireless link of much higher bandwidth to the MTU or master station. Note that the design of the protection agent does not preclude other communication channels such as a fiber link.[3] We can therefore assume that the protection agent has a faster (with a higher bandwidth and a lower latency) and typically more reliable communication channel (for most of the time) with the MTU than the field devices. On the basis of a more powerful machine with a faster communication channel to the MTU, security hardening on the protection agent is much easier. We assume that the protection agent has a secured, authenticated channel with the master station. Multi-factor entity authentication (for example, those based on pre-shared secret keys stored in a tamper-resistant device, physical unclonable functions [15,25], or even new approaches [8] etc.) could be adopted to implement this authenticated channel to strengthen its security assurance. Compared to the field device platforms with little resources for the implementation of cryptographic defence, the protection agent is more ready to implement cryptographic algorithms and protocols, and other security mechanisms requiring more resources (such as firewall or remote code attestation). In short, the protection agent can be viewed as a trusted proxy for the MTU.

On the other hand, the protection agent can be seen as a reliable incognito for the MTU, monitoring what is happening in the field network. It is assumed that the protection agent can interpret the underlying protocol messages (as coded in its design) and can sniff messages in the field network. As discussed in Sect. 2, devices in the same field network are usually connected over a broadcast channel, meaning that such traffic sniffing is a practical assumption. Difference in topology would only affect the number devices that can be eavesdropped. With the protection agent monitoring the traffic in place, the previously observed problem of some legacy SCADA systems that the MTU is not aware of a circuit breaker having been tripped by an attacker since it has not initiated the tripping [11] would not happen if a protection agent is installed in the field network. When the protection agent observes the tripping command in the

---

[3] A wireless channel is assumed here simply because it is one of the common approaches for adding new communication channels between a remote substation and a control centre.

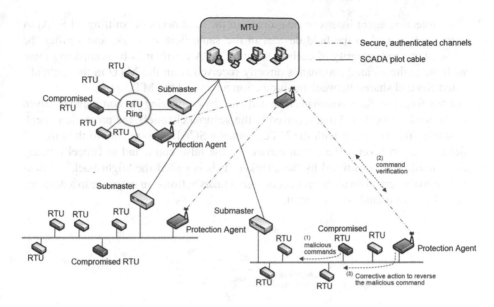

Fig. 5. A SCADA system with protection agents installed

field network but does not receive the same command through the trusted communication channel shared with the MTU, it would report the tripping event back to the MTU, which would then be aware of a possible intrusion. While there is possibility that an attacker might physically remove the protection agent from a field network, security mechanisms could be implemented on the protection agent to detect any malicious removal. For instance, the MTU can run a challenge-response verification protocol with the protection agent by sending a sequence of specially crafted random messages (i.e. nonces)—destined at a void device identity—to the protection agent via the field network; if the protection agent is disconnected from the field network, it would not be able to receive these messages to respond to the MTU's challenge correctly. Besides, remote code attestation could be implemented to provide the assurance that the software being executed on the protection agent has not been tampered with. It should be emphasized that a protection agent offers more resources and flexibility than a typical field device like an RTU or PLC for implementing preventive security measures and intrusion detection mechanisms.

4.2   Detect-and-Respond Defence of Protection Agent

The detect-and-respond mechanism of the protection agent can simply be implemented as a finite state machine as shown in Fig. 6. The basic idea is as follows:

1. Whenever the MTU issues a SCADA command to any field device, it also sends an authenticated message of the same command (protected by a certain cryptographic algorithm such as AES-CCM) to the corresponding protection agent which is connected to the same field network as the concerned field device is in.

2. The protection agent listens or eavesdrops in the field network, sniffing all SCADA commands issued to the field devices in the same field network, and verifies the authenticity and integrity of each of these SCADA commands by comparing them with the authenticated commands directly received from the MTU in the authenticated channel shared between the protection agent and the MTU.

3. For any forged or false command detected (say, by comparing the command received in the field network and that received in the secured channel), the protection agent, possibly after verifying with the MTU, issues a SCADA command to the affected field device to reverse the action caused by the false command to cancel out any undesirable action initiated by the attacker. This is called the "fight-back" or neutralization mechanism as the protection agent takes action—in response to a detected malicious command—to correct it.

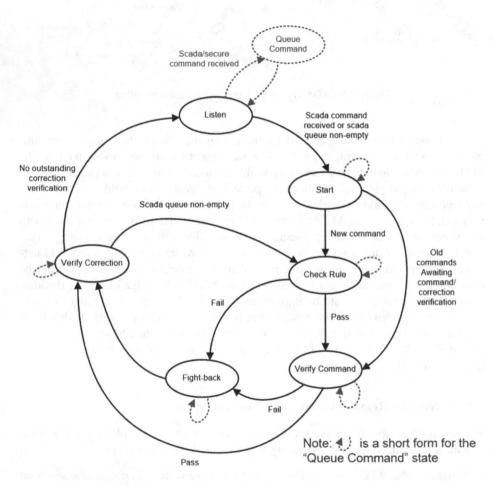

Fig. 6. The state machine diagram of a SCADA protection agent

Table 1. Details of the protection agent implementation as a state machine

State	Description	Tasks
Queue	State to queue newly received SCADA and authenticated commands	- Read commands from the receiving port - Queue the command to the SCADA or authenticated queue accordingly
Listen	Idle state when the SCADA queue is empty	- Check if the SCADA queue is non-empty and trigger the "Start" state when the queue is non-empty
Start	State to tell between a new SCADA command received or an old SCADA command pending the completion and confirmation of corrective actions taken	- Check whether a new SCADA command arrives and trigger command verification if positive
Check Rule	State to check the local rule set to see if the received SCADA command is illegitimate and violates the prescribed rules	- Evaluate the SCADA command against the local rule set - If the SCADA does not pass any of the rules, trigger the correction process. Otherwise, check the authenticity of the SCADA command
Verify Command	State to check whether the received SCADA command is really from the MTU through the use of the authenticated channel	- If the SCADA command has a matched authenticated command received in the authenticated queue, issue a pass, otherwise, request the MTU to verify through the authenticated channel and check again - If the SCADA command fails, trigger the correction process
Fight-back	State to correct or reverse the actions caused by a malicious command	- Look up from a pre-set table for the corrective actions needed for a particular SCADA command - Issue the listed SCADA commands to the affected RTUs to reverse the actions of the malicious command
Verify Correction	State to confirm that the correction is in effect	- Read the status of the affected RTUs to confirm that the corrective actions have been applied

In principle, the neutralization mechanism could invalidate or void out forged commands, restoring the field device to the original state. But the degree of neutralization or residual effect of a false command would depend on the actual implementation of the logic and the SCADA command set of a field device. This defence approach shares some similarities with the fight-back mechanism of OSPF (Open Shortest Path First)—a link state routing protocol used in the Internet—through which an innocent router could publicly renounce a malicious route update forged by an attacker [21].

In case of missing commands, the protection agent can request the MTU to resend a command over the secured, authenticated channel for verification. Besides, the implementation of the protection agent could be further extended by including additional false command detection mechanisms beyond comparison with an authenticated copy of a legitimate command. For example, the detection mechanisms of [13, 18] can possibly be used by the protection agent to trigger neutralization, preferably after confirmation by the MTU. However, in order to respond correctly to any maliciously injected commands, the deployed detection mechanism should provide sufficient details to help identify the commands falsely injected by the attacker.

In some cases, a forged or malicious command could be immediately detected in the local field network without relying on authenticated messages from the MTU. For example, the remote software update of a field device is normally prohibited by most utility operators. However, in some SCADA systems composed of RTUs, the denial of a remote software update request is implemented on the MTU side only, while the RTUs in the field network usually have no mechanism to deny a software update request or distinguish whether it is initiated by the MTU or an intruding device. In other words, a compromised RTU or an intruding attacker device could still initiate a remote software update at any RTU in the same field network, which will not be denied by the latter. This flaw would greatly facilitate the spread of worms or malicious instruction sequences over a field network. In a typical SCADA deployment, a firewall usually only safeguards a field network from external attacks and would not be able to stop such an insider threat since the attack is launched from within the field network by a compromised field device or an intruding device connected to the field network. In contrast, the protection agent could possibly halt the malicious software update. A local rule set can be implemented on the protection agent, explicitly specifying that only manual update is allowed. When the protection agent detects an automatic software update command, it can immediately halt the update by issuing another command, without having to check with the MTU.

The same technique can be used for other clearly harmful actions. For instance, the protection agent can enforce that a certain range of parameters is prohibited in some SCADA commands. With the local rule on protection agents, the damage of the centrifuge equipment caused by the Stuxnet worm could be avoided, since the command with parameters causing excessive spin speed could be invalidated by the protection agent. Similarly, the protection agent can be configured to eliminate or invalidate set point commands—which are used in typical SCADA systems to preset the thresholds on certain measured system variables (such as voltages or phase angles at certain point of a power grid) for triggering protective actions like tripping a circuit breaker—with harmful parameters.

In details, two command queues are implemented in the protection agent, which respectively stores SCADA commands received in the field network and authenticated commands received through the secured, authenticated channel between the MTU and the protection agent. When the SCADA command queue is empty, the protection agent is at the "Listen" state waiting for new SCADA commands. The arrival of a new SCADA command will trigger the protection agent to verify the authenticity of the requested action and reverse it in case it is a fake command. A list of tasks to be implemented at different states of the protection agent is shown in Table 1.

The detect-and-respond strategy deviates from intuition and standard techniques used in securing a communication network. Whereas existing schemes would suggest filtering all bogus messages injected by an attacker, the proposed mechanism aims to tolerate the intrusion for a while if the resulting malicious actions are not critically harmful and then correct or neutralize the malicious actions. For critical actions which are usually banned by norm, the local rule set in the protection agent would stop them immediately from onset. Since the detect-and-respond approach favors local, distributed defence, it is more scalable than centralized defence mechanisms.

4.3   Example Implementation with Siemens Sinaut 8FW Protocol

Table 2 illustrates how the detect-and-respond defence strategy can be implemented with respect to the command set of the Siemens Sinaut 8FW protocol [27], a popular industrial protocol commonly used in legacy SCADA systems. The Sinaut 8FW protocol was the standard protocol used by Siemens devices and systems for communicating control and monitoring messages between MTU systems and RTU devices before being replaced by IEC 60870-5-101. It was broadly supported by devices provided by other manufacturers like ABB and GE. While the principle of the detect-and-respond strategy can be equally applied to newer protocols like IEC 60870-5-101 and 60870-5-104, its implementation with these protocols is outside the scope of this paper, partly because it is possible to implement authentication mechanisms in these protocol [26]. In contrast, the resource constraints of devices running the Sinaut 8FW protocol preclude the possibility of implementing any security mechanism despite that the protocol is still actively used in a non-negligible fraction of systems. In other words, it is more critical to investigate add-on protection for the Sinaut 8FW protocol over others. Each command is enclosed in a control message in the form of a telegram. Table 2 only shows telegram types sent in the control direction (from the MTU to field network), with other telegram types in the monitoring direction (from the field network to the MTU) skipped since these telegram types are largely for messages sent to the MTU.

False commands that may have critical impact on the functioning of a SCADA system are neutralized first and then verified with the MTU, whereas, the less critical ones are corrected upon confirmation from the MTU. Most of the neutralization actions can be readily implemented through the replace command telegram. For commands which switch on/off a certain feature or function, the neutralization can simply be done by toppling the command in the oppositive direction with respect to the false command. For commands which involve updating of parameters like thresholds or set points to trigger preventive actions, the protection agent stores the latest version of all the parameters of a field device (with parameters of different field devices stored in different tables) and apply relevant ones to form a replace command when necessary to revert the parameters affected by a false command.

Experimentation was carried out on an Intel 2.5 GHz Quad Core Celeron CPU (with 8 GB RAM)—which simulates the protection agent—to estimate the response time of the protection agent to issue a neutralization command or telegram for different types of false commands. The protection agent is connected to a server (which simulates the master station) through a WiFi link. On the other side, the protection agent is connected to another single board computer through a RS232 serial port (set at a baud rate of 19200), which simulates a compromised field device (in Scenario 1) or a master station (in Scenario 2) to issue commands to the protection agent. Two types of response time are measured corresponding to two different scenarios. In the first scenario (i.e. Scenario 1), the protection agent is set to receive no message from the master station and the compromised field device (simulated by the single board computer) injects a false

Table 2. Implementation of the detect-and-respond defence on Siemens Sinaut 8FW protocol

Telegram type	Priority to neutralize	Protection agent's actions to neutralize
- Control (Type 64) - Replace command (Type 195)	High	- Topple the command - Report the action back to MTU and wait for acknowledgement. If negative acknowledgement is received, topple the command back
- Analogue/digital set point (Type 65–67/68–70) - Modification of threshold value limit (Type 205) - Modification of smoothing factor (Type 206) - Remote parameterization (Type 212)	High	- Temporarily store a copy of the suspected command - Apply the latest confirmed parameter setting stored in the protection agent to form a command - Use replace command (Type 195) to switch the parameter setting back - Report the action back to MTU and wait for acknowledgement. If negative acknowledgement is received, apply the stored suspected command, otherwise, erase stored command
- Start-up request (start up/restart) (Type 211) - Switch on/off recipient in master station (Type 203) - Switch off record transfer from/to station (Type 204)	Medium	- Report to the MTU and wait for confirmation. If confirmed, topple the command
- Switch on/off for temporal lists (Type 201–202) - Synchronization of fine time (type 207) - Setting of minutes (Type 208) - Setting of calendar (Type 209) - Switch on/off addresses in the lists (Type 210) - 4-byte-storage interrogation control (Type 214) - Interrogation command ZFBIT and STOP-cause (Type 215–222)	Low	- Report to the MTU and wait for confirmation. If confirmed, topple the command or restore the stored parameters
- Check command (Type 192) - Check command (type 192) - Message repeat request/TFK-acknowledge (Type 193) - Start acknowledgement (Type 194) - Single/group interrogation command (Type 196–197) - Multiple request (Type 198–200) - Matrix-check command (Type 213)	Low	- Neutralization is not necessary

command to the serial port to trigger the protection agent to neutralize the command. The response time needed to issue a neutralization command after the injection of a false command is measured. In the second scenario (i.e. Scenario 2), the single board computer simulates an authentic command from the master station. That is, the injected command is authentic but the protection agent mistakenly considers it as a false command. The protection agent first issues a neutralization command and then queries the master station which always returns a negative acknowledgement. That is, the protection agent has to switch back the command and cancel the effects of the neutralization command. The response time for the protection agent to issue the second command after the injection of the first command by the single board computer is measured.

The experimental measurements are presented in Fig. 7. The average response time required for the protection agent to look up the parameter for a particular field device identity and issue a neutralization command or telegram for different types of false commands (at high priority) is 45.52 ms with a standard deviation of 9.28 ms. The average response time required for the protection agent to switch back the command for the second scenario is 175.32 ms with a standard deviation of 27.5 ms. Compared to the maximum tolerable delay for SCADA transactions, which is 0.54 s [5], this processing delay is acceptable (respectively, 8.4% and 32.4% of the maximum tolerable delay).

4.4 Security Analysis

The key assumption for the detect-and-respond mechanism based on a protection agent is that the protection agent is trusted and has a reliable communication channel to the master station. This should be a reasonable assumption in practice.

First, it is considerably harder to compromise a protection agent than a typical field device. But it is easier to detect any compromise of the protection agent. As discussed in Sect. 4.1, since the protection agent is based on a more powerful computing platform compared to a field device, various techniques—such as remote code attestation to ensure that a correct version of software is executed on the protection agent and challenge-response verification to ensure that the protection agent is not disconnected from the field network—can be readily applied to strengthen the security assurance of the protection agent and detect any compromise. Besides, if a protection agent is compromised, the attacker can cause no more harm than what he can achieve with a compromised field device when no protection agent is deployed. Since compromising a protection agent is more difficult than compromising a field device, adding a protection agent would make the job of an attacker more difficult and strengthen system security.

Second, the more powerful platform used for a protection agent (compared to a field device) enables the implementation of common cryptographic primitives, thereby allowing the use of standard protocols such as the TLS (Transport Layer Security) to secure the communication channel between a protection agent and the master station. The confidentiality and authenticity of each message sent over the channel is thus assured. An out-of-band wireless channel is assumed for the communication between a protection agent and the master station because it is the most cost-effective way, and a popular means, to add a new communication channel to a power substation. To address the reliability issues associated with a wireless channel, the protection agent can request the master station to resend any missed command or explicitly acknowledge/confirm

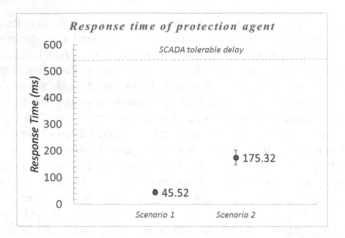

Fig. 7. Response time of the protection agent for: (a) Scenario 1: Neutralization of a malicious command; (b) Scenario 2: Ratification of false neutralization.

any command it has sent through the field network. Since such a channel usually has a higher bandwidth and a lower latency compared to the field network, the processing delay is usually reasonable. As demonstrated by the experimental results, the latency for the confirmation required for a missed command (Scenario 2) seems practically acceptable. Alternatively, an in-band, authenticated communication channel [7] or a more reliable communication channel such as a fiber link could be used.

4.5   Cost and Benefit Analysis

The detect-and-respond strategy embodied by the protection agent offers a number of advantages as follows.

1. The protection mechanism is non-intrusive and truly add-on while strong crypto-graphic mechanisms can be adopted to protect the communications between a field network and the MTU (via a protection agent), without replacing any field devices or modifying their code. No laying of new cables is needed, as wireless links like mobile cellular networks could be used between protection agents and the MTU.
2. Compared to the bump-in-the-wire approach [1, 14] which adds a new cryptographic device per field device, a smaller number of protection agents are required, with one required for each field network in most cases. A typical field network could have at least 30 devices, whereas, the maximum number of field devices per network is limited by the protocol's address space. As an example, up to 128 and 65535 devices per network are allowed for Sinaut 8FW and IEC60870-5-104 respectively. Hence, compared with the bump-in-the-wire approach, the detect-and-respond approach can reduce the number of cryptographic devices by a factor between 1/128 and 1/30. The minimum number of protection agents needed for a SCADA system is roughly equal to the number of its field networks. For instance, less than 100 protection agents are needed to secure the SCADA system of Singapore's 22 kV distribution grid (with

$\sim$10, 000 substations), whereas, 1–2 protection agents suffice to cover that of its 66 kV distribution grid (with $\sim$100 substations).

3. The protection agent would not become a bottleneck since additional protection agents can be deployed to a given field network with many field devices (say, more than 300 devices). In such cases, the set of field devices in a network can be grouped into partitions based on their identities and multiple protection agents could be installed in the network with each responsible for a distinct partition. Since any number of protection agents can be added to a field network and the field devices need not be aware of the presence of a protection agent, the solution is scalable.

4. The detect-and-respond strategy is particularly effective for defending against insider attacks, which existing solutions like firewalls often cannot withhold. A firewall normally cannot filter messages sent from a field device located behind it or forged messages from outside if no authentication mechanism is in place. Unlike a firewall, the protection agent does not present a single point of failure. If it is down, the field network would still operate as usual, which is not the case for a firewall.

5 Conclusions

The instrumentation and control of a power grid is usually carried out by a SCADA system which is a distributed network of cyber-physical devices taking measurements and issuing commands at different parts of a power grid. Obscurity and operation in isolation have long been the security strategy of SCADA systems. However, this is no longer a reasonable assumption for SCADA systems in the smart grid context with the need of connectivity with other relatively open networks. False command injection is a real threat to legacy SCADA systems. While effective security mechanisms and algorithms for command authentication are largely an overkill for implementation on field devices in legacy SCADA systems, these devices would normally take decades to be phased out as they are closely integrated with the power equipment. This paper discusses and compares two different approaches, namely, the data diode strategy and the detect-and-respond strategy, to secure legacy SCADA systems for safe integration with other smart grid systems. A detailed comparison of the two approaches can be found in Table 3.

The detect-and-respond strategy proposed in this paper presents a number of advantages for securing legacy SCADA systems, including scalability and usability for a wide range of smart grid scenarios. The proposed framework is also generally applicable to different SCADA protocols and systems, while a concrete instantiation on Siemens Sinaut 8FW protocol is presented in this paper. While the data diode strategy offers the highest level of security guarantee, it can only be applied to a restricted number of use cases wherein unidirectional data exchange suffices. In contrast, the detect-and-respond strategy is a more flexible approach which can be applied in almost all scenarios but generally offer a lower level of security guarantee and is more complex to design.

Table 3. Comparison between the data diode and detect-and-respond strategy

	Data diode	Detect-and-respond
Security assurance	Highest (EAL7)	Medium to High
Applicable cases	Limited range	Wide range
Pros	- Isolation preserved with a high level of security - No modifications on field devices required - Highly scalable, with only one data diode required per system	- Flexible to incorporate other techniques for attack detection and neutralization - Allow bidirectional data exchange - No modification on field devices required - Scalable
Cons	- Only allow unidirectional data flow from SCADA systems to other systems - Little flexibility	- More complex design required to maintain security - Design strongly dependent on the SCADA protocols in use

References

1. Alcaraz, C., Agudo, I., Nuñez, D., López, J.: Managing incidents in smart grids à la cloud. In: Proceedings of IEEE CloudCom 2011, pp. 527–531 (2011)
2. Alcaraz, C., López, J., Wolthusen, S.D.: Policy enforcement system for secure interoperable control in distributed smart grid systems. J. Netw. Comput. Appl. **59**, 301–314 (2016)
3. Alcaraz, C., López, J., Zhou, J., Roman, R.: Secure SCADA framework for the protection of energy control systems. Concurr. Comput. Pract. Exp. **23**(12), 1431–1442 (2011)
4. Amoah, R., Camtepe, S., Foo, E.: Securing DNP3 broadcast communications in SCADA systems. IEEE Trans. Industr. Inf. **12**(4), 1474–1485 (2016)
5. Bowen, C.L., Buennemeyer, T.K., Thomas, R.W.: Next generation SCADA security: best practices and client puzzles. In: Proceedings of the 6th Annual IEEE SMC Information Assurance Workshop, June 2005
6. Bratus, S., Hansen, A., Shubina, A.: LZfuzz: a fast compression-based fuzzer for poorly documented protocols. Darmouth Computer Science, Technical report TR2008-634, September 2008
7. Castellanos, J.H., Antonioli, D., Tippenhauer, N.O., Ochoa, M.: Legacy-compliant data authentication for industrial control system traffic. In: Gollmann, D., Miyaji, A., Kikuchi, H. (eds.) ACNS 2017. LNCS, vol. 10355, pp. 665–685. Springer, Cham (2017). https://doi.org/10.1007/978-3-319-61204-1_33
8. Chan, A.C.-F., Wong, J.W., Zhou, J., Teo, J.: Scalable two-factor authentication using historical data. In: Askoxylakis, I., Ioannidis, S., Katsikas, S., Meadows, C. (eds.) ESORICS 2016. LNCS, vol. 9878, pp. 91–110. Springer, Cham (2016). https://doi.org/10.1007/978-3-319-45744-4_5
9. Common Criteria. Common methodology for information technology security evaluation, Rev. 5 (ISO/IEC 18045), April 2017
10. de Freitas, M.B., Rosa, L., Cruz, T., Simões, P.: SDN-Enabled virtual data diode. In: Katsikas, S.K., et al. (eds.) SECPRE/CyberICPS -2018. LNCS, vol. 11387, pp. 102–118. Springer, Cham (2019). https://doi.org/10.1007/978-3-030-12786-2_7
11. Hahn, A.: Cyber security of the smart grid: attack exposure analysis, detection algorithms, and testbed evaluation. Iowa State University Graduate Theses and Dissertations (2013)

12. Hasan, M.M., Mouftah, H.T.: Optimization of trust node assignment for securing routes in smart grid SCADA networks. IEEE Syst. J. **13**(2), 1505–1513 (2018)
13. He, Y., Mendis, J., Wei, J.: Real-time detection of false data injection attacks in smart grid: a deep learning-based intelligent mechanism. IEEE Trans. Smart Grid **8**(5), 2505–2516 (2017)
14. Heine, E., Khurana, H., Yardley, T.: Exploring convergence for SCADA networks. In: Proceedings of the ISGT 2011, January 2011
15. Herder, C., Yu, M.-D.M., Koushanfar, F., Devadas, S.: Physical unclonable functions and applications: a tutorial. Proc. IEEE **102**(8), 1126–1141 (2014)
16. Humayed, A., Lin, J., Li, F., Luo, B.: Cyber-physical systems security – a survey. IEEE Internet Things J. **4**(6), 1802–1831 (2017)
17. Langner, R.: Stuxnet: dissecting a cyberwarfare weapon. IEEE Secur. Priv. **9**(3), 49–51 (2011)
18. Lin, H., Slagell, A., Kalbarczyk, Z.T., Sauer, P.W., Iyer, R.K.: Runtime semantic security analysis to detect and mitigate control-related attacks in power grids. IEEE Trans. Smart Grid **9**(1), 163–178 (2016)
19. McLaughlin, S., Konstantinou, C., Wang, X., Davi, L., Sadeghi, A.-R., Karri, R.: The cyber-security landscape in industrial control systems. Proc. IEEE **104**(5), 1039–1057 (2016)
20. Modbus. Modbus over serial line – specification and implementation guide V1.02. Modbus Documentation, December 2006
21. Nakibly, G., Kirshon, A., Gonikman, D., Boneh, D.: Persistent OSPF attacks. In: Proceedings of the NDSS 2012, February 2012
22. Nazir, S., Patel, S., Patel, D.: Assessing and augmenting SCADA cyber security: a survey of techniques. Comput. Secur. **70**, 436–454 (2017)
23. Nourian, A., Madnick, S.: A systems theoretic approach to the security threats in cyber physical systems applied to Stuxnet. IEEE Trans. Dependable Secure Comput. **15**(1), 2–13 (2018)
24. Okhravi, H., Sheldon, F.T.: Data diodes in support of trustworthy cyber infrastructure. In: Proceedings of the CSIIRW 2010, pp. 1–4, April 2010
25. Pappu, R., Recht, B., Taylor, J., Gershenfeld, N.: Physical one-way functions. Science **297**, 2026–2030 (2002)
26. Pidikiti, D.S., Kalluri, R., Kumar, R.K.S., Bindhumadhava, B.S.: SCADA communication protocols: vulnerabilities, attacks and possible mitigations. CSIT **1**, 135–141 (2013)
27. Siemens. SINAUT ST-7 station control system – system manual. SINAUT Documentation, Edition 05/2001, May 2001
28. Tweed, K.: Bulletproofing the grid. IEEE Spectr. **51**(5), 13–14 (2014)
29. Wright, A.K., Kinast, J.A., McCarty, J.: Low-latency cryptographic protection for SCADA communications. In: Jakobsson, M., Yung, M., Zhou, J. (eds.) ACNS 2004. LNCS, vol. 3089, pp. 263–277. Springer, Heidelberg (2004). https://doi.org/10.1007/978-3-540-24852-1_19
30. Yun, J.-H., Chang, Y., Kim, K.-H., Kim, W.: Security validation for data diode with reverse channel. In: Havarneanu, G., Setola, R., Nassopoulos, H., Wolthusen, S. (eds.) CRITIS 2016. LNCS, vol. 10242, pp. 271–282. Springer, Cham (2017). https://doi.org/10.1007/978-3-319-71368-7_23

Cloud S&P – Cloud Security and Privacy

RATLS: Integrating Transport Layer Security with Remote Attestation

Robert Walther[1], Carsten Weinhold[2(✉)], and Michael Roitzsch[2]

[1] Technische Universität Dresden, Dresden, Germany
`robert.walther@mailbox.tu-dresden.de`
[2] Barkhausen Institut, Dresden, Germany
{`carsten.weinhold`,`michael.roitzsch`}`@barkhauseninstitut.org`

Abstract. We present RATLS, a companion library for OpenSSL that integrates the Trusted Computing concept of Remote Attestation into Transport Layer Security (TLS). RATLS builds upon handshake extensions that are specified in version 1.3 of the TLS standard. It therefore does not require any changes to the TLS protocol or the OpenSSL library, which offers a suitable API for handshake extensions. RATLS supports remote attestation as part of a complete TLS handshake for new connections and it augments session resumption by binding session tickets to the platform state of TLS peers. We demonstrate that RATLS enables both client and server to attest their respective software stacks using widely-used Trusted Platform Modules. Our evaluation shows that the number of round trips during handshake is the same as for traditional TLS and that session resumption can reduce cryptographic overhead caused by remote attestation for frequently communicating peers.

Keywords: TLS · TPM · Remote attestation · Trusted computing

1 Introduction

Transport Layer Security (TLS) [10] is the state-of-the-art protocol for securing communication channels between two computers. It uses encryption and message authentication codes (MACs) to ensure confidentiality and integrity for all information that is transmitted over the communication channel. TLS also provides authentication to ensure that only the "right" communication partners can successfully establish a TLS connection. The authentication method used by TLS requires users to trust that the party who operates the remote computer acting as a TLS peer will keep this computer secure. Typically, if Alice wants to exchange data over TLS with a computer operated by Bob, she has to make two assumptions: 1) Bob keeps the cryptographic keys needed for TLS authentication secret, and 2) the software running on Bob's computer does what he claims it does (e.g., not leak data received from Alice).

The Need for Verifiable Trust. Unfortunately, TLS on its own cannot provide a verifiable proof that assumptions 1) and 2) actually hold. In certain highly-critical use cases, such a proof is desirable, though. For example, Alice might

J. Zhou et al. (Eds.): ACNS 2022 Workshops, LNCS 13285, pp. 361–379, 2022.
https://doi.org/10.1007/978-3-031-16815-4_20

want an assurance that her valuable scientific data will only be processed by a certain, trusted analysis program running on the cloud server that Bob rented to her. And in an Internet-of-Things (IoT) scenario, lives might be at stake if an attacker manages to manipulate the firmware of an IoT device. The risk that TLS keys (assumption 1) and software integrity (assumption 2) are compromised are much greater for a connected device that must be installed in a public place, compared to a server behind the walls of a guarded data center. Thus, technical measures are needed to reduce the trust in the operator of a remote computer or the environment that surrounds it.

Trusted Computing. *Remote Attestation* is a cryptographic protocol that can complement TLS by solving the two trust problems described above. First, it is built on top of hardware support that is designed to protect cryptographic secrets. Second, it provides one computer, the *challenger*, with a verifiable proof that software running on another computer, the *attester*, is in a known-good state. It works as follows:

1. **Identifiability:** The attester has a root of trust integrated into its hardware that includes a cryptographic identity that cannot be forged. Through this identity, the challenger can know what the attester device is and what its capabilities are.
2. **Integrity:** The root of trust can create a digital signature over the code of the software that has been started on the attester. Through this signature, the challenger can know, if the software currently running on the attester will be behave as required. Typically, the signature covers both system-level code and applications, including the TLS protocol implementation that protects the communication channel.

Roots of trust are much harder to compromise than pure software solutions because the attacker has to manipulate tamper-resistant hardware. They are available in various forms for many different platforms. A well-known implementation is the Trusted Platform Module (TPM) [4], which is nowadays built into most desktops, laptops, and many servers.

TLS with Remote Attestation. Despite the clear security advantages, Remote Attestation is complicated to deploy for application developers. No standardized protocol suite exists, but different root-of-trust implementations come with their own protocol and software development kit. RATLS intends to simplify the use of attestation by integrating it into the widely-used TLS protocol. The integration leverages a feature of the TLS v1.3 standard [10], where applications can append user-defined extensions to TLS handshake messages. Using this mechanism, RATLS is able to piggyback attestation-related messages onto TLS handshake messages. The RATLS approach can be applied to any TLS implementation that supports handshake extensions. We built RATLS as a companion library for the widely-used OpenSSL [2] implementation, which provides a suitable extensions API. The design of RATLS is also agnostic to the underlying hardware root of trust. In this paper, we describe an RATLS plugin that works with the widely-used TPM v2.0.

Contribution. Our work on RATLS makes the following contributions:

- RATLS integrates remote attestation into TLS, thereby enabling verification of the identity and software integrity of peers communicating via TLS.
- RATLS does not require changes to the TLS protocol nor modifications to OpenSSL, thereby demonstrating that the approach is non-invasive.
- RATLS supports both full handshakes for new connections and TLS session resumption for efficient reconnects.
- We evaluate API usability, security properties, and performance of an RATLS prototype implementation using TPM v2.0-based roots of trust.

In the following Sect. 2, we describe relevant background. Sections 3 and 4 present the design and implementation, respectively, and in Sect. 5, we evaluate RATLS. We discuss related work in Sect. 6 before concluding paper in the Sect. 7.

2   Background

In this section, we describe the basics of TLS. We highlight those features of the standard that are important for RATLS. Furthermore, we give an overview over trusted computing concepts that enable remote attestation and secure storage.

2.1   Transport Layer Security

TLS enables two computers to communicate securely over an untrusted network. The protocol is based on cryptography and it guarantees confidentiality and integrity for all user data that is transmitted through the communication channel. Two computers that wish to communicate over TLS must authenticate themselves to each other. In the most common scenario, one peer, the *server*, proves its identity through possession of the private key of an asymmetric signature key pair. The other communication partner, the *client*, can validate the identity of the server using a publicly-known *server certificate* that contains the public part of said key pair. Optionally, the client can also authenticate itself to the server using its own private key and a corresponding *client certificate*. In so-called zero-trust communication scenarios using *mutual TLS (mTLS)*, certificate-based authentication is mandatory for both peers.

Security Assumptions. For all these variants of TLS, the attacker model assumes that the private key used by a TLS peer is exclusively known to the party that operates this peer. For example, if Bob operates a TLS-protected server, then only Bob shall know the private key used by his server. Likewise, only Alice shall be in possession of the private key used by her TLS client. A computer operated by a third party like Eve can impersonate neither Alice's nor Bob's machines, because she does not know their respective private keys. The encryption and signature algorithms as well as the hash-based MAC schemes in TLS v1.3 are state of the art and considered secure.

TLS Handshake and Extensions. One TLS peer, the client, initiates the secure communication by sending a `ClientHello`. The server replies with a `ServerHello` message, which the client acknowledges in a third message. As part of this three-phase handshake, the client and server present each other their certificates and they negotiate the symmetric *session keys* for encrypting and integrity-protecting the payload data that is transmitted after the channel has been established. In TLS v1.3, an application program can request the TLS implementation to append user-defined extensions to certain TLS messages, including handshake messages[1]. Extensions can contain up 64 KiB of arbitrary data. They must follow a request–response scheme, where a specific extension can only be appended to a reply message, if the previous message also contained an extension of the same user-defined type.

TLS Session Resumption. Creating and validating signatures and exchanging session keys incurs computational overhead. Furthermore, during the three-phase TLS handshake, both client and server must wait for replies to arrive over a potentially slow network, before they can continue with the protocol. To speed up connection establishment between frequently communicating peers, TLS v1.3 supports *session resumption*. Using this optimization, a client can reopen a previously closed TLS session by sending a `ClientHello` message with a *session ticket* that the server issued to the client while the original connection was active. If the server recognizes the session ticket, only one network round trip is needed instead of two round trips for the complete handshake. With session resumption, both client and server skip the certificate exchange and key negotiation, as they can reuse the session keys from the original connection.

2.2 Trusted Computing

The core idea behind *trusted computing* is to verify through technical means that a computer and the software running on it conform to certain security properties. This verification can be performed remotely from a second, already trusted device in the case of *remote attestation*. But given the right hardware and system-software support, trusted-computing concepts can also be used to verify software that is running locally, like in the case of *sealed memory*.

Remote Attestation. In the first use case, a trusted *challenger* device requests an *attestation report* from a remote computer called the *attester*. Like TLS, the underlying cryptographic protocol uses the private part of a signature key pair[2] to prove its identity. However, in contrast to TLS, which is pure software, an implementation of remote attestation typically requires a hardware root of trust that is integrated into the hardware of the attester device.[3] This root of trust

---

[1] TLS v1.2 supports extensions, too, but on fewer message types than TLS v1.3.

[2] Some implementations use symmetric keys or a physically unclonable function (PUF) instead, but the general concept is the same.

[3] There are implementations of remote attestation that are software only, but they assume a weaker attacker model.

hides the private key in hardware to make it more difficult to forge. The root of trust signs the executable code that is currently in control of the attester. If the challenger recognizes that the signature has been created by a root of trust that it deems trustworthy, it will know what kind of device the attester is and what software is running on it. Based on the information in the attestation report (e.g., a hash of the executable code on the attester), the challenger can then decide whether to trust the attester's software for the purpose it is interested in.

Sealed Memory. An attestation can also be done locally by the root of trust on the attester device. Some trusted-computing platforms use local attestation to protect confidentiality of user data by encrypting it with a storage key that is also hidden in the hardware root of trust. The root of trust will only release or *unseal* the plaintext copy of the data to the currently running software, if the identity of this software is the one that has been specified as the "owner" when the data had been *sealed*. Thus, it is possible to *bind* (i.e., restrict access to) user data to a specific, *authorized* software configuration.

Trusted Platform Modules. A widely-used and thoroughly standardized root of trust implementation is the Trusted Platform Module (TPM) [4]. TPMs can create remote attestation reports (called *quotes*) and they support sealed memory. Quotes are computed over a set of *Platform Configuration Registers (PCRs)*, which store hashes of the software stack that has been started (ranging from firmware over bootloader and OS to application programs). Like all roots of trust, TPMs require operating-system support in terms of a device driver and other system-level integration. This support includes the so-called *TPM Software Stack (TSS)* [3] through which applications can interact with the TPM.

In the following, we will refer to the combination of root of trust and its system-level support software as the *Attestation Provider*. We will also use *Quote* as a synonym for "attestation report", as this term is commonly used for many root-of-trust implementations. RATLS integrates remote attestation into the TLS handshake and it uses sealed memory to bind TLS session tickets to the software configuration that was valid at the time of the initial handshake. Sealed memory can also be used to protect TLS private keys, in addition to the identity keys of the root of trust that are already hidden in hardware. Our prototype implementation is based on a TPM v2.0-based attestation provider.

3   Design

TLS already provides confidentiality and integrity for all data sent through the communication channel. Our main goal in improving it is twofold: 1) to enhance authentication of TLS endpoints through additional identity checking, and 2) to provide technical means for verifying the software integrity on these endpoints. Thus, our aim for RATLS is to augment TLS with remote attestation such that it provides additional security guarantees.

3.1 Design Goals

In the following paragraphs, we define security goals as well as functional and non-functional goals for the design of RATLS.

Freshness of Attestation Reports. To prevent replay attacks, it is essential that pre-generation of attestation reports is not possible. Otherwise, an attacker could intercept a valid attestation report and send it again when trying to spoof an identity in an impersonation attack. To prevent replay attacks, RATLS must include a *nonce*, which is generated by the challenger, in each attestation report issued by the attester.

Mutual Attestation. In many distributed-computing use cases, both parties need to trust each other. For example, in so-called zero-trust scenarios in cloud environments, multiple services communicate with each other over TLS and both client and server must authenticate themselves. To fully support such mutual TLS (mTLS) connections, RATLS should enable *mutual attestation* as well. Thus, both the client and the server shall be able to request an attestation report from their respective peer.

Minimal Number of Handshake Messages. Round-trip messages require both client and server to wait, which is particularly costly in case of high-latency networks. Therefore, RATLS should not increase the number of handshake messages that need to be sent and received during handshake. We consider both one-sided and mutual remote attestation for this design goal.

Session Resumption. In environments where connections are opened and closed frequently between the same peers, the TLS standard allows a client to resume a recently-closed session instead of performing the complete TLS handshake with the server again. To keep the benefits of this optimization, RATLS shall support TLS session resumption in a way that minimizes the cryptography-related costs for creating and validating attestation reports.

"Don't Roll Your Own Crypto". The TLS standard and its implementations have been subject to extensive review by a huge number of experts in the fields of computer security and distributed-systems engineering. Therefore, we must avoid changes to the TLS protocol and, ideally, RATLS should even be compatible with an existing TLS implementation without further modifications. These two sub-goals minimize the risk of RATLS introducing new security vulnerabilities. They also reduce maintenance overhead and make it easier to keep RATLS up to date with future TLS standards and implementations thereof.

Low-Barrier Adoption. The API offered by RATLS should be as simple as possible and closely follow the API of the TLS implementation it improves upon. This simplicity will make it easy for application developers to upgrade their communication from traditional TLS to TLS with remote attestation.

Separation of Concept and Realization. Remote attestation is a Trusted-Computing concept, but to use it in practice, it needs to be implemented for a concrete computer platform with a suitable hardware root of trust. Therefore, we aim to integrate the platform-independent concept of remote attestation in RATLS, but keep separate the support for specific attestation providers as "plugins" that extend the RALTS implementation.

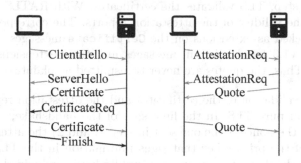

Fig. 1. Simplified visualization of the TLS v1.3 handshake (left) and protocol steps of remote attestation (right)

3.2   High-Level Design

The two sequence diagrams in Fig. 1 show simplified visualizations of the TLS v1.3 handshake (left) and the steps of the remote attestation protocol (right). Groups of arrows pointing in the same direction represent protocol information that can be transmitted in a single batched message. For example, in the TLS handshake, the server can send the `ServerHello`, `Certificate`, and `CertificateReq` messages in a single reply to the `ClientHello` message. The green and blue colors highlight conceptual similarities between establishing a TLS connection and performing a remote attestation. They give an idea of how the two protocols could be folded into one combined handshake, which establishes a mutually-authenticated TLS connection with mutual remote attestation between client and server running in parallel.

Combined RATLS Handshake. RATLS builds upon handshake extensions, which have been standardized in TLS v1.3 [10]. They allow an application to append arbitrary information to the TLS messages that are exchanged during the three-phase TLS handshake. The combined handshake works as follows:

1. At the beginning of the TLS handshake, the client and the server send the `ClientHello` and `ServerHello` messages, respectively. RATLS appends to these messages the attestation requests of both peers. An `AttestationReq` message carries a nonce that the sender picked randomly in its role as a remote-attestation challenger.
2. In their role as the attester in the remote-attestation protocol, the client and server request a quote from the attestation provider of their respective devices. Each quote includes the nonce received from the respective challenger

and the recorded state of the software on the attester. Each attester must also include the public counterpart to its TLS private key in the attestation report. By including the public key, both parts of the combined handshake are cryptographically linked.

3. In the final step, TLS validates the certificates. With RATLS, both parties also check the validity of the attestation reports. The corresponding quotes are piggybacked as extensions on the `Certificate` messages. At this stage of the TLS v1.3 handshake, all messages and their extensions are already encrypted. Thus, the quotes are never transmitted as plaintext.

The combined validation of the certificates and the attestation reports is more complex than in pure TLS. In the final step of the handshake, the challenger verifies that 1) the nonce is the one sent in step 1, and 2) the attester is indeed in possession of the private key that signs information in the TLS part of the handshake. To do that, it compares the public keys (embedded in the client and server certificates) from the `Certificate` message to those in the quote. If the public keys match, the connection is indeed end-to-end encrypted between the client and server. In case of a mismatch of either the nonce or the public key, a man-in-the-middle attack has been attempted and the handshake must be aborted to prevent an insecure (i.e., not end-to-end encrypted) connection.

Properties of the RATLS Handshake. By piggybacking attestation-related information on the three batches of TLS messages, we can integrate remote attestation into TLS without additional network round trips. The combination of both protocols is also convenient from application's point of view. Once the combined RATLS handshake completed, both client-side and server-side applications can be certain that the hardware identity and software integrity of the remote peer have been verified and found to be trustworthy. If one of the peers does not need an attestation report from the other party, it can just omit the `AttestationReq` extension in its `ClientHello` or `ServerHello` message.

Session Resumption. When the client resumes a previously closed TLS session, some parts of the handshake, including certificate exchange, are skipped. Instead, the client presents to the server a session ticket that includes the previously negotiated session keys. This *resume handshake* is shorter and therefore the remote-attestation protocol cannot be piggybacked on it. To provide the additional security guarantees of remote attestation also with session resumption, we borrow from TLS the idea of keeping session secrets for later use. In a nutshell, our variation of the approach in RATLS works as follows:

1. During the lifetime of a TLS session, the server sends a `NewSessionTicket` message to the client. This message carries the session ticket that the client can later use to resume the session. In RATLS, the server creates a pair of additional secrets, namely a *client secret* and a *server secret*. It appends these secrets to the `NewSessionTicket` message and when the client receives this message, it stores the server secret in sealed memory. The server keeps a copy of these secrets, too. It seals the client secret.

2. When an RATLS-enabled client resumes the session at a later point in time, it unseals the server secret. It appends this secret to the `ClientHello` message and sends it to the server. The server does the same with the client secret, which it will send to the client in its `ServerHello` reply. Both client and server then compare the received secrets with their locally stored copies.

We introduce the client and server secrets, because OpenSSL's API does not allow RATLS seal, discard, and later unseal session tickets. By sealing the secrets, the client and server bind them to the software states that have previously been attested as part of the RATLS handshake. The capability of the client and server to unseal the secrets at a later time is used to prove that the session had originally been established between remotely attested RATLS peer.

We discuss further details about RATLS session resumption and all other parts of the implementation in the following Sect. 4.

4   Implementation

In this section, we describe an implementation of RATLS that is compatible with the widely-used OpenSSL library. We describe in detail how the combined RATLS handshake works, both for new connections and for session resumption. We will also describe the plugin API for attestation providers and an example implementation of such a plugin for TPMs.

4.1   Architecture

The general design of RATLS is independent of both the TLS implementation and the attestation provider that is needed for a specific computer platform. Although message extensions are part of the TLS v1.3 standard, not all TLS libraries support them. The OpenSSL library does offer an API, which is based on user-defined callbacks. We therefore built a companion library to OpenSSL that implements our RATLS prototype as a callback-driven state machine on top of this interface.

OpenSSL API for Message Extensions. Whenever OpenSSL creates or consumes a TLS protocol message during the lifetime of a TLS session, it calls a function that RATLS registered for the corresponding OpenSSL session context (`SSLContext`). We refer to these two functions as `AddCallback` and `ParseCallback`, respectively. Before sending a message, OpenSSL invokes the `AddCallback` for any extensions that have been registered for that specific message. The callbacks can specify whether or not to add the extension and what data to populate it with. When receiving a message, OpenSSL calls the `ParseCallback` for all registered extensions. In this `ParseCallback`, we can extract the extension data and also decide whether to abort or continue the handshake. There is no way in OpenSSL to define a callback for a missing extension. If the extension is not set, no callback is invoked. Also, according to the specification, TLS v1.3 does not allow applications to freely add extensions to arbitrary messages. Instead, extensions can only be appended if the same extension has already been added to the corresponding, previously received message. For example, to add an extension to the `Certificate` message on the server side, the same extension must be set in the `ClientHello` message.

RATLS State Management. OpenSSL defines additional callbacks for events such as creation of a new session or certificate verification. RALTLS registers appropriate callback functions for all relevant events. When invoked by OpenSSL, each of these callbacks receives a pointer to the current SSL session object. In this object, the RATLS functions maintain an additional `RASession` that represents the attestation-related state during the lifetime of the session. The complete set of RATLS callback functions implement the generic concept of remote attestation for TLS.

Attestation Provider Callbacks. Each of the RATLS functions invokes another callback function that is implemented by an attestation provider plugin. This second layer of callbacks separates the platform-specific root of trust and its system-level support software from the generic parts of RATLS. When the application initializes OpenSSL and RATLS, it must register the callbacks of the attestation provider with their generic counterparts in the RATLS library.

4.2 RATLS Handshake with Remote Attestation

The sequence diagram in Fig. 2 visualizes the complete, mutual handshake for both client and server attestation. For readability reasons, we explain in the following paragraphs only how the server attests to the client. The steps for attesting the client's identity and software state to the server are analogous and interleaved in the RATLS handshake as shown in Fig. 2.

Request Phase. Each TLS handshake starts with a `ClientHello` message sent by the client to the server. If RATLS has been enabled for the specific `SSLContext`, OpenSSL invokes the `AddCallback` for the remote attestation request (`RA_REQ`) extension. The `AddCallback` invokes another callback function for generating an `RA_REQ`. This `CreateRequest` callback is provided by the attestation provider. It is called in the client's role as the challenger of the remote-attestation protocol and its main purpose is to randomly generate a nonce.

Attestation Phase. Upon receiving the `ClientHello` message, the server detects the `RA_REQ` extension and invokes the `ParseCallback`. The server stores the client's nonce in the `RASession` part of OpenSSL's SSL session object, such that the next RATLS callback function can retrieve the nonce from there. The handshake continues until the server intends to send the `Certificate` message. OpenSSL calls the RATLS `AddCallback`, this time for the remote attestation response (`RA_RES`) extension. From this callback, RATLS invokes the `RemoteAttest` function of the attestation provider plugin with the previously stored nonce as a parameter. In the `RemoteAttest` function, the server's attestation provider creates a quote of the client's nonce, the TLS public key, and the system state. The user-defined data that has been passed via `CreateRequest` will also be included in the quote. RATLS appends the quote to the `Certificate` message.

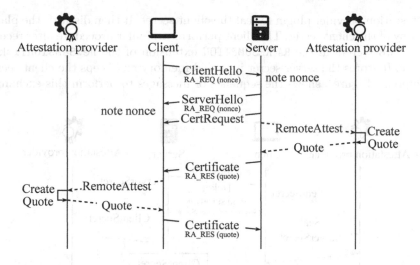

Fig. 2. Remote attested handshake

Verification Phase. When RATLS on the client receives the `Certificate` message via the `ParseCallback`, it stores the server's quote in the client-side `RASession` for later use. Later, OpenSSL invokes the certificate-validation callback of RATLS. Here, RATLS checks if the client application originally requested an attestation. This information is expresses as a flag in the `RASession`. If the flag is true and the server ignored the request, the handshake is aborted. If the server did append an `RA_RES` extension with a quote, RATLS calls the attestation provider's `CheckQuote` function with the original nonce and the received quote as a parameter. In it's role as remote-attestation challenger, it then checks the quote's signature, compares the copies of the public key in the TLS certificate and the quote, and aborts the handshake if there is a mismatch. The `CheckQuote` function also decides whether the server's software state as reported in the quote is acceptable or not.

4.3 RATLS Handshake with Session Resumption

When the client resumes a TLS session, RATLS uses the same callback-based approach to create and inspect message extensions.

Binding Phase. Session resumption requires a preparatory step while a TLS session is active. The specification allows the server to send a `NewSessionTicket` message at any point during the lifetime of this session. When that happens, a server-side RATLS callback function creates and appends two new secrets, the *client secret* and the *server secret*, to this message. On the server, RATLS keeps the server secret in plaintext, but it invokes the `SealSecret` callback function of its attestation provider plugin to seal the client secret. It then discards the plaintext copy of the client secret. The client performs a similar procedure after receiving the two secrets in the RA_RESUMPTION extension of the NewSessionTicket message. It stores the server secret in sealed memory and keeps the client secret in plaintext. Figure 3 shows the sequence of messages to perform this exchange.

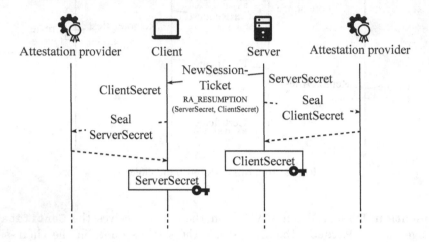

Fig. 3. Attested ticket issuing

Unseal and Resume Phase. As explained at the end of Sect. 3.2, OpenSSL does not allow RATLS to access the session ticket. Instead the client must append the server secret to the ClientHello message when it wants to resume an RATLS-enabled session. Since it discarded the plaintext copy after sealing this secret, RATLS must first unseal it using the UnsealSecret function of its attestation provider plugin. When the server receives the session ticket and the client's copy of the server secret via the ClientHello message, it looks up the secret that matches the session ticket. It then compares the client's version of this secret with its own, locally found copy. It allows the session to resume, if the two copies of the client secret match and the session ticket is valid. As shown in Fig. 4, the server proves the capability to access its previously sealed copy of the client secret in the same way.

Security of Session Resumption. Because of the way the TLS protocol works, the NewSessionTicket message and its RA_RESUMPTION extension are end-to-end encrypted between client and server. However, when resuming, the RA_RESUMPTION extension attached to the ClientHello must be transmitted in plaintext and the server secret is potentially revealed to an observing attacker. Nevertheless, an impersonation attack cannot be mounted using just the server secret:

1. TLS Session tickets are cryptographically bound to the client and server that negotiated a TLS session. Therefore only a specific pair of client and server

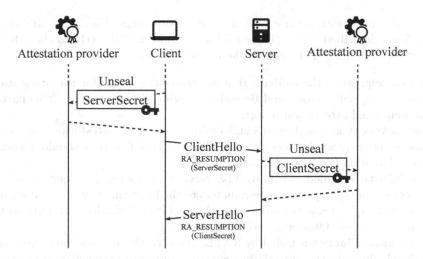

Fig. 4. Resumed attested handshake

processes have access to the pre-shared session keys associated with the session ticket. Well-behaving TLS clients and servers do not compromise session tickets and keys.

2. If there is a client and server secret for a session ticket, this session ticket has been exchanged between two computers whose software stacks have been verified and found to use well-behaving TLS implementations based on remote attestation during the initial, non-resume handshake.

3. The fact that a server secret (or client secret) is presented during a resume handshake means that the software on the client (or server) has been in the correct state at the time of the resumption attempt. Otherwise, the attestation provider of the respective device could not have successfully unsealed the plaintext secret that the well-behaving RATLS implementation discarded before. The pre-shared session key are required to complete the handshake.

Thus, despite their name, the client and server secrets are not used for cryptographic purposes or as an authentication token. Instead, they merely serve as a hint that the session that is being resumed has been previously negotiated with a well-behaving client or server that must still be in the same software and hardware state as at the time of the attestation. An eavesdropper has no use for the secrets as the session is still cryptograhpically bound to the TLS session ticket.

4.4 Attestation Provider Plugins

RATLS integrates the concept of remote attestation into the TLS handshake but leaves the implementation open to a specific attestation provider. All attestation provider-specific functionality is offloaded to callbacks. This allows RATLS to be easily used with a variety of attestation providers. The API callbacks of RATLS are described below. These callbacks could map directly to the attestation provider plugins API, making them trivial to use:

- `CreateRequest` is the callback that generates the nonce for the attestation. Also user specific data could be included, which in turn then is also part of the generated attestation report.
- `RemoteAttest` is called by RATLS upon receiving an attestation request. It passes the requested nonce to the callback. This function should return a quote based on the requested nonce.
- `CheckQuote` is called, when RATLS received a quote. This quote and the expected nonce are passed as parameters to the function. The function returns true, if the quote comes from a trusted attestation provider and matches the requested nonce. Otherwise, false is returned.
- `SealSessionSecret` is called by RATLS upon receiving a session secret. This callback binds the secret to the system state and returns the encrypted session secret.
- `UnsealSessionSecret` is the inverse operation to `SealSessionSecret`. It unseals the secret and returns it as plaintext.

RATLS must register two callback functions in the OpenSSL context to work as intended. If an application registered its own callbacks for the same OpenSSL handshake events, it would disable RATLS. Therefore, RATLS provides the following replacement callbacks, which such an application can use instead:

- `CustomNewSession` mirrors the functionality of the `new_session_cb` callback in OpenSSL. It gets called when a session ticket is issued or received.
- `CustomVerifyCallback` mirrors the `verify_callback` and is invoked when OpenSSL verifies the certificate chain.

Customization. Registering these two callbacks is optional. Furthermore, the behavior of RATLS can be adjusted by the following parameters:

- `maxSessionTicketsNum` specifies the maximum number of session tickets that RATLS should keep stored, making it possible to limit the memory footprint.
- `onlyAllowRemoteAttestedSessionResumption` can be specified on the client side to prevent the use of session tickets that resulted from unattested sessions.
- `forceClientRemoteAttestation` is a server-side parameter. When set to true, the server will abort the handshake, if the client has not attested itself. When false, unattested TLS connections are accepted, too.

RATLS_TPM2. RATLS comes with a sample implementation of an attestation provider plugin for TPM v2.0-based roots of trust. The RATLS_TPM2 plugin is based on Microsoft's TSS.MSR [5] library, which allows communication with both hardware and software TPMs. We use the C++ version of TSS.MSR, which we extended with a driver back-end class for accessing TPMs via the `/dev/tpm0` character device on Linux. RATLS_TPM2 provides all callback functions that

RATLS needs and it performs all TPM_Quote, TPM_Seal, and TPM_Unseal operations that a TPM v2.0 attestation provider must use to fulfill its purpose. It also verifies quotes using TSS.MSR, as a real implementation would do, but with demonstration-only TPM storage and attestation keys.

5   Evaluation

In this section, we evaluate the usability, security, and performance of our RATLS prototype implementation.

5.1   Usability

Activating RATLS for a specific OpenSSL context is as simple as performing one initialization call. After that all handshakes in that context are attested. To use RATLS with a specific attestation provider, the application just needs to register the callback functions of the plugin library.

5.2   Security

RATLS is about integrating the concept of remote attestation into TLS, but its security guarantees build upon the underlying attestation provider and its system-level integration. These lower layers must ensure secure startup of applications that use RATLS. They also provide the functionality that RATLS needs to request quotes that attest identity, integrity, and possession of certain secrets for the system and application using RATLS. However, the specifics of their implementation are out of scope for this paper, as RATLS does not need to alter the quote format employed by the underlying root of trust. It transmits each quote as an opaque piece of data. Furthermore, RATLS does not alter the TLS protocol or its implementation, but rather extends OpenSSL through publicly available interfaces. Therefore, we are confident that RATLS does not individually weaken the security properties of remote attestation or TLS. However, two potential issues remain.

Code Size. First, RATLS itself contributes additional library code to an application using it and therefore increases code complexity. Our prototype implementation adds 1, 145 and 384 lines of C++ code for RATLS and RATLS_TPM2, respectively. OpenSSL is much more complex, as the entire package consists of hundreds of thousands of lines of code. The C++ implementation of TSS.MSR comprises more than 30, 000 lines of code. Weighed against the stronger cryptographic assertions offered by attestation, we consider this a worthwhile addition.

Protocol Composition. Second, although we reuse attestation and TLS without modification, RATLS could introduce weaknesses at the meeting points of both protocols. We performed a manual audit and identified one critical point: Looking at Fig. 2, we observe that a malicious server could try to fake an attestation response in the server-side RemoteAttest step. Instead of asking its local root of trust for a quote, the server could instead become a client to a new attested handshake and pass along the quote obtained from this new connection as its own. The original client would thus receive a valid quote as part of a valid TLS connection, but from different remote machines. RATLS defends against this attack by including the public keys of the TLS certificates in the measurements that are reported by the quote. By comparing the keys in the quote and the certificate, each peer can verify that the quote it received originates from the machine terminating the TLS connection and not from a third party.

5.3 Performance

We evaluate the performance of our RATLS prototype implementation with standard, non-attested TLS as a baseline. The evaluation was carried out on two Raspberry Pi 4 single-board computers acting as client and server. Each Raspberry Pi had an Infineon Optiga SLB 9670 TPM 2.0 plugged onto the GPIO pin header of the device. Both devices were located in the same local-area network with a round-trip latency of less than half a millisecond.

Baseline. We benchmarked four variants for establishing a TLS connection: 1) mutually-attested RATLS handshake, 2) RATLS session resumption using sealing, 3) standard TLS handshakes, and 4) standard TLS session resumption. Variants 3 and 4 represent the baseline, using the same OpenSSL version and parameters as RATLS. All experiments were run 100 times. Table 1 shows the average duration to complete the handshake for all four variants and for both server and client side. Variation was low, as indicated by the standard deviation (STDEV) figures in the table.

Table 1. Comparison of RATLS and TLS handshake duration

Benchmarks	Server		Client	
	Avg. time	STDEV	Avg. time	STDEV
RATLS initial handshake	616.06 ms	2.92 ms	525.30 ms	2.88 ms
RATLS resume handshake	156.23 ms	1.42 ms	114.28 ms	1.30 ms
TLS initial handshake	52.89 ms	2.03 ms	52.60 ms	2.04 ms
TLS resume handshake	2.97 ms	0.38 ms	2.79 ms	0.37 ms

Initial Handshake Measurements. Mutually-attested RATLS handshakes are significantly slower than standard TLS handshakes without remote attestation. The observed 10x overhead is caused almost entirely by cryptographic operations being performed inside the Optiga TPM. On average, TPM_Quote and TPM_Seal operations take 212 and 42 ms, respectively. As the TLS handshake protocol forces client and server to perform their quote operations one after the other (see Fig. 2 on page 11), these costs add up for mutually-attested sessions. The measurements also include the cost for sealing the session secrets on the server. A breakdown of these costs, including the time spent on the TLS part of the protocol, is shown in Fig. 5. Note that the client receives multiple NewSessionTicket messages that trigger TPM_Seal operations. But two of these messages arrives after the handshake already completed on the client side. Hence, their costs are not captured in the client-side figures in the table, but we confirmed that the operations are performed by the client and the costs are as expected.

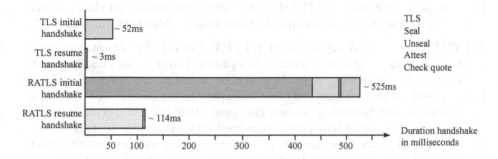

Fig. 5. Duration of client side handshakes in comparison

Resume Handshake Measurements. The TLS-only bars in Fig. 5 show that TLS session resumption can speed up TLS re-connects. Fortunately, RATLS can play the same trick to reduce the attestation-related costs. RATLS session resumption is dominated by the duration of two TPM_Unseal operations, one performed by the client and one on the server. As unsealing is cheaper on the Optiga TPM than generating a quote, RATLS re-connects are about four times faster than a complete RATLS handshake. On the server, we measured 156 ms, whereas the client finishes the resume handshake after 114 ms. Like above, for the complete handshake, this difference is caused by session-ticket messages arriving after the client-side finished the handshake.

Discussion. We acknowledge that RATLS takes significantly more time to establish a secure connection than standard TLS. However, our benchmarks represent a worst-case scenario, because discrete TPM chips like the ones we used are among the slowest roots of trust that are available. Also, the relative performance benefits of session resumption would be greater in higher-latency networks (e.g., over the Internet); we used an Ethernet link with 0.5 ms latency. The additional costs pay for the additional security guarantees that remote attestation provides.

6 Related Work

RATLS integrates remote attestation into the TLS handshake. Other works have explored integration at levels below or above the TLS protocol layer with resulting differences in usability or generality.

SGX Remote Attestation with TLS. Knauth et al. integrated attestation for Intel SGX enclaves with TLS [9]. They chose not to change or extend the TLS protocol or implementation, but included an attestation quote into the X.509 certificate used for authentication. A certificate extension is used to carry the additional information. This method of integration is fully transparent to the TLS layer and therefore works with any TLS implementation. However, a new certificate must be minted for every attestation, complicating the interaction with existing TLS certificate hierarchies. The paper therefore restricts its scope to self-signed certificates. RATLS does not alter certificates and thus can fully reuse existing certificate chains and the trust relationships they encode.

HTTPA. King and Wang proposed HTTPA, the HTTPS Attestable Protocol [8]. This work integrates attestation in a protocol layer above TLS, by proposing changes to the HTTP layer. New HTTP messages are used to exchange bidirectional attestation information. Consequently, no changes to TLS implementations or certificates are needed. However, attestation is specific to HTTP and must be integrated into application-level code. By encapsulating attestation in TLS, RATLS gives developers TLS encryption with automatic remote attestation for any application-layer protocol with just a few lines of code.

DECENT. Zheng and Arden published DECENT [11], which is an attestation system for decentralized applications consisting of multiple distributed components. These components mutually authenticate and attest themselves. In order to save expensive attestation operations, DECENT proposes mechanisms to perform attestation only once at component launch. TLS-based protocols like RATLS would have to re-attest components for every established connection. However, because we integrated session resumption, RATLS can keep attestation information alive and reusable, similarly saving expensive operations.

LightBox. Duan et al. describe an example of how trusted execution environments can be used to protect metadata of network applications. Their network middlebox system, called LightBox [6], tightly integrates with Intel SGX [1]. Their proposed design is highly optimized for operation in SGX enclaves to avoid computational overhead when handling packet routing inside an SGX enclave. Although RATLS could use SGX as an attestation provider for an application running in an SGX enclave, its goals are orthogonal. Namely, RATLS aims to integrate the concept of remote attestation into the TLS protocol, so that it can be used in a variety of applications with minimal effort on behalf of the application developer.

Benefits of Remote Attestation. Other works point out security benefits of trusted execution environments and using their roots-of-trust for remote attestation. For example, Kim et al. published [7] case studies for leveraging of SGX for privacy sensitive applications. In their use cases, they introduce attestation schemes for inter-domain routing, mix relays like TOR, and other types of middle boxes. The goals and benefits of RATLS are similar to what they present in terms of establishing a secure channel between attested endpoints or middle boxes. RATLS could be used as a building block to implement such use cases and because of its modular design, it is compatible with a variety of attestation providers besides SGX. But most importantly, our work aims to be a general solution that is easy to use. Thus, by integrating remote attestation into the TLS Handshake, RATLS makes it trivial to upgrade existing TLS connections to remote attested sessions in many other application scenarios.

7   Conclusions

In this paper, we presented the design and implementation of RATLS, which integrates the concept of Remote Attestation into the Transport Layer Security (TLS) protocol. RATLS provides additional security guarantees for authentication and software integrity of TLS endpoints. Our implementation builds upon message extensions in v1.3 of the TLS standard. This approach requires no modifications to the TLS protocol or its implementation, thereby minimizing the risk of introducing new security weaknesses. Our prototype is compatible with Trusted Platform Modules (TPMs), but thanks to a modular design, other hardware roots of trust could be supported via attestation provider plugins.

Acknowledgements. This research was co-financed by public funding of the state of Saxony/Germany. It has also received funding from the European Union's Horizon 2020 research and innovation program under grant agreement No. 957216.

References

1. Intel Software Guard Extensions (Intel SGX). https://www.intel.com/content/www/us/en/architecture-and-technology/software-guard-extensions.html. Accessed 1 May 2022
2. OpenSSL. https://www.openssl.org/
3. The Trusted Computing Group - TPM Software Stack (TSS). https://trustedcomputinggroup.org/work-groups/software-stack/
4. The Trusted Computing Group - Trusted Platform Module (TPM). https://trustedcomputinggroup.org/work-groups/trusted-platform-module/
5. TSS.MSR. https://github.com/microsoft/TSS.MSR
6. Duan, H., Wang, C., Yuan, X., Zhou, Y., Wang, Q., Ren, K.: LightBox: full-stack protected stateful middlebox at lightning speed, pp. 2351–2367 (2019). https://doi.org/10.1145/3319535.3339814
7. Kim, S., Shin, Y., Ha, J., Kim, T., Han, D.: A first step towards leveraging commodity trusted execution environments for network applications (2015). https://doi.org/10.1145/2834050.2834100
8. King, G., Wang, H.: HTTPA: HTTPS attestable protocol. CoRR **abs/2110.07954** (2021). https://arxiv.org/abs/2110.07954
9. Knauth, T., Steiner, M., Chakrabarti, S., Lei, L., Xing, C., Vij, M.: Integrating remote attestation with transport layer security. CoRR **abs/1801.05863** (2018). http://arxiv.org/abs/1801.05863
10. Rescorla, E.: The transport layer security (TLS) protocol version 1.3. RFC 8446, RFC Editor, August 2018. https://www.rfc-editor.org/rfc/rfc8446.txt
11. Zheng, H., Arden, O.: Building secure distributed applications the DECENT way. CoRR **abs/2004.02020** (2020). https://arxiv.org/abs/2004.02020

DLPFS: The Data Leakage Prevention FileSystem

Stefano Braghin$^{(\boxtimes)}$, Marco Simioni, and Mathieu Sinn

IBM Research Europe, Dublin, Ireland
{stefanob,marcosim,mathsinn}@ie.ibm.com

Abstract. Shared folders are still a common practice for granting third parties access to data files, regardless of the advances in data sharing technologies. Services like Google Drive, Dropbox, Box, and others, provide infrastructures and interfaces to manage file sharing. The human factor is the weakest link and data leaks caused by human error are regrettable common news. This takes place as both mishandled data, for example stored to the wrong directory, or via misconfigured or failing applications dumping data incorrectly. We present Data Leakage Prevention FileSystem (DLPFS), a first attempt to systematically protect against data leakage caused by misconfigured applications or human error. This filesystem interface provides a privacy protection layer on top of the POSIX filesystem interface, allowing for seamless integration with existing infrastructures and applications, simply augmenting existing security controls. At the same time, DLPFS allows data administrators to protect files shared within an organisation by preventing unauthorised parties to access potentially sensitive content. DLPFS achieves this by transparently integrating with existing access control mechanisms. We evaluate the impact of DLPFS on system's performances to demonstrate the feasibility of the proposed solution.

Keywords: Data leakage prevention · Filesystem · Data management

1 Introduction

Most of today's data breaches are due to human error caused by insiders (e.g. misconfiguration, poor data governance), rather than attacks by hackers from outside an organization[1]. Incorrectly configured applications and bugs are an ever present threat to confidentiality of sensitive data. Examples of these scenarios include log files, which might contain incorrectly handled log level messages, and thus potentially leaking sensitive information such as usernames and passwords, and stack traces or core dumps of crashed applications.

Several approaches [7,19,21] aim to address the issue, mainly through access control or encryption, hence by restricting who can access specific storage structures (e.g. partitions, mount points, directories, files and/or zones). This is still

---

[1] Fugue Survey Finds Widespread Concern Over Cloud Security Risks During the COVID-19 Crisis, https://tinyurl.com/46zj4hwh.

J. Zhou et al. (Eds.): ACNS 2022 Workshops, LNCS 13285, pp. 380–397, 2022.
https://doi.org/10.1007/978-3-031-16815-4_21

not sufficient if data are meant to be shared among various principals in a platform, in case of data that is required to be accessible for various reasons (e.g. log files that need to be accessible both for audit and debugging purposes), or if datasets are incorrectly stored in locations not initially envisioned – like public nodes of a Hadoop cluster in a hybrid cloud setting.

Several common use cases require data, possibly containing sensitive information, to be accessible from different user/roles with different granularity/level of completeness. Currently, the solution most used in practice is to create different versions of the dataset for each purpose, which is expensive or even impractical if large volumes of data need to be replicated. Alternatives, such as utilization of techniques based on fully or partially homomorphic encryption have been proposed [16]. These solutions incur significant performance penalties, however, caused by the mathematical complexity of the algorithms required to achieve required levels of security. As the adoption of tools like Dropbox[2], Google Drive[3], and Box[4] suggests, file systems offer a very popular approach to data sharing across applications [13] and across systems [2].

Therefore, we propose Data Leakage Prevention FileSystem (DLPFS), a novel mechanism to share data across multiple applications and systems leveraging state-of-the-art data type identification and de-identification technologies. DLPFS exposes a POSIX file system API to applications accessing a protected subtree of the file system. Practically, DLPFS acts as a middleware between applications and the actual file systems, identifying and protecting sensitive data on both read and write paths.

DLPFS allows data users to share data in a privacy preserving fashion across multiple systems without the need to create bespoke copies of the data for the target application. Moreover, DLPFS allows legacy applications to operate on data de-identified on the fly, without the need of modifying the original applications. This removes the burden of modifying legacy and mission critical applications from the developers, allowing DevOps and SecOps teams to define fine grained access control and privacy profiles, according to application and context requirements.

The rest of the paper is organized as follows. Section 2 introduces the design principles of DLPFS and its operational steps. Section 3 and 4 present the implementation of the DLPFS prototype and discuss empirical performance evaluations. Finally, Sect. 5 compares our solution with the state of the art and Sect. 6 summarizes the contribution and depicts possible future directions.

2   Data Leakage Prevention FileSystem in Practice

DLPFS operates as a middleware between a software application and the file system stack. The DLPFS conceptual architecture is shown in Fig. 1.

---

[2] https://www.dropbox.com.

[3] https://www.google.com/drive.

[4] https://www.box.com/.

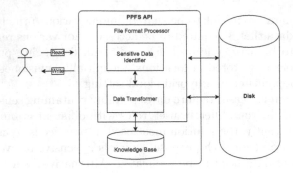

Fig. 1. Overall modules architecture

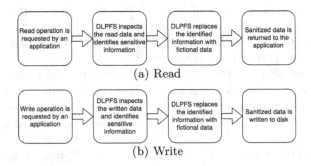

(a) Read

(b) Write

Fig. 2. Data flows

The system exposes a POSIX filesystem API that proxies all requests performed by a client application to the actual filesystem. DLPFS intercepts all read and write operations and acts on the transferred data according to the instructions specified in the knowledge base. The two supported read and write flows are sketched in Fig. 2a and Fig. 2b.

The key idea behind DLPFS is to intercept and analyse data as it is transferred between the data storage and applications. Inspection and transformation operations can generally be applied to streams of raw data. Hence, there is no strict need for DLPFS to be aware of the format of the files where the data is being read from or written to, or their structure.

However, having knowledge of the file structure improves how information is handled in specific scenarios, leading to more accurate data detection and data transformation. As an example, consider an application that loads data from a Comma-Separated Values (CSV) file into memory by sequentially reading blocks of 1,024 bytes of data. According to the CSV format, information is stored within data fields that are separated by a comma character (',') and groups of fields, i.e. rows, must be terminated with a newline character ('\n'). Ignoring such terminators and processing data in blocks with a fixed size of 1,024 bytes can result in a high probability of processing truncated data, which might lead to incorrect classification of the represented information. Therefore, identification and transformation must be performed on the data in a format dependent and semantically consistent manner, and DLPFS achieves this by loading and processing data with a strategy respecting file format specifications and encoding.

For this reason, minimal support for common file formats like CSV, XLS, or JSON positively impacts the precision of detection and utility preservation, by reducing the risk of incorrect classification of data blocks, and the probability of damaging the file structure.

When a read or write operation is intercepted, DLPFS inspects the raw data that is being read (or written) in order to identify potentially sensitive information. On read, DLPFS retrieves a certain amount of bytes before and after the buffer requested by the client application. We call this additional amount of bytes *guard*. This allows the identification of sensitive patterns that are expanding beyond the acquired buffer. The application of guards is in addition to the ability to support specific file formats, allowing DLPFS to also handle exotic file formats. The client application receives only the amount of data initially requested while the other bytes are kept internally by DLPFS as a cache. Thus, improving retrieval time for sequential read.

On the other hand, on write, DLPFS delays the flush operation to be able to perform detection of sensitive information beyond the individual buffer.

These operations require DLPFS of being aware of all applications accessing files within the directory exposed by DLPFS, basically mimicking the behaviour of modern operating systems. The size of the left and right guards can be defined by the user based on empirical observations, or be predefined by the file type. The latter strategy allows better precision and utility preservation, while requiring the ability to correctly identify file types with extensive work to expand the support for unconventional, or custom file types.

The definition of sensitive information is provided through a Knowledge Base (KB). The KB contains information about the definition of sensitive information, and instructions on how the identified information should be treated. DLPFS supports several types of data transformation, ranging from simple redaction, where the identified values are being replaced with blanks or '*', to semantic and format preserving masking [5] and anonymisation techniques such as data generalisation and local differential privacy.

The main advantage of the proposed approach lies in the transparency that the solution provides. DLPFS can be deployed as a protection layer in order to reduce the privacy risk in a number of scenarios. For example, by providing access to data files for monitoring purposes to a third party system, while preventing leakage of incorrectly handled information produced by applications in testing or debug mode. This way, it is not required to modify the application consuming the data, as DLPFS can be transparently deployed to inspect, and redact, the data that such an application is consuming and/or producing within a specific portion of file system. The sole effort required is to properly define and validate in the KB the specifications for detection and transformation of sensitive information.

As an example of such validation, transformations applied need to be consistent with the original data format, if the expected applications are sensitive to data format.

3   Implementation Details

A prototype has been implemented to validate the feasibility of DLPFS and to test its impact on performance. The code is available as open source[5] for community validation.

Following agile best practices, we concentrated on creating a proof of concept implementation. This means leveraging languages and framework that would speed up the development and testing of the system.

For this reason, we created a prototype using `Python` (version 3.8) and `python-fuse` as main development library.[6] This library exposes the Python bindings of FUSE [20]. The reasons behind these choices are as follows. Python is a popular language for rapid prototyping, thus allowing fast experimentation of various strategies for rules and transformation application. Similarly, File system in User Space (FUSE) is the de-facto standard for user-space applications exposing a filesystem interface.

These implementation choices have known drawbacks. Namely, using Python as main language introduces performance penalties, which can be overcome by implementing the application in a more canonical system language (mainly C or C++). Similarly, the fact that the main functionality of DLPFS are executed in user space introduces another performance penalty, as we will present and discuss in the evaluation section. An implementation in a more canonical system language would have yielded better performance, however, we are accounting for this in the evaluations. Nonetheless, these design choices come with advantages. We want to highlight two in particular. First particular, the simplicity and rapidity of development overtake performance consideration at prototype stage. Making this solution easily extensible for further developments. Secondly, the fact that the system runs in user space fosters for its utilization in low privileges container environments, thus further reducing the security risk of running application in environments like Kubernetes.

The prototype consists of a main application that is in charge of running FUSE. Invoking the `dlpfs` module from Python requires three mandatory parameters, namely: `-t`, specifying the file system type; `-r`, specifying the root directory; `-m`, specifying the mounting point; and optionally `-s`, that is the path to the *behaviour specification file*.

Currently, the prototype supports two types of file systems: (i) `dlpfs`, and (ii) `LoopBack`. The latter is a simple LoopBack (LB) file system that mirrors the content of the root directory to the mounting directory, and its purpose is only to fairly benchmark DLPFS, as will be discussed in Sect. 4. The former, `dlpfs`, is the actual implementation of the method presented in Sect. 2.

---

[5] https://github.com/IBM/data-leakage-prevention-filesystem.
[6] https://github.com/libfuse/python-fuse.

The behaviour specification file contains instructions to DLPFS regarding which data flow to protect (write, read, or both), which patterns to protect and what transformation to apply to the detected patterns. A simple example of this specification file is presented in Fig. 3. The structure of the file is simple. It consists of a JavaScript Object Notation (JSON)[7] object containing the following fields:

- `do_read`, a boolean value indicating if read data flow should be protected
- `do_write`, a boolean value indicating if write data flow should be protected
- `rules`, a list of rules to be applied on read and/or write operations.

Each rule is a JSON object containing two fields:

- `patterns`, a list of patterns identified within this rule
- `transformation`, the transformation to apply to the detected bytes

Currently, DLPFS supports two types of patterns: regular expressions – implemented using the Python wrapper for `re2`[8] – and lookup tables. Other types of patterns – for instance those presented in [5] – are envisioned to be added to the system according to the needs presented in use cases.

DLPFS currently supports a small but functional set of transformations: redaction, masking, generalisation, and anonymisation. Redaction is implemented as a specialisation of masking where the detected bytes are replaced with a predefined character, set as default to '*', preserving the length of the replaced bytes. Masking, on the other hand, replaces the value with another fictionalised value within the same domain [5,22]. Generalisation is a special type of masking, where the identified value is replaced with a more generic value within the same domain, for example replacing the value "Single" with "Not Married", when protecting values within the *Marital Status* domain. Generalisations are performed using external knowledge bases like type hierarchies. Finally, DLPFS supports a lightweight form of local differential privacy. This is achieved by replacing numerical values with the output of the application of a differential privacy mechanism [11].

4   Experimental Evaluation

This section describes the evaluation setup used to validate the performance of DLPFS.

4.1   Setup

A number of experiments have been conducted in order to assess the impact of DLPFS on the performance of read and write operations. The benchmarks

---

[7] https://www.json.org.
[8] https://github.com/google/re2/.

```
{
    "do_read": true,
    "do_write": false,
    "rules": [{
        "patterns": [{
                "type": "re",
                "spec": "(:?\\w|\\.)+@(?:\\w|\\.)+\\.\\w{2,4}
                "
        }],
        "transformation": {
            "type": "redact"
        }}, {
        "patterns":[{
            "type":"re",
            "spec": "Account\\s+total:\\s+(-?\\d+\.\\d{2})"
        }],
        "transformation": {
            "type": "diff_priv",
            "mechanism": "laplace",
            "e": 0.01,
            "d": 0.2
        }
    }]
}
```

Fig. 3. Example of behaviour specification file content

presented and discussed in the remainder of this section have been executed on a Virtual Machine (VM), equipped with an Intel® Xeon® Gold 6140 CPU 2.30 GHz vCPU with 4 vcores, 8 GB of RAM, and Storage Area Network (SAN) drives.

This scenario mimics a common production environment, where applications are running in a virtualised environment and the hardware stack is abstracted to the user. It is not uncommon for the storage system of such virtualised environments to be mounted as a remote filesystem, leveraging technologies such as Network FileSystem (NFS)[9].

Thanks to this approach, for instance, directories can be easily shared across different virtual machines within the same cloud infrastructure, and data can easily migrate across different environments. This introduces additional penalties to the performance of read and write operations through network factors such as latency, jitter, and congestion. Therefore, it is paramount to define an unbiased and clear baseline for performing objective and accurate benchmark measurements.

---

[9] https://tools.ietf.org/html/rfc7530.

As described in Sect. 3, the initial DLPFS prototype has been developed by extending the `fusepy`[10] library. The performance impact of the protection offered by DLPFS has then been measured by comparing its throughput with that obtained from a simple LoopBack (LB) filesystem implementation that also extends the `fusepy` library.

A *LoopBack* file system is a simple pseudo-file system implementation that accesses content from a storage device at a given path, and renders it available at a different path. In other words, it simply forwards read and write operations without introducing any additional computational steps. For any given benchmark test, the performance of such LB implementation has been used as a baseline for the experiments, thus accounting in the comparison for the computational overhead caused by using `fusepy` library and network delays.

4.2   Methodology

The experiments have been conducted as follows.

First, a number of synthetic datasets have been generated using the Python library `faker`[11], a popular open source library for the generation of synthetic data. The data schema of these datasets is the following:

- `id` contains a monotonically increasing sequence number. It reflects the typical row identifier present in most datasets. Its values range from 0 to $N-1$, where N is the number of rows contained in the dataset.
- `icd` contains a valid International Classification of Diseases (ICD) value with probability 0.05, or an empty string. The ICD is an international coding standard maintained by the World Health Organization (WHO), which is globally used as diagnostic standard for epidemiology, health management, and clinical purposes. This field contains valid values for the version 10 of the standard.[12]
- `amount` contains a randomly generated currency value. Its values range from 1 to 1,000 US dollars, with up to 2 decimal places. The values are sampled uniformly from the domain.
- `message` contains a variable length string representing a text message, or a comment, and it is composed by concatenating: (i) A randomly generated sentence, with length varying between 3 and 9 words. (ii) A first keyword with probability 0.01. (iii) A second keyword with probability 0.1. (iv) A randomly generated email address with probability 0.05. (v) Another randomly generated sentence, comprised of 3 to 9 words.

The test data is then represented in CSV format[13] and an excerpt of a test dataset is shown in Fig. 4.

---

[10] https://github.com/fusepy/fusepy.
[11] https://faker.readthedocs.io.
[12] https://icd.who.int/browse10/2019/en.
[13] https://tools.ietf.org/html/rfc4180.

```
...
124,"G30.1","$683.91","Force food second. Direction note his finish case."
125,"C00.6","$3.97","Carry wish quickly industry... International visit..."
126,"F71.8","$355.56","The politics mother resource... Charge fill that..."
127,"D51.3","$93.64","Born industry here... Health ever nearly achieved..."
128,"G29.3","$87.94","Role method must... FrequentKeyword. Late why hold..."
129,"F71.1","$159.71","Father go everybody... Big according he move."
130,"B20.3","$874.19","Chance data under line left... FrequentKeyword..."
131,"C00.2","$825.05","Nation cut last old... vanessa36@cox-mata.net..."
...
```

Fig. 4. Example of generated data.

We created several of such CSV test datasets with sizes ranging from 1 to 20,000 rows, where each row amounts to approximately 100 bytes, and we then performed two main batches of experiments.

The first batch concentrates on exploring the performance impact of DLPFS on read operations, while the second one concentrates on measuring the impact on write operations.

Read Strategies. We tested a number of read strategies, with the objective of simulating behaviours that are commonly followed by applications while reading the content of an input file. Namely, we simulated the following scenarios:

– Entire file content loaded in memory as **pandas**[14] dataframe, this strategy replicates the usual behaviour of a data scientist or machine learning practitioner.
– Entire file content entirely copied in memory, another common practice to load and process the content of files
– Scan file content one row at a time, delegating to Python the identification of row boundaries, typically via the new line character (\n). This is the behaviour of row-oriented programs or scripts.
– Read file content using Operating System (OS) operations with varying read buffer size between 10, 100, 1,000, and 10,000 bytes. This strategy simulates sequential access to file when loading fixed size buffers, for example when data objects are deserialised from disk.

Write Strategies. Similarly to how the read performances were tested, we also executed benchmarks of different behaviours with respect to writing files to disk. Namely, we simulated the following writing patterns:

– Entire file content written to disk as **pandas** dataframe, this strategy replicates the usual behaviour of a data scientist or machine learning practitioner who is storing the result of a computation to disk.
– Entire file at once, this pattern simulates an application saving the all the output at once, or a program faulting and creating a memory dump.

---

[14] https://pandas.pydata.org/.

- Row by row, this pattern mimics the behaviour of an application periodically logging messages to disc.
- Field by field, this pattern replicates the behaviour of an application incrementally writing the produced output.

DLPFS Configuration. As we will show later in this section, the most important factor on the performance of DLPFS resides in its configurations, in terms of identification pattern and guard sizes. We tested numerous configurations. First of all, we tested the overhead caused by the DLPFS architecture. This has been done providing a configuration with no patterns or transformation. After that we tested with different types of patterns, namely regular expressions of various complexity and coverage. We tested the impact of an administrator specifying not optimised regular expressions (i.e. containing unnecessary greedy operators, or containing overlapping parts) against precise patterns. We then tested the performance impact of using different guard sizes, ranging from 0 (i.e. no guard) to 256 bytes. Note that the effectiveness of guard size relates to the block size of the Hard Disk Drive (HDD), or in our case of the SAN. Generally, modern HDD block size is set to a value between 512 bytes to 4,096 bytes, while the SAN block size is generally between 4 kilobytes to 1,024 kilobytes.

Matching Cases. The last variable in our evaluation is the percentage of matches encountered by the privacy protection policies when executing the read or write operation. More precisely, we tested several policies that differ in the number of matching patterns with the file that is being read or written. As it will be presented in Sect. 4.3, this is one of the factors that most impacted performance of the system. We tested three main cases:

- **No matches.** Thus, specifying patterns that were by design not existing in the test data.
- **Few matches.** In this case we used a set of patterns having a low probability of match within the test data. More precisely, we tested patterns with probability 0.01 of being present in the test data, according to both data construction and post data generation assessment.
- **Many matches.** In this case we used a set of patterns having a higher probability of match within the test data. Specifically, we tested patterns with probability 0.10 of being present in the test data, according to both data construction and post data generation assessment.

Finally, we also tested different strategies in terms of how the patterns are matched, and how the patterns behave. For example, we noticed in the preliminary evaluation how the structure of patterns implemented as regular expression produced very different results depending on whether the regular expression itself had certain characteristics. As one would expect, optimised regular expressions with less overlapping parts and less greedy operators were performing better.

Table 1. Transformations time.

Transformation	Time (ms)
No transformation	3.459
Redaction	6.113
Masking	151.982
DP noise	319.207

4.3   Results and Discussion

We repeated executions of the experiments 30 times, and report mean, 10th, and 90th percentile of the execution time.

Before analyzing the performance of DLPFS, let us argue about more general observations. First of all, the experimental evaluation clearly shows the importance of the correct selection of the detection engine. One might notice how, with no detection, DLPFS behaves exactly as the LB baseline, which means that the additional buffering is not impacting overall read/write performances. Let us also remark that the time taken by the actual transformation is negligible when compared with the detection, as demonstrated by preliminary execution of DLPFS with configuration specifying no transformation, redact, masking (randomisation) or differential privacy noise addition. Table 1 presents the average of 30 runs over randomly generated 20,000 numerical values transformed with the strategies supported by DLPFS. In fact, the average time required for processing 20,000 numerical values takes is, 3.459, 6.113, 151.982, and 319.207 milliseconds. The only exception is the application of noise addition in a differentially private fashion. This is caused by two factors. The first one relates to the fact that the used framework has been designed to operate on vectors of values, not individual ones. Secondly, the framework is designed to sample noise from a distribution in a secure manner (see [10,14]), a procedure that introduces additional complexity.

On the other hand, as patterns are detected the reader should notice an increment in execution time. The amount of execution time directly depends on the amount of matches the pattern has in the file, as one would expect. Moreover, the engine actually used for the detection of the patterns greatly impacts the amount of time spent in this phase. This analysis of difference in performance, for example between re and re2, is beyond the scope of this paper and it has been previously discussed.[15] For the rest of this we will present only the best performing detection engine configuration.

Similarly, the strategy of operation affects the performance. For example, Fig. 5 shows the difference in time required to process different files reading, or writing, using the different strategies.

A common pattern that can be observed, is that the time increases linearly as the file sizes increase. This is an expected behavior, and follows the trend of the baseline, even if generally with a more steep slope. This is shown in Fig. 6,

---

[15] https://pypi.org/project/re2/#performance.

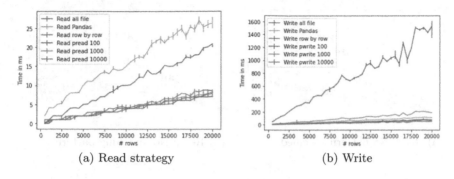

(a) Read strategy   (b) Write

Fig. 5. LB performance, varying file size, all strategies

where we present the trend for two special cases. The first one, Fig. 6a, where the protection policy is set to empty, and a second one, Fig. 6b, where the policy has no match in the processed data. The experiments performed on the write path provide a similar picture, although the overhead of validating data on write is greater than for read, as shown in Fig. 6c and Fig. 6d.

Figure 7 shows the execution time of the introduced policies when the entire file is read as a block of data. The first observation is that the guard size does not seem to impact significantly the performance. On the other hand, the specified patterns greatly impact the overall performance, as clearly shown in Fig. 7 and following. A poorly optimised set of patterns, as shown in Fig. 7a, reduces the system performance greatly, while a set of patterns with similar hit ratio but with more optimised regular expressions still shows a significant but from a practical viewpoint acceptable overhead (see Fig. 7b). On the other hand, in case of patterns with few hits in the data, the performances are affected by less then 30%, as shown in Fig. 7c and Fig. 7d.

Figure 8 shows how the performance changes with the guard size. Once can notice how there is no significant variation as the guard, which we remind is the amount of bytes DLPFS reads before and/or after the buffer required by the user, ranges from 0 to 256 bytes. One might only notice a shift on the y-axis caused by the different number of matches between Fig. 8a, having many matches, and Fig. 8b, having fewer matches.

Similar as for read, also the write pattern performances are mostly influenced by the pattern itself and the privacy protection policy enforced. Figure 9 presents an overview of the impact. The performance can degrade up to twice in case of many matches, as shown in Fig. 9b, but can be deemed generally acceptable for non real-time services.

After this analysis, we can conclude the DLPFS has known costs in terms of performance, but compares favourably considering the additional protection provided. In fact, the mentioned motivating scenario assumes DLPFS to be deployed as additional protection layer, thus generally providing a minimal impact on application's performance as shown in Fig. 6, while providing additional guarantees in rare but critical events. This is further corroborated by

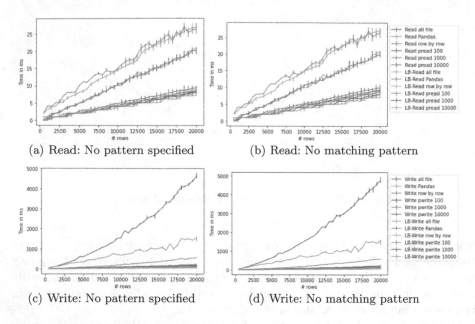

(a) Read: No pattern specified

(b) Read: No matching pattern

(c) Write: No pattern specified

(d) Write: No matching pattern

Fig. 6. Minimum penalty of DLPFS over LB

Fig. 10, where we present the throughput of an application reading (Fig. 10a) and writing (Fig. 10b) data. This application behaves according to the following pattern: first it reads(/writes) non sensitive data. At $t = 100$ the application accesses a protected pattern, after which it resumes normal operation.

5   Related Work

Properly protecting data outsourcing or sharing, even locally, is an open issue. Several works have been proposed to address these issues in specific context, with particular focus on context where sensitive data are pervasive, like in the healthcare domain [6]. The majority of the proposed approaches leverage, one way or another, cryptographic-based techniques. For example, [21] presents a cryptographic-based access control mechanism to selectively limit access to sensitive parts of the file. Similarly, [7,19] describe a system, and associated architecture, to introduce cryptography-based techniques in federated health information systems. The authors show the feasibility of improving the security of such systems by adopting proper mechanisms to protect the exchanged data and the provided functionalities from malicious manipulations. Still in the healthcare domain, other approaches – like the one presented in [23] – tackle the problem of data sharing using a microservice approach. Hence, data is provided on demand using highly restricted access control rules, to reveal data on a need-to-know bases, and transforming the data in an abstract data format before release, thus limiting the risk of data leakage.

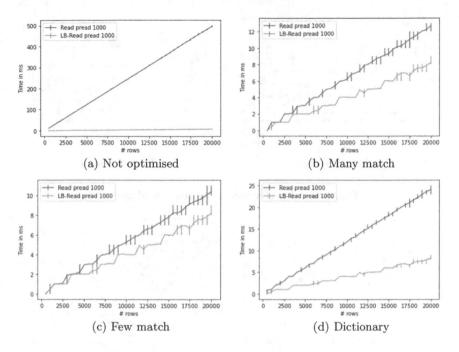

(a) Not optimised   (b) Many match

(c) Few match   (d) Dictionary

Fig. 7. Read performance, varying file size, pread-1000

Other approaches rely on different ways to encode the files on storage. For example, [18] presents a new file system that focuses on the privacy protection of the on-disk state. This is achieved by re-ordering data in user files at the bit level, and storing bit slices at distributed locations in the storage system. On the other hand, [8] presents a stackable filesystem that leverages trusted hardware to provide confidentiality and integrity for user files stored on untrusted platforms. A similar idea is presented in [15], where the authors propose a technique that involves using a hash function that uniquely identifies the data and then splitting data across multiple cloud providers. This is done following a "Good Enough" approach to privacy-preserving cloud data storage, which has been proven to be both technologically feasible and financially advantageous. Moreover, [3] presents a statistical Data Leakage Prevention (DLP) model to classify data on the basis of semantics. This study contributes by using data statistical analysis to detect evolved confidential data. A fairly a summary and comparison of DLP systems, techniques and research directions is also provided in [4].

The work the most similar to DLPFS is presented in [17]. The authors analyse and propose mechanisms to enhance the disclosure control of personal data. The scheme, called the Hippocratic Filesystem, stores personal data's purpose and use limitation as the data's label, propagates the label as the information flows from one place to another, and enforces the label to prevent accidental disclosures. DLPFS, on the other hand, presents a complementary method, where data is transformed either at reading or writing time. Similarly, [1] proposes the

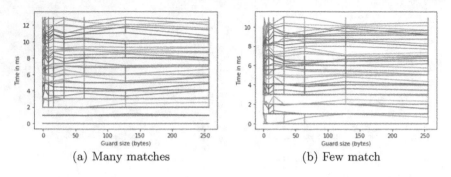

(a) Many matches   (b) Few match

Fig. 8. Read performance, varying guard size

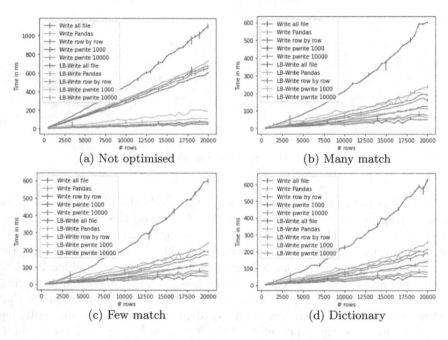

(a) Not optimised   (b) Many match

(c) Few match   (d) Dictionary

Fig. 9. Write performance, varying file size

so called Hippocratic databases (HDB), which presents similar concept to the filesystem approach previously presented, but in the context of a centralised database. Moreover, [24] presents a Windows file system that transparently encrypts files automatically according to encryption strategies. This work is complementary to the approach here presented. The main differentiation is that in DLPFS it is not mandatory to access the protected data through DLPFS itself. A file directory can be protected while accessed from some applications, while others can access the data without interacting with DLPFS, thus introducing a performance penalty only when deemed necessary. Leveraging HDB, a P2P-based solution to tackle the private data sharing problem in social networks

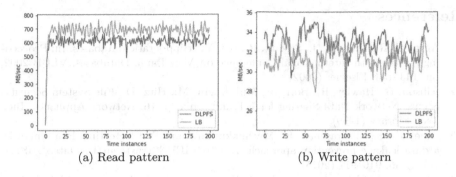

(a) Read pattern   (b) Write pattern

Fig. 10. Throughput of the test application

has been presented [12]. The identification and transformation capabilities of DLPFS are inspired by the work in [5], which presents a toolkit that contains functionality for the detection and format preserving transformation of values.

Finally, an extensive survey of masking anonymisation and cryptographic-based methods for outsourced data storage is presented in [9]. This survey was instrumental to the design of DLPFS because, even if the application scenario is different, the referenced techniques can be ported to DLPFS.

6 Conclusions and Future Work

We presented DLPFS, a novel data leakage prevention file system middleware, to protect sensitive information potentially stored in shared systems. We demonstrated the technical feasibility and experimentally evaluated the performance impact of the system. In particular, the evaluation demonstrated that little to none overhead is introduced by DLPFS on normal file-based operations, with reductions in performance detected only when sensitive data is protected.

Future work can focus on four main aspects. First, scaling up the concepts illustrated here in a purely distributed setting, for example by porting the prototype to Java to enhance HDFS. Second, the extension of the capabilities offered by DLPFS in terms of data transformation. This could materialise as an integration with more established data privacy frameworks. Third, to extend data detection capabilities, for example with the integration of contextual information, such as file metadata, application and user operation, during the detection process. Fourth and finally, we envision to integrate DLPFS with conventional access control frameworks, to simplify configuration management and deployment.

Acknowledgments. The authors would like to thank Spiros Antonatos, Andrea Reale, and Kostas Katrinis for suggestions and support during the conceptualization of this work, and to Vassilis Vassiliadis for helping reviewing the writing.

References

1. Agrawal, R., Kiernan, J., Srikant, R., Xu, Y.: Hippocratic databases. In: Proceedings of the 28th International Conference on Very Large Databases, VLDB 2002, pp. 143–154. Elsevier (2002)
2. Allison, B., Hawley, R., Borr, A., Muhlestein, M., Hitz, D.: File System Security: Secure Network Data Sharing for NT and Unix, p. 16. Network Appliance, Inc., Tech Library (1999)
3. Alneyadi, S., Sithirasenan, E., Muthukkumarasamy, V.: Detecting data semantic: a data leakage prevention approach. In: 2015 IEEE Trustcom/BigDataSE/ISPA, vol. 1, pp. 910–917 (2015)
4. Alneyadi, S., Sithirasenan, E., Muthukkumarasamy, V.: A survey on data leakage prevention systems. J. Netw. Comput. Appl. **62**, 137–152 (2016)
5. Antonatos, S., Braghin, S., Holohan, N., Gkoufas, Y., Mac Aonghusa, P.: PRIMA: an end-to-end framework for privacy at scale. In: 34th IEEE International Conference on Data Engineering, ICDE 2018, Paris, France, 16–19 April 2018. IEEE Computer Society (2018). https://doi.org/10.1109/ICDE.2018.00171
6. Appari, A., Johnson, M.E.: Information security and privacy in healthcare: current state of research. Int. J. Internet Enterp. Manag. **6**(4), 279–314 (2010)
7. Ciampi, M., De Pietro, G., Esposito, C., Sicuranza, M., Donzelli, P.: A federated interoperability architecture for health information systems. Int. J. Internet Protocol Technol. **7**(4), 189–202 (2013)
8. Djoko, J.B., Lange, J., Lee, A.J.: Nexus: practical and secure access control on untrusted storage platforms using client-side SGX. In: 2019 49th Annual IEEE/IFIP International Conference on Dependable Systems and Networks (DSN), pp. 401–413. IEEE (2019)
9. Domingo-Ferrer, J., Farràs, O., Ribes-González, J., Sánchez, D.: Privacy-preserving cloud computing on sensitive data: a survey of methods, products and challenges. Comput. Commun. **140**, 38–60 (2019)
10. Holohan, N., Braghin, S.: Secure random sampling in differential privacy. arXiv preprint arXiv:2107.10138 (2021)
11. Holohan, N., Braghin, S., Mac Aonghusa, P., Levacher, K.: Diffprivlib: the IBM differential privacy library. CoRR abs/1907.02444 (2019)
12. Jawad, M., Serrano-Alvarado, P., Valduriez, P.: Supporting data privacy in P2P systems. In: Chbeir, R., Bouna, B.A. (eds.) Security and Privacy Preserving in Social Networks. LNSN, pp. 195–244. Springer, Vienna (2013). https://doi.org/10.1007/978-3-7091-0894-9_7
13. Lim, S.H., Sim, H., Gunasekaran, R., Vazhkudai, S.S.: Scientific user behavior and data-sharing trends in a petascale file system. In: Proceedings of the International Conference for High Performance Computing, Networking, Storage and Analysis, SC 2017. Association for Computing Machinery, New York (2017). https://doi.org/10.1145/3126908.3126924
14. Mironov, I.: On significance of the least significant bits for differential privacy. In: Proceedings of the 2012 ACM Conference on Computer and Communications Security, CCS 2012, pp. 650–661. Association for Computing Machinery, New York (2012). https://doi.org/10.1145/2382196.2382264
15. Paul, M., Collberg, C., Bambauer, D.: A possible solution for privacy preserving cloud data storage. In: 2015 IEEE International Conference on Cloud Engineering, pp. 397–403. IEEE (2015)

16. Samanthula, B.K., Howser, G., Elmehdwi, Y., Madria, S.: An efficient and secure data sharing framework using homomorphic encryption in the cloud. In: Proceedings of the 1st International Workshop on Cloud Intelligence, Cloud-I 2012. Association for Computing Machinery, New York (2012). https://doi.org/10.1145/2347673.2347681
17. Sar, C., Cao, P., Dean, D.: The Hippocratic file system: protecting privacy in networked storage. Technical report, Computer Science Department, Stanford University (2005)
18. Sheng, Z., Ma, Z., Gu, L., Li, A.: A privacy-protecting file system on public cloud storage. In: 2011 International Conference on Cloud and Service Computing, pp. 141–149. IEEE (2011)
19. Sicuranza, M., Ciampi, M., De Pietro, G., Esposito, C.: Secure healthcare data sharing among federated health information systems. Int. J. Crit. Comput.-Based Syst. 4(4), 349–373 (2013)
20. Vangoor, B.K.R., Tarasov, V., Zadok, E.: To {FUSE} or not to {FUSE}: performance of user-space file systems. In: 15th {USENIX} Conference on File and Storage Technologies ({FAST} 2017) (2017)
21. Wang, H., Yi, X., Bertino, E., Sun, L.: Protecting outsourced data in cloud computing through access management. Concurr. Comput.: Pract. Experience 28(3), 600–615 (2016)
22. Weiss, M., Rozenberg, B., Barham, M.: Practical solutions for format-preserving encryption. arXiv preprint arXiv:1506.04113 (2015)
23. Yang, Y., Zu, Q., Liu, P., Ouyang, D., Li, X.: MicroShare: privacy-preserved medical resource sharing through microservice architecture. Int. J. Biol. Sci. 14, 907–919 (2018). https://doi.org/10.7150/ijbs.24617
24. Zhang, X., Liu, F., Chen, T., Li, H.: Research and application of the transparent data encryption in intranet data leakage prevention. In: 2009 International Conference on Computational Intelligence and Security, vol. 2. IEEE (2009)

Privacy-Preserving Record Linkage Using Local Sensitive Hash and Private Set Intersection

Allon Adir[1], Ehud Aharoni[1], Nir Drucker[1]([✉]), Eyal Kushnir[1],
Ramy Masalha[1], Michael Mirkin[2], and Omri Soceanu[1]

[1] IBM Research, Haifa, Israel
drucker.nir@gmail.com
[2] Technion - Israel Institute of Technology, Haifa, Israel

Abstract. The amount of data stored in data repositories increases
every year. This makes it challenging to link records between different
datasets across companies and even internally, while adhering to privacy
regulations. Address or name changes, and even different spelling used
for entity data, can prevent companies from using private deduplication or record-linking solutions such as private set intersection (PSI). To
this end, we propose a new and efficient privacy-preserving record linkage (PPRL) protocol that combines PSI and local sensitive hash (LSH)
functions, and runs in linear time. We explain the privacy guarantees
that our protocol provides and demonstrate its practicality by executing the protocol over two datasets with 2^{20} records each in 11–45 min,
depending on network settings.

Keywords: Privacy-preserving record linkage · Entity resolution ·
Private set intersection · Local sensitive hash · Information privacy ·
Data security and privacy · Secure two-party computations

1 Introduction

Entity resolution (ER) is the process of identifying similar entities in several
datasets, where the datasets may belong to different organizations. While these
organizations would like to join hands and analyzes the behavior of matching customers, they may be restricted by law from sharing sensitive client-data such as
medical, criminal, or financial information. The problem of matching records in
two or more datasets without revealing additional information is called privacy-
preserving record linkage (PPRL) [11] or blind data linkage (BDL) [10] and is
the focus of this paper. A survey of PPRL methods is available in [18]. The
importance of finding efficient and accurate PPRL solutions can be observed,
for example, in the establishment of a special task team by the Interdisciplinary
Committee of the International Rare Diseases Research Consortium (IRDiRC)
to explore different PPRL approaches [1].

M. Mirkin—The work for this paper was done while Michael Mirkin was with IBM
Research.

The PPRL problem is a generalization of the well-studied private set intersection (PSI) problem in which two parties with different datasets would like to know the intersection or the size of the intersection of these datasets without revealing anything else about their data to the other party. Examples for PSI solutions include [5,6,12,21,33,35]. With PSI, the two parties compute the intersection of their respective sets, which can be used to identify matches by looking for records that share the same identifying field e.g., PSI over social security numbers (SSNs). However, in reality, such identifying fields do not always exist, and even when they do exist, their content may be entered incorrectly or differently. For example, consider two parties that perform PSI on entity names. A single user may register himself in different systems under the names: 'John doe', 'John P Doe', 'john doe', just 'John', or even 'Jon ode' by mistake. A general PPRL solution may attempt to consider all of the above names as matching.

In some cases, more than one data field is used to match two records, e.g., first name, last name, addresses, and dates of birth. These fields are known as quasi-identifiers (QIDs), which may hold private information. In this paper, we assume that the parties are allowed to learn data by matching QIDs. In other cases, one can use a masking method e.g., as in [27] to maintain the users' privacy.

Non-exact matching is commonly performed using ER solutions that employ a local sensitive hash (LSH) function (e.g., as in [19,32]). Unlike cryptographic hash functions, this technique permits collisions by deliberately hashing similar inputs to a single digest. For example, consider a hash function that hashes all the above names to a single digest value or to lists of digests with non-empty intersection. Different LSH functions with different parameters allow us to fine-tune the results in different ways. We provide more details in Sect. 2.2.

Unfortunately, few practical protocols exist that can securely perform such "fuzzy" record linkage without revealing some private data of the parties, and do so in a linear time frame. See Sect. A for a review of the different approaches. Many involve a third-party (e.g., [25]), which we aim to avoid, while other works do not provide a thorough leakage analysis that would help evaluate the security of the solution. To this end, we constructed a new and efficient PPRL solution that runs in $\mathcal{O}(n)$. We describe its performance and discuss its security characteristics.

The goal of our solution is to compose a PSI with an LSH function. The dataset fields are first locally hashed by both parties using the LSH and then checked for matches using PSI. The choice of PSI algorithm can only affect the performance (latency and bandwidth) of our solution but does not affect the amount of leaked information that can be tuned using the different parameters of the LSH. Figure 1 illustrates a high-level view of our solution. For completeness, we provide a short related work survey in Appendix A.

Our Contribution. Our contributions can be summarized as follows:

- We introduce a novel and efficient PPRL protocol that combines LSH and PSI, and analyze its security against semi-honest adversaries. It does not involve third parties. Specifically, due to the use of LSH, our protocol has a low probability of revealing the data of non-matched records and thereby provides better privacy guarantees.

- We implemented the model and suggest several low-level optimizations.
- We evaluated our implementation over a dataset with 2^{20} records and demonstrated its practical advantage when the execution took 11–45 min, depending on network settings.
- Our program is freely available for testing at [23].
- We present and discuss several formal definitions of PPRL protocols in Appendix C.

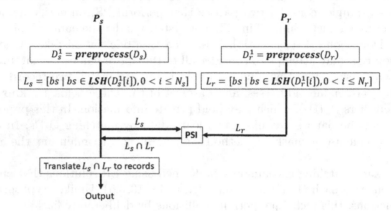

Fig. 1. A high level illustration of our PPRL protocol. The parties P_s and P_r hold datasets D_s and D_r. They preprocess the data for every record and then feed the results into an LSH that outputs an ordered list of digest vectors L_s and L_r, respectively. These are fed into a PSI black box. Finally, P_s translates the PSI output to the matching record IDs.

Organization. The paper is organized as follows. Section 2 provides some background notation and describes the required preliminaries for this work. Due to page limit, we defer the presentation and discussion of several possible definitions of PPRL protocols to Appendix C. We provide a high level description of our solution in Sect. 3 and provide further details about our implementation in Sect. 4. We report our experimental setup and results in Sect. 5 and conclude in Sect. 6.

2   Preliminaries and Notation

We denote the concatenation of two strings by $s_1 \mid s_2$. The function $Eq(s, r)$ returns 1 when two strings are equal and 0 otherwise. An ordered list of elements A is marked with square brackets, e.g., $A = [5, 3, 8]$ and we access its ith element by $A[i]$. A permutation π can either return a permuted list when operating on an ordered list, or the index of a permuted element within that list when the input is another index. For example, let $\pi : x \mapsto x + 1 \pmod 4$ be a permutation, then $\pi([5, 6, 7, 8]) = [8, 5, 6, 7]$, $\pi(2) = 3$, and $\pi(3) = 0$. Uniform random sampling from a set U is denoted by $u \xleftarrow{\$} U$.

2.1   Entity Resolution (ER)

An ER method gets as input two datasets of N_s and N_r records from record spaces $\mathcal{R}$: $D_s = \{s_1, s_2, \ldots, s_{N_s}\}$ and $D_r = \{r_1, r_2, \ldots, r_{N_r}\}$, respectively. It evaluates the similarity of every two records using a similarity measure $\mu : \mathcal{R} \times \mathcal{R} \to [0,1]$ and an associated similarity indicator

$$I_t^\mu : \mathcal{R} \times \mathcal{R} \longrightarrow \{0,1\}$$

$$(s,r) \longmapsto \begin{cases} 1 & \mu(s,r) \geq t \\ 0 & otherwise \end{cases}$$

The ER method uses the similarity indicator to facilitate a bipartite graph $G = (U, V, E)$, where the nodes of U, V are the records of D_s, D_r, respectively, and for every two nodes ($u \in U$, $v \in V$), an edge exists in E if $I_t^\mu(u,v) = 1$.

PPRL. Informally, a PPRL protocol is an ER method executed by two parties: a sender P_s and a receiver P_r, who privately hold D_s and D_r, respectively. At the end of the protocol, P_r learns the similarity edges E while P_s learns nothing. We provide a formal definition in Appendix C. Specifically, our PPRL solution uses the LSH and PSI primitives, described next.

2.2   Local Sensitive Hash (LSH)

An LSH [31] is a hash function that deliberately hashes *similar* inputs to the same output hash value. We are interested in the similarity of strings i.e., the content of the record fields. Therefore, we use the LSH from [31], which is based on the Jaccard index and on *Min-Hashes*, as demonstrated in Fig. 2.

Jaccard index (a.k.a. the Jaccard similarity coefficient) is a similarity measure for strings. The procedure for computing the Jaccard index of two inputs strings (s,r) splits each normalized string into the set of all overlapping sub-strings of given lengths, termed *k-shingles* (or *k-grams*), where k is the length of the sub-strings. We use small letters to denote strings or the corresponding records, and capital letters to denote their associated sets of k-shingles. The Jaccard index for records s, r is

$$J(s,r) = \frac{|S \cap R|}{|S \cup R|} \tag{1}$$

when the context is clear we use J instead of $J(s,r)$.

Example 1. Consider the strings:

$$s = \text{'Sunset Blvd, Los Angeles'}$$
$$r = \text{'Sunet Blvd, Los Angeles'}$$

that are normalized into

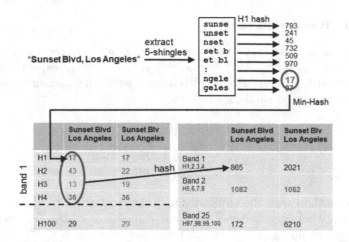

Fig. 2. Computing the LSH for a string: shingles are extracted from the normalized string, and then min-hashes are evaluated and grouped into bands that are hashed to a list of signatures.

'sunset blvd los angeles'

'sunet blvd los angeles'

and then split into the set of 19 and 18 shingles of length $k = 5$, respectively:

$$S = \{\text{'sunse'}, \text{'unset'}, \text{'nset'}, \text{'set b'}, \ldots, \text{'ngele'}, \text{'geles'}\}$$
$$R = \{\text{'sunet'}, \text{'unet'}, \text{'net b'}, \text{'et bl'}, \ldots, \text{'ngele'}, \text{'geles'}\}$$

Here, the Jaccard index is $J = \frac{15}{22} \approx 0.68$. Using longer shingles of length $k = 11$ would result in a lower Jaccard index of $J = 0.56$.

It is possible to instantiate a PPRL solution that relies on the Jaccard index. The drawback of such a protocol is that it has quadratic complexity in the size of the datasets. For linear complexity, we use Min-Hash.

Definition 1 (Min-Hash [31]). *For a collision-resistant hash function H with an integer output digest and an integer k, a Min-Hash function receives a string s as input, converts it to a k-shingles set S, and returns*

$$MinH_k^H(s) = \min_{e \in S} H(e)$$

When the context is clear we write MinH instead of $MinH_k^H$.

Observation 1 ([31]). *For two normalized records s and r, a collision resistant hash function H, and $k > 0$, it follows that $Pr\left[MinH_k^H(s) = MinH_k^H(r)\right] = J(s,r)$.*

An LSH involves applying P different Min-Hash functions to a string s. The outputs are split into B *bands* of R digests ($P = BR$). The concatenation of the R digests of each band is again hashed to produce the *signature* of the band, where the same signature hash function is used for all bands. An LSH output is a tuple with these band signatures.

Definition 2 (LSH). *For $k, R, B \in \mathbb{N}$, $P = RB$, distinct collision-resistant hash functions H_i, $1 \leq i \leq P$ and another collision-resistant hash functions G, a band b_j, $1 \leq j \leq B$ over a string s is the concatenation*

$$b_j(s) = MinH_k^{H_{R \cdot (j-1)+1}}(s) \mid \cdots \mid MinH_k^{H_{R \cdot (j-1)+R}}(s)$$

and the LSH output over a string s is the ordered list

$$LSH(s) = \left[G\left(b_1(s)\right), G\left(b_2(s)\right), \ldots, G\left(b_B(s)\right) \right]$$

Two LSH tuples are considered to be a match if they share at least one common signature. We denote this by the indicator function

$$\texttt{LSHMatch} : \mathcal{R} \times \mathcal{R} \longrightarrow \{0, 1\}$$

$$(s, r) \longmapsto \begin{cases} 1 & 1 \leq \sum_{i=1}^{B} Eq\left(LSH(s)[i], LSH(r)[i]\right) \\ 0 & otherwise \end{cases}$$

Observation 2 ([31]). *For two records s, r,*

$$Pr[\texttt{LSHMatch}(s, r) = 1] = 1 - (1 - J^R)^B \tag{2}$$

Example 2. Figure 2 demonstrates an LSH with $P = 100$, $B = 25$, $R = 4$, where $MinH_5^{H_1}(s_1) = 17$, $MinH_5^{H_2}(s_1) = 43$, etc. Subsequently, every sequence of R digests is concatenated and hashed to produce a band signature, with a total of B band signatures, which form the LSH of s_1, $LSH(s_1) = (865, 1082, \ldots, 172)$. Repeating the process for s_2, we observe a match in the signature of the second band for the two compared strings; this means that the two LSHs match and the strings match with a high probability.

2.3   Private Set Intersection (PSI)

PSI is a cryptographic protocol that allows two parties to compute the intersection of their private sets without revealing anything beyond this fact or beyond the size of the intersected sets to the other party. PSI is a special case of PPRL, which considers only exact matches. Some variations of PSI allow the parties to learn just the cardinality of the intersection.

Many PSI solutions exist (see Appendix A). In this work, we use a unidirectional variant of the Diffie-Hellmann (DH)-PSI [33], as presented in Fig. 3. The two parties P_s and P_r first agree on a group $\mathbb{G}$ and a collision-resistant hash function H, and each party generates its own secret key sk_s and sk_r, respectively.

Subsequently, both parties hash and encrypt their records using their private keys and send them to the other party. In addition, P_r encrypts the output of P_s using its secret key and sends the results back to P_s. Finally, P_s learns the intersection of the two datasets.

$$\underline{P_s\ (sk_s)} \hspace{8cm} \underline{P_r\ (\ sk_r)}$$

$$D_s' = \{H(s)^{sk_s} | s \in D_s\}$$

$$\xrightarrow{\hspace{3cm} D_s' \hspace{3cm}}$$

$$D_r' = \{H(r)^{sk_r} | r \in D_r\}$$
$$D_s'' = \{(s')^{sk_r} | s' \in D_s'\}$$

$$\xleftarrow{\hspace{2cm} D_r'\ \text{and}\ D_s'' \hspace{2cm}}$$

$$D_r'' = \{(r')^{sk_s} | r' \in D_r'\}$$
$$\text{Output } D_s'' \cap D_r'' \hspace{6cm} \text{Output } \{\}$$

Fig. 3. One side DH-PSI

Informally, the security of these protocols against semi-honest adversaries is guaranteed by the one-way property of the hash function, the computational hardness of the decisional DH, and the one-more-DH [17] assumptions (see definitions in Appendix B). The decisional DH is used to hide the data in transit from eavesdroppers, while the one-more-DH assumption is used to prevent P_s from generating new records in the name of P_r.

One DH-PSI variant is the mutual DH-PSI, which includes one extra round: P_s sends D_r'' to P_r so that P_r can also compute the intersection. However, here an eavesdropper learns both D_s'' and D_r'' and can therefore learn the cardinality of the intersection $D_s'' \cap D_r''$.

One issue with DH-PSI is that it is susceptible to man-in-the-middle attacks [13]. To mitigate this attack and the leakage of the mutual DH-PSI's intersection cardinality, we assume that the transportation is encrypted and authenticated using TLS 1.3.

3   Our Solution

Our PPRL solution (hereafter: LSH-PSI PPRL) is an ER protocol that uses LSHMatch as its similarity indicator, where for privacy reasons, the parties cannot directly share the LSH results. The reason depends on whether the LSH is a preimage-resistant hash function or not. When it is not, P_r and P_s can simply inverse the LSH results for records that are not in the intersection and reveal private information of P_s, P_r, respectively. But even when it is, the solution's privacy depends on the LSH input entropy, where the parties can maintain an offline brute force attack against the LSH records of the other party.

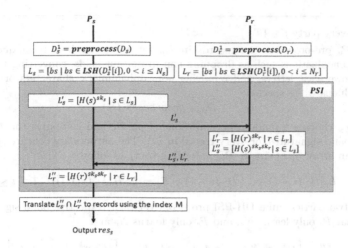

Fig. 4. Schematic of the LSH-PSI PPRL protocol.

To mitigate the privacy issue, we use a PSI protocol. The two parties first compute the LSH band signatures of all their records and then apply a PSI protocol over these signatures. Finally, P_s maps back the intersected signatures to the original records to learn the set of similar records. The concrete properties of LSHMatch can be tuned using the B and R LSH parameters. Figure 5 presents the LSH-PSI protocol, and Fig. 4 illustrates it schematically.

Our protocol is defined against semi-honest (honest-but-curious) adversaries, where all parties do not deviate from the protocol, and their inputs are genuine. Nevertheless, they may record and analyze all the intermediate computations and messages from the other parties to get more information.

To increase the efficiency of the underlying ER method, the two parties must use the same preprocessing techniques. In addition, the LSH-PSI protocol assumes that the pre-processing phase runs some deduplication protocol on the dataset of every party. Otherwise, P_s can extract information from pairs of matching records $s_1, s_2 \in D_s$, where s_1 matches a record in D_r but s_2 does not. Finally, the PSI protocol is executed for all records at once and not per record, therefore it is critical to preserve the order of the signatures exchanged between the parties, i.e., of $L_s^{'}$ and $L_s^{''}$ in Fig. 4. Otherwise, it will be impossible to match the records in Step 4 of Fig. 5. In Sect. 3.1, we discuss the case where P_r does *not* preserve the order of P_s encrypted signatures.

The purpose of using the permutation π_p in Step 1b is to avoid the case where the other party learns information about "missing" records. For example, suppose that the records in D_r are ordered alphabetically according to a first name QID, and that P_s learns that *Jerry* and *Joseph* are in the intersection. If *Jerry* and *Joseph* happen to belong to adjacent records in D_r, then an honest but curious P_s learns that P_r has no record for *John*. When using a permutation, the only way for P_s to deduce the same information is by learning all the records in D_r. A concrete example of Steps 1.b - 3 is given in Appendix D.

1. For every party $p \in \{s, r\}$
   (a) P_p pre-processes the records in D_p by using standard techniques and canonizations such as dropping non-important fields, converting texts to lower-case letters, and removing non-alphanumeric characters or superfluous white spaces.
   $$D_p^1 = preprocess(D_p)$$
   (b) P_p chooses a random permutation π_p on D_p^1 and computes the B LSH band signatures for every record in D_p^1. The outputs are concatenated in an array L_p of size $B \cdot N_p$ according to π_p as follows
   $$L_p[B \cdot (i - 1) + 1 : B \cdot (i - 1) + B] = LSH(D_p^1(\pi_p(i))) \quad 1 \leq i \leq N_p$$

2. The two parties run a DH-PSI protocol over their respective band signatures so that P_r only learns N_s, and P_s only learns N_r and
   $$L_s'' = \left[H(s)^{sk_s sk_r} \mid s \in L_s \right] \qquad L_r'' = \left[H(r)^{sk_s sk_r} \mid r \in L_r \right]$$

3. P_s generates the array
   $$M[i] = \begin{cases} 1 & L_s''[i] \in L_r'' \\ 0 & otherwise, \end{cases} \qquad 1 \leq i \leq |L_s''|$$

4. P_s returns the matching records
   $$res_s = \{r \mid r = D_s[\pi_s^{-1}(i)], \ 1 \leq i \leq N_s, \ 1 \leq \sum_{j=1}^{B} M[B \cdot (i - 1) + j]\}$$

Fig. 5. The LSH-PSI PPRL protocol.

Theorem 1. *The LSH-PSI PPRL protocol is a PPRL protocol according to Definition 6 from Appendix C where the similarity indicator is* LSHMatch. *This protocol is secure against semi-honest adversaries.*

Proof. **Correctness.** The correctness of the protocol follows from the fact that the intersection $L_s \cap L_r$ has a one-to-one correlation with the encrypted band signatures $L_s'' \cap L_r''$.

Privacy of P_s. By the discrete-log assumption, P_r only gets to see N_s elements that are indistinguishable from random values. Thus, P_r only learns N_s.

Privacy of P_r. P_s gets from P_r the values of L_s' and L_r raised to the power of P_r's secret key. By the discrete-log assumption, these values are indistinguishable from random to P_s. Except that P_s can raise L_r' values to the power of its own secret key and then intersect the results with L_s''. This intersection of random values is used by P_s to identify matching signatures, which is expected by Definition 6. Because P_s learns nothing from values outside the intersection, we say that it only learns res and N_r as expected. $\square$

Remark 1. Similar to the DH-PSI case, the use of TLS 1.3 allows the parties to mutually authenticate themselves and to avoid the attack presented in [13]. Still, as a defense-in-depth mechanism, the parties in every PPRL session should avoid reusing secret keys to avoid man-in-the-middle attacks.

3.1   PPRL Variants

Based on the above protocol, we construct three other protocols: a mutual PPRL protocol, where both parties learn the intersection; an N-PPRL protocol, where the parties only learn the cardinality of the intersection; and a revealing PPRL protocol, where the latter immediately follows the definition. Appendix C provides formal abstract definitions of these protocols.

A Mutual PPRL Protocol. To establish a mutual PPRL protocol, we modify Step 2 of Fig. 5 to use the mutual DH-PSI protocol of Sect. 2.3. The security of the protocol follows from either the security of the mutual DH-PSI, or from the fact that the mutual protocol is equivalent to running the original PPRL protocol twice: first between P_s and P_r, and subsequently between P_r and P_s. Note that P_s cannot reduce the communication by sending only records that are in the intersection because then an eavesdropper can learn the intersection size. This claim is valid even when using a secure communication channel (e.g., TLS 1.3).

An N-PPRL Protocol. To achieve an N-PPRL protocol, we could have simply counted the number of elements in the intersection set *res*, but this would reveal to P_s more information beyond $N_{s \cap r}$. Instead, we suggest reordering the encrypted band signatures during the DH-PSI in a way that hides the identity of the matched records but still enables them to be counted. Specifically, we ask P_r to apply a secret permutation to L_s'' before sending it to P_s. This permutation has a special property that permutes together the groups of adjacent B signatures that originate from the same record, otherwise, P_s will not be able to distinguish between the cases

1. $|LSH(s_1) \cap LSH(r_1)| = 1$ and $|LSH(s_2) \cap LSH(r_2)| = 1$
2. $|LSH(s_1) \cap LSH(r_1)| = 2$ and $|LSH(s_2) \cap LSH(r_2)| = 0$

We call the above permutation an intra-permutation of records. In addition, we apply an inter-permutation of records, where we separately permute the B signatures in each group of signatures in L_s'' that originate from the same record.

4   Our Implementation

For reproducibility, we provide concrete details about our LSH implementation. We start by explaining the concept of relative weighting of the record fields.

4.1 Relative Weighting of the Record Fields

Some record fields may be more indicative of identity than other fields. For example, an SSN field is very indicative (though it may also include typos), and a similarity of the full names is more indicative of identity than the similarity of zip codes. A simple method of weighting the effect of the different fields on the matching process is to duplicate the shingles originating from a field for a predefined number of times. We call this number the field weight. For example, consider a PPRL that operates over records with two fields: name and zip code. We use $k = 6$ and $k = 7$ shingles for these fields and set their weights to be 3 and 1, respectively. Then, the 6-shingle 'John S' extracted from the name field 'John Smith' will be duplicated into three separate shingles 'John S1', 'John S2', 'John S3', whereas the zip-code 7-shingle '2304170' will not be duplicated. This causes shingles originating from the name to be three times more likely than zip-code shingles to be the minimum value used by the Min-Hashes of the LSH (see Sect. 2.2). This will make the band signatures more likely to match if name shingles are identical than if zip-code shingles are identical.

The problem with this shingle duplication weighting method is that the extra shingles slow down the PPRL process because more shingles need to be hashed by the many Min-Hashes. To this end, we present a novel method for weighting the shingles, which yields the same results as the shingle duplication method but is much faster. The idea is to reduce the hash value of a shingle according to the shingle's weight, to directly increase its chance of being the shingle that receives the minimal value by the Min-Hashes.

We view the hash code h of a shingle as a discrete random variable with uniform distribution over some integer range $[0, maxVal]$. Thus, $x = h/maxVal$ is approximately a random variable with a continuous uniform distribution over $[0, 1]$. Our method relies on this being a good approximation.

Our method is as follows: instead of duplicating a shingle w times, we compute the shingle's hash-code h, normalize it $x = h/maxVal$, then apply the transformation $y = 1 - (1 - x)^{1/w}$, and finally return back to the original scale $h' = \lfloor y * maxVal \rfloor$. Lemma 1 shows that this results with a variable h' whose distribution is the same as the minimum of w independent hashes.

Lemma 1. *Let H_1, H_2, ..., H_n be i.i.d. random variables with uniform distribution over $[0, 1]$. Let $Y = min(H_1, H_2, \ldots, H_w)$. Then $X = 1 - (1 - H_1)^{1/w}$ has the same distribution as Y.*

Proof. Let F_H be the cumulative distribution function (CDF) of each H_i, i.e., $F_H(h) = h$ in the range $[0, 1]$. Let F_Y be the CDF of Y, i.e., $F_Y(y) = 1 - (1 - F_H(y))^w = 1 - (1 - y)^w$ and its inverse is $F_Y^{-1}(p) = 1 - (1 - p)^{1/w}$, so $X = F_Y^{-1}(H_1)$. The CDF of X is therefore

$$F_X(x) = P(X \leq x) = P(F_Y^{-1}(H_1) \leq x) = P(H_1 \leq F_Y(x)).$$

Since H_1 is a uniform variable over $[0, 1]$, this means $F_X(x) = F_Y(x)$.   □

Algorithm 1. Compute the LSH for a given DB record

Input: *record*, a map of fields to values (strings) and *conf* a list of tuples (F, k, w) where F is a set of field names, and $k, w \in \mathbb{N}$ are the shingles length and the fields weight, respectively.

Output: $lsh = [b_1, b_2, \ldots, b_B]$.

1: **procedure** LSH(*record*, *conf*)
2:     $FG = \emptyset$
3:     **for** $t \in conf$ **do**
4:         $s =$ ""
5:         **for** $f \in t.F$ **do**
6:             $s = s \mid record[f]$
7:         $FG = FG \cup (s, t.k, t.w)$
8:     **return** $LshFG(FG)$

We observed a 9% speedup when comparing the computation time (ignoring communications) of our PPRL solution using the shingle duplication method versus the above hash-dropping method.

Remark 2. The work in [24] also describes a method of computing a 'Weighted MinHash' over multisets with duplicated elements, but the universe of all possible items (or dimension for vectors) is assumed to be known in advance.

4.2 LSH Description

We are now ready to describe our LSH implementation. The algorithms below use a data structure that we call the field-group data structure FG, which is a list of tuples (s, k, w), where s is a string, $k \in \mathbb{N}$ is the shingles length, and $w \in \mathbb{N}$ is a vector with the shingles' weights, respectively. Algorithm 1 computes the LSH for a given record *record*. First, it concatenates together strings from fields that belong to the same group according to the configuration variable *conf* (Lines 5–6). Then, it attaches to every concatenated string the k, w values of its group as defined by *conf* (Line 7). The algorithm returns the output of the LshFG function on the generated field-group data structure FG (Line 8).

The LshFG algorithm uses the auxiliary functions getWeigthedShingles, which we describe in Algorithm 2. Its input is a field-group data structure and its output is a list of pairs of k-shingles and their respective weights.

Algorithm 3 describes the function LshFG, which basically follows the LSH definition. First, the strings are converted to shingles by invoking Algorithm 2. The loop of lines 8–14 generates the signature bands in M. It starts by computing a 32-bit hash for every shingle (lines 10–11), and then uses them to construct R different hashes for each of the shingles. The R hash values are then reduced according to the shingle weight using the function CalcH. This function is based on Lemma 1, where the equation in Line 3 can be modified when $w \leq 2$ to avoid the division and save computations. The resulting R minimal hash values are kept in the M array. To generate fast hash values, we replaced the intermediate

Algorithm 2. Returns weighted shingles for given strings
___
Input: FG a field-group data structure.
Output: res an ordered list of pairs (sh, w) where sh is a string and $w \in \mathbb{N}$.
1: **procedure** GETWEIGTHEDSHINGLES(FG)
2:     $res = \emptyset$
3:     **for** $(s, k, w) \in FG$ **do**
4:         $S = \texttt{getShingles}(s, k)$ ▷ Returns an ordered list of the k-shingles of s.
5:         $res = res.append\left([(sh, w) \mid sh \in S]\right)$
6:     **return** res
___

Algorithm 3. Compute the LSH for a given record field group
___
Constants: MP $= 2^{61} - 1$, a Mersenne prime, and $maxVal = 2^{32}$
Input: $h, c, d, w \in \mathbb{N}$.
Output: an integer.
1: **procedure** CALCH(h, c, d, w)
2:     $h = \left[h \cdot c + d \ (\text{mod } MP)\right] \ (\text{mod } maxVal)$
3:     **return** $maxVal \cdot \left(1 - (1 - \frac{h}{maxVal})^{\frac{1}{w}}\right)$ ▷ based on Lemma 1.

Input: $B, R \in \mathbb{N}$, and FG a field-group data structure.
Output: $L = [b_1, b_2, \ldots, b_B]$.
4: **procedure** LSHFG(B, R, FG)
5:     $C \xleftarrow{\$} \{1, \ldots, MP\}^R$
6:     $D \xleftarrow{\$} \{0, \ldots, MP\}^R$
7:     $wS = \texttt{getWeightedShingles}(FG)$
8:     **for** $b = 1, \ldots, B$ **do**
9:         $i = 1$
10:         **for** $(sh, w) \in wS$ **do**
11:             $H[i++] = (\textsc{Trunc}_{32}(\textsc{SHA256}(sh)), w)$
12:         **for** $r = 1, \ldots, R$ **do**
13:             $M[r] = \min_i\{\textsc{CalcH}(H[i].sh, C[r], D[r], H[i].w)\}$
14:         $L[b] = \textsc{SHA256}(M)$
15:     **return** L
___

SHA256 calls with a Mersenne twister, which uses random numbers. The algorithm generates and holds these numbers in the arrays C and D. Finally, using SHA256, we concatenate and hash the values of M to create the band signature (Line 14).

5   Experiments

Experimental Setup. We carried out the experiments on two machines that are located in different local area networks (LANs). We measured an average of 65 ms round-trip latency between them.

Table 1. Accuracy of our PPRL protocol over the NCVR snapshots.

Set size	FN	FP	TP	Precision (%)	Recall (%)	F1 (%)
10^4	19	21	653	96.88	97.17	97.03
10^5	1,369	1,665	55,682	97.1	97.6	97.35
10^6	22,233	19,365	847,724	97.77	97.44	97.61

- Machine A has an Intel® Xeon® CPU E5-2620 v3 @ 2.40 GHz, with 12 physical cores and 377 GB of RAM.
- Machine B has an Intel® Xeon® CPU E5-2699 v4 @ 2.20 GHz, with 44 physical cores and 744 GB of RAM.

We set machine A to run P_s and machine B to run P_r with $N_s \approx N_r$.

Our code is written in C++ and runs on Ubuntu 20.04. It uses OpenSSL version 1.1.1f to establish secure TLS 1.3 connections between the two parties. In addition, it uses OpenSSL hash function implementation (concretely, H = SHA256) and DH operations (concretely, elliptic curve DH operations over the NIST P-256 curve). We report communications in KB and running time in seconds. We also provide a breakdown of the different running time phases: communication and computations per party. For the measurements, we separated the communication phases from the computation phases, which in a real scenario can be pipelined to run in parallel.

For the evaluations, we considered two dataset cases: a) The North Carolina voter register (NCVR) dataset[1], which is commonly used for PPRL evaluations; b) a synthetic dataset that we generated and made available in [23].

NCVR Datasets. We used the November 2014 and November 2017 snapshots of the NCVR datasets. Prior to running the PPRL protocol, we deduplicated the snapshots by eliminating duplicate records with identical "NCID" or with identical values in the 'first_name', 'last_name', 'midl_name', 'birth_place' and 'age' fields. Subsequently, we removed the NCID field from the two snapshots, and ran our PPRL protocol on the two snapshots. A reported matching pair was considered to be a true-positive event if the two reported records share the same NCID value. Table 1 shows the accuracy breakdown of the LSH we used by reporting the number of false-negative (FN), false-positive (FP), and true-positive (TP) events, together with the precision, recall, and F1 results when sampling sets of fixed sizes from the above snapshots. Note that while the precision is high, the absolute number of false-positives may be regarded as too high for some users. See Sect. E.1 for ways to tune the process and balance the number of false positive and false negative cases while considering the protocol performance.

Synthetic Dataset. We generated two synthetic datasets using IBM InfoSphere® Optim^{TM} Test Data Fabrication [22] with the following fields: 'first

---

[1] https://www.ncsbe.gov/results-data/voter-registration-data,lastaccessedMar2022.

Table 2. Performance results on the synthetic dataset for different samples of the original dataset.

Set sizes	Comm. (KB)	Comm. time (s)	Offline time (s)	Total time (s)
2^8	$5.68 \cdot 10^3$	3	1	4
2^{12}	$9.04 \cdot 10^4$	17	2	19
2^{16}	$1.44 \cdot 10^6$	237	36	273
2^{20}	$1.19 \cdot 10^7$	1,959	608	2,567

name', 'last name', 'email', 'email domain', 'address number', 'address location', 'address line', 'city', 'state', 'country', 'zip base', 'zip ext', 'phone area code', 'phone exchange code' and 'phone line number', where $N_s \approx N_r \approx 1,000,000$. We generated the datasets in a way that only 100 records in the two datasets represent identical entities. The pairs of records that describe these shared entities sometimes have identical fields and sometimes fields with minor typos, different styles, and other types of minor differences, which are still small enough to warrant the assumption that the similar records in fact describe the same entity. Our PPRL protocol identified all the matching records. The performance evaluation of the protocol is given in Table 2.

6   Conclusion

We presented a novel PPRL solution that relies on LSH to identify similar records while using PSI to ensure privacy. We formally defined the privacy guarantees that such a protocol provides and evaluated its efficiency. Our results show that it takes 11–45 min (depending on network settings) to perform a PPRL solution comparing two large datasets with 2^{20} records per dataset. Note that none of the results presented in Sect. A reported comparable speeds for such large datasets. This makes our solution practical and attractive for companies and organizations. We made our implementation available for testing at [23].

We proposed a PPRL framework that can use different PSI protocols as long as they provide the same security guarantees defined above. We demonstrated our solution using an ECDH PSI protocol. It may be an interesting direction to implement and test the protocol using other solutions that can further improve its performance and overall bandwidth.

A   Related Work

To demonstrate our solution, we use a PSI instantiation that uses public-key cryptography; specifically, we use one that leverages the commutative properties of the DH key agreement scheme. This PSI construction was introduced in

[21] with a similar construction even before that in [33]. Subsequent PSI works consider other, more complex cryptographic primitives such as homomorphic encryption (HE) [6] and oblivious transfer (OT) [35]. While the latter solutions may offer an interesting tradeoff in terms of performance and security, we decided to stick with the basic DH-style protocol due to its simplicity and the fact that its primitives were already standardized [2]. Because we use PSI as a blackbox, we can also benefit from most of the advantages that the other methods provide such as performance and security guarantees.

Our solution follows previous works in considering a *balanced* case, where the two datasets are roughly equal in size. An example, for a PSI over unbalanced sets was studied in [5]. In fact, there were attempts to use PSI for PPRL before this paper. However, they were either noted to be inefficient [40] or relied on a different techniques such as term frequency-inverse document frequency (TF-IDF) [37], which is more appropriate for comparing documents, rather than short record fields (such as names or addresses). Furthermore, the protocol of [37] can only compare given record pairs. This implies the need for $\mathcal{O}(n^2)$ operations, in contrast to our method, which requires $\mathcal{O}(n)$ operations.

A complete survey of PPRL techniques and challenges is available at [18, 40], in which we observed solutions that use different cryptographic primitives. For example, [14, 41] relies on HE, which is known for its high computational cost. For example, [14] reports that it took somewhat less than two hours to evaluate 20,000 patient records, which is less records than in our evaluations by several orders of magnitude. Other works [4, 38] use garbled circuits, which can still be inefficient, while other multi-party computation (MPC) solutions such as [28] can incur high communication costs [7]. Another example is the fuzzy volts approach, which uses secure polynomial interpolations [34], but only reports results for around 1,000 records.

Other solutions [20, 36] overcome the privacy issue by using differential privacy (DP), which provides some level of anonymization. In [36], the two parties partition the dataset into blocks of records and compare only records in corresponding blocks via an MPC process that computes the distance function. In contrast, in [20], for every block, the parties compute a private "synopsis" and send it to a third party, which uses this information to identify when blocks are too far from each other to justify a comparison of their records. In both [20, 36], the scheme privacy comes from DP, while the scheme security comes from the MPC process used to compare the pairs of records. The two solutions use MPC protocols for comparing integers while our record matching metric relies on LSH, which is a more appropriate comparison method for longer texts such as addresses. In addition, the complexity of our solution is linear in the total number of records since we do not separately compare every pair of records in the two data sets or even in pre-arranged blocks, which requires a sub-quadratic complexity. Unlike [20], our solution does not require the presence of a third party. Finally, it is possible to enhance the privacy of our scheme by adding a preprocessing DP layer as in [20, 36]. Thus, we view the usage of DP as orthogonal to our approach.

Many PPRL works use Bloom filter encodings [39], which use a locality preserving hash (LPH) function over the data. The main advantage of the Bloom filter is speed. The difference between LPH and LSH is that LPH is data-dependent, i.e., for three records p, q, r, a metric d, and an LPH function l_p

$$d(p,q) < d(q,r) \implies d(l_p(p), l_p(q)) < d(l_p(q), l_p(r))$$

This relation complicates the evaluation of the protocol leakage. The lack of a formal analysis for Bloom filter based solutions caused several attacks on them [8,9,29,30]. A survey of attacks and countermeasures for this method can be found in [15]. Our solution's use of LSH has an advantage over Bloom filters as it is data-independent and more robust against the above attacks. A method that combines Bloom filters and LSH was presented in [16,26]. In contrast to this one, our solution only uses LSH, which simplifies the privacy analysis. Moreover, our use of PSI hides the LSH output and thus prevents offline attacks. In addition, [26] requires use of a third-party and demonstrates a solution that took more than an hour to match $300K$ records. Another recent example is [28], which runs in $\mathcal{O}(n \cdot polylog(n))$ and proved to be cryptographically secure in the semi-honest security model. However, the method analyzed $4,096$ records in 88 min and it is not clear whether this method can scale to handle more than $100K$ records.

B Security Assumptions

Definition 3 (Decisional DH (DDH)). *For a cyclic group $\mathbb{G}$, a generator g, and integers $a, b, c \in \mathbb{Z}$, the decisional DH problem is hard, if for every probabilistic polynomial-time (PPT) adversary $\mathcal{A}$*

$$|Pr[A(g, g^a, g^b, g^{ab}] = 1) - $$
$$Pr[A(g, g^a, g^b, g^c) = 1]| < negl(),$$

where the probability is taken over (g, a, b, c).

Definition 4 (Computational DH (CDH)). *For a cyclic group $\mathbb{G}$, a generator g, and integers $a, b \in \mathbb{Z}$, the computational DH problem is hard, if for every PPT adversary $\mathcal{A}$*

$$Pr[A(g, g^a, g^b] = g^{ab}) < negl(),$$

where the probability is taken over (g, a, b).

Definition 5 (One-more-DH (OMDH) [17]). *Let $\mathbb{G}$ be a cyclic group. The one-more-DH problem is hard, if for every PPT adversary $\mathcal{A}$ that gets a generator $g \in \mathbb{G}$ together with some power g^a and who has access to two oracles: $h^a = CDH_{g,g^a}(h)$ for some $h \in \mathbb{G}$, and $r \xleftarrow{\$} C()$ a challenge oracle that returns a random challenge point $r \in G$ and can only be invoked after all calls to the CDH_{g,g^a}, it follows that*

$$Pr[A(g, g^a, r \leftarrow C()) = r^a] < negl()$$

where the probability is taken over (g, a).

C   Privacy-Preserving Record Linkage

PPRL [11] is an ER protocol between two parties P_s and P_r, with private datasets D_s and D_r of sizes N_s and N_r, respectively; these records have a similarity measure $\mu(\cdot, \cdot)$, and some additional privacy requirements. These requirements may lead to several security models and several formal definitions of PPRL.

The most intuitive way to define privacy for PPRL is by following the PSI privacy notion: P_s only learns N_r and the intersection $D_s \cap D_r$, i.e., all records that exactly match in all fields while P_r only learns N_s. Note that in both PSI and PPRL, P_s and P_r need to share the nature of the information contained in their datasets with each other to decide which QIDs they can validly compare.

The difference between PSI and PPRL is that PSI only returns exact matches according to some uniquely identifying QIDs, while PPRL returns matching records up to some similarity indicator and according to non-unique QIDs. For example, a PSI protocol may rely on users' SSNs, while a PPRL protocol may compare first and last names. Thus, a PPRL may inadvertently match "David Doe" with "Davy Don" even if they represent different entities (users).

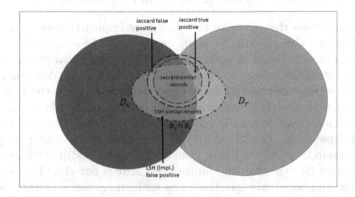

Fig. 6. A Venn diagram of different ER outputs applied on two datasets D_s and D_r. The ER methods are: matching only identical pairs of records (purple), matching pairs of records with a Jaccard index above some threshold (green), and matching pairs of records with matching LSH indicators (yellow). (Color figure online)

Figure 6 shows a Venn diagram for the output of different ER solutions on D_s and D_r datasets. With the exact matching method ($D_s \cap D_r$) no privacy risks occur since it only reveals the agreed-upon intersection[2]. In contrast, when using the Jaccard similarity to compute the matches, the parties learn: a) records

---

[2] In practice, if P_s learns that both parties share a record with the same SSN and at a later stage learns that the other record fields do not match, then it may deduce that D_r contains a record with a very close SSN that leaks information. Following previous studies, we only consider leaks that occur as a result of the protocol itself.

in $D_s \cap D_r$, which is ok; b) records outside $D_s \cap D_r$ that represent the same entity (true-positive), which is also ok; c) records outside $D_s \cap D_r$ that represent different entities (false-positive), which may break the privacy of the parties. In general, any PPRL protocol must assume this kind of leakage, and should do its best to quantify it, e.g., by assuming the existence of a bound τ on the similarity false-positive rate.

Definition 6 (PPRL). *A PPRL protocol* $\mathcal{P}$ *between two parties* P_s, P_r *with datasets* D_s, D_r, *respectively, a similarity measure* μ, *a measure indicator* I_t^{μ} *for a fixed threshold* t *with a false-positive rate bounded by* τ, *has the following properties.*

– **Correctness:** $\mathcal{P}$ *is correct if it outputs to* P_s *the set*

$$res = \{(s, Enc(r)) \mid s \in D_s, r \in D_r, I_t^{\mu}(s,r) = 1\},$$

  where $Enc(r)$ *is an encryption of* r *under a secret key of* P_r.
– **Privacy:** $\mathcal{P}$ *maintains privacy if* P_s *only learns* res *and* N_r, *and* P_r *only learns* N_s.

Corollary 1. *The leaked information of* P_r *in* $\mathcal{P}$ *is bounded by* $\tau \cdot \frac{|res|}{N_r}$.

Definition 6 assumes the existence of τ but only implicitly uses it. The reason is that τ does not always exist. In many cases, it can be empirically estimated based on prior data or based on perturbed synthetic data. However, relying solely on empirical estimates increases the ambiguity of the privacy definition for such protocols. Moreover, in many cases, τ depends on data from the two datasets that have different distributions, which none of the parties know in advance. Another reason for only implicitly relying on τ is that the leaked information in Corollary 1 depends on res and can only be computed after running the protocol.

While τ bounds the privacy leak from above, there is still the issue of quantifying the exact leakage after the protocol ends. It is not clear how the parties can verify the number of false-positive cases without revealing private data. Usually, an ER protocol is used when the compared records do not include uniquely identifying fields (such as an SSN) and thus the parties cannot compute the exact matches using PSI. Consequently, their only way to verify matches is by revealing their private data. To assist in this task, we define a protocol called a revealing PPRL.

Definition 7 (Revealing PPRL). *A revealing PPRL protocol* $\mathcal{P}$ *is a PPRL protocol* $\mathcal{P}'$, *where* P_r *also learns* $u = \{Enc(r) \mid (s, Enc(r)) \in \mathcal{P}'.res\}$ *and* P_s *also learns*

$$res' = \{(r, Enc(r)) \mid (s, Enc(r)) \in \mathcal{P}'.res\},$$

In words, P_r learns which of its own records are matched, and P_s learns the field content of the matched records of the other party. The simplest way to achieve a revealing PPRL is for P_s to send u to P_r, who will then decrypt its values and hand them back to P_s. The difference between Definitions 6 and 7 is that in the latter, P_s learns the values of P_r's records instead of just their encryption. While this definition leaks more data from P_r to P_s, it is easier to analyze because now P_s can verify the matches with some probability and learn the estimated number of false-positives. We also consider the definitions of the associated mutual PPRL and the mutual revealing PPRL.

Definition 8 (Mutual PPRL). *A PPRL protocol $\mathcal{P}$ between two parties P_s, P_r with datasets D_s, D_r, respectively, a similarity measure μ, a measure indicator I_t^μ for a fixed threshold t with a false-positive rate bounded by τ, has the following properties.*

- **Correctness:** *$\mathcal{P}$ is correct if it outputs res_s (resp. res_r) to P_s (resp. P_r), where*
$$res_s = \{(s, Enc(r)) \mid s \in D_s, r \in D_r, I_t^\mu(s,r) = 1\}$$
$$res_r = \{(r, Enc(s)) \mid s \in D_s, r \in D_r, I_t^\mu(s,r) = 1\},$$
and $Enc(r)$ (resp. $Enc(s)$) is an encryption of r (resp. s) under a secret key of P_r (resp. P_s).
- **Privacy:** *$\mathcal{P}$ maintains privacy if P_s only learns res_s and N_r, and P_r only learns res_r and N_s.*

The mutual revealing PPRL is similarly defined. The difference between the mutual PPRL and the revealing PPRL in terms of privacy is that in the mutual PPRL, P_r can match the encryption of P_s records to its records and therefore gains more information while P_s only learns the encryption of P_r records.

In the PPRL protocols described above, the two parties learn the intersection of their datasets. However, in some scenarios, the parties merely need to learn the *number* of matches and do not wish to reveal the identity of the matched records to the other party. To this end, we define an N-PPRL protocol.

Definition 9 (N-PPRL). *A PPRL protocol $\mathcal{P}$ between two parties P_s, P_r with datasets D_s, D_r, respectively, a similarity measure μ, a measure indicator I_t^μ for a fixed threshold t with a false-positive rate bounded by τ, has the following properties.*

- **Correctness:** *$\mathcal{P}$ is correct if it outputs to P_s the value*
$$N_{s \cap r} = |\{(s,r) \mid s \in D_s, r \in D_r, I_t^\mu(s,r) = 1\}|,$$
- **Privacy:** *$\mathcal{P}$ maintains privacy if P_s, (resp. P_r) only learns $N_{s \cap r}$, N_r (resp. N_s).*

The mutual N-PPRL protocol is similarly defined.

D   Example of the LSH-PSI Protocol

A concrete example of Steps 1.b - 3 of the LSH-PSI PPRL protocol (Fig. 5) is given in Fig. 7. Suppose that $v = H(455)^{sk_s sk_r}$ then P_s learns via the PSI process that P_r also has a band signature with the same value 455. P_r took care to preserve the order of P_s's encrypted band signatures during the PSI, so P_s can map the shared value v back to the band signature for Band 1 of record N_s, and deduce that P_r has some unknown record that is similar to her own record N_s.

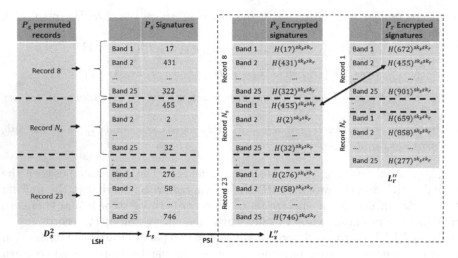

Fig. 7. Steps 1.b - 3 of our protocol. P_s learns via the PSI protocol that the signature for Record N_s Band 1 is shared with P_r.

E   Using the Jaccard Indicator

Theorem 1 shows that the LSH-PSI PPRL protocol follows Definition 6 when considering the LSH as the similarity indicator. This means that security reviewers need to accept the privacy leakage that occurs when using an LSH, something that is already done by many organizations that perform RL. However, some reviewers may instead prefer to trust the Jaccard index due to its wide acceptance.

Figure 6 shows two ways to define LSH false-positive events: in relation to exact matches of entire records as in the LSH-PSI PPRL, or in relation to the method of matching pairs of records with a high enough Jaccard index. Thus according to the latter definition an LSH false-positive happens only when a pair of records are matched due to having at least one shared LSH band, and yet they do not have a high enough Jaccard index to justify a claim of similarity.

Bounding the false-positive events rate τ' based on the latter definition will allow us to define an LSH-PSI PPRL related to the Jaccard index metric but with a different bound $\tau \cdot \tau'$, where τ is the Jaccard original false-positive bound. In this section, we further discuss the relation between the LSH and the Jaccard index.

For two records s, r with Jaccard index J, Fig. 8 shows the probability for an LSHMatch $= 1$ event according to Eq. 2 with $R = 200$ and $B = 20$. In standard ER solutions, it is the role of the domain expert to decide the specific Jaccard index that would indicate enough similarity between the two records. For example, in the figure the targeted Jaccard index is 0.78. The figure shows the cumulative probability of getting true-positives ($J(s,r) > 0.78$ and LSHMatch$(s,r) = 1$), true-negatives ($J(s,r) \leq 0.78$ and LSHMatch$(s,r) = 0$), and the corresponding false-positive and false-negative cumulative probabilities.

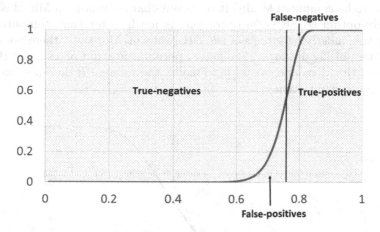

Fig. 8. The function $F(J) = 1 - (1 - J^R)^B$ from Eq. 2, where $R = 20$ and $B = 200$. The black vertical line is the Jaccard index threshold.

The above example shows that when $B = 20$ and $R = 200$, it is possible to close the gap between the Jaccard index and the LSH by choosing the Jaccard threshold to be below 0.5. In that case, the probability for a false-positive event is less than 0.0001, which means that one in every ten-thousand records leaks. However, using such a Jaccard threshold will yield many false-positive cases relative to exact record matching, which is less desirable in terms of privacy.

It turns out that it is possible to tune the slope of the accumulated probability function. Figure 9 compares the probability functions in four different setups $B = 20, R = 200$ (setup 1) $B = 100, R = 100$ (setup 2) $B = 14, R = 30$ (setup 3) and $B = 120, R = 18$ (setup 4). Here, we see that replacing setup 1 with setup 2 allows us to set the Jaccard threshold at 0.78 while reducing the LSH false-positive rate to as low as 10^{-8}. However, setup 2 dramatically increases the LSH false-negative rate. Note however that false negatives affect the security less than false-positives, and in addition, users are often much more reluctant to report false positives than to miss reports due to false negatives. Setup 2 may also increase the overall performance of the protocol relative to setup 1 because there are many more bands to encrypt and communicate, as described in the following section.

E.1   Optimizing the Protocol

Setup 4 in Fig. 9 probably results in more false-positive and false-negative cases than setup 1, and the low slope of the curve implies a larger region of uncertainty. However, the PSI for setup 4 runs more than 6 times faster than the PSI for setup 1, because there are just 20 rather than 180 band signatures that need to be encrypted and communicated. The change in the R parameter does not affect the performance as much, since it merely determines the number of Min-Hashes that need to be computed locally. It turns out that computing a Min-Hash (like the highly optimized SHA-256 operation) is much faster than computing the power in the underlying groups of the DH protocol. Moreover, there are known methods for quickly producing R different permutations out of a single SHA-256 call such as the Mersenne twister [3]. Finally, the value of R does not affect the size of the communication.

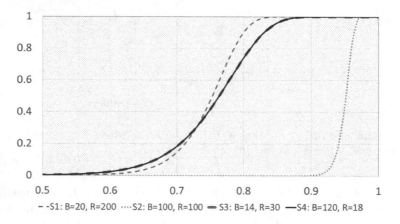

- -S1: B=20, R=200   ····S2: B=100, R=100   — S3: B=14, R=30   —S4: B=120, R=18

Fig. 9. A comparison of four probability functions $F(J) = 1 - (1 - J^R)^B$ (see Eq. 2) with different B and R values.

We use the B and R parameters to control the curve, which in turn affects the protocol's accuracy and performance. Reducing B makes it less likely to find a matching band signature, thus increasing the false-negative probability, but improving performance. The rate of false-negatives can be reduced by decreasing R, thus making it more probable for two bands to match. Conversely, if the false-positive rate is too high, then one can increase R with little performance penalty. We therefore optimize the process by searching for values of B and R that have the minimal B value (for best performance) while more or less preserving the targeted curve shape.

Suppose for example that setup 1 has the targeted probability function. The figure shows the probability function for setup 3, which runs almost twice as fast as setup 1 and has an almost identical probability function. Setup 4 has an almost identical curve as setup 3 so it gives an almost identical accuracy, but it runs much slower because it requires almost 8 times more bands.

E.2   Scoring the Reported Matches

When a PPRL protocol relies on the Jaccard index but its implementation uses LSH, it may be in the users' interest to quantify the number of false-positive events. To this end, we present a way to estimate the Jaccard index based on the LSH results.

Estimating the Jaccard Index for Matching Pairs. When using LSH with B band signatures, it is possible to estimate the actual Jaccard index J by using a binomial confidence interval. By Observation 1, the probability for a matching band (i.e. the probability for a match in all R Min-Hashes of the band) is $p = J^R$. Suppose that P_s learns that there are h matching band signatures and $t = B - h$ non-matching band signatures. Using a 95% confidence interval, the Jaccard index lies in the range

$$\left[\sqrt[R]{\left| \frac{h}{B} - 1.96\sqrt{t\frac{h}{B^3}} \right|}, \ \sqrt[R]{\left| \frac{h}{B} + 1.96\sqrt{t\frac{h}{B^3}} \right|} \right] \tag{3}$$

In some cases this interval is too wide, and the users may prefer using a different approach, such as a revealing PPRL. In a revealing PPRL, the two parties learn the intersection of their datasets as in a standard PPRL but they also learn the records of the other parties that are involved in of the intersection. Thus, the leaked information in a revealing PPRL is higher than in a PPRL. Below, we propose an approach with privacy leakage that lies between the leakage of a revealing PPRL and a PPRL, where we compute the Jaccard index only for matching pairs, without revealing the exact shingles.

Computing the Precise Jaccard Index for Matching Pairs. Suppose that at the end of the LSH-PSI PPRL protocol, P_s learns the matching pair $(s, Enc(r))$. P_s can ask P_r to participate in another PSI process over the set of shingles of (s, r), where P_s knows s and P_r knows r. In this PSI, P_s only learns the intersection size of the associated shingles $|S \cap R|$ and the size $|R|$, so it can compute $J(s, r) = \frac{|S \cap R|}{|S| + |R| - |S \cap R|}$. Note that learning only the intersection size and not the intersection itself makes it harder for P_s to guess P_r's record.

These additional PSIs are relatively expensive in terms of performance, but we only need to carry them out for the reported matches, which are presumably only a very small fraction of all possible pairs of records. P_s and P_r can decide to perform such PSIs for every matching pair or for selected pairs of special interest, or for pairs selected after estimating the Jaccard index as described above. As mentioned in Sect. C performing a selective PSIs leaks the size of the selection to an eavesdropper **and this should be taken into account in the application threats model.**

References

1. Baker, D.B., et al.: Privacy-preserving linkage of genomic and clinical data sets. IEEE/ACM Trans. Comput. Biol. Bioinf. **16**(4), 1342–1348 (2019). https://doi.org/10.1109/TCBB.2018.2855125
2. Barker, E., Chen, L., Moody, D.: Recommendation for Pair-Wise Key-Establishment Schemes Using Integer Factorization Cryptography (Revision 1) (2014). https://doi.org/10.6028/NIST.SP.800-56Br1
3. Carter, J.L., Wegman, M.N.: Universal classes of hash functions. J. Comput. Syst. Sci. **18**(2), 143–154 (1979)
4. Chen, F., et al.: Perfectly secure and efficient two-party electronic-health-record linkage. IEEE Internet Comput. **22**(2), 32–41 (2018). https://doi.org/10.1109/MIC.2018.112102542
5. Chen, H., Huang, Z., Laine, K., Rindal, P.: Labeled PSI from fully homomorphic encryption with malicious security. In: Proceedings of the 2018 ACM SIGSAC Conference on Computer and Communications Security, CCS 2018, pp. 1223–1237. Association for Computing Machinery, New York (2018). https://doi.org/10.1145/3243734.3243836
6. Chen, H., Laine, K., Rindal, P.: Fast private set intersection from homomorphic encryption. In: Proceedings of the 2017 ACM SIGSAC Conference on Computer and Communications Security, CCS 2017, pp. 1243–1255. Association for Computing Machinery, New York (2017). https://doi.org/10.1145/3133956.3134061
7. Chen, Y.: Current approaches and challenges for the two-party privacy-preserving record linkage (PPRL). In: Collaborative Technologies and Data Science in Artificial Intelligence Applications, pp. 108–116 (2020). https://codassca2020.aua.am/wp-content/uploads/2020/09/2020_Codassca_Chen.pdf
8. Christen, P., Ranbaduge, T., Vatsalan, D., Schnell, R.: Precise and fast cryptanalysis for bloom filter based privacy-preserving record linkage. IEEE Trans. Knowl. Data Eng. **31**(11), 2164–2177 (2019). https://doi.org/10.1109/TKDE.2018.2874004
9. Christen, P., Schnell, R., Vatsalan, D., Ranbaduge, T.: Efficient cryptanalysis of bloom filters for privacy-preserving record linkage. In: Kim, J., Shim, K., Cao, L., Lee, J.-G., Lin, X., Moon, Y.-S. (eds.) PAKDD 2017. LNCS (LNAI), vol. 10234, pp. 628–640. Springer, Cham (2017). https://doi.org/10.1007/978-3-319-57454-7_49
10. Churches, T., Christen, P.: Blind data linkage using n-gram similarity comparisons. In: Dai, H., Srikant, R., Zhang, C. (eds.) PAKDD 2004. LNCS (LNAI), vol. 3056, pp. 121–126. Springer, Heidelberg (2004). https://doi.org/10.1007/978-3-540-24775-3_15
11. Clifton, C., et al.: Privacy-preserving data integration and sharing. In: Proceedings of the 9th ACM SIGMOD Workshop on Research Issues in Data Mining and Knowledge Discovery, DMKD 2004, pp. 19–26. Association for Computing Machinery, New York (2004). https://doi.org/10.1145/1008694.1008698

12. Cong, K., et al.: Labeled PSI from homomorphic encryption with reduced computation and communication. In: Proceedings of the 2021 ACM SIGSAC Conference on Computer and Communications Security, CCS 2021, pp. 1135–1150. Association for Computing Machinery, New York (2021). https://doi.org/10.1145/3460120.3484760

13. Cui, H., Yu, Y.: A Not-So-Trival Replay Attack Against DH-PSI. Cryptology ePrint Archive, Report 2020/901 (2020). https://ia.cr/2020/901

14. Essex, A.: Secure approximate string matching for privacy-preserving record linkage. IEEE Trans. Inf. Forensics Secur. **14**(10) (2019). https://doi.org/10.1109/TIFS.2019.2903651

15. Franke, M., Rahm, E.: Evaluation of Hardening Techniques for Privacy-Preserving Record Linkage (2021)

16. Franke, M., Sehili, Z., Rahm, E.: Parallel privacy-preserving record linkage using LSH-based blocking. In: International Conference on Internet of Things, Big Data and Security (IoTBDS) (2018). https://www.scitepress.org/Papers/2018/66827/66827.pdf

17. Freeman, D.: Pairing-based identification schemes. Cryptology ePrint Archive, Report 2005/336 (2005). https://ia.cr/2005/336

18. Gkoulalas-Divanis, A., Vatsalan, D., Karapiperis, D., Kantarcioglu, M.: Modern privacy-preserving record linkage techniques: an overview. IEEE Trans. Inf. Forensics Secur. **16**, 4966–4987 (2021). https://doi.org/10.1109/TIFS.2021.3114026

19. Gyawali, B., Anastasiou, L., Knoth, P.: Deduplication of scholarly documents using locality sensitive hashing and word embeddings. In: Proceedings of The 12th Language Resources and Evaluation Conference, Marseille, France, pp. 894–903. European Language Resources Association (2020). https://oro.open.ac.uk/70519/

20. He, X., Machanavajjhala, A., Flynn, C., Srivastava, D.: Composing differential privacy and secure computation: a case study on scaling private record linkage. In: Proceedings of the 2017 ACM SIGSAC Conference on Computer and Communications Security, CCS 2017, pp. 1389–1406. Association for Computing Machinery, New York (2017). https://doi.org/10.1145/3133956.3134030

21. Huberman, B.A., Franklin, M., Hogg, T.: Enhancing privacy and trust in electronic communities. In: Proceedings of the 1st ACM Conference on Electronic Commerce, EC 19999, pp. 78–86. Association for Computing Machinery (1999). https://doi.org/10.1145/336992.337012

22. IBM: IBM InfoSphere® Optim^{TM} Test Data Fabrication (2022). https://www.ibm.com/products/infosphere-optim-test-data-fabrication

23. IBM Research: Helayers (2022). https://hub.docker.com/r/ibmcom/helayers-pylab

24. Ioffe, S.: Improved consistent sampling, weighted MinHash and L1 sketching. In: 2010 IEEE International Conference on Data Mining, pp. 246–255 (2010)

25. Karapiperis, D., Gkoulalas-Divanis, A., Verykios, V.S.: FEDERAL: a framework for distance-aware privacy-preserving record linkage. IEEE Trans. Knowl. Data Eng. **30**(2), 292–304 (2018). https://doi.org/10.1109/TKDE.2017.2761759

26. Karapiperis, D., Verykios, V.S.: A distributed near-optimal LSH-based framework for privacy-preserving record linkage. Comput. Sci. Inf. Syst. **11**(2), 745–763 (2014). https://doi.org/10.2298/CSIS140215040K

27. Kargupta, H., Datta, S., Wang, Q., Sivakumar, K.: Random-data perturbation techniques and privacy-preserving data mining. Knowl. Inf. Syst. **7**(4), 387–414 (2005). https://doi.org/10.1007/s10115-004-0173-6

28. Khurram, B., Kerschbaum, F.: SFour: a protocol for cryptographically secure record linkage at scale. In: 2020 IEEE 36th International Conference on Data Engineering (ICDE), pp. 277–288 (2020). https://doi.org/10.1109/ICDE48307.2020.00031

29. Kroll, M., Steinmetzer, S.: Automated cryptanalysis of bloom filter encryptions of health records. In: Proceedings of the International Joint Conference on Biomedical Engineering Systems and Technologies, BIOSTEC 2015, vol. 5, pp. 5–13. SCITEPRESS - Science and Technology Publications, Lda, Setubal, PRT (2015). https://doi.org/10.5220/0005176000050013

30. Kuzu, M., Kantarcioglu, M., Durham, E., Malin, B.: A constraint satisfaction cryptanalysis of bloom filters in private record linkage. In: Fischer-Hübner, S., Hopper, N. (eds.) PETS 2011. LNCS, vol. 6794, pp. 226–245. Springer, Heidelberg (2011). https://doi.org/10.1007/978-3-642-22263-4_13

31. Leskovec, J., Rajaraman, A., Ullman, J.D.: Finding similar items. In: Mining of Massive Datasets, pp. 73–130 (2014). https://infolab.stanford.edu/~ullman/mmds/ch3a.pdf

32. Li, Y., Xia, K.: Fast video deduplication via locality sensitive hashing with similarity ranking. In: Proceedings of the International Conference on Internet Multimedia Computing and Service, ICIMCS 2016, pp. 94–98. Association for Computing Machinery, New York (2016). https://doi.org/10.1145/3007669.3007725

33. Meadows, C.: A more efficient cryptographic matchmaking protocol for use in the absence of a continuously available third party. In: 1986 IEEE Symposium on Security and Privacy, p. 134 (1986). https://doi.org/10.1109/SP.1986.10022

34. Mullaymeri, X., Karakasidis, A.: A two-party private string matching fuzzy vault scheme. In: Proceedings of the 36th Annual ACM Symposium on Applied Computing, pp. 340–343. Association for Computing Machinery (2021). https://doi.org/10.1145/3412841.3442079

35. Pinkas, B., Schneider, T., Zohner, M.: Faster private set intersection based on OT extension. In: 23rd USENIX Security Symposium (USENIX Security 2014), San Diego, CA, pp. 797–812. USENIX Association (2014). https://www.usenix.org/conference/usenixsecurity14/technical-sessions/presentation/pinkas

36. Rao, F.Y., Cao, J., Bertino, E., Kantarcioglu, M.: Hybrid private record linkage: separating differentially private synopses from matching records. ACM Trans. Priv. Secur. 22(3) (2019). https://doi.org/10.1145/3318462

37. Ravikumar, P., Cohen, W.W., Fienberg, S.E.: A secure protocol for computing string distance metrics. PSDM held at ICDM (2004). https://www.cs.cmu.edu/afs/cs.cmu.edu/Web/People/wcohen/postscript/psdm-2004.pdf

38. Saleem, A., Khan, A., Shahid, F., Masoom Alam, M., Khan, M.K.: Recent advancements in garbled computing: how far have we come towards achieving secure, efficient and reusable garbled circuits. J. Netw. Comput. Appl. 108(January), 1–19 (2018). https://doi.org/10.1016/j.jnca.2018.02.006

39. Schnell, R., Bachteler, T., Reiher, J.: Privacy-preserving record linkage using Bloom filters. BMC Med. Inform. Decis. Mak. 9(1), 41 (2009). https://doi.org/10.1186/1472-6947-9-41

40. Vatsalan, D., Sehili, Z., Christen, P., Rahm, E.: Privacy-preserving record linkage for big data: current approaches and research challenges. In: Zomaya, A.Y., Sakr, S. (eds.) Handbook of Big Data Technologies, pp. 851–895. Springer, Cham (2017). https://doi.org/10.1007/978-3-319-49340-4_25

41. Wong, K.S.S., Kim, M.H.: Privacy-preserving similarity coefficients for binary data. Comput. Math. Appl. 65(9), 1280–1290 (2013). https://doi.org/10.1016/j.camwa.2012.02.028

SCI – Secure Cryptographic
Implementation

UniqueChain: Achieving (Near) Optimal Transaction Settlement Time via Single Leader Election

Peifang Ni[1,2,3] and Jing Xu[1(✉)]

[1] Institute of Software, Chinese Academy of Sciences, Beijing 100190, China
{peifang2020,xujing}@iscas.ac.cn
[2] State Key Laboratory of Cryptology, Beijing 100878, China
[3] Hangzhou Innovation Institute, Beihang University, Hangzhou 310051, China

Abstract. Leader election in most existing blockchain consensus protocols is probabilistic (i.e. based on proof-of-work or proof-of-stake) and results in the differences in honest parties' selection of local leaders, which further leads to the inconsistency among honest parties' local chains and high latency in terms of transaction settlement time.

In this work, we study the impact of probabilistic leader election on transaction settlement time and propose a new structure of two-chain blockchain, called UniqueChain, which, for the first time, presents a general way to achieve single leader election under the mildly adaptive adversary. Precisely, UniqueChain provides the honest parties with a same and unique local leader. To showcase the usability of UniqueChain, we apply it in the proof-of-stake setting to obtain a provably secure blockchain consensus protocol π_{uc}. Specifically, π_{uc} achieves the property of uniqueness and exhibits (near) optimal transaction settlement time.

Keywords: Two-chain blockchain · Single leader election · Uniqueness · Optimal transaction settlement time

1 Introduction

To coordinate with the communication network latency Δ and maintain a lower chain forking rate, blockchain protocol should adjust difficulty target T properly to maintain a relatively low block production rate, where the expected time interval d to elect a leader to generate the next block in the whole network satisfies $d >> \Delta$, and this is the basic security guarantee in blockchain protocol design. As a result, the time interval from generating a block B to the time that B has been received by all the honest parties is lower-bounded by $d + \Delta$ and upper-bounded by $\frac{1}{\alpha_H}d + \Delta$, where $\alpha_H \in (\frac{1}{2}, 1]$ denotes the ratio of overall resources (i.e., the computational power or stake) that are held by honest parties.

This work is supported in part by the National Key R&D Program of China (No. 2020YFB1005801), in part by the National Natural Science Foundation of China (No. 62172396), and in part by Hangzhou Innovation Institute, Beihang University (No. 2020-Y10-A-013).

Probabilistic leader election provides honest parties with uncertain local leaders and hence the inconsistency of the latest several blocks, where block final confirmation with an exponential error in the number of blocks accumulated beyond this block [1,6,11,13,21,25]. These existing works only guarantee that the chains held by honest parties satisfy common prefix property with parameter $K \in \mathbb{N}$. Consequently, the time interval from generating a block B to the time that B is confirmed finally by honest parties is lower-bounded by $(K+1)\cdot(d+\Delta)$ and upper-bounded by $(K+1)\cdot(\frac{1}{\alpha_H}d + \Delta)$.

We can further conclude that block production speed and block confirmation latency are the most two major factors in transaction settlement time. The objective communication network latency Δ determines that we cannot shorten the time interval of block production to achieve $d < \Delta$ (i.e., via lowering difficult target T) and the only improvement we can make is to minimize the waiting time of confirming blocks. It is meaningful to ask the question: *Is it possible to confirm a valid block finally as soon as it has been received by all the honest parties?*

1.1   Our Contributions

We propose UniqueChain, a new structure of two-chain blockchain, that achieves (near) optimal transaction settlement time. Our main results are briefly summarized in the following outline.

Single Leader Election. UniqueChain consists of two closely linked chains: one is leader-chain consisting of leader-blocks; and the other is transaction-chain consisting of transaction-blocks. To see how to maintain uniqueness of honest parties' local transaction-chains during protocol execution: informally, transaction-block with payloads links to a confirmed empty leader-block instead of a newly generated one. By PoW or PoS, the leader is allowed to generate an empty leader-block and the leader of issuing transaction-block is the issuer of the newly confirmed leader-block.

Obviously, if all the honest parties hold an unique view of the current leader, then they will hold a same view of the current valid block. In UniqueChain, the newly confirmed leader-block determines a deterministic leader to generate the next transaction-block. Thanks to the common prefix property of leader-chains held by honest parties, there is exactly one eligible party to extend transaction-chain in honest parties' views at any time, which determines the uniqueness of valid transaction-block. Roughly, in UniqueChain, the leader-chain executes in the traditional way called *first writing and then consensus*, while the transaction-chain executes in the way called *first consensus and then writing*.

With UniqueChain, we obtain the following result: once an honest leader-block has been confirmed finally, then, under the mildly adaptive adversary, the corresponding transaction-block will be received and confirmed finally by all the honest parties within time Δ. Actually, UniqueChain achieves optimal transaction settlement time, which is upper-bounded by the time interval between two consecutive confirmed honest leader-blocks and network latency Δ.

A PoS-Based Protocol π_{uc}. To show case the usability of UniqueChain, we present a provably secure PoS-based blockchain protocol π_{uc} to achieve optimal transaction settlement time, where honest parties hold the forked local leader-chains that share a common prefix and an unique transaction-chain that is at least K blocks shorter than the corresponding leader-chain.

1.2 Related Work

The core of bitcoin system [25] has been extracted as bitcoin backbone and analyzed [15,16,20,27]. Considering the well-known painpoint of PoW-based protocols that enormous energy waste [5,26], a sequence of works aim to study the PoS-based ones [1,2,6,17,21].

However, both the PoW and PoS based blockchain protocols exhibit an inherent speed-security trade-off. Later efforts to improve performance mainly adopt one of the four strategies to handle transactions: (1) extend Nakamoto-style structure to select temporary leaders to generate blocks with transactions - exemplified by [11,13,30]; (2) redefine the underlying blockchain protocol structure (i.e., DAG-based structure) - exemplified by [3,23,29]; (3) delegate block generation to an eligible set of parties (named committee)- exemplified by [17,18,22,28]; and (4) adopt layer-2 payment [9] or state [8,10] channels that enables users to perform off-chain transactions. The first two strategies focus on improving transaction throughput via fasting the block generation and still need to wait K blocks to confirm the current valid block. The third strategy delegates block generation to a small set of parties to achieve quick transaction confirmation, but it can only resist against $\frac{1}{3}$ adversary and create undesirable hierarchies among parties. The last strategy is only suitable for the transactions with small value.

Two-chain and parallel-chain blockchain protocols [7,11–14,24,30] str-ength system security and improve performance. 2-hop [7] combines PoW and PoS to achieve high level of security where the adversary can succeed if it controls majority of the collective resources. iChing [12] mimics Nakamoto's protocol via PoS. Bitcoin-NG [11] designs two types of blocks called *key*-block and *micro*-block, in which the current leader do not stop handling transactions (issuing *micro*-blocks) until the next leader is elected (*key*-block). Parallel Chains [13], OHIE [30],Ledger Combiners [14] and TaiJi [24] execute $m > 1$ instances of an underling blockchain protocol in parallel via parallel composition. In these works, the eligible parties to handle transactions are elected by the newly generated empty blocks (i.e., [7,11,12]) or the mechanisms PoW and PoS (i.e., [13,30]). Due to the instability of the latest several empty blocks and the probabilistic leader election, honest parties hold inconsistent views of the latest several blocks that contain payloads (transactions) and adopt different valid ones to extend local chains. So a long time is required to wait the corresponding block being confirmed finally and further confirm the transactions.

2 Preliminaries

2.1 The Model of Protocol Execution

- *Epoch-Based Execution.* UniqueChain executes in disjoint and consecutive time intervals called *epoch*. Concretely, time is divided into fixed size unites called slot (denoted by *sl*) and each epoch consists of $R \in \mathbb{N}$ slots.

- *The Parties.* In UniqueChain, we use the flat model of [15] that assumes each party owns one unite of resource and security holds if $\alpha_H \geq \frac{1+\varphi}{2+\varphi}$ for a constant $\varphi > 0$, where α_H denotes the ratio of resource that honest parties hold and hence, the number of honest parties in the whole network.
- *The (Mildly) Adaptive Adversary.* The adversary is allowed to dynamically corrupt parties that its *corrupt* instruction takes effect after $\delta \geq W + \varsigma$ slots since it is sent. Parameter W guarantees that the adversary cannot control the leaders of current epoch, even if he knows the leaders at the beginning of an epoch, and secure duration ς ensures the block generated by the last leader of an epoch can be confirmed finally before the *corrupt* instruction takes effect. Note that we do not consider the malicious leader, who execute nothing-at-stake attack in PoS setting to issue and broadcast multiple valid blocks at the same time.
- *Synchronous Communication Network.* UniqueChain allows synchronous communication among the honest parties via a diffusion mechanism that guarantees the sent honest messages to be delivered within Δ slots. We assume the parties have access to functionality $\mathcal{F}_{net}$ (Fig. 1).

$\mathcal{F}_{net}$ is parameterized by Δ, interacts with an ideal adversary $\mathcal{S}$ and a set of parties $\mathbb{P}$. At slot $sl \in e_i$ $(i \in \mathbb{N})$, it proceeds as follows:
- Upon receiving input $(Broadcast, m, P_{i'})$ from a party $P_{i'} \in \mathbb{P}$ $(i' \in \mathbb{N})$, sends $(Broadcast, m, P_{i'})$ to $\mathcal{S}$ and records $(P_{i'}, m, b = 0, sl)$.
- Upon receiving $(Broadcast, m, P'_{i'}, t)$ from $\mathcal{S}$, where $P'_{i'} \in \mathbb{P}$, then

  - if there is a record $(\cdot, m, b = 0, sl)$ and $t \leq sl + \Delta$, then sends $(m, P'_{i'})$ to all the other parties at time t and sets $b = 1$;
  - else, if $t > sl + \Delta$, then sends $(m, P'_{i'})$ to all the other parties at time $sl + \Delta$ and sets $b = 1$;
  - else, ignores the message.

Fig. 1. The communication network functionality $\mathcal{F}_{net}$

3   The Single Leader Election

Definition 1 (Transaction Settlement Time (TST)). *Blockchain consensus protocol achieves (θ, α_H)-TST with parameters $\theta \in [1, K+1]$ and $\alpha_H \in (\frac{1}{2}, 1]$ iff the time interval for a block being generated and confirmed finally is upper-bounded by $\theta \cdot (\frac{1}{\alpha_H}d + \Delta)$ slots, where $K \in \mathbb{N}$ is the parameter of common prefix property.*

Note that $(K+1) \cdot (d+\Delta)$ slots and $(K+1) \cdot (\frac{1}{\alpha_H}d + \Delta)$ slots describe the lower-bound and upper-bound of transactions settlement time of some existing protocols (i.e., bitcoin, Ouroboros system, Snow White). Under honest majority assumption that $\alpha_H \in (\frac{1}{2}, 1]$, the optimal TST achieves when θ approaches to 1.

3.1   Two-Chain Blockchain

Notations. Blockchain is a sequence of well connected blocks denoted by $\mathcal{C} :=$ $B_0, B_1, ..., B_n$. Genesis block B_0 is generated during the initial epoch e_0 and contains the initial state. The number of blocks except the genesis block is the length of $\mathcal{C}$ denoted by $len(\mathcal{C}) = n$. $\mathcal{C}^{\lceil \kappa}$ is a chain by pruning the κ rightmost blocks of $\mathcal{C}$ and if $\kappa \geq len(\mathcal{C})$, then $\mathcal{C}^{\lceil \kappa} = \epsilon$ is an empty string. $\mathcal{C}_1 \preceq \mathcal{C}_2$ means that $\mathcal{C}_1$ is a prefix of $\mathcal{C}_2$. $\mathcal{C}^{sl}$ denotes the subpart of $\mathcal{C}$ with time before slot sl. Chain $\mathcal{C}$ is valid if each $B \in \mathcal{C}$ satisfies $\mathcal{V}(B) = 1$, where $\mathcal{V}(\cdot)$ is a function that specifies the conditions that a valid block should satisfy.

Precisely, UniqueChain $\mathcal{C} = \{\bar{\mathcal{C}}, \tilde{\mathcal{C}}\}$ (Fig. 2) consists of two chains called leader-chain $\bar{\mathcal{C}} = B_0, \bar{B}_1, ..., \bar{B}_n$ and transaction-chain $\tilde{\mathcal{C}} = \tilde{B}_1, ..., \tilde{B}_m$, where $n - m \geq K$ (K is the parameter of common prefix property). $\mathcal{C}$ is valid if $\bar{\mathcal{V}}(\bar{B}_{\bar{i}}) = 1$ and $\tilde{\mathcal{V}}(\tilde{B}_{\tilde{j}}) = 1$, where $\bar{B}_{\bar{i}} \in \bar{\mathcal{C}}$ ($\bar{i} \in \{1, ..., n\}$) and $\tilde{B}_{\tilde{j}} \in \tilde{\mathcal{C}}$ ($\tilde{j} \in \{1, ..., m\}$). For clarity, we use letters with bar to denote the leader-chain parameters and the letters with tilde to denote the transaction-chain parameters.

Leader-block $\bar{B} = (\bar{h}_{-1}, \bar{\tau})$ is an empty block generated by the elected parties of slot sl and transaction-block $\tilde{B} = (\tilde{h}_{-1}, \tilde{\tau})$ contains transactions $\tilde{X}$ generated by a party whose leader-block $\bar{B}$ has been confirmed finally.

1. $\bar{B}_{\bar{i}} = (\bar{h}_{-1}, \bar{\tau}_{\bar{i}})$ is valid (denoted as $\bar{\mathcal{V}}(\bar{B}_{\bar{i}}) = 1$ ($\bar{i} \in \mathbb{N}$)) if:
   (1) $\bar{h}_{-1} = \mathcal{H}(\bar{B}_{\bar{i}-1})$. $\bar{B}_{\bar{i}}$ links to its parent leader-block $\bar{B}_{\bar{i}-1}$ correctly;
   (2) $\bar{\tau}_{\bar{i}} = (sl, \bar{\omega}_{\bar{i}})$:
      - $\bar{B}_{\bar{i}}.sl > \bar{B}_{\bar{i}-1}.sl$. Leader-chain with strictly increasing sequence of time;
      - $\bar{\omega}_{\bar{i}}$ is witness to show that $P_{i'}$ is a leader of slot $sl \in e_i$ and $\bar{B}_{\bar{i}}$ is indeed generated by $P_{i'}$. Let $nonce_i \in_R \{0,1\}^k$ be random value to determine the current hash function $\mathcal{H}$ and T_i is difficulty target of epoch e_i. Formally, in PoS setting, $\bar{\omega}_{\bar{i}} = (pk_{i'}, s_{i'}, \bar{\sigma}_{\bar{i}})$, where $\mathcal{H}(nonce_i, pk_{i'}, sl) < s_{i'} \cdot T_i$ denotes that $P_{i'}$ with account $(pk_{i'}, s_{i'})$ is a leader of slot sl and $Ver_{pk_{i'}}([\bar{B}_{\bar{i}}], \bar{\sigma}_{\bar{i}}) = 1$ denotes the signature $\bar{\sigma}_{\bar{i}}$ on $(\bar{h}_{-1}, sl)$ under verifying key $pk_{i'}$ is correct to ensure that $\bar{B}_{\bar{i}}$ is generated by $P_{i'}$; in PoW setting, $\bar{\omega}_{\bar{i}} = (c\bar{t}r_{\bar{i}}, pk_{i'}, \bar{\sigma}_{\bar{i}})$, where $\mathcal{H}(nonce_i, c\bar{t}r_{\bar{i}}, pk_{i'}) < T_i$ denotes that $P_{i'}$ with $pk_{i'}$ is elected as leader of slot sl and $Ver_{pk_{i'}}([\bar{B}_{\bar{i}}], \bar{\sigma}_{\bar{i}}) = 1$ denotes the signature $\bar{\sigma}_{\bar{i}}$ on $(\bar{h}_{-1}, sl, c\bar{t}r_{\bar{i}})$ under verifying key $pk_{i'}$ is correct to guarantee that $\bar{B}_{\bar{i}}$ is generated by $P_{i'}$.
2. $\tilde{B}_{\tilde{j}} = (\tilde{h}_{-1}, \tilde{\tau}_{\tilde{j}})$ is valid (denoted as $\tilde{\mathcal{V}}(\tilde{B}_{\tilde{j}}) = 1$ ($\tilde{j} \in \mathbb{N}$)) if:
   (1) $\tilde{h}_{-1} = \mathcal{H}(\tilde{B}_{\tilde{j}-1})$. $\tilde{B}_{\tilde{j}}$ links to its parent transaction-block $\tilde{B}_{\tilde{j}-1}$ correctly;
   (2) $\tilde{\tau}_{\tilde{j}} = (sl, \tilde{X}, \tilde{r}_{\tilde{j}}, \tilde{\omega}_{\tilde{j}})$
      - $\tilde{B}_{\tilde{j}}.sl > \tilde{B}_{\tilde{j}-1}.sl$. Transaction-chain with strictly increasing sequence of time;
      - $V(\tilde{X}) = 1$. The set of transactions X is valid;
      - $\tilde{r}_{\tilde{j}} \in_R \{0,1\}^k$. $\tilde{r}_{\tilde{j}}$ is used for generating $nonce_{i+1}$ ($i > 0$);
      - $\tilde{\omega}_{\tilde{j}} = (\bar{h}, pk_{j'}, \tilde{\sigma}_{\tilde{j}})$
         (a) $Fresh(\bar{B}) = 1$. $\bar{B}$ is the newly confirmed leader-block in honest party $P_{i'}$'s local leader-chain $\mathcal{C}_{i'}$ at slot sl^* and $\tilde{B}_{\tilde{j}}.sl - \Delta \leq sl^* \leq \tilde{B}_{\tilde{j}}.sl + \Delta$;

(b) $\bar{h} = \mathcal{H}(\bar{B})$. $\tilde{B}_{\tilde{j}}$ links to its parent leader-block $\bar{B}$ correctly;

(c) $(\tilde{B}_{\tilde{j}}.pk = \bar{B}.pk) \wedge (Ver_{pk_{j'}}([\tilde{B}_{\tilde{j}}], \tilde{\sigma}_{\tilde{j}}) = 1)$. The blocks $\tilde{B}_{\tilde{j}}$ and $\bar{B}$ are generated by a same party $P_{j'}$ ($pk_{j'}$), and the signature $\tilde{\sigma}_{\tilde{j}}$ on $(\tilde{h}_{-1}, \bar{h}, sl, \tilde{X}, \tilde{r}_{\tilde{j}})$ under verifying key $pk_{j'}$ is correct.

The items in red guarantee that, at any slot sl, the party who is eligible to generate transaction-block $\tilde{B}_{\tilde{j}}$ is the one whose leader-block $\bar{B}$ is just in the common prefix of honest parties' local leader-chains at the onset of slot sl, which provides exactly one leader and, under the mildly adaptive adversary, this leader will be honest if it is not corrupted when generated the leader-block.

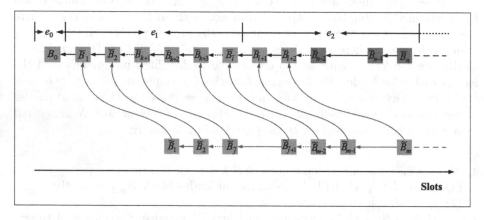

Fig. 2. The black arrows denote leader-chain $\bar{C}$ and the blue arrows denote transaction-chain $\tilde{C}$. The green blocks are the confirmed ones and the red blocks are the unstable ones. Note that $\bar{C}$ and $\tilde{C}$ may not grow synchronously at some slots, in that, at some slots, there may be no party being elected to generate leader-block or the elected adversary may not generate block honestly. (Color figure online)

3.2 The Resource Procedure

The resource procedure functionality $\mathcal{F}_{res}$ shows how UniqueChain executes. At slot $sl \in e_i$, $\mathcal{F}_{res}$ grants each registered party with one unit of resource denoted by $s = 1$ and sets one party as leader to generate the leader-block with probability $p_i = \frac{T_i}{2^k}$. Especially, $\mathcal{F}_{res}$ maintains a set $(Ctr, \mathcal{P}) = \{(Ctr_{i,j}, \mathcal{P}_{i,j})\}_{i>0,\ j\in\{1,...,R\}}$, where $Ctr_{i,j}$ is a counter and initialized as 0, and $\mathcal{P}_{i,j}$ is a set of elected parties and initialized as an empty set ϕ of slot $sl_{i,j}$ (the jth slot of epoch e_i). If at least one parties are elected at slot $sl_{i,j}$, then set $Ctr_{i,j} = Ctr_{i,j-1} + 1$ or $Ctr_{i,j} = Ctr_{i-1,R} + 1$ for $j = 1$ and add the corresponding elected parties to $\mathcal{P}_{i,j}$, otherwise, set $Ctr_{i,j} = Ctr_{i,j-1}$ or $Ctr_{i,j} = Ctr_{i-1,R}$ for $j = 1$ and $\mathcal{P}_{i,j} = \phi$. Furthermore, if $Ctr_{i,j} - K = Ctr_{i,\xi} > 0$ (or $Ctr_{i,j} - K = Ctr_{i-1,\xi} > 0$) and $\mathcal{P}_{i,\xi} \neq \phi$ (or $\mathcal{P}_{i-1,\xi} \neq \phi$), then $\mathcal{F}_{res}$ uniformly selects a party $P \in \mathcal{P}_{i,\xi}$ (or $\mathcal{P}_{i-1,\xi}$) to generate a transaction-block with slot $sl_{i,j}$, where $Ctr_{i,j}$ is the current counter and $\xi \in \{1,...,R\}$. At any time, each party has access to the verification process of $\mathcal{F}_{res}$ to verify blocks. The detailed description of $\mathcal{F}_{res}$ is showed in Fig. 3.

$\mathcal{F}_{res}$ with security parameter $k \in \{0,1\}^*$ and probability $p_i = \frac{T_i}{2^k} \in (0,1)$, interacts with the ideal adversary $\mathcal{S}$, parties $P_{i'}$ and $P_{i''}$.

- **Registration.**
  1. Upon receiving $(Register, P_{i'})$ from $P_{i'}$, if there is a record $(P_{i'}, re_{i'} = 1)$, then ignore. Otherwise, send $(Register, P_{i'})$ to $\mathcal{S}$. Upon receiving $(Registered, P_{i'})$ from $\mathcal{S}$, record $(P_{i'}, re_{i'} = 1)$ and send $(Registered, P_{i'})$ to $P_{i'}$.
  2. Upon receiving $(Unregister, P_{i'})$ from $P_{i'}$, if there is no record $(P_{i'}, re_{i'} = 1)$, then ignore the message. Otherwise, update record $(P_{i'}, re_{i'} = 0)$ and send $(Unregistered, P_{i'})$ to $P_{i'}$.
- **Chain Extension.** At slot $sl_{i,j} \in e_i$ $(i > 0, j \in \{1, ..., R\})$.
  1. **Generating Leader-Block:** set $Ctr_{1,1} = 0$ and $Ctr_{i,j} = Ctr_{i,j-1}$ or $Ctr_{i,j} = Ctr_{i-1,R}$ for $i > 1, j = 1$, and $\mathcal{P}_{i,j} = \phi$. Every registered party $P_{i'}$ is granted with one unite resource $s_{i,j,i'} = 1$.
     - Upon receiving $(L\text{-}Elect, P_{i'})$ from $P_{i'}$, proceed as follows:
       * if there is a record $(P_{i'}, re_{i'} = 1, s_{i,j,i'} = 1)$, then
         · with probability p_i, set $\mathcal{P}_{i,j} = \mathcal{P}_{i,j} \cup \{P_{i'}\}$, update $((P_{i'}, re_{i'} = 1, s_{i,j,i'} = 0), \mathcal{P}_{i,j})$ and send $(L\text{-}Elected, P_{i'}, \bar{f} = 1)$ to $P_{i'}$; ($P_{i'}$ is elected)
         · with probability $1 - p_i$, update $((P_{i'}, re_{i'} = 1, s_{i,j,i'} = 0), \mathcal{P}_{i,j})$ and send $(L\text{-}Elected, P_{i'}, \bar{f} = 0)$ to $P_{i'}$. ($P_{i'}$ is not elected)
       * otherwise, send $(L\text{-}Elected, P_{i'}, f = 0)$ to $P_{i'}$. ($P_{i'}$ is not elected) If $\mathcal{P}_{i,j} \neq \phi$, then set $Ctr_{i,j} := Ctr_{i,j} + 1$. Otherwise, $Ctr_{i,j} := Ctr_{i,j}$. Update record as $(Ctr_{i,j}, \mathcal{P}_{i,j})$. (Record the counter $Ctr_{i,j}$ and elected parties $\mathcal{P}_{i,j}$ of slot $sl_{i,j}$.)
     - Upon receiving $(Compute, \bar{B}_{-1}, P_{i'})$ from $P_{i'}$: (Compute index of the parent leader-block $\bar{B}_{-1}$)
       * If $P_{i'} \in \mathcal{P}_{i,j}$ and there is a record $(\bar{B}_{-1}, \bar{h}_{-1})$, then send $(Computed, \bar{h}_{-1})$ to $P_{i'}$. Otherwise, choose $\bar{h}_{-1} \in_R \{0,1\}^k$, record $(\bar{B}_{-1}, \bar{h}_{-1})$ and send $(Computed, \bar{h}_{-1})$ to $P_{i'}$;
       * Otherwise, send $(Error)$ to $P_{i'}$.
     - Upon receiving $(Sign, \bar{B}, P_{i'})$ from $P_{i'}$: (Compute signature of $\bar{B}$)
       * if $P_{i'} \in \mathcal{P}_{i,j}$, then send $(Sign, P_{i'}, \bar{B})$ to $\mathcal{S}$. Upon receiving $(Signed, P_{i'}, (\bar{B}, \bar{\sigma}))$ from $\mathcal{S}$, record $(\bar{B}, \bar{\sigma})$ and send $(Signed, (\bar{B}, \bar{\sigma}))$ to $P_{i'}$;
       * otherwise, send $(Error)$ to $P_{i'}$.
  2. **Generating Transaction-Block:**
     - Upon receiving $(T\text{-}Elect, P_{i'})$ from $P_{i'}$, compute $Ctr_{i,j} - K = Ctr_{i,\xi}$ (or $Ctr_{i,j} - K = Ctr_{i-1,\xi}$). If $Ctr_{i,j} > 0$ (or $Ctr_{i-1,\xi} > 0$) and $\mathcal{P}_{i,\xi} \neq \phi$ (or $\mathcal{P}_{i-1,\xi} \neq \phi$), then uniformly choose $P_{j'} \in_R \mathcal{P}_{i,\xi}$ (or $P_{j'} \in_R \mathcal{P}_{i-1,\xi}$). (Only party $P_{j'}$ is elected to generate the transaction-block of slot $sl_{i,j}$.)
       * if $P_{i'} = P_{j'}$, then record $(P_{i'}, Ctr_{i,j}, Ctr_{i,\xi})$ (or $(P_{i'}, Ctr_{i,j}, Ctr_{i-1,\xi})$) and send $(T\text{-}Elected, P_{i'}, \tilde{f} = 1)$ to $P_{i'}$; ($P_{i'}$ is elected)
       * otherwise, send $(T\text{-}Elected, P_{i'}, \tilde{f} = 0)$ to $P_{i'}$. ($P_{i'}$ is not elected)
     - Upon receiving $(Compute, \tilde{B}_{-1}, \bar{B}, P_{i'})$ from $P_{i'}$: (Compute index of the parent transaction-block $\tilde{B}_{-1}$ and the corresponding leader-block $\bar{B}$)
       * if there is a record $(P_{i'}, Ctr_{i,j}, Ctr_{i,\xi})$ (or $(P_{i'}, Ctr_{i,j}, Ctr_{i-1,\xi})$), then if there is a record $((\tilde{B}_{-1}, \tilde{h}_{-1}), (\bar{B}, \bar{h}))$, send $(Computed, \tilde{h}_{-1}, \bar{h})$ to $P_{i'}$. Otherwise, choose $\tilde{h}_{-1}, \bar{h} \in_R \{0,1\}^k$, record $((\tilde{B}_{-1}, \tilde{h}_{-1}), (\bar{B}, \bar{h}))$ and send $(Computed, \tilde{h}_{-1}, \bar{h})$ to $P_{i'}$;
       * otherwise, send $(Error)$ to $P_{i'}$.
     - Upon receiving $(Sign, \tilde{B}, P_{i'})$ from $P_{i'}$: (Compute the signature of $\tilde{B}$)
       * if there is a record $(P_{i'}, Ctr_{i,j}, Ctr_{i,\xi})$ (or $(P_{i'}, Ctr_{i,j}, Ctr_{i-1,\xi})$), then send $(Sign, P_{i'}, \tilde{B})$ to $\mathcal{S}$. Upon receiving $(Signed, P_{i'}, (\tilde{B}, \tilde{\sigma}))$ from $\mathcal{S}$, then record $(\tilde{B}, \tilde{\sigma})$ and send $(Signed, (\tilde{B}, \tilde{\sigma}))$ to $P_{i'}$;
       * otherwise, send $(Error)$ to $P_{i'}$.
- **Verification.** Upon receiving $(Verify, \bar{B}$ (or $\tilde{B}))$ from party $P_{i''}$:
  1. If there is a record of $(\bar{B}$ (or $\tilde{B}), \bar{\sigma}$ (or $\tilde{\sigma}))$, then send $\bar{f}'(or \tilde{f}') = 1$ to $P_{i''}$;
  2. Otherwise, send $\bar{f}'(or \ \tilde{f}') = 0$ to $P_{i''}$.

Fig. 3. Resource functionality $\mathcal{F}_{res}$

4 Protocol π_{uc}: UniqueChain in the PoS Setting

We present protocol π_{uc} in the $\{\mathcal{F}_{init}, \mathcal{F}_{net}, \mathcal{F}_{res}\}$-hybrid model (Fig. 6). First, the initial parties generate genesis block B_0 via $\mathcal{F}_{init}$ (Fig. 4); then, each party fetches information from the network via $\mathcal{F}_{net}$ (Fig. 1); and finally, each party performs validations locally via $BestValid$ (Fig. 5) and try to extend local chain via $\mathcal{F}_{res}$ (Fig. 3). The security properties that π_{uc} satisfies presented as follows.

Definition 2 *(Uniqueness of Transaction-Chain $\mathcal{Q}_{utc}$). Let any two honest parties* P_1, P_2 *hold local transaction-chain* $\tilde{\mathcal{C}}_1$ *and* $\tilde{\mathcal{C}}_2$ *at the onset of slot* $sl + \Delta$ *respectively.* $\mathcal{Q}_{utc}$ *states that* $\tilde{\mathcal{C}}_1^{sl} = \tilde{\mathcal{C}}_2^{sl}$.

Definition 3 *(Common Prefix of Leader-Chain $\mathcal{Q}_{cplc}$). Let any two honest parties* P_1, P_2 *hold local leader-chain* $\bar{\mathcal{C}}_1$ *and* $\bar{\mathcal{C}}_2$ *at the onset of slot* sl_1 *and* sl_2 *($sl_1 + \Delta \leq sl_2$) respectively.* $\mathcal{Q}_{cplc}$ *with parameter* $K \in \mathbb{N}$ *states that* $\bar{\mathcal{C}}_1^{\lceil K} \preceq \bar{\mathcal{C}}_2$.

$\mathcal{F}_{init}$ is parameterized by initial parties $P_1, ..., P_n$ and stakes $s_1, ..., s_n$. It gets the current slot and, upon receiving $(Initialize, P_{i'}, s_{i'})$ from $P_{i'}$ at slot sl:
– if $sl = 0$, then compute target T_1 according to $\mathbb{S}_0 = \{s_1, ..., s_n\}$, sample $nonce_1 \in_R$ $\{0,1\}^k$ and generate $B_0 = (\mathbb{S}_0, nonce_1)$. It stores B_0, sends $(Initialized, B_0)$ to $P_{i'}$ and set $isInit \leftarrow true$;
– else, if $sl > 0$ and $isInit = true$, then send $(Initialized, B_0)$ to $P_{i'}$.
– else, send $(Error)$ to $P_{i'}$.

Fig. 4. Initialization functionality $\mathcal{F}_{init}$

$BestValid$ with parameter $K \in \mathbb{N}$ and two content validation predicates $\bar{\mathcal{V}}(\cdot)$ and $\tilde{\mathcal{V}}(\cdot)$. At slot $sl \in e_i$ ($i > 0$), it takes a set of chains $\mathbb{C}$ and party $P_{i'}$'s local chain $\mathcal{C}_{loc} := (\bar{\mathcal{C}}, \tilde{\mathcal{C}})$ as inputs and proceeds as follows:
1. For each $\mathcal{C}_{\bar{i}} = (\bar{\mathcal{C}}_{\bar{i}}, \tilde{\mathcal{C}}_{\bar{i}}) \in \mathbb{C}$, if $\bar{\mathcal{C}}_{\bar{i}}$ forks from $\bar{\mathcal{C}}$ with more than K blocks or $\tilde{\mathcal{C}}_{\bar{i}}$ forks from $\tilde{\mathcal{C}}$ with more than one blocks, then remove $\mathcal{C}_{\bar{i}}$ from $\mathbb{C}_{i,j}$ and set $\mathbb{C}_1 := \mathbb{C}/\{\mathcal{C}_{\bar{i}}\}$;
2. For each $\mathcal{C}_{\bar{i}} = (\bar{\mathcal{C}}_{\bar{i}}, \tilde{\mathcal{C}}_{\bar{i}}) \in \mathbb{C}_1$, if $(\bar{\mathcal{V}}(\bar{B}) \neq 1)$ or $(\tilde{\mathcal{V}}(\tilde{B}) \neq 1)$, then remove $\mathcal{C}_{\bar{i}}$ from $\mathbb{C}_1$ and set $\mathbb{C}_2 = \mathbb{C}_1/\{\mathcal{C}_{\bar{i}}\}$, where $\bar{B} \in \mathcal{C}_{\bar{i}}$ and $\tilde{B} \in \tilde{\mathcal{C}}_{\bar{i}}$;
3. For each $\mathcal{C}_{\bar{i}} = (\bar{\mathcal{C}}_{\bar{i}}, \tilde{\mathcal{C}}_{\bar{i}}) \in \mathbb{C}_3$ and $\mathcal{C}_{loc} := (\bar{\mathcal{C}}, \tilde{\mathcal{C}})$. if $len(\bar{\mathcal{C}}_{\bar{i}}) > len(\mathcal{C})$ or $len(\tilde{\mathcal{C}}_{\bar{i}}) - len(\tilde{\mathcal{C}}) = 1$, then set $\mathcal{C}_{loc} := \mathcal{C}_{\bar{i}} = (\bar{\mathcal{C}}_{\bar{i}}, \tilde{\mathcal{C}}_{\bar{i}})$; otherwise, set $\mathcal{C}_{loc} := \mathcal{C}_{loc}$.

Fig. 5. The best valid chain algorithm $BestValid$

Definition 4 *(Chain Growth $\mathcal{Q}_{cg}$). Honest party* P *holds local chain* $\mathcal{C} = (\bar{\mathcal{C}}, \tilde{\mathcal{C}})$ *at the onset of slot* sl, *and chains* $\mathcal{C}_1 = (\bar{\mathcal{C}}_1, \tilde{\mathcal{C}}_1)$ *and* $\mathcal{C}_2 = (\bar{\mathcal{C}}_2, \tilde{\mathcal{C}}_2)$ *at the onset of slot* sl_1 *and* sl_2 *respectively, where* $sl_1 + t \leq sl_2 \leq sl$ *and* $t \in \mathbb{N}$. $\mathcal{Q}_{cg}$ *with parameters* $\bar{g} \in (0,1]$ *and* $\tilde{g} \in (0,1]$ *states that* $len(\bar{\mathcal{C}}_2) - len(\bar{\mathcal{C}}_1) \geq \bar{g} \cdot t$ *and* $len(\tilde{\mathcal{C}}_2) - len(\tilde{\mathcal{C}}_1) \geq \tilde{g} \cdot t$, *where* $\bar{g}$ *and* $\tilde{g}$ *are the lower bounds of leader-chain and transaction-chain growth rate respectively.*

Definition 5 *(Chain Quality $\mathcal{Q}_{cq}$).* *Honest party* P *holds chain* $\mathcal{C} = (\bar{\mathcal{C}}, \tilde{\mathcal{C}})$ *at the onset of slot sl.* $\mathcal{Q}_{cq}$ *with parameters* $\bar{L} > K, \tilde{L} \in \mathbb{N}$, $\bar{\mu} \in [0,1)$ *and* $\tilde{\mu} \in [0,1)$ *states that, for any portion of* $\bar{\mathcal{C}}$ *and* $\tilde{\mathcal{C}}$ *with length* $\bar{L}$ *and* $\tilde{L}$ *respectively, the ratio of blocks generated by the adversary are at most* $\bar{\mu}$ *and* $\tilde{\mu}$ *respectively.*

π_{uc} is parameterized by two content validation predicates $\bar{V}(\cdot)$, $\tilde{V}(\cdot)$, interacts with party $P_{i'}$, the adversary $\mathcal{A}$ and the environment $\mathcal{Z}$. It proceeds as follows:

1. **Initialization.**
   * if $sl = 0$, then $P_{i'}$ sends $(Initialize, P_{i'}, s_{i'})$ to $\mathcal{F}_{init}$ and gets $(Initialized, B_0)$;
   * else, return $(Error)$.
2. **Fetch Messages from the Network.** Each party fetches a set of messages $\mathcal{M}_{i,j}$ from network at slot $sl_{i,j} \in e_i$ via $\mathcal{F}_{net}$:
   * the elected parties of $sl_{i,j}$ extract the set of chains $\mathbb{C}_{i,j}$ from $\mathcal{M}_{i,j}$;
   * the parties whose former leader-blocks have been backed by K blocks extract the set of chains $\mathbb{C}_{i,j}$ and the set of transactions $\mathbb{T}$ from $\mathcal{M}_{i,j}$.
3. **Update Local State.** After receiving the messages from network, each party updates local chain as $\mathcal{C}_{loc} := BestValid(\mathcal{C}_{loc}, \mathbb{C}_{i,j})$.
4. **Extend Chain.** Each party $P_{i'}$, who has registered to $\mathcal{F}_{res}$ and been granted with stake $s_{i,j,i'} = 1$, tries to extend local chain $\mathcal{C}_{loc} = \{\bar{\mathcal{C}}, \tilde{\mathcal{C}}\}$:
   * Upon receiving $(Input\text{-}Stake, P_{i'})$ from $\mathcal{Z}$, $P_{i'}$ extends $\bar{\mathcal{C}}$:
     − send $(L\text{-}Elect, P_{i'})$ to $\mathcal{F}_{res}$ and then receive $(L\text{-}Elected, P_{i'}, f)$;
     − if $f = 1$,then,
       ⋆ send $(Compute, \bar{B}_{-1}, P_{i'})$ to $\mathcal{F}_{res}$ and receive $(Computed, \bar{h}_{-1})$;
       ⋆ send $(Sign, \bar{B}, P_{i'})$ to $\mathcal{F}_{res}$ and receive $(Signed, (\bar{B}, \bar{\sigma}))$;
       ⋆ set $\bar{\mathcal{C}} := \bar{\mathcal{C}} \| \bar{B}$, $\mathcal{C}_{loc} := \{\bar{\mathcal{C}}, \tilde{\mathcal{C}}\}$ and send $(Broadcast, \mathcal{C}_{loc}, P_{i'})$ to $\mathcal{F}_{net}$.
   * Upon receiving $(Input\text{-}Stake, \mathbb{T}, P_{i'})$ from $\mathcal{Z}$, $P_{i'}$ extends $\tilde{\mathcal{C}}$:
     − send $(T\text{-}Elect, P_{i'})$ to $\mathcal{F}_{res}$ and receive $(T\text{-}Elected, P_{i'}, \tilde{f})$;
     − if $\tilde{f} = 1$, then,
       ⋆ send $(Compute, \tilde{B}_{-1}, \bar{B}, P_{i'})$ to $\mathcal{F}_{res}$ and receive $(Computed, \tilde{h}_{-1}, \bar{h})$;
       ⋆ send $(Sign, P_{i'}, \tilde{B})$ to $\mathcal{F}_{res}$ and receive $(Signed, (\tilde{B}, \tilde{\sigma}))$;
       ⋆ set $\tilde{\mathcal{C}} := \tilde{\mathcal{C}} \| \tilde{B}$, $\mathcal{C}_{loc} := \{\bar{\mathcal{C}}, \tilde{\mathcal{C}}\}$ and send $(Broadcast, \mathcal{C}_{loc}, P_{i'})$ to $\mathcal{F}_{net}$.

Fig. 6. Blockchain protocol π_{uc}

5 Security Analysis of π_{uc}

1. $f = 1 - (1-p)^{|\mathbb{E}|}$ is the probability that at least one party elected to generate leader-block at a given slot and $(1-f)^\Delta \geq \frac{1}{2}$, where $\mathbb{E}$ is the set of all parties;
2. $\bar{\alpha} = \alpha_H f$ is the probability that at least one honest party is elected to generate leader-block at a given slot;
3. $\bar{\beta} = (1 - \alpha_H)f$ is the probability that the adversary is elected to generate leader-block at a given slot.

The Security Analysis of Leader-Chain

1. Achieving Chain Growth Property $\mathcal{Q}_{cglc}$.

Theorem 1. *For parameters $k, K, \Delta \in \mathbb{N}$, $\varepsilon_1 \in (0, \frac{1}{2}]$, let an honest party P_1 holds local leader-chain $\bar{C}$ at slot sl, and $\bar{C}_1$ and $\bar{C}_2$ at slots sl_1 and sl_2 respectively, where $sl_1 + t \leq sl_2 \leq sl$. Then protocol π_{uc} achieves chain growth property with $\bar{g} = (1 - \varepsilon_1) \cdot \bar{\gamma}$, where $\bar{\gamma} = \frac{\alpha_H f}{1 + \alpha_H f \Delta}$, except with error probability $p_{cglc} = \exp(-\frac{\varepsilon_1^2 \cdot \bar{\gamma} t}{2})$.*

Proof. We set $\bar{\gamma} = \frac{\alpha_H f}{1 + \alpha_H f \Delta}$, a "discounted" version of $\bar{\alpha}$, to denote the lower bound of honest parties' power and the number of newly added leader-blocks in honest parties' local leader-chains during time interval $I = [sl_1, sl_2]$ is lower-bounded by $\bar{\gamma} \cdot t$. By the Chernoff bound, we thus have the chain growth property holds with $\bar{g} = (1 - \varepsilon_1) \cdot \bar{\gamma}$ except with error probability

$$p_{cglc} = \Pr\left[len(\bar{C}_2) - len(\bar{C}_1) \leq (1 - \varepsilon_1)\bar{\gamma} t\right] \leq \exp(-\frac{\varepsilon_1^2 \cdot \bar{\gamma} t}{2})$$

2. Achieving Chain Quality Property $\mathcal{Q}_{cqlc}$.

Theorem 2. *For the fix parameters $\bar{L}$, $K \in \mathbb{N}$, $\varepsilon_2, \varepsilon_3, \varepsilon_4 \in (0, \frac{1}{2}]$, let an honest party P holds local leader-chain $\bar{C}$ at the onset of slot sl. Then for any $\bar{L} \geq 2K$ consecutive blocks of $\bar{C}$, the ratio of blocks created by the adversary is at most $\bar{\mu} = 1 - (1 - \varepsilon_4) \cdot \frac{\bar{\gamma}}{f}$, except with error probability $p_{cqlc} = \exp(-\frac{\varepsilon_4^2 \bar{\gamma}}{3f})$.*

Proof. Let $\bar{I}$ be the slot interval in which these $\bar{L}$ blocks generated, we have $\Pr[|\bar{I}| > (1 - \varepsilon_2) \cdot \frac{\bar{L}}{f}] > 1 - \exp(-\frac{\varepsilon_2^2 \bar{L}}{3f})$. Let $\bar{X}$ denote the number of blocks generated by the honest parties during $\bar{I}$, we have $\Pr[\bar{X} > (1 - \varepsilon_3) \cdot \bar{\gamma}|\bar{I}|] > 1 - \exp(-\frac{\varepsilon_3^2 \cdot \bar{\gamma}|\bar{I}|}{3})$. Thus, the number of blocks generated by the adversary is upper-bounded by $\bar{Y} \leq \bar{L} - \bar{X} \leq \bar{L} - (1 - \varepsilon_3) \cdot \bar{\gamma}|\bar{I}|$ and $\bar{\mu} = \frac{\bar{Y}}{\bar{L}} \leq \frac{\bar{L} - (1 - \varepsilon_3) \cdot \bar{\gamma}|\bar{I}|}{\bar{L}} \leq 1 - (1 - \varepsilon_3)(1 - \varepsilon_2) \cdot \frac{\bar{\gamma}}{f} = 1 - (1 - \varepsilon_3)(1 - \varepsilon_2) \cdot \frac{\alpha_H}{f + \alpha_H f^2 \Delta}$.

By picking sufficiently small ε_2 and ε_3, it follows that $\bar{\mu} \leq 1 - (1 - \varepsilon_4) \cdot \frac{\bar{\gamma}}{f}$ for some constant $\varepsilon_4 \in (1, \frac{1}{2}]$, except with error probability $p_{cqlc} = \exp(-\frac{\varepsilon_4^2 \bar{\gamma}}{3f})$.

3. Achieving Common Prefix Property $\mathcal{Q}_{cplc}$.

Lemma 1. *Assume $\bar{\gamma} \geq (1+\delta)\bar{\beta}$ for $\delta \in (0, 1)$, the adversary generates a leader-chain $\bar{C}$ with length $l > K$ at slot sl. Then it holds that honest party holds local leader-chain $\bar{C}'$ at slot $sl' \geq sl + \delta_1 t$ $(\delta_1 \in (0, 1))$ with length $len(\bar{C}') \geq l$.*

Proof. Let block $\bar{B}$ be the latest common honest block of leader-chain $\bar{C}$ and $\bar{C}'$ (if no such block, then let $\bar{B} = B_0$), where $len(B_0, ..., \bar{B}) = l - K \in \mathbb{N}$ and $\bar{B}.sl = sl'' \leq sl$. Thus at least $\delta_2 t$ slots has been passed from slot sl'' to sl'. By theorem 1, the leader-chain growth rate is lower-bounded by $(1 - \varepsilon_1)\bar{\gamma}$ except with error probability $\exp(-\frac{\varepsilon_1^2 \cdot \bar{\gamma} t}{2})$. Thus we have that $K \geq (1 - \varepsilon_1) \cdot \bar{\gamma} \delta_1 t$ and the number of blocks generated by the adversary in these $\delta_1 t$ slots is upper-bounded by $(1 + \varepsilon_1') \cdot \beta \delta_1 t$ for some $\varepsilon_1' \in (0, 1)$ except with error probability $\exp(-\frac{\varepsilon_1'^2 \cdot \beta t}{2})$.

We set $(1 + \varepsilon_1') \cdot \beta \delta_1 t \geq K \geq (1 - \varepsilon_1) \cdot \bar{\gamma} \delta_1 t$ and get $\bar{\gamma} \leq \frac{(1 + \varepsilon_1')}{(1 - \varepsilon_1)} \beta$. Picking sufficiently small ε_1 and ε_1', we have $\bar{\gamma} \leq (1 + \delta)\beta$ for $\delta \in (0, 1)$.

Lemma 2. *Assume* $(1 - 2(\Delta + 1)\bar{\alpha})\bar{\alpha} \geq (1 + \delta_2)\bar{\beta}$ *for* $\delta_2 \in (0, 1)$*, honest parties* P_1 *and* P_2 *hold local leader-chains* $\bar{C}_1$ *and* $\bar{C}_2$ *at slots* sl_1 *and* sl_2 *($sl_1 \geq sl_2 + \Delta$) respectively. It holds that* $\bar{C}_1$ *and* $\bar{C}_2$ *cannot diverge at slot* $sl'' = sl_1 - t$*, except with error probability* $p_{cplc} = \exp(-\frac{\delta_1'^2 \cdot \bar{\beta} t}{3})$.

Proof. We consider the set of slots $SL = \{sl | sl'' \leq sl \leq sl_1\}$ that satisfies: (1) lasting for at least Δ slots before slot sl that have no honest leaders; (2) there is exactly one honest leader at slot sl; and (3) lasting for at least Δ slots after slot sl that have no honest leaders. After such a slot, unless the adversary have succeed between slot $sl''' \geq sl + \Delta - t$ and $sl + \Delta$, the honest parties will agree on the newly generated leader-block and further hold an identical local leader-chain.

Then we show that the number of such slots increases faster than the number of blocks generated by the adversary even if it has the additional $\delta_1 t$ slots to withhold some generated leader-blocks.

- Let $\mathcal{O}$ denotes the number that honest parties are elected during slot sl'' to slot sl_1. We have $\Pr[\mathcal{O} \geq (1 - \varepsilon_5) \cdot \bar{\alpha} t]$ except with error probability $\exp(-\frac{\varepsilon_5^2 \cdot \alpha t}{2})$;
- Let $Q_0 > 0$ be the number of slots from slot sl'' to the first honest successful slot, where *honest successful slot* is the slot that some honest party is elected;
- For each $j \in [1, \ldots, \mathcal{O}]$:
  - Let Q_j be the number of slots between the jth honest successful slot and the $j + 1^{th}$ honest successful slot, and $\mathcal{Q}_j = 1$ if $q_j \geq \Delta$;
  - Let $X_j = 1$ if there is exactly one honest party elected at the 1th honest successful slot;
  - Let $\mathcal{X}_j = 1$ if $(X_j = 1) \wedge (\mathcal{Q}_j = 1)$;
  - Let $Y_1 = 1$ if $\mathcal{X}_1 = 1$ and $Y_j = 1$ $(j > 1)$ if $(\mathcal{X}_j = 1) \wedge (\mathcal{X}_{j-1} = 1)$.

Note that when $Y_j = 1$ $(j \in [1, \ldots, \mathcal{O}])$ and without interference of the adversary, honest parties converge at a single block and we call such an event as a convergence opportunity. Let $\mathbf{Y} = \sum_{j=1}^{\mathcal{O}} Y_j$, each $\mathcal{X}_j = 0$ can ruin at most two convergency opportunities, we have $\mathbf{Y} \geq \mathcal{O} - 2\sum_{j=1}^{\mathcal{O}}(1 - \mathcal{X}_j) = 2\sum_{j=1}^{\mathcal{O}} \mathcal{X}_j - \mathcal{O}$. As $\Pr[\mathcal{X}_j = 0] \leq (\Delta + 1)\bar{\alpha}$ and $\Pr[\mathcal{X}_j = 1] \geq 1 - (\Delta + 1)\bar{\alpha}$, with error probability $\exp(-\frac{\varepsilon_5'^2 \cdot \bar{\alpha} t}{2})$ for $\varepsilon_5' \in (0, 1)$, we have $2\sum_{j=1}^{\mathcal{O}} \mathcal{X}_j - \mathcal{O} \geq 2(1 - \varepsilon_5')[1 - (\Delta + 1)\bar{\alpha}]\mathcal{O} - \mathcal{O} \geq [1 - 2\varepsilon_5' - 2(\Delta + 1)\bar{\alpha}] \cdot [(1 - \varepsilon_5) \cdot \bar{\alpha} t]$.

It follows that for constant $\varepsilon_5'' \in (0, 1)$, by picking sufficiently small ε_5 and ε_5', the number of convergence opportunity is at least $(1 - \varepsilon_5'') \cdot (1 - 2(\Delta + 1)\bar{\alpha}) \cdot \bar{\alpha} t$. During SL and $\delta_1 t$ slots, the number of adversarial blocks is upper-bounded by $(1 + \delta_1')(1 + \delta_1)(t + 1)\bar{\beta} \leq \frac{(1 + \delta_1')(1 + \delta_1)}{(1 + \delta_2)} \cdot (1 - 2(\Delta + 1)\bar{\alpha})(t + 1)\bar{\alpha}$ for $\delta_1' \in (0, 1)$, except with error probability $\exp(-\frac{\delta_1'^2 \cdot \bar{\beta} t}{3})$. This follows that $\bar{C}_1$ and $\bar{C}_2$ diverge at slot sl'' with probability $\exp(-\frac{\delta_1'^2 \cdot \bar{\beta} t}{3})$.

Theorem 3. *For parameters $\Delta \in \mathbb{N}, \varepsilon_5 \in (0, \frac{1}{2}]$, let any two honest parties P_1 and P_2 hold local leader-chain $\bar{C}_1$ and $\bar{C}_2$ at slot sl_1 and sl_2 ($sl_1 \geq sl_2 + \Delta$) respectively, then $\bar{C}_2^{\lceil K} \preceq \bar{C}_1$, where $K \leq (1+\varepsilon_5) \cdot ft$, except with error probability $p_{cplc} = \exp(-\frac{\varepsilon_5^2 \cdot ft}{3})$.*

Proof. In these t consecutive slots, the total number of leader-blocks are generated is upper-bounded by $(1+\varepsilon_5) \cdot ft$, except with error probability $\exp(-\frac{\varepsilon_5^2 \cdot ft}{3})$. Thus we have that leader-chain $\bar{C}_2$ is a prefix of $\bar{C}_1$ except the latest $K \leq (1 + \varepsilon_5) \cdot ft$ blocks with error probability $p_{cplc} = \exp(-\frac{\varepsilon_5^2 \cdot ft}{3})$.

The Security Analysis of Transaction-Chain

1. Achieving Chain Growth Property $\mathcal{Q}_{cgtc}$

Lemma 3. *Suppose that a leader-block B is backed by K blocks at the onset of slot sl held by honest parties and issued by an honest party P. Then the transaction-chain held by each honest party must be extended with one valid transaction-block $\tilde{B}$ within the following 2Δ slots.*

Proof. Based on common prefix property of leader-chain held by honest parties, at the onset of $sl + \Delta$, B must has been in the common part of honest parties' local chains. Hence P realizes that he is eligible to issue a transaction-block $\tilde{B}$ no later than slot $sl + \Delta$ and there is only one valid transaction-block linked to leader-block B received by all honest parties within the following Δ slots.

Theorem 4. *For parameters $\Delta \in \mathbb{N}, \varepsilon_6 \in (0, \frac{1}{2}]$, let honest party P holds transaction-chains $\tilde{C}$, $\tilde{C}_1$ and $\tilde{C}_2$ at the onset of slot sl, sl_1 and sl_2 respectively, where $sl_1 + t \leq sl_2 \leq sl$ and $t > 0$. Then protocol π_{uc} achieves chain growth property with $\tilde{g} = (1 - \varepsilon_6) \cdot \frac{\alpha_H \bar{g}}{1 + \alpha_H \bar{g} \Delta}$, such that $len(\tilde{C}_2) - len(\tilde{C}_1) \geq \tilde{g} \cdot t$ except with error probability $p_{cgtc} = \exp(-\frac{\varepsilon_6^2}{2} \cdot \frac{\alpha_H \bar{g} t}{1 + \alpha_H \bar{g} \Delta})$.*

Proof. First, the growth rate of confirmed leader-block is lower-bounded by $\bar{g} = (1 - \varepsilon_1) \cdot \bar{\gamma}$. Second, the slot interval between two consecutive honest confirmed leader-blocks is upper-bounded by $\frac{1}{\alpha_H \bar{g}}$ and the corresponding transaction-block will be added to all the honest parties' local transaction-chains within the following Δ slots. Actually, the transaction-chain held by honest parties will be increased by one block once in at most $\frac{1}{\alpha_H \bar{g}} + \Delta$ slots. Thus, the chain growth property holds with $\tilde{g} = (1 - \varepsilon_6) \cdot \frac{\alpha_H \bar{g}}{1 + \alpha_H \bar{g} \Delta}$ except with error probability

$$p_{cgtc} = \Pr\left[len(\tilde{C}_2) - len(\tilde{C}_1) < (1 - \varepsilon_6) \cdot \frac{\alpha_H \bar{g}}{1 + \alpha_H \bar{g} \Delta} \cdot t\right] \leq \exp(-\frac{\varepsilon_6^2}{2} \cdot \frac{\alpha_H \bar{g} t}{1 + \alpha_H \bar{g} \Delta}).$$

2. Achieving Chain Quality Property $\mathcal{Q}_{cqtc}$

Theorem 5. *For parameters* $\tilde{L}, \Delta \in \mathbb{N}$, $\varepsilon_4 \in (0, \frac{1}{2}]$, *let honest party* P *with transaction-chain* $\tilde{C}$ *at the onset of slot sl. Then for any* $\tilde{L}$ *consecutive blocks of* $\tilde{C}$, *the ratio of blocks created by the adversary is at most* $1 - (1 - \varepsilon_4) \cdot \frac{\tilde{\gamma}}{f}$ *except with error probability* $p_{cqtc} = \exp(-\frac{\varepsilon_4^2 \tilde{\gamma}}{3f})$.

Proof. These $\tilde{L}$ transaction-blocks correspond to $\tilde{L}$ independent confirmed leader-blocks in honest parties' local chains. We observe that as long as the confirmed leader-blocks are generated by honest parties, then under the mildly adaptive adversary, the corresponding transaction-blocks must be generated by honest parties. Hence, the chain quality property of transaction-chain fully relies on chain quality property of the confirmed part in honest parties' local leader-chain.

Since, except with error probability $\exp(-\frac{\varepsilon_4^2 \tilde{\gamma}}{3f})$, the adversary can generate at most $\bar{Y} \leq \tilde{L} - (1 - \varepsilon_4) \cdot \frac{\tilde{\gamma}}{f} \tilde{L}$ blocks in $\tilde{L}$ consecutive leader-blocks. Additionally, these $\tilde{L}$ consecutive leader-blocks may contain some unstable blocks, which may be discarded by honest parties in the future slots. Thus, the actual number of confirmed leader-blocks generated by the adversary in $\tilde{L}$ satisfies $\bar{Y}' \leq \bar{Y}$. Furthermore, in these $\tilde{L}$ consecutive transaction-blocks, the adversary can generate at most $\tilde{Y} \leq \bar{Y}'$ transaction-blocks. We obtain that $\tilde{\mu} = \frac{\tilde{Y}}{\tilde{L}} \leq \frac{\bar{Y}'}{\tilde{L}} \leq 1 - (1 - \varepsilon_4) \cdot \frac{\tilde{\gamma}}{f}$ except with error probability $p_{cqtc} = \exp(-\frac{\varepsilon_4^2 \tilde{\gamma}}{3f})$.

3. Achieving Uniqueness Property $\mathcal{Q}_{utc}$

Lemma 4. *There is at most one valid transaction-block with slot sl.*

Proof. Consider a contradiction that there are two different valid transaction-blocks $\tilde{B}_1$ and $\tilde{B}_2$ with slot *sl*. Let $\bar{B}_1$ and $\bar{B}_2$ are the corresponding leader-blocks that are linked by $\tilde{B}_1$ and $\tilde{B}_2$ respectively. Based on protocol execution, $\bar{B}_1$ and $\bar{B}_2$ must be the newly confirmed blocks at the onset of slot *sl*, which have been backed by K blocks in honest parties' local leader-chains. So that $\bar{B}_1$ and $\bar{B}_2$ are in two different leader-chains. Suppose that honest parties P_1 and P_2 with local leader-chains $\bar{C}_1$ and $\bar{C}_2$ at slot $sl + \Delta$ respectively, where $\bar{B}_1 \in \bar{C}_1$ and $\bar{B}_2 \in \bar{C}_2$. Hence we get that $\bar{C}_1^{\lceil K} \not\preceq \bar{C}_2$ and $\bar{C}_2^{\lceil K} \not\preceq \bar{C}_1$, which contradicts the common prefix property of leader-chains held by honest parties.

Theorem 6. *For parameter* $\Delta \in \mathbb{N}$, *let any two honest parties* P_1 *and* P_2 *hold local transaction-chains* $\tilde{C}_1$ *and* $\tilde{C}_2$ *at slot* $sl + \Delta$ *respectively. Then it holds that* $\tilde{C}_1^{sl} = \tilde{C}_2^{sl}$ *except with error probability* $p_{cutc} = \tilde{p}_1 + p_{cplc}$.

Proof. Observe that the blocks generated and receive by some honest parties before slot *sl* must be received by all the honest parties at slot $sl + \Delta$. Consider a contradiction that $\tilde{C}_1^{sl} \neq \tilde{C}_2^{sl}$, so $len(\tilde{C}_1^{sl}) \neq len(\tilde{C}_2^{sl})$ or there are some different blocks in these two chains.

For condition 1, we assume that $len(\tilde{C}_1^{sl}) < len(\tilde{C}_2^{sl})$. Without loss of generality, let $len(\tilde{C}_2^{sl}) - len(\tilde{C}_1^{sl}) = 1$. It must be the case that the last block $\tilde{B}_{len(\tilde{C}_2^{sl})} \in \tilde{C}_2^{sl}$ is not accepted or received by P_1 at slot $sl + \Delta$. First, we can see that $\tilde{B}_{len(\tilde{C}_2^{sl})}$ must be valid in that it has been accepted by P_2. Second, in synchronous network, $\tilde{B}_{len(\tilde{C}_2^{sl})}$ must have been received by all the honest parties at slot $sl + \Delta$. As a result, if a valid transaction-block $\tilde{B}_{len(\tilde{C}_2^{sl})}$ has been received by an honest party, then it must be confirmed by all the honest parties within Δ slots. So that condition 1 happens with negligible probability $\tilde{p}_1$.

For condition 2, assume that the last blocks of $\tilde{C}_1^{sl}$ and $\tilde{C}_2^{sl}$ are different (denoted by $\tilde{B}_1, \tilde{B}_2$). During protocol execution, $\tilde{B}_1$ and $\tilde{B}_2$ must be valid and received by all the honest parties at the end of $sl + \Delta$, which contradicts to the result of Lemma 4 and happens with error probability p_{cplc}.

6. Achieving (Near) Optimal Transaction Settlement Time

Theorem 7. *For parameters* $\Delta \in \mathbb{N}, \varepsilon_1, \varepsilon_6, \varepsilon_7 \in (0, \frac{1}{2}], \alpha_H \in (\frac{1}{2}, 1], \theta \in [1, K+1]$, *protocol* π_{uc} *achieves* (θ, α_H)-*transaction settlement time with* $\theta = \frac{1}{(1-\varepsilon_1)(1-\varepsilon_6)\alpha_H^3 f \Delta} + \frac{1}{2}$, *except with error probability* $\exp(-\frac{\varepsilon_7^2}{3} \cdot (\frac{1}{(1-\varepsilon_1)(1-\varepsilon_6)\alpha_H^3 f \Delta} + \frac{1}{2}))$.

Proof. Intuitively, the optimal time in transaction-block confirmation is $\frac{1}{g} + \Delta$ slots. As the honest transaction-block generated once in $\frac{1}{\alpha_H \tilde{g}}$ slots on expectation and will be received by all the honest parties within Δ. Hence, we conclude that once in $\frac{1}{\alpha_H \tilde{g}} + \Delta$ slots on expectation there will be a honest transaction-block, which must be received and confirmed finally by all the honest parties. Thus, with error probability $\exp(-\frac{\varepsilon_7^2}{3} \cdot (\frac{1}{(1-\varepsilon_1)(1-\varepsilon_6)\alpha_H^3 f \Delta} + \frac{1}{2}))$, a transaction-block can be generated and confirmed finally within slot interval:

$$
\begin{aligned}
\tilde{I} &= \frac{1}{\alpha_H \tilde{g}} + \Delta = \frac{1 + (1-\varepsilon_1)\alpha_H^2 f \Delta}{(1-\varepsilon_1)(1-\varepsilon_6)\alpha_H^3 f} + \Delta \\
&\leq \frac{2}{(1-\varepsilon_1)(1-\varepsilon_6)\alpha_H^3 f} + \Delta \\
&= \left[\frac{2}{(1-\varepsilon_1)(1-\varepsilon_6)\alpha_H^3 f \cdot (\frac{1}{\alpha_H}d + \Delta)} + \frac{\Delta}{\frac{1}{\alpha_H}d + \Delta} \right] \cdot (\frac{1}{\alpha_H}d + \Delta) \\
&\leq \left[\frac{1}{(1-\varepsilon_1)(1-\varepsilon_6)\alpha_H^3 f \Delta} + \frac{1}{2} \right] \cdot (\frac{1}{\alpha_H}d + \Delta)
\end{aligned}
$$

6   Conclusion

In this work, we propose a new structure of two-chain blockchain and based on which we propose a provably secure PoS-based blockchain protocol π_{uc}. Under honest majority assumption, except for the three fundamental security properties, the uniqueness of chains that contain transactions held by the honest parties is achieved in a slot-synchronous network, which guarantees the low latency in transactions confirmation. We note that there may be ways to further optimize UniqueChain, e.g., improving it by allowing the adversary to be fully adaptive and partition the network for an arbitrarily longtime.

A   The Implementation of $\mathcal{F}_{init}$

We denote φ_{init} as the ideal protocol of $\mathcal{F}_{init}$, where the parties are dummy that they only forward messages sent by environment $\mathcal{Z}$ to $\mathcal{F}_{init}$ and then forward the messages sent by $\mathcal{F}_{init}$ to environment $\mathcal{Z}$. Further, we denote Π_{init} (Fig. 7) as the protocol that implements φ_{init} securely.

Let $EXEC^{\mathcal{F}_{init}}_{\varphi_{init},\mathcal{S},\mathcal{Z}}$ be the random variable that denotes the joint outputs of all the parties by executing φ_{init} with adversary $\mathcal{S}$ and environment $\mathcal{Z}$. Let $EXEC^{\mathcal{F}_{net}}_{\Pi_{init},\mathcal{A},\mathcal{Z}}$ be the random variable that denotes the joint outputs of all the parties by executing Π_{init} with adversary $\mathcal{A}$ and environment $\mathcal{Z}$.

Lemma 5. $EXEC^{\mathcal{F}_{net}}_{\Pi_{init},\mathcal{A},\mathcal{Z}}$ and $EXEC^{\mathcal{F}_{init}}_{\varphi_{init},\mathcal{S},\mathcal{Z}}$ are indistinguishable.

Proof. Consider the adversary $\mathcal{A}$ for Π_{init}, we construct the adversary $\mathcal{S}$ with a local table $\mathcal{T}$ for φ_{init}. Upon receiving $(Initialize, P_{i'}, s_{i'})$ from $\mathcal{A}$, if it has record $B_0 \in \mathcal{T}$, then send $(Initialized, B_0)$ to $\mathcal{A}$; otherwise, pass message to $\mathcal{F}_{init}$ and receive $(Initialized, B_0)$, then record B_0 and send $(Initialized, B_0)$ to $\mathcal{A}$. We can see that for each query from $\mathcal{A}$, the form of output is $(Initialized, B_0)$, where $B_0 = (\mathcal{S}_0, nonce_1)$, $nonce_1$ is sampled uniformly from $\{0, 1\}^k$. Therefore, $EXEC^{\mathcal{F}_{net}}_{\Pi_{init},\mathcal{A},\mathcal{Z}}$ and $EXEC^{\mathcal{F}_{init}}_{\varphi_{init},\mathcal{S},\mathcal{Z}}$ are indistinguishable.

B   The Implementation of $\mathcal{F}_{res}$

As described above, we denote φ_{res} as the ideal protocol of $\mathcal{F}_{res}$ and Π_{res} as the protocol that implements φ_{res}. We show Π_{res} in the $\{\mathcal{F}_{RO}, \mathcal{F}_{SIG}\}$-*hybrid* model (Fig. 8), where functionalities $\mathcal{F}_{RO}$ and $\mathcal{F}_{SIG}$ have been well defined in [4, 19].

Let $EXEC^{\mathcal{F}_{res}}_{\varphi_{res},\mathcal{S},\mathcal{Z}}$ be the random variable that denotes the joint outputs of all the parties by executing protocol φ_{res} with adversary $\mathcal{S}$ and environment $\mathcal{Z}$. Let $EXEC^{\mathcal{F}_{RO},\mathcal{F}_{SIG}}_{\Pi_{res},\mathcal{A},\mathcal{Z}}$ be the random variable that denotes the joint outputs of all the parties by executing protocol Π_{res} with adversary $\mathcal{A}$ and environment $\mathcal{Z}$.

Lemma 6. $EXEC^{\mathcal{F}_{res}}_{\varphi_{res},\mathcal{S},\mathcal{Z}}$ and $EXEC^{\mathcal{F}_{RO},\mathcal{F}_{SIG}}_{\Pi_{res},\mathcal{A},\mathcal{Z}}$ are indistinguishable.

Proof. Consider the adversary $\mathcal{A}$ for Π_{res}, we construct the adversary $\mathcal{S}$ with a local table $\mathcal{T}$ for φ_{res}. At slot $sl_{i,j}$ ($i \in \mathbb{N}, j \in \{1, ..., R\}$), it proceeds as follows:

- Simulating Registration Phase.
  - *Upon receiving $(Register, P_{i'})$ from $\mathcal{A}$, send $(Register, P_{i'})$ to $\mathcal{F}_{res}$ and obtain $(Registered, P_{i'})$, then send $(Registered, P_{i'})$ to $\mathcal{A}$;
  - * Upon receiving $(Unregister, P_{i'})$ from $\mathcal{A}$, send $(Unregister, P_{i'})$ to $\mathcal{F}_{res}$ and obtain $(Unregistered, P_{i'})$, then send $(Unregistered, P_{i'})$ to $\mathcal{A}$.
- Simulating Chain Extension Phase.
  - * Generating Leader-Block.
    - Upon receiving $(L\text{-}Elect, P_{i'})$ from $\mathcal{A}$, if there is a record $(P_{i'}, \bar{\mathbf{h}})$, then send $\bar{\mathbf{h}}$ to $\mathcal{A}$. Otherwise, send $(L\text{-}Elect, P_{i'})$ to $\mathcal{F}_{res}$ and obtain $(L\text{-}Elected, P_{i'}, \bar{f})$. If $\bar{f} = 1$, choose $\bar{\mathbf{h}} \in \{0,1\}^k$ such that $\bar{\mathbf{h}} \le T_i$. Otherwise, choose $\bar{\mathbf{h}} \in \{0,1\}^k$ such that $\bar{\mathbf{h}} > T_i$. Then record $(L\text{-}Elected, P_{i'}, \bar{\mathbf{h}})$ and send $\bar{\mathbf{h}}$ to A;
    - Upon receiving $(Compute, \bar{B}_{-1}, P_{i'})$ from $\mathcal{A}$, if their is a record $(\bar{B}_{-1}, \bar{h}_{-1})$, then send $\bar{h}_{-1}$ to $\mathcal{A}$. Otherwise, send $(Compute, \bar{B}_{-1}, P_{i'})$ to $\mathcal{F}_{res}$ and obtain $(Computed, \bar{h}_{-1})$, then record $(\bar{B}_{-1}, \bar{h}_{-1})$ and send $\bar{h}_{-1}$ to $\mathcal{A}$;
    - Upon receiving $(Sign, \bar{B}, P_{i'})$ from $\mathcal{A}$, if there is a record $(\bar{B}, \bar{\sigma})$, then send $(Signed, (\bar{B}, \bar{\sigma}))$ to $\mathcal{A}$. Otherwise, send $(Sign, \bar{B}, P_{i'})$ to $\mathcal{F}_{res}$ and obtain $(Signed, (\bar{B}, \bar{\sigma}))$, record $(\bar{B}, \bar{\sigma})$ and send $(Signed, (\bar{B}, \bar{\sigma}))$ to $\mathcal{A}$.
  - * Generating Transaction-Block.
    - Upon receiving $(T\text{-}Elect, P_{j'})$ from $\mathcal{A}$, if there is a record $(P_{j'}, \tilde{f})$, then send $\tilde{f}$ to $\mathcal{A}$. Otherwise, send $(T\text{-}Elect, P_{j'})$ to $\mathcal{F}_{res}$ and obtain $(T\text{-}Elected, P_{j'}, \tilde{f})$, then record $(P_{j'}, \tilde{f})$ and send $\tilde{f}$ to $\mathcal{A}$.
    - Upon receiving $(Compute, \tilde{B}_{-1}, \bar{B}, P_{j'})$ from $\mathcal{A}$, if there is a record $(\tilde{B}_{-1}, \bar{B}, \tilde{h}_{-1}, \bar{h})$, then send $(\tilde{h}_{-1}, \bar{h})$ to $\mathcal{A}$. Otherwise, send $(Compute, \tilde{B}_{-1}, \bar{B}, P_{j'})$ to $\mathcal{F}_{res}$ and obtain $(Computed, \tilde{h}_{-1}, \bar{h})$, then record $(\tilde{B}_{-1}, \bar{B}, \tilde{h}_{-1}, \bar{h})$ and send $(\tilde{h}_{-1}, \bar{h})$ to $\mathcal{A}$;
    - Upon receiving $(Sign, \tilde{B}, P_{j'})$ from $\mathcal{A}$, if there is a record $(\tilde{B}, \tilde{\sigma})$, then send $(Signed, (\tilde{B}, \tilde{\sigma}))$ to $\mathcal{A}$. Otherwise, send $(Sign, \tilde{B}, P_{j'})$ to $\mathcal{F}_{res}$ and obtain $(Signed, (\tilde{B}, \tilde{\sigma}))$, record $(\tilde{B}, \tilde{\sigma})$ and send $(Signed, (\tilde{B}, \tilde{\sigma}))$ to $\mathcal{A}$.

– Simulating Verification Phase.
  • Upon receiving $(Verify, \bar{B})$ from $\mathcal{A}$, if there is a record $((P'_{i'}, \bar{f}), (\bar{B}, \bar{\sigma}))$, then send $\bar{y}'_{i'} = \bar{f}$ to $\mathcal{A}$. Otherwise, then send $\bar{y}'_{i'} = 0$ to $\mathcal{A}$;
  • Upon receiving $(Verify, \tilde{B})$ from $\mathcal{A}$, if there is a record $((P'_{i'}, \tilde{f}), (\tilde{B}, \tilde{\sigma}))$, then send $\tilde{y}'_{i'} = \tilde{f}$ to $\mathcal{A}$. Otherwise, send $\tilde{y}'_{i'} = 0$ to $\mathcal{A}$.

Now, we can see that the environment $\mathcal{Z}$ gets what it can get in the real protocol execution. Precisely, for each L-$Elect$ query, based on $\mathcal{F}_{res}$'s response, $\mathcal{S}$ responds with messages chosen uniformly from $\{0,1\}^k$; for each T-$Elect$, $Compute$ and $Sign$ query, $\mathcal{S}$ responds as $\mathcal{F}_{res}$ does; for each $Verify$ query, $\mathcal{S}$ responds according to the records in $\mathcal{T}$, which also come from $\mathcal{F}_{res}$. In fact, $\mathcal{S}$ just transfers messages between $\mathcal{Z}$ and $\mathcal{F}_{res}$. Thus, we have that $EXEC^{\mathcal{F}_{res}}_{\varphi_{res}, \mathcal{S}, \mathcal{Z}}$ and $EXEC^{\mathcal{F}_{RO}, \mathcal{F}_{SIG}}_{\Pi_{res}, \mathcal{A}, \mathcal{Z}}$ are indistinguishable.

Π_{init} is parameterized by security parameter k, interacts with initial party $P_{i'}$ ($i' \in \{1, 2, ...\}$), adversary $\mathcal{A}$ and environment $\mathcal{Z}$. For each $P_{i'}$, it proceeds as follows. Upon receiving $(Initialize, P_{i'}, s_{i'})$ from $\mathcal{Z}$, $P_{i'}$ gets the current slot $sl_{i,j}$ ($i \in \mathbb{N}, j \in \{1, ..., R\}$) from the local clock.

– If $i = 0$ and $j = 1$, then chooses random values $r'_{i'}, r_{i'} \in \{0,1\}^k$, computes commitment as $C_{i'} := Com(s_{i'}, r_{i'}; r'_{i'})$ and sends $(Broadcast, P_{i'}, C_{i'})$ to $\mathcal{F}_{net}$.
  • collects all the received commitments $C := \{C_{i'}, i' \in \{1, 2, ...\}\}$, opens commitment as $(s_{i'}, r_{i'})$ and sends $(Broadcast, P_{i'}, (s_{i'}, r_{i'}))$ to $\mathcal{F}_{net}$ at $sl_{0,2}$.
  • collects all the valid openings $O := \{(s_{i'}, r_{i'}), i' \in \{1, 2, ...\}\}$, computes the difficulty target T_1 according to the distribution of stakes $\{s_{i'}, i' \subset \{1, 2, ...\}\}$ and the random value $nonce_1 := \oplus_{i'} r_{i'}$;
  • set $B_0 = (\mathcal{S}_0, nonce_1)$;

Output $(Initialized, B_0)$ to the environment $\mathcal{Z}$.

Fig. 7. The initialization protocol Π_{init}

Π_{res} is parameterized by probability p, security parameter k, interacts with parties $P_{i'}, P_{i''}$, adversary $\mathcal{A}$ and environment $\mathcal{Z}$. At slot $sl_{i,j}$, it proceeds as follows:

1. **Registration.**
1) Upon receiving $(Register, P_{i'})$ from $\mathcal{Z}$, if $P_{i'}$ has registered with $re_{i'} = 1$, then ignore the message. Otherwise, record $(P_{i'}, re_{i'} = 1)$ and send $(Registered, P_{i'})$ to $\mathcal{Z}$;
2) Upon receiving $(Unregister, P_{i'})$ from environment $\mathcal{Z}$, if $P_{i'}$ has not registered with $re_{i'} = 1$, then ignore the message. Otherwise, record $(P_{i'}, re_{i'} = 0)$ and send $(Unregistered, P_{i'})$ to $\mathcal{Z}$.

2. **Chain Extension.**
1) **Generating Leader-Block:** $P_{i'}$ with one unite stake $s_{i,j,i'} = 1$ proceeds as follows:

- Upon receiving $(L\text{-}Elect, P_{i'})$ from $\mathcal{Z}$:
  - If there is a record $(P_{i'}, re_{i'} = 1, s_{i,j,i'} = 1)$, then query $\mathcal{F}_{RO}$ with input $(pk_{i'}, sl_{i,j})$ and obtain $\bar{h}$. If $\bar{h} \leq T_i$, send $(L\text{-}Elected, P_{i'}, \bar{f} = 1)$ to $\mathcal{Z}$, otherwise, send $(L\text{-}Elected, P_{i'}, \bar{f} = 0)$ to $\mathcal{Z}$.
  - Otherwise, send $(L\text{-}Elected, P_{i'}, \bar{f} = 0)$ to $\mathcal{Z}$.
- Upon receiving $(Compute, \bar{B}_{-1}, P_{i'})$ from $\mathcal{Z}$, query $\mathcal{F}_{RO}$ with $\bar{B}_{-1}$ and obtain $\bar{h}_{-1}$, then send $(Computed, \bar{h}_{-1})$ to $\mathcal{Z}$.
- Upon receiving $(Sign, \bar{B}, P_{i'})$ from $\mathcal{Z}$, send $(Sign, \bar{B}, P_{i'})$ to $\mathcal{F}_{SIG}$, obtain $(Signed, (\bar{B}, \bar{\sigma}))$, then send $(Signed, (\bar{B}, \bar{\sigma}))$ to $\mathcal{Z}$.

2) **Generating Transaction-Block:** if a leader-block $\bar{B}$ is backed by K' blocks issued by $P_{i'}$, then $P_{i'}$ proceeds as follows:

- Upon receiving $(T\text{-}Elect, P_{i'})$ from $\mathcal{Z}$, if $K' = K$, then send $(T\text{-}Elected, P_{i'}, \tilde{f} = 1)$ to $\mathcal{Z}$. Otherwise, send $(T\text{-}Elected, P_{i'}, \tilde{f} = 0)$ to $\mathcal{Z}$.
- Upon receiving $(Compute, \tilde{B}_{-1}, \bar{B}_1, P_{i'})$ from $\mathcal{Z}$, query $\mathcal{F}_{RO}$ with $(\tilde{B}_{-1}, \bar{B}_{-1})$ and obtain $(\tilde{h}_{-1}, \bar{h})$, then send $(Computed, \tilde{h}_{-1}, \bar{h})$ to $\mathcal{Z}$.
- Upon receiving $(Sign, \tilde{B}, P_{i'})$ from $\mathcal{Z}$, then send $(Sign, \tilde{B}, P_{i'})$ to $\mathcal{F}_{SIG}$ and obtain $(Signed, (\tilde{B}, \tilde{\sigma}))$, then send $(Signed, (\tilde{B}, \tilde{\sigma}))$ to $\mathcal{Z}$.

3. **Verification.** Upon receiving $(Verify, \bar{B})$ or $(Verify, \tilde{B})$ from $\mathcal{Z}$, $P_{i''}$ proceeds as follows:
1) Send $(pk'_{i'}, sl_{i,j})$ to $\mathcal{F}_{RO}$ and obtain $\bar{h}$, if $\bar{h} \leq T_i$, then set $\bar{y}_{i'} = 1$, otherwise set $\bar{y}_{i'} = 0$;
2) Send $(Verify, (\bar{B}, P'_{i'}, \bar{\sigma}))$ or $(Verify, (\tilde{B}, P'_{j'}, \tilde{\sigma}))$ to $\mathcal{F}_{SIG}$ and obtain $\bar{y}'_{i'}$ or $\tilde{y}'_{i'}$;
3) If $(\bar{y}_{i'} = 1 \wedge \bar{y}'_{i'} = 1)$ or $\tilde{y}'_{i'} = 1$, then send $(Verified, \bar{f}' = 1)$ or $(Verified, \tilde{f}' = 1)$ to $\mathcal{Z}$. Otherwise, send $(Verified, \bar{f}' = 0)$ or $(Verified, \tilde{f}' = 0)$ to $\mathcal{Z}$.

Fig. 8. The resource protocol Π_{res}

References

1. Badertscher, C., Gai, P., Kiayias, A., Russell, A., Zikas, V.: Ouroboros genesis: composable proof-of-stake blockchains with dynamic availability. In: the 2018 ACM SIGSAC Conference (2018)
2. Bentov, I., Pass, R., Shi, E.: Snow white: Provably secure proofs of stake. IACR Cryptology ePrint Archive **2016**, 919 (2016)
3. Boyen, X., Carr, C., Haines, T.: Graphchain: a blockchain-free scalable decentralised ledger. In: the 2nd ACM Workshop (2018)

4. Canetti, R.: Universally composable signature, certification, and authentication. In: IEEE Workshop on Computer Security Foundations (2004)
5. Croman, K., et al.: On scaling decentralized blockchains. In: Clark, J., Meiklejohn, S., Ryan, P.Y.A., Wallach, D., Brenner, M., Rohloff, K. (eds.) FC 2016. LNCS, vol. 9604, pp. 106–125. Springer, Heidelberg (2016). https://doi.org/10.1007/978-3-662-53357-4_8
6. David, B., Gaži, P., Kiayias, A., Russell, A.: Ouroboros praos: an adaptively-secure, semi-synchronous proof-of-stake blockchain. In: Nielsen, J.B., Rijmen, V. (eds.) EUROCRYPT 2018. LNCS, vol. 10821, pp. 66–98. Springer, Cham (2018). https://doi.org/10.1007/978-3-319-78375-8_3
7. Duong, T., Fan, L., Veale, T., Zhou, H.: Securing bitcoin-like backbone protocols against a malicious majority of computing power. IACR Cryptology ePrint Archive **2016**, 716 (2016)
8. Dziembowski, S., Eckey, L., Faust, S., Hesse, J., Hostáková, K.: Multi-party virtual state channels. In: Ishai, Y., Rijmen, V. (eds.) EUROCRYPT 2019. LNCS, vol. 11476, pp. 625–656. Springer, Cham (2019). https://doi.org/10.1007/978-3-030-17653-2_21
9. Dziembowski, S., Eckey, L., Faust, S., Malinowski, D.: Perun: virtual payment hubs over cryptocurrencies. In: 2019 IEEE Symposium on Security and Privacy (SP) (2019)
10. Dziembowski, S., Faust, S., Hostakova, K.: General state channel networks. In: the 2018 ACM SIGSAC Conference (2018)
11. Eyal, I., Gencer, A.E., Sirer, E.G., Van Renesse, R.: Bitcoin-NG: a scalable blockchain protocol, pp. 45–59 (2016)
12. Fan, L., Zhou, H.: iChing: a scalable proof-of-stake blockchain in the open setting (or, how to mimic nakamoto's design via proof-of-stake). IACR Cryptology ePrint Archive **2017**, 656 (2017)
13. Fitzi, M., Gazi, P., Kiayias, A., Russell, Λ.: Parallel chains. improving throughput and latency of blockchain protocols via parallel composition. IACR Cryptology ePrint Archive **2018**, 1119 (2018)
14. Fitzi, M., Gaži, P., Kiayias, A., Russell, A.: Ledger combiners for fast settlement. In: Pass, R., Pietrzak, K. (eds.) TCC 2020. LNCS, vol. 12550, pp. 322–352. Springer, Cham (2020). https://doi.org/10.1007/978-3-030-64375-1_12
15. Garay, J., Kiayias, A., Leonardos, N.: The bitcoin backbone protocol: analysis and applications. In: Oswald, E., Fischlin, M. (eds.) EUROCRYPT 2015. LNCS, vol. 9057, pp. 281–310. Springer, Heidelberg (2015). https://doi.org/10.1007/978-3-662-46803-6_10
16. Garay, J., Kiayias, A., Leonardos, N.: The bitcoin backbone protocol with chains of variable difficulty. In: Katz, J., Shacham, H. (eds.) CRYPTO 2017. LNCS, vol. 10401, pp. 291–323. Springer, Cham (2017). https://doi.org/10.1007/978-3-319-63688-7_10
17. Gilad, Y., Hemo, R., Micali, S., Vlachos, G., Zeldovich, N.: Algorand: scaling byzantine agreements for cryptocurrencies. In: Symposium on Operating Systems Principles 2017, pp. 51–68 (2017)
18. Goyal, V., Li, H., Raizes, J.: Instant block confirmation in the sleepy model. In: Borisov, N., Diaz, C. (eds.) FC 2021. LNCS, vol. 12675, pp. 65–83. Springer, Heidelberg (2021). https://doi.org/10.1007/978-3-662-64331-0_4
19. Hofheinz, D., Müller-Quade, J.: Universally composable commitments using random oracles. In: Naor, M. (ed.) TCC 2004. LNCS, vol. 2951, pp. 58–76. Springer, Heidelberg (2004). https://doi.org/10.1007/978-3-540-24638-1_4

20. Kiayias, A., Panagiotakos, G.: Speed-security tradeoffs in blockchain protocols (2015)
21. Kiayias, A., Russell, A., David, B., Oliynykov, R.: Ouroboros: a provably secure proof-of-stake blockchain protocol. In: Katz, J., Shacham, H. (eds.) CRYPTO 2017. LNCS, vol. 10401, pp. 357–388. Springer, Cham (2017). https://doi.org/10.1007/978-3-319-63688-7_12
22. Kokoriskogias, E., Jovanovic, P., Gailly, N., Khoffi, I., Gasser, L., Ford, B.: Enhancing bitcoin security and performance with strong consistency via collective signing, pp. 279–296 (2016)
23. Li, C., Li, P., Zhou, D., Xu, W., Long, F., Yao, A.: Scaling nakamoto consensus to thousands of transactions per second (2018)
24. Li, S., Tse, D.: TaiJi: longest chain availability with BFT fast confirmation. arXiv preprint arXiv:2011.11097 (2020)
25. Nakamoto, S.: Bitcoin: a peer-to-peer electronic cash system. Consulted (2008)
26. Odwyer, K.J., Malone, D.: Bitcoin mining and its energy footprint, pp. 280–285 (2014)
27. Pass, R., Seeman, L., Shelat, A.: Analysis of the blockchain protocol in asynchronous networks. In: Coron, J.-S., Nielsen, J.B. (eds.) EUROCRYPT 2017. LNCS, vol. 10211, pp. 643–673. Springer, Cham (2017). https://doi.org/10.1007/978-3-319-56614-6_22
28. Pass, R., Shi, E.: Hybrid consensus: Efficient consensus in the permissionless model, p. 16 (2017)
29. Sompolinsky, Y., Zohar, A.: Accelerating bitcoin's transaction processing. fast money grows on trees, not chains. IACR Cryptology ePrint Archive **2013**, 881 (2013)
30. Yu, H., Nikolic, I., Hou, R., Saxena, P.: OHIE: blockchain scaling made simple. In: 2020 IEEE Symposium on Security and Privacy (SP) (2020)

PEPEC: Precomputed ECC Points Embedded in Certificates and Verified by CT Log Servers

Guangshen Cheng[1,5], Jiankuo Dong[2](✉), Xinyi Ji[2], Bingyu Li[3], Haoling Fan[4], and Pinchang Zhang[2]

[1] School of Cyber Security, University of Science and Technology of China, Hefei, China
[2] School of Computer Science, Nanjing University of Posts and Telecommunications, Nanjing, China
djiankuo@njupt.edu.cn
[3] School of Cyber Science and Technology, Beihang University, Beijing, China
[4] Institute of Information Engineering, Chinese Academy of Sciences, Beijing, China
[5] Beijing Research Institute, University of Science and Technology of China, Beijing, China

Abstract. Elliptic curve cryptography (ECC) is respected in public key infrastructures (PKIs) due to its high performance and small key size. However, for some client devices with limited computing resources, signature verification and key agreement using the ECC public key is computationally difficult which mainly due to the complexity of scalar multiplication. The window non-adjacent form algorithm can be used to improve the performance of the elliptic curve public key operation, which is combining the window method with the Non-adjacent form representation (w-NAF). Compared with fixed-point scalar multiplication using the offline precomputed table, for the unknown-point multiplication of ECC public key operation, a pre-computed table needs to be generated online. In this paper, a novel efficient certificate scheme called PEPEC (Precomputed ECC Points Embedded in Certificates) is proposed to integrate the w-NAF into CT (Certificate Transparency) which is a trusted enhancement for PKI. By using the PEPEC certificate, the client can improve the performance of the public key operation by more than 10%, with the offline-generated precomputed table of the w-NAF algorithm. The correctness of the precomputed table is provided by CT. Our PEPEC certificate is compatible with the existing standardized PKI system. The client can select the optimal window size of the w-NAF algorithm according to the current situation of computing resources to improve the performance of the public key operation.

Keywords: ECC · Certificate Transparency · PKI · Certificate · w-NAF

This work was supported in part by Key RD Plan of Shandong Province under Grant No. 2020CXGC010115; in part by the National Natural Science Foundation of China under Grant 62002011; in part by the China Postdoctoral Science Foundation under Grant 2021T140042 and Grant 2021M690304.

J. Zhou et al. (Eds.): ACNS 2022 Workshops, LNCS 13285, pp. 447–460, 2022.
https://doi.org/10.1007/978-3-031-16815-4_24

1   Introduction

With the rapid development of public key cryptography, Public Key Infrastructure was formed to provide comprehensive security services for the Internet and Internet-related facilities. PKI [28] uses public key cryptography and digital certificates to ensure the security of system information and is responsible for verifying the identity of the digital certificate holder. At present, PKI can be used for security services such as identity authentication, non-repudiation of operations, information transmission, storage integrity and confidentiality.

Although PKI technology is relatively mature and has entered the stage of large-scale application, the security governance of the PKI trust system faces many new opportunities and challenges. In recent years, a large number of new PKI technology research results have emerged one after another, dedicated to overcoming various difficulties in application promotion and deployment. Some focus on enhancing the credibility of PKI, like CT [24], DANE [17], CAA [14]. Some focus on optimizing certificate revocation such as CRLite [23], PKISN [34]. But there are few related kinds of research on improving the performance of public key usage, which is one of the main contents of a digital certificate.

In 1987, the elliptic curve cryptography public key cryptography algorithm [21] was first proposed. Compared with RSA, elliptic curve cryptography has a shorter key length and faster computing speed. It has attracted extensive attention from academia and industry. It is reported that ECC is the most widely used public key cryptography algorithm at present [16]. Among the international public key cryptographic algorithms, the mainstream elliptic curve algorithms include NIST-P series [29], Brainpool [27], etc. Affected by the Snowden incident, some new elliptic curve curves with higher security and more efficient performance have received attention, including Curve25519/448 [22], Edwards25519/448 [19], FourQ [8], etc.

The public key cryptography algorithm structure based on the elliptic curve discrete logarithm problem (ECDLP) is complex, and the computing performance is an important bottleneck in practical application. With the promotion of IoT applications in smart transportation, smart medical care and other fields, users are extremely demanding on the computing power of ECC cryptographic algorithms. Researchers have carried out a lot of works on the acceleration of elliptic curve cryptographic algorithms on various computing platforms, including GPU [13], CPU [6], Embedded CPU [26], FPGA [18], etc. Liu et al. [26] improved the scalar multiplication implementation of FourQ elliptic curve on three resource-constrained embedded platforms (AVR, MSP430, ARM Cortex M4). Considering the sufficient memory resources of the GPU platform, Dong et al. [9] used a fixed window and a portion-by-portion addition method for EdDSA signature and verification, respectively. These works use the idea of combining software and hardware to improve the performance of the ECC algorithm and do not take into account the performance breakthrough brought by optimizing the PKI certificate.

In this paper, we propose a novel improved X.509v3 certificate, named Precomputed ECC Points Embedded in Certificates (short for PEPEC), which contains a validated w-NAF precomputed table related to the certificate public key. Each Domain owner who uses a PEPEC certificate will establish a faster but still secure communication with clients. The offline precomputed table of PEPEC can improve the performance of ECC public key operation by about 10%. Even clients with limited performance can load the appropriate size of precomputed table according to their situation. Moreover, a PEPEC certificate is fully applicable to the current CT environment, and the log servers of CT can also ensure the correctness of the w-NAF precomputed table.

The rest of our paper is organized as follows. Section 2 covers the basic knowledge. Section 3 gives an overall architecture of our CT-based efficient ECC certificate scheme. Section 4 presents a comparative analysis in terms of computational costs and security. Section 5 concludes the paper.

2   Preliminaries

2.1   PKI and CT

In traditional PKI, TLS Server (domain owner for example) generates its private and public key first. Then Server will encode the public key and identifying attributes into a Certificate Signing Request (CSR), sign the CSR with its private key and send the signature and CSR to the Certificate Authority (CA). The issuing CA validates the request and signs the certificate with the CA's private key. Once the domain owner obtains the certificate, it can communicate confidentially with the TLS client. Anyone including the TLS client can use the public portion of a certificate to verify that it was issued by the CA. The whole process is shown in Fig. 1:

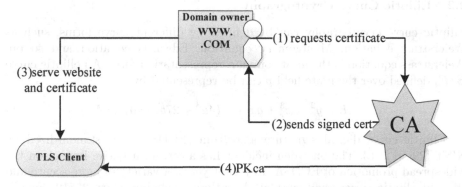

Fig. 1. The structure of PKI

A certificate, the important trust credential in PKI, is issued by the CA. Therefore, as a trust anchor, CA is usually considered to be completely trusted. However, a series of security incidents have shown that, as trust anchors in PKI systems, CAs are not as reliable as people think. CAs may issue "fake" certificates due to mismanagement or attacks [7,36]. The fake certificate is issued by a trusted CA, so it can pass the certificate verification so that it can be used by the adversary to launch malicious websites, man-in-the-middle, or impersonation attacks without any warning of the target. In this regard, relevant technical achievements in attack detection and protection have been proposed to detect fake certificates in time and restrict the rights of CA agencies [10,20,33]. At present, the most mainstream trust enhancement mechanism is Certificate Transparency (CT), which was led by Google in 2013. It has been officially adopted as the IETF RFC 6962 standard [24] and is supported by browsers and TLS software, including Firefox [5], Apple platforms [2], Chrome [4], Nginx [30], OpenSSL [35]. Compared to traditional PKI, the CT solution adds two main components, including *log server* and *monitor*:

Log Server. A Log server maintains append-only logs to record certificates, which means that once a certificate is added to the log, it cannot be removed or modified. These logs are publicly visible so that anyone can audit the logged certificates by calling the port provided by the log server. Once the certificate submitted to the Log Server is verified to be valid, the Log Server needs to generate a Signature Timestamp (SCT), which proves that the relevant certificate has been stored on the Log Server. The SCT contains the SCT version number, log Id, timestamp and a signature containing the above contents and the received certificate. The signature ensures that the certificate cannot be modified after it is submitted to the Log Server.

Monitor. Monitors regularly query public logs and can download and store certificates for subsequent reporting. There are also third-party monitors which process the records in public to provide certificate search services for users [25].

2.2 Elliptic Curve Cryptography

Elliptic curve cryptography can be defined by different curve forms, such as Weierstrass equation, Montgomery equation, Edwards equation and so on. Weierstrass equation is the most common representation form. An elliptic curve E/F_p defined over the finite field p can be represented by

$$E: \ y^2 = x^3 + ax + b \ (4a^3 + 27b^2 \neq 0) \tag{1}$$

Elliptic curve digital signature algorithm (ECDSA) was standardized by NIST [29] in 2013. The Snowden incident has a certain negative impact on the widespread promotion of ECDSA. In recent years, a variety of more secure and efficient elliptic curve cryptography algorithms, including Curve25519, FourQ, have been proposed and applied. The Edwards-curve Digital Signature Algorithm (EdDSA) is a variant of Schnorr's signature system with Edwards curves. EdDSA is a popular choice to improve the traditional ECDSA (elliptic curve digital signature algorithm) signature algorithm, which has the characteristics of high performance and high security. At present, EdDSA has been added to TLS 1.3 [32]. A variety of cryptographic algorithm libraries including OpenSSL [12] have support EdDSA.

Algorithm 1. ECC Signature Verification Sample (EdDSA)

Input:
    256-bit Message Digest M, 32-octet public key U, 64-octet signature (R, S), the fixed based point G, the order of edwards25519 L.
Output:
    Accept or reject the signature
1: $k =$SHA-512$(R||U||M)$ mod L
2: accept if $[2^c S]G = [2^c](\texttt{Decode}(R) + [k]\texttt{Decode}(U))$; otherwise reject.

From the bottom to the top, elliptic curve cryptography can be divided into: finite field layer, point arithmetic layer and scalar multiplication layer. The scalar multiplication is to compute $kP = P + ... + P$. The implementation of scalar multiplication is directly specific to the performance of elliptic curve cryptography algorithm. The common algorithms mainly include Double-and-add, Montgomery Ladder, Non-adjacent form (NAF) and so on. There are also methods of using space for time, such as fixed window method, sliding window method and w-NAF. According to different base points P, the scalar multiplication kP can be simply divided into two types:

- *Fixed-point Scalar Multiplication*: the base point P of kP is fixed (the scalar multiplication $[2^c S]G$ in Algorithm 1), and is able to use one offline precomputed table for accelerations of different keys, such as portion-by-portion addition method in [31]. Because all keys share one precomputed table, it only needs to be generated once. And the calculation time of the precomputed table can be ignored.
- *Unknown-point Scalar Multiplication*: the base point P of kP is unfixed(the scalar multiplication $[k]Decode(U)$ in Algorithm 1). To use the space-for-time acceleration methods, the existing works always calculate the precomputed table online.

Figure 2 presents the relationship between ECC signature operations and scalar multiplications. Compared with ECC key generation and signature generation, the signature verification operation of elliptic curve cryptography is more complex, which requires not only a fixed-point scalar multiplication, but also an unknown-point one.

2.3 w-NAF

Window Non-adjacent form combines the Non-adjacent method with a window method, which processes w digits of k at a time. In the width-w NAF of length l, a positive integer k is an expression $k = \sum_{i=0}^{l-1} k_i 2^i$, where each nonzero coefficient k_i is odd, $|k_i| \leq 2^{w-1}$ and $k_{l-1} \neq 0$. It must be sure that at most one of any w consecutive digits is nonzero and the window size must be greater than or equal to 2. If the window size is 2, $\text{NAF}_2(k)$ is equal to $\text{NAF}(k)$.

A positive integer k has a unique $\text{NAF}_w(k)$, which can be efficiently computed, leading to Algorithm 2, where the value of k *mods* 2^w is mapped to the range

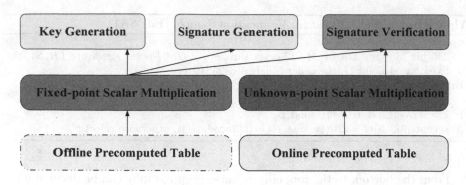

Fig. 2. Scalar multiplication & ECC signature operation

Algorithm 2. Computing the width-w NAF of a positive integer

Input:
    Window width w, a positive integer k.
Output:
    $\text{NAF}_\omega(k)$.
1: $i \leftarrow 0$
2: **while** $k \leftarrow 0$ **do**
3:     **if** k is odd **then**
4:         $k_i \leftarrow k \bmod s\ 2^w$, $k \leftarrow k - k_i$
5:     **else**
6:         $k_i \leftarrow 0$
7:     **end if**
8:     $k \leftarrow k/2$, $i \leftarrow i + 1$
9: **end while**
10: $\text{Return}(k_{i-1}, k_{i-2}, \cdots, k_1, k_0)$

---

of $[-2^{(w-1)}, 2^{(w-1)} - 1]$. The digits of $\text{NAF}_\omega(k)$ are generated by repeatedly dividing k by 2, allowing remainders r in $[-2^{(w-1)}, 2^{(w-1)} - 1]$. If k is odd, then remainder $r = k \bmod s\ 2^w$ is chosen so that $(k - r)/2$ will be divisible by 2^{w-1}, ensuring that the next $w - 1$ digits are 0 [15].

Algorithm 3 generalizes the binary NAF method for point multiplication by using $\text{NAF}_\omega(k)$. When executing the algorithm, we need to preprocess $P_i = iP$ for $i \in \{1, 3, \cdots, 2^{w-1} - 1\}$.

3   PEPEC Design

Although the w-NAF algorithm can speed up the calculation of the public key point, the calculation of the precomputed table is time-consuming. If the TSL client calculates the precomputed table, it will perform $2^{w-2} - 1$ point double operations. An idea that comes to our mind is to move this part of the calculation to the CA side. As mentioned above, the CA may not be trusted, we believe that the log server is also needed to verify the generated precomputed table.

Algorithm 3. Window NAF method for point multiplication

Input:
    Window width w, positive integer k, $P \in E(\mathbb{F}_q)$
Output:
    $Q = kP$.
1: Use Algorithm 2 to compute $\mathrm{NAF}_2(k) = \sum_{i=0}^{l-1} k_i 2^i$
2: $Q \leftarrow \propto$
3: **for** $i = l - 1$ to 0 **do**
4:     $Q \leftarrow 2Q$
5:     **if** $k_i \neq 0$ **then**
6:         **if** $k_i > 0$ **then**
7:             $Q \leftarrow Q + P_{k_i}$
8:         **else**
9:             $Q \leftarrow Q - P_{-k_i}$
10:         **end if**
11:     **end if**
12: **end for**
13: Return(Q)

Combining the above two aspects, we design a PEPEC certificate which brings the main changes to CT are reflected in three stages: 1) Generating PEPEC Certificates, 2) Verifying PEPEC Certificates, 3) Utilizing PEPEC Certificates. We named this improved CT model PEPEC-CT, as shown in Fig. 3:

3.1 Generating PEPEC Certificates

In PEPEC-CT, the whole process still starts with the domain owner submitting the request. The domain owner generates the public key, constructs the CSR with a flag, applies for the CA to generate a precomputed table, added and signs it. Then the CA can generate a precomputed table for the domain owner's public key after validating the request. The window size of the precomputed table is determined by CA according to its computing ability. Finally, a TBSCertificate [3] containing a precomputed table will be constructed with the following structure (Fig. 4):

Referring to the RFC 5280, we put the precomputed table into the certificate as an X.509v3 extension. The window size of w-NAF w is also needed to notify Log Server and client so that they can verify or use the precomputed table properly. These should be a non-critical extension which means it can be ignored if clients don't support such extension. According to the requirements of RFC9162, a precertificate in Cryptographic Message Syntax (CMS) format will be constructed and sent to at least two different logs.

3.2 Verifying PEPEC Certificates

Log Server maintains a list of trusted certificates, which is obtained out-of-band and should include the set of root CAs trusted by mainstream browsers. Once

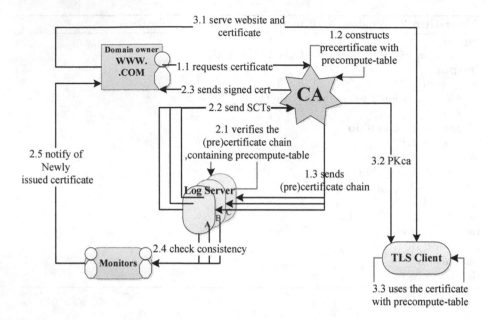

Fig. 3. The structure of PEPEC-CT

the precertificate chain or certificate chain is submitted by CA, the Log Server will verify it. The verification includes two aspects: 1) Each certificate: check the certificate encoding format, the Key Usage extension, the Basic Constraints extension to verify that the certificate on the chain is valid, or a badCertificate identifier will return to the CA. 2) Between certificates: check whether each certificate on the chain except the first certificate is the issuer of its previous certificate, otherwise return the bad Chain identifier; check whether the last certificate on the chain is in the list of trusted certificates in the log, otherwise the unknown Anchor identifier is returned.

In PEPEC-CT, Log Server only needs to perform additional verification on the precomputed table when checking each certificate. If the verification fails, the badCertificate will also be returned, or else, the Log Server should issue an SCT, which ensures the correctness and read-only of the precomputed table. Finally, CA signs the PEPEC certificate and sends the SCT along with the PEPEC certificate to the domain owner, and then the domain owner can communicate confidentially with the TLS client. As for step 2.4 and 2.5 in the PEPEC-CT, Monitors play their part periodically, therefore these two steps do not have to be performed in order.

3.3 Utilizing PEPEC Certificates

From the side of the client, the TLS client will first validate the SCTs and the inclusion proofs to make sure the certificate from the domain owner is valid.

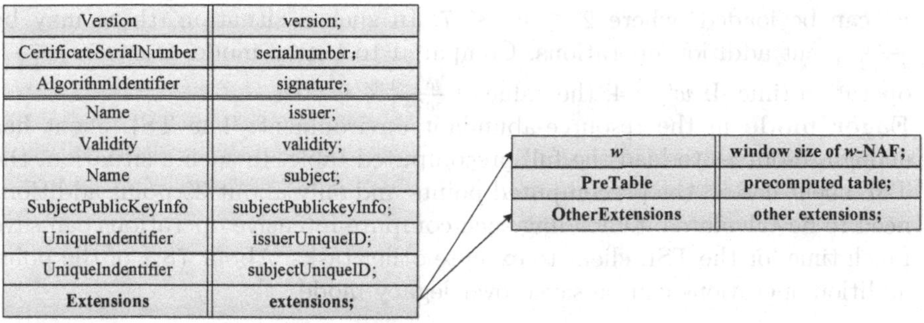

Version	version;
CertificateSerialNumber	serialnumber;
AlgorithmIdentifier	signature;
Name	issuer;
Validity	validity;
Name	subject;
SubjectPublicKeyInfo	subjectPublickeyInfo;
UniqueIdentifier	issuerUniqueID;
UniqueIdentifier	subjectUniqueID;
Extensions	**extensions;**

w	window size of w-NAF;
PreTable	precomputed table;
OtherExtensions	other extensions;

Fig. 4. New structure of PEPEC certificates

Then the precomputed table will come into play. According to Algorithm 3, accelerated computations can be performed everywhere public keys are used, including certificate authentication and key exchange.

Table 1 shows performance differences caused by different width-w. Owing to the point P as the public key has been loaded, we don't need to store it. For example, when the window width is 2, the number of precomputed points is 0. And, it is quite clear from the number of point addition that the larger the window width is, the less the number of point addition operations required.

Table 1. Performance variation of different width-w

Window size w	2	3	4	5	6	7	8
Number of precomputed points[a]	0	1	3	7	15	31	63
Number of point addition[b]	86	64	52	43	37	32	29
Precomputed table size/B[c]	0	64	192	448	960	1984	4032

[a]As introduced in Sect. 2.3, we can get it with the formula $2^{w-2} - 1$.
[b]In general, the type of k is 256 bits. The number of point addition can be calculated utilizing the Hamming Weight, where the Hamming Weight is $\frac{k}{w+1}$.
[c]We reserve 64B for a single point P.

In actual situations, the following three modes in Fig. 5 may appear when the TLS client applies the precomputed table:

- **Legacy mode** in the unsupported environment: The TSL client does not support certificate authentication and key exchange with PEPEC Certificates. This means that it will directly ignore the relevant content of the precomputed table extension in the certificate. For a 256-bit value of k, even though it guarantees zero memory usage to store precomputed tables, it requires extra computing power to compute 128 point additions.
- **Hit mode** in the resource-restricted environment: Due to limited resources in TSL client, such as insufficient memory space, only suitable window size

w' can be loaded, where $2 \leq w' \leq 7$. In such a situation, there may be $\frac{256}{w'+1}$ point addition operations. Compared to legacy mode, it saves $\frac{w'-1}{w'+1}\%$ operation time. If $w' = 4$, the value of $\frac{w'-1}{w'+1}\%$ is 60%.

- **Eager mode** in the resource-abundant environment: The TSL client has enough resources to load the full precomputed table. In such a situation, the TSL client has all the precomputed points and only about 29 point additions need to be calculated. Offloading such compute-intensive operations can save much time for the TSL client to execute other tasks. About 78% of the point addition operations can be saved over legacy mode.

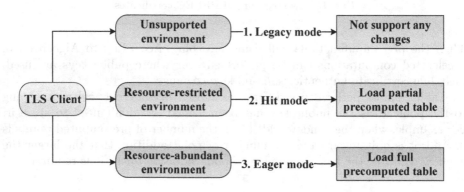

Fig. 5. Three modes of utilizing PEPEC certificates

4   Evaluation

In this section, We mainly introduce the security and performance of the PEPEC certificate.

4.1   Security Evaluation

In this part, we analyze the security of the PEPEC certificate from the three security elements: 1) Confidentiality, 2) Integrity, and 3) Availability.

Confidentiality. Our major optimizations are for the certificate public key, which is public. And the corresponding precomputed table can be constructed by everyone. So we don't involve a discussion of confidentiality for the PEPEC certificate.

Integrity. For a PEPEC certificate, the client will check integrity from two aspects. The first one is to verify the CA signature which can be found in the signatureValue field according to the RFC 5280 [3]. The CA signature for the TBSCertificate including precomputed table guarantees that the precomputed table has not been tampered with. The second one is to verify SCTs from different Log Servers. Each SCT contains a signature for the received certificate where the precomputed table is on. We don't need extra resources for integrity because these two signatures are provided by CT.

Availability. Log Servers will verify the precomputed table in the PEPEC certificate by recalculating the precomputed table based on the w value. Since it is almost impossible for CA to collude with all logs in CT, we can assume that all precomputed tables in the PEPEC certificate passed to the client are correct. In addition, the client can load precomputed tables of the corresponding size according to their own needs, as mentioned above. We believe that TLS clients have a better experience when using PEPEC certificates.

4.2   Performance Evaluation

In this section, we take Signature Verification via EdDSA as an example to analyze the efficiency improvement brought by the use of PEPEC certificates to the client. We compared the amount of computation required in the two cases of using the PEPEC certificate and using the standard X.509v3 certificate and found that the performance improved by at least 11%.

As shown in Fig. 2, Signature Verification can be divided into fixed-point scalar multiplication and unknown-point scalar multiplication. To simplify the analysis, we use the w-NAF algorithm with a window size of 8 for both sides, which will produce a 4 KB precomputed table to be embedded in a PEPEC certificate. This is a reasonable size since the average size of a certificate in actual delivery is around 4 KB [11]. In the case of IoT devices using the communication module ATK-M751C provided by ALIENTEK, the network transmission rate is between 7.5 Mbit/s and 10 Mbit/s [1], which means we only need to spend an extra 4.26 ms to transfer a PEPEC certificate. Then we need 29 point additions and 256 point doublings for fixed-point scalar multiplication because we ignore the calculation time of the precomputed table. This part of the calculation is fixed, whether a PEPEC certificate is used or not. As for unknown-point scalar multiplication, we can save 63 point additions if we use a PEPEC certificate, which is shown in Table 2.

Table 2. Complexity comparison of X.509 and PEPEC

Types	Fixed-point scalar multiplication		Unknown-point scalar multiplication	
	Point addition	Point double	Point addition	Point double
X.509	29	256	29 + **63**	256
PEPEC	29	256	29	256

According to the RFC 8032 [19], 9 multiplications are required for each point doubling and 11 for each point addition. Using the standard X509v3 certificate, we need to do 5939 multiplications, while the times of multiplication will reduce to 5246 if we use the PEPEC certificate. In the general case, we got an 11% performance boost, but if we convert multiply by 2 into shift left operation which means 8 multiplications for each point doubling and 9 for each point addition, we will get a 13% performance boost. And if We optimize the algorithm for this part of the fixed point calculation by using methods in [9,13], clients will get a 19% computing performance boost.

5   Conclusion

In this paper, We integrate w-NAF and CT into a novel efficient certificate called PEPEC, which accelerates the client to use the certificate public key to perform related calculations. As an innovative efficient certificate, PEPEC satisfies clients vary from high-memory to low-memory while ensuring the correctness of the precomputed table. Due to this efficient certificate compatibly working with current CT, we plan to do a simple implementation of the PEPEC certificate in the future. Then we can further study how this certificate improves client computing performance.

References

1. ALIENTEK: 4G Cat1 DTU communication module ATK-IDM751C (2022). https://detail.tmall.com/item.htm?id=669018761342
2. Apple-Inc.: Apple's Certificate Transparency policy (2019). https://support.apple.com/en-us/HT205280
3. Boeyen, S., Santesson, S., Polk, T., Housley, R., Farrell, S., Cooper, D.: Internet X.509 public key infrastructure certificate and certificate revocation list (CRL) profile. RFC 5280, May 2008. https://doi.org/10.17487/RFC5280. https://www.rfc-editor.org/info/rfc5280
4. Certificate-Transparency-Policy: Certificate Transparency Enforcement in Google Chrome (2018). https://groups.google.com/a/chromium.org/g/ct-policy/c/wHILiYf31DE/m/iMFmpMEkAQAJ
5. Certificate-Transparency-Policy: Mozilla CT Policy (2019). https://groups.google.com/a/chromium.org/forum/m/#!topic/ct-policy/Xx1bv8r33ZE
6. Cheng, H., Großschädl, J., Tian, J., Rønne, P.B., Ryan, P.Y.A.: High-throughput elliptic curve cryptography using AVX2 vector instructions. In: Dunkelman, O., Jacobson, Jr., M.J., O'Flynn, C. (eds.) SAC 2020. LNCS, vol. 12804, pp. 698–719. Springer, Cham (2021). https://doi.org/10.1007/978-3-030-81652-0_27
7. Comodo: Comodo report of incident (2011). https://www.comodo.com/Comodo-Fraud-Incident-2011-03-23.html
8. Costello, C., Longa, P.: FourQ: four-dimensional decompositions on a Q-curve over the Mersenne prime. In: Iwata, T., Cheon, J.H. (eds.) ASIACRYPT 2015. LNCS, vol. 9452, pp. 214–235. Springer, Heidelberg (2015). https://doi.org/10.1007/978-3-662-48797-6_10
9. Dong, J., Zheng, F., Lin, J., Liu, Z., Xiao, F., Fan, G.: EC-ECC: accelerating elliptic curve cryptography for edge computing on embedded GPU TX2. ACM Trans. Embedded Comput. Syst. (TECS) 21(2), 1–25 (2022)

10. Evans, C., Palmer, C., Sleevi, R.: Public key pinning extension for HTTP. RFC 7469, April 2015. https://doi.org/10.17487/RFC7469. https://www.rfc-editor.org/info/rfc7469

11. Forsby, F., Furuhed, M., Papadimitratos, P., Raza, S.: Lightweight X.509 digital certificates for the Internet of Things. In: Fortino, G., et al. (eds.) InterIoT/SaSeIoT -2017. LNICST, vol. 242, pp. 123–133. Springer, Cham (2018). https://doi.org/10.1007/978-3-319-93797-7_14

12. OpenSSL Software Foundation: OpenSSL Cryptography and SSL/TLS Toolkit (2016). http://www.openssl.org/

13. Gao, L., Zheng, F., Emmart, N., Dong, J., Lin, J., Weems, C.: DPF-ECC: accelerating elliptic curve cryptography with floating-point computing power of GPUs. In: 2020 IEEE International Parallel and Distributed Processing Symposium (IPDPS), pp. 494–504. IEEE (2020)

14. Hallam-Baker, P., Stradling, R.: DNS Certification Authority Authorization (CAA) resource record. RFC 6844, January 2013. https://doi.org/10.17487/RFC6844. https://www.rfc-editor.org/info/rfc6844

15. Hankerson, D., Vanstone, S., Menezes, A.J.: Guide to Elliptic Curve Cryptography. Springer, New York (2004). https://doi.org/10.1007/b97644

16. Harkanson, R., Kim, Y.: Applications of elliptic curve cryptography: a light introduction to elliptic curves and a survey of their applications. In: Proceedings of the 12th Annual Conference on Cyber and Information Security Research, p. 6. ACM (2017)

17. Hoffman, P.E., Schlyter, J.: The DNS-based Authentication of Named Entities (DANE) Transport Layer Security (TLS) protocol: TLSA. RFC 6698, August 2012. https://doi.org/10.17487/RFC6698. https://www.rfc-editor.org/info/rfc6698

18. Järvinen, K., Miele, A., Azarderakhsh, R., Longa, P.: FourQ on FPGA: new hardware speed records for elliptic curve cryptography over large prime characteristic fields. In: Gierlichs, B., Poschmann, A.Y. (eds.) CHES 2016. LNCS, vol. 9813, pp. 517–537. Springer, Heidelberg (2016). https://doi.org/10.1007/978-3-662-53140-2_25

19. Josefsson, S., Liusvaara, I.: Edwards-Curve Digital Signature Algorithm (EdDSA). RFC 8032, January 2017. https://doi.org/10.17487/RFC8032. https://rfc-editor.org/rfc/rfc8032.txt

20. Kasten, J., Wustrow, E., Halderman, J.A.: CAge: taming certificate authorities by inferring restricted scopes. In: Sadeghi, A.-R. (ed.) FC 2013. LNCS, vol. 7859, pp. 329–337. Springer, Heidelberg (2013). https://doi.org/10.1007/978-3-642-39884-1_28

21. Koblitz, N.: Elliptic curve cryptosystems. Math. Comput. 48(177), 203–209 (1987)

22. Langley, A., Hamburg, M., Turner, S.: Elliptic Curves for Security. RFC 7748, January 2016. https://doi.org/10.17487/RFC7748. https://rfc-editor.org/rfc/rfc7748.txt

23. Larisch, J., Choffnes, D., Levin, D., Maggs, B.M., Mislove, A., Wilson, C.: CRLite: a scalable system for pushing all TLS revocations to all browsers. In: 2017 IEEE Symposium on Security and Privacy (SP), pp. 539–556 (2017). https://doi.org/10.1109/SP.2017.17

24. Laurie, B., Langley, A., Kasper, E.: Certificate Transparency. RFC 6962, June 2013. https://doi.org/10.17487/RFC6962. https://www.rfc-editor.org/info/rfc6962

25. Li, B., et al.: Certificate transparency in the wild: exploring the reliability of monitors. In: Proceedings of the 2019 ACM SIGSAC Conference on Computer and Communications Security, pp. 2505–2520 (2019)

26. Liu, Z., Longa, P., Pereira, G.C., Reparaz, O., Seo, H.: FourQ on embedded devices with strong countermeasures against side-channel attacks. IEEE Trans. Dependable Secure Comput. **17**(3), 536–549 (2018)

27. Lochter, M., Merkle, J.: Elliptic curve cryptography (ECC) brainpool standard curves and curve generation. Technical report (2010)

28. Monton, A.L.: History of the Internet (2021). https://www.globalsign.com/en-sg/blog/history-internet-development-pki

29. National Institute of Standards and Technology: Digital Signature Standard (DSS) (2013). https://doi.org/10.6028/NIST.FIPS.186-4.pdf

30. NGINX: NGINX Unit Now Supports TLS (2018). https://www.nginx.com/blog/nginx-unit-1-5-available-now/

31. Pan, W., Zheng, F., Zhu, W., Jing, J.: An efficient elliptic curve cryptography signature server with GPU acceleration. IEEE Trans. Inf. Forensics Secur. **12**(1), 111–122 (2017)

32. Rescorla, E.: The transport layer security (TLS) protocol version 1.3. RFC 8446(1-160), p. 10, 2018.17487/RFC8446. https://doi.org/10.17487/RFC8446

33. Szalachowski, P., Matsumoto, S., Perrig, A.: PoliCert: secure and flexible TLS certificate management. ACM (2014)

34. Szalachowski, P., Chuat, L., Perrig, A.: PKI safety net (PKISN): addressing the too-big-to-be-revoked problem of the TLS ecosystem. In: 2016 IEEE European Symposium on Security and Privacy (EuroSP), pp. 407–422 (2016). https://doi.org/10.1109/EuroSP.2016.38

35. The-OpenSSL-Project-Authors: Certificate transparency in OpenSSL (2018). https://www.openssl.org/docs/man3.0/man7/ct.html

36. Wikipedia: Flame (malware) (2022). https://en.wikipedia.org/wiki/Flame_(malware)

Efficient Software Implementation of GMT6-672 and GMT8-542 Pairing-Friendly Curves for a 128-Bit Security Level

Zihao Song[1], Junichi Sakamoto[1,2], Shigeo Mitsunari[3], Naoki Yoshida[1],
Riku Anzai[1], and Tsutomu Matsumoto[1(✉)]

[1] Yokohama National University, 79-7 Tokiwadai, Hodogaya-ku,
Yokohama 240-8501, Japan
tsutomu@ynu.ac.jp
[2] National Institute of Advanced Industrial Science and Technology,
2-3-26 Aomi, Koto-ku, Tokyo 135-0064, Japan
[3] Cybozu Labs, Inc, Tokyo Nihombashi Tower 27F, 2-7-1 Nihombashi,
Chuo-ku, Tokyo 103-6028, Japan

Abstract. A Bilinear pairing on an elliptic curve defined over a finite field provides an attractive prospect for designing cryptographic schemes with various functionalities. An elliptic curve over which a computationally efficient bilinear pairing can be defined is called a "pairing-friendly curve". Finding families of pairing-friendly curves with sufficient anticipated bit security has attracted significant research attention. For example, the Barreto-Neahrig (BN) and Barreto-Lynn-Scott (BLS) curves, are existing curves of this type. However, there is a need for alternatives to back up these already evaluated curves. In 2020 Guillevic, Masson, and Thomé (GMT) proposed pairing-friendly curves with embedding degrees 5 to 8 range. GMTk denotes curves with an embedding degree k. A composite k is preferred from the efficiency viewpoint. However, to the best of the GMT6 and GMT8 curves have been reported in the literature. In this paper, novel field-towering methods using two types of extension method and constructions are developed. These methods are applied to efficiently implement and analyze the bilinear pairings based on the GMT6 curve over a 672-bit prime field and the GMT8 curve over a 542-bit prime field. The pairing-computation times of our developed software evaluated using an Intel Core i7-8700 (@4.3 GHz Turbo Boost on) is computer are 0.987 ms and 1.12 ms for GMT6-672 and GMT8-542, respectively indicating the practicality of these curves.

Keywords: Software implementations · Bilinear pairings · Type-I AOPF

1 Introduction

A Bilinear pairing (hereafter simply "pairing") over an elliptic curve is valuable for implementing advanced cryptography, such as aggregate signatures [1],

J. Zhou et al. (Eds.): ACNS 2022 Workshops, LNCS 13285, pp. 461–478, 2022.
https://doi.org/10.1007/978-3-031-16815-4_25

homomorphic encryption [2], etc. One of the recent innovative protocols based on pairing is the zero-knowledge succinct noninteractive argument of knowledge (zk-SNARKs) [3]. Pairing is a nondegenerate bilinear map obtained from the direct product of two additive groups $\mathbb{G}_1$ and $\mathbb{G}_2$, resulting in a multiplicative group $\mathbb{G}_3$. The groups $\mathbb{G}_1$ and $\mathbb{G}_2$ are generally subgroups obtained from elliptic curve groups $E(\mathbb{F}_p)$ and $E(\mathbb{F}_{p^k})$, where E, p, and k denote an elliptic curve, field characteristic, and embedding degree, respectively. Pairings constructed over elliptic curves require different properties and security levels depending on the particular application. Therefore, the investigation of new curves of efficient pairing computation (called "pairing-friendly" curves) constitutes a significant research area. The Barreto-Naehrig (BN) curves [5], Barreto-Lynn-Scott curves (BLS) [6], and Kachisa-Schaefer-Scott (KSS) curves are the most well-known families of pairing-friendly curves, which have been widely studied as efficient candidates for 128-bit level security pairings. Besides, there is an attack reported in [7] improves the number field sieve algorithm in discrete-logarithm problems in extension fields and affects the security level of many pairing-friendly curves. Hence, the parameters of pairing-friendly curves are forced to be replaced with their parameters for 128-bit security levels with enough margin. This parameter replacement has been studied only for a short period since the year 2016, after it the performance and security assessment for the well-known curves appear vague. In 2020, Guillevic, Masson, and Thomé (GMT) [8] proposed new curves generated by a modified Cocks-Pinch method. These curves satisfy the 128-bit level security against the attack mentioned in [7]. We refer to the paper [8] as "the GMT paper". Moreover, we denote the curves with $k = 6, 8$ proposed in [8] as the GMT6 and GMT8 curves, respectively. The GMT paper presented algorithms for fast pairing calculation. A simple model estimates the computational timings of pairing computation over the GMT6 and GMT8, where both results are 1.5 ms using an Intel Core i7-8700@3.2 GHz computer. Although the results reported in the GMT paper are promising, to the best of our knowledge, there is no study on rigorous software implementation for these curves. For this purpose, this paper aims to provide the first and efficient software implementation of the GMT curves with a detailed cost analysis.

Our Contributions. The following three main contributions are present in this paper. First, two types of efficient field towering methods for the GMT6 and GMT8 curves with the type-I all-one polynomial field (AOPF) [11] and the optimal extension field (OEF) [12] are proposed. These fields are used as the first subextension fields for fast paring calculation. Furthermore, the number of arithmetic operations of the proposed extension field towering is investigated and a new GMT8 curve parameter optimized for our extension fields is provided. Second, an unique detailed cost at the algorithm level is provided for implementing Miller's algorithm [4] with twists [13], and the required cost is reevaluated using an accurate expression. Moreover, the polynomials suggested by the GMT paper are reviewed for calculating the fast final exponentiation calculation and revised for efficiently calculating the orders of both curves. Finally, the experimental results obtained from the implemented software regarding the pairings over the GMT6 and GMT8 curves based on the proposed constructions are presented. The software implementations, which are based on the crypto library [14] and the GNU MP library (GMP) version 6.2.1, give rise to pairing computation of the GMT6 and GMT8 curves in 0.987 ms and 1.12 ms, respectively, using an i7-8700 (@4.3 GHz Turbo Boost enabled) computer without using the lazy reduction technique.

Related Research Works. Lavice et al. [9] proposed a small-area pairing-computation architecture using the FPGA for the updated 128-bit level pairing-friendly curves. They also proposed an attractive formula for calculating the squaring in the quadratic cyclotomic subgroup. We adopt this suggested squaring method employed in the quadratic cyclotomic subgroup and use it in our proposed tower of extension fields to reduce the calculation cost.

Notation. In this paper, a multiplication, squaring, and inversion cost in $\mathbb{F}_{p^k}$ is denoted as m_k, s_k, and i_k, respectively. The symbol a_k denotes an addition cost in $\mathbb{F}_{p^k}$, where it is assumed that subtraction, left-shift, and right-shift costs in $\mathbb{F}_{p^k}$ are identical to a_k. $\mathbf{m}$ is used with m_1, and s_1 summarizes the total cost of $m_1 + s_1$ in $\mathbb{F}_p$. To distinguish parameters with different characteristics with the same embedding degree, each curve parameter is given a different designation using a bit length of characteristic p as the suffix, such as the GMT8-544 and GMT8-542.

2   Preliminaries

The GMT curves with embedding degrees $k = 6, 8$ and ate pairing over the GMT curves are reviewed in this section.

2.1   Guillevic-Masson-Thomé (GMT) Curves with Embedding Degrees 6 and 8

Guillevic, Masson, and Thomé [8] proposed pairing-friendly elliptic curves based on the Cocks-Pinch algorithm with embedding degrees $k = 5, 6, 7, 8$. The curves with even embedding degrees $k = 6$ and 8 (GMT6 and GMT8) are capable of calculating pairing efficiently. The parameters of the GMT curves (field characteristic $p(u)$, order $r(u)$, and Frobenius trace $t(u)$ with coefficient h_t, h_y) are given by the following polynomials, where the integer parameters $u, h_y, h_t \in \mathbb{Z}$ are selected as p and r are prime numbers. The complex multiplication (CM) discriminant of the GMT6 curve is $D = 3$ with elliptic curve $E : y^2 = x^3 + b$ where $x, y \in \mathbb{F}_{p^6}$ with non-zero coefficient $b \in \mathbb{F}_p$. The ρ-value= $log(p)/log(r)$ of GMT6 is 2.63. For GMT8 curve, the CM discriminant is $D = 4$ with the elliptic curve $E : y^2 = x^3 + ax$ where $x, y \in \mathbb{F}_{p^8}$ with the nonzero coefficient $a \in \mathbb{F}_p$. For $k = 8$, the obtained GMT8-542 curve has a slightly better ρ-value= 2.12 than the GMT6 curve.

Algorithm 1. Ate pairing over the GMT6 and GMT8 curves using a 2-NAF loop parameter expression

---

Require: $T, P \in \mathbb{G}_1, Q \in \mathbb{G}_2$
Ensure: $f_{T,Q}(P) \in \mathbb{F}_{p^k}^*$

1 $f \leftarrow 1, R \leftarrow Q$
2: **for** $i = \lfloor \log_2(T) \rfloor - 1$ down to 0 **do**
3:        $\lambda \leftarrow l_{R,R}(P), R \leftarrow 2R$ ▷ //DBLLine
4:        $f \leftarrow f^2 \cdot \lambda$ ▷ //UPDATE1
5:        **if** $T[i] = 1$ **then**
6:            $\lambda \leftarrow l_{R,Q}(P), R \leftarrow R + Q$ ▷ //ADDLine
7:            $f \leftarrow f \cdot \lambda$ ▷ //UPDATE2
8:        **if** $T[i] = -1$ **then**
9:            $\lambda \leftarrow l_{R,-Q}(P), R \leftarrow R - Q$ ▷ //ADDLine
10:           $f \leftarrow f \cdot \lambda$ ▷ //UPDATE2
11: $f \leftarrow f^{(p^k-1)/r}$
12: **return** f

The number of rational points on the elliptic curve E over the finite field $\mathbb{F}_p$ is expressed as $\#E(\mathbb{F}_p) = p + 1 - t$ according to the Hasse's theorem. The elliptic curve E also forms an additive group in the extension field $E(\mathbb{F}_{p^k})$, where k is the embedding degree of the curve. The order of $E(\mathbb{F}_{p^k})$ is $\#E(\mathbb{F}_{p^k}) = p^k + 1 - t_k$, where $t_k = \alpha^k + \beta^k$ and α and β are complex conjugate numbers. The r-torsion subgroup of E, which is defined as $E[r] := \{P | P \in E, [r]P = \mathcal{O}\}$ has two unique subgroups of order r. These subgroups are useful for efficient pairing computation. Let the π_p be Frobenius endomorphism and the first subgroup $\mathbb{G}_1 = E[r] \cap \ker(\pi_p - [1]) \subset E(\mathbb{F}_p)[r]$, which is defined over $\mathbb{F}_p$. The second subgroup $\mathbb{G}_2 = E[r] \cap \ker(\pi_p - [p]) \subset E(\mathbb{F}_{p^k})[r]$, which is defined over $\mathbb{F}_{p^k}$. The subgroup order r satisfies the condition $r|(p^k - 1)$, $r|\#E(\mathbb{F}_p)$, $r^2|\#E(\mathbb{F}_{p^k})$ which are important for pairing computation optimization.

2.2   Ate Pairing over the GMT6 and GMT8 Curves

Let $\mathbb{G}_3$ be a multiplicative subgroup defined as

$$\mathbb{G}_3 = \mathbb{F}_{p^k}[r] \tag{1}$$

where k is the embedding degree of the pairing-friendly curve. For three Abelian groups $\mathbb{G}_1, \mathbb{G}_2, \mathbb{G}_3$, an ate pairing a_T can be defined as follows:

$$a_T : \mathbb{G}_2 \times \mathbb{G}_1 \rightarrow \mathbb{G}_3, \tag{2}$$

$$(Q, P) \mapsto (f_{T,Q}(P))^{(p^k-1)/r} \tag{3}$$

where $T = u - 1$ and $f_{T,Q}$ is a rational function with a divisor $\mathrm{div}(f_{T,Q}) = T(Q) - ([T]Q) - (T-1)(\mathcal{O})$. Ate pairing for the GMT6 and GMT8 curves is calculated by using Algorithm 1.

In Algorithm 1, the calculation steps 1 to 10 are identified as Miller's algorithm, where steps 2 to 10 are particularly called Miller's loop. Steps 3, 6 and 9 describe the calculations of the rational functions $l_{R,R}, l_{R,Q}$ together with the elliptic curve doubling (ECD) and elliptic curve addition (ECA) calculations. We call the calculations of $l_{R,R}$ together with the ECD as DBLLine. Similarly, we call the calculations of and $l_{R,Q}$ together with the ECA as ADDLine. UPDATE1 and UPDATE2 are "sparse" multiplications in $\mathbb{F}_{p^k}$ with less computational load than the standard multiplication in $\mathbb{F}_{p^k}$.

The input $T = u - 1$ is expressed in a nonadjacent form (NAF), which represents integers in certain conditions as three value types of $1, 0, -1$, rather than a binary form for efficient pairing calculating. Miller's algorithm is also known as an algorithm capable of using a 2-NAF since the inversion operation $l_{R,-Q}(P)$ can be easily calculated in this case.

Step 11 is known as the final exponentiation, the details of the final exponentiation calculation for the GMT6 and GMT8 curves are described in Sect. 5.2.

2.3 Ate Pairings over GMT Curves with Twists

The **GMT6** curve with the CM discriminant $D = 3$ and input $Q \in \mathbb{G}_2$ used for ate paring over the elliptic curve $E : y^2 = x^3 + b$ known as having an isomorphism ψ. The isomorphism ψ projects the subgroup $\mathbb{G}_2 \subset E(\mathbb{F}_{p^6})$ to a same order subgroup $\mathbb{G}'_2 \subset E'(\mathbb{F}_p)$ where the sextic twist $E' : y^2 = x^3 + b/z, z \in \mathbb{F}_p$. Since two subgroups have the same information, the required cost heavy arithmetics in $\mathbb{F}_{p^6}$ can be replaced by the simple calculations in $\mathbb{F}_p$. The isomorphism ψ from the twisted curve to the original curve can be defined as follows:

$$\psi : E' \to E, \tag{4}$$

$$Q'(x, y) \mapsto Q(xz^{-1/3}, yz^{-1/2}) \tag{5}$$

With assuming that both $P \in \mathbb{G}_1 \subset E(\mathbb{F}_p)$ and $Q \in \mathbb{G}'_2 \subset E'(\mathbb{F}_p)$, the twisted ate pairing for the GMT6 curve can be computed as follows:

$$a_T : \mathbb{G}'_2 \times \mathbb{G}_1 \to \mathbb{G}_3, \tag{6}$$

$$(Q', P) \mapsto (f_{T,\psi(Q')}(P))^{(p^6-1)/r} \tag{7}$$

In this case, the ADDLine and DBLLine can be computed in $\mathbb{F}_p$.

The **GMT8** curve $E : y^2 = x^3 + ax$ with a CM discriminant $D = 4$ has a different type of twist called "quartic twist". The map φ from the twisted elliptic curve E' to the original curve E is defined as follows:

$$\varphi : E' \to E, \tag{8}$$

$$Q'(x, y) \mapsto Q(xz^{-1/2}, yz^{-3/4}) \tag{9}$$

where $z \in \mathbb{F}_{p^2}$ is a quadratic non-residue in $\mathbb{F}_p$, $x^4 - z \in \mathbb{F}_{p^2}[x]$ is irreducible, the twisted curve $E' : y^2 = x^3 + ax/z$, and $Q' \in \mathbb{G}'_2 \subset E'(\mathbb{F}_{p^2})$. Similar to the GMT6 curve, ate pairing with the quartic twist for the GMT8 curve can be computed as follows:

$$a_T : \mathbb{G}'_2 \times \mathbb{G}_1 \rightarrow \mathbb{G}_3, \tag{10}$$

$$(Q', P) \mapsto (f_{T,\varphi(Q')}(P))^{(p^8-1)/r} \tag{11}$$

In this case, the GMT8 curves with embedding degree 8 can compute the ADDLine and DBLLine functions of ate pairing in $\mathbb{F}_{p^2}$ arithmetics. Even though the twist maps reduce the number of arithmetic operations in the pairing, the total cost of Miller's algorithm depends on other elements, such as the Miller's loop parameter T and the coordinate system. Furthermore, optimizing the final exponentiation calculation and not only Miller's algorithm (for example, factorizing the polynomial $(p^k - 1)/r$ $(k = 6, 8)$ and performing fast squaring in the extension fields), is also a key component for fast pairing computations.

3 Review of Extension Field Classes

For fast pairing computation, the efficiency of the multiplication over the extension fields heavily decides it's efficiency. To construct an extension field, first the primitive root c of $f(x)$ is preferred to choose from the twist curve parameter z [13]. Second, the primitive root of $f(x)$ is preferred to be as simple as possible (for example $c = 2$). These constraints make impose a difficulty to find efficient irreducible polynomials for pairing. A tower of extension fields that have nested structures is proposed based on [10]. In this section, the existing classes of practical extension fields are initially reviewed and then the candidates for the tower of fields available for the GMT curves are indicated.

3.1 Optimal Extension Fields

Bailey and Paar [12] introduced the following formal definition for constructing extension fields consisting of a polynomial basis:

Definition 1 (Optimal extension fields, OEFs). *OEFs are the extension fields satisfying the following three properties.*

1. **Characteristic:** *A pseudo-Mersenne prime number p of the form $p = 2^l \pm c$, where $l, c \in \mathbb{Z}$.*
2. **Modular Polynomial:** *An irreducible binomial $x^m - s$, where $s \in \mathbb{F}_p$ and m is the extension degree.*
3. **Basis:** *A set $\{1, \omega, \omega^2, ..., \omega^{m-1}\}$, where ω is a primitive root of the modular polynomial.*

   Although the characteristic p is a pseudo-Mersenne prime number in the OEF definition, it is known that an OEF is actually capable of general prime numbers. An OEF has several fast multiplication algorithms for different degrees m, such as Karatsuba method [19], the Karatsuba-like method [20], and Toom-Cook method [21]. Specifically $m = 2$ and $s = -1$ constitute the most important variant, where the squaring computation in $\mathbb{F}_{p^2}$ requires only two multiplications in $\mathbb{F}_p$, using the Karatsuba method. We call this technique "Karatsuba complex method," which is a famous and standard technique for accelerating pairing calculation.

3.2 All-One Polynomial Extension Fields

Unlike an extension field such as the polynomial based OEF described above, a special extension with a Gaussian normal basis was introduced by Nogami et al. [11]. This field is called all-one polynomial field (AOPF). Later Nekado et al. extended its definition and classified several types of AOPFs, such as type-I X [18] and type-II X [15,17]. The definition of Type-I AOPF is given as follows:

Definition 2 (Type-I All-one polynominal Fields). *Type-I AOPFs are the extension fields satisfying the following three properties.*

1. **Characteristic:** *A pseudo-Mersenne prime number p of the form $p = 2^l \pm c$, where $l, c \in \mathbb{Z}$.*
2. **Modular Polynomial:** *An all-one irreducible polynomial $(x^{m+1} - 1)/(x - 1)$, where $s \in \mathbb{F}_p$ and $m + 1$ is a prime number.*
3. **Basis:** *A pseudo basis $\{\omega, \omega^2, , \omega^3 ..., \omega^m\}$ is equivalent to the normal basis $\{\omega, \omega^p, \omega^{p^2}, ..., \omega^{p^{m-1}}\}$ where ω is a primitive root of the modular polynomial.*

Although the characteristic p is a pseudo-Mersenne prime number in the Definition 2, it is known that an AOPF is actually capable of general prime numbers. An efficient way to calculate the multiplication in an AOPF is to use the cyclic vector multiplication algorithm (CVMA), which is more efficient than the multiplication in an OEF. According to Nekado et al. [18], the squaring in the quadratic type-I AOPF: $\mathbb{F}_{p^2} = \mathbb{F}_p[\omega]/(\omega^2 + \omega + 1)$ only requires two multiplications in $\mathbb{F}_p$ as follows:

$$\alpha = (a_0, a_1), \quad \alpha^2 = \beta = (b_0, b_1), \tag{12}$$

$$b_0 = \{-a_1(a_0 - a_1) + a_0\}, \quad b_1 = \{-a_0(a_0 - a_1) - a_1\} \tag{13}$$

where $\alpha, \beta \in \mathbb{F}_{p^2}$ and $a_0, a_1, b_0, b_1 \in \mathbb{F}_p$. Unlike the OEF, the type-I AOPF has much constraints. For example, $m + 1$ must be a prime number, which restricts the degree of AOPF extension to an even number only. Furthermore, since the degree of type-II AOPF, the squaring in $\mathbb{F}_{p^2}$ requires three multiplications in $\mathbb{F}_p$, which is less efficient compared with the type-I AOPF or the adapted $z = s = -1$ OEF in Karatsuba complex method. In addition, if the probability of a general prime number to construct a degree-2 type-I AOPF is at most 50%. Still, the 2 m cost squaring, the quadratic extension field of both OEF with $s = -1$ and type-I AOPF are still good candidates for a fast pairing calculation.

4   Proposal of Efficient GMT6 and GMT8 Curve Parameters and Their Field-Towering Schemes

As described in Sect. 3, building an efficient tower of an extension field with twist capability has a few constraints regarding the selection of the polynomial primitive root. Although the field towering system reduces the degree of irreducible polynomials to be explored, finding the curve parameters with an efficient computation cost is still complicated. In this section, the parameter selection for both GMT6 and GMT8 curves is described, and new curve parameters and tower construction methods for efficient pairing computation over GMT curves are proposed.

4.1   GMT6 Curve Parameters and Towers

The GMT paper [8] suggests the use of parameters for the GMT6 curve, as shown in Table 1. These parameters are denoted as GMT6-672. The GMT paper suggests the direct sextic extension using the irreducible polynomial $x^6 - s, s = 2 \in \mathbb{F}_p$ for the pairing computation over GMT6-672. Since 2 is a quadratic non-residue (QNR) and a cubic non-residue (CNR) in $\mathbb{F}_p$, the twist parameter z can be equivalent to $z = 2$. In this work, a field towering scheme τ_1 based on the extension proposed in the GMT paper was derived, as shown in Table 3. However, we found that the suggested τ_1 cost 2 extra addition in $\mathbb{F}_{p^2}$ squaring compare to $z = s = -1$; therefore, the arithmetic costs in τ_1 is not the best for pairing calculation.

We propose a new variant of field towering scheme τ_2 for efficient pairing computation over the GMT6 curve using both the sextic twist and Karatsuba complex techniques. -1 is not CNR in $\mathbb{F}_p$. Therefore, we had to find an alternative, QNR and CNR elements in $\mathbb{F}_p$ for the twist parameter z without changing the entire tower construction. Using numerical experiments, we found that the element $-4 \in \mathbb{F}_p$ satisfies the requirements. The cost estimations presented in Table 3 show that the extension field construction τ_2 exhibits less $\mathbb{F}_p$ addition costs in $\mathbb{F}_{p^6}$ than τ_1.

4.2   GMT8 Curve Parameters and Towers

The GMT8-544 curve proposed in [8] with the extension Field $\mathbb{F}_{p^8} = \mathbb{F}_p[x]/(x^8 - 5)$ which only capable with OEF and Type-II AOPF. We present an alternative characteristic p for the GMT8 curve with both OEF and Type-I AOPF construction available which can achieve flexible and efficient implementation. To find such a characteristic, we focus on finding a prime number available with either the Karatsuba complex or type-I AOPF. According to the GMT paper [24], the 2-NAF weight of some parameters is required for efficient computation over the GMT8-544 curves as follows:

$$u : \text{2-naf weight} \leq 5, h_y : \text{2-naf weight} \leq 7, h_t : \text{2-naf weight} \leq 4 \qquad (14)$$

Table 1. GMT6-672 parameters [8]

Param	2-NAF weights	Bit length	Value
u	2	128	0xefffffffffffffe00000000000000000
h_t	1	–	-1
h_y	4	–	0xffbbffffffffffffc020
p	–	672	0x9401ff90f28bffb0c610fb10bf9e0fefd59211629a7991 563c5e468d43ec9cfe1549fd59c20ab5b9a7cda7f27a0067 b8303eeb4b31555cf4f24050ed155555cd7fa7a5f8aaaaaa ad47ede1a6aaaaaaaab69e6dcb

In the GMT paper, the evaluated security level of the proposed GMT8-544 curve is 131-bits. We investigated for new parameters which satisfies approximately the 128-bit security level by focusing the characteristic search in the 525 - 544 bit range. Looking for only the characteristic satisfying the condition above for quadratic type-I AOPF and OEF construction could be obtained. The parameters found are denoted as GMT8-542; these are presented in Table 2. The subgroup security and twist subgroup security of our GMT8-542 are the same with original GMT8-544; $\mathbb{G}_1, \mathbb{G}_2$ subgroup-security are confirmed, the twist-subgroup is not secure.

Compared to the original GMT8-544 curve, h_y in the proposed curve has 2 more weights in the 2-NAF. A part from this disadvantage, the proposed GMT8-542 parameters are available only with the type-I AOPF, and 1/3 cost reduction is achieved for the squaring operation in the extension fields. Based on the extension proposed in the GMT paper, we derived a field-towering scheme τ_3 as shown in Table 3. In this case, the element 3 is a QNR in $\mathbb{F}_p$, and the square root of 3 in $\mathbb{F}_{p^2}$ is also a QNR element which makes the quartic twist available for this tower.

We propose a more efficient towering scheme τ_4, where the first subextension field $\mathbb{F}_{p^2}$ is constructed using the type-I AOPF method. A simple QNR element $(1, -1) \in \mathbb{F}_{p^2}$ for the second and third stage OEFs is selected. Since $(1, -1)$ is QNR, the quartic twist is also available in τ_4. Two towers of extension fields and their arithmetic costs for each curve are summarized in Table 3. The newly proposed towers τ_2 and τ_4 exhibit less number of arithmetic operations for the squaring and the cyclotomic subgroup squaring in $\mathbb{F}_{p^2}$, $\mathbb{F}_{p^6}$, and $\mathbb{F}_{p^8}$.

The final exponentiation raising power of $(p^k - 1)/r$ is heavily dependent on the squaring cost in $\mathbb{F}_{p^k}$. We can use two strategies to accelerate the final exponentiation: compressed squaring introduced by Karabina [25] and cyclotomic subgroup squaring [9,26]. Both algorithms are efficient compared with the regular squaring in the extension fields; however, the compressed squaring requires inversion operation in $\mathbb{F}_p$, which could be the bottleneck of pairing computation.

In Table 3, the s_k^{cyclo} is represented by the square in the cyclotomic subgroup of extension field $\mathbb{F}_{p^k}$. s_k^{cyclo} represents the cost of the cyclotomic subgroups

Table 2. GMT8-542 parameters

Param	2-NAF weights	Bit length	Value
u	4	64	0xffc0000004020002
h_t	1	–	-1
h_y	6	–	0x7452
p	–	542	0x347111bfc75e57d130de7be68437c8d75455d209459d42 1455023bee14df9fe75aa4734686ca3d08c1fa594100d794 21d56c53899ee0f066fad9eb45b0985dbdbba2dcc1

squaring in $\mathbb{F}_{p^k}$. The cyclotomic subgroup squaring equation for τ_1 and τ_2 was adopted from [26, Sect. 3.2]. For τ_3, we adopt the cyclotomic subgroup squaring equation from [26, Sect. 3] was adopted, whereas for τ_4, the equation from a recent work [9] was selected to prevent the multiplication with $(\omega^2 + \omega)^{-1}$ in the $\mathbb{F}_{p^4}$ multiplication.

5   Implementation of Ate Pairing over the GMT6 and GMT8 Curves

In this section, the details of the proposed pairing implementation are presented. Among the proposed towers of the extension fields, τ_2 and τ_4 are the best constructions for the GMT6 and GMT8 curves, respectively. This section provides a detailed calculation of pairing cost based on these towers.

5.1   Implementation of Miller's Algorithm

In previous studies, many sophisticated techniques were proposed to improve the performance of Miller's algorithm. For example, the optimal coordinate system depends on the type of the underlying elliptic curves. Base on the GMT paper [8, Table 5], the homogeneous projective coordinate system (weight[1:1])) for the GMT6-672 curve was adopted. This system was proposed by Costello et al. in [23] and later modified in [22, Section 5].

For the proposed GMT8-542 curve, the Miller's algorithm with the projective coordinate system (weight[1:2]) was adopted. This is also suggested by Costello et al. in [22, Sect. 4]. As a Miller's loop parameter, the GMT6-672 has 129-bit $T = u - 1$ with a 2-NAF weight of 2, whereas the GMT8-542 curve has a 65-bit $T = u - 1$ with a 2-NAF weight = 4. The cost of the implemented functions in Miller's loop based on the τ_2 and τ_4 field-towering schemes is summarized in Table 4.

In Table 4, the column "Call" indicates the number of function calls per Miller's algorithm execution. Since DBLLine does not require UPDATE1 in the first loop of Miller's algorithm, UPDATE1 has one less call than DBLLine. Two ADDLine functions are denoted "ADDLine" and "ADDLine'" in Table 4. Due to

$3i_1$ and $1m_1$ precomputation, ADDLine in Miller's loop can be replaced with "ADDLine'''". Although the pairings and applications employ "ADDLine'''", the only functional with constant P, Q is the subgroup generator of $\mathbb{G}_1$ and $\mathbb{G}'_2$. Thus, pairings without restricting any of the application functionalities were implemented.

5.2   Implementation of Final Exponentiation

In the second part of pairing calculation, the result of Miller's algorithm is raised to the power of $(p^k - 1)/r$. This is also known as final exponentiation $(p^k - 1)/r$ can be separated into two parts; the easy part and the hard part. The complexity of the final exponentiation largely depends on the curve parameters, especially the polynomials of characteristic $p(u)$, order $r(u)$, and Frobenius trace $t(u)$.

Table 3. Arithmetic calculation costs in the tower of the extension fields

Curve and tower	Extension fields	Operation	m_1	s_1	a_1	i_1	Note
GMT6, τ_1 $E(\mathbb{F}_p): y^2 = x^3 - 1$ $E'(\mathbb{F}_p): y^2 = x^3 - v^{-6}$	$\mathbb{F}_{p^2}: \mathbb{F}_p[i]/(i^2 - 2)$	m_2	3	0	6	0	
		s_2	2	0	5	0	
	$\mathbb{F}_{p^6}: \mathbb{F}_{p^2}[v]/(v^3 - i)$, where $i^2 = 2$	m_6	18	0	76	0	
		s_6	12	0	47	0	
		s_6^{cyclo}	6	0	37	0	[26] Sect. 3.2
		f_6	4	0	0	0	
		i_6	35	1	102	1	
GMT6, τ_2 $E(\mathbb{F}_p): y^2 = x^3 - 1$ $E'(\mathbb{F}_p): y^2 = x^3 - v^6$	$\mathbb{F}_{p^2}: \mathbb{F}_p[i]/(i^2 + 1)$	m_2	3	0	5	0	
		s_2	2	0	3	0	
	$\mathbb{F}_{p^6}: \mathbb{F}_{p^2}[v]/(v^3 - 2i)$, where $i^2 = -1$	m_6	18	0	64	0	
		s_6	12	0	41	0	
		s_6^{cyclo}	6	0	29	0	[26] Sect. 3.2
		f_6	4	0	0	0	
		i_6	36	1	80	1	
GMT8, τ_3 $E: y^2 = x^3 + x$ $E'(\mathbb{F}_{p^2}): y^2 = x^3 + ix$	$\mathbb{F}_{p^2}: \mathbb{F}_p[i]/(i^2 - 3)$	m_2	3	0	7	0	
		s_2	2	0	5	0	
	$\mathbb{F}_{p^4}: \mathbb{F}_{p^2}[v]/(v^2 - i)$	m_4	9	0	33	0	
		s_4	6	0	25	0	
	$\mathbb{F}_{p^8}: \mathbb{F}_{p^4}[g]/(g^2 - v)$, where $i^2 = 3$	m_8	27	0	121	0	
		s_8	18	0	93	0	
		s_8^{cyclo}	12	0	69	0	[26] Sect. 3.1
		f_8	6	0	0	0	
		i_8	46	1	169	1	
GMT8, τ_4 $E: y^2 = x^3 + x$ $E'(\mathbb{F}_{p^2}): y^2 = x^3 + v^2x$	$\mathbb{F}_{p^2}: \mathbb{F}_p[\omega]/(\omega^2 + \omega + 1)$	m_2	3	0	4	0	
		s_2	2	0	3	0	Type-I AOPF
	$\mathbb{F}_{p^4}: \mathbb{F}_{p^2}[v]/(v^2 - (\omega^2 + \omega))$	m_4	9	0	26	0	
		s_4	6	0	21	0	
	$\mathbb{F}_{p^8}: \mathbb{F}_{p^4}[g]/(g^2 - v)$, where $(1, -1) \in \mathbb{F}_{p^2}$ $\omega + \omega^p = 1$	m_8	27	0	102	0	
		s_8	18	0	83	0	
		s_8^{cyclo}	12	0	66	0	[9] Sect 3.3
		f_8	9	0	12	0	
		i_8	49	0	132	1	

Using the following equation, the GMT curves feature a very unique and efficient construction [8]:

$$t' \equiv u^i + 1 \ \equiv p + 1 \ (\text{mod } r), (i = 1) \tag{15}$$

$$j = \frac{p + 1 - t'}{r}, \tag{16}$$

GMT6-672 Final Exponentiation

As mentioned above, the final exponentiation can be separated into two parts such as follows:

$$\frac{p^6 - 1}{r} = (p^3 - 1)(p + 1) \times \frac{(p^2 - p + 1)}{r} \tag{17}$$

The easy part $(p^3 - 1)(p+1)$ requires two Frobenius endomorphism calculations f_6 for p and p^3. The Frobenius endomorphism for the raised power of $p^k/2$ does not require any multiplication when k is even. Moreover, as shown in Table 3, the OEF nested tower of the extension field only requires 4 **m** for the Frobenius endomorphism f_k.

For the hard part, using the replacement technique given in (17) and (18) where $c = j$ (where $\Phi_6(x)$ is the 6-th cyclotomic polynomial), $\frac{(p^2-p+1)}{r}$ can be broken down to:

$$\frac{\Phi_6(t' - 1)}{r} + (p + t' - 2)c = 1 + (p + t' - 2)c \tag{18}$$

The hard part can be multiplied by a small integer, which does not change the bilinear pairing integrity. In this case, a multiplication by 3 is recommended, so that the polynomial $3c$ does not have any fraction terms, such as

$$3(1 + (p + t' - 2)c) = 3 + 3c(p + u - 1) \tag{19}$$

Table 4. Cost of miller's loop in τ_2 and τ_4

Curve: tower	Function	m_1	s_1	Total **m**	Call
GMT6-672: τ_2	DBLLine	4	7	11 **m**	128
	UPDATE1	25	0	25 **m**	127
	ADDLine	13	2	15 **m**	2
	ADDLine'	12	2	14 **m**	0
	UPDATE2	13	0	13 **m**	2
	Miller's loop	3739	900	4639 **m**	1
GMT8-542: τ_4	DBLLine	26	0	26 **m**	64
	UPDATE1	42	0	42 **m**	63
	ADDLine	44	0	44 **m**	4
	ADDLine'	41	0	41 **m**	0
	UPDATE2	24	0	24 **m**	4
	Miller's loop	4582	0	4582 **m**	1

However, bilinearity could not be achieved using (19) with the polynomial $3c$ provided in Sect. 5.2 (3) of the GMT paper. Thus, our version of $3c$ was recalculated and corrected as follows:

$$3c = ((1 + 3w + 9w^2)(u - 1) + (6w + 9w^2))(u - 1) + 9w + 9w^2, \qquad (20)$$

where $w = h_y/2$. We propose an efficient calculation order for $3c$, which is shown in Table 5. However, we realize Nanjo et al. [16] already proposed the same equation in their paper's TABLE IX. The final exponentiation costs using the above $3c$ calculation based on τ_2 are summarized in Table 7. Compare with the original GMT672 final exponentiation hard part, our calculation order reduced $4m_6$ and s_6.

GMT8-542 Final Exponentiation

Similar to the GMT6-672 curve, the power of the GMT8-542 final exponentiation can also be divided into two parts as follows:

$$\frac{p^8 - 1}{r} = (p^4 - 1) \times \frac{(p^4 + 1)}{r} \qquad (21)$$

In this case the easy part $(p^4 - 1)$ only requires $1\ m_6$ and $1\ i_6$. Using again the replacement technique given in (17) and (18) with parameter $u' = u - 1$. The hard part of GMT8-542 can be broken down as follows:

$$\frac{(p^4 + 1)}{r} = \frac{\Phi_8(t' - 1)}{r} + d(p + t' - 1)(p + (t' - 1)^2) = 1 + d(p + u)(p^2 + u^2) \quad (22)$$

Table 5. Calculation of the raised power of GMT6-672 hard part-$3c$

Computation	Term computed	Cost
Input: $M \in \mathbb{F}_{p^6}, w, u' \in \mathbb{F}_p$		
Output: $M^{3c} \in \mathbb{F}_{p^6}$		
Temp. var: t_0, t_1, t_2		
$t_0 \leftarrow M^w$	M^w	c_w
$t_1 \leftarrow t_0^2$	M^{2w}	s_6^{cyclo}
$t_0 \leftarrow t_0 t_1$	M^{3w}	m_6
$t_1 \leftarrow t_0 M$	M^{3w+1}	m_6
$t_1 \leftarrow t_1^w$	M^{3w^2+w}	c_w
$t_2 \leftarrow t_1^2$	M^{6w^2+2w}	s_6^{cyclo}
$t_1 \leftarrow t_2 t_1$	M^{9w^2+3w}	m_6
$t_2 \leftarrow t_1 t_0$	M^{9w^2+6w}	m_6
$t_1 \leftarrow t_1 M$	M^{9w^2+3w+1}	m_6
$t_1 \leftarrow t_1^{u'}$	$M^{(9w^2+3w+1)u'}$	$c_{u'}$
$t_1 \leftarrow t_1 t_2$	$M^{(9w^2+3w+1)u'+9w^2+6w}$	m_6
$t_1 \leftarrow t_1^{u'}$	$M^{((9w^2+3w+1)u'+9w^2+6w)u'}$	$c_{u'}$
$t_1 \leftarrow t_1 t_2$	$M^{((9w^2+3w+1)u'+9w^2+6w)u'+9w^2+6w}$	m_6
$t_0 \leftarrow t_1 t_0$	$M^{((9w^2+3w+1)u'+9w^2+6w)u'+9w^2+9w}$	m_6
return t_0		

According to the GMT paper, thr hard part of embedding degree 8 is multiplied by 4 as follows:

$$4 + 4d(p + u)(p^2 + u^2) \tag{23}$$

Similar to the GMT6-672, $4d$ was recalculated and corrected as follows:

$$4d = ((((4n^2 + 1)u - 4n)u + 4n + 1)u - 4)u + 4n^2, \tag{24}$$

where $n = h_y$. We propose an efficient calculation algorithm for $4d$, as shown in Table 6. The total calculation costs of the final exponentiation are summarized in Table 7. Compare with the original GMT672 final exponentiation hard part, our calculation order increased $2s_6$ reduced $5m_6$.

6   Implementation Results

To confirm the efficiency of the proposed methods, all the towers shown in Table 3 were implemented for ate pairing cost and speed comparison. The software developed computes bilinear pairings based on the algorithms introduced in Sect. 2.3. In this section, the features of the software libraries used are initially introduced. Furthermore, the pairing implementation results with detailed calculation costs are presented.

Table 6. Calculation of the raised power of GMT8-542 hard part-$4d$

Computation	Term computed	Cost
Input: $M \in \mathbb{F}_{p^8}, u, n \in \mathbb{F}_p$		
Output: $M^{4d} \in \mathbb{F}_{p^8}$		
Temp. var: t_0, t_1, t_2, t_3		
$t_0 \leftarrow M^2$	M^2	s_8^{cyclo}
$t_0 \leftarrow t_0{}^2$	M^4	s_8^{cyclo}
$t_1 \leftarrow t_0{}^n$	M^{4n}	c_n
$t_2 \leftarrow t_1{}^n$	M^{4n^2}	c_n
$t_3 \leftarrow t_2 M$	M^{4n^2+1}	m_8
$t_3 \leftarrow t_3{}^u$	$M^{(4n^2+1)u}$	c_u
$t_3 \leftarrow t_3 t_1{}^{-1}$	$M^{(4n^2+1)u-4n}$	m_8
$t_3 \leftarrow t_3{}^u$	$M^{((4n^2+1)u-4n)u}$	c_u
$t_3 \leftarrow t_3 t_1$	$M^{((4n^2+1)u-4n)u+4n}$	m_8
$t_3 \leftarrow t_3 M$	$M^{((4n^2+1)u-4n)u+4n+1}$	m_8
$t_3 \leftarrow t_3{}^u$	$M^{(((4n^2+1)u-4n)u+4n+1)u}$	c_u
$t_3 \leftarrow t_3 t_0{}^{-1}$	$M^{(((4n^2+1)u-4n)u+4n+1)u-4}$	m_8
$t_3 \leftarrow t_3{}^u$	$M^{((((4n^2+1)u-4n)u+4n+1)u-4)u}$	c_u
$t_0 \leftarrow t_3 t_2$	$M^{((((4n^2+1)u-4n)u+4n+1)u-4)u+4n^2}$	m_8
return t_0		

6.1   Multi-precision Libraries and Implementation Features

As mentioned above, two libraries (mcl [14] and GMP) are used, which are combined in this work. mcl is a library for pairing-based cryptography, mainly supporting the optimal ate pairing over BN curves and BLS12-381 curves. This library is available on almost all x32 and x64 architecture available platforms. The implementation conducted in this work mainly uses the mpn function group of the GNU multiple precision (GMP) Library called by the C++ language, although some core operations such as multiplication, modulo, addition and bit shift are replaced by mcl functions. The multiplication in $\mathbb{F}_p$ is performed using the Montgomery multiplication techniques.

6.2   Pairing Benchmark Results

Miller's algorithm and final exponentiation costs are summarized in Table 8. It can be observed that the proposed towers τ_2 and τ_4 exhibit lower costs than τ_1 and τ_3 by applying all the techniques previously described. Specifically, compared with τ_1 and τ_2, they are addition almost 6% more efficient because of the addition cost reduced Karatsuba complex method. Although, τ_4 exhibits an approximate 2% higher costs due to the specially of type-I AOPF but it has lower addition in total. The implementation results are presented in Table 9. The program was compiled using the Clang++12 with the compile option -Ofast -march=native. The benchmarks were obtained using an i7-8700 (base clock 3.2 GHz, boost 4.3 GHz) computer.

Table 7. τ_2 and τ_4 final exponentiation costs.

Curve: tower	Part	m_6	s_6^{cyclo}	f_k	f_k^2	i_6	c_u	$c_{u-1}{}^a$	$c_w{}^a$	$c_n{}^a$	Total m
GMT6-672 : τ_2	Easy	2	0	1	0	1	0	0	0	0	77 m
	Hard (without 3c)	4	1	1	0	0	1	0	0	0	886 m
	3c	8	2	0	0	0	0	2	2	0	2892 m
	Total	14	3	2	0	1	1	2	2	0	3855 m
GMT8-542 : τ_4	Easy	1	0	0	0	1	0	0	0	0	76 m
	Hard (without 4d)	3	2	1	1	0	3	0	0	0	2748 m
	4d	6	2	0	0	0	4	0	0	2	4320 m
	Total	10	4	1	1	1	7	0	0	2	7144 m

[a] GMT6-672:τ_2, the costs for the raised power of $u, u-1$ and w are $c_u = 804$ m , $c_{u-1} = 822$ m , $c_w = 546$ m respectively. For the GMT8-542:τ_4 case the costs for raised power of u and n are $c_u = 876$ m, $c_n = 315$ m respectively.

Table 8. Pairing total costs

Tower	Miller's algorithm cost	Final Exponentiation cost	Total Pairing cost
τ_1	4902 m	3854 m $+i_1$	8774 m $+i_1$
τ_2	4639 m	3855 m $+i_1$	8494 m $+i_1$
τ_3	4310 m	7135 m $+i_1$	11445 m $+i_1$
τ_4	4582 m	7144 m $+i_1$	11726 m $+i_1$

Table 9. Implementation results obtained using an i7-8700 CPU (3.2 GHz Turbo Boost off, 4.3 GHz on) computer compared with the GMT paper estimation results

Curve	Tower	MP library	Miller's algorithm [μs]	Final exponentiation [μs]	Pairing [μs]	Turbo Boost
GMT6-672	$\tau 1$	mcl	772	722	1494	Off
		mcl	539	503	1042	On
	$\tau 2$	mcl	721	693	1410	Off
		mcl	505	481	987	On
	–	RELIC (estimation)	800	700	1500	Off
GMT8-542	$\tau 3$	mcl	589	1050	1639	Off
		mcl	411	731	1142	On
	$\tau 4$	mcl	569	1050	1616	Off
		mcl	398	730	1120	On
GMT8-544	–	RELIC (estimation)	600	900	1500	Off

The proposed pairing computation over the GMT6-672 and GMT8-542 curves is achieved in 0.99 and 1.12 ms, respectively, with Turbo Boost enabled. The construction of tower τ_2 is 5.2% faster than τ_1. Moreover, the construction of tower τ_4 is 2% faster than that of τ_3 due to the addition reduction. It is also observed that τ_4 has this feature which does not require any squaring in $\mathbb{F}_p$, which is an interesting result. A comparison with the GMT paper estimation results is also provided. A comparison between our implementation result and the GMT paper estimation results is provided in Table 9.

Our implementation results are Benchmarked in the same environment as the GMT paper estimation results. It is observed that the GMT6-672 curve with tower τ_2, our results are achieved faster by approximately 6% than the GMT paper estimation results. For the GMT8-542 curve with tower τ_4, our results are achieved by 0.116 ms slower than the GMT paper estimation results.

7   Conclusion and Future Work

The following results can be concluded:

1. After reviewing the GMT6 and GMT8 curve parameters and classes of the existed extension fields, two different types of towers for newly emerged pairing-friendly curves were proposed. Since the GMT6 curve original characteristic is considered sufficiently efficient, a unique and efficient tower construction consisting of nested OEF was proposed. This scheme is suitable to the minimal addition karatsuba complex method. For the GMT8 curve, the existed parameters cannot achieve the best performance. Thus, we reexplored the characteristic and proposed a new set of parameters with only 2 less bits suitable with the type-I AOPF.
2. To the best of the authors' knowledge, complete and efficient software implementations of pairings for the GMT6 and GMT8 curves have not been reported. The cost of the recommended Miller's algorithm with a twist on

the available rational functions of pairings was presented. For the final exponentiation, the polynomials were recalculated, and the costs for both curves were re-evaluated. The implementation results suggested that the GMT6 and GMT8 curves are excellent and efficient candidates for 128-bit security pairing applications.

Acknowledgments. A part of this work was supported by the Cabinet Office (CAO), Cross-ministerial Strategic Innovation Promotion Program (SIP), "Cyber Physical Security for IoT Society", JPNP18015 (Funding agency: NEDO). The authors thank Tadanori Teruya of CPSEC, AIST, for his assistance with the towering construction, and Yuki Nanjo of Okayama University for her comments on improving the manuscript.

References

1. Boneh, D., Gentry, C., Lynn, B., Shacham, H.: Aggregate and verifiably encrypted signatures from bilinear maps. In: Biham, E. (ed.) EUROCRYPT 2003. LNCS, vol. 2656, pp. 416–432. Springer, Heidelberg (2003). https://doi.org/10.1007/3-540-39200-9_26

2. Naehrig, M., Lauter, K., Vaikuntanathan, V.: Can homomorphic encryption be practical?. In: Proceedings of the 3rd ACM Workshop on Cloud Computing Security Workshop (CCSW 2011). Association for Computing Machinery, pp. 113–124 (2011)

3. Abdolmaleki, B., Baghery, K., Lipmaa, H., Zając, M.: A Subversion-Resistant SNARK. In: Takagi, T., Peyrin, T. (eds.) ASIACRYPT 2017. LNCS, vol. 10626, pp. 3–33. Springer, Cham (2017). https://doi.org/10.1007/978-3-319-70700-6_1

4. Boxall, J., El Mrabet, N., Laguillaumie, F., Le, D.-P.: A variant of Miller's formula and algorithm. In: Joye, M., Miyaji, A., Otsuka, A. (eds.) Pairing 2010. LNCS, vol. 6487, pp. 417–434. Springer, Heidelberg (2010). https://doi.org/10.1007/978-3-642-17455-1_26

5. Barreto, P.S.L.M., Naehrig, M.: Pairing-friendly elliptic curves of prime order. In: Preneel, B., Tavares, S. (eds.) SAC 2005. LNCS, vol. 3897, pp. 319–331. Springer, Heidelberg (2006). https://doi.org/10.1007/11693383_22

6. Barreto, P.S.L.M., Lynn, B., Scott, M.: Constructing elliptic curves with prescribed embedding degrees. In: Cimato, S., Persiano, G., Galdi, C. (eds.) SCN 2002. LNCS, vol. 2576, pp. 257–267. Springer, Heidelberg (2003). https://doi.org/10.1007/3-540-36413-7_19

7. Kim, T., Barbulescu, R.: Extended tower number field sieve: a new complexity for the medium prime case. In: Robshaw, M., Katz, J. (eds.) CRYPTO 2016. LNCS, vol. 9814, pp. 543–571. Springer, Heidelberg (2016). https://doi.org/10.1007/978-3-662-53018-4_20

8. Guillevic, A., Masson, S., Thomé, E.: Cocks-Pinch curves of embedding degrees five to eight and optimal ate pairing computation. Des. Codes Crypt. **88**(6), 1047–1081 (2020). https://doi.org/10.1007/s10623-020-00727-w

9. Lavice, A., Mrabet, N.E., Berzati, A., Rigaud, J., Proy, J.: Hardware implementations of pairings at updated security levels. In: Grosso, V., Pöppelmann, T. (eds.) CARDIS 2021. LNCS, vol. 13173, pp. 189–209. Springer, Cham (2021). https://doi.org/10.1007/978-3-030-97348-3_11

10. Benger, N., Scott, M.: Constructing tower extensions of finite fields for implementation of pairing-based cryptography. In: Hasan, M.A., Helleseth, T. (eds.) WAIFI 2010. LNCS, vol. 6087, pp. 180–195. Springer, Heidelberg (2010). https://doi.org/10.1007/978-3-642-13797-6_13

11. Nogami, Y., Saito, A., Morikawa, Y.: Finite extension field with modulus of all-one polynomial and representation of its elements for fast arithmetic operations. IEICE Trans. Fundam. Electron. Commun. Comput. Sci. **86**(9), 2376–2387 (2003)
12. Bailey, D.V., Paar, C.: Optimal extension fields for fast arithmetic in public-key algorithms. In: Krawczyk, H. (ed.) CRYPTO 1998. LNCS, vol. 1462, pp. 472–485. Springer, Heidelberg (1998). https://doi.org/10.1007/BFb0055748
13. Scott, M. (2009): A note on twists for pairing friendly curves. Personal. ftp://ftp.computing.dcu.ie/pub/resources/crypto/twists.pdf
14. Mitsunari, S.: A portable and fast pairing-based cryptographic library. https://github.com/herumi/mcl. Accessed 14 Jan 2021
15. Nanjo, Y., Kodera, Y., Matsumura, R., Shirase, M., Kusaka, T., Nogami, Y.: Evaluation of a pairing on elliptic curves of embedding degree 15 with type-II all-one polynomial extension field of degree 5. In: 2020 Symposium on Cryptography and Information Security (2020)
16. Nanjo, Y., Khandaker, M.M., Kusaka, T, Nogami, Y.: Consideration of efficient pairing applying two construction methods of extension fields. In: 2018 Sixth International Symposium on Computing and Networking Workshops (CANDARW), pp. 445–451 (2018)
17. Kato, H., Nogami, Y., Yoshida, T., Morikawa, Y.: A multiplication algorithm in Fpm such that p¿ m with a special class of gauss period normal bases. EICE Trans. Fundam. Electron. Commun. Comput. Sci. **92**(1), 173–181 (2009)
18. Kato, H., Nogami, Y., Yoshida, T., Morikawa, Y.: Cyclic vector multiplication algorithm based on a special class of Gauss period normal basis. ETRI J. **29**(6), 769–778 (2007)
19. Karatsuba, A., Ofman, Y.: Multiplication of many-digital numbers by automatic computers. In: Proceedings of the USSR Academy of Sciences, vol. 145, pp. 595–596 (1963). Translation in the academic journal Physics-Doklady, pp. 293–294
20. Montgomery, P.L.: Five, six, and seven-term Karatsuba-like formulae. IEEE Trans. Comput. **54**(3), 362–369 (2005)
21. Toom, A. L.: The complexity of a scheme of functional elements realizing the multiplication of integers. In: Soviet Mathematics Dok-Lady, vol. 3, no. 4, pp. 714–716 (1963)
22. Costello, C., Lange, T., Naehrig, M.: Faster pairing computations on curves with high-degree twists. In: Nguyen, P.Q., Pointcheval, D. (eds.) PKC 2010. LNCS, vol. 6056, pp. 224–242. Springer, Heidelberg (2010). https://doi.org/10.1007/978-3-642-13013-7_14
23. Costello, C., Hisil, H., Boyd, C., Gonzalez Nieto, J., Wong, K.K.-H.: Faster pairings on special weierstrass curves. In: Shacham, H., Waters, B. (eds.) Pairing 2009. LNCS, vol. 5671, pp. 89–101. Springer, Heidelberg (2009). https://doi.org/10.1007/978-3-642-03298-1_7
24. Masson, S.: Cocks-Pinch variant. https://gitlab.inria.fr/smasson/cocks-pinch-variant. Accessed 14 Jan 2021
25. Karabina, K.: Squaring in cyclotomic subgroups. Math. Comput. **82**(281), 555–579 (2013)
26. Granger, R., Scott, M.: Faster squaring in the cyclotomic subgroup of sixth degree extensions. In: Nguyen, P.Q., Pointcheval, D. (eds.) PKC 2010. LNCS, vol. 6056, pp. 209–223. Springer, Heidelberg (2010). https://doi.org/10.1007/978-3-642-13013-7_13

SecMT – Security in Mobile Technologies

Leaky Blinders: Information Leakage in Mobile VPNs

Thijs Heijligenberg[1]($\boxtimes$), Oualid Lkhaouni[2], and Katharina Kohls[1]

[1] Radboud University, Nijmegen, The Netherlands
{theijligenberg,kkohls}@cs.ru.nl
[2] Ruhr University, Bochum, Germany
oualid.lkhaouni@rub.de

Abstract. In the mobile domain, VPN applications promise an additional layer of protection for wireless connections. They offer users the choice to improve the security of their connections, however, we only have very limited knowledge about the technical implications that the shift from desktop to mobile applications brings. In this work, we conduct a quantitative analysis of selected Android VPNs and demonstrate how all of them leak packets during an active tunnel. We conduct these measurements for different phones and in varying use case scenarios, including the comparison of Wi-Fi and 4G connections, to get a better understanding of how the mobile setting influences the security of a VPN. While we observe leaks in *all* combinations, some settings particularly cause the transmission of thousands of unprotected packets. We further conduct a series of case studies to provide some first insights on the *causes* for the observed leakage.

Keywords: VPN · Mobile · Information leakage

1 Introduction

VPN applications provide an additional layer of protection to Internet connections. The market size of VPNs is expected to grow from 25 million USD in 2019 up to 75 million USD in 2027 [17], indicating a high commercial potential. VPNs are beneficial in various use case scenarios ranging from casual convenience, e.g., circumventing geofencing for online content, over adding more security to standard Internet connections, to gaining protection from censorship authorities [19]. While conventional VPN applications are well-researched in the context of desktops [9,13,15], we only have limited knowledge about their performance in the mobile domain.

Mobile devices introduce constraints that are not present when running a VPN application on a desktop computer. In most cases, a mobile device has less computational power. It runs on a battery and uses a wireless network connection to either a Wi-Fi or a mobile network. All of these constraints have in common that they limit the performance of an application, e.g., optimizing the battery usage

© The Author(s), under exclusive license to Springer Nature Switzerland AG 2022
J. Zhou et al. (Eds.): ACNS 2022 Workshops, LNCS 13285, pp. 481–494, 2022.
https://doi.org/10.1007/978-3-031-16815-4_26

makes active applications and processes compete for the available resources. Due to these constraints, we assume consequences for *mobile* VPN applications, especially concerning their power and data consumption. Prior work provides different static and dynamic analyses of Android-based VPN apps [8]. However, they mainly focus on the characteristics of the various applications and ignore influencing factors that are critical for the mobile domain. The results of these studies indicate different security issues involving malware in officially accessible Playstore apps, occurrences of TLS interception, or information leakage due to the transmission of untunneled traffic. However, these results are obtained through stationary setups that ignore the critical characteristics in the mobile domain. Examples of this are operating devices without any power connection or connecting to a mobile network instead of a Wi-Fi connection. Both characteristics are directly related to the power and traffic optimizations of a mobile device, and we must assume an impact on the behavior of mobile VPN apps.

In this work, we analyze Android VPN apps with a focus on the key influencing factors of the *mobile domain*. More precisely, we test three popular apps (Turbo VPN, Thunder VPN, Orbot) on three mobile devices that represent different ages of smartphones. Our primary focus is on information leakage, i.e., traffic that leaves or reaches the device without being protected by the active VPN tunnel. We use leakage to indicate how well an application handles a use case scenario in our experimental setup. Our quantitative evaluation demonstrates that *all* apps and devices in our setup transport unprotected traffic while the VPN is supposed to be active. This leakage can result in thousands of unprotected packets that carry potentially sensitive information.

Our setup covers various use case scenarios and combinations of influencing factors. Besides comparing devices and the individual VPN applications, we further investigate the differences between devices with and without an available USB power supply. In another experiment, we evaluate the differences between a network connection through Wi-Fi versus a mobile network connection using 4G. We apply these combinations to typical usage scenarios that resemble varying types of user data traffic, including simple browsing under varying link qualities or data-intensive streaming of multimedia content. Our case studies support our initial assumptions and indicate that the internal performance optimizations affect the security of mobile VPNs.

Our experimental evaluation prepares different starting points for future work on the performance of VPN apps in the mobile domain. This includes various technical aspects derived from our quantitative and qualitative evaluation findings, e.g., the internal resource optimization under varying constraints or the internal dependencies of operating systems and VPN apps that require a proxy interface for tunneling traffic. Finally, we point out user discrepancies that can arise from the consistent leakage of all apps in our test set. Overall, we make the following core contributions.

1. Quantitative analysis: We test three commercial smartphones and three Android-based VPN apps in four scenarios. We use the results of these experiments to compare the traffic leakage under various influencing factors.

2. Qualitative analysis: In a smaller set of targeted measurements, we investigate the performance of VPN apps in characteristic setups, including a lockdown setting and DNS specifics.
3. We provide a detailed discussion of our technical findings and identify different starting points for future work in this context.

2 Technical Background

A Virtual Private Network (VPN) tunnels traffic through a TCP or UDP connection between the user's system and a remote network, which allows access to services and devices in the remote network. Optional encryption through IPSec [6], TLS, or Wireguard [3] provides an additional level of confidentiality.

2.1 Mobile Devices

Mobile devices use the same architecture of processes, network devices etc.. as home computers, e.g., most mobile devices run on a version of the Linux kernel [7]. The fact that there are different underlying components for Wi-Fi, mobile data, or Bluetooth is abstracted away from applications running in userspace.

Differences to Desktops. Mobile devices are typically more resource-constrained than laptops or desktop computers. High screen resolutions and intensive applications draw power and produce heat, and applications differ by their performance requirements [14]. In addition to the graphical processing and the CPU in the phone's chipset, there are different chips for Wi-Fi or mobile connections that increase the overall load on the available resources. On the network side, mobile devices receive a higher number of unsolicited incoming connections, mainly from mobile network sources. While these incoming connections are technically also established by the mobile device after an indication from the network, the phone user has little control over this in practice.

Based on the particular characteristics of the mobile domain, we expect differences in the performance of mobile applications, including VPNs. Due to the additional layer of encryption and the tunneling of user traffic, a VPN introduces a significant overhead for the device. Limited resources might affect the performance of such apps, which eventually leads to security flaws.

Mobile VPN Apps. The Android operating system allows apps to register as a VPN by creating a *VpnService* [1]. The developer can provide an IP address of the tunnel endpoint, a route for the traffic (generally expected to be the default route for all traffic), and a DNS server. After establishment, this gives the app a filehandle from which reading equates to getting a message sent into the tunnel, and writing equates to sending a message out of the tunnel. The Android API also allows the application to set allowed or disallowed apps explicitly or enable apps to bypass the VPN.

Modern Android versions provide two additional settings that the user can set for an individual VPN from the settings menu: the option to always have the VPN enabled and to block traffic outside the tunnel, which in the android source code is referred to as *lockdown*. The Android operating system handles these settings, but apps must provide specific functionality relating to device startup to allow the always-on option to work.

2.2　Networks

Mobile devices use either an available Wi-Fi connection or refer to the mobile network made available through an active data plan with one of the network operators. While this wireless Internet connection is transparent to the user, the internal connection handling introduces some technical differences.

Wi-Fi. Wi-Fi networks in their most common simple form, as provided by a Raspberry Pi 4 in our test network (Sect. 3), are a transmission modem and a gateway behind a NAT (Network Address Translation). The modem is responsible for communicating with the connected devices, which have been appointed individual IP addresses in the local network. The gateway aggregates all traffic and forwards it to the Internet or the encompassing network.

The operating system implements its protocol stack to handle Ethernet connections on the mobile device. The underlying Wi-Fi protocol stack is implemented in either the application processor or a dedicated Wi-Fi chip and resembles the same reference model as other network devices.

Mobile Networks. Mobile networks consist of multiple base stations and the core network. A base station handles the radio connection with connected mobile devices and sends/receives the traffic to/from the core network. The core network provides a link to the Internet and manages the phone's registration status. It also includes identity management and cryptographic procedures, and handles mobility between base stations or gateways.

On mobile devices, a separate baseband processor implements the mobile network stack. In the case of a mobile network connection, this stack takes over the processing of traffic on the network layer and handles the traffic from that point on.

3　Experimental Setup

The main focus of our analysis is on the volume of leaked traffic during an *active* VPN connection.

3.1　Network Setup

The network setup describes how we provide a wireless access point for the devices under test (cf. Fig. 1). This access point is either a Wi-Fi access point (Sect. 3.1), or serves as a 4G (LTE) mobile network base station (Sect. 3.1).

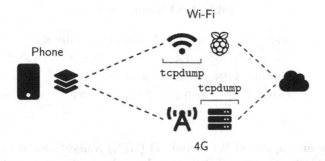

Fig. 1. Experimental setup. The phone connects through a VPN to a wireless access point. We capture traffic at the wireless interface (Wi-Fi) or the core's Internet gateway (4G).

Table 1. Devices and capabilities.

Name	Device			Experiments			
	Short	Android	Chipset	Wi-Fi	4G	Unplugged	Lockdown
Oneplus 8	O8	11	SM8250	●	●	●	●
Poco F2 Pro	PO	10	Qualcomm SM8250	●	●	○	●
Samsung Galaxy S9	S9	10	Exynos 9810	●	●	○	●

Wi-Fi Setup. For the Wi-Fi setup, we use a Raspberry Pi 4 that offers network access through a `hostapd` service. The Pi is connected to the Internet and provides a dedicated Wi-Fi network for the devices in our test set. To record traffic, we run `tcpdump` on the wireless interface of the access point and save the resulting PCAP traces on a second machine to avoid any additional file writing load on the Pi. We have complete control over the access point, and we can adjust the network link according to our scenarios.

4G Setup. The wireless access point is a base station for our mobile network setup and offers connectivity through a mobile network. To this end, we use an Amarisoft callbox classic [2] configured to a 4G setup. The callbox is connected to the Internet and offers connectivity through the core network's serving gateway. More precisely, the mobile network serves as a NAT providing the connected device with an internal IPv4 address and making requests through its external address. We record traffic using `tcpdump` at the *external* interface of the callbox and apply traffic shaping to the internal interface if necessary for a scenario.

3.2 Devices and App Setup

Our experiments cover devices released between 2018 and 2020, as summarized in Table 1. These devices differ in their hardware capabilities and enable us to analyze the performance of VPN apps on different host machines. All devices in

Table 2. VPN apps used

App	Version	Downloads	Protocol
Turbo VPN	3.7.4	100 m+	ESP
Thunder VPN	4.1.2	50 m+	SSL
Orbot	16.5.2	10 m+	TCP

our test setup are capable of Wi-Fi and 4G (LTE) connections. We control each phone using ADB, either via USB (in the plugged experiments) or via a network connection (in the unplugged experiments).

The Xiaomi and Samsung provide a relatively clean setup with only a handful of apps installed or activated, representing a realistic but controlled environment. The Oneplus has around 300 popular apps installed to simulate a setting where background traffic and heavy CPU load can occur.

Each device installs the same set of VPN apps as specified in Table 2. The apps in our setup represent different popular choices of free VPN services, with two offering a paid premium option (we refer to the basic service). Despite some conceptual and technical differences, all apps have in common that they route network traffic through at least one additional proxy on the transmission path (cf. Sect. 2).

3.3 Parameter Setup

We test three different devices and applications in four use case scenarios. If not noted otherwise, each experiment covers *all* 36 combinations of these parameters. We apply these combinations to different setups that focus on relevant influencing factors.

Scenarios. The four different scenarios in our setup represent individual use cases that result in characteristic user data traffic.

Reference. The reference scenario covers simple web browsing where we open the Alexa top 10 websites in individual tabs of the device's standard browser and wait 1 s between new page loads. This setup serves as a reference with a moderate amount of traffic generated. We use the same browsing procedure in the following *link failure* setups.

Link Failure. In the *link failure* scenarios, we artificially add *delay* or *loss* to the transmission link. To this end, we use different combinations of the Linux traffic control settings tc. In the Wi-Fi setup, we apply the delay and loss rules to the wireless interface of the Raspberry Pi; in the mobile setting, we select the internal tunnel interface of the callbox. The tunnel interface represents the internal address of the serving gateway, i.e., the gateway that a mobile phone uses for an outbound connection from the core network to the Internet. The assumption behind this scenario is that we force the device into compensating for the lost or delayed traffic, e.g., through initiating retransmissions of packets.

Stress. The *stress* scenario aims to create a high overall burden for the device. This is achieved by opening a webpage with eight embedded 8K videos, resulting in the network link being fully used. The assumption behind this scenario is that by interfering with the limited resources of a device, eventual optimization steps by the operating system might affect the performance of the VPN. Furthermore, the high amount of traffic might affect the internal policies of a VPN app.

Influencing Factors. We identify two key influencing factors that are characteristic of the mobile domain. To get a better understanding of these factors, we apply them to *all* of the above combinations. For example, to compare different network setups, we conduct the 36 permutations of devices, apps, and scenarios on a Wi-Fi and a 4G setting, resulting in 72 experiments in total.

Network Setup. We test two different variants of wireless network access. The device connects to our access point and receives an Internet connection through the wireless interface in the Wi-Fi setting. We connect the device to our mobile network in the LTE setting. The assumption behind this comparison is to vary the received signals and trigger the operating system's optimization of the traffic consumption.

Power Supply. As mobile devices only have a limited battery capacity, the power consumption of different apps and services is the target of optimization. To cover the differences between mobile and stationary usage of a device, we conduct experiments in both a plugged-in and plugged-out setting. The assumption behind these two variants is that energy optimization might also affect a VPN app and lead to side effects for tunneled traffic.

4   Dynamic Analysis

In our dynamic analysis, we look at the volume of leaked packets in different combinations of our parameters and setups.

4.1   Metrics

Our primary focus is on the amount of leaked information, i.e., the number and volume of packets that are processed outside the tunnel while a VPN app is active. We define and measure leakage as follows. When a device starts the VPN app, a `VPN connection established` message is sent to the Android log. We take this event as the starting point of the VPN and note the start time. As soon as the VPN app terminates, the log documents a `VPN disconnected` message. We use this timestamp as the end time. In the next step, we filter captured traffic and keep those packets sent between the recorded start and end times. We assume this to be the window in which the VPN tunnel is supposed to be active.

To determine leakage, we then document all IP addresses that transmit traffic using the protocol used by the VPN app (cf. Table 2). All traffic sent to and

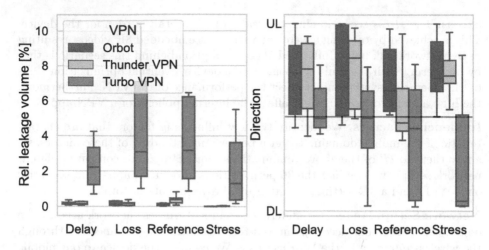

Fig. 2. Relative leakage (left) and distribution of traffic up/downlink (right). We compare the performance of the three VPN apps in our test setup.

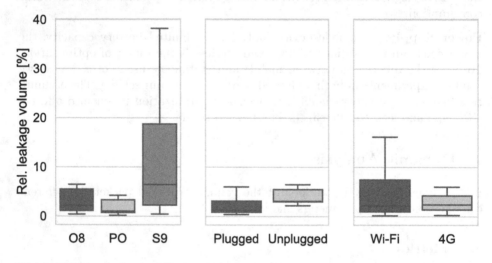

Fig. 3. Relative leakage of Turbo VPN traffic. Plots show the comparison of different devices (left), power supply (middle), and network connections (right).

received from these addresses is considered VPN traffic, and all other transmissions (IP address $\neq$ VPN IP) are untunneled traffic. The main metric of interest is the leak's volume, i.e., the sum of the sizes of all packets outside the tunnel. We document the leakage relative to the overall volume of traffic sent while the VPN is active.

We conduct five repetitions for all experiments for each parameter combination and aggregate the results accordingly.

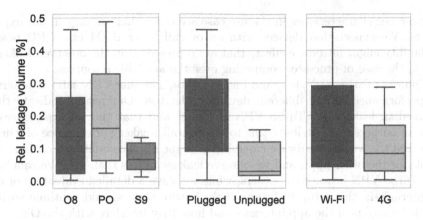

Fig. 4. Relative leakage of Orbot and Thunder VPN traffic. Plots show devices (left), power (middle), and network (right); results are merged for both apps.

4.2 Experiments

Our experiments provide a step-by-step analysis of the different influencing factors. We first give a general comparison of apps and continue with devices, power supply, and network connection. As Turbo VPN has a significantly higher leakage than the other apps, we separate all results after inspecting the apps.

Apps. Our experiments cover three popular (by download numbers) VPN apps from the Android Play Store. While some apps compensate for the free usage model with advertisements (Turbo VPN, Thunder VPN), the Orbot app provides its core service without any additional content. For our measurements, we focus on the free variants of the apps and compare their performance in our set of four use case scenarios.

Figure 2 summarized the relative leakage per app and further documents the transmission direction of leaked traffic. In our results, it is evident that Turbo VPN causes a significantly higher leakage. While the other apps provide a much lower number and volume of leaked packets, it is worth mentioning that *all* experiments (combinations and repetitions) contain leakage.

We further observe that Turbo VPN traffic consists of significantly more downlink traffic. This indicates that Turbo VPN constantly receives traffic, even though the app operates in the same settings as other candidates. To avoid any bias in the next steps of our evaluation, we separate the results of Turbo VPN from the other apps. This allows us to discuss the factors that influence the heavy leakage in Turbo VPN while also allowing us to look at the results of the other apps without the outliers introduced by Turbo VPN.

Devices. The devices in our test setup provide different hardware specifications and were released during the last four years. Consequently, we expect individual performance characteristics in the use case scenarios that we vary in our experiments. We expect that devices with an overall lower RAM and CPU power availability might introduce effects that are represented in the observed leakage, e.g., in the case of processes competing over the available resources.

Figure 3 (Turbo VPN, left) and Fig. 4 (Orbot, Thunder VPN; left) summarize the performance for the different devices under test. Our results indicate that the median leakage for Turbo VPN is higher and that the S9 experiences a series of outliers. We attribute this to the overall weaker performance of Turbo VPN and the weaker hardware capabilities of the S9. No significant outliers are visible for the other apps, and we observe leakage of less than 1%. We conclude that Turbo VPN introduces outliers, while we leave a detailed evaluation of the S9 internals in this setup to future work. Future work should continue with a detailed analysis of the app internals and how they interfere with the OS.

Power. We compare the performance differences for plugged and unplugged setups, e.g., the devices receive power via USB or are unplugged from any power source. In these experiments, we limit ourselves to the Oneplus 8. We perform a full test of scenarios for the Wi-Fi setup.

Again, we observe how Turbo VPN differs from the results of the other apps, as it indicates a higher leakage for the unplugged setting. In all other cases, a constant power supply leads to more unprotected traffic. We assume that battery power leads to a higher degree of performance optimizations in the OS, which eventually leads to more constraints for the VPN apps. Future work should investigate OS optimizations and how they affect different apps, e.g., categorized by access and interface usage.

Network. Next, we analyze the differences between a Wi-Fi and a 4G mobile network setup. While we do not expect significant differences on the packet level (the underlying network connection is invisible to the VPN app), mobile traffic might lead to a different optimization strategy for the operating system. An example of this is minimizing mobile traffic consumption for specific use cases.

In our experiments, the use of 4G resulted in less leakage. The hypothesis can explain that the phone is more stringent with giving resources to background processes while leaving the VPN app untouched. Future work should continue this by monitoring the power consumption and device battery status.

4.3   Case Study: Lockdown Option

In addition to the quantitative evaluation of the above parameter combinations, we conduct targeted case studies for specific VPN characteristics. We begin with the lockdown function that blocks all traffic outside a VPN tunnel. Figure 5 provides a comparison of scenarios with and without the lockdown function enabled. We observe that the option drastically reduces leakage in all scenarios. However, none of the setups yielded truly zero leakage, and further research is required to investigate what information the leaked packets contain. We did

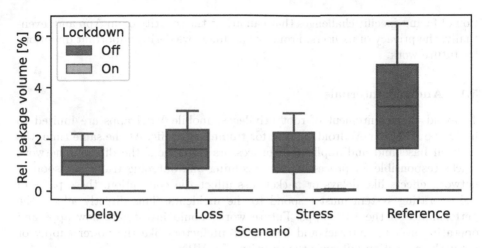

Fig. 5. Comparison of different scenarios with the lockdown option disabled and enabled.

not test Thunder VPN in this variation as it does not support the prerequisite *always-on* option.

4.4 Case Study: DNS Traffic

A portion of the leaked traffic consists of DNS messages bypassing the VPN. As a second case study, we test whether a domain responds to a DNS request. This gives us a strong indication that this domain serves as a name server. In all our experiments, the combined DNS traffic amounted to around 1% of traffic by packet count. This indicates that while DNS is part of the leaked traffic, it is not the leading cause. Unprotected DNS messages, when sniffed, can lead to a privacy leak as they do give a hint on the user's behavior, but further research is required to ascertain how impactful the DNS traffic leaked from the DNS apps is.

Conclusion. From the analysis of different influencing factors, we can conclude that the choice of a VPN app serves as an amplifier for the observed characteristics. All setups have in common that they do not function *without* any leakage, and even the otherwise effective lockdown function does not entirely prevent this. Less reliable VPN apps lead to more downlink traffic, which indicates that incoming traffic is less likely to be protected by the tunnel. Our evaluation is a first starting point and helps identify future work directions. In particular, the dependencies between operating systems and applications should be analyzed in settings characteristic of mobile usage.

5 Directions for Future Work

Our work indicates that the mobile domain introduces different influencing factors that affect the performance of VPN apps. This underlines the initial assumption of facing specific challenges that can affect the security of an App and, eventually, the privacy of its users. From our findings, we derive important directions for future work.

5.1   Android Internals

To avoid the requirement of root privileges, mobile VPN apps are limited to using the API that Android exposes for tunneling traffic. At the same time, the internal baseband and application processors implement the different network stacks responsible for processing the incoming and outgoing traffic. As soon as network effects like delays or packet loss affect the connection, these parts of the operating system must respond to the incidents. This directly affects the performance of the VPN apps. Future work should investigate how apps and operating systems interact and how different factors like the power supply or network connection influence the security of a VPN.

5.2   VPN App Internals

Similar to the impact of the operating system, the specific implementation of an app influences how different use case scenarios can be handled. As we observed significant differences between the VPN apps in our experiments, a valuable next step is an evaluation of the internals of such apps. While prior work already covers static analyses, a dynamic approach would allow for covering relevant characteristics of the mobile domain.

5.3   User Expectations

Besides the technical aspects of apps and their host devices, users' expectations are a critical factor in assessing the security of mobile VPNs. Our experiments show constant leakage for all combinations of scenarios and parameters. Although the relative amount of leaked packets can be low, all untunnelled data has the potential to carry sensitive information. This might cause discrepancies with user expectations and emphasizes the fact that a mobile OS is mostly opaque to users [11]. Future work must analyze such user expectations, the technical understanding of VPN apps, and differences between the perception of mobile versus desktop VPN solutions.

6   Related Work

Prior work provides an extensive measurement study on more than 200 commercial VPN providers that involves static and dynamic analyses of the apps and the resulting traffic [8]. While their work demonstrates how the VPN permissions of Android facilitate different kinds of information leakage or connection manipulations, this existing study only covers a stationary, single-device setup using a Wi-Fi connection. In contrast, our work focuses on the specific characteristics of a *mobile* setting. More precisely, we incorporate different network setups and the capabilities of different classes of devices, all in the presence of individual use case scenarios. Our results underline the assumption that these influencing factors affect the performance of a mobile VPN and should not be isolated in quantitative analyses.

There are different reasons to use a VPN application. Tunneling traffic through a trusted party can help to improve the overall privacy, e.g., by avoiding tracking [4] or fingerprinting [16] attacks. Another use case scenario is the circumvention of Internet censorship, where the authorities of a jurisdiction limit the access to certain services and information sources on the Internet. Prior work monitors worldwide incidents of Internet censorship [18] and investigates ways to circumvent the resulting limitations [10,12].

A different line of work focuses on the manual inspection of popular VPN services regarding their network characteristics or the infrastructure of the different providers. Results indicate misconfigurations and bugs that lead to leakage of DNS and IPv6 information [5,13]. Follow-up work repeats this with a specific focus on VPN applications in the Android ecosystem [8,20]. These studies show different instances of malware, manipulation of connections and TLS interception, or traffic leakage. The findings of these studies were later confirmed [9].

7   Conclusion

VPNs offer an additional layer of protection for user traffic. While such apps are increasingly popular, we only have limited knowledge about the implications of switching from stationary to mobile settings. Optimization strategies of operating systems that aim to reduce the battery usage and consumed traffic when connected to a mobile network might impact the protection capabilities of a VPN, leading to traffic and, thus, information leakage. In this work, we analyze the information leakage of Android VPN apps in different use case setups to assess the impact of critical characteristics of the mobile domain. Our results indicate that in *all* combinations of devices, apps, and scenarios, a certain amount of traffic remains unprotected by the tunnel. In some cases, the combination of influencing factors leads to thousands of leaked packets. Our results indicate different directions for future work and emphasize the need to consider the unique aspects of mobile VPN usage.

References

1. VpnService reference (2022). https://developer.android.com/reference/android/net/VpnService
2. Amarisoft callbox series (2022). https://www.amarisoft.com/products/test-measurements/amari-lte-callbox/
3. Donenfeld, J.A.: Wireguard: next generation kernel network tunnel. In: NDSS, pp. 1–12 (2017)
4. Englehardt, S., Narayanan, A.: Online tracking: a 1-million-site measurement and analysis. In: Proceedings of the 2016 ACM SIGSAC Conference on Computer and Communications Security, CCS 2016, New York, NY, USA, pp. 1388–1401. Association for Computing Machinery (2016). https://doi.org/10.1145/2976749.2978313

5. Fazal, L., Ganu, S., Kappes, M., Krishnakumar, A.S., Krishnan, P.: Tackling security vulnerabilities in VPN-based wireless deployments. In: 2004 IEEE International Conference on Communications (IEEE Cat. No. 04CH37577), vol. 1, pp. 100–104. IEEE (2004)
6. Frankel, S., Kent, K., Lewkowski, R., Orebaugh, A.D., Ritchey, R.W., Sharma, S.R.: Guide to IPsec VPNs (2005)
7. GlobalStats statcounter: Mobile operating system market share worldwide (2022). https://gs.statcounter.com/os-market-share/mobile/worldwide. Accessed 4 Feb 2022
8. Ikram, M., Vallina-Rodriguez, N., Seneviratne, S., Kaafar, M.A., Paxson, V.: An analysis of the privacy and security risks of android VPN permission-enabled apps. In: Proceedings of the 2016 Internet Measurement Conference, pp. 349–364 (2016)
9. Khan, M.T., DeBlasio, J., Voelker, G.M., Snoeren, A.C., Kanich, C., Vallina-Rodriguez, N.: An empirical analysis of the commercial VPN ecosystem. In: Proceedings of the Internet Measurement Conference 2018, pp. 443–456 (2018)
10. Khattak, S., Javed, M., Khayam, S.A., Uzmi, Z.A., Paxson, V.: A look at the consequences of internet censorship through an ISP lens. In: Proceedings of the 2014 Conference on Internet Measurement Conference, pp. 271–284 (2014)
11. Liu, B., et al.: Follow my recommendations: a personalized privacy assistant for mobile app permissions. In: Symposium on Usable Privacy and Security (2016)
12. Nobori, D., Shinjo, Y.: VPN gate: a volunteer-organized public VPN relay system with blocking resistance for bypassing government censorship firewalls. In: 11th USENIX Symposium on Networked Systems Design and Implementation (NSDI 2014), pp. 229–241 (2014)
13. Perta, V.C., Barbera, M., Tyson, G., Haddadi, H., Mei, A., et al.: A glance through the VPN looking glass: IPv6 leakage and DNS hijacking in commercial VPN clients (2015)
14. How much RAM do you need in a smartphone? (2019). https://www.androidauthority.com/how-much-ram-do-you-need-in-smartphone-2019-944920/
15. Ramesh, R., Evdokimov, L., Xue, D., Ensafi, R.: VPNalyzer: systematic investigation of the VPN ecosystem. In: Network and Distributed Systems Security, NDSS 2022. ISOC (2022)
16. Rimmer, V., Preuveneers, D., Juarez, M., Van Goethem, T., Joosen, W.: Automated website fingerprinting through deep learning. In: Network and Distributed System Security Symposium, NDSS 2018, San Diego, CA, USA. The Internet Society, February 2018
17. Statista: Size of the virtual private network (VPN) market worldwide in 2019 and 2027 (2022). https://www.statista.com/statistics/542817/worldwide-virtual-private-network-market/
18. Sundara Raman, R., Shenoy, P., Kohls, K., Ensafi, R.: Censored planet: an internet-wide, longitudinal censorship observatory. In: ACM SIGSAC Conference on Computer and Communications Security (CCS) (2020)
19. Wired: The attack on global privacy leaves few places to turn (2017). https://www.wired.com/story/china-russia-vpn-crackdown/
20. Zhang, Q., Li, J., Zhang, Y., Wang, H., Gu, D.: Oh-Pwn-VPN! Security analysis of OpenVPN-based android apps. In: Capkun, S., Chow, S.S.M. (eds.) CANS 2017. LNCS, vol. 11261, pp. 373–389. Springer, Cham (2018). https://doi.org/10.1007/978-3-030-02641-7_17

Instrumentation Blueprints: Towards Combining Several Android Instrumentation Tools

Arthur van der Staaij and Olga Gadyatskaya(✉) (iD)

LIACS, Leiden University, Leiden, The Netherlands
a.j.w.van.der.staaij@umail.leidenuniv.nl,
o.gadyatskaya@liacs.leidenuniv.nl

Abstract. The explosive growth of the amount of Android apps has given rise to a pressing need to analyse these apps, most importantly for security purposes. Many Android app analysis and hardening tools rely on *bytecode instrumentation*: the modification of the compiled app code. App instrumentation tools have all kinds of purposes, ranging from the measurement of code coverage to placing probes for malware detection. Given this variety, it may be useful to work with multiple tools that rely on instrumentation at the same time. The composition of such tools can however lead to issues, since their changes to the applications under analysis may conflict with each other. To facilitate the composition of multiple instrumentation tools, we propose a two-step approach involving *instrumentation blueprints*, reports of the instrumentation changes a tool needs to apply. We have designed a prototype syntax for these blueprints, adapted a modern instrumentation tool to emit them and implemented a prototype blueprint application program. Our evaluation shows that the proposed approach is viable.

Keywords: Android · App instrumentation · Instrumentation blueprints

1 Introduction

Over the last few years, the smartphones market has continued to grow. According to Statcounter, today Android is the most popular mobile operating system today, with a market share exceeding 70%[1]. Many apps are released for this operating systems every day: according to Statista, approximately 81,000 apps were released on Google Play only during February 2022[2]. As the size of the Android ecosystem grows, so does the demand for tools that analyze its apps. And indeed, in the recent years many such tools have become available.

---

[1] https://gs.statcounter.com/os-market-share/mobile/worldwide Data for February 2022; last accessed on March 18, 2022.

[2] https://www.statista.com/statistics/1020956/android-app-releases-worldwide/ Last accessed on March 18, 2022.

© The Author(s), under exclusive license to Springer Nature Switzerland AG 2022
J. Zhou et al. (Eds.): ACNS 2022 Workshops, LNCS 13285, pp. 495–512, 2022.
https://doi.org/10.1007/978-3-031-16815-4_27

Android app analysis tools often use a technique called *instrumentation*: they modify the (compiled) code of the application in order to gather information while it is running. Even though a multitude of systems and frameworks related to instrumentation is continually being developed (e.g., [6–8, 23, 26, 34]), a topic that has not been considered in detail in the community is the *composition* of instrumentation tools: using multiple such tools at once.

Indeed, given the variety of the available instrumentation tools, it may be useful to work with multiple of them at the same time. Example use cases are composing multiple analysis tools to scan for different kinds of behavior at the same time, combining a tool that looks for malicious behavior with a code coverage tool in order to gain information on how complete the results are, and composing multiple app hardening tools to gain the benefits of each of them. To the best of our knowledge, not much research has been done in this area.

For dynamic analysis tools, a simple approach to composition would be to repeat the same input for differently instrumented versions of an app. This is however not always possible: even with the same input, apps do not always behave in the same way (see, e.g., [23]), since they may use some form of external input like the internet or may just contain random elements. The time overhead of such a scheme might also be quite large. And of course, it does not apply at all in the case of app hardening.

Instrumenting an application with multiple tools may cause problems, as instrumentation tools generally assume that no changes have been applied to the application before, and no changes will be applied after. Applying instrumentation tools one after the other will cause the later tools to instrument the code added by the earlier ones, which may result in undesired behavior: we do not want to measure the coverage of the code inserted by other tools, or to analyze such inserted code for malicious behavior. It may even lead to a combinatorial explosion of added code, significantly increasing the overhead of the instrumentation. Multiply instrumented apps may also fail to run altogether, since it is known that success rate of individual tools is often much lower than 100% [23].

In order to facilitate the composition of instrumentation tools, this work introduces the concept of *instrumentation blueprints*: specifications of the instrumentation changes applied by a tool. Instead of instrumenting applications directly, tools can output a blueprint, and a dedicated *applicator* system can subsequently apply multiple such blueprints at once. Because the applicator has knowledge of all the required code changes of the different tools at once, it can avoid issues that would otherwise be caused by the composition of the tools.

The contributions of this work are:

1. The design of an approach for the composition of instrumentation tools, based on instrumentation blueprints.
2. The definition of a prototype syntax for instrumentation blueprints.
3. The proof-of-concept implementation of a blueprint output for ACV-Tool [23][3].

---

[3] Available at https://gitlab.com/avdstaaij-academic/citfaa-acvtool-fork.

4. The implementation of a prototype blueprint applicator program released open-source for the community to build on this work[4].
5. Evaluation of the prototypes on a case study.

2 Instrumentation Tools in the Literature

2.1 Taxonomy of Instrumentation Tools

We can distinguish two different types of app bytecode instrumentation: *static instrumentation* and *dynamic instrumentation* (not to be confused with static and dynamic *analysis*). With static instrumentation, applications are modified in one go, prior to analysis. With dynamic instrumentation on the other hand, the app is continuously modified as it runs. Dynamic instrumentation is more complex and appears to be less frequently used.

Examples of analysis tools that use static instrumentation are ICCInspect [17], AspectDroid [2], DroidFax [7], APIMonitor [34] (a system that was used in a version of DroidBox [19,35]) and other unnamed tools [15,27,32]. AppTrace [24] is an example of a dynamic instrumentation tool.

The contributions of this work apply to only the static instrumentation approaches. From this point on, we will refer tools that use some form of static Dalvik bytecode instrumentation as simply *instrumentation tools*.

Instrumentation tools have a variety of purposes. DroidFax [7] and the tool developed by Somarriba et al. [27] monitor and visualize the runtime behavior of apps. ICCInspect [17] provides statistics and visualizations for the runtime usage of the Android ICC system. The tool from Hu et al. [15] analyzes the energy consumption of methods and API calls, helping developers with the optimization of their apps.

Another common use for instrumentation is *taint tracking*. AspectDroid [2], DroidBox [19] and the tool developed by Will [32] are examples of taint tracking tools that rely on app instrumentation.

There are also a number of frameworks for development of instrumentation tools. Examples are Apkil [34], I-ARM-Droid [8] and InsDal [20]. An interesting system that also somewhat fits in this category is Repackman [26], which can repackage apps with arbitrary payloads in order to evaluate other tools that detect such repackaging.

Some instrumentation tools instrument apps in order to *improve* them, usually focusing on security and privacy. If instrumentation is used for this purpose, it is often called *bytecode rewriting* or *app hardening*. One such tool is introduced by [4], describing the use cases of advertisement removal and the injection of a more fine-grained permission system. The system from [18] also involves bytecode instrumentation to make the Android permission system more fine-grained. Aurasium [33] is yet another example. An overview of techniques of this family is given by [13].

---

[4] https://gitlab.com/avdstaaij-academic/citfaa-blueprint-applicator.

Finally, an interesting group of instrumentation tools is formed by tools that measure black-box code coverage, i.e. how much of the bytecode of the application under test is actually executed during analysis. Examples of instrumentation tools that measure code coverage are Ella [3], CovDroid [36], the tools described in [16] and [14], ACVTool [23], and COSMO [25]. ACVTool appears to be the most mature tool of this group, and [22, 23] describe many more tools, alternative approaches and uses for code coverage measurements.

2.2 Limitations of Instrumentation

Although bytecode instrumentation is used by a variety of tools, it does have some significant limitations. Instrumented apps must be repackaged, and malicious apps could detect this repackaging and then not execute any malicious code (again capitalizing on the general weakness of dynamic analysis). Apps can, for example, verify their own signature: changing the bytecode of an application invalidates its signature, so instrumentations tools must re-sign them before installation. Another limitation is that instrumentation may sometimes break the application under test: Pilgun et al. report that instrumentation success rates (the fraction of apps that remains functional after instrumentation) of older code coverage tools lie between 36% and 65% [23]. ACVTool and COSMO have much higher success rates, but they cannot successfully instrument every app either.

As an alternative to bytecode instrumentation, many tools (e.g. [5,10,29]) instead change or substitute some component of the Android operating system itself, like the Android Runtime or the API framework. Usually, these tools use an emulator to run the modified operating system. A notable disadvantage of these techniques compared to bytecode instrumentation is that the tools need to be updated as the Android OS changes. The bytecode specification is sometimes changed in updates as well, but these changes are usually fairly small.

To summarize, a rich variety of instrumentation tools exist in the literature, but, even though many of their goals are complimentary, to the best of our knowledge, nobody has investigated composing several tools. This is the gap that we start to address with this work.

3 Background

Applications for Android come in the form of an Android Package, or APK for short. An APK contains all components that make up an application, such as Dalvik bytecode, native code and assets like images and XML files. They also include a manifest file, which is an XML file that holds the name of the package, its components, required permissions and other metadata.

Dalvik Bytecode and the Smali Representation. Dalvik bytecode is in many ways similar to machine code, consisting of low-level instructions like add and goto [9]. The full instruction list can be found in [1]. There are, however, some significant

Table 1. Example register layout (adapted from [32])

v0	First local register
v1	Second local register
v2 = p0	First parameter register (*this*)
v3 = p1	Second parameter register
v4 = p2	Third parameter register

differences as well. For example, the Android Runtime is a *register-based* virtual machine [9]. This means that there are no memory access instructions in the bytecode, and there is no stack. Instead, functions have parameter registers and declare the amount of *local registers* they need. A total number of 65 536 registers is supported, far more than most real-world machines have.

Because Dalvik bytecode representation is too low-level, instrumentation tools usually do not deal with it directly. Instead, a human-readable assembly-like representation of it is used. There are two such representations that are commonly used: Smali [12] and Jimple [31]. Smali, the output of Gruver's `smali/baksmali` tool, has been designed specifically for Dalvik bytecode and stays very close to it. Jimple is a bit more abstract, and was primarily created for Java bytecode. This work uses the Smali representation.

In this work we use Apktool [30], which relies on `smali/baksmali`, to disassemble APKs into Smali files. A separate file is used for every Java class. Figure 1 shows an example of a Java class and its Smali representation. For clarity, we have removed some debug information and optional reflection metadata from the Smali code. Note how the class `Foo`, its methods `bar` and `baz` (and its implicit constructor) and its field `value` can all still be identified. The lines that start with a dot are called *directives*.

For each method in the original Java code, there is a corresponding `.method/.end method` block. Such a block begins with a header containing the method descriptor: the name of the method, its parameters and its return type. For example, the descriptor of `bar` is `bar(I)V`, as it requires one parameter of type `int` (`I`), and its return type is `void` (`V`). The first line after the method header declares how many local register the method uses. All methods in the example use one. Instead of using `.locals`, as in the example, methods can also use `.registers` to specify the *total* number of registers (local and parameter). Inside a function, local registers are referenced with `v<number>`. The registers containing the method's parameters use the `p` prefix instead. All non-`static` methods also have an implicit *this*-parameter, which is placed in `p0`.

Although local and parameter registers use different names, there is actually no distinction: parameters are simply placed in the last registers of the method. If a method has `n` local registers, the first parameter register is `vn`. The `p`-names refer to the exact same registers; they are merely aliases. Table 1 shows the relation between the `v`- and `p`-registers for a non-static method with two local registers and three parameters (including the *this*-parameter).

```
1   package com.example;
2
3   public class Foo {
4     private void bar(int count) {
5       for(int i = 0; i < count; i++) {
6         baz(i);
7       }
8     }
9
10    private void baz(int i) {
11      value += i;
12    }
13
14    private int value = 0;
15  }
```

```
1   .class public Lcom/example/Foo;
2   .super Ljava/lang/Object;
3   .source "Foo.java"
4
5   # instance fields
6   .field private value:I
7
8   # direct methods
9   .method public constructor <init>()V
10      .locals 1
11      invoke-direct {p0}, Ljava/lang/Object;-><init>()V
12      const/4 v0, 0x0
13      iput v0, p0, Lcom/example/Foo;->value:I
14      return-void
15  .end method
16
17  .method private bar(I)V
18      .locals 1
19      const/4 v0, 0x0
20      :goto_0
21      if-ge v0, p1, :cond_0
22      invoke-direct {p0, v0}, Lcom/example/Foo;->baz(I)V
23      add-int/lit8 v0, v0, 0x1
24      goto :goto_0
25      :cond_0
26      return-void
27  .end method
28
29  .method private baz(I)V
30      .locals 1
31      iget v0, p0, Lcom/example/Foo;->value:I
32      add-int/2addr v0, p1
33      iput v0, p0, Lcom/example/Foo;->value:I
34      return-void
35  .end method
```

(a) Java   (b) Smali

Fig. 1. Example of a Java file and the corresponding Smali code

A challenge that nearly all instrumentation tools face is the management of registers. Because Dalvik bytecode is register-based, almost any meaningful addition to it will require a register. Instrumentation code could use the existing local registers if the method already has enough of them, but unless code is added only at the beginning or at the end of the method, doing so without disturbing the original code is very difficult, and not always possible. In most cases, additional registers have to be allocated. For the lack of space we only discuss how we approached the register management in this work (Sect. 5.2). The challenges of register management and an alternative solution are discussed in detail in [22,28].

4 Instrumentation Blueprints

In order to better facilitate the composition of instrumentation tools, we will now introduce our main contribution: the concept of *instrumentation blueprints*.

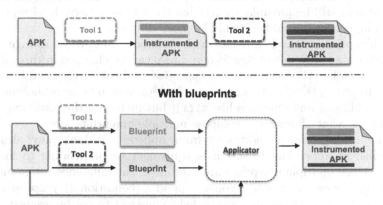

Fig. 2. Process flow for instrumentation composition with and without blueprints

As stated in Sect. 1, the main disadvantage of using instrumentation tools one after the other is that they will instrument each other's changes. In order to avoid these problems, we essentially need to instrument an application with both tools *at the same time*. This is exactly what we aim to make possible by using instrumentation blueprints. Figure 2 shows a diagram of how instrumentation tool composition works with and without instrumentation blueprints. Without blueprints, the tools are used one after the other. The use of the second tool may break the changes of the first tool, or lead to the instrumentation of the first tool's instrumentation code. With blueprints, each tool first outputs a blueprint individually, and the applicator then applies these blueprints at the same time. Since the applicator has knowledge of all the changes that need to be made, it is able to avoid certain problems that would otherwise arise, or to at least warn the user in the case that composition is not possible.

4.1   Blueprint Design

Practically, an instrumentation blueprint is a file that contains all changes that an instrumentation tool wants to apply to the bytecode. It is essentially a kind of `diff`, but a bit richer. Our main goal when designing a prototype syntax for instrumentation blueprints was to make them highly expressive in order to support as many instrumentation tools as possible, while at the same time giving them enough structure to actually help with composition.

Blueprints represent code using the Smali representation, because it makes the code human-readable and easier to work with while still remaining very close to the original bytecode. It may be harder to implement blueprint output for instrumentation tools that are based on a more abstract representation like

Jimple, but since all representations must eventually be converted back to byte-code, it should still be possible. Converting changes at a lower-level representation to a higher-level would certainly be more difficult.

The blueprint syntax is line-based: the smallest unit whose change can be represented is a single line of Smali code. Lines can be changed in three distinct ways: code can be *prepended* to them, *appended* to them, or they can be entirely *replaced*. In principle, all code changes can be represented using replacements (or by using additions and deletions like `diff`), but including the intention behind the change is what allows us to compose multiple blueprints.

Distinguishing prepend-additions from append-additions may also seem superfluous, as appending to line n is equivalent to prepending to line n+1. However, when multiple blueprints are combined, the difference can actually be meaningful. For example, a tool could append a (conditional) `jump` instruction after line n that may cause code prepended to line n+1 to not be reached. Again, we aim to capture the intention behind the code changes, and separating *prepend* from *append* yields more expressivity in that regard.

Currently, the only requirement for two blueprints to be composable is that they do not include a replacement for the same line. We believe that many instrumentation tools do not need to replace lines, since they usually aim to analyze the code that already exists in a *transparent* manner (i.e. without changing its behavior). We expect that replace-conflicts are only unavoidable when tools are inherently not composable, for example when two app hardening tools try to modify the same part of a program, but we did not investigate this thoroughly.

There is however one important exception to this: tools may need to replace lines of code whose behavior they do not intend to change for the purpose of register management. For example, ACVTool needs to change every line that contains a parameter register [23]. For this reason, we designed the blueprint syntax to abstract register management away.

Blueprints consist of a series of *method entries*, each containing the line changes for a single method. Every method entry specifies how many additional registers the instrumentation code needs. The included Smali code can then refer to these additional *instrumentation registers* using the names i0, i1, i2 and so on (the i stands for instrumentation). Of course, the normal v- and p-registers can still be used as well. The applicator program will then ensure that the registers are managed correctly (described in Sect. 5.2).

4.2   The Syntax

All instrumentation changes to an APK file are condensed into a single blueprint file. As we already touched upon, blueprint consist of a list of *method entries*. These method entries consist of a header, followed by a list of *line entries*. Line entries have a header as well, and optionally Smali code contents.

The format of these entries is shown in Fig. 3. The `<method>` field specifies the fully qualified descriptor of the method, and the `<register-count>` field

```
@@<method>:<register-count>           @<line-number>:<operation>
<line entry>                          <content>
<line entry>
...
```

      (a) Method entry   (b) Line entry

Fig. 3. Formats of method and line entries

Table 2. Possible line entry operations

Character	Operation	Description
a	Append	Add `<content>` after the line
p	Prepend	Add `<content>` before the line
r	Replace	Replace the line with `<content>`

specifies the required number of instrumentation registers. Lines are identified by their line number relative to the method (starting at zero), which is placed in the `<line-number>` field. The `<operation>` field contains a character that identifies type of line operation. The options are shown in Fig. 2. Finally, the `<content>` field may consist of any amount of Smali instructions, optionally using i-registers. Multiple method entries for the same method, or multiple line entries for the same line and operation, are permitted.

Both method and line entry headers can appear directly after a line of Smali code, so we have to be able to distinguish these headers from Smali. This is achieved by beginning both headers with an @-character, since beginning a line with one is not legal in Smali. Its "*at*"-meaning also fits rather well. Method entry headers have an additional @ to distinguish them from line entry headers.

Because we identify lines using their line number, we need to be very precise about which lines are counted. Generally, the fewer lines are counted, the easier the implementation of blueprint output for instrumentation tools becomes, but changes to lines that are not counted cannot be represented in a blueprint. We decided to count every line, except for (1) empty lines; (2) the line containing `.locals` or `.registers`; (3) lines containing debug information.

The lines that we consider to be debug lines are those containing a `.line`, `.local` or `.prologue` directive. We do not count these lines because they are optional, they do not alter the state of the program, and we cannot think of any reason to instrument them: they are equivalent to empty lines. Any change to a debug line can instead be represented as a prepend entry for the line that comes after it.

The syntax is still a prototype: there are multiple code modifications that it currently cannot represent. We will discuss these shortcomings in Sect. 5.4. A concrete example of the blueprint syntax will be given in Sect. 5.1.

5   Implementation

We have implemented our blueprint system from two directions: we extended
ACVTool [23] to generate blueprints, and we created a program that can apply
blueprints to Smali files. In this section, we describe how we went about each of
these directions.

5.1   Generation of Instrumentation Blueprints for ACVTool

We have extended ACVTool to generate a blueprint as a side-effect of instrumentation[5]. Because ACVTool uses Smali and instruments almost every line, it
is a good test of both the expressivity of our syntax and the correctness of our
applicator (discussed in Sect. 5.2).

ACVTool is written in Python and its source code is publicly available [21].
We refer the interested reader to [22] for the detailed explanation of the ACVTool
instrumentation process. The tool uses a modified version of Apkil, a bytecode
instrumentation library that was originally created for APIMonitor [34]. Apkil
discards lines containing debug information at an early stage, which partly influenced our decision to not count those lines for the blueprint syntax.

We identified all locations in the ACVTool code where Smali was inserted into
the application and added blueprint generation code for each of them. ACVTool
creates an auxiliary `.pickle` file, used to generate a report from the analysis
results. We made ACVTool additionally create a blueprint file at the same location.

Figure 4 shows the blueprint segment for an ACVTool instrumentation example. The lines that are highlighted[6] in Fig. 4b which also appear in Fig. 4c are
highlighted there as well.

The blueprint begins with a header specifying the method `baz(I)V` from
`com/example/Foo`. ACVTool needs three instrumentation registers per method,
so the header ends with `:3`. Below that, the blueprint contains five line entries:
`@0:p`, `@0:a`, `@1:a`, `@2:a` and `@3:a`. The first entry contains the prepended lines
that load in the coverage array and mark the method as covered. The other
entries contain the appended lines that mark each of the original instructions
as covered. Note that the blueprint uses the `i0`, `i1` and `i2` registers where the
instrumented code uses `v3`, `v4` and `v5`. The first two instructions added by ACV-
Tool are omitted, since they only served to copy the values of the parameters
to their original positions, in order to free up the `v3`, `v4` and `v5` registers. Since
register management has been abstracted away by the `i`-register system, these
two instructions should not be included in the blueprint.

---

[5] Our extension of ACVTool is available at https://gitlab.com/avdstaaij-academic/
citfaa-acvtool-fork.

[6] Highlighted in yellow lines are those added by ACVTool during instrumentation.

```
1  .method private baz(I)V
2    .locals 1
3    iget v0, p0, Lcom/example/Foo;->value:I
4    add-int/2addr v0, p1
5    iput v0, p0, Lcom/example/Foo;->value:I
6    return-void
7  .end method
```

(a) Original bytecode

```
1  .method private baz(I)V
2    .locals 4
3    move-object/16 v1, p0
4    move/16 v2, p1
5    sget-object v3, Ltool/acv/AcvReporter
       ↪ ;->LcomexampleFoo583:[Z
6    const/16 v4, 0x1
7    const/16 v5, 0xe
8    aput-boolean v4, v3, v5
9    iget v0, v1, Lcom/example/Foo;->value
       ↪ :I
10   goto/32 :goto_hack_2
11   :goto_hack_back_2
12   add-int/2addr v0, v2
13   goto/32 :goto_hack_1
14   :goto_hack_back_1
15   iput v0, v1, Lcom/example/Foo;->value
       ↪ :I
16   goto/32 :goto_hack_0
17   :goto_hack_back_0
18   return-void
19   :goto_hack_0
20   const/16 v5, 0xb
21   aput-boolean v4, v3, v5
22   goto/32 :goto_hack_back_0
23   :goto_hack_1
24   const/16 v5, 0xc
25   aput-boolean v4, v3, v5
26   goto/32 :goto_hack_back_1
27   :goto_hack_2
28   const/16 v5, 0xd
29   aput-boolean v4, v3, v5
30   goto/32 :goto_hack_back_2
31 .end method
```

(b) Instrumented by ACVTool bytecode

```
1  @@Lcom/example/Foo;->baz(I)V:3
2  @0:p
3  sget-object i0, Ltool/acv/AcvReporter;-
       ↪ >LcomexampleFoo583:[Z
4  const/16 i1, 0x1
5  const/16 i2, 0xe
6  aput-boolean i1, i0, i2
7  @0:a
8  goto/32 :goto_hack_2
9  :goto_hack_back_2
10 @1:a
11 goto/32 :goto_hack_1
12 :goto_hack_back_1
13 @2:a
14 goto/32 :goto_hack_0
15 :goto_hack_back_0
16 @3:a
17 :goto_hack_0
18 const/16 i2, 0xb
19 aput-boolean i1, i0, i2
20 goto/32 :goto_hack_back_0
21 :goto_hack_1
22 const/16 i2, 0xc
23 aput-boolean i1, i0, i2
24 goto/32 :goto_hack_back_1
25 :goto_hack_2
26 const/16 i2, 0xd
27 aput-boolean i1, i0, i2
28 goto/32 :goto_hack_back_2
```

(c) Blueprint segment

Fig. 4. An example blueprint segment for ACVTool

5.2   Blueprint Applicator

Besides designing a prototype blueprint syntax and extending ACVTool to generate blueprints, we also created the prototype blueprint applicator program applybp[7]. It has two functions: apply and merge. The primary function apply is capable of applying any amount of blueprints to a specified set of Smali files. The additional function merge merges multiple blueprints into a single one and outputs the result. This allows us to examine the result of combining two blueprints without actually applying them.

For either function, before looking at any Smali file, applybp first parses all specified blueprint files and merges them into a single data structure. We

---

[7] https://gitlab.com/avdstaaij-academic/citfaa-blueprint-applicator.

do this primarily for register management purposes and to detect incompatible blueprints early, but it has performance advantages as well. If the original program consists of n lines, and the blueprints to apply have a total sum of m line entries, the simple approach of looking up all line entries that affect a Smali line for every line would result in a time complexity of $O(n \cdot m)$. By first merging all blueprints into a single data structure, we can improve on this.

The blueprint syntax has a natural *"method entry → Smali line number → line operation"* tree structure. The blueprint data structure stores this tree using lookup maps (`std::map`). Creating the structure therefore has a time complexity of $O(m \log(m))$: inserting an element into the tree has a complexity of $O(\log(m))$, and there are m lines to insert. After parsing all the blueprint files, applying them to the Smali code has a time complexity of $O(n \log(m))$: looking up a line entry in the data structure is logarithmic. The total complexity therefore becomes $O(m \log(m) + n \log(m))$. If we assume that m grows about as fast as n, which seems realistic (more lines means more instrumented lines), then $O(m \log(m) + n \log(m)) = O(n \log(n))$, which is better than $O(n \cdot m) = O(n^2)$.

If multiple method entries for the same method are encountered, they are merged together. When method entry B is merged into method entry A, the instrumentation register count of A is set to the sum of the counts of A and B. Every line entry from B is added to A, but all instrumentation register indices are increased with the original instrumentation register count of A. For example, if A used three instrumentation registers (`i0`, `i1` and `i2`) and B used two (`i0` and `i1`), the combined method entry uses five, and all line entries that came from B refer to `i3` and `i4` instead of `i0` and `i1`. This ensures that the added lines from each of the method entries do not affect each other.

If multiple line entries for the same line and operation type (*append/prepend/replace*) are encountered, one of two things happens: If the operation is *append* or *prepend*, the Smali contents are simply concatenated. However, like we stated in Sect. 4.1, if there are two replacements for the same line, the blueprints are considered non-composable, and `applybp` aborts with an error message.

Note that the blueprint syntax does not prohibit multiple method entries for the same method or multiple line entries for the same line, so merges (and even replace-conflicts) can occur within a single blueprint. In fact, concatenating multiple blueprint files and then passing them to `applybp` as one large file is equivalent to passing them separately. Using `applybp`'s `merge` function with only a single blueprint as input will squash all duplicate entries. If the `merge` function was chosen, `applybp` prints the result from the merge and exits.

Figure 5 shows an example result of merging two blueprints. Both blueprints have a method entry for `Lcom/example/Foo;->bar(I)V`. Blueprint 1's version uses three instrumentation registers and blueprint 2's version uses two. In the merged blueprint, this method entry therefore uses $3 + 2 = 5$ of them. The `@0:a` line entry from blueprint 2 is added to the `@0:p` and `@0:r` line entries from blueprint 1 without problems. Both `Lcom/example/Foo;->bar(I)V` method entries have a `@1:a` line entry, so the merged blueprint contains the contents of

```
1  @@Lcom/example/Foo;->bar(I)V      1  @@Lcom/example/Foo;->bar(I)V      1  @@Lcom/example/Foo;->bar(I)V
        ↪ :3                              ↪ :2                              ↪ :5
2  @0:p                              2  @0:a                              2  @0:p
3  add-int i0, i1, i2                3  div-int i0, i1, v0                3  add-int i0, i1, i2
4  @0:r                              4  @1:a                              4  @0:r
5  sub-int i0, i1, i2                5  rem-int i0, i1, v0                5  sub-int i0, i1, i2
6  @1:a                              6  @@Lcom/example/Foo;->baz(I)V      6  @0:a
7  mul-int i0, i1, i2                      ↪ :1                         7  div-int i3, i4, v0
                                     7  @0:a                              8  @1:a
                                     8  neg-int i0, v0                    9  mul-int i0, i1, i2
                                                                         10  rem-int i3, i4, v0
                                                                         11  @@Lcom/example/Foo;->baz(I)V
                                                                               ↪ :1
                                                                         12  @0:a
                                                                         13  neg-int i0, v0
```

      (a) Blueprint 1   (b) Blueprint 2   (c) Merged

Fig. 5. The result of merging two blueprints

both. Note how the indices of all instrumentation registers used by the line entry contents that came from blueprint 2's Lcom/example/Foo;->bar(I)V method entry have been incremented by three. A method entry for baz only appears in blueprint 2, so it is included in the merged blueprint without any modifications.

If the apply function was chosen, applybp will proceed with applying the merged blueprint to the specified Smali targets. Targets can be either files or directories: in the case of directory, applybp applies the blueprints to all files in the directory recursively.

Register Management Approach. To manage registers, applybp uses the same method as ACVTool [22] and the tool described by Will [32], because Pilgun has shown that this method is very robust [22]. We increment the number of local registers by the amount of instrumentation registers, then copy the values of the parameters to the v-registers corresponding to their original positions, and then replace all p- and i-register references with their v-equivalents. Figure 6 illustrates the register management process for an example method with one original local register, two parameter registers and three instrumentation registers. Initially, the method has three registers in total, and p0 and p1 are aliases of v1 and v2. After incrementing the local register count with three, there are five registers in total, and the parameter registers point to v4 and v5. The values of the parameter registers are copied back to v1 and v2, leaving v3, v4 and v5 available as instrumentation registers.

When applying the merged blueprint, applybp will read the Smali files line by line, generally copying them directly to its output. When it encounters a method, it will look up if the blueprint contains an entry for it, and if it does, it will apply its line entries. The number in the .locals/.registers line is incremented as specified by the method entry, and move instructions are added to move the parameters to v-registers. Dalvik contains a few different move instructions; the specific one to use depends on the type of the parameter.

The application of line entries is straightforward: prepend contents are added before the line, append contents are added after, and if there is a replace entry,

```
        v0                    v0                    v0
        v1 = p0               v1                    v1 = p0
        v2 = p1               v2                    v2 = p1
                              v3                    v3 = i0
                              v4 = p0               v4 = i1
                              v5 = p1               v5 = i2
```

(a) Initial layout   (b)   Additional   local   (c) Parameters moved
                      registers

Fig. 6. Register management process

the line is replaced with its contents. For every line of Smali written in an instrumented method, whether it comes from the original code or from the blueprint, all p- and i-registers are replaced with their v-equivalents (Fig. 6c).

Our program needs to parse two languages: the blueprint language, and Smali (the blueprint language also contains a subset of the Smali language). We wrote two simple recursive descent parsers for this purpose. Our Smali parser is very limited: it only parses exactly what applybp needs to function, and leaves everything else as strings. An advantage of this is that the parser is fairly future-proof. For example, it does not care about specific instructions, so it will not be affected if new instructions are added to Dalvik.

We ran into quite a few issues while implementing the application part of applybp, mostly because the Smali syntax lacks extensive documentation. We used the Android Emulator in combination with the debug tool logcat [11] to discover and fix any issues we came across. Some notable examples are:

- Two of the types supported Smali, *long* and *double*, are "*wide*": their values occupy two registers instead of one. We had to take this into account for the code that copies p-registers to v-registers.
- Methods that are abstract or native (implemented in native code) are empty in Smali: they do not even contain a .locals/.registers line. Our program ignores these methods when applying blueprints.
- Instead of the operation arg1, arg2, arg3 syntax that is used by almost all Smali instructions, method calls use lists of registers. For example: invoke-direct {p0, v0}, <method-descriptor> (see Fig. 1b). The variant {v0 .. v3} is sometimes used as well.
- Before we clearly defined our policy of which lines are counted for the purpose of blueprint line entry line numbers, some "*block-directives*" caused the counts of applybp and our ACVTool blueprint output to become mismatched. An example of such a block-directive is .packed-switch/.end packed-switch, which corresponds to the packed-switch-payload as described in [1].

Our program is still a prototype, and as such, it still has a few limitations discussed in Sect. 5.4. Our prototype is released to the community[8].

---

[8] https://gitlab.com/avdstaaij-academic/citfaa-blueprint-applicator.

5.3   Evaluation

We tested the correctness of our ACVTool blueprint-generation extension and our blueprint application program `applybp` in a case study, using an app from F-droid[9]. For the case study, we used *Lesser Pad*, a simple note-taking app from F-droid[10]. We generated a blueprint for the it, applied it to the original app using `applybp` and checked whether the resulting app ran without problems on the Android Emulator. As a result, the app, which ran successfully with ACVTool's instrumentation, also did so after being instrumented according the above procedure.

To verify whether ACVTool's coverage-measuring code still functioned correctly when applied through `applybp`, we generated a code coverage report with both a directly instrumented version and an `applybp`-instrumented version of *Lesser Pad*. For both versions, we installed the app on the Android Emulator, opened it, interacted with it for a few seconds, closed it, and then made ACVTool generate a coverage report using the gathered data. The obtained coverage reports were identical. Screenshots of the generated reports can be inspected in [28]. We note that the experiment was rather informal: we did not use a testing framework to repeat the exact same inputs for each version.

We must note that the performance of the blueprint parsing step of `applybp` is rather bad. We expected the difference in speed of the parsing and the application steps to be a small constant factor (see the time complexity discussion in Sect. 5.2). The blueprint application step is virtually instant, so we expected the parsing step to be similarly fast. However, the parsing step takes significantly longer. On our machine, it took ACVTool 8.29 seconds to instrument Lesser Pad (including the unpacking, repacking and re-signing steps) and it took our program 9.91 seconds to parse the blueprint. As the size of the instrumented application increases, the blueprint application time seems to grow faster than the instrumentation time, but we did not investigate this in detail.

The bad blueprint parsing performance may be caused by the fact that the blueprint files generated by ACVTool are extremely large: the blueprint for Lesser Pad consisted of 619 235 lines. The reason for this size is that ACVTool instruments every method, even those from additional libraries provided by Google. Only 29 384 of the 619 235 blueprint lines (about 5%) were for Lesser Pad-specific code. Perhaps the blueprint parsing performance could be improved if blueprints were split into separate files for every class. Do note that the bad parsing performance is not a huge issue, since it only affects the offline blueprint application time. There is no difference in the runtime performance of directly instrumented and `applybp`-instrumented apps.

5.4   Limitations

Although we believe that our blueprint composition approach is promising, it does have a number of limitations. Our blueprint system can only be used

---

[9] https://www.f-droid.org/.

[10] https://f-droid.org/en/packages/org.pulpdust.lesserpad/.

with static instrumentation, since all instrumentation changes have to be known before they are combined. It also requires internal changes to existing instrumentation tools (although a limited form of automatic blueprint generation may be possible). Furthermore, since we use the Smali representation, the implementation of blueprint output will be more difficult for tools that are based on other representations like Jimple. We stated our reasons for using Smali in Sect. 4.1. It may be possible to integrate a translation of Jimple changes to Smali changes into our system, since Jimple is more high-level than Smali.

We already mentioned the limitations of our prototype blueprint syntax in Sect. 5.3. Blueprints can currently only represent changes to method contents: they cannot represent changes to classes, method descriptors, fields or any other components of Smali. They also cannot represent changes to an application's manifest file. Many instrumentation tools need to change the manifest file in order to function. Our current blueprint prototype cannot represent added or removed files either.

These syntax limitations can likely all be alleviated by extending the blueprint syntax. Special entry types could be added to represent added or removed methods, fields or classes (files), and method entry headers could be given additional fields for information such as return value and parameter modifications. The manifest file has a well-defined structure, so a more semantical syntax could be created to represent changes to it, with entries such as *"add <contents> to <xml element>"*.

A minor limitation of our prototype applicator program is that application unpacking and repacking are currently not built in: it can only operate on Smali files or directories thereof. Users have to manually unpack, repack, re-sign and install `applybp`-instrumented apps. This shortcoming can be addressed with updates to the program. Another limitation is the bad blueprint parsing performance. This could be improved by further optimizing the program or by redesigning blueprints to use multiple files.

A general limitation of our work is that we did not perform extensive experiments, and that the experiments we did perform only involved a single instrumentation tool. We therefore do not yet have empirical evidence that shows whether our approach works for most tools, nor whether it actually improves the success rate of instrumentation composition. We plan to address this limitation in the future work.

6   Conclusions and Future Work

To address problems that may occur from the composition of instrumentation tools, we have proposed a two-step approach involving instrumentation blueprints and the application thereof. We have defined a prototype syntax for these blueprints, we have extended the code coverage tool ACVTool [23] to emit blueprints, and we have implemented the program `applybp` that can apply them. We have performed a case study showing that our approach can work in practice. Our proposed blueprint system may offer benefits for the creation of new instrumentation frameworks or the meta-analysis of instrumentation tools.

There are still many aspects that can be explored in future work. First of all, improving the prototype will improve the practical usability of our system. Furthermore, we have only implemented blueprint output for a single instrumentation tool, so a larger-scale investigation of the effectiveness of our system, involving multiple instrumentation tools, is in order. Finally, it would be interesting to explore automated generation of blueprints and to empirically assess challenging arising from combining multiple instrumentation tools.

Acknowledgements. We thank the anonymous reviewers for their useful comments.

References

1. Dalvik bytecode. https://source.android.com/devices/tech/dalvik/dalvik-bytecode
2. Ali-Gombe, A., Ahmed, I., Richard, G.G., Roussev, V.: AspectDroid: Android app analysis system. In: Proceedings of the CODASPY, pp. 145–147 (2016)
3. Anand, S.: ELLA: a tool for binary instrumentation of Android apps. https://github.com/saswatanand/ella
4. Bartel, A., Klein, J., Martin, M., Allix, K., Traon, Y.L.: Improving privacy on Android smartphones through in-vivo bytecode instrumentation. arXiv abs/1208.4536 (2012)
5. Bläsing, T., Batyuk, L., Schmidt, A.D., Camtepe, S., Albayrak, S.: An Android application sandbox system for suspicious software detection. In: Proceedings of Malware, pp. 55–62 (2010)
6. Cai, H., Meng, N., Ryder, B., Yao, D.: DroidCat: effective Android malware detection and categorization via app-level profiling. IEEE Trans. Inf. Forensics Secur. **14**(6), 1455–1470 (2018)
7. Cai, H., Ryder, B.G.: DroidFax: a toolkit for systematic characterization of Android applications. In: Proceedings of ICSME, pp. 643–647 (2017)
8. Davis, B., Sanders, B., Khodaverdian, A., Chen, H.: I-ARM-Droid: a rewriting framework for in-app reference monitors for Android applications. Mob. Secur. Technol. **2012**(2), 1–7 (2012)
9. Ehringer, D.: The Dalvik virtual machine architecture 4(8), 72 (2010). Technical report, March 2010
10. Enck, W., et al.: TaintDroid: an information-flow tracking system for realtime privacy monitoring on smartphones. ACM Trans. Comput. Syst. **32**(2), 1–29 (2014)
11. Google: Logcat command-line tool. https://developer.android.com/studio/command-line/logcat
12. Gruver, B.: Smali/baksmali. https://github.com/JesusFreke/smali
13. Hao, H., Singh, V., Du, W.: On the effectiveness of API-level access control using bytecode rewriting in Android. In: Proceedings of ASIACCS, pp. 25–36 (2013)
14. Horváth, F., Bognár, S., Gergely, T., Rácz, R., Beszédes, Á., Marinkovic, V.: Code coverage measurement framework for Android devices. Acta Cybernet. **21**, 439–458 (2014)
15. Hu, Y., Yan, J., Yan, D., Lu, Q., Yan, J.: Lightweight energy consumption analysis and prediction for Android applications. Sci. Comput. Program. **162**, 132–147 (2017)
16. Huang, C.Y., Chiu, C.H., Lin, C., Tzeng, H.W.: Code coverage measurement for android dynamic analysis tools. In: Proceedings of MobServ, pp. 209–216 (2015)

17. Jenkins, J., Cai, H.: ICC-inspect: supporting runtime inspection of Android inter-component communications. In: Proceedings of MOBILESoft, pp. 80–83 (2018)
18. Jeon, J., et al.: Dr. Android and Mr. Hide: fine-grained permissions in Android applications. In: Proceedings of SPSM, pp. 3–14 (2012)
19. Lantz, P.: Droidbox. https://github.com/pjlantz/droidbox
20. Liu, J., Wu, T., Deng, X., Yan, J., Zhang, J.: InsDal: a safe and extensible instrumentation tool on Dalvik byte-code for Android applications. In: Proceedings of SANER, pp. 502–506 (2017)
21. Pilgun, A.: Acvtool. https://github.com/pilgun/acvtool
22. Pilgun, A.: Instruction coverage for Android app testing and tuning. Ph.D. dissertation, University of Luxembourg (2020)
23. Pilgun, A., Gadyatskaya, O., Zhauniarovich, Y., Dashevskyi, S., Kushniarou, A., Mauw, S.: Fine-grained code coverage measurement in automated black-box Android testing. ACM Trans. Softw. Eng. Methodol. (TOSEM) **29**(4), 1–35 (2020)
24. Qiu, L., Zhang, Z., Shen, Z., Sun, G.: AppTrace: dynamic trace on Android devices. In: Proceedings of ICC, pp. 7145–7150 (2015)
25. Romdhana, A., Ceccato, M., Georgiu, G.C., Merlo, A., Tonella, P.: COSMO: code coverage made easier for Android. In: Proceedings of ICST, pp. 417–423 (2021)
26. Salem, A., Paulus, F.F., Pretschner, A.: Repackman: a tool for automatic repackaging of Android apps. In: Proceedings of A-Mobile, p. 25–28 (2018)
27. Somarriba, O., Zurutuza, U., Uribeetxeberria, R., Delosières, L., Nadjm-Tehrani, S.: Detection and visualization of Android malware behavior. J. Electr. Comput. Eng. **2016**, 1–17 (2016)
28. van der Staaij, A.: Composing instrumentation tools for Android apps. Bachelor's thesis, Leiden University (2021). https://theses.liacs.nl/2176
29. Tam, K., Khan, S., Fattori, A., Cavallaro, L.: CopperDroid: automatic reconstruction of Android malware behaviors. In: Proceedings of NDSS (2015)
30. Tumbleson, C., Wiśniewski, R.: Apktool. https://ibotpeaches.github.io/Apktool/
31. Vallée-Rai, R., Hendren, L.: Jimple: simplifying Java bytecode for analyses and transformations (1998)
32. Will, C.: A framework for automated instrumentation of Android applications (2013)
33. Xu, R., Saïdi, H., Anderson, R.J.: Aurasium: practical policy enforcement for Android applications. In: Proceedings of USENIX Security (2012)
34. Yang, K.: apkil. https://github.com/kelwin/apkil
35. Yang, K.: Beta release of DroidBox for Android 2.3 and APIMonitor. https://web.archive.org/web/20161219204143/. https://www.honeynet.org/node/940
36. Yeh, C.C., Huang, S.K.: CovDroid: a black-box testing coverage system for Android. In: Proceedings of COMPSAC, vol. 3, pp. 447–452 (2015)

SiMLA – Security in Machine Learning and its Applications

A Siamese Neural Network for Scalable Behavioral Biometrics Authentication

Jesús Solano[3], Esteban Rivera[1]([✉]), Lizzy Tengana[4], Christian López[1], Johana Flórez[1], and Martín Ochoa[2]

[1] Appgate Inc., Bogotá, Colombia
{esteban.rivera,christian.lopez,johana.florez}@appgate.com
[2] Department of Computer Science, ETH Zürich, Zürich, Switzerland
[3] University College London, London, UK
[4] Aalto University, Espoo, Finland

Abstract. The rise in popularity of web and mobile applications brings about a need of robust authentication systems. Behavioral Biometrics Authentication has emerged as a complementary risk-based authentication approach which aims at profiling users based on their interaction with computers/smartphones. In this work we propose a novel approach based on Siamese Neural Networks to perform a few-shot verification of user's behavior. We develop our approach to authenticate either human-computer or human-smartphone interaction. For computer interaction, our approach learns from mouse and keyboard dynamics, while for smartphone interaction it learns from holding patterns and touch patterns. The proposed approach requires only one model to authenticate all the users of a system, as opposed to the one model per user paradigm. This is a key aspect with respect to the scalability of our approach. The proposed model exhibits a few-shot classification accuracy of up to 99.8% and 90.8% for mobile and web interactions, respectively. We also test our approach on a database that contains over 100K interactions collected in the wild.

Keywords: Risk-based authentication · Behavioral biometrics · Deep learning · Siamese networks

1 Introduction

Although password authentication is the most popular authentication mechanism, it has several drawbacks [8,45]. Biometric authentication has emerged as a complement to traditional authentication systems [28,29,43]. The main advantage of such systems is that they rely on user's information that can not easily be stolen or crafted. Most active fields of biometric authentication in academia and industry are related to face authentication or fingerprint authentication, with a recent increase in interest on behavioral biometrics. Behavioral Biometrics authentication refers to the use of human-device interaction features to grant access to a specific service. This interaction could include, but is not

J. Zhou et al. (Eds.): ACNS 2022 Workshops, LNCS 13285, pp. 515–535, 2022.
https://doi.org/10.1007/978-3-031-16815-4_28

limited to, typing patterns [21,37], mouse dynamics [36], smartphone holding patterns [1,5,16,24], voice recognition, gait recognition [19,44], etc.

Machine learning algorithms have been proposed to verify users' identity using behavioral biometrics features. Regarding behavioral biometrics in web environments (Human-Computer interaction), most of the work has focused on the use of Support Vector Machine and Random Forest classifiers to analyze mouse and keyboard interaction [21,37]. Alternatively, some works have proposed to use built-in sensors available in mobile devices (i.e. sensors information, touch interaction etc.) for authentication purposes [1,5,31,32,44]. However, previous works in behavioral biometrics usually have three main drawbacks: (1) they need long interactions (minutes) in order to learn accurately the user behavior; (2) they need a model per user to improve system accuracy; or (3) they require ad-hoc interaction challenges.

In this paper, we present a Siamese One-Shot Neural Network (SOS-NN) which is able to assess a risk score after only one observation (i.e. enrollment behavior) of a given user. To achieve this, we propose a Siamese Neural Network architecture that assesses whether two behaviors belong to the same user. We present a similar network architecture for user verification for both web and mobile environments. In web environments, we create a set of features from raw mouse movements and keyboard strokes. On the other hand, for the mobile environment our SOS-NN analyzes features created from touch interaction and motion sensors on the smartphone. For both environments, the proposed set of features successfully built a suitable feature representations of human-device interactions from different behavioral sources (mouse, keyboard, mobile sensors). This feature representation enables the generation of an effective latent space for one-shot biometric authentication.

In sum, the contributions of our work are:

- An accurate few-shot model based on behavioral biometrics information to authenticate users after only 5 s of user interaction;
- A unified neural network architecture to authenticate user's behavior for both mobile and web environments that is able to achieve an accuracy of up to 99.8% and 90.8% respectively;
- A scalable framework which is able to accurately authenticate users without requiring to retrain the model for new users;
- A systematic measurement study to understand the impact of the parameters to SOS-NN based on the authentication time window length and the n number in the n-shot test
- A practical study in the intersection of biometric data and Deep Learning which evaluates in-the-wild our SOS-NN over thousands of users from real financial services.

2   Background

In the field of biometric-based authentication, many sources of information have been proposed. These could be physical (facial recognition, fingerprint scanning, retina scan, etc.) or behavioral patterns (signature verification, mouse dynamics, gait analysis, voice recognition, etc.). Behavioral biometrics has gained increased attention since reproducing the behavior of a legitimate user constitutes an unconventional challenge for attackers. While substantial advances have been achieved, there is still a gap to make such systems widely adopted in practice. We define as 'practical' methods that demand short periods of interaction per user (both for model training and for authentication), and simple architectures that ease deployment and maintenance. This paper proposes a few-shot learning novel approach, which complements traditional authentication in web and mobile environments, considering practical implementation characteristics and scalability constraints.

Web Environment. Multiple previous studies have employed multimodal biometrics in desktop environments to identify user's behaviour [6,14,27,37,40]. These studies propose to integrate, either at the feature or decision level, information from keyboard interaction, mouse dynamics and others. Most of these studies have evaluated classic machine learning classification models (e.g. support vector machine (SVM), Naive Bayes, Random forest and J48 algorithms). Few others [20,21], have explored the use of shallow neural networks.

Regarding user interaction, we highlight that, in multiple real-world applications there is a practical limit to the length of the interaction and amount of data that can be collected before deploying an authentication model. Therefore, we compared previous approaches on the amount of interaction required, per user, to train the model. We are comparable to few studies, that require between 2 min to approximately 30 min of user interaction to train the model. As an illustration, Khan et al. [21] reported an accuracy of 97.3% using an SVM model per user, however, their approach would require recording at least 30 previous login attempts (≈15 min) to train each user's model. A more recent approach proposed by Neha et al. [27] achieves an accuracy of 95.6% after training a multilayer perceptron (MLP) for each user but they required 50 logins (≈25 min) for training phase.

On the scalability perspective, previous studies use authentication paradigms that involve one model per user or multiclass classification, these methods translate into large infrastructure, deployment, monitoring and maintenance challenges. In contrast, our SOS-NN model generates a measure of similarity between two behaviors in a latent feature space. In this case, the question is not whether the sample belongs to a particular user, but rather if the samples are similar enough to conclude that the user is the same. This one-model-for-all (OfA) paradigm facilitates deployment and avoids further training for every new user registered in the system. Acien et al. [2] implements an OfA paradigm as well, but they require longer interactions, like writing an email, instead of just a login, and they save and process the value of the pressed keys, which is completely unacceptable in a banking login environment, where the privacy of the users must be protected above all other aspects.

Mobile Environment. Likewise, behavioral biometrics for authentication has also been implemented for mobile environments. Such models complement traditional authentication by taking advantage of the multiple built-in sensors available in mobile devices, being able to capture user behavior through several modalities. Some modalities rely on the use of mobile keyboard dynamics [11]; touchscreen interaction [31,32]; or embedded motion sensors data [1] to authenticate users. In order to strengthen security, especially against ad-hoc adversarial attacks, multimodal authentication frameworks have been proposed by researchers [3,10,23,25,34,35,38,42]. Those methods rely on the fusion of multiple modalities of behavioral information (i.e. keyboard, sensors, touch, etc.) with the goal of having a better performance. Previous works, have achieved low False Acceptance Rate (FAR) and False Rejection Rates (FRR). However, they require a one-model-per-user paradigm (OpU) and long user interaction times (>10 min), which makes them challenging to use in real world scenarios. In our review, one of the best comparable performances was reported by Stanciu et al. [38], with FAR and FRR equal to 0.14%, nonetheless, the system would require one K-Nearest Neighbors (KNN) model per user and 20 previous logins from the user to train each model. The performance of [12], namely a 97.1% TAR (True Acceptance Rate) at 0.1 % FAR is impressive as well, however, they need to train one model for each of the eight features they process.

Table 3 presents a detailed comparison between the main state-of-the-art studies developed for both web and mobile behavioral biometrics in terms of the classification methods used, the authentication paradigm, user interaction required and model performance.

Siamese Networks. Siamese Neural Networks were first introduced by Bromley et al. [9] to verify hand-written signatures. In general, Siamese networks are composed of two twin sub-networks and a similarity module which compares the outputs of both sub-networks. Consequently, Siamese networks are trained by feeding a pair of inputs which are processed by each twin in the network. Siamese networks have been used for verification tasks because of their capabilities to create embedding representations which minimizes similarity between samples from different classes [7,26]. In the field of behavioral biometrics, Siamese networks have been implemented to approach different behavioral modalities, like face recognition [33,39], signature recognition [13], gait recognition [44], among others. Regarding the use of Siamese networks for behavioral biometrics authentication in web and mobile environments, [10] used Siamese networks along with convolutional neural networks (CNNs) as a tool to create embeddings from motion sensors plots, and then feed them into a one-class SVM classifier. More recently, [15] proposed the use of Siamese networks to approach static authentication model using keyboard dynamics in web environments.

Moreover, Siamese networks have been extensively used to approach classification problems in which the few samples of each class are available to learn from (i.e. *Few-shot Learning*) [18]. Particularly, it is possible to go as far as to limit the number of available samples to only one (*one-shot learning*). In one-shot learning literature, Siamese networks have shown promising results in tackling classification tasks, under the restriction of observing only one sample before making a prediction over a test instance [22, 41]. Even though Siamese Neural Networks have been previously studied, and other applications in different domains have been presented, our novelty relies on proposing a methodology that couples previous knowledge related to architecture, losses, sample generation and data structures, producing a well-performing model in a new domain. The behavioral domain presents its own difficulties inherent to the nature of biometric data, different from the challenges present in other tasks such as object tracking and face recognition tasks.

To the best of our knowledge there are no previous works on the use of Siamese networks to approach multimodal behavioral biometrics authentication agnostic to web or mobile environments. Specifically, our approach differs from others in that it (1) focuses on one-shot learning, (2) implements semi-hard pair selection, (3) learns from different behavioral sources in both web and mobile environment, and (4) needs only one model to process all the feature types. Additionally, this paper is the first to propose an OfA paradigm for web behavioral mouse and keyboard biometric data. Furthermore, we test our approach in a real production case with thousands of users, which has never been reported before.

2.1   Attacker and System Model

System Model. We assume a system where a Monitor ($\mathbb{M}$) on the client-side receives raw mouse and keyboard events as inputs, that is a series $\mathcal{S}_\mathcal{M}$ of mouse events (tuples (x, y, a, t)) where x and y are positions, a is an action and t is a timestamp and a series $\mathcal{S}_\mathcal{K}$ of keyboard events (tuples (k, a, t) where k is the key identifier, a is an action (click, scroll, key-press, key-release, etc.) and t is a timestamp). $\mathbb{M}$ pre-processes each of those traces at a given time interval and ultimately communicates with our SOS-NN, which is in the server-side, by sending the processed feature vectors. Notice that we transform raw sequences into processed features on the client-side in order to ensure privacy of sensitive information. For the scope of this paper, we assume that the classifier resides in a server outside the end-user's device and that communication cannot be tampered with (because security keys are stored in a trusted computing instance for example, or other software protection mechanisms are in place).

Attacker Model. We consider an attacker ($\mathcal{A}$) who is interested in impersonating a user ($\mathcal{U}$) while authenticating into a sensitive service. For the scope of this paper we assume the attacker will manually interact with the system and will behave as they would normally behave when interacting with their laptop or mobile. Replay attacks or more sophisticated automatic impersonation attacks (such as adversarial machine learning attacks for instance) are out of scope of this work.

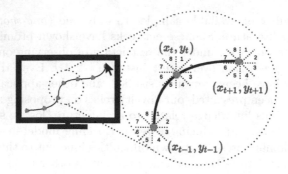

Fig. 1. Features engineering illustration for mouse analysis in web environment.

3   Approach

In this work we propose a deep learning framework to complement traditional authentication systems by analyzing behavioral biometric features. Such framework aims to learn and analyze inherent user behavior while interacting with a device in a few-shot fashion. In particular, we analyze two different environments to learn from users: *Web environments* and *Mobile environments*. For the Web environment we are interested in authenticating users using information from mouse and keyboard dynamics; while for the Mobile environment we focus on the physical sensors like touch, accelerometer, gyroscope and magnetometer.

3.1   Feature Engineering

As we are interested in behavior verification, the first step consists in processing continuous raw data sequences, recorded from the machine-user interaction, and then transform them into readable features for the model. These features do not contain sensitive information like usernames or passwords. Recorded sequences are split into multiple fixed length interaction windows for all the modalities recorded. In this paper we explored the performance of the model for multiple fixed-time windows varying from 5 s to 60 s of user interaction.

Web Environment. For the Web environment, we start out from the raw sequences of mouse movements and key presses. The raw mouse data includes timestamp, pointer coordinates (x, y) and the type of interaction (i.e. click, mouse movement, etc.). We transform the mouse raw data by designing two sets of features, inspired in [4, 36]. These features build a mouse dynamics profile over the movements performed by a user in a fixed-time window. We perform this test by getting and analyzing the next pointer's position (See Fig. 1). To calculate features that capture the direction of the mouse moment, the angular space is split into eight equal bins of 45° and each mouse event in the fixed-time window is classified into one bin. Then, the first set of features is calculated by finding the average movement speed in each of those direction partitions. The second set is the proportion of movements performed in each direction along the

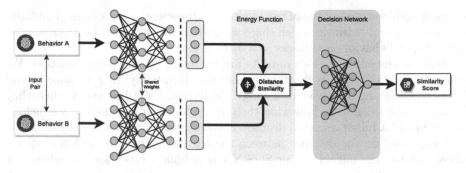

Fig. 2. SOS-NN architecture.

fixed-time window. Mouse dynamics were captured from 16 features (2 sets × 8 directions).

In a similar manner, the keyboard raw data includes the timestamp, key and key interaction (i.e. Press or release). Four sets of keyboard features were created: (1) the length of time from a key is pressed until it is released; (2) the latency from one key is released until the next key is released; (3) the latency between two consecutive keys are pressed; and (4) the length of time from one key is released until the next key is pressed. As a result, for the keyboard dynamics information we build a set of 12 features (4 sets × 3 metrics). Altogether, the feature vector for the web environments contains 28 elements.

Mobile Environment. For the Mobile environment, the raw data is represented by (1) measurements from sensors (gyroscope, magnetometer and accelerometer) and (2) touch inputs performed by the user along the fixed-time window. Regarding the sensor's measurements, we record values in X, Y and Z axes for each sensor. Consequently, we have 9 sequences of sensor measurements (3 sensors x 3 axes). For each sensor sequence, we compute 5 measures of central tendency of the data distribution: mean, standard deviation, median, minimum and maximum. On the other hand, for the touch interaction we record raw data from the touch's center, the touch's pressure and the touch's size. From these records we compute 4 features: mean touch duration, the average number of changes in pressure or touch center within the same touch (down-up) interaction, standard deviation of touch's center (x, y) and mean finger size (touch size area). We added two features related to mobile keyboard interaction, based on latency between consecutive touches. Altogether, for each fixed-time window we have a vector containing 52 features (45 sensors + 5 touch + 2 keyboard).

3.2 Siamese Neural Network

Our Deep Learning framework evaluates if two recorded behaviors belong to the same user. To that end our SOS-NN computes the similarity between two behavior inputs. In that sense, if two inputs are similar enough, our system concludes that the incoming behavior belongs to the legitimate user. The siamese network architecture is made of two identical sub-networks; in our case, two fully-connected neural networks which share weights. Each sub-network processes one of the input behaviors and works as a feature extractor.

Both of the sub-network's outputs are bounded by an energy function. We compute a L_1 *distance* as the energy function. Intuitively, this distance should be large when input behaviors belong to different users but small when they belong to the same user. Following the energy function calculation, we include in our model a fully-connected decision network, which makes the classification decision based on the distance between the feature vectors in the latent space. Consequently, the output of our SOS-NN is a binary classification, where the output is One if behaviors belong to the same user, and Zero otherwise. Figure 2 depicts an illustration of the architecture of the proposed SOS-NN.

Sample Generation. The Siamese networks learn from comparing pairs of behaviors. A positive pair is defined as a pair of two behaviors which belong to the same user, whereas a pair of behaviors from different users is labeled as a negative pair. The model is trained by presenting multiple samples of these pairs, the training goal is to minimize the energy function (i.e. L_1 *distance*) between behaviors in positive pairs, and to maximize the energy function for negative pairs. The quality of retrieved pairs in training will determine the quality of our SOS-NN. The naive selection of those positive and negative pairs is a random selection. This naive approach is fine for the positive pairs but for the negative samples it is crucial to select high quality pairs.

More advanced techniques can be used to select the training samples, like triplet loss technique, which uses simultaneously 3 examples to optimize every training step [17]. For instance, these 3 examples could be carefully selected so that the first two of them belong to a positive match (i.e. two examples that correspond to the same class, namely an anchor *(A)* and a positive example *(P)*) and the last one corresponds to a different class, being a negative example *(N)*. The goal is to minimize the distance in the feature space between examples of the same class and maximize the distance between examples of different classes, which can be expressed as:

$$|f(x_A) - f(x_P)|^2 + \alpha < |f(x_A) - f(x_N)|^2 \tag{1}$$

where α is a margin parameter related to the difficulty of the examples. The final loss can be represented as:

$$L(A, P, N) = max(|f(x_A) - f(x_P)|^2 + \alpha - |f(x_A) - f(x_N)|^2, 0) \tag{2}$$

As in the pair generation, the three examples per triplet can be generated randomly as long as they fulfill the previously named condition. Nevertheless, this strategy would deliver most of the time a small loss, because it is expected that many negative examples produce features with larger distances from the anchors, whose loss ends up adding nothing to the training. A better approach is to pre-select the triplets, by controlling the distances within the triplets. Therefore, the pre-selection could be performed by choosing two kinds of triplets: Hard negatives and Semi-hard negatives. Hard negatives are examples whose feature distances with the anchor are strictly smaller than the distance between the positive example and the anchor [33]. Semi-hard negatives are examples whose distance with the anchor is greater than the positive example, but still inside the margin α [17]. In principle, the Hard negatives deliver the greatest losses, and therefore the strongest convergence, but in practice they could be too aggressive and collapse the loss function. Consequently, we use Semi-hard negatives as our strategy to populate triplets in training phase. On the evaluation we compare two pair generation strategies to feed with the Siamese networks, namely (1) Naive Pair and (2) Semi-hard Triplets.

4   Evaluation

4.1   Experimental Setup

Web Environment Dataset. We collected two datasets under *controlled* and *uncontrolled* conditions. For the *controlled setting*, we used data acquired through the *'Amazon Mechanical Turk' service*[1] by submitting a task of logging on a website designed to capture mouse and keyboard events. Here we collected interactions from 89 worldwide workers who introduced fictitious credentials on the login website. A total of 1374 full login interactions were obtained with an average duration of 26.7 s per session. As for the *uncontrolled setting*, a monitoring system was appended into two real banking login web pages where mouse and keyboard events were recorded. To protect users privacy, the raw data was transformed into features on the client-side before they were sent to the server. In this setting, $\approx$800K sessions worth of interactions were collected from $\approx$125K users, with an average of 22.4 s per session.

Mobile Environment Dataset. We developed a realistic looking Android application simulating different banking activities and equipped with an event logger to record information related to touch, accelerometer, magnetometer and gyroscope events. For keyboard touch events, the timestamp and key value were logged. We collected data from 35 volunteers performing sessions lasting 10 min on average and making up to 372 min in total. Moreover, the volunteers used more than 20 different smartphone devices. Volunteers were mostly IT workers with ages ranging from 20 to 50 years.

Privacy Concerns. Collecting behavior sequences could lead to privacy concerns as personal data like passwords patterns (Keyboard dynamics), user location (Sensor analysis), among others, is being recorded. To ensure privacy of the

---

[1] A service where human workers perform a certain task following instructions defined by the task requester.

information, we transform the raw sequences in the client-side so that no sensitive information leaves the device and send the behavioral biometrics features to be analyzed by our SOS-NN model in the server-side.

Feature Engineering. The behavioral data gathered in controlled settings was subsequently merged into a continuous interaction for each user. Afterwards, the full history per user was split into fixed-time windows. We analyzed time windows of 5, 10, 20, 30 and 60 s of interaction. Next, for each fixed-time window we calculate the features following the methodology described in Sect. 3.1. Regarding the data collected in the wild from real banking domains, since features are pre-computed on the client-side, we collected login sessions with arbitrary durations. Finally, we randomly split the dataset by users, since we wanted to avoid validating with behaviors similar to the ones observed in training. Splitting the dataset by users has been shown to perform better than other train-test schemes in previous verification tasks [22]. Once the features have been calculated, we split the dataset into three disjoint set of users: 64% of the users for training, 16% for validation and 20% for test. Finally, the features were transformed in order to follow a normal distribution by using a non-linear transformation on each feature independently (Quantile Transformation in Scikit-learn [30]).

Networks Configuration. The feature extraction and classification decision is made by a siamese network and decision network respectively, both were built using fully connected architectures. The feature extractor was composed by a couple of dense layers with *ReLU* activation and a last layer with a *Sigmoid* activation. For the decision module, another fully connected network was implemented whose input was the L_1 distance layer between the features in the latent space. We also tested other distances as energy function, like L_2, *Manhattan* and *Cosine* distances as well, but L_1 showed the best results. Regularization, batch normalization and dropouts were also tested for both networks. For the triplet loss we used the `SemiHardTriplets` implementation available on Tensorflow Addons [17]. The best parameter configuration was a mini batch of 100 samples, a learning rate of 0.001, an Adam Optimizer and 200 steps per epoch. Weights were initialized following a normal distribution with zero-mean and standard deviation 0.01. For the feature extraction training with triplet configuration, we use a L_2 distance for triplet loss schema ($\alpha = 1.0$). We implemented our approach using the Tensorflow framework.

Training Strategies. The training procedure depends on the sample generation strategy (naive or triplet). For the naive pair strategy, we train our SOS-NN using a cross entropy objective loss on our binary classifier (same or different user). Therefore, for the naive strategy, we perform the weights optimization over the full network (including both siamese and decision networks), using standard back propagation. Notice that gradient is additive over the tied sub-networks. On the other hand, for the triplet strategy the training is done in two steps: (1) Siamese Network training and (2) decision layer training. To train the Siamese Network, we use the Semi-Hard Triplets procedure [17]. Once the feature extractor is trained, their weights are frozen and the fully connected decision layer is

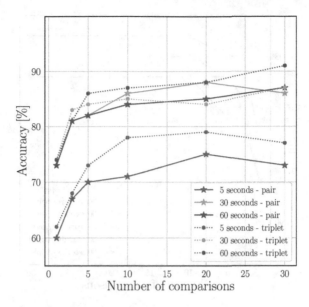

Fig. 3. Accuracy for evaluation over several n-shot comparisons and time window inter-action in web environment

appended to complete the SOS-NN. Lastly, we train the decision layer by using binary cross-entropy as a loss function.

4.2 Results

To understand the capabilities and robustness of our proposed SOS-NN we per-form a systematic evaluation over the model performance for different setups in the training and verification phase. Variables included in this systematic evalua-tion are the sample generation scheme (pair o triplet), interaction time required (fixed-time window length) and the number of samples (n) from previous history to compare with (n-shot testing). For the n-shot testing, the output consists in the average of each individual pair-comparison. At the end of the section, we show an evaluation of our SOS-NN for web environments over a large scale experiment ($\approx$125K of users) to verify that performance remains at the same level under uncontrolled conditions.

Web Environment Results. Figure 3 illustrates the model accuracy in web environments for different configurations. It can be seen, that the verification accuracy is consistently higher for longer time windows in the verification phase. The best verification accuracy obtained for web environment is 90.8%. More-over, we also found a gradual rise in the verification accuracy when the number of comparisons increases. In the *1-shot* and *5-shot* verification tasks our app-roach achieves up to 74% and 86% in verification accuracy respectively. Table 1 summarizes the accuracies for different verification windows requirements with

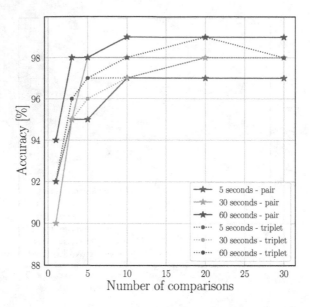

Fig. 4. Accuracy for evaluation over several n-shot comparisons and time window interaction in mobile environment

higher values in darker color. As we expected, the performance of our model is better when analyzing longer times in verification phase. However, more comparisons seems to have a larger effect on accuracy than longer interactions times. For instance, 10 comparisons (*10-shot*) for window lengths of 5 s is better than one comparison (*1-shot*) of 60 s, as can be observed in Table 1b. We believe this is due to multiple comparisons smoothing the score of the incoming fixed-time windows.

Moreover, we observe an improvement of around 4% when using triplet setup for training phase. This improvement is a consequence of better negative sample choices in the training phase, which leads to a more powerful feature extraction at the bottom of our SOS-NN. Consequently, our results confirm that a better choice of behavioral positive and negative samples could moderately improve the performance of our SOS-NN for web environments. Furthermore, the verification accuracy reaches the best values after 10 comparisons (*10-shot*) as it starts fluctuating close to the maximum obtained performance. As can be observed from Fig. 6, the FAR and FRR are 9.8% and 16.2% respectively for classification threshold equal to 0.45.

Table 1. Accuracies for test in Web environment

(a) Accuracies for pair training.

		Time Length [sec]				
		5	10	20	30	60
Comparisons	1	0.60	0.64	0.67	0.73	0.73
	3	0.67	0.71	0.74	0.81	0.81
	5	0.70	0.75	0.78	0.82	0.82
	10	0.71	0.78	0.79	0.86	0.84
	20	0.75	0.80	0.81	0.88	0.85
	30	0.73	0.80	0.82	0.86	0.87

(b) Accuracies for triplet training.

		Time Length [sec]				
		5	10	20	30	60
Comparisons	1	0.62	0.66	0.71	0.74	0.74
	3	0.68	0.75	0.80	0.83	0.81
	5	0.73	0.74	0.79	0.84	0.86
	10	0.78	0.79	0.85	0.85	0.87
	20	0.79	0.80	0.88	0.84	0.88
	30	0.77	0.81	0.86	0.87	0.91

Mobile Environment Results. Results for the mobile environment can be found on Fig. 4. The best verification accuracy obtained is 99.8%. We found a considerable accuracy improvement (5%) when the number of n comparisons increases from 1 to 10 comparisons. However, from 10 comparisons until 30, for all window lengths the accuracy is saturated around 98% for a 60 s window and 97% for a 5 s window. Besides, a 1% difference between a 5 and a 60 s-window suggests that the information collected in the first seconds gives already a satisfactory description of user behavior. The difference between pair and triplet training is not significant. This suggests for high validation accuracy (i.e. >90%), the performance depends more on the architecture of the sub-networks or on data structure aspects instead of the sample generation strategy.

Table 2. Accuracies for test in mobile environment.

(a) Accuracies for pair training.

		Time Length [sec]				
		5	10	20	30	60
Comparisons	1	0.92	0.90	0.93	0.90	0.94
	3	0.95	0.95	0.94	0.95	0.98
	5	0.95	0.95	0.97	0.98	0.98
	10	0.97	0.96	0.98	0.98	0.99
	20	0.97	0.96	0.99	0.98	0.99
	30	0.97	0.97	0.99	0.98	0.99

(b) Accuracies for triplet training.

		Time Length [sec]				
		5	10	20	30	60
Comparisons	1	0.92	0.92	0.91	0.92	0.92
	3	0.96	0.96	0.94	0.95	0.96
	5	0.97	0.97	0.96	0.96	0.97
	10	0.97	0.98	0.97	0.97	0.98
	20	0.98	0.98	0.98	0.98	0.99
	30	0.98	0.99	0.98	0.98	0.98

Finally, if we focus on an ideal setting where there are no restrictions on how much data can be sampled from each user, meaning no limit on comparisons or windows lengths, we achieve a validation accuracy up to 98% for all with windows above 20 comparisons (See Table 2). Nevertheless, in the case of a practical solution (i.e. a company's product) there are some limitations to be taken into account. Here, waiting too much to gather several 60-s windows can compromise the security of the system. In this case, the lesser the time the better: even for

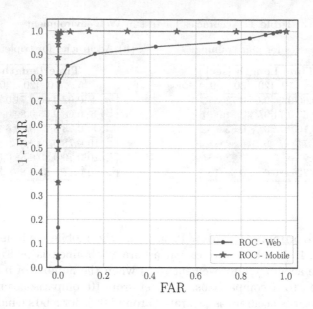

Fig. 5. Receiver Operative Curve (ROC) for the best setup for Web (20 s) and Mobile (5 s) environments. Notice that the True Positive Rate (TPR) is equal to $1 - FRR$ and that FAR is equivalent to the False Negative Rate (FNR).

the case of a 5-s window and only one comparison, namely one-shot inference, we achieve an accuracy of 92%. Our preferred case would be using 3 comparisons, which corresponds to 15 s of interaction, easily collected after only one login session of the user; in this scenario our accuracy is 96%. Figure 5 shows the ROC curve and Fig. 6 shows the FAR and FRR for the best setup in web and mobile environments. The best FAR and FRR are 0.01% and 0.22% respectively for threshold classification equal to 0.4. Remarkably, our SOS-NN achieves an AUC of 0.99 in mobile environment (See Fig. 5).

Evaluation in the Wild. In order to reach a deep understanding on how our SOS-NN behaves in the wild at a large scale, we tested the framework with over 100 thousand real users from legitimate banking domains. Figure 7 depicts the verification accuracy of our approach evaluated in real web sessions. First of all, we simulated the same setting we had in the controlled experiment: we trained with 50 users and tested with the remaining users. In this baseline, the verification accuracy for *1-shot* testing is 63% and 68% for pair and triplet training respectively. Notice that this performance value is very close to metrics we had for the controlled dataset for a time window length of 10 s. Recall that 75% of sessions in the uncontrolled dataset lasted less than 10 s. In like manner, the accuracy when testing in a *5-shot* and a *10-shot* fashion is up to 75% and 79% respectively.

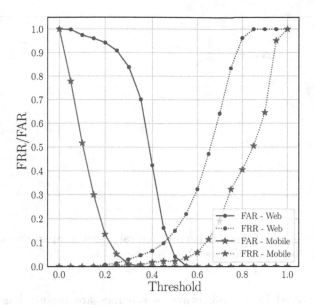

Fig. 6. FAR and FRR for all classification thresholds for the best setup for Web (20 s) and Mobile (5 s) environments.

More importantly, we investigated how the model performance increases when more data is considered to train it. Accordingly, we study the verification accuracy or our SOS-NN when behavioral data from 25K, 75K or 100K different users is included in the training set. Figure 7 shows the verification accuracy for different *n-shot* configurations when different amounts of users in training data are used. From Fig. 7 we can observe that model performance jumps when more user's behaviors are in the training phase. In general, the rise in verification accuracy when training with 25K in comparison with 50 users is about 9%. In addition, we do not observe sharp improvements when training with more than 25K users. We believe this is happening because the behavior of 25K users is complex enough to force the network to learn the differences in the latent space among a diverse spectrum of user behaviors. This finding suggests that, for behavioral biometric data, there could be a limit to the representational power of the data in the latent space, this is an interesting insight for future research on siamese neural networks applied to structured data.

Discussion. As shown, our SOS-NN is able to accurately classify behaviors for short and long interaction windows, and therefore it is suitable as a competitive, maintainable and lightweight mechanism for authentication in contrast to previous works. Table 3 shows a detailed comparison of our SOS-NN with previous works in terms of model inputs, model performance, authentication paradigm, required amount of user interaction to train the model and required amount of interaction to authenticate the user, once the model has been trained. Firstly,

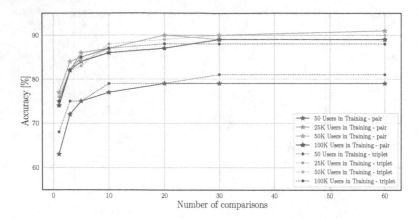

Fig. 7. Accuracy results for evaluation over several n-shot comparisons for web behaviors collected in the wild (125K users).

as can be observed in Table 3, previous schemes are mainly based on either one model per user or a multiclass classification, which could result in a resource intensive implementation in the real world and arguably not as scalable for thousands or even millions of users as our proposed one-for-all approach. In fact, for multiclass classification paradigm the model has to be re-trained every time a new user is added; while for the one-model-per-user a model has to be trained for new user in the service (requiring high volumes of data for each new user). By comparison, after training with a certain quantity of data our SOS-NN is ready to be deployed and used with any user, even if it has not seen before by the system.

Additionally, we studied the system performance in a real authentication scenario, where requiring short interaction windows and rapidly deploy a model that can assess a risk score for the user can be a large advantage. The majority of examples in the related work require minutes or even hours of interactions or tenths of logins to achieve their performance (See Table 3). Alternatively, our approach could authenticate the user after only 25 s to 3 min with an accuracy of 92% to 99% in Mobile environment, while for Web environment it is between 73% to 85%. We understand the performance achieved in Web Environment could seem relatively low, but that is because we push to the limit the capabilities of the model to learn behaviors even from very short interactions as a trade-off between accuracy and promptness of assessment.

Finally, the difference of performance between web and mobile environments is noteworthy. The complete framework behaves way better with mobile data, even when the architecture and training procedure are the same. Recall that for the mobile environment a few seconds of interaction are enough for the model to achieve 99% of accuracy. This can be explained given that our model receives the devices' sensors input even when the user is not actively interacting with the application and is only holding the device. On the other hand, the web

Table 3. Related work - Web and mobile behavioral biometric authentication

	Reference	Input	Paradigm	Performance	Training & authentication interaction per user
Web	[20]	K, M	OpU	Acc. 82.2%	Tr: ≈11 min Auth: ≈30 s
	[14]	K, M, St	MC	FAR 0.004% FRR 0.01%	Tr: 33.6 h Auth: 30 s
	[21]	K, M	OpU	Acc. 97.3%	Tr: ≈17 min Auth: ≈30 s
	[27]	K, M	MC	Acc. 95.6%	Tr: ≈25 min Auth: ≈30 s
	[37]	K, M	OpU	Acc. 85%	Tr: 2 min Auth: 30 s
	[2]	K	OfA	EER 3.35%	Tr: 3 min Auth: 3 min
	Ours	K, M	**OfA**	FAR 3.62% FRR 27.3% EER 13.1% Acc. 88.4%*	Tr: 6.6 min Auth: 20 s
Mobile	[35]	K, TI	OpU	EER 7.16 %	Tr: ≈10 min Auth: ≈20 s
	[34]	TI, MS	OpU	FRR 6.85% FAR 5.01%	Tr: ≈250 min Auth:3 s
	[38]	K, MS	OpU	EER 0.14%	Tr: ≈3 min Auth: ≈15 s
	[10]	MS	OpU	Acc 95.8%	Tr: ≈4.5 min Auth:2 s
	[42]	MS, TI	OpU	EER 15%	Tr:≈ 80 min Auth: ≈ 9 min
	[12]	EMS, TI, GPS	SfA	TAR 97.1% FAR 0.1%	Tr: 20 s Auth: 3 s
	Ours	MS, K, TI	**OfA**	FAR 0.01% FRR 0.22% EER: 0.10% Acc. 96.2%*	Tr: 15 s Auth: 5 s

Input: K: Keyboard Interaction, M: Mouse Dynamics, MS: Motion Sensors, EMS: Extended Motion Sensors, TI: Touchscreen Interaction, GPS: Global Positioning System, GUI: Gui Features, St: Stylometry Features, AppU: App-usage time.
Paradigm: OpU: One Model per User, MC: Multi-Class Classification, OfA: One Model for All, SfA: Several models for All
Performance: EER: Equal Error Rate, FAR: False Acceptance Rate, FRR: False Rejection Rate, TAR: True Acceptance Rate, Acc.: Accuracy.
Tr/Auth Interaction: ME: Mouse Events, KS: Key strokes.
***For both web and mobile, those are not the best accuracies that we could achieve, but they are the best trade-off between interaction time and performance.**

environment depends on the user interacting with the peripherals (mouse & keyboard), otherwise the system goes blind due to insufficient input data to make a valuable prediction, as seen in Fig. 3. This means that our web system needs more data, and therefore more time to be able to complement the authentication, but nonetheless can achieve reasonable performances of up to 90% of accuracy.

Scalability. Besides the advantages in data required for training and inference, our SOS-NN is a scalable framework ready to be deployed to millions of users without increasing the deployment complexity. Firstly, as our SOS-NN is based on the one-model-for-all (OfA) users paradigm it is only necessary to train/store one model. Consequently, the system architecture is simplified due to the fact that only one universal service is required to be available. Furthermore, no re-training is needed when new users are added to the systems, which is particularly important when scaling a computing cluster both horizontal and vertically. More-over, it is required that a scalable framework handles a high volume of request (millions) simultaneously. One way to accomplish this requirement while mini-mizing the computing resources could be by decreasing the inference time of the model, so the system could process more request per second. The inference time of our SOS-NN is 17 ms, which faster (44%) than inference times reported in the literature [37].

On the other hand, this model not only is accurate but also light, ≈120 Kb and ≈70 Kb for mobile and web, respectively. In that sense, the storage required to serve 1M of users in our SOS-NN is ≈1 GB, which is the sum of ≈100 Kb of the model plus the store of the enrollment behaviors ($1'000.000 x 1$ Kb). Previous works in literature developed one-model-per-user strategies where each model size is about ≈ 100 Kb per user, which means that for a system of 1M of users 100 GB are required [37].

5   Conclusion

In this paper we have presented an effective feature representation for human-device interactions from different behavioral sources (mouse, keyboard, mobile sensors), that enables the generation of a latent space effective for biometric authentication. Our approach is based on Siamese Neural Network models to learn user behavior in both web and mobile environments. Remarkably, our model obtained high accuracy even when tested in a few-shot fashion, that is, needing only a few behavior samples per user. We also showed that the proposed feature representation and model architecture can be easily adapted to both web and mobile interactions. Furthermore, our methodology has been proved in large scale in-the-wild scenarios and over different behavioral sources. Our system exhibits the potential to rapidly scale in production environments because it needs only one model to evaluate behavior of many users. Besides, as we do not process the key values of the keyboard, and all the features can be calculated on the client side, our system protects the privacy and data of the users, which is essential for login in banking applications, our principal use case. Finally, we evaluated our approach on various datasets, including production data from thousands of users in a web-application. Finally, our proposed methodology exhibits interesting insights about how biometric data and Deep Learning could be integrated in realistic scenarios, setting a precedent for future studies in the field.

References

1. Abuhamad, M., Abuhmed, T., Mohaisen, D., Nyang, D.H.: AUToSen: deep learning-based implicit continuous authentication using smartphone sensors. IEEE Internet of Things J. **7**, 5008–5020 (2020)
2. Acien, A., Monaco, J.V., Morales, A., Vera-Rodríguez, R., Fiérrez, J.: TypeNet: scaling up keystroke biometrics. CoRR abs/2004.03627 (2020). https://arxiv.org/abs/2004.03627
3. Acien, A., Morales, A., Vera-Rodriguez, R., Fierrez, J., Tolosana, R.: Multilock: mobile active authentication based on multiple biometric and behavioral patterns. In: 1st International Workshop on Multimodal Understanding and Learning for Embodied Applications, pp. 53–59 (2019)
4. Ahmed, A.A.E., Traore, I.: A new biometric technology based on mouse dynamics. IEEE Trans. Dependable Secure Comput. **4**(3), 165–179 (2007)
5. Amini, S., Noroozi, V., Pande, A., Gupte, S., Yu, P.S., Kanich, C.: DeepAuth: a framework for continuous user re-authentication in mobile apps. In: Proceedings of the 27th ACM International Conference on Information and Knowledge Management, pp. 2027–2035 (2018)
6. Bailey, K.O., Okolica, J.S., Peterson, G.L.: User identification and authentication using multi-modal behavioral biometrics. Comput. Secur. **43**, 77–89 (2014)
7. Boenninghoff, B., Nickel, R.M., Zeiler, S., Kolossa, D.: Similarity learning for authorship verification in social media. In: 2019 IEEE International Conference on Acoustics, Speech and Signal Processing (ICASSP), ICASSP 2019, pp. 2457–2461. IEEE (2019)
8. Bonneau, J., Herley, C., van Oorschot, P.C., Stajano, F.: The quest to replace passwords: a framework for comparative evaluation of Web authentication schemes. Technical report. UCAM-CL-TR-817, University of Cambridge, Computer Laboratory (2012). https://www.cl.cam.ac.uk/techreports/UCAM-CL-TR-817.pdf
9. Bromley, J., Guyon, I., LeCun, Y., Säckinger, E., Shah, R.: Signature verification using a "Siamese" time delay neural network. In: Advances in Neural Information Processing Systems, pp. 737–744 (1994)
10. Centeno, M.P., Guan, Y., van Moorsel, A.: Mobile based continuous authentication using deep features. In: Proceedings of the 2nd International Workshop on Embedded and Mobile Deep Learning, pp. 19–24 (2018)
11. Cilia, D., Inguanez, F.: Multi-model authentication using keystroke dynamics for smartphones. In: 2018 IEEE 8th International Conference on Consumer Electronics-Berlin (ICCE-Berlin), pp. 1–6. IEEE (2018)
12. Deb, D., Ross, A., Jain, A.K., Prakah-Asante, K.O., Prasad, K.V.: Actions speak louder than (pass)words: passive authentication of smartphone users via deep temporal features. CoRR abs/1901.05107 (2019). http://arxiv.org/abs/1901.05107
13. Dey, S., Dutta, A., Toledo, J.I., Ghosh, S.K., Lladós, J., Pal, U.: SigNet: convolutional siamese network for writer independent offline signature verification. arXiv preprint arXiv:1707.02131 (2017)

14. Fridman, L., et al.: Multi-modal decision fusion for continuous authentication. Comput. Electr. Eng. **41**, 142–156 (2015)
15. Giot, R., Rocha, A.: Siamese networks for static keystroke dynamics authentication. In: 2019 IEEE International Workshop on Information Forensics and Security (WIFS), pp. 1–6. IEEE (2019)
16. Ehatisham-ul Haq, M., Azam, M.A., Naeem, U., Amin, Y., Loo, J.: Continuous authentication of smartphone users based on activity pattern recognition using passive mobile sensing. J. Netw. Comput. Appl. **109**, 24–35 (2018)
17. Hermans, A., Beyer, L., Leibe, B.: In defense of the triplet loss for person re-identification. arXiv preprint arXiv:1703.07737 (2017)
18. Hindy, H., et al.: Leveraging Siamese networks for one-shot intrusion detection model. arXiv preprint arXiv:2006.15343 (2020)
19. Hoang, T., Nguyen, T.D., Luong, C., Do, S., Choi, D.: Adaptive cross-device gait recognition using a mobile accelerometer. JIPS **9**(2), 333 (2013)
20. Jagadeesan, H., Hsiao, M.S.: A novel approach to design of user re-authentication systems. In: 2009 IEEE 3rd International Conference on Biometrics: Theory, Applications, and Systems, pp. 1–6. IEEE (2009)
21. Arif Khan, F., Kunhambu, S., Chakravarthy G, K.: Behavioral biometrics and machine learning to secure website logins. In: Thampi, S.M., Madria, S., Wang, G., Rawat, D.B., Alcaraz Calero, J.M. (eds.) SSCC 2018. CCIS, vol. 969, pp. 667–677. Springer, Singapore (2019). https://doi.org/10.1007/978-981-13-5826-5_52
22. Koch, G., Zemel, R., Salakhutdinov, R.: Siamese neural networks for one-shot image recognition. In: ICML Deep Learning Workshop, Lille, vol. 2 (2015)
23. Lamiche, I., Bin, G., Jing, Y., Yu, Z., Hadid, A.: A continuous smartphone authentication method based on gait patterns and keystroke dynamics. J. Ambient. Intell. Humaniz. Comput. **10**(11), 4417–4430 (2018). https://doi.org/10.1007/s12652-018-1123-6
24. Li, Y., Hu, H., Zhou, G.: Using data augmentation in continuous authentication on smartphones. IEEE Internet Things J. **6**(1), 628–640 (2018)
25. Lin, H., Liu, J., Li, Q.: TDSD: a touch dynamic and sensor data based approach for continuous user authentication. In: PACIS, p. 294 (2018)
26. Melekhov, I., Kannala, J., Rahtu, E.: Siamese network features for image matching. In: 2016 23rd International Conference on Pattern Recognition (ICPR), pp. 378–383. IEEE (2016)
27. Neha, Chatterjee, K.: Continuous user authentication system: a risk analysis based approach. Wirel. Pers. Commun. **108**(1), 281–295 (2019). https://doi.org/10.1007/s11277-019-06403-0
28. Nishiuchi, N., Aoki, S.: Study on soft behavioural biometrics to predict consumer's interest level using web access log. Int. J. Biometrics **11**(3), 243–256 (2019). https://doi.org/10.1504/IJBM.2019.100838
29. Patel, Y.: The state of play - traditional versus behavioural biometrics. Biometric Technol. Today **2019**(2), 5–7 (2019). https://doi.org/10.1016/S0969-4765(19)30024-4
30. Pedregosa, F., et al.: Scikit-learn: machine learning in Python. J. Mach. Learn. Res. **12**, 2825–2830 (2011)
31. Rauen, Z.I., Anjomshoa, F., Kantarci, B.: Gesture and sociability-based continuous authentication on smart mobile devices. In: Proceedings of the 16th ACM International Symposium on Mobility Management and Wireless Access, pp. 51–58 (2018)

32. Rocha, R., Carneiro, D., Costa, R., Analide, C.: Continuous authentication in mobile devices using behavioral biometrics. In: Novais, P., Lloret, J., Chamoso, P., Carneiro, D., Navarro, E., Omatu, S. (eds.) ISAmI 2019. AISC, vol. 1006, pp. 191–198. Springer, Cham (2020). https://doi.org/10.1007/978-3-030-24097-4_23

33. Schroff, F., Kalenichenko, D., Philbin, J.: FaceNet: a unified embedding for face recognition and clustering. In: Proceedings of the IEEE Conference on Computer Vision and Pattern Recognition, pp. 815–823 (2015)

34. Shen, C., Yu, T., Yuan, S., Li, Y., Guan, X.: Performance analysis of motion-sensor behavior for user authentication on smartphones. Sensors **16**(3), 345 (2016)

35. Sitová, Z., et al.: HMOG: new behavioral biometric features for continuous authentication of smartphone users. IEEE Trans. Inf. Forensics Secur. **11**(5), 877–892 (2015)

36. Solano, J., Camacho, L., Correa, A., Deiro, C., Vargas, J., Ochoa, M.: Risk-based static authentication in web applications with behavioral biometrics and session context analytics. In: Zhou, J., et al. (eds.) ACNS 2019. LNCS, vol. 11605, pp. 3–23. Springer, Cham (2019). https://doi.org/10.1007/978-3-030-29729-9_1

37. Solano, J., Tengana, L., Castelblanco, A., Rivera, E., Lopez, C., Ochoa, M.: A few-shot practical behavioral biometrics model for login authentication in web applications. In: NDSS Workshop on Measurements, Attacks, and Defenses for the Web (MADWeb 2020) (2020)

38. Stanciu, V.D., Spolaor, R., Conti, M., Giuffrida, C.: On the effectiveness of sensor-enhanced keystroke dynamics against statistical attacks. In: Proceedings of the Sixth ACM Conference on Data and Application Security and Privacy, pp. 105–112 (2016)

39. Taigman, Y., Yang, M., Ranzato, M., Wolf, L.: DeepFace: closing the gap to human-level performance in face verification. In: Proceedings of the IEEE Conference on Computer Vision and Pattern Recognition, pp. 1701–1708 (2014)

40. Traore, I., Woungang, I., Obaidat, M.S., Nakkabi, Y., Lai, I.: Combining mouse and keystroke dynamics biometrics for risk-based authentication in web environments. In: 2012 Fourth International Conference on Digital Home, pp. 138–145. IEEE (2012)

41. Triantafillou, E., Zemel, R., Urtasun, R.: Few-shot learning through an information retrieval lens. In: Advances in Neural Information Processing Systems, pp. 2255–2265 (2017)

42. Volaka, H.C., Alptekin, G., Basar, O.E., Isbilen, M., Incel, O.D.: Towards continuous authentication on mobile phones using deep learning models. Procedia Comput. Sci. **155**, 177–184 (2019)

43. Yampolskiy, R.V., Govindaraju, V.: Behavioural biometrics: a survey and classification. Int. J. Biometrics **1**(1), 81–113 (2008). https://doi.org/10.1504/IJBM.2008.018665

44. Zhang, C., Liu, W., Ma, H., Fu, H.: Siamese neural network based gait recognition for human identification. In: 2016 IEEE International Conference on Acoustics, Speech and Signal Processing (ICASSP), pp. 2832–2836. IEEE (2016)

45. Zheng, N., Paloski, A., Wang, H.: An efficient user verification system via mouse movements. In: Proceedings of the 18th ACM Conference on Computer and Communications Security, pp. 139–150. ACM (2011)

A Methodology for Training Homomorphic Encryption Friendly Neural Networks

Moran Baruch[1,2] (ID), Nir Drucker[1(✉)] (ID), Lev Greenberg[1] (ID),
and Guy Moshkowich[1] (ID)

[1] IBM Research, Haifa, Israel
nir.drucker@ibm.com
[2] Bar Ilan University, Ramat Gan, Israel

Abstract. Privacy-preserving deep neural network (DNN) inference is a necessity in different regulated industries such as healthcare, finance, and retail. Recently, homomorphic encryption (HE) has been used as a method to enable analytics while addressing privacy concerns. HE enables secure predictions over encrypted data. However, there are several challenges related to the use of HE, including DNN size limitations and the lack of support for some operation types. Most notably, the commonly used ReLU activation is not supported under some HE schemes.

We propose a structured methodology to replace ReLU with a quadratic polynomial activation. To address the accuracy degradation issue, we use a pre-trained model that trains another HE-friendly model, using techniques such as 'trainable activation' functions and knowledge distillation. We demonstrate our methodology on the AlexNet architecture, using the chest X-Ray and CT datasets for COVID-19 detection. Experiments using our approach reduced the gap between the F_1 score and accuracy of the models trained with ReLU and the HE-friendly model to within a mere 0.32–5.3% degradation. We also demonstrate our methodology using the SqueezeNet architecture, for which we observed 7% accuracy and F_1 improvements over training similar networks with other HE-friendly training methods.

Keywords: Deep learning · Homomorphic encryption · HE-friendly neural networks · DNN training · AlexNet · SqueezeNet

1 Introduction

The ability to run deep neural network (DNN) inference on untrusted cloud environments is becoming critical for many industries such as healthcare, finance, and retail. Doing so while adhering to privacy regulations such as HIPAA [7] and GDPR [15] is not trivial. For example, consider a hospital that wishes to analyze and classify medical images (e.g., [20,43]) on the cloud. Regulations may force the hospital to encrypt these images before uploading them to the cloud; this would normally require that the data first be decrypted before any analytical evaluation can be done.

© The Author(s), under exclusive license to Springer Nature Switzerland AG 2022
J. Zhou et al. (Eds.): ACNS 2022 Workshops, LNCS 13285, pp. 536–553, 2022.
https://doi.org/10.1007/978-3-031-16815-4_29

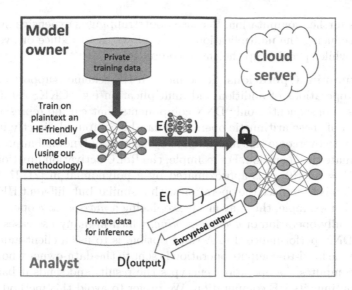

Fig. 1. This paper focuses on the model-owner training task. A typical flow for running DNN over HE spans over three entities: a model owner, a cloud server, and an analyst. The model owner **trains an unencrypted HE-friendly DNN model**, encrypts it, and uploads it to the cloud. Next, the analyst encrypts some private samples and also uploads them to the cloud. Finally, the cloud processes the encrypted data using the encrypted model and returns the results to the analyst for decryption.

Homomorphic encryption (HE), which allows computation over encrypted data, is one of the recent promising approaches to help maintain the confidentiality of private data in untrusted environments. At its core, an HE scheme provides three capabilities: encryption (Enc), evaluation ($Eval$), and decryption (Dec). The data owner, say the hospital in our example, can encrypt a message m by invoking $c = Enc(m)$ and then upload the ciphertext c to the cloud, together with some function f that it wishes to evaluate on m. Subsequently, the cloud evaluates $c' = Eval(f, c)$ without learning anything about m or the value that c' encrypts. The function returns the encrypted results to the data-owner, who can decrypt it using $m' = f(m) = Dec(c')$ and get the desired results. For further information on HE, see [17].

HE for DNN inference is an active research topic [18,21,36] focused on using a trained DNN model to classify encrypted data. Figure 1 illustrates the overall process and highlights the training phase; this training is done by the model owner on unencrypted data and is the focus of this paper. In practice, the training task is not trivial due to possible limitations of the HE scheme. We describe two principal challenges of HE inference.

Multiplication Depth. Multiplication depth is defined as the longest chain of sequential multiplication operations in the HE evaluated function. Some HE schemes only allow for a certain number of consecutive multiplication operations. To tackle this challenge, such schemes use a *bootstrapping* operation [16] that allows further computation. Because bootstrapping is expensive in terms of run-time, reducing the multiplication depth allows us to reduce or avoid bootstrapping, while speeding up the entire computation.

Non-polynomial Operations. Some modern HE schemes support only basic arithmetic operations of addition and multiplication e.g., CKKS [8] and BGV [6] schemes. Consequently, only DNN components that can be represented as a composition of these arithmetic operations can be computed directly in HE.

One way to overcome this limitation is by using a polynomial approximation to approximate the operation. For example, the ReLU activation function defined as $ReLU(x) = max(0, x)$ is approximated by a polynomial in [21, 27, 35, 41]. A second option is to replace the operation with a similar but different HE-friendly operation. For example, this may involve replacing a *max-pooling* operation with the HE-friendly operation of *average-pooling*, which in many use cases does not affect the DNN performance [18]. A third option, is to use a client-aided design [31], where the hard-to-compute operation is sent to the data-owner who decrypts the data, computes the operation, encrypts the result, and sends it back to the cloud to continue its HE computation. We prefer to avoid this method because, in addition to the communication complexity, it increases the attack surface and opens the door to theoretical attacks such as those suggested by Akavia et al. [3] or model-extraction attacks as presented by Li [28]. We summarize our research question.

Research Question. Can we find a methodology for modifying DNN architectures and their training process to produce a HE-friendly model with similar prediction accuracy as the original DNN?

1.1   Our Contributions

We propose a new methodology that combines several techniques for adapting and training HE-friendly DNNs on the plaintext, to enable homomorphic inference over encrypted data. In these DNNs, we replace the ReLU activations by customized quadratic polynomial activation functions. Our methodology also enables the entire inference process to occur in the cloud environment, without interaction with the data-owner. We show empirically that the resulting inference accuracy is comparable with the inference accuracy of our *baseline*, the original DNN with the ReLU activation function.

Our customized activation functions apply the following techniques:

- Low-degree polynomial activation functions with trainable coefficients
- Method for gradual replacement of the original activation functions during the training phase
- Adaptation of the knowledge distillation (KD) technique [22] to train an HE-friendly model from a pre-trained baseline model in its vanilla settings

We evaluated the efficiency of our method on two different model architectures, AlexNet [25] and SqueezeNet [23], for the task of COVID-19 detection over CT and chest X-ray (CXR) images of size $224 \times 224 \times 3$. We chose these datasets for their relevance to the current pandemic, as it may enable hospitals to evaluate COVID-19 cases on the cloud, and analyze them globally. In addition, we prefer these datasets over more standard datasets such as MNIST or CIFAR-10, which have much smaller image sizes: $28 \times 28 \times 1$ and $32 \times 32 \times 3$, respectively; as a result, their DNN models are also much smaller. For completeness, we also evaluated our methodology on CIFAR-10 images that were resized to $224 \times 224 \times 3$, and showed that our methodology outperforms previous works, even when using the original AlexNet.

Our results for AlexNet demonstrated a minimal degradation of up to 5.3% in the F_1 score, compared to the original baseline models. For both architectures, we improved the F_1 score by 4%–10% compared with HE-friendly networks that we trained using state-of-the-art methods. Note that we chose to demonstrate our methodology on AlexNet and SqueezeNet as these are, to the best of our knowledge, the deepest HE-friendly architectures that were demonstrated to run encrypted within a reasonable amount of time over large images. Other architectures such as VGG-16, MobileNet, and ResNet-20 were either demonstrated for non-HE-friendly, client-aided solutions [5] or over datasets with smaller images such as CIFAR-10 with images of size $32 \times 32 \times 3$ as in [33]. Our trained models are available online[1].

Organization. The paper is organized as follows. Section 2 surveys the relevant literature. Section 3 presents our methodology and the techniques we used. We present our experiments in Sect. 4 and conclude in Sect. 5.

2   Related Work

The ReLU function uses the non-polynomial *max* operation, which is not supported by some HE schemes such as CKKS. These schemes can only address this limitation using methods such as lookup tables and polynomial approximations.

Using lookup tables to approximate ReLU was introduced in [26,37], and was used to homomorphically train DNNs in [32,36]. One disadvantage of this approach is the low resolution of the lookup table, which is limited by the number of lookup table entries. This number is significantly lower than the number of values possible in a single or double floating-point number. In addition, this technique is not available for all HE schemes, such as CKKS.

The second approach involves techniques to replace the ReLU activation function with a polynomial approximation function. This can be done using an analytical method to approximate the polynomial or machine learning to train the polynomial coefficients. The work of Cheon et al. [9] describes a method for approximating the generic *max* function. However, using this method often leads to a high degree polynomial approximation, which increases the multiplication depth and the accumulated noise. In addition, this approximation is applicable only when the input operands are limited to a specific range. Unlike

---

[1] https://ibm.ent.box.com/folder/161803670185?v=fhe-friendly-models.

the above methods that can approximate generic functions, we are interested in ReLU. ReLU is a special case of the *max* function, where one of the *max* input operands is fixed to zero. Hence, it is possible to use other approximation methods that yield polynomials with even lower degrees and better performance, while improving the overall efficiency.

The square function $(square(x) = x^2)$ [18] is a well-known low-degree polynomial replacement for the ReLU function. However, when the number of layers in the model grows, the accuracy of the model degrades significantly. To mitigate this degradation, several works [21,27,35,41] suggested using a higher-degree polynomial, which again leads to high multiplication depth. For example, Lee et al. [27] used polynomial approximation with degrees 15 and 27. However, these polynomials had to use bootstrapping twice for each activation function. The excessive use of bootstrapping caused them to report the results only for a 98-bit secure solution. In contrast, our method enabled the authors of [2] to run the AlexNet model on large images using 128-bit security and without any bootstrap operations.

Another mitigation suggested by Wu et al.[41] approximated ReLU using the quadratic polynomial $0.00047x^2 + 0.5x$ instead of a simple square function. To evaluate the performance of their methods, the authors use a lighter variant of AlexNet [25] with images of size $32 \times 32 \times 3$. We tested their approach on the original AlexNet architecture with larger images of size $224 \times 224 \times 3$. As reported in Sect. 4, this approximation suffers from a degradation in accuracy of up to 35%.

The studies above searched for a ReLU replacement that would serve as a good polynomial approximation. They then replace all the ReLU occurrences in a model with this approximation. In contrast, we consider a fine-tuning approach, in which we use a different activation per layer, without necessarily approximating the ReLU activation function. To this end, we used a DNN to train the coefficients of the different polynomials. We call this technique 'trainable activation'[2].

A similar approach was suggested in other works [37,39,45], in which the authors trained a polynomial per neuron in small networks of several dozens of neurons. Clearly, this approach is not feasible in modern networks, where the number of neurons is in the order of millions and the number of parameters requiring optimization is huge.

Instead of training a polynomial per neuron, Wu et al. [44] suggested training a polynomial per layer, for all channels together. They evaluated their activation functions on 3 models, where the largest model has 4 convolutional layers, 2 average-pooling layers, 2 fully-connected layers, and 3 polynomial activations, accompanied by a batch normalization layer. The experiments were applied on the MNIST dataset, which consists of images of size $28 \times 28 \times 1$. We scaled up this approach by using a larger model (see Appendix A), over larger images, and extended their methodology by combining additional techniques to help the

---

[2] Other names suggested in previous works are "parametric activation" [44] and "adaptive polynomial activation" [37,39,45].

model converge better. Our evaluation shows that we were able to narrow down the accuracy gap between the HE-friendly AlexNet and SqueezeNet, trained using the approach of [44] with our baseline. Our experiments show that we improved the performance of the model by up to 12.5% compared to their approach.

3   Methodology

Our goal was to replace the ReLU function with a polynomial activation function. This section describes the training methodology we used to achieve comparable performance with the baseline model, as presented in Fig. 2.

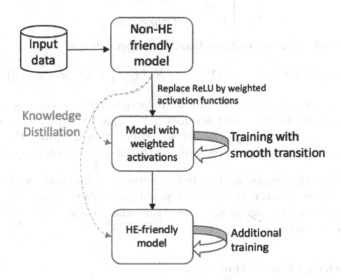

Fig. 2. Training methodology for HE-friendly DNNs.

3.1   Trainable Polynomial Activation

Based on our approach, we wanted to design a trainable polynomial that would replace the ReLU activation, without approximating it. Recent papers suggested approximating ReLU using high-degree polynomials to achieve a good approximation. However, for a polynomial of degree n, this requires an order of $log_2(n)$ multiplications [40], which significantly increases the computation depth as the number of multiplications grows.

Therefore, we suggest using a trainable polynomial activation of a 2nd degree polynomial without the constant term. We used the form $ax^2 + bx$, where a and b are trainable coefficients, which we trained individually **per layer**. A similar approach was presented by Wu et al. [44], where each such activation layer only increments the multiplication depth by 1.

3.2 Smooth-Transition

Applying such a significant architectural change to a complex model, without first adapting the model weights, can lead to a steep drop in accuracy. Hence, we designed a new approach that we call *smooth-transition*. We start by training a model that includes ReLU activation layers for e_0 epochs. Over the next d epochs, we smoothly transition from the ReLU functions to the polynomial activation functions $poly\_act()$. Then, we continue to train the model on the transitioned HE-friendly architecture. To model this, we use the ratio parameter λ_e per epoch e.

$$\lambda_e = \begin{cases} 0, & (e - e_0) \leq 0 \\ \dfrac{e - e_0}{d} & 0 < (e - e_0) < d \\ 1 & Otherwise \end{cases}$$

and set the **weighted activation function** at epoch e as

$$weighted\_act_{\lambda_e}(x) := (1 - \lambda_e) \cdot ReLU(x) + \lambda_e \cdot poly\_act(x).$$

To help the network converge, we initiated the quadratic function $poly\_act(x) = ax^2 + bx$ as a linear function that is somewhat similar to ReLU, by setting $a = 0$ and $b = 1$. We stress that the weight λ_e is not trained during the transition phase, instead it is predefined according to the smooth-transition policy.

Remark 1. We tried replacing the ReLU activation functions with quadratic polynomials layer-by-layer, instead of replacing all layers in parallel. However, it did not provide any significant advantage, and in some cases even showed performance degradation.

3.3 Knowledge Distillation

Using polynomial activations instead of ReLU activations is less suitable for the classification task. To strengthen the model, we adopted the well known KD [22] technique.

KD enables a knowledge transfer from a stronger pre-trained 'teacher' model to a weaker 'student' model. In practice, the student model is usually smaller than the teacher [34]. In our case, replacing ReLU by a polynomial activation weakens the HE-friendly model; therefore, the original model is used as a 'teacher' model to assist in training the 'student' HE-friendly model.

We used the response-based KD approach, one of the simplest KD methods [19]. Here, an additional term is added to the loss function to measure discrepancies between the predictions of the teacher and student models. We also employed the *soft target* technique [22], in which *soft targets* are used instead of the original predictions of the teacher and student models:

$$Q^\tau[i] = \frac{\exp\left(z_i/\tau\right)}{\sum_j \exp\left(z_j/\tau\right)}$$

where $Q^\tau[i]$ is the *soft target* version of the prediction for the class i, z_i are the original prediction logits, and τ is the *temperature* [22]. With $\tau = 1$, the above formula becomes the standard "softmax" output: using a higher temperature value ($\tau > 1$) produces a more uniform distribution of the probabilities over the classes. The resulting loss function becomes [29,30]:

$$L_{KD} = \alpha\tau^2 \cdot CE(Q_s^\tau, Q_t^\tau) + (1 - \alpha) \cdot CE(Q_s^1, y_{true})$$

where Q_s^τ and Q_t^τ are vectors of the soft target predictions of the student and teacher models with the same temperature $\tau > 1$, Q_s^1 is the "softmax" student prediction, y_{true} is the original labels, CE is the cross-entropy loss function, and α is the hyperparameter controlling the relative weight of the additional KD loss term.

4 Experiments

4.1 Datasets

Our experiments use two datasets: COVIDx and COVIDx CT-2A.

- **COVIDx** [43]. This is a dataset of CXR images labeled as: *Normal, Pneumonia*, or *COVID-19*. It is an open access benchmark dataset comprising ~20,000 CXR images, with the largest number of publicly available COVID-19 positive cases. This dataset collects its data from 6 chest X-Ray datasets [1,10–12,38,42] and combines them into a big dataset that is updated over time with more COVID-19 positive CXR images. The number of images we used per class is depicted in Table 1. When creating this dataset, we verified that there are no patients overlapping between the train, test, and validation subsets. We applied an augmentation process to the data, similar to Wang et al. [43].
- **COVIDx CT-2A** [20]. This dataset contains 194,922 chest CT slices from 3,745 patients, with the same classes as in the previous dataset. We used a random balanced subset of the original dataset, as depicted in Table 1. Each image was augmented as follows: resize to 224 × 224 × 3, random rotation, horizontal flip, vertical flip, color jitter, and normalize.

4.2 Model

For evaluation, we used the AlexNet [25] and SqueezeNet [23] models. We chose AlexNet because it was the deepest network that was tested for non-interactive HE solutions [2]. We also used SqueezeNet, which was designed as a light version of AlexNet with 50× fewer parameters. Although lighter, it is a much deeper network with 40 layers instead of 21. The models were originally pretrained on the ImageNet [14] dataset, and then fine-tuned on the COVIDx datasets. Because both original models are not HE-friendly, we describe the steps to transform the original models into HE-friendly models.

Table 1. COVIDx and COVIDx CT-2A data sizes used per class

		Normal	Pneumonia	COVID-19	Total
COVIDx	Train	7966	5475	4303	17744
	Validation	797	534	559	1871
	Test	88	60	61	209
COVIDx CT-2A	Train	10000	10000	10000	30000
	Validation	1000	1000	1000	3000
	Test	100	100	100	300

AlexNet. We implemented an AlexNet model based on PyTorch[3], and added a batch normalization layer after every activation layer. To avoid additional multiplication depth, after the training process ended, we absorbed the coefficients of the batch normalization into the weights of the next layer, as suggested by Ibarrondo and Onen [24]. Appendix A presents the network architecture.

HELayers [2] is an AI over HE framework. Following the pre-print version of this paper [4], the developers of HELayers tested our methodology for AlexNet. Their results showed a speedup for time and accuracy over encrypted input when using large networks (in terms of HE) and large image sizes of $224 \times 224 \times 3$.

SqueezeNet. The SqueezeNet model [23] aims to achieve AlexNet-level accuracy with $50\times$ fewer parameters. This comes at the cost of significantly increasing the multiplication depth, from 21 layers to 40 layers. Unlike our approach for AlexNet, we did not add *batch normalization* for SqueezeNet, as we did not observe significant performance improvement when using it. Our model architecture is the SqueezeNet version 1.0 implemented in PyTorch.

A lighter HE-Friendly version of SqueezeNet tailored for CIFAR-10 with 23 layers instead of 40 over small images of size $32 \times 32 \times 3$ was implemented and evaluated by Dathathri et al. [13]. The successful implementation of this lighter version increased our motivation to offer a method that can also successfully train the original (larger) SqueezeNet over larger images while achieving acceptable accuracy.

Our evaluation is focused on AlexNet and SqueezeNet as these are the largest model architectures that were demonstrated to run over HE in a non-interactive mode, i.e., without using client-aided designs. We are not aware of other attempts to use larger networks while also considering large image sizes as in our case.

4.3 Experimental Results

AlexNet. Table 2 summarizes our experimental results using different methods on the COVIDx and COVIDx-CT-2A datasets. In every experiment, we measured the accuracy and macro-average of the F_1 scores on all of the three

---

[3] https://pytorch.org.

Table 2. A comparison of our suggested methods and their contributions to previous works, over the AlexNet model. The results are reported for the test data of COVIDx and COVIDx CT-2A images. The baseline network is the original network with max pooling and ReLU. For all columns, higher values are better. We use the term TP for Trainable Polynomials, ST for Smooth-Transition and KD for Knowledge Distillation.

Technique	COVIDx CT-2A		COVIDx	
	Accuracy	F_1	Accuracy	F_1
Square [18]	0.435 ± 0.11	0.429 ± 0.13	0.378 ± 0.06	0.372 ± 0.08
Approx. ReLU [41]	0.706 ± 0.02	0.703 ± 0.09	0.696 ± 0.01	0.670 ± 0.01
TP [44]	0.806 ± 0.03	0.807 ± 0.03	0.811 ± 0.02	0.809 ± 0.04
Our method TP+ST	0.837 ± 0.01	0.835 ± 0.10	0.881 ± 0.12	0.878 ± 0.14
Our method TP+ST+KD	$\mathbf{0.848 \pm 0.04}$	$\mathbf{0.847 \pm 0.09}$	$\mathbf{0.913 \pm 0.10}$	$\mathbf{0.907 \pm 0.16}$
Baseline	0.893 ± 0.03	0.892 ± 0.08	0.916 ± 0.01	0.915 ± 0.03

classes. We repeated every experiment five times with different seeds and report the average results and the standard deviation. For more details regarding the training setup, see Appendix B.

As can be seen from Table 2, the **trainable activation** improved the results by 14–20% when compared to the quadratic approximated ReLU. The **smooth-transition (ST)** approach, which gradually changes the activation function over 10 epochs starting from the 3rd epoch, further improved the results by 3.4–8.6% when compared to replacing all activations at once. Finally, combining both approaches with **Knowledge Distillation (KD)**, where the original AlexNet with ReLU was used as a teacher to the new adapted architecture, performed even better with an improvement of 1.3–3.6% (baseline divided by our method). This almost closed the gap with the original reference model, with only 0.32–5.3% degradation.

Table 3. A comparison of our suggested methods and their contributions to previous works over the SqueezeNet architecture. The results are reported on the test data of COVIDx CT-2A images. The baseline network is the original network with max-pooling and ReLU; we also added a reference model with average-pooling and ReLU. For all columns, higher values are better.

Technique	Accuracy	F_1
Square	0.33 ± 0.00	0.33 ± 0.00
Approx. ReLU	0.740 ± 0.15	0.728 ± 0.15
TP	0.754 ± 0.05	0.742 ± 0.06
Our method TP+ST	0.806 ± 0.23	0.800 ± 0.05
Our method TP+ST+KD	$\mathbf{0.820 \pm 0.23}$	$\mathbf{0.816 \pm 0.02}$
Baseline (ReLU + Avgool)	0.825 ± 0.23	0.826 ± 0.31
Baseline (ReLU + Maxpool)	0.898 ± 0.01	0.897 ± 0.05

SqueezeNet. Table 3 summarizes the results of using different methods on the COVIDx-CT-2A dataset. The results are reported in a similar format as in Table 2. The only difference is that in this table we also added a baseline model, which consists of the original model of SqueezeNet with ReLU but with average-pooling. The reason is that when we replaced the max-pooling layer with an average-pooling layer, both the F_1 scores and the accuracy scores went down by around 8%. This observation is interesting because it shows that the claim of Gilad-Backrach et al. [18] does not hold for all models. This may also open the door for a new line of research that focuses not only on the activation layers but also on max-pooling layers.

We compared the accuracy and F_1 score of models with average-pooling, where one is trained using our methodology and the other using the standard methodologies. The results showed almost the same performance as with AlexNet, with 0.6–1.2% degradation in the former model. Interestingly, the smooth-transition technique played an important role, and improved the results by 6.9%–7.8%. Interestingly, when we evaluated a model with square activations, the model did not converge at all.

CIFAR-10 for AlexNet. For completeness, we also evaluated our methodology on the well-known CIFAR-10 dataset over the AlexNet model. We resized the images to $224 \times 224 \times 3$ to fit the input size required by the model. The baseline network with ReLU reached an accuracy of 0.901, and the accuracy of the HE-friendly model using our full methodology was only slightly lower at 0.872 (and 0.869 without KD). Using non-smooth trainable activation functions resulted in a low accuracy of 0.751, and with an approximated ReLU it reached 0.7405. Again, we see that our methodology outperforms previous works, especially when evaluating on the original AlexNet model without modifications, and over large images.

Varying Polynomial Activations per Layer. To better understand the final activation polynomials ($ax^2 + bx$), we analyzed the ranges of their coefficients. For AlexNet, we got $a \in [0.003, 0.010]$, with a standard deviation of 32% of the 0.0065 average value and $b \in [0.057, 0.110]$, with a standard deviation of 20% of the 0.0830 average value. We got similar results for SqueezeNet. Figure 3 presents a sample of the activation function graphs of different layers next to the graphs of the ReLU, square, and the ReLU approximation functions. The large variance between the polynomials may explain the accuracy advantage we see when using several different polynomial activations compared to using only one fixed approximation for all layers.

In our experiments, the inputs to the AlexNet activation functions were in the range $[-90, 90]$, the average input value for most layers was close to zero with standard deviations in the range $[4, 18]$. In contrast, in SqueezeNet, the input to the activation functions were in $[-100, 100]$ for the first 18 activations, and in $[-1506, 1356]$ otherwise. Here too, the average input value for most layers was close to zero with standard deviations of less than 20 for the first 18 layers and around 180 for the other layers. Thus, Fig. 3 shows the graphs for small

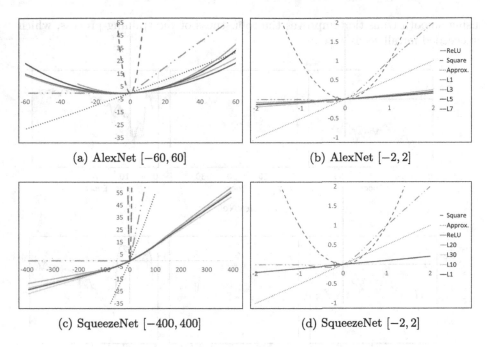

(a) AlexNet $[-60, 60]$ (b) AlexNet $[-2, 2]$

(c) SqueezeNet $[-400, 400]$ (d) SqueezeNet $[-2, 2]$

Fig. 3. Different activation functions: ReLU, Square function, ReLU approximation and the resulted trainable polynomials for several layers of AlexNet (top panels) and SqueezeNet (bottom panels). In panel (d) the curves of L1-L30 coincide.

inputs in $[-2, 2]$ but also in wide ranges $[-60, 60]$ and $[-400, 400]$ for AlexNet and SqueezeNet, respectively.

The graphs show that, unlike ReLU, the square function grows and even explodes for negative inputs, therefore it is less likely to cause a network to converge. In contrast, compared to ReLU, the ReLU approximation outputs lower values for both negative and positive inputs. This allows the network to converge, but the increased weight it gives to negative inputs might be the reason for the observed lower accuracy. Interestingly, our trainable functions happen to be closer to ReLU, at least in the range $[-2, 0]$ and starts to deviate from it when extending the input range. It seems that in $[-2, 2]$ with small inputs, our trainable functions almost agree on their outputs, but for distant inputs, they uniquely define the characteristics of the layers. In our experiments, we did not observe that the order of layers dictates some order on the trained functions.

Smooth Transition and Training Robustness. Figure 4 compares the robustness of the previous methods for replacing the ReLU activations with our smooth transition approach over five different seeds. The graphs show that using approximated ReLU or trainable activations without smooth transition leads to a wide deviation of the final accuracy results and training failures. In contrast, using smooth transition improves the robustness of the training process, which succeeded for all seeds.

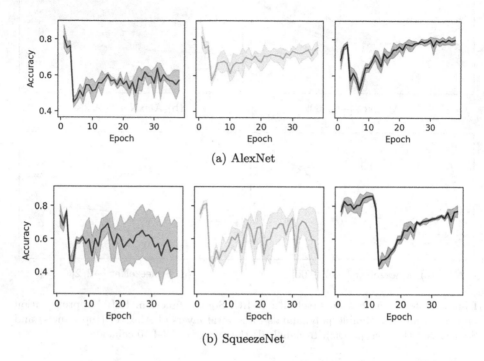

(a) AlexNet

(b) SqueezeNet

Fig. 4. Test accuracy for the AlexNet (top) and SqueezeNet (bottom) architectures trained with the approximated ReLU (left, orange), trainable polynomial without smooth-transition (middle, green), and trainable polynomial with smooth-transition (right, red) – our method. The graphs show the average and spread of five different runs with different seeds. A smaller spread indicates a more stable training method. (Color figure online)

As described in Sect. 3.2, the smooth transition starts at epoch 3 and progresses over 10 epochs. This explains the immediate accuracy drop at epoch 3 for the left and middle graphs in Fig. 4. The rightmost graphs show the training process with a smooth transition, where the accuracy drop is delayed to the last transition epoch (around epoch 13) or stretched during epochs 3–13. One explanation for the accuracy drop in the rightmost graph is that the graphs of the trainable activations lay below the ReLU graph, see Fig. 3. Therefore, when we set the activation to $\lambda_e \times trainable + (1 - \lambda_e) \times ReLU$, the ReLU term is larger than the trainable term. Once the transition ends, we remove the ReLU term, which causes the model to respond with an accuracy drop. However, as we see in the graphs, the transition period helps stabilize the final accuracy. We also evaluated a smoother version of the transition, where we split the last 2 epochs into 10 smaller epochs with an increment of 0.02 for λ_e; but we did not observe any improvement.

5   Conclusions

We introduced a new methodology for training HE-friendly models that replaces the ReLU activation functions with a trainable quadratic approximation. Our approach uses techniques such as polynomial activation functions with trainable coefficients, gradual replacement of activation layers during training, and KD. In addition, our methodology can be automated and thus simplifies the way data scientists generate HE-friendly networks. Moreover, it allows them to avoid many struggles in achieving models with relatively good accuracy. We stress again that the entire training phase is done by the data owners on unencrypted data. Only when the model is ready the data owner encrypts it and uploads it to the cloud.

We tested our methodology on chest CT and CXR image datasets using the AlexNet architecture, and showed that the performance of our trained model is only 0.32–5.3% less accurate than the reference model, making it at least 15% better than all previously suggested HE-friendly training methods. We achieved similar results for SqueezeNet, which is a deeper network with 40 layers. Finally, we note that the authors of [2] used our methodology to train AlexNet. Subsequently, they used their HELayers framework to demonstrate running it *over encrypted data* in less than five minutes without any degradation in accuracy.

Secure computations using HE is a rapidly growing domain and there are already several HE frameworks that enable private DNN computations on untrusted systems such as [2,13]. However, they can provide accurate and usable solutions only in the presence of accurate HE-friendly models. This puts our study on the critical path of deploying non-interactive HE-based solutions. In future work, we plan to further evaluate our methodology on more complicated models and domains. In addition, in the light of the results from SqueezeNet, we would like to design an approach for replacing max-pooling that will offer less accuracy degradation.

A   AlexNet Network Architecture

Our AlexNet architecture is the original implementation of PyTorch, where we added a batch normalization layer after every activation layer as our baseline. Here, all convolution layers use padding='same'. Note that the original model implemented by PyTorch has a *Global Average Pooling* layer with an output size that is 6×6. For input images of size 224×224, it is equivalent to the identity function so we ignored it in our experiments.

Our Variant of AlexNet

1. Conv2d(3, 64, kernel=11×11, stride=4, trainable_polynomial)
2. AvgPool2d(3×3, stride=2)
3. BatchNorm2d(64)
4. Conv2d(64, 192, kernel=5×5, stride=1, trainable_polynomial)
5. AvgPool2d(kernel=3×3, stride=2)
6. BatchNorm2d(192)

7. Conv2d(192, 384, kernel=3 × 3, stride=1, trainable_polynomial)
8. Conv2d(384, 256, kernel=3 × 3, stride=1, trainable_polynomial)
9. Conv2d(256, 256, kernel=3 × 3, stride=1, trainable_polynomial)
10. AvgPool2d(kernel=3 × 3, stride=2)
11. BatchNorm2d(256)
12. Dropout(p=0.2)
13. Flatten()
14. FC(in=256, out=4096, activation=trainable_polynomial)
15. Dropout(p=0.2)
16. FC(in=4096, out=4096, activation=trainable_polynomial)
17. FC(in=4096, out=3)

Total number of layers, including the activation layers and ignoring the dropout layers: 21.

B   Model Hyperparameters

We evaluated each experiment with 5 different seeds: 111, 222, 333, 444, 555. During the training process, we loaded images in mini-batches of size 32, and optimized the loss function using Adam optimizer. The number of epochs differs for each task, as does the learning rate, which was usually 3e−5 or 3e−4.

The activation replacement started at epoch 3, and in case of smooth transition it was gradually replaced for 10 epochs. We replaced all ReLU activations in parallel. We found that it is better to initialize the coefficients with values similar to the form of ReLU, and that when the coefficients are scaled by a predefined number (s_1, s_2), the network converges better. Therefore, the coefficients of each trainable activation were initialized as $s_1 \times 0.0X^2 + s_2 \times 1.1x$ or $s_1 \times 0.0X^2 + s_2 \times 1.1x$, where (s_1, s_2) are set to either $(0.1, 0.1)$ or $(0.01, 0.1)$.

For the distillation process described in Sect. 3.3, we set the temperature value to 10, and the α parameter was set to 0.1.

References

1. AC: Actualmed COVID-19 chest X-ray data initiative (2020). https://github.com/agchung/Actualmed-COVID-chestxray-dataset
2. Aharoni, E., et al.: HeLayers: a tile tensors framework for large neural networks on encrypted data. https://arxiv.org/abs/2011.01805
3. Akavia, A., Vald, M.: On the privacy of protocols based on CPA-secure homomorphic encryption. Cryptology ePrint Archive: Report 2021/803 (2021). https://eprint.iacr.org/2021/803
4. Baruch, M., Greenberg, L., Moshkowich, G.: Fighting COVID-19 in the Dark: Methodology for Improved Inference Using Homomorphically Encrypted DNN (2021)
5. Boemer, F., Costache, A., Cammarota, R., Wierzynski, C.: NGraph-HE2: a high-throughput framework for neural network inference on encrypted data. In: Proceedings of the 7th ACM Workshop on Encrypted Computing & Applied Homomorphic Cryptography, WAHC 2019, pp. 45–56. Association for Computing Machinery, New York (2019). https://doi.org/10.1145/3338469.3358944

6. Brakerski, Z., Gentry, C., Vaikuntanathan, V.: (Leveled) fully homomorphic encryption without bootstrapping. ACM Trans. Comput. Theory (TOCT) **6**(3), 1–36 (2014). https://doi.org/10.1145/2633600
7. Centers for Medicare & Medicaid Services: The Health Insurance Portability and Accountability Act of 1996 (HIPAA) (1996). https://www.hhs.gov/hipaa/
8. Cheon, J.H., Kim, A., Kim, M., Song, Y.: Homomorphic encryption for arithmetic of approximate numbers. In: Takagi, T., Peyrin, T. (eds.) ASIACRYPT 2017. LNCS, vol. 10624, pp. 409–437. Springer, Cham (2017). https://doi.org/10.1007/978-3-319-70694-8_15
9. Cheon, J.H., Kim, D., Kim, D., Lee, H.H., Lee, K.: Numerical method for comparison on homomorphically encrypted numbers. In: Galbraith, S.D., Moriai, S. (eds.) ASIACRYPT 2019. LNCS, vol. 11922, pp. 415–445. Springer, Cham (2019). https://doi.org/10.1007/978-3-030-34621-8_15
10. Chowdhury, M.E.H., et al.: Can AI help in screening viral and COVID-19 pneumonia? IEEE Access **8**, 132665–132676 (2020). https://doi.org/10.1109/ACCESS.2020.3010287
11. Clark, K., et al.: The cancer imaging archive (TCIA): maintaining and operating a public information repository. J. Digit. Imaging **26**(6), 1045–1057 (2013). https://doi.org/10.1007/s10278-013-9622-7
12. Cohen, J.P., Morrison, P., Dao, L., Roth, K., Duong, T.Q., Ghassemi, M.: Covid-19 image data collection: prospective predictions are the future. arXiv preprint (2020). https://arxiv.org/abs/2006.11988
13. Dathathri, R., et al.: Chet: an optimizing compiler for fully-homomorphic neural-network inferencing. In: Proceedings of the 40th ACM SIGPLAN Conference on Programming Language Design and Implementation, PLDI 2019, pp. 142–156. Association for Computing Machinery (2019). https://doi.org/10.1145/3314221.3314628
14. Deng, J., Dong, W., Socher, R., Li, L.J., Li, K., Fei-Fei, L.: ImageNet: a large-scale hierarchical image database. In: 2009 IEEE Conference on Computer Vision and Pattern Recognition, pp. 248–255 (2009). https://doi.org/10.1109/CVPR.2009.5206848
15. EU General Data Protection Regulation: Regulation (EU) 2016/679 of the European Parliament and of the Council of 27 April 2016 on the protection of natural persons with regard to the processing of personal data and on the free movement of such data, and repealing Directive 95/46/EC (General Data Protection Regulation). Official Journal of the European Union 119 (2016). http://data.europa.eu/eli/reg/2016/679/oj
16. Gentry, C.: Fully homomorphic encryption using ideal lattices. In: Proceedings of the Forty-First Annual ACM Symposium on Theory of Computing, pp. 169–178 (2009). https://doi.org/10.1145/1536414.1536440
17. Gentry, C.: Computing arbitrary functions of encrypted data. Commun. ACM **53**(3), 97–105 (2010). https://doi.org/10.1145/1666420.1666444
18. Gilad-Bachrach, R., Dowlin, N., Laine, K., Lauter, K., Naehrig, M., Wernsing, J.: CryptoNets: applying neural networks to encrypted data with high throughput and accuracy. In: International Conference on Machine Learning, pp. 201–210 (2016). https://proceedings.mlr.press/v48/gilad-bachrach16.html
19. Gou, J., Yu, B., Maybank, S.J., Tao, D.: Knowledge distillation: a survey. Int. J. Comput. Vis. **129**(6), 1789–1819 (2021). https://doi.org/10.1007/s11263-021-01453-z

20. Gunraj, H., Wang, L., Wong, A.: COVIDNet-CT: a tailored deep convolutional neural network design for detection of COVID-19 cases from chest CT images. Front. Med. **7** (2020). https://doi.org/10.3389/fmed.2020.608525
21. Hesamifard, E., Takabi, H., Ghasemi, M.: CryptoDL: deep neural networks over encrypted data. arXiv preprint (2017). https://arxiv.org/abs/1711.05189
22. Hinton, G., Vinyals, O., Dean, J.: Distilling the knowledge in a neural network. In: NIPS Deep Learning and Representation Learning Workshop (2015). https://arxiv.org/abs/1503.02531
23. Iandola, F.N., Han, S., Moskewicz, M.W., Ashraf, K., Dally, W.J., Keutzer, K.: SqueezeNet: AlexNet-level accuracy with 50x fewer parameters and <0.5 mb model size. arXiv preprint arXiv:1602.07360 (2016)
24. Ibarrondo, A., Önen, M.: FHE-compatible batch normalization for privacy preserving deep learning. In: Garcia-Alfaro, J., Herrera-Joancomartí, J., Livraga, G., Rios, R. (eds.) DPM/CBT -2018. LNCS, vol. 11025, pp. 389–404. Springer, Cham (2018). https://doi.org/10.1007/978-3-030-00305-0_27
25. Krizhevsky, A., Sutskever, I., Hinton, G.E.: ImageNet classification with deep convolutional neural networks. In: Advances in Neural Information Processing Systems, vol. 25, pp. 1097–1105 (2012). https://proceedings.neurips.cc/paper/2012/file/c399862d3b9d6b76c8436e924a68c45b-Paper.pdf
26. Kumar Meher, P.: An optimized lookup-table for the evaluation of sigmoid function for artificial neural networks. In: 2010 18th IEEE/IFIP International Conference on VLSI and System-on-Chip, pp. 91–95 (2010). https://doi.org/10.1109/VLSISOC.2010.5642617
27. Lee, J.W., et al.: Privacy-preserving machine learning with fully homomorphic encryption for deep neural network. arXiv preprint (2021). https://arxiv.org/abs/2106.07229
28. Lehmkuhl, R., Mishra, P., Srinivasan, A., Popa, R.A.: Muse: secure inference resilient to malicious clients. In: 30th USENIX Security Symposium (USENIX Security 2021), pp. 2201–2218. USENIX Association (2021). https://www.usenix.org/conference/usenixsecurity21/presentation/lehmkuhl
29. Li, H.: Exploring knowledge distillation of DNNs for efficient hardware solutions (2018). http://cs230.stanford.edu/files_winter_2018/projects/6940224.pdf
30. Li, H.: Exploring knowledge distillation of DNNs for efficient hardware solutions (2021). https://github.com/peterliht/knowledge-distillation-pytorch, gitHub repository, commit:ef06124d67a98abcb3a5bc9c81f7d0f1f016a7ef
31. Lloret-Talavera, G., et al.: Enabling homomorphically encrypted inference for large DNN models. IEEE Trans. Comput. 1 (2021). https://doi.org/10.1109/TC.2021.3076123
32. Lou, Q., Feng, B., Fox, G.C., Jiang, L.: Glyph: fast and accurately training deep neural networks on encrypted data. arXiv preprint (2019). https://arxiv.org/abs/1911.07101
33. Meftah, S., Tan, B.H.M., Mun, C.F., Aung, K.M.M., Veeravalli, B., Chandrasekhar, V.: Doren: toward efficient deep convolutional neural networks with fully homomorphic encryption. IEEE Trans. Inf. Forensics Secur. **16**, 3740–3752 (2021). https://doi.org/10.1109/TIFS.2021.3090959
34. Mirzadeh, S.I., Farajtabar, M., Li, A., Levine, N., Matsukawa, A., Ghasemzadeh, H.: Improved knowledge distillation via teacher assistant. In: Proceedings of the AAAI Conference on Artificial Intelligence, vol. 34, pp. 5191–5198 (2020). https://doi.org/10.1609/aaai.v34i04.5963

35. Mohassel, P., Zhang, Y.: SecureML: a system for scalable privacy-preserving machine learning. In: 2017 IEEE Symposium on Security and Privacy (SP), pp. 19–38 (2017). https://doi.org/10.1109/SP.2017.12
36. Nandakumar, K., Ratha, N., Pankanti, S., Halevi, S.: Towards deep neural network training on encrypted data. In: Proceedings of the IEEE Conference on Computer Vision and Pattern Recognition Workshops (2019). https://openaccess.thecvf.com/content_CVPRW_2019/html/CV-COPS/Nandakumar_Towards_Deep_Neural_Network_Training_on_Encrypted_Data_CVPRW_2019_paper.html
37. Piazza, F., Uncini, A., Zenobi, M.: Neural networks with digital LUT activation functions. In: Proceedings of 1993 International Conference on Neural Networks (IJCNN-93-Nagoya, Japan), vol. 2, pp. 1401–1404 (1993). https://doi.org/10.1109/IJCNN.1993.716806
38. Rahman, T., et al.: Exploring the effect of image enhancement techniques on Covid-19 detection using chest X-ray images. Comput. Biol. Med. **132**, 104319 (2021). https://doi.org/10.1016/j.compbiomed.2021.104319
39. Scardapane, S., Scarpiniti, M., Comminiello, D., Uncini, A.: Learning activation functions from data using cubic spline interpolation. In: Esposito, A., Faundez-Zanuy, M., Morabito, F.C., Pasero, E. (eds.) WIRN 2017 2017. SIST, vol. 102, pp. 73–83. Springer, Cham (2019). https://doi.org/10.1007/978-3-319-95098-3_7
40. Schönhage, A.: A lower bound for the length of addition chains. Theor. Comput. Sci. **1**(1), 1–12 (1975). https://doi.org/10.1016/0304-3975(75)90008-0
41. Takabi, D., Podschwadt, R., Druce, J., Wu, C., Procopio, K.: Privacy preserving neural network inference on encrypted data with GPUs. CoRR (2019). https://arxiv.org/pdf/1911.11377.pdf
42. Tsai, E.B., et al.: The RSNA international COVID-19 open annotated radiology database (RICORD). Radiology 203957 (2021). https://doi.org/10.1148/radiol.2021203957
43. Wang, L., Lin, Z.Q., Wong, A.: Covid-net: a tailored deep convolutional neural network design for detection of Covid-19 cases from chest X-ray images. Sci. Rep. **10**(1), 1–12 (2020). https://doi.org/10.1038/s41598-020-76550-z0
44. Wu, W., Liu, J., Wang, H., Tang, F., Xian, M.: PPolyNets: achieving high prediction accuracy and efficiency with parametric polynomial activations. IEEE Access **6**, 72814–72823 (2018). https://doi.org/10.1109/ACCESS.2018.2882407
45. Zhang, M., Xu, S., Fulcher, J.: Neuron-adaptive higher order neural-network models for automated financial data modeling. IEEE Trans. Neural Netw. **13**(1), 188–204 (2002). https://doi.org/10.1109/72.977302

Scalable and Secure HTML5 Canvas-Based User Authentication

Esteban Rivera[1](✉), Lizzy Tengana[4], Jesús Solano[3], Christian López[1],
Johana Flórez[1], and Martín Ochoa[2]

[1] Appgate Inc., Bogotá, Colombia
{esteban.rivera,christian.lopez,johana.florez}@appgate.com
[2] Department of Computer Science, ETH Zürich, Zürich, Switzerland
[3] University College London, London, UK
[4] Aalto University, Espoo, Finland

Abstract. Although browser fingerprinting has been widely studied from a privacy angle, there is also a case for fingerprinting in the context of risk-based authentication. Given that most browser-context features can be easily spoofed, APIs that potentially depend both on software and hardware have gained interest. HTML5 Canvas has been shown to provide a certain degree of characterization of a browser. However, multiple research questions remain open. In this paper, we study how to use this API for browser fingerprinting in a scalable way by means of a Siamese deep neural network. We also explore the limits of this technique on modern browsers that are progressively standardizing the Canvas outputs. On our evaluation using over 200 browser instances, we obtain an 82% accuracy in distinguishing browser instances in our dataset and 92% if the model only distinguishes between users with a different browser or OS. Our model has a 0% false-rejection rate and up to 36% average false acceptance rate on simulated attacks, that occurs mostly when victims and attackers share the same browser model and version and the same OS.

Keywords: Risk-based authentication · Machine learning · Deep learning · Computer vision · Siamese networks · HTML5 Canvas

1 Introduction

Browser fingerprinting, the ability to remotely recognize or identify a browser or sets of browsers with similar intrinsic characteristics, has been studied in the literature for various reasons. On the one hand, browser fingerprinting can be used to track and identify users, and as such it poses a risk to user's privacy [1,15,33,35]. Also, browser fingerprinting can be a useful tool to enforce risk-based authentication and protect users specially for websites that require very sensitive information, like email accounts or credit card numbers [5,13,31]. If we are used to seeing legitimate users accessing our web services from a given set of browsers, sudden changes (i.e. a never seen before browser) could trigger 2-factor authentication mechanisms or other checks.

Several features have been considered so far to characterize browsers, ranging from the browser-declared user agent, to checks on installed fonts and browser family specific implementations that can be distinguished via JavaScript. Among proposed features, the use of HTML5 Canvas, first proposed by [24], stands out given that it has been shown that Canvas rendering can depend on both software implementations (browser family) and hardware (graphic cards). So far, this feature has been leveraged in two ways in order to build a fingerprint: a) originally, a hash was computed out of a given generated picture on a browser, which can be stored and used later for comparison on freshly generated hashes of the same image and b) machine learning classifiers have been proposed to distinguish images generated in a given browser from those generated in other browsers.

There are however so far unanswered questions in three important respects: 1) How secure is a fingerprinting solution based on HTML5 Canvas with respect to replay attacks? 2) Is it possible to build a secure solution that also scales to thousands, even millions of system users? and 3) Are the early observations on HTML5 Canvas still valid in modern browsers, as standardization efforts progress?

In this paper we study the above research questions and propose a fingerprint-based authentication protocol that uses HTML5 Canvas and a Siamese neural network with the following characteristics. First, it relies on a freshness factor (a randomly generated text) to validate a fingerprinting which defends against replay attacks. Second, it only needs a single Siamese network to evaluate a freshly generated fingerprint that can be used for all users in a system. Similar for example to a face detection network that compares a stored picture of a user against a freshly taken one, this paradigm avoids the necessity of storing and training a classifier for each user in a system (as opposed to closely related work), and only requires to store previously generated canvases in order to authenticate fresh instances.

We evaluate our approach on a dataset consisting of 1'374.000 images generated on 239 different browsers and 80 distinct machines. As a result of our training we obtain a network that has 82% accuracy with 0% false-rejection rate (FRR) and 36% false-acceptance rate (FAR), a 30 ms of inference time and requires 9.7 MBs of storage. Note that the high FAR is an average value that includes simulated attacks using all possible combinations of browser and OS, and that instance of false acceptance occur mostly when attackers use the same browser type and version and operating system as the victim. Moreover, our analysis indicates that recent versions of browsers based on Chromium yield identical canvases and it is thus impossible to distinguish them using this feature, although they are still distinguishable from other browser families.

In summary, our contributions are as follows:

- We propose a single Siamese neural network to classify randomly generated canvas images as generated by a given known browser or not, obtaining an accuracy of 82%.
- Based on this network, we propose a browser fingerprinting protocol that is resistant to replay attacks.
- We evaluate our approach on a dataset consisting of 1'374.000 images generated with HTML5 Canvas on 239 distinct browsers.
- We discuss the effectiveness of HTML5 Canvas as a fingerprinting technique in modern browsers, concluding that the Chromium-based family has effectively standardized this API rendering, making it an ineffective browser for fingerprinting purposes, and observing a similar trend in other browser families as well.

2   Background

In computer science, a fingerprinting algorithm is a mechanism to extract a unique signature to identify a trait from a specific user, such as human fingerprints uniquely identify people. These traits can contain features from one or several sources. For example, iris images, fingerprint scanners, heartbeat signals, and face photographs are information on the biological aspects of the user known as biometrics [7,8,26]. For instance, User-Agent string, HTTP request headers, cookies enabled, time zone, screen size, browser plugins, and their versions, and the list of system fonts are features that describe the interaction between a user with a browser [16,20]. Recent research applies the described features and others generated by HTML5 requirements (see Sect. 2.2) to identify a user uniquely as a browser fingerprinting [1,10,13,15,23,29].

2.1   Browser Fingerprinting

With the well-known *Panopticlick*[1] experiment, Eckersley [14] investigated the potential of fingerprinting using the browser features given the absence of standard tracking technologies like cookies and achieve an 84% of unique identification of the participants from a collection of hundreds of thousands of submissions when data came from HTTP headers, using JavaScript and plugins like Flash or Java. Panopticlick is a usual acquisition tool used by several authors [16,20,23].

Later studies found that fingerprinting in the browser environment has several applications with benign and malign proposes.

On one hand, for harmless applications, Al-Fannah [3] classify them into four applications: target advertising [9], social media sharing [27], analytics services [1], and web security. From the last application, there is the study of Nikiforakis in 2013 [25] where he discovered 40 pages (0.4% of the Alexa top 10,000) utilizing fingerprinting with commercial code and related to web tracking to detect shared or stolen credentials of paying members and user identification in dating

---

[1] https://coveryourtracks.eff.org/.

sites to ensure that attackers do not create multiple profiles for social engineering purposes. Mowery [24] also mentions that current approaches include fingerprinting a user's machine by a bank to require additional authentication for login attempts from systems whose fingerprint does not match.

For the aim of this paper, fingerprinting is treated as a web security service focused on authentication processes. It is known that the main challenge with browser fingerprinting is that most collected attributes of a browser are static and could easily be modified and replayed, enabling attackers to impersonate users [6]. In contrast to active fingerprinting techniques like canvas (see Sect. 2.2), WebGL, audio, or crypto fingerprinting which are valuable tools for creating challenge/response-based authentication protocols [10,12,22,31].

On the other hand, when fingerprint use is destructive, users do not benefit from being tracked or do not wish to be tracked. In that case, users can attempt to avoid tracking by using their browsers' "private browsing" modes [17] or addons [2] intended to hide the user preferences.

Due to the detrimental approach of fingerprinting, community research has developed tools to detect, quantify, and characterize emerging online tracking behaviors, as Englehardt presents in [15] with an open-source web privacy measurement tool. Similarly, Vastel [35] tested a suite to evaluate fingerprinting countermeasures and resilience against an adversarial crawler developer that tries to modify its crawler fingerprints to bypass security checks. Furthermore, Reitinger [30] explored in his work blocking canvas fingerprinting using a machine-learning-based approach, and Al-Fannah [4] presented a comprehensive and structured discussion of measures to limit or control browser fingerprinting.

In addition, recent works like Gomez et al. [18] evaluate the uniqueness of the browser fingerprinting, finding that from 2,067,942 fingerprints collected from one of the top 15 French websites, only 33.6% of fingerprints are unique in contrast to results published by Eckersley [14]. Authors of [18] attribute this gap to the fact that users do not need to play with their browsers to change their configuration and produce different fingerprints to protect their privacy, as is suggested in the *Panopticlick* experiment.

2.2   HTML5 Canvas

Browser features from Flash and Java plugins have shown that they are not enough to obtain a unique user identification. Also, the browser user should accept the use of the plugins to achieve a high degree of uniqueness [14], and some of the Flash applications are currently obsolete [11]. Late approaches prefer the use of canvases which differentiate from their conventional counterparts by their potential to circumvent users' tracking preferences, being hard to discover and resilient to removal [1,31]. Besides, works like [19,32] research into the identification performance increment using machine learning techniques, extracting a relation among the existing browser features and HTML5 canvases.

Mowery et al. [24] suggest that current browsers are increasing their sophistication in their application platforms which implies additional requirements and resources to the operating system, in contrast to traditional functionalities. The

HTML5 suite with its specifications is guilty of many sophistications such as programmatic drawing surfaces (canvas), three-dimensional graphics (WebGL), structured client-side data-store, geolocation services, the ability to manipulate browser history together with the browser cache, audio and video playback, and more.

The natural way for browsers to implement such features is to draw on the host operating system and hardware. They use the GPU for 2D or 3D graphics, improving visual performance and saving battery on mobile devices. Moreover, using the operating system's font-rendering code for text means that browsers automatically display text in a way that is optimized for the display and consistent with the user's expectations.

Differences among user's machines generated by a list of fonts (a particular case of canvas fingerprinting called canvas font fingerprinting [16]), font rendering, smoothing, and other device features cause a drawing of a particular image where the resulting pixels can be part of a canvas fingerprinting [15].

3   Approach

In the following, we will discuss the protocol and machine learning classifier design that we will later evaluate on data collected from several browser instances. To guide our discussions, we will start by stating the research questions we want to answer in this work.

GRQ: *Is it possible to enhance risk-based authentication through canvas based fingerprinting in today's browsers?*

- **RQ1:** How dependent are canvases on hardware and software nowadays?
- **RQ2:** Can a unique canvas-fingerprint be created for each browser instance?
- **RQ3:** Is it possible to build a system that scales to thousands/millions of users?
- **RQ4:** Is it possible to design a system that is secure against replay attacks?

3.1   System and Attacker Model

We assume an attacker $\mathcal{A}$ wants to impersonate a victim V on an online service. The attacker is in possession of the victim's credentials and can therefore successfully login at the target service. An attacker can spoof any value transmitted over to the server, including HTTP parameters as usually declared by a browser or other readings collected by JavaScript on behalf of the service. The service will collect such information to profile legitimate users through a risk-based authentication module. The service will assume that all legitimate clients can run HTML 5 Canvas calls on their browsers and thus request them to do so for (benign) profiling purposes.

We do not rule out that an attacker might be in possession of old legitimate communications between a victim and the service and therefore access to past rendered images on the victim's browser and other context information on the victim.

The attacker's goal is to successfully evade a risk-based authentication system that considers the profiling information of a legitimate user. The system may challenge users with a 2-factor authentication method in case of suspicious activity, and we assume attackers do not have access to this additional authentication mechanism.

3.2   Authentication Protocol Design

The system design corresponds to an authentication scenario where a user attempts to gain access to secured resources from a web server. The user must solve particular challenges, such as enter a combination of username and password, to authenticate him/her into the server. In the background, the user's device is required to authenticate by rendering an HTML5 Canvas image on the user's browser. If it can be ascertained that the image comes from one of the user's registered devices, the authentication is complete.

The authentication process followed by our system is shown in Fig. 1. First, to authenticate a user's device, the server generates a fresh scripting recipe for an image and challenges the user's browser to render it and send the result back to the server. In HTML5 Canvas, a fresh recipe means asking a browser to draw graphics via scripting where the script contains a randomness source. Including a source of randomness in the system, such as random text strings, is essential to avoid replay attacks. To ensure no replay attack is able to bypass authentication, both the server and the client generate images based on the same fresh challenge, then the images are compared through a classical image-similarity approach. If both images contain the same text, the mean difference should be smaller than the case where the images represent different text, which is the scenario when an attacker steals a previously generated canvas by the victim and tries to input into the system. Length and complexity of the random string determines the theoretical security of the protocol (secret's entropy).

After filtering replay attacks, the next step is to compare the image generated by the user's browser against a previous instance of an image from the same user's device (reference image). To extend the system to users with multiple devices, at least one reference image per device should be saved, and the whole process should be executed for each image. Through this comparison the system assess if the new login is suspicious or not. The key challenge of such a multi-user system is to devise a scalable strategy to determine whether two different images come from the same user device. It is not practical to create a single model that would need to be retrained when a new user is registered. On the other hand, a one-model-per-user approach usually requires large amounts of data per user that is hard to collect in the short-term (as in [31]), affecting the model reliability due to users constantly updating devices. Moreover, users may log in from multiple devices that might be constantly or sporadically used. Therefore

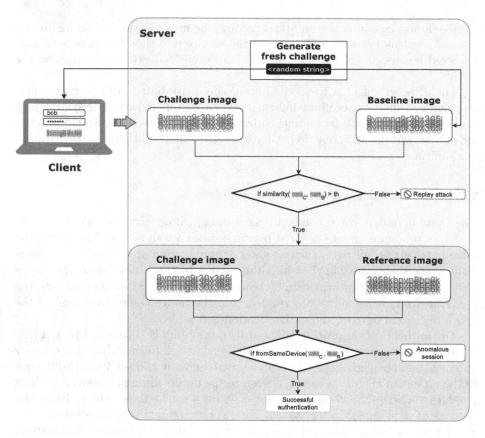

Fig. 1. The authentication process begins with the delivery of a fresh challenge to a client. The similarity of the client's image is compared against a baseline image generated on the server-side using the same random text. If the similarity between both images surpasses a given threshold, the client's image is now compared against a reference image previously generated from the user device (e.g. when registering or a previous login). If both images were generated from the same device, the authentication is successful and the most recent challenge becomes the new reference image.

a model-per-user would need retraining, or enough data must be collected to create a model per user device. We solve this scalability challenge by means of a Siamese deep neural network.

3.3 Machine Learning Classifier Design

Feature Engineering: For the purpose of fingerprinting, exploring various canvas styles is fundamental to establish which graphic features better highlight the differences among images rendered with different devices. Experimenting with multiple curves, text strings and visual effects as in [10,22] provides key insights represented in Fig. 2. Here, we generated 300 different canvas styles

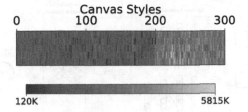

Fig. 2. Canvas style comparison. The color represents the mean absolute difference between two samples coming from different users of the *same* canvas.

(X-axis) for 5 different pages (Y-Axis). Each cell represents the mean canvas difference between 2 random sampled users. The 0–200 canvases only contained colored curves and shadows, the 200–300 contained colored texts. As it can be seen, the greatest differences appear for the canvases containing text, therefore, those types of canvases were used later for our main experiment.

These findings corroborate the positive results yielded by SWAT [31]. Thus, the same configuration of fonts, colors, and design were used in our subsequent experiments as we focused on going one step forward to develop a scalability strategy that can make this graphic approach suitable for real production environments. An example of the resulting images can be seen in Fig. 3.

Fig. 3. Example of an image generated on the client-side using Canvas API (35 × 280 px).

Siamese Neural Network: In order to go further than previous approaches [10,31] in the task of user authentication through the canvas, we implemented a Siamese network [21] as a way of using only one model to identify if two images were rendered by the same device instead of training one model for every single user. Therefore, the inputs of our system are two images, and the output corresponds to a binary similarity score stating whether they belong to the same device or not. In addition, we wanted to use fresh challenges so the system was not weak against replay attacks. Hence it was trained with different images with randomly generated text for the positive class.

The overall design of the architecture used in the classification process is depicted in Fig. 4. The main idea is to implement a Siamese network, this is, two networks sharing their weight values. For the implementation we used two different network architectures: a convolutional neural network (CNN) followed by a fully connected or dense network. The outputs for both networks in the Siamese architecture are then compared using an energy function represented by a similarity distance between both outputs. This similarity distance feeds a

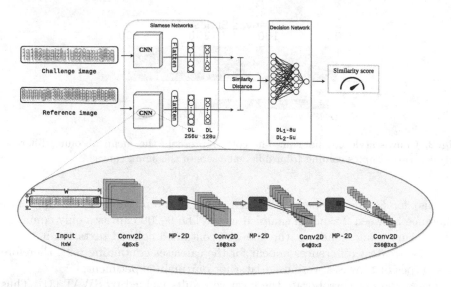

Fig. 4. Model architecture used for the classification of generated canvas images.Conv2D: 2D Convolution layer, MP: MaxPooling layer, DL: Dense Layer, u: units.

subsequent decision network which consists of a fully connected or dense neural network whose output will measure the similarity distance between both canvas or inputs.

Using too deep network architectures led to the vanishing gradient problem, which could be reduced with the inclusion of residual blocks. However, the results are similar to those obtained using shallower networks, but the time involved in the training process increases significantly with the inclusion of more layers. In the decision process, the decision network, which corresponds to a fully connected neural network, was included to obtain a higher performance in the classification results than those obtained using only the energy function (represented by the similarity distance in Fig. 4).

3.4 Training Procedure

For training the negative class, we generated the inputs from the random images in two different ways: Easy and Random generators. The easy one selects a pair of images from users who did not share at least one feature: Browser or OS. The random generator did not filter the users at all. The approach was always the same for the positive class: Select a random couple of images from the same user.

To optimize the process, the training was performed in an easy-to-difficult way. The first batches of data were small, and as soon as the metrics achieved a specific value, a new bigger batch was sampled. Incidentally, the firsts batches were generated with the easy generator and the last ones with the random generator. In this way, it should have been easier for the optimizer to find the local minima for the first epochs, and the last epochs were used as a fine-tuner of the model. This approach did not do not only help the speed of training but the convergence itself. To ensure the generalization results, we split the users into train and test sets, so both of them were in principle independent and gave us insights on the performance of the model on unseen data.

3.5 Evaluation Strategy

We wanted to test if the model was really learning features related to the rendering of the canvases or learning other aspects related to the string written on the canvas or its colors. To accomplish this, we proposed the following evaluation approach: For the positive class, we used different images from the same user, which would have different strings. For the negative class, we would pick the same image from two different users. In this way, we are sure that, the positive class images are more dissimilar than the negative class images in a pixel-wise manner, so the evaluation tests the image rendering in the worst case possible. This would give us a lower bound for the accuracy and recall of the system in the real world because in the actual environment would be expected that the images coming from different devices will have different texts.

4   Evaluation

In this section we discuss our evaluation efforts, based on the previously discussed strategy. We will also discuss the results of our evaluation in the context of the larger objective which is risk-based authentication.

4.1   Datasets

A dataset was collected to train and evaluate the approach. For this purpose, we designed a login web page where users provided a unique username. In one login, a user's browser built 6000 images in the background through the Canvas API. 3000 images were generated from canvases with random text strings. The other 3000 images were generated from canvases with fixed text strings, which means that the 3000 strings were the same for all users. Nevertheless, all of the canvases shared font colors and sizes. The only randomness source was the text string in the image, see Fig. 3.

The random images are used to train the models and the fixed images are used to evaluate them and gain insights from a pixel-wise analysis.

The data collection was performed with the help of 80 volunteers that collaborated with the experiment, but each of them could perform the login from different browsers. We usually collected information from three browsers from each user, giving us a total of 239 pairs browser-devices to be identified. The information was collected only for computers for this experiment, leaving mobile devices for the next steps.

The OS-Browser distribution can be seen in Fig. 5. There is an obvious prevalence of Windows devices as expected [34], followed by Mac-OS. Ubuntu is also present in our sample almost as much as Mac-OS, maybe because there are several developers in the company who prefer this operative system. The most used browser of the sample is Google Chrome, followed by Mozilla Firefox. Safari only appears for Mac-OS users and Microsoft Edge is prevalent for Windows users and a marginal quota for Ubuntu and Mac-OS users. Our sample appears to be close to what we would find in the real world [34], therefore, we consider it is a adequate representation of data in a bigger scale, and additionally, it has the heterogeneity we look for identifying all the cases we want to analyze.

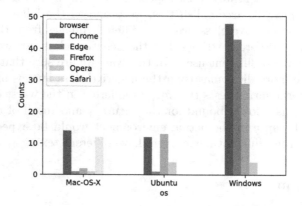

Fig. 5. OS-Browser distribution for the collected dataset

4.2   Results

To characterize the reach of our approach, we tested the pixel-wise difference for canvases between different types of users. This classification was made with the browser and OS information from the collected user agents. As we collected the data in a controlled environment, we are sure that none of the participants tried to hide or modify their user agent data polluting the dataset.

For this step, we used the fixed canvas part of the dataset, meaning that all the 3000 images were different between them, but *similar* between users. Their color and text were the same, but it was expected that the rendering made from each browser was going to make them different to a small extent.

We took the difference between two images and summed all the resulting matrix elements in a single number. Then the mean for all the entries with the same pair Browser-OS was calculated. The results can be seen in Fig. 6.

One of the most important insights from this plot is the diagonal: The comparisons between users with the same Browser-OS configuration. For this type of comparison, the mean difference is close to zero. It means that the unique fingerprint per user is rather difficult for this case. Additionally, for comparisons

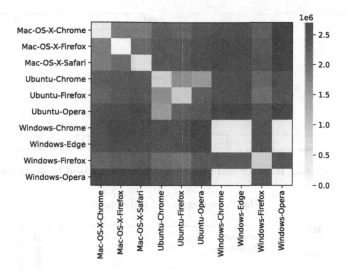

Fig. 6. Mean pixel-wise differences for users grouped by Browser-OS configuration.

between Chromium-based browsers, the mean difference is slight, suggesting that these browsers use the same engine to render the canvases, which would be an issue towards a unique fingerprint.

To see more closely those cases, the histogram of differences for same configuration comparison is shown in Fig. 7a. Although some samples are above zero, the great majority of the data is centered at exactly zero. There are no differences between canvases of users with the same configuration, which could mean that no unique fingerprint can be forged for those users.

Following the hint given by Fig. 6, we wanted to check what was happening with the comparison of devices with Chromium-based browsers like Chrome, Edge and Opera. Those results are seen in Fig. 7b. The histogram looks similar to the one in Fig. 7a, with the majority of mean differences at exactly zero. This results tells us that Chromium-based browsers tend to generate the exact same canvas and therefore, it is impossible to distinguish devices using the latest versions of those browsers through a canvas fingerprint.

Next, we wanted to test how our system would defend against replay attacks, as explained in Sect. 3.2. Our key assumption is that a couple of images containing the same text, rendered with different devices, are more similar than two images containing different texts. In this way, if an attacker returns an image with a text different from the one the server sent as a challenge, it would be labeled as an attack. We tested both cases, calculating the similarity between two images with the Structural Similarity Function from Sklearn [28]. The only preprocessing done was a Gaussian blur. The resulting histograms can be seen in Fig. 8. This outcome supports our hypothesis. We can certainly distinguish between pairs of images with the same and different texts. Consequently, our system should be robust against replay attacks.

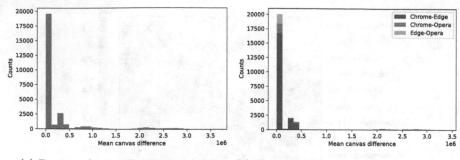

(a) Devices sharing Browser and OS   (b) Chromium-based browser comparisons

Fig. 7. Histogram of differences

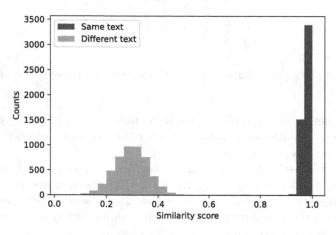

Fig. 8. Histogram of scores for images compared with the Structural similarity function

Given the concerns expressed about the canvases generated by users with the same Browser-OS configuration, the first evaluation over the canvases was made for the negative class scenario, as seen in Fig. 9a. Here we present a histogram of scores for couples of the negative class, meaning two images generated from different devices. If those devices share neither browser nor OS, the score is mostly zero or close to it. However, when they share both of those properties, the score becomes higher than 0.7. This insight was expected because of the previously performed analysis. If the images are pixel-wise equal, there is *no* way to distinguish them through any computer vision algorithm by itself. However, for actually different images, the neural network does a good job separating the classes. Moving the threshold between 0.1 and 0.7 does not make any difference, which makes the output relatively stable. We would suggest using 0.4 as threshold, because is the mean value between both positive and negative distributions.

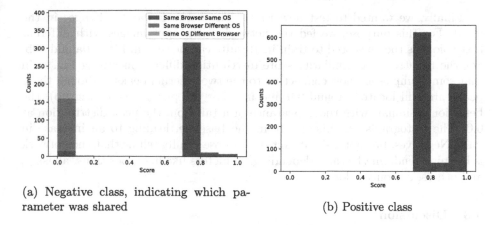

(a) Negative class, indicating which parameter was shared

(b) Positive class

Fig. 9. Score histograms

On the other hand, for the case where we have different images generated by the same device, namely the positive class, the histogram is presented in Fig. 9b. It can be seen that all of the scores are above 0.7, so every threshold below would assure that no positive attempt would be labeled as a false negative.

Summarizing, for a threshold of 0.4, we achieved the following metrics: Accuracy: 0.82, Precision: 0.73, Recall: 1.00. The worst value is the precision because of the common appearance of false positives. In contrast, the perfect recall means that in a real-world application, the model would present no friction at all for users trying to authenticate or access some service.

Taking this into account, we present the metrics for an implementation for which it is not necessary to identify a single user through a unique fingerprint but to identify the configuration they have and raise the alarm if something is off. For this case, the metrics are: Accuracy: 0.92, Precision: 0.86, Recall: 1.00. The precision increases substantially because the system is not presented in the case where the input images come from devices with the same configuration. However, it is still low. We believe the explanation lies in Fig. 5 and Fig. 7b. First, from the distribution of our data, there are a lot of Chrome and Edge users, and marginally some Opera users. In the histogram of Fig. 7b it is seen that the behavior for users of different but Chromium-based browsers is similar to the behavior of entries from the same browser: The canvases are equal pixelwise. Again, there is no way to distinguish those kinds of images.

Now, to see how well our system behaves for images that are not the same, we propose the following scenario: The inputs are canvases coming from devices which did not share at least one feature (OS or Browser) and Chromium-based browsers (Chrome-Edge-Opera) were grouped as one. In this case the metrics are: Accuracy: 0.99, Precision: 0.99, Recall: 1.00. We achieve an almost perfect performance. The Siamese network successes separating canvas that are actually different.

Finally, we wanted to test how robust the network was to changes in the input. For this purpose, we fed the network with input images with different text colors as the ones used to train it. Results can be seen in Figs. 10a and 10b. For the negative case, similarity score distribution differs concerning Fig. 9a in that some samples are now connecting to the two external peaks, although those peaks are still located around 0.0 and 0.7. For the positive case (Fig. 9b), the behavior is similar, with the appearance of a tail from the peak distribution at 0.0. The histograms are different from the baseline, leading to an increase in False Negatives, but not a significant one. Those results tell us that the network is learning rendering features depending on factors like lines, positions, aliasing, and others, not only colors.

4.3   Discussion

Regarding **RQ1**, some previous works imply that the canvas generation depends on software and hardware stacks [10,31]. This premise is the basis for arguing that a unique canvas fingerprint would be possible, or at least unique enough to distinguish devices with different software or hardware. Nevertheless, the results in Fig. 6 point otherwise. It is clear that the values on the diagonal are much lower than the other ones, suggesting that devices with the same browser are more similar between them than devices with other browsers families. But with the Fig. 7a the analysis can go further. It can be seen that the majority of pixel-wise comparisons between devices with the same OS and browser family lies at exactly zero. It could be thought that several users from our dataset shared a similar hardware configuration, and therefore the canvases were generated so that their pixel-wise difference was zero. Nonetheless, along with their canvas and user-agents, some WebGL hardware features were collected as well. Those WebGL features gave us information about the rendering stack that each device owned, which could be an external GPU or the integrated graphics rendered of the CPU. Even though this is not necessarily the device that renders the canvas, this information could be indirectly related to the hardware stack of each user's device.

When joining the user-agent information, JS browser-navigator, and WebGL hardware features, we found that from about 17K possible user combinations, only 14 showed the exact same software and hardware stacks, less than 0.1%. This indicates that there are limits in the granularity of hardware/software combinations that can be distinguished using images generated by the HTML5 canvas API.

Together with the information in Fig. 7a, it could be assessed that the hardware stack is not a determining parameter at the moment of canvas generation. For different hardware stacks but same software configurations, the result was that the canvas difference was mostly zero. This means that the software stack is the determinant factor when generating canvas, and devices with the same OS-Browser combination tend to produce the exact same image.

RQ2 addresses this particular challenge. If our results show that different hardware configurations generate the same canvas, then creating a unique fin-

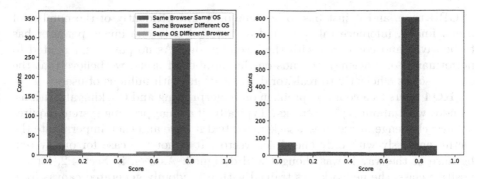

(a) Score histogram for the negative class with different input text colors on test

(b) Score histogram for the positive class with different input text colors on test

Fig. 10. Score histograms for images with different font colors as in the training set.

gerprint based *only* on canvas and computer vision is not possible. It does not matter if the most complex image classification architecture is used or trained with millions of examples if the images contain the same information pixel-wise. This is a limitation observed in the latest browser versions, which are trying to protect users from tracking [17]. They try to hide the most features that can be used to fingerprint them on the web [18], or those features become obsolete, like flash fonts [11], so it is no surprise that they are standardizing canvas rendering to avoid tracking. In this case, it is impracticable to have a canvas-only-based system that provides a unique fingerprint given the current browsers, but as shown in our results, our system has an almost perfect performance to distinguish different types of software configurations. We believe an upper bound has been achieved to distinguish the canvases, and no computer vision strategy could improve it.

Even though the unique fingerprint is not feasible, our system can be used as a first filter to identify attackers, checking if an impersonation attempt is made from a device with a different configuration than the victim's one. In a real scenario, there can be millions of users and thousands of requests per day; **RQ3** relates to this situation. Our system is based on the One-for-all approach. A single Siamese network is used to assess whether two input canvases belong to the same device or not, compared to [31], which trains one model per user. For our case, we do not need to train and allocate *millions* of models.

Additionally, the volume of images needed for training decreases considerably because the entries of all users can be used to train the model, compared to the one-model-per-user approach, which needs many examples of the same user to achieve acceptable accuracy. To bring down this discussion, here are some numbers of our approach: Our model requires less than 140 images per user to train the positive class, in the extreme case that we only want the positive class to be trained with one user; otherwise, that number goes further down; each of those images weights around 25Kb; training of the model requires around 5 min of GPU time, and it just has to be done once independently of the number of users; finally, inference takes around 30 ms, and only one image per user has to be saved and compared with the incoming one. As no parameter related to performance or efficiency depends on the number of users, we believe that the system scales efficiently to real-world applications with millions of users.

RQ4 refers to a common problem on fingerprinting and tracking algorithms, namely, what about replay attacks? Typically, if a fingerprinting system requires a *static* challenge, it requires attackers to steal it once and then impersonate the victim endlessly with only one stolen vector. It is not the case for our system because of the way it was thought and designed. As seen in Sect. 4.2, for the positive class, the network was trained with a randomly generated canvas from each user, with different texts. At the test, it is shown that even when two images had different texts if the same user-generated them, the system assesses this almost perfectly. Thus, the idea for the implementation is to ask the user to generate a random image to compare each time but generate a similar (Same text) image in the server to compare it to whatever the user returns. Both images, generated by the user and the server, should be similar because they represent the same text, which could be tested with a classic image-similarity approach. However, if an attacker tries to use a previously generated image by the user, it would not have the same text as the generated by the server, and it would be easily recognized as an attack. This imposed freshness implies that the system is not vulnerable to replay attacks, in comparison to canvas approaches that depend on hashes [10] because they need to compare between equally generated images.

Lastly, **RQG** asks about the conclusion from the specific research questions. Knowing the reach and limitations of our system, it can be answered that certain types of impersonation attacks can be detected through canvas-based authentication. Namely, attackers with a different OS or Browser family can be opportunely detected even if they modify their user-agent or other browser features.

Nevertheless, it was proven that attackers or users with the same OS-Browser configuration in most cases could not be distinguished, as their pixel-wise difference is frequently zero. Creating a unique fingerprint for each device based only on this type of canvas is not possible. Therefore, we propose our system only to complement other subsystems or features that perform the users' authentication. We distance our goal from scripts that use fingerprints for targeted advertising and other privacy-concerning objectives. Our work aims to provide an extra layer of protection in authentication procedures, looking for canvas-noticeable anomalies. Accordingly, we see no use of models like ours to consistently track users to fill them with advertising or to collect sensitive data from them. However, tracking and fingerprint authentication are for browser developers two sides of the same coin. Consequently, they are still going to make fingerprinting difficult, looking forward to protecting user's privacy.

In sum, although the proposed protocol and underlying classifier have shortcomings in terms of authentication accuracy, we believe that our analysis shows that they constitute a promising building block in the context of a risk-based authentication toolkit. In fact, accuracy can be further improved by taking into account other traditional fingerprinting features (such as installed fonts, declared HTTP parameters, etc.) or other hardware-based features (such as the WebGL API). Given that most of those features are not secure against replay attacks, our technique can complement them by raising the bar against such advanced attacks. Being a complement for the authentication process, the 82% accuracy together with the 0% FRR are encouraging results, because this guarantees low or no friction on legitimate user, while detecting most attacks coming from different browser and OS combinations.

5   Related Work

There are three works that attack the problem of browser fingerprinting exclusively through the canvas API, namely Picasso [10], SWAT [31], and *Morellian* Analysis [22]. Picasso is a protocol to fingerprint browsers based on canvas and hashes. The idea is to create images that maximize the entropy between data from users with different OS or Browser when compared, and minimize the entropy between users who share the same combination. Those images are hashed together with a seed and the generated hash would then be compared to the expected response for that OS-Browser combination. Before Picasso could be launched, a bootstrap step had to be performed: They had to generate themselves a sufficiently large sample of images and expected responses from each combination so that it is not feasible for an attacker to brute force a replay attack on them. This process needs to be repeated every time a new browser or OS version is on the market, because they cannot directly verify the user's response. They presented an accuracy of 100% between users with different OS or Browser but did not analyze Chromium-based browsers other than Google Chrome.

Secondly, SWAT appears as the first contribution that does not use a pixelwise comparison between a trustworthy canvas and a new attempt but a similarity score to compare them. Here, a neural network is trained for each user to assess if an input canvas was generated by the user's device or not. They achieve up to 95% accuracy in the median case, compared to 82% in our case. However, they acknowledge that their False Positive Rate is vast for some scenarios. As discussed in Sect. 4.2 those scenarios refer to users who share either Browser or OS which are sometimes impossible to distinguish. Additionally, they have to train one model per user, with training times between 1–3 min and at least 2000 images per user. This fact may be inconvenient for large-scale implementation, firstly because it requires time and computational resources to train each model, and secondly because collecting 2000 images per user can take a considerable amount of time, compared to the minimum of two images per user necessary for our approach. It would require either increasing the friction to users, make them wait until all the canvases are rendered in one session, or collecting the canvases through several sessions before the SWAT system can be initialized.

Finally, the *Morellian* Analysis paper [22] is a canvas-based fingerprinting technique that generates a challenge on the server-side as an authentication protocol. The comparison is made pixel-wise, so they have an utterly binary response, either both images are equal or not. To avoid replay attacks, they ask the client to generate two random canvases each time he/she wants to authenticate, one for the current login and one to compare the next login. In this way, an attacker must steal the correct canvas to be able to impersonate the victim. In contrast, in our work users always receive fresh challenges in a single session, further raising the bar against replay attacks.

In sum, to the best of our knowledge ours is the first work to propose a Canvas based authentication protocol using machine-learning that is secure against replay attacks and is by design scalable to a large user base, by requiring only one model for all users in a system. Additionally, we prove that for current browsers, the previous works on canvas fingerprinting based on hashes or similarity can not be longer applied to create a unique fingerprint because the generated canvases for same-browser-OS devices are *exactly* the same.

6   Conclusions

In this paper, we present a canvas-based system to help authenticate users. We also analyze the generated text-based canvases in a pixel-wise manner to show that some devices could not be distinguished when they share OS and Browser configuration because their canvases are exactly equal. Nevertheless, comparing random users, we achieve an accuracy of 82%, and comparing users with either different browsers or OS an accuracy of 92%. Specifically, we present virtually no friction for the users for the positive class, with a recall of 100%. Given the nature of our system, the One model for All approach is easily scalable to millions of users without the need to train the same number of models and requiring much fewer images to accomplish the training. Similar to other Risk-based Authentication approaches, we propose our system as a complement, not a replacement of other types of authentication systems, enhancing the security level without compromising the scalability of the system and the overall user experience.

References

1. Acar, G., Eubank, C., Englehardt, S., Juarez, M., Narayanan, A., Diaz, C.: The web never forgets: persistent tracking mechanisms in the wild. In: Proceedings of the 2014 ACM SIGSAC Conference on Computer and Communications Security, pp. 674–689. ACM, New York (2014). https://doi.org/10.1145/2660267.2660347
2. Addons Mozilla: CanvasBlocker (2021). https://addons.mozilla.org/en-US/firefox/addon/canvasblocker/
3. Al-Fannah, N.M., Li, W., Mitchell, C.J.: Beyond cookie monster amnesia: real world persistent online tracking. In: Chen, L., Manulis, M., Schneider, S. (eds.) ISC 2018. LNCS, vol. 11060, pp. 481–501. Springer, Cham (2018). https://doi.org/10.1007/978-3-319-99136-8_26
4. Al-Fannah, N.M., Mitchell, C.: Too little too late: can we control browser fingerprinting? J. Intellect. Capital 21(2), 165–180 (2020). https://doi.org/10.1108/JIC-04-2019-0067. https://www.emerald.com/insight/content/doi/10.1108/JIC-04-2019-0067/full/html

5. Alaca, F., van Oorschot, P.: Device fingerprinting for augmenting web authentication. In: Proceedings of the 32nd Annual Conference on Computer Security Applications, vol. 5-9-Decemb, pp. 289–301. ACM, New York (2016). https://doi.org/10.1145/2991079.2991091

6. Andriamilanto, N., Allard, T., Guelvouit, G.L.: FPSelect: low-cost browser fingerprints for mitigating dictionary attacks against web authentication mechanisms. In: ACM International Conference Proceeding Series, vol. 1, no. 1, pp. 627–642 (2020). https://doi.org/10.1145/3427228.3427297. https://arxiv.org/abs/2010.06404

7. Bharadwaj, S., Vatsa, M., Singh, R.: Biometric quality: a review of fingerprint, iris, and face. EURASIP J. Image Video Process. **2014**(1), 1–28 (2014). https://doi.org/10.1186/1687-5281-2014-34

8. Blanco-Gonzalo, R., Lunerti, C., Sanchez-Reillo, R., Guest, R.: Biometrics: accessibility challenge or opportunity? PLOS ONE **13**(4), 1 (2018). https://doi.org/10.1371/journal.pone.0196372

9. Boerman, S.C., Kruikemeier, S., Borgesius, F.J.Z.: Online behavioral advertising: a literature review and research agenda. J. Advertising **46**(3), 363–376 (2017)

10. Bursztein, E., Malyshev, A., Pietraszek, T., Thomas, K.: Picasso: lightweight device class fingerprinting for web clients. In: Proceedings of the 6th Workshop on Security and Privacy in Smartphones and Mobile Devices, pp. 93–102. ACM, New York (2016). https://doi.org/10.1145/2994459.2994467

11. Cao, Y., Li, S., Wijmans, E.: (Cross-)Browser fingerprinting via OS and hardware level features. In: Proceedings 2017 Network and Distributed System Security Symposium. Internet Society, Reston (2017). https://doi.org/10.14722/ndss.2017.23152

12. Daud, N.I., Haron, G.R., Othman, S.S.S.: Adaptive authentication: implementing random canvas fingerprinting as user attributes factor. In: 2017 IEEE Symposium on Computer Applications & Industrial Electronics (ISCAIE), pp. 152–156. IEEE (2017). https://doi.org/10.1109/ISCAIE.2017.8074968. https://ieeexplore.ieee.org/document/8074968/

13. Durey, A., Laperdrix, P., Rudametkin, W., Rouvoy, R.: FP-redemption: studying browser fingerprinting adoption for the sake of web security. In: Bilge, L., Cavallaro, L., Pellegrino, G., Neves, N. (eds.) DIMVA 2021. LNCS, vol. 12756, pp. 237–257. Springer, Cham (2021). https://doi.org/10.1007/978-3-030-80825-9_12

14. Eckersley, P.: How unique is your web browser? In: Atallah, M.J., Hopper, N.J. (eds.) PETS 2010. LNCS, vol. 6205, pp. 1–18. Springer, Heidelberg (2010). https://doi.org/10.1007/978-3-642-14527-8_1

15. Englehardt, S., Narayanan, A.: Online tracking. In: Proceedings of the 2016 ACM SIGSAC Conference on Computer and Communications Security, pp. 1388–1401. ACM, New York (2016). https://doi.org/10.1145/2976749.2978313

16. Fifield, D., Egelman, S.: Fingerprinting web users through font metrics. In: Böhme, R., Okamoto, T. (eds.) FC 2015. LNCS, vol. 8975, pp. 107–124. Springer, Heidelberg (2015). https://doi.org/10.1007/978-3-662-47854-7_7

17. Firefox Help: Firefox's protection against fingerprinting. https://support.mozilla.org/en-US/kb/firefox-protection-against-fingerprinting

18. Gómez-Boix, A., Laperdrix, P., Baudry, B.: Hiding in the crowd. In: Proceedings of the 2018 World Wide Web Conference on World Wide Web, WWW 2018, pp. 309–318. ACM Press, New York (2018). https://doi.org/10.1145/3178876.3186097

19. Iqbal, U., Englehardt, S., Shafiq, Z.: Fingerprinting the fingerprinters: learning to detect browser fingerprinting behaviors. In: 2021 IEEE Symposium on Security and Privacy (SP), pp. 1143–1161 (2020). https://doi.org/10.1109/SP40001.2021.00017

20. Jiang, W., Wang, X., Song, X., Liu, Q., Liu, X.: Tracking your browser with high-performance browser fingerprint recognition model. China Commun. **17**(3), 168–175 (2020). https://doi.org/10.23919/JCC.2020.03.014

21. Koch, G., Zemel, R., Salakhutdinov, R.: Siamese neural networks for one-shot image recognition. In: 32nd International Conference on Machine Learning, Lille, France, vol. 37, pp. 1–8 (2015). https://doi.org/10.1136/bmj.2.5108.1355-c. https://www.bmj.com/lookup/doi/10.1136/bmj.2.5108.1355-c

22. Laperdrix, P., Avoine, G., Baudry, B., Nikiforakis, N.: Morellian analysis for browsers: making web authentication stronger with canvas fingerprinting. In: Perdisci, R., Maurice, C., Giacinto, G., Almgren, M. (eds.) DIMVA 2019. LNCS, vol. 11543, pp. 43–66. Springer, Cham (2019). https://doi.org/10.1007/978-3-030-22038-9_3

23. Laperdrix, P., Bielova, N., Baudry, B., Avoine, G.: Browser fingerprinting: a survey. ACM Trans. Web **14**(2), 1–33 (2020). https://doi.org/10.1145/3386040

24. Mowery, K., Shacham, H.: Pixel perfect: fingerprinting canvas in HTML5. In: Web 2.0 Security & Privacy 20 (W2SP), pp. 1–12 (2012)

25. Nikiforakis, N., Kapravelos, A., Joosen, W., Kruegel, C., Piessens, F., Vigna, G.: Cookieless monster: exploring the ecosystem of web-based device fingerprinting. In: 2013 IEEE Symposium on Security and Privacy, pp. 541–555. IEEE (2013). https://doi.org/10.1109/SP.2013.43

26. Pagnin, E., Mitrokotsa, A.: Privacy-preserving biometric authentication: challenges and directions. Secur. Commun. Netw. **2017**(1), 9 (2017). https://doi.org/10.1155/2017/7129505

27. Pasquini, C., Amerini, I., Boato, G.: Media forensics on social media platforms: a survey. EURASIP J. Inf. Secur. **2021**(1), 1–19 (2021). https://doi.org/10.1186/s13635-021-00117-2

28. Pedregosa, F., et al.: Scikit-learn: machine learning in Python. J. Mach. Learn. Res. **12**, 2825–2830 (2011)

29. Pugliese, G., Riess, C., Gassmann, F., Benenson, Z.: Long-term observation on browser fingerprinting: users' trackability and perspective. Proc. Priv. Enhancing Technol. **2020**(2), 558–577 (2020). https://doi.org/10.2478/popets-2020-0041

30. Reitinger, N., Mazurek, M.L.: ML-CB: machine learning canvas block. Proc. Priv. Enhancing Technol. **2021**(3), 453–473 (2021). https://doi.org/10.2478/popets-2021-0056. https://www.sciendo.com/article/10.2478/popets-2021-0056

31. Rochet, F., Efthymiadis, K., Koeune, F., Pereira, O.: SWAT: seamless web authentication technology. In: The World Wide Web Conference on WWW 2019, vol. 2, pp. 1579–1589. ACM Press, New York (2019). https://doi.org/10.1145/3308558.3313637

32. Samizade, S., Shen, C., Si, C., Guan, X.: Passive browser identification with multi-scale convolutional neural networks. Neurocomputing **378**, 238–247 (2020). https://doi.org/10.1016/j.neucom.2019.10.028

33. Solomos, K., Kristoff, J., Kanich, C., Polakis, J.: Tales of favicons and caches: persistent tracking in modern browsers. In: Proceedings 2021 Network and Distributed System Security Symposium, p. 18. Internet Society, Reston (2021). https://doi.org/10.14722/ndss.2021.24202

34. StatCounter Global Stats: Desktop browser market share worldwide. https://gs.statcounter.com/browser-market-share/desktop/worldwide

35. Vastel, A., Rouvoy, R., Rudametkin, W.: Tracking versus security: investigating the two facets of browser fingerprinting. Ph.D. thesis, Université de Lille (2019)

Android Malware Detection Using BERT

Badr Souani[1]([✉]), Ahmed Khanfir[1], Alexandre Bartel[2], Kevin Allix[1],
and Yves Le Traon[1]

[1] University of Luxembourg, Esch-sur-Alzette, Luxembourg
{badr.souani,ahmed.khanfir,kevin.allix,yves.letraon}@uni.lu
[2] Umeå University, Umeå, Sweden
alexandre.bartel@cs.umu.se

Abstract. In this paper, we propose two empirical studies to (1) detect
Android malware and (2) classify Android malware into families. We
first (1) reproduce the results of MalBERT using BERT models learning
with Android application's manifests obtained from 265k applications
(vs. 22k for MalBERT) from the AndroZoo dataset in order to detect
malware. The results of the MalBERT paper are excellent and hard to
believe as a manifest only roughly represents an application, we therefore
try to answer the following questions in this paper. Are the experiments
from MalBERT reproducible? How important are Permissions for malware detection? Is it possible to keep or improve the results by reducing
the size of the manifests? We then (2) investigate if BERT can be used to
classify Android malware into families. The results show that BERT can
successfully differentiate malware/goodware with 97% accuracy. Furthermore BERT can classify malware families with 93% accuracy. We also
demonstrate that Android permissions are not what allows BERT to
successfully classify and even that it does not actually need it.

1 Introduction

Android malware are malicious applications aiming at attacking the end-users'
devices, data, money, software or third party applications and services [5]. With
the democratization of smartphones, virtually everyone nowadays carries every-
day a device that can access, store, and manipulate sensitive and private data.
Android, being the most used smartphone operating system, is a target of choice
for attackers, who create malicious applications that aim to obtain financial gains
from often unsuspecting users.

In fact, new Malware are constantly being released [19], causing a constant
threat and challenge for the users, the application-markets maintainers, and the
security researchers.

Consequently, much effort and resources are spent to develop approaches
that are able to automatically detect Malware in the unstopping flow of new
applications. This includes detection approaches at the app store level such as
Google PlayStore [2], or at the device level via anti-viruses [5]. Practitioners and
researchers are in a constant race with the load of appearing Malware, thus, trying to detect not only previously identified Malware but also new ones. For this

J. Zhou et al. (Eds.): ACNS 2022 Workshops, LNCS 13285, pp. 575–591, 2022.
https://doi.org/10.1007/978-3-031-16815-4_31

purpose, they propose approaches that classify the applications into Malware or not depending on relevant suspiciousness-related components appearing in the applications. Those approaches are classified into two main categories: static and dynamic analysis techniques. The approaches based on static analysis aim at identifying Malware by parsing and evaluating the syntax of the application while the dynamic-based approaches extract information about application by instrumenting and running them in order to capture any eventual malicious/suspicious behavior of the application through its execution. Additionally, a third approach category – a hybrid one – consists of combining both static and dynamic analysis, in the hope of obtaining more and better information that could be leveraged to determine the maliciousness of a given application.

The growing interest and evolution of the machine learning techniques have engendered significant advances in the security field in general [13] and in malware detection particularly [27]. Obviously, it is more interesting and even more cost-effective [27] to save expensive human computing effort by letting the machine capture the malicious characteristics of malware, instead. In this regard, previous research has focused on defining the key-components that are the most relevant to malware detection, to better guide the learning and detection abilities of the approaches. Notably, the exotic or unexpected usage of API-calls such as the data-transfer via insecure web urls can be a determinant symptom of an eventual malicious behavior [4,23,29]. Leveraging this extra knowledge of historical malware specifications boosted the capabilities of machine learning techniques towards higher performances.

Recently Rahali et al. [24] have trained a model MalBERT based on BERT [9] – a language representation model, originally only intended for natural text processing – in order to determine whether an Android application is malicious or not by processing applications' Manifest file. More precisely, they fine-tune a pre-trained BERT model on the Manifest files of the malicious and benign Android applications included in an Android dataset collected from public resources. Their evaluation of the proposed approach shows promising results, achieving 97% of prediction accuracy. This high performance could be explained by: (1) first, the relevance of the manifest information – including the configuration and descriptive data of the application – in hinting at the presence or absence of malicious behavior in the application and (2) second, the ability of BERT in differentiating between the malicious and safe variants of these relevant components.

In this same line of research, we drive an empirical study on a large-scale dataset AndroZoo [5], where we: (1) reproduce the training and evaluation experiments of Rahali et al. [24], (2) investigate the impact of the manifest permissions on the Malware detection, (3) evaluate the xml-tags noise effect on the model performance, and finally (4) discuss the capability of the proposed approach in classifying malware by families.

Our results confirm the ones published by the authors in the original paper [24], where MalBERT achieves 97% of prediction accuracy. Surprisingly, our results show that MalBERT's representation of the Manifests is not restricted to particular components of the Manifest. In fact, the model differentiates correctly between malware and benign applications even when fed with only the permissions, or when excluding the permissions, with almost 90% of recall and more than 93% of accuracy. Similarly, reducing the size of the input Manifests by considering only the xml values (without the tags), improves very slightly the results by 0,003% for the accuracy and 0,008% for the recall. Finally, we show that MalBERT can also be used to predict Malware families with an accuracy varying between 0,81 and 0,995.

In this paper we make the following contributions:

- A reproducibility study of MalBERT using a dataset an order of magnitude bigger (265k Android applications vs. 22k);
- An ablation study where we study the impact of different elements of the Android Manifest on the malware detection rate;
- An empirical study of the usefulness of BERT to classify Android malware into families. Results show that the approach can classify malware with 93% accuracy.

The remainder of the paper is organized as follows. In Sect. 2 we describe the background information necessary to understand the paper. In Sect. 3, we present our experimental setup. Next, in Sect. 4, we analyze the empirical results. We discuss the results in Sect. 5 and present the related work in Sect. 6. Finally, we conclude in Sect. 7.

2   Background

2.1   Malware Detection

To detect malware with machine learning, practitioners traditionally have to extract a list of features from the applications, and to represent apps as a vector. These features can be extracted using two main approaches: static analysis and dynamic analysis.

Static Analysis. Static Analysis consists of analyzing an application without executing it. It can extract features such as binary signatures, the list of used libraries, or code structures. More advanced analyses generate information about the code such as a call-graph (i.e., the relationship between callee and caller functions) or control flow graphs to understand, for instance, how data flows in a function or the whole program. The power of static analysis comes from the fact that, contrary to dynamic analysis, the whole code can be reached and analyzed. This also comes with a cost in term of precision and run-time. Many static analyses have a high false positive rate since paths which cannot be executed in practice might also be analyzed. A static analysis often does not scale well and thus might take a long time to execute on realistic applications. In our experiments, we statically extract features from Android applications' manifests.

Dynamic Analysis. In a dynamic analysis, the application is executed to understand its behavior. In the case of malware analysis, executions are typically performed in an isolated sandbox to prevent the malicious code from spreading to the machine running the dynamic analysis or to machines on the network. The main challenge is to find input to the application to execute as much as possible of the application's code. Extracted features could be a list of API calls or a list of DNS requests.

2.2 Android Package

Android applications are zip files whose names end with the `.apk` (Android PacKage) extension. It is a container that includes the application's code, resources, certificates, assets and a manifest. The manifest is an XML file which contains metadata describing among others the structure of the application, its name and version. Furthermore, it also includes the permissions that the application requires. Thus, a manifest is a high-level representation of an Android application. We extract features from Android applications' manifest as input for our experiments.

2.3 Transformer

More recently, researchers have tried to automate the extraction of manually-defined features, or to by-pass this step altogether.

The Transformer [28] is an architecture designed to handle sequential data. It excels in the field of NLP (Natural language processing) such as translation, question and answer, paraphrasing, and text summarization. Transformers quickly became the foundation of several impressive improvements over the previous state of the art. Introduced in 2017, Transformers have been the subject of many research papers. A Transformer consists of an Encoder and a Decoder. The Encoder, takes a sequence in input and transforms it into a continuous sequence. The Decoder then generates a sequences element by element using the previous one at each step, and the sequence generated by the encoder.

2.4 BERT

BERT [9] is an approach based on transformers and has been created for text processing tasks such as translation [34], question answering [32], text classification [14, 26] or text comprehension [30]. With its impressive performance, BERT had a massive impact, and has served as the basis for many other models such as Roberta [21] which is a version of BERT model with carefully selected key hyperparameters to improve its performance, Deberta [11] that improves BERT and Roberta models by changing its attention mechanisms and masking, or Code-Bert [10] that achieves great results on both natural language code search and code documentation generation tasks. BERT (and its descendants) divides its training in two stages, Pre-training and Fine-Tuning. BERT is able to capture high-level concepts from sentences, one of its main novelty being its use of context from sentences in both directions, forward and backward, which may explains its state-of-the-art results on NLP tasks. The **pre-training** phase consists in training the model from scratch using non-labeled data such as the Wikipedia Corpus (2500M words) [1]. The pre-training performs two "fake" tasks, i.e., tasks that have no real purpose other than to force the model to learn to capture high-level concepts:

- **Masked Language Model:** In order to exercise the model's ability to consider the context of a sentence, random words from the input sentences are masked, and BERT tries during this process to infer (i.e.,recover) the words that have been masked.
- **Next Sentence Prediction:** It consists in making BERT tries to infer whether two sentences given as input are likely to be a valid sequence of sentences. This allows BERT to learn the link between sentences, which is very useful for tasks such as questions and answers.

The **fine-tuning** phase adapts an already-trained, task-agnostic BERT model to a specific task. In practice, layers of neurons are added as output, to use the output of BERT. During the fine-tuning phase, the weights of the existing BERT model are fixed, but the weights of the newly added, task-specific layers are trained in order to obtain the desired performance on the task at hand.

This separation in two phases (pre-training and fine-tuning) is a significant advantage of BERT (and of similar approaches): The pre-training, while extremely computationally expensive, only has to be done once. The resulting pre-trained model can then be put to use in a variety of tasks, after a much less computationally expensive fine-tuning.

3 Experimental Setup

In this section, we present the experimental setup we use in our study. A high-level overall representation of the entire process is depicted in Fig. 1. The process features three main steps: (1) the creation of the dataset explained in Sect. 3.1, (2) the pre-processing step described in Sect. 3.2 and (3) the fine-tuning step explained in Sect. 3.3.

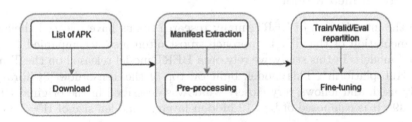

Fig. 1. Experiment representation

3.1 Dataset

In our experiments we use Android applications from AndroZoo [5]. AndroZoo is a dataset of Android apps made available to the research community, and that contains, at the time of writing, more than 19 million Android applications. All applications in AndroZoo are analyzed with several antivirus software using VirusTotal[1] in order to determine whether they are malware.

We randomly selected 265 000 Android applications released in 2019 or after, and we downloaded them from AndroZoo. The resulting dataset is composed of around 30% malware (77 768) mainly containing malware from three families[2]:

– **Jiagu** is a large family of malware. This family includes many variants that exhibit malicious behaviors such as unwanted advertisement, or *Trojan clicking*, i.e., clicking on ads without user's consent. Approximately 60% (47 522) of the malware in our dataset are of the jiagu family.
– **Dnotua** is the second largest family of malware in our dataset, representing 2% (1443) of the malware samples. Apps that are members of the Dnotua family can perform a variety of malevolent actions such as installing other apps or collecting network information.
– **Secneo** is the third largest malware family in our dataset, with 1% (674) of malware samples. Secneo apps can perform many nefarious tasks, such as sending SMS, collecting contacts, or placing phone calls.

In addition to these three families, the remaining 31% (25 182) of the malware in our dataset are either a) members of a family that contains only a small number of samples, or b) malware that do not seem to be members of a family. For our experiments, we construct training, validation, and evaluation sets, by drawing apps from the global dataset. Each experiment is conducted with a different shuffle for training, validation, and evaluation sets in order to report the most faithful values possible during evaluations. For the ground Truth of the malware detection experiments, we rely on the reports obtained from VirusTotal. For the malware family classification, we leveraged the AVclass tool [25] that can take a detection report from VirusTotal, and compute the name of the family of the sample, or a unique identifier for APKs that cannot be linked to a family.

3.2 Pre-trained Model

Since the introduction of BERT, many research teams have released their own implementation of the BERT approach, most often also accompanied by pre-trained models. In this study, we rely on a BERT model released on the Tensor-Flow Hub platform[3]. This model, built on top of the Tensorflow [3] library, is widely used, and follows very closely what was described in the original BERT paper [9]: It is composed of $L = 12$ hidden layers, a hidden size of $H = 768$ and

---

[1] https://www.virustotal.com.
[2] To obtain information about malware families, we rely on the AVclass tool [25].
[3] https://tfhub.dev.

$A = 12$ attention heads[4]. It has been pre-trained for English on Wikipedia [1] and BooksCorpus (110M parameters)[5].

3.3 Fine-Tuning

We perform two different fine-tunings for two different tasks: malware detection and malware family classification. The first tasks we investigate is malware detection. In this setting, models are fine-tuned with the aim of discriminating benign applications from malicious ones. The fine-tuning step is performed on a training-set composed of 132 500 (i.e., half the dataset) APKs from AndroZoo [5] with 30% malware. The second task we investigate, malware family classification, is different than malware detection while being closely related. The models, whose objective is to detect whether an application is part of a malware family or not, are fine-tuned with a dataset of 77 768 malware, i.e., all the malware samples of our dataset. The training, validation and test sets are distributed as 50%, 20% and 30% respectively. The training, validation and test sets are stratified, which means that each set has the same malware/goodware ratio as the whole dataset.

Regarding the parameters, the models are fine-tuned for 20 epochs with a batch size set to 32, using Adam as the optimizer function, and with a learning rate of $3e^{-5}$. All training phases and inference phases are performed on one NVIDIA Tesla V100 GPU with 32 GB of memory. As an indication, one complete experiment (i.e., fine-tuning on a training set for 20 epochs, and inferring on the test set for one given type of input) takes between 10 to 16 hours each. In addition, each complete experiment is performed ten times using a different seed (i.e., a different shuffle for Train/Validation/Test sets), in order to obtain an average of performance as representative as possible of the models.

4 Empirical Results

In this section, we investigate to the following research questions:

- RQ1: Are the experiments from MalBERT reproducible?
- RQ2: How important are Permissions for malware detection?
- RQ3: Is it possible to keep or improve the results by reducing the size of the manifests?
- RQ4: Can BERT classify families of malware?

---

[4] The exact model we used can be found at https://tfhub.dev/tensorflow/bert_en_uncased_L-12_H-768_A-12/4?tf-hub-format=compressed. We note that we also relied on the matching BERT Pre-processor available at https://tfhub.dev/tensorflow/bert_en_uncased_preprocess/3?tf-hub-format=compressed.

[5] More information about this model as well as about the other available models of this collection can be found at https://tfhub.dev/google/collections/bert.

4.1   RQ1: Are the Experiments from MalBERT Reproducible?

While reading the literature, we observed a large number of papers discussing various techniques for Android malware detection [15,16,33]. The objective was to study an Android malware detection technique using BERT. MalBERT [24], which uses BERT with as an embedding technique for manifests from APKs achieves very good results with 97% accuracy. It is not surprising to see BERT perform very well on tasks involving text such as manifests that, while being XML data, contain nonetheless mostly textual data. However, these results might be considered quite hard to believe. Indeed, obtaining such high performance with so little information—Manifest are at most a few tens of kilobits—seems at first sight both surprising and highly promising. Our objective here is therefore to first check if the manifests are really enough to represent an application in order to determine if it is malware or not.

Table 1. Results of Bert model malware detection

Model	Application	Accuracy	Loss	F_1 score
MalBERT	22 000	0.9761	0.1274	0.9547
Our study	265 000	0.970	0.183	0.949

Like in MalBERT, the BERT model we rely on was already pre-trained for English on Wikipedia [1] and BooksCorpus. The experiments are run using the previously mentioned dataset of 265 000 different manifests with 30% malware, and with 20 epochs of fine-tuning. The dataset is divided into three stratified sets as detailed above: training, validation and testing set contain respectively 50%, 20% and 30% of the dataset.

Regarding the results in Table 1, our model has a slightly lower accuracy with 0.970 opposed to 0.976 and F1 score with 0.949 in our results, and 0.9547 with MalBERT. This can be explained by the fact that their dataset consists of only 22.000 manifests with about 45% malware which is a rather different scale. MalBERT's results have therefore been successfully reproduced, it seems that it is indeed possible to identify malware using manifests.

4.2   RQ2: How Important are Permissions for Malware Detection?

As shown above, MalBERT seems to be able to differentiate malware from benign APKs simply by using the manifests. One immediate question that follows from this observation is: What parts of the Manifest files are enabling such performance?

Permissions is the first component of a manifest we investigate the discriminating power of. Several papers [6,8,18] show experiments carried out on the permissions of the manifests to detect malware because this is likely to be the factor that differentiates the category to which an APK belongs. Indeed, some permissions are more dangerous than others because they give more possibilities to the application, such as accessing sensitive information or performing actions that can alter the Android system.

In order to answer this research question, two different pre-processing were done on the manifests in order to create two new types of manifests, one with only the permissions (*Permission Only*), and one composed of manifests without the permissions (*No Permission*). Two different models were fine-tuned like before using the two new manifest types and the same parameters. The results are shown in Table 2.

Table 2. Results of Bert models malware detection with pre-processed Permissions

Pre-process	Accuracy	Loss	F_1 score	Precision	Recall
Full	**0.970**	0.183	**0.949**	0.957	0.941
Permission only	0.930	0.228	0.879	0.897	0.861
No permission	0.967	0.193	0.943	0.952	0.933

The fine-tuned model using manifests with only the requested permissions shows an accuracy of 0.93 and an F1 score of 0.879. Permissions do allow BERT to differentiate malware from benign APKs, but permissions do not seem to be the only part of the manifest that BERT uses for malware detection as shown by the lower results of this training compared to the one using the full manifest. It can be inferred that the permissions do indeed contain information that is very relevant for a malware detector, but that the other information in the manifests also contain additional information that could be leveraged for malware detection.

Next, the results of the fine-tuning using the manifests without the permissions are 0.967 for the accuracy and 0.943 for the F1 Score. Manifests without permissions have a very slightly lower result than the originals. This proves that permissions are not necessary for BERT to get good results. One can assume that something else in the manifests allows to differentiate malware from benign applications quite accurately. Further experiments with more precise ablations will be necessary to define which part of the manifest allows BERT to operate.

4.3   RQ3: Is it Possible to Keep or Improve the Results by Reducing the Size of the Manifests?

To determine what helps BERT to detect malware using the manifests, an intermediate step can be to remove what might be suspected of simply interfering with the learning process. For this purpose, two new variants of manifests have been created by performing a pre-processing on the manifests as before.

For the first variant, a deny list is created with words and characters arbitrarily considered as useless for learning. This list is quite short and consists

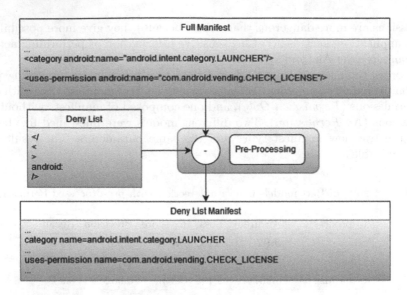

Fig. 2. Pre-process on the manifests using the deny list

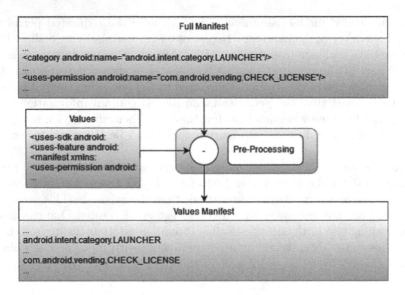

Fig. 3. Pre-process on the manifests removing tag names

of words like 'android:' which is repeated many times in the manifests, or the less-than and greater-than signs that are heavily used to construct the XML elements. These words and letters are simply removed from the manifests and this process can be observed on Fig. 2. We will refer to this manifest variant as (Deny List) For the second variant, referred to as Values, XML tag names are removed to keep only the XML values as shown in Fig. 3. This would allow BERT to focus on what matters most. The results are presented in Table 3 and the experiments are made with the same parameters as before.

Table 3. Results of Bert models for malware detection with pre-processed manifests for Permissions and Noises

Pre-process	Accuracy	Loss	F_1 score	Precision	Recall
Full	0.970	0.183	0.949	0.957	0.941
Permission only	0.930	0.228	0.879	0.897	0.861
No permission	0.967	0.193	0.943	0.952	0.933
Deny list	0.972	0.168	0.951	0.961	0.942
Values	**0.973**	0.155	**0.954**	0.959	0.949

The results of the pre-precessing deny list consisting in removing the redundant words judged as being useless for the learning process allow to obtain slightly better results than the previous fine-tuning phases with an accuracy of 0.0972 and an F1 score of 0.951. This shows that reducing the "noise" indeed seems to help BERT, and that nothing necessary for its classification has been removed.

Finally, the model trained with the manifests without most of the tags but keeping the values shows the best results with 0.973 of accuracy and 0.954 of F1 score. As with the deny list, reducing the noise in the file by deleting tag names makes BERT concentrate more on what helps it to classify.

4.4 RQ4: Can BERT Classify Families of Malware?

It makes sense to say that BERT can detect quite accurately whether an APK is a malware using its manifest. But can BERT determine which family an application labeled as malware belongs to? In order to answer this question, the malware of the dataset have been used in order to construct a new dataset composed exclusively of malware. The experiments are carried out with the same parameters as before with the difference that the dataset is composed as explained above of 77 768 manifests. The tests and fine-tuning are carried out exclusively on the three families of malware the most present in the dataset as a consequence of the too weak presence of the other families in the dataset. These three families are Jiagu, Dnotua and Secneo with respectively 60%, 2% and 1% of presence in the dataset. The tests are performed only on the best models of each category for each family. The best model is selected by taking the one with the lowest loss value on the validation set test. The tests on the validation set are done at the end of each epoch.

Table 4. Results of Bert models Jiagu malware detection with pre-processed manifests

Pre-process	Accuracy	Loss	F$_1$ score	Precision	Recall
Full	0.81	0.43	0.86	0.78	0.958
Permission only	0.758	0.522	0.827	0.734	0.946
No permission	0.81	0.435	0.86	0.783	0.953
Deny list	0.813	0.423	0.863	0.782	0.963
Values	0.813	0.426	0.862	0.785	0.956

Table 5. Results of Bert models Dnotua malware detection with pre-processed manifests

Pre-process	Accuracy	Loss	F$_1$ score	Precision	Recall
Full	0.994	0.015	0.836	0.927	0.762
Permission only	0.989	0.023	0.765	0.627	0.979
No permission	0.995	0.013	0.865	0.902	0.831
Deny list	0.994	0.014	0.854	0.843	0.866
Values	0.992	0.019	0.822	0.719	0.958

Table 6. Results of Bert models Secneo malware detection with pre-processed manifests

Pre-process	Accuracy	Loss	F$_1$ score	Precision	Recall
Full	0.995	0.025	0.682	0.852	0.569
Permission only	0.993	0.035	0.464	0.683	0.351
No permission	0.994	0.032	0.641	0.732	0.683
Deny list	0.995	0.025	0.657	0.768	0.574
Values	0.996	0.023	0.723	0.843	0.639

Among these tables, it is important to pay attention to the F1 score which expresses more accurately the results than the accuracy, since the datasets are very unbalanced for Dnotua (Table 5) and Secneo (Table 6) unlike Jiagu (Table 4).

Table 7. Average of BERT models performance for families binary classification with pre-processed manifests

Pre-process	Accuracy	Loss	F$_1$ score
Full	0.933	0.232	0.793
Permission only	0.913	0.193	0.685
No permission	0.932	0.164	0.789
Deny list	0.934	0.154	0.791
Values	0.934	0.156	0.802

Overall, according to the F1 scores, it seems that BERT manages to classify the families: F1 scores reach on average 0.854 for Jiagu and 0.823 for Dnotua. The inferior results of Secneo with an F1 score of 633 is certainly explained by its too weak presence in the dataset, which unbalances the training and reduces its efficiency. These results are interesting but cannot be considered as a generalization as detection from manifests can be more complex or simpler for other malware families.

Table 7 showing the average of the three family tables tells that permissions are not necessary for the detection of malware families either. This is also easily seen in Tables 4, 5, and 6 which show lower results for the experiments where only the permissions are used.

5 Discussion

As shown in MalBERT [24], the results of the models trained on manifests give very good results slightly exceeding 97% accuracy for the malware/benign differentiation. The reason why this study was done is to define what exactly allows the manifests to teach BERT so well since a manifest is not enough to faithfully represent an application as manifests files are orders of magnitude smaller than applications. Moreover the approach is relatively light and easy to set up, all of the heavy lifting being already done in the BERT pre-training.

When we successfully replicated the MalBERT experiments, we expected that the manifests, once deprived of permissions would give bad results, we thought that permissions were what BERT used to differentiate malware/goodware. This information is important, since an approach relying only (or mostly) on permissions is likely to be unsuitable for real-world malware detection. Indeed, attackers can request as many permissions as they wish, and they would be quick to find combinations of permissions that are not detected as malware. But it turned out that the opposite might be true.

MalBERT seems to not use only permissions, but to also integrate in its *reasoning* other elements of the manifests as the results in Table 2 show. A further ablation study on the manifests would be interesting to understand what correlation BERT finds between the malware manifests, or the goodware ones to get its results.

It should also be noted that BERT differentiates fairly well one family from another based on the manifests, at least for the Dnotua and Jiagu families. The Secneo family does not show such good results, but this can be explained by the dataset which is rather unbalanced for this family. This remains a speculation and it is possible that BERT is simply not as effective in detecting the Secneo family as Dnotua or Jiagu. This is also true for other malware families on which further experiments would be interesting.

6 Related Work

Liu et al. [20] present different Android malware detection approaches based on machine learning. This review goes through the Android system architecture, security mechanisms, and classification of Android malware but also machine learning techniques such as data-preprocessing, feature selection and algorithms.

Similar to our paper, transformers [28] are used in MalBERT [24] in order to detect malicious software. Specifically, it uses BERT [9] based model with static analysis of Android applications to perform binary and multiclass classification. Also called MalBERT but oriented to the detection of malware affecting windows systems using BERT, *MalBERT: A novel pre-training method for malware detection* [31] uses dynamic analysis with two different datasets with more than 40 000 samples. Their results show 99.9% detection rate on their datasets and more than 98% under different robustness tests.

Malware Detection on highly imbalanced data through sequence modeling [22] also performs Android malware detection but using dynamic analysis. Furthermore, sequence activities are generated by launching the applications, and by recording their behavior. Since only a small portion of real-world applications are malicious, they recreate a real-world scenario by taking a low rate of malware in their training and testing set. Both static and dynamic analysis can lead to high performance as shown with DL-Droid [7] with deep learning systems up to 99.6% detection rate.

In a recent paper [12], the authors present an approach for malware detection using manifest permissions but without using deep-learning in contrast to us. They investigates four different machine learning algorithms, Random Forest, Support Vector Machine, Gaussian Naive Bayes and K-Means. On a test set consisting of 5243 samples, they manage to obtain results above 80%. The most effective being Random Forest with 82.5% precision and 81.5% accuracy.

CatBERT [17] is a BERT [9] model for detecting social engineering emails. They fine-tuned a BERT model with half of transformer blocks replaced with simple adapters to learn the representations of the syntax and semantics of the natural language. The model detects social engineering emails with 87% accuracy as compared to DistilBERT or LSTM which achieve 83% and 79%, respectively.

7   Conclusion

The technique used in this paper to detect Android malware and classify Android malware into families is straightforward. It uses only a BERT model and Android manifests to work. In our experiments, BERT works well for malware detection with 97% accuracy and an F1 score of 94.9%. The same goes for classification of families with on average 93.3% accuracy and 79.3% F1 score. Our experiments have shown that for malware detection, permissions alone give lower results with 93% accuracy and 87.9% F1 score, furthermore that the absence of permissions does not significantly impact the performance of the models since it obtains 96.7% accuracy and 94.3% F1 score. Finally, it is also notable that reducing the noise in the manifests used for training the models by removing redundant characters or words that are not useful for training allows BERT to obtain slightly better results. MalBERT seems to have good results and a further ablation study on the manifests would be interesting. It would help to understand what correlation BERT finds between the malware manifests, or the goodware ones to get its results.

Reproduction Package

The code used for the experiments, and the list of APKs in our dataset can be found at https://github.com/BadrSouani/BERT_Manifest.

Acknowledgment. This work was supported by the Luxembourg National Research Fund (FNR) (12696663). This work was partially supported by the Wallenberg AI, Autonomous Systems and Software Program (WASP) funded by the Knut and Alice Wallenberg Foundation.

References

1. The free encyclopedia. https://www.wikipedia.org/
2. Google play store. https://play.google.com/
3. Tensorflow. https://www.tensorflow.org/
4. Alazab, M., Alazab, M., Shalaginov, A., Mesleh, A., Awajan, A.: Intelligent mobile malware detection using permission requests and API calls. Future Gener. Comput. Syst. **107**, 509–521 (2020). https://doi.org/10.1016/j.future.2020.02.002, https://www.sciencedirect.com/science/article/pii/S0167739X19321223
5. Allix, K., Bissyandé, T.F., Klein, J., Le Traon, Y.: AndroZoo: collecting millions of android apps for the research community. In: 2016 IEEE/ACM 13th Working Conference on Mining Software Repositories (MSR), pp. 468–471. IEEE (2016)
6. Alsoghyer, S., Almomani, I.: On the effectiveness of application permissions for android ransomware detection. In: 2020 6th Conference on Data Science and Machine Learning Applications (CDMA), pp. 94–99 (2020). https://doi.org/10.1109/CDMA47397.2020.00022
7. Alzaylaee, M.K., Yerima, S.Y., Sezer, S.: DL-droid: deep learning based android malware detection using real devices. Comput. Secur. **89**, 101663 (2020). https://doi.org/10.1016/j.cose.2019.101663, https://www.sciencedirect.com/science/article/pii/S0167404819300161
8. Arora, A., Peddoju, S.K., Conti, M.: PermPair: android malware detection using permission pairs. IEEE Trans. Inf. Forensics Secur. **15**, 1968–1982 (2020). https://doi.org/10.1109/TIFS.2019.2950134
9. Devlin, J., Chang, M.W., Lee, K., Toutanova, K.: BERT: pre-training of deep bidirectional transformers for language understanding, pp. 4171–4186 (2019). https://doi.org/10.18653/v1/N19-1423, https://aclanthology.org/N19-1423
10. Feng, Z., et al.: CodeBERT: a pre-trained model for programming and natural languages. arXiv e-prints arXiv:2002.08155 (2020)
11. He, P., Liu, X., Gao, J., Chen, W.: DeBERTa: decoding-enhanced BERT with Disentangled Attention. arXiv e-prints arXiv:2006.03654 (2020)
12. Jeffrey, M., Nathan, H., William, G., Ryan, B.: Machine learning-based android malware detection using manifest permissions (2021). https://doi.org/10.24251/HICSS.2021.839

13. Jimenez, M., Rwemalika, R., Papadakis, M., Sarro, F., Le Traon, Y., Harman, M.: The importance of accounting for real-world labelling when predicting software vulnerabilities. In: Proceedings of the 2019 27th ACM Joint Meeting on European Software Engineering Conference and Symposium on the Foundations of Software Engineering, pp. 695–705 (2019)

14. Jin, D., Jin, Z., Zhou, J.T., Szolovits, P.: Is BERT really robust? Natural language attack on text classification and entailment. arXiv preprint arXiv:1907.11932 (2019)

15. Karbab, E.B., Debbabi, M., Derhab, A., Mouheb, D.: MalDozer: automatic framework for android malware detection using deep learning. Digit. Invest. **24**, S48–S59 (2018). https://doi.org/10.1016/j.diin.2018.01.007, https://www.sciencedirect.com/science/article/pii/S1742287618300392

16. Kim, T., Kang, B., Rho, M., Sezer, S., Im, E.G.: A multimodal deep learning method for android malware detection using various features. IEEE Trans. Inf. Forensics Secur. **14**(3), 773–788 (2019). https://doi.org/10.1109/TIFS.2018.2866319

17. Lee, Y., Saxe, J., Harang, R.: CATBERT: context-aware tiny BERT for detecting social engineering emails. arXiv e-prints arXiv:2010.03484 (2020)

18. Li, J., Sun, L., Yan, Q., Li, Z., Srisa-an, W., Ye, H.: Significant permission identification for machine-learning-based android malware detection. IEEE Trans. Industr. Inf. **14**(7), 3216–3225 (2018). https://doi.org/10.1109/TII.2017.2789219

19. Liu, K., Xu, S., Xu, G., Zhang, M., Sun, D., Liu, H.: A review of android malware detection approaches based on machine learning. IEEE Access **8**, 124579–124607 (2020)

20. Liu, K., Xu, S., Xu, G., Zhang, M., Sun, D., Liu, H.: A review of android malware detection approaches based on machine learning. IEEE Access **8**, 124579–124607 (2020). https://doi.org/10.1109/ACCESS.2020.3006143

21. Liu, Y., et al.: RoBERTa: a robustly optimized BERT pretraining approach. arXiv e-prints arXiv:1907.11692 (2019)

22. Oak, R., Du, M., Yan, D., Takawale, H., Amit, I.: Malware detection on highly imbalanced data through sequence modeling. In: Proceedings of the 12th ACM Workshop on Artificial Intelligence and Security, AISec 2019, pp. 37–48. Association for Computing Machinery, New York (2019). https://doi.org/10.1145/3338501.3357374

23. Peiravian, N., Zhu, X.: Machine learning for android malware detection using permission and API calls, pp. 300–305 (2013). https://doi.org/10.1109/ICTAI.2013.53

24. Rahali, A., Akhloufi, M.A.: MalBERT: using transformers for cybersecurity and malicious software detection (2021)

25. Sebastián, M., Rivera, R., Kotzias, P., Caballero, J.: AVCLASS: a tool for massive malware labeling. In: Monrose, F., Dacier, M., Blanc, G., Garcia-Alfaro, J. (eds.) RAID 2016. LNCS, vol. 9854, pp. 230–253. Springer, Cham (2016). https://doi.org/10.1007/978-3-319-45719-2_11

26. Sun, C., Qiu, X., Xu, Y., Huang, X.: How to fine-tune BERT for text classification? arXiv e-prints arXiv:1905.05583 (2019)

27. Sun, T., Daoudi, N., Allix, K., Bissyandé, T.F.: Android malware detection: looking beyond Dalvik bytecode. In: 2021 36th IEEE/ACM International Conference on Automated Software Engineering Workshops (ASEW), pp. 34–39. IEEE (2021)

28. Vaswani, A., et al.: Attention is all you need. **30** (2017). https://proceedings.neurips.cc/paper/2017/file/3f5ee243547dee91fbd053c1c4a845aa-Paper.pdf

29. Wu, D.J., Mao, C.H., Wei, T.E., Lee, H.M., Wu, K.P.: DroidMat: android malware detection through manifest and API calls tracing, pp. 62–69 (2012). https://doi.org/10.1109/AsiaJCIS.2012.18

30. Xu, H., Liu, B., Shu, L., Yu, P.S.: BERT post-training for review reading comprehension and aspect-based sentiment analysis. arXiv e-prints arXiv:1904.02232 (2019)

31. Xu, Z., Fang, X., Yang, G.: Malbert: a novel pre-training method for malware detection. Comput. Secur. **111**, 102458 (2021). https://doi.org/10.1016/j.cose.2021.102458, https://www.sciencedirect.com/science/article/pii/S0167404821002820

32. Yang, W., et al.: End-to-end open-domain question answering with BERTserini. arXiv e-prints arXiv:1902.01718 (2019)

33. Yuan, Z., Lu, Y., Wang, Z., Xue, Y.: Droid-sec: deep learning in android malware detection. SIGCOMM Comput. Commun. Rev. **44**(4), 371–372 (2014). https://doi.org/10.1145/2740070.2631434

34. Zhu, J., et al.: Incorporating BERT into neural machine translation. arXiv e-prints arXiv:2002.06823 (2020)

POSTERS

POSTER: A Transparent Remote Quantum Random Number Generator over a Quantum-Safe Link

Sergejs Kozlovičs[✉] and Juris Vīksna

Institute of Mathematics and Computer Science, University of Latvia,
Raiņa bulv. 29, Riga 1459, Latvia
sergejs.kozlovics@lumii.lv

Abstract. We address the problem of sharing an expensive hardware-based high-entropy quantum random number generator (QRNG) among multiple users connected to it via the network. We demonstrate how to 1) divide the limited bandwidth of the QRNG device among multiple clients, 2) secure network communication between the QRNG and its users by applying quantum-safe algorithms, and 3) switch existing client-side applications to use randomness received from the remote QRNG without the need to recompile their code.

Keywords: Random number generator · QRNG · Quantum random number generator · QRNG · Quantum-safe

1 Motivation

Unpredictable random numbers are required in many cryptographic operations such as key generation, key exchange, randomization-based encryption, and even mechanisms for attacking cryptosystems. True randomness is also important to other applications such as simulation of physical, chemical and biological processes, probabilistic algorithms, sampling, and testing.

While there are different kinds of hardware random number generators[1], it is considered that the only true random number generators (RNG-s) are quantum-based (QRNG-s) [3]. QRNG-s are expected to pass NIST and Dieharder statistical tests.

Due to a high price and specific hardware and OS requirements, it is not feasible to install a QRNG device into every computer. Nevertheless, it is possible to make that device available as a shared resource via a web service (the "QRNG web service"). Still, we face the following challenges:

---

[1] For instance, TrueRNG v3 (https://ubld.it/truerng_v3) uses the avalanche effect in a semiconductor junction; HotBits (https://www.fourmilab.ch/hotbits/) rely on radioactive decay; https://www.random.org is based on atmospheric noise; Intel CPU instructions RDRAND and RDSEED are based on thermal noise within the silicon.

© The Author(s), under exclusive license to Springer Nature Switzerland AG 2022
J. Zhou et al. (Eds.): ACNS 2022 Workshops, LNCS 13285, pp. 595–599, 2022.
https://doi.org/10.1007/978-3-031-16815-4_32

- dividing the QRNG random data into multiple isolated streams to be sent to different users according to fairness principles;
- leveling out the response time during peak request rates and avoiding blocking;
- applying post-quantum cryptography (PQC) to secure communication between the QRNG web service and its clients;
- transparently switching existing applications (without the need to recompile them) to the new QRNG web service.

The following sections provide solutions to all these challenges.

2   The Overall Architecture

Our solution is based on the architecture depicted in Fig. 1.

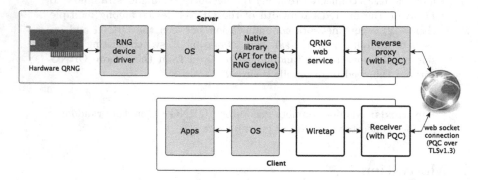

Fig. 1. The overall architecture for accessing the hardware QRNG via a quantum-safe link. White bold boxes constitute our contribution. (Color figure online)

We hide our **QRNG web service** behind a **reverse proxy**, which factors out user authentication, load balancing, and server-side certificate management. Within X.509 certificates, we use PQC algorithms for both the key and the signature chain. In our testbed, we used HAProxy as a reverse proxy. We compiled[2] it with PQC support implemented in liboqs from the Open Quantum Safe (OQS) project[3].

Clients connect to the web service via bi-directional web sockets. That not only simplifies data streaming but also requires only one initial TLS handshake per client, which is important since PQC keys are longer than classical RSA/ECC keys and require more computation power.

On the client side, we introduce a native library (called the **receiver**) that can establish a quantum-safe TLSv1.3 web socket connection with the server for

---

[2] we contribute our script at https://github.com/LUMII-Syslab/oqs-haproxy.git.
[3] https://openquantumsafe.org.

receiving random data from it. The receiver behaves similarly on different platforms; only the byte code varies. We also introduce an OS-specific module (called the **wiretap**) that replaces the default OS-level random number generator with ours.

The QRNG web service, the receiver, and the wiretap constitute our contribution. The following three sections provide the details.

3   The QRNG Web Service

The QRNG web service cannot be launched in the cloud since it needs to access a physical QRNG device attached directly. Besides, it should not be launched in a virtual environment since it is difficult to "passthrough" devices from the host OS to the guest OS, PCI devices being the hardest. Thus, the QRNG web service is launched on a real (non-virtualized) OS with the corresponding QRNG device drivers installed.

In our laboratory, we have tested IDQ Quantis PCIe 40 Mbps QRNG devices on Windows 10 and Ubuntu 18.04-22.04. Since Java bindings for the native QRNG API were also available from IDQ, our design choice was to implement the QRNG web service as a cross-platform Java program using Jetty as an embedded web server. HAProxy was configured to forward web socket connections to the QRNG web service backend.

The QRNG web service maintains a synchronized buffer (called the Big Buffer) of random bytes generated by the QRNG. The Big Buffer is constantly replenished by a specific "charger" thread at a fixed rate. Our experiments with IDQ Quantis show that the best QRNG speed is achieved when large ($>$ 1 MiB or 8 Mpbs) portions of random bytes are requested. Since our Quantis QRNG device has a rate of 9.6 Mbps $\pm$ 5% (with post-processing), we replenish the buffer once a second. If there are multiple QRNGs installed, multiple charger threads are launched. Let S denote the maximal number of bytes per second that can be appended to the Big Buffer by all threads when all clients are idle.

The Big Buffer is consumed by 1 KiB **blocks**, which are distributed among the connected users. The fair bandwidth distribution is ensured by the rule: each next 1 KiB block is sent to the user who has not been served the longest. In order to guarantee the 1 KiB/s = 8 Kbps rate, we must limit the number of simultaneously connected users to $S/1024$. However, the actual speed will be higher since (a) users request random bytes depending on their needs, (b) on peek requests, the Big Buffer allows us to sustain low response time by consuming the content loaded into the buffer earlier. We are going to compute the expected mean response time as we get more users registered for our service.

There are several existing HTTP GET-based QRNG services such as RandomNumbers.info[4], the Ruđer Bošković Institute service[5], the Humboldt-

---

[4] http://www.randomnumbers.info (operating on Quantis QRNG PCIe Legacy).
[5] http://random.irb.hr/index.php (operating on QRBG121).

Universität zu Berlin service[6], the Australian National University service[7], and QRate qrng.cloud (not launched yet). Sadly, some of these services use insecure HTTP, and none of them can establish a quantum-safe TLS connection. Those services that support HTTPS require a TLS handshake on each request. In contrast, our service is quantum-safe and relies on more efficient web sockets.

4   The Receiver

The receiver is a native library for accessing a remote QRNG via a quantum-safe web socket. The following arguments must be provided:

- the server web socket URL (`wss://`);
- the authorization token (unique for each client);
- the trusted CA certificate signed with a PQC algorithm (e.g., SPHINCS+-SHA256-128f-robust) for validating the server.

We implemented the receiver in Java and compiled it using `native-image` from the GraalVM JDK. Thus, we have the same code base for different platforms. Besides, we do not have a dependency on the OQS version of OpenSSL.

However, while OQS provides Java bindings for invoking OQS PQC algorithms, the standard Java `javax.net.ssl.SSLSocket` class is unaware of them. The Bouncy Castle library[8] implements *some* PQC algorithms but still they are not integrated with Java Secure Socket Extension (JSSE). By thoroughly investigating the Bouncy Castle TLSv3 code, analyzing TLS handshake dumps, and trial-and-error, we found that OQS uses specific code points (marked "for private use" by NIST) for both key-exchange and signature algorithms. We had to modify the Bouncy Castle TLSv3 handshake process by adding support for OQS code points, validating PQC server certificates, and negotiating the cipher in a quantum-safe way (previously, only RSA- and ECC-based key exchange methods were supported). In our testbed, we used Frodo640AES for key exchange and Rainbow-I-Classic to sign and validate the CA+server certificate chain. We also implemented in Java a PQC-aware TLS1.3-based SSLSocket that is able to communicate with an OQS-OpenSSL-based C endpoint (HAProxy).

Sadly, Rainbow is vulnerable to MinRank-based attacks [1]. Thus, we continue our experiments by replacing Rainbow with SPHINCS+, which is another family of algorithms supported by both OQS and Bouncy Castle.

5   The Wiretap

In Windows, the wiretap is a DLL that re-implements Windows API functions CryptGenRandom, BCryptGenRandom, and RtlGenRandom by returning the randomness obtained from the receiver. We use the Microsoft Detours[9] library to

---

[6] http://qrng.physik.hu-berlin.de/download (operating on PicoQuant PQRNG 150).

[7] https://qrng.anu.edu.au (own equipment for measuring quantum fluctuations of the vacuum with the potential to achieve the 70 Gbit/s rate) [2].

[8] provides pure Java implementations of cryptographic primitives, https://www.bouncycastle.org.

[9] https://github.com/microsoft/Detours.

replace the original Windows functions with ours. In order to force a particular program (such as `openssl.exe`) to use our randomization functions, we launch it with the help of `withdll.exe` (from the Detours library). Other DLL injection techniques (such as listing the wiretap DLL in the correct Windows registry key or manipulating existing processes with `CreateRemoteThread`) are also possible.

In GNU/Linux, the wiretap consists of 2 modules:

- a Linux kernel module that creates and manages a new device file with the default name `/dev/qrandom0`;
- a simple C program that is launched as a systemd service; it fetches random numbers (by means of the receiver) and writes them to `/dev/qrandom0`, which stores them in a buffer until someone reads them.

In order to force applications to use `/dev/qrandom0`, we backup the existing `/dev/random` file and create the symlink `/dev/random`→`/dev/qrandom0`.

Since version 5.6, the Linux kernel implements its own cryptographically secure RNG that is used as a non-blocking entropy source for both `/dev/random` and `/dev/urandom`. Additional entropy can be added by writing into `/dev/random` (with a subsequent `ioctl` call). Thus, for Linux kernel v5.6+, our GNU/Linux wiretap could consist only of the systemd service, which fetches random numbers from the QRNG web service and writes them into `/dev/random` on a regular basis.

6   Conclusion

The proposed QRNG web service with the corresponding client-side modules will be available in June 2022 at qrng.lumii.lv. We also look forward to experimenting with hybrid RSA/ECC and PQC algorithms and integrating them into our web application infrastructure webAppOS [4].

Acknowledgements. Research supported by the European Regional Development Fund, project No. 1.1.1.1/20/A/106 "Applications of quantum cryptography devices and software solutions in computational infrastructure framework in Latvia".

References

1. Beullens, W.: Breaking rainbow takes a weekend on a laptop (2022). Cryptology ePrint Archive, Report 2022/214
2. Haw, J.Y., et al.: Maximization of extractable randomness in a quantum random-number generator. Phys. Rev. Appl. Am. Phys. Soc. **3**(5), 12 (2015)
3. Jacak, M.M., Jóźwiak, P., Niemczuk, J., Jacak, J.E.: Quantum generators of random numbers. Sci. Rep. **11**(1), 1–21 (2021)
4. Kozlovičs, S.: The web computer and its operating system: a new approach for creating web applications. In: Proceedings of the 15th International Conference on Web Information Systems and Technologies, Vienna, Austria, pp. 46–57. SCITEPRESS (2019)

POSTER: Enabling User-Accountable Mechanisms in Decision Systems

Rosario Giustolisi[(✉)] and Carsten Schürmann

IT University of Copenhagen, Copenhagen, Denmark
Rosg@itu.dk

Abstract. Decision systems are at the core of our democratic and meritocratic processes. Systems for voting, procurement, grant management, and competitive examinations all rest on *submission, evaluation,* and *ranking.* Computer assistance is a critical part of modern decision systems and so are cybersecurity challenges. As decision systems get increasingly complex, the classic approach of enforcing security through fail-safe mechanisms *preventing* cybersecurity attacks becomes infeasible. A recent trend in cybersecurity is to disincentivize potential attacks by using deterrence-based mechanisms that make stakeholders accountable for their actions. However, using such mechanisms requires knowledge of the underlying technology, which is not accessible to all people.

This poster looks at ways to extend decision systems with *user-accountable mechanisms* enabling users to verify correct executions and provide dispute resolution capabilities by combining cryptographic techniques for human senses with advanced cryptographic protocols. If successful, this line of work will provide novel ways to secure decision systems by creating disincentivizing mechanisms that are accessible to any human user.

1 Motivation

Currently, decision systems require user expertise in the auditing technology. It is an open question on how to make auditing accessible to everyone. End-to-end verifiable voting schemes, which allow voters to check that the outcome of an election is correct, have no user-friendly mechanisms for dispute resolution in case of incorrect tallying, hence they do not provide adequate attack deterrence [8]. Current systems for procurement, grant management, and competitive examinations heavily rely on trusted parties that run core parts of the system as black boxes at the price of a lack of transparency [6]. We challenge such design in favour of a trust-no-one and user-accountable design. Moreover, general approaches for algorithmic accountability have been recently proposed in the context of AI, machine learning, and secure multi-party computation (MPC) [7], but the verification procedures require relevant expertise in the underlying technology to accomplish auditing.

The verification procedures for accountability should essentially be a human task. State-of-the-art technologies only provide guarantees for machines, while

J. Zhou et al. (Eds.): ACNS 2022 Workshops, LNCS 13285, pp. 600–605, 2022.
https://doi.org/10.1007/978-3-031-16815-4_33

leaving out human users. This undermines public confidence in the system's reliability and in the end affects negatively the trustworthiness of decision systems. We thus need to design accountability mechanisms that can be used by humans.

We observe that existing cryptographic techniques for human senses, such as visual cryptography and hash visualization, can achieve classic security goals such as confidentiality and authentication. We aim at exploring whether a combination of cryptographic techniques for human senses with state-of-the-art cryptographic protocols enables user-accountable mechanisms in decision systems. We deem the following combinations to be of particular relevance:

Cryptographic techniques for human senses		Protocols
Visual cryptography [9]		Zero-knowledge proofs
Audio cryptography [3]	✕	Oblivious transfer schemes
Lound-and-clear [5]		Identity-based encryption
Hash visualization [10]		Homomorphic schemes
EyeDecrypt [4]		

Building user-accountable mechanisms for decision systems will give: (i) a concrete method to design accountable decision systems, in the age of pervasive security attacks aiming at breaking down public trust; (ii) a novel security paradigm that revisits the established view of "users being the weakest link *in* security" in to "users as the needed link *for* security"; (iii) new research directions in cybersecurity aimed at reconciling the mathematical guarantees of cryptography with the public confidence in democratic and meritocratic processes.

2   Approach

Figure 1 presents our approach to design accountable mechanisms for decision systems. We consider potential misbehaving parties willing to attack one or more

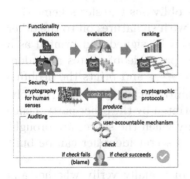

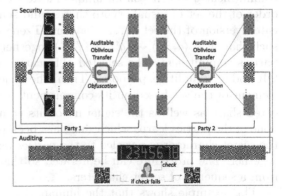

Fig. 1. Design approach for user-accountable mechanism in decision systems.

Fig. 2. A user-accountable mechanism for verifying the correct generation of anonymous identifiers.

functionalities in a decision system. We identify the needed security guarantees and choose accordingly cryptographic protocol and technique for human sense. We want to allow a user to detect the failure of a functionality requirement and to find the misbehaving parties who caused that failure. We model a user-accountable mechanism by intertwining the chosen protocol and technique in order to provide evidence that can be used by humans. Below we show how one can construct a user-accountable mechanism by combining visual cryptography and an oblivious transfer scheme.

2.1   User-Accountable Anonymous Identifiers

One of the core functionalities of a decision system is to guarantee anonymous submissions. For example, in voting, this is equivalent to ballot privacy. The goal is to generate identifiers to anonymise submissions *and* to make their construction user-accountable in case of a dispute. In a trustless environment, anonymous identifiers can be normally built using secret sharing. We describe how one can design a user-accountable mechanism for anonymous identifiers by combining oblivious transfer schemes, visual cryptography, digital signatures, and QR codes (cf. Fig. 2). We note that the combination of digital signatures and oblivious transfer can provide auditability. In a two-party setting, an auditable oblivious transfer enables one party to generate a secret random permutation of the set of possible identifiers, and the other party to obliviously select one random element of the permutation. Parties can send each other encrypted audits, which can be encoded as QR codes. Also, each party encodes their secrets using visual cryptography, and only when the secrets are brought together the identifier is determined.

More specifically, to encode a single secret visual character c, one party generates a random visual crypto image share α, prints it, and generates a complementary set of visual crypto shares $\beta_1, \ldots, \beta_k$ for each of the possible $c_1, \ldots, c_k$ characters, such that $\beta_i \leftarrow_{\pi_{\mathcal{R}}} (\alpha \oplus c_i)$, with $\pi_{\mathcal{R}}$ being a random permutation of the list of characters. The same party receives from the other party a Pedersen commitment $y = g^x h^\gamma$ on an unique index $\gamma \in_{\mathcal{R}} [1, k]$, randomly permutes the order of the set of visual crypto shares, and sends to the other party an obfuscated version of the set $\omega_1, \ldots, \omega_k$ using Tzeng's oblivious transfer scheme [12], such that $\omega_i = \langle a_i, b_i \rangle \leftarrow \langle g^{r_i}, \beta_i \left(\frac{y}{h}\right)^{r_i} \rangle$ together with signatures on to the other party's commitment. The selected obfuscation can be signed and printed as a QR code for auditing purposes. Then, the other party deobfuscates a random element of the set based on its commitment $\beta = \frac{b_\gamma}{(a_\gamma)^x}$ and prints the deobfuscated share as well as the signature on its commitment as QR code. Notably, none of the parties learns which share has been printed by the other party, hence the secret character is revealed to the parties only when the shares are brought together. The procedure can be iterated so that a secret identifier can be built from a sequence of secret characters.

This example shows that the human user can visually verify whether any of the parties misbehaved since no intelligible identifier would be determined if any of the parties misprints their visual shares. Thanks to the digital signatures encoded in the QR code, the user can also blame which parties misprinted their share, making them accountable for the generation of anonymous identifiers.

3 Challenges and Potential

One of the main challenges is that a single user-accountable mechanism might not fit all situations. We can address this by investigating several alternative combinations of protocols and techniques, and by developing specialised mechanisms for specific systems. Having defined a way to design user-accountable mechanisms and to add them to decision systems, we will first implement our user-accountable mechanisms in a mock voting system. Then, we will test whether our user-accountable mechanisms can be integrated into existing secure decision systems such as Helios [1], Prêt à Voter [11], and Confichair [2]. This will convince us whether our approach can scale up to any other decision systems.

Also, privacy and accountability are intuitively two contrasting requirements: accountability demands for more evidence to accomplish the verification procedures aiming at increase confidence in the decision outcome; privacy demands for minimising such evidence. For example, a voting system should provide high confidence in the result of the election even for voters who do not necessarily trust the voting authority. On the other hand, failing to provide vote privacy opens to effective manipulation of voters and to control the outcome of the election. While it is challenging designing mechanisms that maximise both accountability and privacy, one can explore mechanisms that allow one to set an appropriate trade-off between privacy and accountability.

Providing a practical design for user-accountable mechanisms enables people to audit the system and fosters public trust in accepting computer assistance in decision systems. This has the potential not only to pave the way for an exciting research agenda in developing a new generation of decision systems, but it can provide new directions in securing distributed systems and MPC. Also, the field of AI and machine learning, whose current efforts are aimed at helping the machines to understand and interpret humans, can eventually benefit from this line of work, which is about helping humans to interpret the machines.

4 Conclusion and Open Questions

This work explores ways for building verification mechanisms for accountability in decision systems by combining existing cryptographic techniques for human senses with state-of-the-art cryptographic protocols. The ultimate goal of this line of work is to enable human users to directly execute the verification mechanism themselves without the need of relying on trusted computer parties. This poster also provides a practical example on how one can implement such a mechanism.

Although our example works for generating verifiable anonymous identifiers for submissions, it may not work to address any requirement of decision systems. Still, with this work, we challenge the established position of minimising people involvement in cybersecurity by building methods that enable people to understand *when* the underlying technology works, rather than *how* it works.

This line of work can provide a practical way to build and strengthen public confidence in decision systems technology. The need for user-accountable mechanisms is concrete and actual, as it could be readily used in today's challenges, such as providing credible elections. This can also inspire addressing future challenges, such as allowing any user to audit AI-powered decision systems.

Some open questions can be easily drafted. An obvious one comes from observing that some decision systems are very different from each other, and a user-accountable mechanism may not be used in, e.g., both voting and procurement systems. In fact, there are obvious differences in the requirements among categories and also within a single category. One can address this question by focusing on the core functionalities and related requirements, which exist among all decision systems. We believe that even a limited number of user-accountable mechanisms provide some guarantees to the users and deters attacks, unlike current decision systems.

Finally, we observe that security researchers have not looked at this before for some reason. The cryptographic community focuses on making highly secure and efficient algorithms for machines while usable security community focuses on how to make secure technologies more human-centric. The two communities do not collaborate often. This line of work also aims to bridge the gap.

References

1. Adida, B.: Helios: web-based open-audit voting. In: USENIX (2008)
2. Arapinis, M., Bursuc, S., Ryan, M.: Privacy supporting cloud computing: confichair, a case study. In: Degano, P., Guttman, J.D. (eds.) POST 2012. LNCS, vol. 7215, pp. 89–108. Springer, Heidelberg (2012). https://doi.org/10.1007/978-3-642-28641-4_6
3. Desmedt, Y., Hou, S., Quisquater, J.-J.: Audio and optical cryptography. In: Ohta, K., Pei, D. (eds.) ASIACRYPT 1998. LNCS, vol. 1514, pp. 392–404. Springer, Heidelberg (1998). https://doi.org/10.1007/3-540-49649-1_31
4. Forte, A.G., Garay, J.A., Jim, T., Vahlis, Y.: EyeDecrypt — private interactions in plain sight. In: Abdalla, M., De Prisco, R. (eds.) SCN 2014. LNCS, vol. 8642, pp. 255–276. Springer, Cham (2014). https://doi.org/10.1007/978-3-319-10879-7_15
5. Goodrich, M.T., Sirivianos, M., Solis, J., Tsudik, G., Uzun, E.: Loud and clear: human-verifiable authentication based on audio. In: ICDCS (2005)
6. Kanav, S., Lammich, P., Popescu, A.: A conference management system with verified document confidentiality. In: Biere, A., Bloem, R. (eds.) CAV 2014. LNCS, vol. 8559, pp. 167–183. Springer, Cham (2014). https://doi.org/10.1007/978-3-319-08867-9_11
7. Kroll, J.A.: Accountable algorithms. Ph.D. thesis, Princeton (2015)
8. Küsters, R., Truderung, T., Vogt, A.: Accountability: definition and relationship to verifiability. In: CCS (2010)
9. Naor, M., Shamir, A.: Visual cryptography. In: De Santis, A. (ed.) EUROCRYPT 1994. LNCS, vol. 950, pp. 1–12. Springer, Heidelberg (1995). https://doi.org/10.1007/BFb0053419

10. Perrig, A., Song, D.: Hash visualization: a new technique to improve real-world security. In: International Workshop on Techniques and E-Commerce (1999)
11. Ryan, P.Y.A., Schneider, S.A.: Prêt à voter with re-encryption mixes. In: ESORICS (2006)
12. Tzeng, W.G.: Efficient 1-out-of-n oblivious transfer schemes with universally usable parameters. IEEE Trans. Comput. 53(2), 232–240 (2004)

Poster: Key Generation Scheme Based on Physical Layer

Hong Zhao (ID) and Chunhua Su(⊠) (ID)

Division of Computer Science, University of Aizu, Aizuwakamatsu, Japan
{d8231109,chsu}@u-aizu.ac.jp

Abstract. Key generation from the randomness of wireless channels is a promising technology for the establishment of cryptographic keys between any two users. This paper introduces the wireless key generation technology based on physical layer. Aiming at the shortcomings of the existing key generation scheme, we have done optimization work in the quantization algorithm and preprocessing. We design an iterative lossless quantization algorithm, which is a multi-round lossless quantization algorithm to make full use of the collected measurements. To enhance the randomness of the generated keys, an adaptive quantization algorithm is designed, which enlarges the quantization intervals in the quantization algorithm. In addition, according to the characteristics of the measurements of static and dynamic scenario, we adopt suitable filtering methods for the respective scenario. At last we concludes with some suggestions for future studies.

Keywords: Wireless network security · Physical layer security · Physical layer key generation

1 Introduction

1.1 Wireless Network Security

In today's world, wireless communication technology has quietly entered all levels of people's lives, the footprint of wireless communication technology can be seen everywhere in modern production and life. However, due to the inherent broadcast nature of wireless channels, attackers can launch various attacks such as passive eavesdropping, traffic analysis and monitoring, etc., which makes wireless communication security a major issue related to people's livelihood. Establishing communication keys between wireless devices is an effective way to protect wireless network security. Currently, there are two methods to generate keys in wireless network, one is classical encryption method and the other method is physical layer method.

The classical encryption for establishing key is achieved by public key cryptography, which is generally based on the unproven assumptions of the hardness of some problems, such as integer factorization and discrete logarithm [3]. However, a public key encryption system can be broken if the adversary has enough

J. Zhou et al. (Eds.): ACNS 2022 Workshops, LNCS 13285, pp. 606–610, 2022.
https://doi.org/10.1007/978-3-031-16815-4_34

computing power. Moreover, such method consumes too many resources and might require a key management center.

In contrast, key generation leveraging wireless channel reciprocity is considered as a promising alternative to public key cryptography. Physical layer method achieves the goal of secure communication by utilizing the unpredictability and randomness of the existing wireless channel by both legitimate communication parties [1,2]. The encryption and decryption keys of both parties Alice and Bob come from the generation of the wireless channel, and do not need to be obtained through a third-party key distribution center.

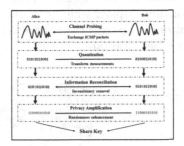

Fig. 1. Schematic of key generation.

1.2 Key Generation Method Based on Physical Layer

As a promising technique achieves wireless network security, the design of key generation method based on physical layer consists of four parts: Channel Probing, Quantization, Information Reconciliation and Privacy Amplification. Figure 1 illustrates the process of key generation based on physical layer. In the Channel Probing, the wireless devices use wireless network cards to obtain the channel measurements. The measurements are converted into bitstream after Quantization. The output of Quantization serves as input of the Information Reconciliation, the inconsistent bits from wireless devices can be removed. In order to enhance the security of the generated keys, Privacy Amplification phase is implemented.

2 Our Work

Although the physical layer-based key generation method is accepted in wireless networks, there are still problems such as low key generation rate and weak randomness that need to be optimized. In view of the existing problems, we have done optimization work in the quantization algorithm and preprocessing. The specific details are described as follows.

2.1 Optimization of Quantization Algorithms

Aiming at the shortcomings of the existing quantization algorithms, we have successively designed two optimization algorithms: iterative quantization algorithm [5] and adaptive quantization algorithm [4,6]. Most of the existing quantization algorithms are based on one round of lossy quantization. The main purpose of the optimization algorithm is to design a multi-round lossless quantization algorithm to make full use of the collected measurements. Therefore, we design an iterative lossless quantization algorithm, which is a multi-round lossless quantization algorithm to make full use of the collected measurements [5]. The specific details are shown in the Fig. 2(a). There are multiple rounds of quantification in the algorithm display, which can quantify all the input measurement values. This not only improves the utilization of the measured value, but also improves the key generation rate.

Algorithm 1: The iterative lossless quantization.

```
Input  : X=[x_1, x_2, x_3, ..., x_m].
Output: B_X. (the bit stream generated by Alice)
L = Length(X);
while Length(X) > 0 do
    μ_k ← mean(X), σ_k ← std(X);
    q_k^+ ← μ_k + α * σ_k, q_k^- ← μ_k - α * σ_k;
    for i= 1 to L do
        if X(i) ⩽ q_k^-  then   X(i) ← 0;
        else if X(i) ⩾ q_k^+ then   X(i) ← 1;
        else   X(i) ← X(i);
        end
    end
end
B_X ← 0 0 1 1 0...1 1 0
```

(a) The iterative lossless quantization.

Algorithm 2: The adaptive quantization.

```
Input: T = [ t_1, t_2... t_s] : s groups of the collected RSS measurements
       l : the length of each group
       s : the number of groups
Output: B = Q_1, Q_2, ..., Q_s the generated bit streams
for j= 1 to s do
    while l > 0 do
        μ_k ← mean(t), max_k ← max(t), min_k ← min(t);
        q_k^+ ← μ_k + α × (max_k + min_k), q_k^- ← μ_k - α × (max_k − min_k);
        for k= 1 to l do
            if t(i) ⩽ q_k^-  then   t(i) ← 0;
            else if t(i) ⩾ q_k^+ then   t(i) ← 1;
            else   t(i) ← t(i);
            end
    Q_j ← 0 0 1 1 0...1 1 0
B ← Q_1, Q_2, ..., Q_s
```

(b) The adaptive quantization.

Fig. 2. The details of the optimization algorithm.

After repeated experiments and tests, it is found that privous work cannot adapt to different scenarios to generate keys with strong randomness. Since the measurements show different characteristic trends, if the same quantization threshold is used to quantize the measured values of different characteristics, the probability of consecutive 0 s and 1 s appearing in the generated key will be high. Therefore, we design an adaptive quantization algorithm to solve the above problems. The details of algorithm is given in the Fig. 2(b). The difference from the work [5] is the design of the quantization algorithm. The specific detail is shown in the quantization reference levels, which enlarges the quantization intervals in the quantization algorithm. The design of the quantization reference levels makes the generated keys more random and avoids consecutive zeros or ones in the generated keys.

In addition, we have extended on the basis of these two algorithms, and optimized the group quantization for the measurements in different scenarios [6]. Based on the paper [4], according to the characteristics of different scenarios, we design a method based on group quantization. This is because that RSS

measurements in static and dynamic scenarios are different and cannot be quantified by using the same quantification standard. Additionally, in the experimental implementation, we collect measurements of different network cards in static and dynamic scenarios to verify the feasibility of the method.

2.2   Preprocessing of Measurements in Different Scenarios

Due to the absence of environmental noise and the influence of hardware devices, the reciprocity of the wireless channel measurements of both parties will be affected, which will affect the final key. In order to reduce the influence of the external environment and the device itself on the measurements, it is necessary to preprocess the collected measurements before key generation. Filtering the collected measurements is a particularly effective method. Filtering is the operation of filtering out specific frequency bands in the signal, and it is an important measure to suppress and prevent interference. According to the characteristics of the measurements of static scenario and dynamic scenario, we adopt filtering methods suitable for the respective scenarios. In our work, according to the characteristics of the measurements of static and dynamic scenario, we adopt suitable filtering methods for the respective scenario. The purpose of preprocessing in static scenario is to filter out outliers, so we use a clipping filter to ensure the removal of abnormally mutated data. In dynamic scenario, the main purpose is to remove the high-frequency noise, and we use the method of wavelet transform or discrete cosine transform. Figure 3 shows the preprocessing of measurements in different scenarios.

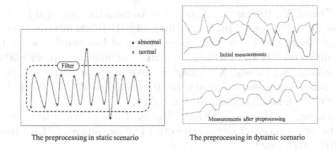

The preprocessing in static scenario   The preprocessing in dynamic scenario

Fig. 3. The preprocessing of measurements in different scenarios.

3   Future Research

Though the physical layer-based key generation scheme has great potential in the security of future wireless communication systems, there are still open questions to be resolved in order to make key generation more robust. Future research work can be carried out from the following aspects.

- Pre-judgment of wireless channel measurements. From the characteristics of static scenarios and dynamic scenarios, the differences in the measurements of different scenes are obvious. Therefore, it is necessary to perform a preliminary analysis of the collected measurements and to select an appropriate preprocessing and key generation scheme.
- Optimizing the key generation algorithm in static and dynamic scenarios. In practical scenarios, the differences in measurements lead to a lack of emphasis on key generation requirements. Therefore, the general key generation process is not necessarily suitable for specific application scenarios.
- Regular update keys. At present, most key generation schemes remain in the successful establishment of a single key, and it is still a blank stage for using the physical layer to periodically update the key for wireless devices. Regularly updating the keys of wireless devices can ensure the timeliness of wireless network security and resist potential attacks.

References

1. Jorswieck, E., Tomasin, S., Sezgin, A.: Broadcasting into the uncertainty: authentication and confidentiality by physical-layer processing. Proc. IEEE **103**(10), 1702–1724 (2015)
2. Yang, N., Wang, L., Geraci, G., Elkashlan, M., Yuan, J., Di Renzo, M.: Safeguarding 5G wireless communication networks using physical layer security. IEEE Commun. Mag. **53**(4), 20–27 (2015)
3. Zhang, J., Rajendran, S., Sun, Z., Woods, R., Hanzo, L.: Physical layer security for the internet of things: authentication and key generation. IEEE Wirel. Commun. **26**(5), 92–98 (2019)
4. Zhao, H., Zhang, Y., Huang, X., Xiang, Y.: An adaptive physical layer key extraction scheme for smart homes. In: Proceedings of 2019 IEEE International Conference On Trust, Security and Privacy in Computing and Communications/ IEEE International Conference On Big Data Science and Engineering, pp. 499–506 (2019)
5. Zhao, H., Zhang, Y., Huang, X., Xiang, Y.: An adaptive secret key establishment scheme in smart home environments. In: Proceedings of 2019 IEEE International Conference on Communications, pp. 1–6 (2019)
6. Zhao, H., Zhang, Y., Huang, X., Xiang, Y., Su, C.: A physical-layer key generation approach based on received signal strength in smart homes. IEEE Internet Things J. **9**(7), 4917–4927 (2022)

POSTER: ODABE: Outsourced Decentralized CP-ABE in Internet of Things

Mohammed B. M. Kamel[1,2,3(✉)], Peter Ligeti[1], and Christoph Reich[2]

[1] Faculty of Informatics, Eötvös Loránd University, Budapest, Hungary
{mkamel,ligetipeter}@inf.elte.hu
[2] Institute of Data Science, Cloud Computing and IT Security,
Furtwangen University, Furtwangen im Schwarzwald, Germany
{mkamel,christoph.reich}@hs-furtwangen.de
[3] Department of Computer Science, University of Kufa, Najaf, Iraq

Abstract. The 'things' layer in Internet of Things (IoT) consists of a massive number of devices, many of which are power and resource constrained. Decentralized Attribute-based Encryption (DABE) provides a one-to-many scheme that fits the distributed nature of IoT, however requires extensive computation power which makes its adoption difficult. In this work, we proposed an encryption model in DABE utilizing a single node, without revealing the secrets to the outsider node. The results showed that our model significantly improved the DABE.

1 Introduction

In public key cryptography, the data owner encrypts the data based on the identity of the data consumer in a one-to-one scheme. This scheme might not be suitable in some environments such as IoT where there are many data consumers and the data encryptor might not know the exact decryptors. Attribute-based Encryption (ABE) [5] provides a one-to-many scheme by allowing the data owner to define a policy in which the decryptors with given attributes can decrypt the data, even if the attribute has been gained after the data encryption.

While the original ABE proposal by Sahai and Waters [3] consists of a centralized entity, Lewko and Waters proposed Decentralized ABE [1] that removes any

---

This research was partially supported by Application Domain Specific Highly Reliable IT Solutions project which has been implemented with the support provided from the National Research, Development and Innovation Fund of Hungary, financed under the Thematic Excellence Programme TKP2020-NKA-06 (National Challenges Subprogramme) funding scheme, Project no. TKP2021-NVA-29 has been implemented with the support provided by the Ministry of Innovation and Technology from the National Research, Development and Innovation Fund and by ÚNKP-20-4 New National Excellence Program of the Ministry for Innovation and Technology from the source of National Research, Development and Innovation Fund.

J. Zhou et al. (Eds.): ACNS 2022 Workshops, LNCS 13285, pp. 611–615, 2022.
https://doi.org/10.1007/978-3-031-16815-4_35

centralized managing or attribute authority. Compared to public key cryptography, ABE suffers from more extensive computations of expensive exponentiation which limits its deployment in distributed systems with resource-constrained nodes. Many efforts tried to decrease the computation power by various techniques such as outsourcing to more powerful nodes or introducing a trusted third party to perform the encryption. In this paper, we proposed Outsourced Decentralised ABE (ODABE) to perform the heavy computations during encryption in a single external node, without revealing the secret data.

2   Literature Review

ABE [3] extends the concept of identities in Identity Based Encryption (IBE) by proposing a new term of attribute. Due to its heavy computations, several authors proposed lightweight model [2,4] to improve the ABE algorithms. The proposed models for lightweight ABE rely on a centralized entity as part of their algorithms. The existence of a centralized single entity in a model makes its adoption in a large-scale distributed system harder.

Authors in [1] proposed a model to decentralizing ABE [3], which comes with significant overhead. ODABE resembles [2] to outsource the heavy computations during encryption computational node. However, unlike the model in [2] that outsources the computations of Ciphertext-Policy Attribute-based Encryption (CP-ABE) with a central attribute authority and a central Key Distribution Center (KDC), our model distributes the computations of Decentralized ABE to an outsider node without introducing a centralized managing entity.

3   Outsourced Encryption

Our proposed solution utilizes the Decentralized ABE cryptographic protocol.

Protocol 1 (Decentralized ABE [1]). *The protocol consists of the following five algorithms:*
Global Setup: *on the security parameter as input this algorithm generates the public parameters GP that include two cyclic groups G, G_T, a generator g in the group G, a bilinear mapping $e : G \times G \to G_T$ and a hash function $\mathcal{H}(.)$ that maps a given identifier to a member in G.*
Attribute Setup: *in this protocol a new attribute authority takes the public parameters GP as input and chooses random private parameters $PR = (\alpha, \beta)$, and computes its public parameters $PK = (e(g, g)^\alpha, g^\beta)$.*
Key Generation: *an attribute authority takes the general identifier I_u of the user as input and using PR generates the secret key $sk = g^{\alpha_i} \mathcal{H}(I_u)^{\beta_i}$ of the attribute.*
Encrypt: *It takes the public parameters GP, the set of public keys of the involved attribute authorities, the access structure Γ along with the message m as inputs, and generates the ciphertext c.*
Decrypt: *It takes all the secret keys sk of the attributes of a single user as input and computes a message m.*

In DABE, first the global parameters (cyclic groups G, G_T, a generator $g \in G$, bilinear pairing $e : G \times G \to G_T$, and hash function $\mathcal{H} : \{0,1\}^* \to G$ are generated. Each attribute authority i generates and publishes its public parameters $e(g,g)^{\alpha_i}$ and g^{β_i}. The encryption algorithm in DABE takes the message m, the access structure Γ, and the public parameters $Q = \{\{e(g,g)^{\alpha_1}, g^{\beta_1}, \dots\}, \{G, G_T, g \in G, \mathcal{H}(.)\}\}$, and outputs the ciphertext c, i.e. $Encrypt(m, \Gamma, Q) = c$.

Our model consists of three disjoint sets of participants. The set $\mathcal{U}$ consists of members that uses three of the DABE algorithms: *Keygeneration()*, *Encrypt()* and *Decrypt()*. The attribute authorities reside in $\mathcal{A}$ set that includes independent nodes. During the model life cycle new attribute authorities can joint $\mathcal{A}$ independently. The nodes in $\mathcal{A}$ generate their private keys, publish their public keys, and generate secret keys for any node in $\mathcal{U}$ that has the relevant attributes. The set $\mathcal{P}$ includes the computational nodes with high computational power that can execute heavy computational operations. In IoT environment, the data producers might be resource-constrained with limited computation power, while the data consumers are mostly clients with proper computation power. Due to that, we focus on the encryption algorithm of DABE that is done by the data producers.

The members of $\mathcal{A}$ that handle attributes T_u of the user $u \in \mathcal{U}$ are considered semi-honest. Additionally, the chosen members in $\mathcal{P}$ from the point of view of members of $\mathcal{U}$ are defined as semi-honest nodes, and all other members in $\mathcal{U}$ might be considered malicious. We assume that each user $u \in \mathcal{U}$ has a unique global identifier I_u, and secure channels between the encryptor and the involved members of $\mathcal{A}$ and at least one member in $\mathcal{P}$ are established. As shown in Fig. 1, these channels will be used to securely generate the secret parameters and distribute the heavy computations.

Protocol 2 (ODABE Secret parameter generation). *A user $u \in \mathcal{U}$ randomly chooses a number $x_i, y_i, z_i \in \mathbb{Z}_p$, for the attribute i. An attribute authority $a_i \in \mathcal{A}$ receives the values x_i, y_i, z_i from the user, and generates and sends the following to the user:*

$$g^{y_i}, \quad g^{z_i}, \quad g^{\beta_i z_i}, \quad e(g,g)^{x_i}, \quad e(g,g)^{\alpha_i z_i}$$

Protocol 3 (ODABE encryption). *The proposed outsourced encryption works as follows:*
Step 1: *The encryptor $u \in \mathcal{U}$ randomly chooses $s \in \mathbb{Z}_p$, and calculates:*

$$\gamma = (s, \dots), \quad \omega = (0, \dots)$$

Step 2: *For each row i in $\mathcal{M}(\Gamma)$ generates:*

$$\gamma_i = \mathcal{M}(\Gamma)_i \cdot \gamma, \quad \omega_i = \mathcal{M}(\Gamma)_i \cdot \omega, r_i \in \mathbb{Z}_p$$

Step 3: *Chooses a computational node $P_0 \in \mathcal{P}$ and sends:*

$$\Gamma, \forall i : \quad \gamma_i' \equiv \gamma_i - x_i \mod p, \quad \omega_i' \equiv \omega_i - y_i \mod p, \quad r_i' \equiv r_i - z_i \mod p$$

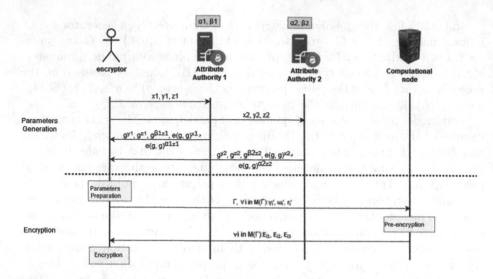

Fig. 1. ODABE encryption overview

Step 4: *The computational node P_0 for each leaf i in Γ computes the following three parameters and sends the results ($\forall i : \{\mathcal{E}_{i1}, \mathcal{E}_{i2}, \mathcal{E}_{i3}\}$) back to the encryptor:*

$$\mathcal{E}_{i1} = e(g,g)^{\gamma_i'}e(g,g)^{\alpha_i r_i'}, \quad \mathcal{E}_{i2} = g^{r_i'}, \quad \mathcal{E}_{i3} = g^{\beta_i r_i'}g^{\omega_i'}$$

.

Step 5: *The encryptor u calculates the final ciphertext of the message m as follows:*

$$C_0 = m \cdot e(g,g)^s, \forall i : C_{i1} = \mathcal{E}_{i1}e(g,g)^{x_i} \; e(g,g)^{\alpha_i z_i}, \quad C_{i2} = \mathcal{E}_{i2} \; g^{z_i}, \quad C_{i3} = \mathcal{E}_{i3} \; g^{y_i} \; g^{\beta_i z_i}$$

4   Analysis

ODABE is secure if a PPT adversary getting the values $\forall i : \gamma_i'$ has negligible probability of guessing $\forall i : \gamma_i$, and thereafter the secret value s.

Lemma 1. *Let $\mathbb{G}$ be a cyclic group of prime order p, and $r \in \mathbb{G}$ be uniformly distributed over $\mathbb{G}$, then given a number $n \in \mathbb{G}$ the value $n + r \bmod p$ is uniformly distributed over $\mathbb{G}$.*

As a result of applying Lemma 1 to the step 3, the values $\forall i : \gamma_i', \omega_i', r_i'$ are uniformly distributed over $\mathbb{Z}_p$. Therefore, a PPT adversary can guess the used values γ_i, ω_i, r_i during encryption with negligible probability only. The proposed model has been validated in a setup including a Raspberry Pi running at 1000 MHz MHz as the encryptor, a computer running at 1800 MHz MHz as a computational node in $\mathcal{P}$ on a communication link with 20 ms delay, and the result is shown in Fig. 2.

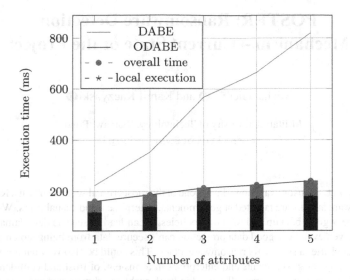

Fig. 2. Encryption execution time

5   Conclusion

In this paper we proposed a lightweight encryption model for DABE. During encryption in ODABE the required computation in the encryptor is minimized, and the heavy computations are outsourced to an outsider computational node, without revealing the secret data. The encryption is done without involving any centralized managing entity, through a single external node.

References

1. Lewko, A., Waters, B.: Decentralizing attribute-based encryption. In: Paterson, K.G. (ed.) EUROCRYPT 2011. LNCS, vol. 6632, pp. 568–588. Springer, Heidelberg (2011). https://doi.org/10.1007/978-3-642-20465-4_31
2. Nguyen, K.T., Oualha, N., Laurent, M.: Securely outsourcing the ciphertext-policy attribute-based encryption. World Wide Web **21**(1), 169–183 (2017). https://doi.org/10.1007/s11280-017-0473-x
3. Sahai, A., Waters, B.: Fuzzy identity-based encryption. In: Annual International Conference on the Theory and Applications of Cryptographic Techniques, pp. 457–473. Springer, Heidelberg (2005). https://doi.org/10.1007/11426639_27
4. Tian, H., Li, X., Quan, H., Chang, C.-C., Baker, T.: A lightweight attribute-based access control scheme for intelligent transportation system with full privacy protection. IEEE Sens. J. **21**(14), 15793–15806 (2021)
5. Yan, Y., Kamel, M.B., Ligeti, P.: Attribute-based encryption in cloud computing environment. In: 2020 International Conference on Computing, Electronics & Communications Engineering (ICCECE), pp. 63–68. IEEE (2020)

POSTER: Ransomware Detection Mechanism – Current State of the Project

Michał Glet$^{(\boxtimes)}$ ⓘ and Kamil Kaczyński ⓘ

Military University of Technology, Warsaw, Poland
michal.glet@wat.edu.pl

Abstract. Ransomware nowadays is one of the most critical security threats. Ransomware attacks are targeted at governments, enterprises, and casual users. Without very good backup and retention policies, it can lead to serious data damage. However, even very good data protection can't secure data from being stolen and revealed after a successful ransomware attack. This could be also very dangerous, especially for governments and enterprises in terms e.g. of trust and confidence. We have seen many times all these kinds of problems during our professional activity. We have helped recover from many ransomware attacks. Sometimes we were able to recover almost all of the encrypted data, sometimes not even a single one. That is why we have started the project that will end with specifications and working Proof-of-Concept of the ransomware detection mechanism.

Keywords: Ransomware · Cryptovirus · Detection

1 Introduction

The project is being led by the Military University of Technology in Warsaw and TiMSI Sp. z o.o. Some of the results of the project will be published in the public domain and will be available free of charge for every polish citizen. The project is addressing the topic of the early detection of the activity of the ransomware software and will end with specifications and working Proof-of-Concept of the ransomware detection mechanism. This mechanism would be able to detect ransomware activity at the very beginning stage and thus minimize the possible losses that this attack could have caused.

The project consists of three main phases. The first one is an analysis. The second one is development. The third one is implementation and testing. We are at the beginning of phase number two. We have analyzed ransomware samples and Windows mechanisms, provided ransomware general characteristics, and developed ideas for the detection indicators. Now we are creating a detailed description of the indicators and shortly, we will develop the detection mechanism that will use those indicators. In the next phases, we will create a working Proof-of-Concept, conduct some tests and implement necessary tweaks and improvements.

What is more, the project covers some topics that are not being connected with ransomware detection (like locality-preserving hashing) and in detail consider topics that were not analyzed in the literature very well (like using Windows drivers/drivers

© The Author(s), under exclusive license to Springer Nature Switzerland AG 2022
J. Zhou et al. (Eds.): ACNS 2022 Workshops, LNCS 13285, pp. 616–620, 2022.
https://doi.org/10.1007/978-3-031-16815-4_36

filters in term of ransomware detection). In our work, we are also using results presented in papers e.g. written by Scaife et al. [1], Continella et al. [2], Kharraz et al. [3], Palisse et al. [4] and [5], Kolodenker et al. [6], Lee et al. [7], etc.

In this paper, we briefly summarize the current status of the project and mention the main challenges that we will deal with shortly.

2   Current State

The project started in the summer of 2021. Since then we have done a lot of analysis, mind-storming, and engineering work. The important results are:

- Working environment and procedures – the project started with preparations of the working environment and working procedures. The prepared working environment consists of virtual machines for running and for analyzing ransomware software. The main tools to disassemble and decompile ransomware binary code are a very powerful Hex-Rays IDA Pro and Hex-Rays IDA Decompiler. We use also other assisting software like e.g. APIMonitor, WinDbg, Ghidra, Binary Ninja, Autopsy, etc. What is more, we have created a set of procedures for maintaining working environments and for analyzing the binary code of the ransomware. The procedures consist of steps and expected results. This approach speeded up the analysis process and ensured that results from different versions of the ransomware are measurable and comparable.
- Analyzed samples – samples that we have used were collected from malware repositories like MalwareBazaar (https://bazaar.abuse.ch/), MalShare (https://malshare.com/) or Bleeping Computer (https://www.bleepingcomputer.com). We have downloaded, analyzed, or tried to run (debug) ransomware from many families, e.g.: Avaddon, BlackMatter, Chaos, Conti, Darkside, Hanta, Hive, Kaseya, Lockbit, LokiLocker, Magniber, MedusaLocker, MountLocker, Nefilim, Nitro, Sodinokibi, Stop, Thanos, White Rabbit. The results from this phase were crucial in terms of further analysis and preparation of the ransomware detection mechanism.
- Analyzed Windows OS mechanisms – during the first stage of the project, we analyzed many different mechanisms available in the Windows OS. We have analyzed them for two purposes: to better understand mechanisms that are used by ransomware and to find the best suitable mechanisms for detection mechanism. We have analyzed e.g.: Windows API functions, Windows drivers, Windows driver filters, PE files, DDL files, process injection techniques, DLL injection techniques, Windows API hooks, kernel mode, etc.
- Ransomware characteristics – the results from conducted ransomware samples analysis were used to prepare generic ransomware characteristics. Those characteristics include behavior like destroying backup resources, stopping system processes, stopping system services, filesystem operations, cryptography operations, privileges escalations, threads/processes management, and local and network resources discovery.

2.1   Indicators

The indicators are among the most important results of the project that have been achieved so far. The basic specification of the indicators has been developed during the last phase of the project. Indicators use characteristics and behaviors that were observed during ransom-ware samples analysis. The task of every indictor would be to provide some measurements and inform detection mechanisms when orange or red levels are exceeded. For every indicator, we have defined warning levels. Indicators can have defined green, orange, and red levels. The green level means that indicators do not recognize any suspicious behavior. The orange level means that the process could be suspicious and that other measurements should be taken into the consideration. The red level means that the process is probably ransomware.

We have developed the following indicators:

- Cryptography API usage – this indicator will monitor and measure the usage of the most popular cryptography functions available in the API provided by a Windows OS. Monitoring will include functions like CryptAcquireContextW, CryptDestroyKey, CryptDuplicateKey, CryptEncrypt, CryptExportKey, CryptGenKey, CryptImportKey, CryptReleaseContext, CryptSetKeyParam. For this indicator, we have defined green, orange, and red warning levels.
- File API usage – this indicator will monitor and measure the usage of the most popular file functions available in the API provided by a Windows OS. Monitoring will include functions like CopyFileW, CreateFileW, FindClose, FindFirstFileExW, FindFirstFileW, FindFirstVolumeW, FindNextFileW, FindNextVolumeW, FindVolumeClose, GetFileAttributesW, GetFileSizeEx, GetFileType, GetVolumeInformationW, GetVolumePathNamesForVolumeNameW, MoveFileExW, ReadFile, SetFileAttributesW, SetFilePointerEx, SetVolumeMountPointW, WriteFileCryptSetKeyParam. For this indicator we have defined green, orange and red warning levels.
- Process/thread API usage – this indicator will monitor and measure the usage of the most popular process/threads management functions available in the API provided by a Windows OS. Monitoring will include functions like CreateThread, ExitProcess, ExitThread, GetCurrentProcess, GetCurrentProcessId, GetCurrentThread, GetCurrentThreadId, GetExitCodeThread, GetProcessAffinityMask, GetProcessHeap, GetThreadContext, GetThreadPriority, GetThreadTimes, OpenProcess, OpenProcessToken, Process32FirstW, Process32NextW, SetThreadAffinityMask, SetThreadPriority, TerminateProcess. For this indicator we have defined green and orange warning levels.
- Settings API usage – this indicator will monitor and measure the usage of the most popular system settings management functions available in the API provided by a Windows OS. Monitoring will include functions like GetCommandLineW, GetComputerNameA, GetDateFormatW, GetDiskFreeSpaceW, GetEnvironmentStringsW, GetEnvironmentVariableW, GetStartupInfoW, GetSystemInfo, IsProcessorFeaturePresent, IsValidCodePage, RegCloseKey, RegOpenKeyExW, RegSetValueExW. For this indicator we have defined green and orange warning levels.
- Other API usages – this indicator will monitor and measure the usage of functions available in the API provided by a Windows OS that was identified by us as unusual in normal programs. Monitoring will include functions like AdjustTokenPrivileges, CheckRemoteDebuggerPresent, GetCommandLineA, GetCommandLineW, GetLocaleInfoA, GetLocaleInfoW, GetProcAddress, IsDebuggerPresent, IsProcessorFeaturePresent, IsValidCodePage, IsValidLocale, LoadLibraryExW, LoadLibraryW. For this indicator, we have defined green and orange warning levels.

- Privilege escalation – this indicator will monitor active processes if there were execution privileges changes since the process started. The indicator will also monitor the changes in the state of the Windows UAC mechanism. For this indicator, we have defined green and orange warning levels.
- Level of randomness change – this indicator will monitor and measure the level of the change in the randomness of the file content. To do this it will combine file entropy with some high-speed statistical functions. For this indicator, we have defined green, orange, and red warning levels.
- Bucket change – this indicator will monitor and measure if the content of the file belongs to the same category (bucket) as before the changes. To do this it will use a specially crafted locality-preserving hash function. This function will ensure that minor changes to original content result in no or minor changes in the hash value. For this indicator, we have defined green and orange warning levels.
- Decoy files access – this indicator will monitor and measure the access to specially prepared decoy files. Decoy files will be created and distributed randomly within system resources – every computer will have different files in different locations. For this indicator, we have defined green and red warning levels.
- Decoy files changes – this indicator will monitor and measure the changes in the content of the specially prepared decoy files. Decoy files will be created and distributed randomly within system resources – every computer will have different files in different locations. For this indicator, we have defined green and red warning levels.

3   Upcoming Challenges

The final results of this project will be a working Proof-of-Concept of the ransomware detection mechanism and a set of specifications. Those specifications will describe in detail proposed indicators, mechanisms, and detection use cases. Specifications will have an implementation-ready description. This should speed up deployments in production environments. Below we have described the main challenges we will deal with in the nearest future:

- Detection mechanism – The ransomware detection mechanism will use proposed indicators. Proposed indicators will work mainly as a part of analyzed Windows mechanisms. E.g. indicator "decoy file access" will use Windows drivers and Windows driver filters to measure and detect ransomware activity. In this phase of the project, we will propose and technically specify the ransomware detection mechanism. For every indicator, we will provide a detailed explanation of how it should be used within the detection mechanism. For the detection mechanism, we will provide a detailed description of how it should work, how it should react to measurements from indicators, and how it should react in the most common scenarios.
- Proof-of-Concept – the proof-of-Concept will be a crucial part of this project in terms of assessing the effectiveness and the accuracy of the ransomware detection level. All tests and further improvements will be conducted on this working PoC. PoC will be also used as a reference implementation of the indicators and the detection mechanism.

- Testing and improvements – the testing process will involve PoC and ransomware samples running in the test environment. We will use well-known samples, as well as samples gathered during the whole project lifecycle. This approach will allow checking how well the PoC of the detection mechanism will deal with new and unknown during the analysis phases versions of ransomware. The test result will be used to add some final tweaks and improvements in the PoC, specification of the detection mechanism, and specification of the indicators.

Acknowledgment. This work is partially funded by The National Centre for Research and Development, Poland. The project number is CYBERSECIDENT/490737/IV/NCBR/2021. The project will last till the end of the year 2023.

References

1. Scaife, N., Carter, H., Traynor, P., Butler, K.R.B.: CryptoLock (and drop it): stopping ransomware attacks on user data. In: IEEE 36th International Conference on Distributed Computing Systems (ICDCS), pp. 303–312, June 2016
2. Continella, A., et al.: ShieldFS: a self-healing, ransomware-aware filesystem. In: Proceedings of the 32nd Annual Conference on Computer Security Applications, pp. 336–347. ACM, New York (2016)
3. Kharraz, A., Kirda, E.: Redemption: real-time protection against ransomware at end-hosts in research in attacks, intrusions, and defenses. In: Dacier, M., Bailey, M., Polychronakis, M., Antonakakis, M. (eds.) Research in Attacks, Intrusions, and Defenses, vol. 10453, pp. 98–119. Springer, Cham (2017). https://doi.org/10.1007/978-3-319-66332-6_5
4. Palisse, A., Durand, A., Le Bouder, H., Le Guernic, C., Lanet, J.-L.: Data aware defense (DaD): towards a generic and practical ransomware countermeasure. In: Lipmaa, H., Mitrokotsa, A., Matulevičius, R. (eds.) Secure IT Systems, vol. 10674, pp. 192–208. Springer, Cham (2017). https://doi.org/10.1007/978-3-319-70290-2_12
5. Palisse, A., Le Bouder, H., Lanet, J.-L., Le Guernic, C., Legay, A.: Ransomware and the legacy crypto API. In: Cuppens, F., Cuppens, N., Lanet, J.L., Legay, A. (eds.) Risks and Security of Internet and Systems, vol. 10158, pp. 11–28. Springer, Cham (2016). https://doi.org/10.1007/978-3-319-54876-0_2
6. Kolodenker, E., Koch, W., Stringhini, G., Egele, M.: Paybreak: defense against cryptographic ransomware. In: Proceedings of the 2017 ACM on Asia Conference on Computer and Communications Security, pp. 599–611. ACM, New York (2017)
7. Lee, J., Lee, J., Hong, J.: How to make efficient decoy files for ransomware detection? In: Proceedings of the International Conference on Research in Adaptive and Convergent Systems, pp. 208–212. ACM, Krakow (2017)

Author Index

Printed in the United States
by Baker & Taylor Publisher Services

Printed in the United States
by Baker & Taylor Publisher Services